Communications in Computer and Information Science 2463

Rationale
The CCIS series is devoted to the publication of proceedings of computer science conferences. Its aim is to efficiently disseminate original research results in informatics in printed and electronic form. While the focus is on publication of peer-reviewed full papers presenting mature work, inclusion of reviewed short papers reporting on work in progress is welcome, too. Besides globally relevant meetings with internationally representative program committees guaranteeing a strict peer-reviewing and paper selection process, conferences run by societies or of high regional or national relevance are also considered for publication.

Topics
The topical scope of CCIS spans the entire spectrum of informatics ranging from foundational topics in the theory of computing to information and communications science and technology and a broad variety of interdisciplinary application fields.

Information for Volume Editors and Authors
Publication in CCIS is free of charge. No royalties are paid, however, we offer registered conference participants temporary free access to the online version of the conference proceedings on SpringerLink (http://link.springer.com) by means of an http referrer from the conference website and/or a number of complimentary printed copies, as specified in the official acceptance email of the event.

CCIS proceedings can be published in time for distribution at conferences or as post-proceedings, and delivered in the form of printed books and/or electronically as USBs and/or e-content licenses for accessing proceedings at SpringerLink. Furthermore, CCIS proceedings are included in the CCIS electronic book series hosted in the SpringerLink digital library at http://link.springer.com/bookseries/7899. Conferences publishing in CCIS are allowed to use Online Conference Service (OCS) for managing the whole proceedings lifecycle (from submission and reviewing to preparing for publication) free of charge.

Publication process
The language of publication is exclusively English. Authors publishing in CCIS have to sign the Springer CCIS copyright transfer form, however, they are free to use their material published in CCIS for substantially changed, more elaborate subsequent publications elsewhere. For the preparation of the camera-ready papers/files, authors have to strictly adhere to the Springer CCIS Authors' Instructions and are strongly encouraged to use the CCIS LaTeX style files or templates.

Abstracting/Indexing
CCIS is abstracted/indexed in DBLP, Google Scholar, EI-Compendex, Mathematical Reviews, SCImago, Scopus. CCIS volumes are also submitted for the inclusion in ISI Proceedings.

How to start
To start the evaluation of your proposal for inclusion in the CCIS series, please send an e-mail to ccis@springer.com.

Enrico Borgogno-Mondino · Paola Zamperlin
Editors

Geomatics for Green and Digital Transition

27th Italian Conference, ASITA 2024
Padua, Italy, December 9–13, 2024
Proceedings, Part I

Springer

Editors
Enrico Borgogno-Mondino
University of Torino
Grugliasco, Italy

Paola Zamperlin
University of Firenze
Florence, Italy

ISSN 1865-0929 ISSN 1865-0937 (electronic)
Communications in Computer and Information Science
ISBN 978-3-031-91140-8 ISBN 978-3-031-91141-5 (eBook)
https://doi.org/10.1007/978-3-031-91141-5

This Springer imprint is published by the registered company Springer Nature Switzerland AG
The registered company address is: Gewerbestrasse 11, 6330 Cham, Switzerland

Preface

The Italian Conference on Geomatics and Geospatial Technologies is a biennial event whose 2024 edition was held in Padua (Italy) from the 9th to the 13th of December 2024, offering an important opportunity to share the latest developments in Geomatics, with a particular reflection on the Italian context in terms of technology transfer and innovation proposals.

Participation exceeded expectations and involved prestigious representatives of official institutions and public administration (at various levels of governance), the public and private research sector, and the business world. Over 130 speakers animated the parallel sessions and the poster session with their contributions.

Some remarkable contents were as follows: (i) the initial findings from the ongoing national projects developed within the Next Generation EU framework (Piano Nazionale di Ripresa e Resilienza - PNRR in Italy); (ii) transferability and exploitability of new official geographical products and services provided by institutional entities (e.g., Copernicus); (iii) the need for a definition of adequate standardized procedures for producing and validating geographical and Earth Observation data, products, and services with special concerns about their potential roles in monitoring and control activities from institutional players; (iv) concerns about the disruptive role of Artificial Intelligence in Geomatics-related applications and human job markets.

These two volumes collect 54 selected articles organized into five sections, presenting an in-depth exploration of innovative geospatial analysis and technology in tackling key natural or human environmental challenges, including climate change impacts, urban ecosystem planning and management, emergency response effectiveness, and advancements in complex systems monitoring.

With its particular perspective, each paper contributes to the broader objective of supporting technology transfer of innovative methodologies to improve understanding, preparedness, and response to environmental, cultural heritage, and urban management.

Collectively, these studies emphasize the integration of advanced remote sensing technologies, spatial analysis and GIS, and photogrammetry, always highlighting the critical role of data accuracy, standardization, and accessibility.

In the first chapter, **Natural Hazards and Emergencies**, the papers explore innovative geomatic techniques and remote sensing technologies for environmental monitoring, disaster management, and risk assessment. Key topics include soil moisture estimation, wildfire and flood mapping, landslide susceptibility, and ground deformation analysis using InSAR and GIS-based methods. Applications range from UAV support in firefighting to geospatial assessments of antimicrobial resistance and out-of-hospital cardiac arrests. All works are based on the integration of advanced data processing, satellite monitoring, and field sensors to enhance emergency response, infrastructure resilience, and environmental sustainability.

Studies collected in the second chapter, **Urban Systems: Structures, Cities, and Infrastructure**, present innovative geomatic techniques and approaches for urban planning, sustainability, and public safety. Key themes include digital twins, urban heat island analysis, accessibility evaluation, and crime mapping, alongside assessments of ecosystem services and industrial recycling dynamics. Advanced methodologies, such as AI-driven spatial analysis, groupware planning tools, and satellite data integration for urban efficiency, environmental resilience, and safety perception, are presented here. These approaches contribute to sustainable urban development, inclusive design, and data-driven decision-making for city planning and regeneration.

The third chapter, **Cultural Heritage and Landscape Management**, groups papers where geomatics, GIS, and remote sensing are used for historical, cultural, and environmental preservation and interpretation. Key topics include digitalizing World War I cartography, participatory mapping for education, and advanced surveying of cultural heritage sites using BIM-GIS integration and multispectral imaging. Innovative methods for monitoring coastal and marine areas and changes in land use with artificial intelligence-based techniques are central to the research presented. The interdisciplinary approach that characterizes the articles enhances historical research, urban planning, and conservation efforts through advanced geospatial technologies.

The fourth chapter, **Agriculture and Forests**, collects articles related to the application of remote sensing, UAVs, and satellite imagery in agriculture and environmental monitoring. The main topics include crop stress analysis, drought impact assessment, soil erosion mapping, and irrigation modeling using advanced geospatial technologies, highlighting the integration of LiDAR, multispectral data, and satellite analysis to support sustainable farming and land management.

The works grouped in the fifth and last chapter, **Environmental Applications of Geomatics**, refer to vertical domains of applications of Geomatics with special concerns about automated habitat mapping, glacier and coastal monitoring, deformation analysis of the MOSE system in Venice, and marine pollution response.

The importance and effectiveness of collaborative approaches among groups and skills can be explicitly recognized in all the selected papers, demonstrating the high added value that such approaches, based on interdisciplinarity and plurality of players from different institutions/academies/companies, can bring.

As Editors and members of the Italian and International community of geomaticians, we hope for the continuation of this trend in the future. We further recognize that only a wise and open dialogue among research, politics, and companies can drive a proper response to the global challenges that different human communities are facing.

As Editors of the 4th collection of ASITA Proceedings in Springer's CCIS series, we warmly express our thanks to all those who have contributed, as authors and reviewers, to make both the Conference and these Proceedings successful.

March 2025

Enrico Borgogno-Mondino
Paola Zamperlin

Organization

Program Committee Chairs

Enrico Borgogno Mondino	Università di Torino, Italy
Paola Zamperlin	Università di Firenze, Italy

Program Committee

Filiberto Chiabrando	Politecnico di Torino, Italy
Elena Dai Prà	Università di Trento, Italy
Andrea Fiduccia	AMFM GIS Italia, Italy
Antonio Ganga	Università di Sassari, Italy
Fabio Giulio Tonolo	Politecnico di Torino, Italy
Michele Grimaldi	Università di Salerno, Italy
Maria Teresa Melis	Università di Cagliari, Italy
Giovanni Pugliano	Università degli Studi di Napoli Federico II, Italy
Monica Sebillo	Università di Salerno, Italy
Domenico Visintini	Università di Udine, Italy

Additional Reviewers

Andrea Ajmar
Marco Anibaldi
Alessandro Auzzas
Mirco Balin
Caterina Balletti
Rafael Barroca Silva
Elena Belcore
Camillo Berti
Angelo Besana
Stefano Bilotta
Sandro Bimonte
Massimo Blandino
Giuseppe Borruso
Mariano Bresciani
Samuele Bumbaca
Alessio Calantropio
Andrea Cantile
Alessandra Capolupo
Vittorio Marco Casella
Enrica Caporali
Enrico Chiesa
Alberto Cina
Elisabetta Colucci
Paolo Dabove
Samuele De Petris
Maria A. Dessena
Marco Devecchi
Vincenzo Di Pietra
Alessandro Farbo
Sergio Farrugia
Giorgio V. Federici
Monica Franzini

Vanina Fissore
Nicola Gabellieri
Arturo Gallia
Chiara Garau
Federica Ghilardi
Marco Gianinetto
Claudia Giardino
Fabio Giulio Tonolo
Nives Grasso
Francesco Guerra
Alessandro L. Ipsaro Palesi
Andrea Lingua
Andrea Lombardelli
Antonino Maltese
Pierpaolo Milan
Giuseppe Modica
Stefano Nicolodi
Tommaso Orusa
Gianni Pantaleo
Francesco Parizia
Davide Pavia
Luigi Perotti
Silvia Elena Piovan
Francesco Pirotti
Chiara Richiardi
Alessandro Rissone
Antonello Romano
Giulia Sammartano
Filippo Sarvia
Marco Scaioni
Domenico Sguerso
Alessandra Spreafico
Deodato Tapete
Davide Travaglini
Annalisa Viani
Andrea Virano
Domenico Visintini
Alfonso Vitti

Contents – Part I

Natural Hazards and Emergencies

Contents – Part II

Natural Hazards and Emergencies

Surface Soil Moisture Estimate by Integration of Optical Remote Sensing and Low-Cost Field Sensor Network: The Case Study of Ceriana-Mainardo (Liguria, Italy)

Alessandro Iacopino(✉), Rossella Bovolenta, and Bianca Federici

Department of Civil, Chemical and Environmental Engineering (DICCA), University of Genoa, Genoa, Italy
{alessandro.iacopino,rossella.bovolenta, bianca.federici}@unige.it

Abstract. Surface Soil Moisture (SSM) is a fundamental information in various research contexts. The monitoring of soil moisture variations can be performed through an accurate use of sensors calibrated and distributed over the study areas. Also, remote sensing techniques can be used to estimate SSM, analyzing wide areas automatically. Starting from previous studies about the response of capacitive soil moisture sensors (WaterScout SM100) installed in the study area of Ceriana-Mainardo (Liguria, Italy), the present work aims to investigate the correlation between ground-based soil moisture data and reflectance extracted from Sentinel-2 images in a study area characterized by sparsely vegetated surfaces. Despite S-2 limitations due to sensitivity to atmospheric obstacles, they provide very effective monitoring of vegetation conditions, thanks to the Red Edge bands. In fact, Reflectance – Soil Moisture correlation analysis highlighted a better response for Red Edge 2, Red Edge 3, Broad Near Infrared and Near Infrared bands, being the vegetation cover spectral response an indirect indicator of soil moisture in the investigated depths. The best correlation is found referring to soil moisture at 10 cm depth and considering the mean reflectance of the four mentioned bands. This kind of dependency allows to have a quite good correlation ($R^2 = 0.56$, RES STD = 3.3% θ (m^3/m^3), MAE = 2.1% θ (m^3/m^3)), comparable with the accuracy of the ground soil moisture sensors (3% θ), hence useful to extract spatially distributed information of Volumetric Water Content (θ [m^3/m^3%]) from S-2 images. The results of the analysis appear encouraging. The workflow, implemented on an area mostly characterized by complex cultivations, could be replicated on other vegetated land uses in presence of field soil moisture data in the study area.

Keywords: Volumetric Water Content · Monitoring Network · Multispectral Images

E. Borgogno-Mondino and P. Zamperlin (Eds.): ASITA 2024, CCIS 2463, pp. 3–19, 2025.
https://doi.org/10.1007/978-3-031-91141-5_1

1 Introduction

Knowledge of Soil Moisture (SM) (typically referred to the upper meter depth) is useful in several research fields, particularly in hydrological balances [1–3] and precision agriculture [4], but also in the analysis of the mechanical behavior of partially saturated soils on slopes susceptible to surface landslides [5, 6]. It can be distinguished in Surface Soil Moisture (SSM, referring to the first 5–10 cm depth from ground level) and Root Zone Soil Moisture (RZSM, referring to depths between 50–100–200 cm) [7, 8]. SSM estimate (typically expressed in Volumetric Water Content, θ [$m^3/m^3\%$]) can be carried out using sensors (direct measurements) installed in the ground or remote sensing techniques.

Soil moisture sensors, often integrated in monitoring networks consisting of many measuring points (nodes), provide information on the volumetric soil water content locally. Such systems differ based on sensor complexity, accuracy and cost. Some typical examples of soil moisture sensors are gamma-ray transmission, electrical resistance, soil heat flux, time-domain reflectometry (TDR), and frequency-domain reflectometry (FDR) [9, 10]. However, capacitive sensors are more suited for automated applications because of their more straightforward data output, the reduced power consumption, and the lower costs [11].

In order to obtain a spatially distributed estimate of SSM, remote sensing products derived by multispectral optical or microwave radar images, that differ mainly in spatial resolution and sensitivity to atmospheric obstacles [12], can be used. Copernicus Sentinel mission, developed by the European Commission and the European Space Agency for the Copernicus Global Earth Observation Project, have been providing Earth Observation (EO) products for almost a decade. The Sentinel-1 (S-1) imaging system operates in the C-band and has four imaging modes, providing technical support for long-term monitoring of a given region due to its dual polarization capability, short revisit period, and fast processing of products [13]. Sentinel-2 (S-2) satellite carries a high-resolution MultiSpectral Imager (MSI) with 13 spectral bands, three of which are specialized Red Edge bands, particularly effective for monitoring vegetation healthy state [14]. Several studies have relied on the combined use of S-1 and S-2 products to assess surface soil characteristics such as water content, but also organic carbon and total nitrogen [15–17]. However, in this work, because of the marked presence of low vegetation, i.e. herbaceous and shrub species in the study area, classified in the Land Cover cartography [18] as *complex agriculture*, only the potential of S-2 is investigated. Moreover, since the vegetation can be considered homogeneous in the study area, its spectral response can also be considered homogeneous, simplifying the analysis, as described in the following.

The analyzed study area is Ceriana-Mainardo (IM), in the western side of the Ligurian Region, in Italy. The site has been monitored placing in field a network of capacitive sensors (WaterScout SM100), because the area was subject to shallow landslides induced by changes in soil moisture. This occurred, for example, during intense rainfall in 2018, causing road disruption and substantially isolating the population, that was then evacuated from their houses for safety reasons. In such cases, the analysis of the evolution of soil moisture (in the upper meter depth) over time could be useful to assess when conditions become stable again, allowing people to return to their houses.

This paper aims at defining an expeditious methodology for large-scale and high spatial resolution estimate of Surface Soil Moisture, based on the integration of direct ground-based measurements and S-2 multispectral images. The combined use of these resources could lead to a detailed estimate of spatial-temporal variation of SSM, useful for the implementation of geotechnical models for shallow landslide analysis.

The specific goals of the present work can be summarized as follows:

- Correct functionality assessment of the ground-based soil moisture monitoring network; this crucial phase aims to establish the ground-truth, necessary to correlate the satellite images reflectance with the soil moisture measurements.
- Definition of the Reflectance – SM correlation at different multispectral bands, and determination of the spectral bands providing the statistically best correlation (evaluated based on the highest coefficient of determination R^2 values from linear regressions).
- Creation of SM maps from multispectral images, here proposed with reference to homogeneous land uses.

2 Study Area and Ground-Based Data

The Ceriana Mainardo site is one of five landslide areas selected in the Ad-Vitam project (Analysis of the Vulnerability of the Mediterranean Alpine Territories to natural risks), financed within the Interreg V-A France–Italie, ALCOTRA 2014–2020. The aim was to increase the resilience of territories affected by rain-induced shallow landslides through the implementation of a forecasting system based on low-cost environmental monitoring that would provide near-real-time data of slope moisture conditions referred to the first meter of depth [19]. The installation of a monitoring network in this area made it possible to obtain a volumetric soil water content dataset, characterized by sufficient continuity over three years of observation (2020–2021–2022), on the basis of which it was possible to perform analyses on the correlation between soil moisture and multispectral satellite images.

2.1 Soil Moisture Monitoring Network: Characteristics and Reliability Analysis

The soil moisture monitoring network installed at the Ceriana-Mainardo site (Fig. 1) is composed of five measurement nodes (C1, C2, C3, C4 and C5), each equipped with four WaterScout SM100 sensors placed at depths of approximately −10 cm, −30 cm, 50 cm and −80 cm. The nodes are connected to a Retriever and a Modem for remote transmission of soil moisture monitoring [20] (Fig. 2).

In order to improve ground-based measurement reliability- soil moisture sensors were calibrated on the basis of the soil-specific characteristics of the area. The adopted calibration procedure is simplified and operative, as it does not properly take into account the soil porosity (for the results refer to [20, 21]). However, the monitoring network was verified to be capable of detecting the infiltration of water into the ground following a rainfall. This analysis was realized in Mendatica (Liguria, Italy), another site selected in the Ad-Vitam project, by analysing the correlation between precipitation variations (mm/h) and the volumetric water content θ (m^3/m^3%) recorded by the four sensors along

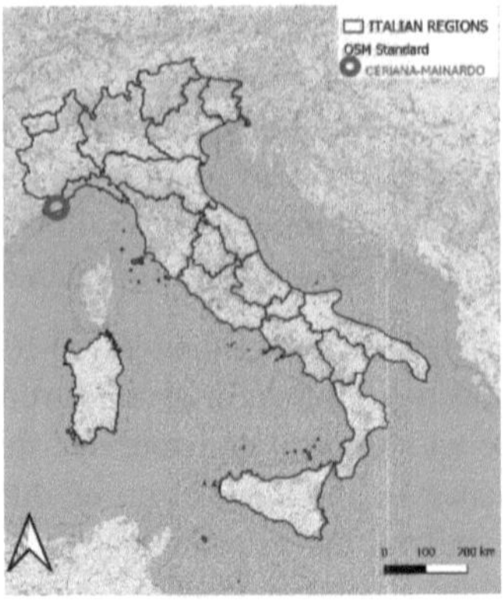

Fig. 1. Ceriana-Mainardo location.

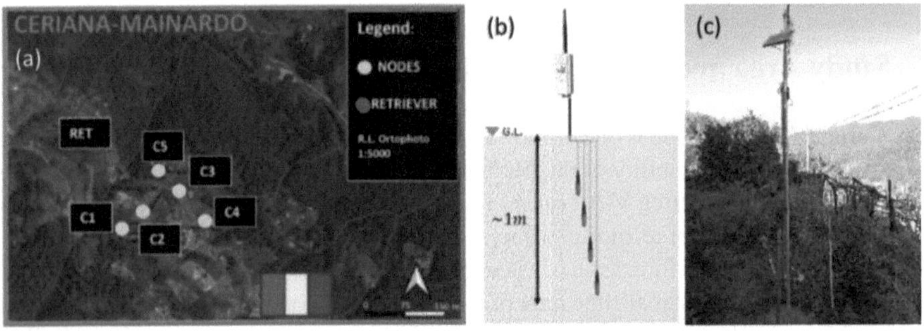

Fig. 2. (a) Soil moisture monitoring network installed in Ceriana-Mainardo. (b) Soil Moisture vertical installation mode. (c) A measurement node (C2) in *complex agriculture* Land Cover.

the vertical, forming a measurement node (called M1). Figure 3a shows an example of temporal evolution of rainfall and soil moisture measurements at the four analysed depth in January 2021. The cross-covariance (Matlab command *xcov(x,y)* [22]) between rainfall (x) and θ (y) shifted (lagged) in time, was calculated. As expected, a higher similarity between rainfall and soil moisture is evident in the shallower sensors, with maximum Pearson's coefficient (ρ) positioned at short lags (3 h). Deepest sensors show a decrease of the Pearson's coefficient (ρ), with a progressive delay of the peaks (10 cm depth: 3 h, 30 cm depth: 5 h, 50 cm depth: 6 h, 80 cm depth: 8 h), as shown in Fig. 3b for the rainfall event occurred in January 2021.

The correct functionality of the soil moisture monitoring network can be considered verified. Such an analysis makes it possible to conclude that the soil moisture dataset obtained by the described monitoring network can represent the ground-truth for further analyses. The four soil moisture datasets (concerning the four considered depths) relative to the Ceriana-Mainardo network were organized in terms of a daily median.

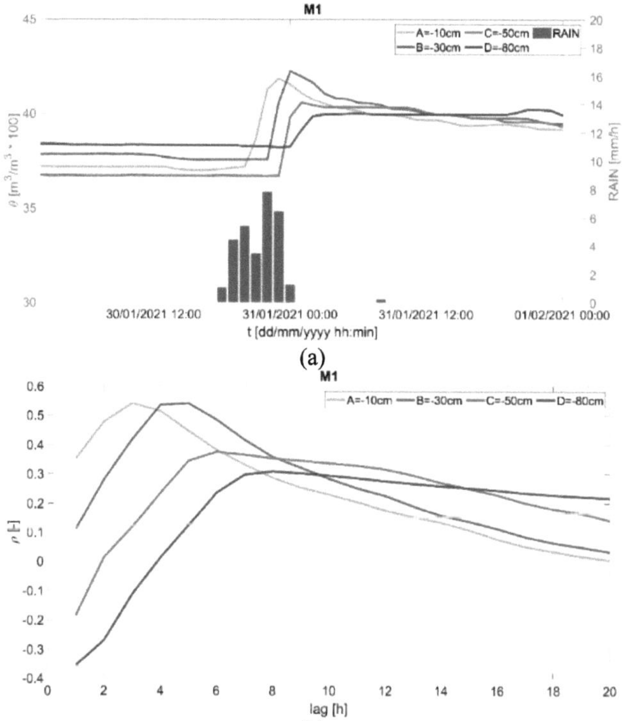

(b)

Fig. 3. (a) Rainfall and soil moisture referred to M1 node (Jan. 30–31, 2021). (b) Correlation between rainfall and soil moisture referred to M1 node (Jan. 30–31, 2021) (y-axis: Pearson's correlation coefficient ρ).

The considered time window includes the years 2020, 2021 and 2022, as it was during this period that the monitoring network operated most with the lowest number of interruptions.

3 Multispectral Images Analysis

3.1 Dataset Preprocessing

Sentinel-2 (S-2) A/B multispectral images were used in the present analysis. Automatic download of the Bottom of Atmosphere (BOA), clear sky satellite images was performed through the free script (GNU General Public License) SAme-Day SAtellite DAta Mosaics (SADASADAM) [23]. It uses the python package EODAG, distributed by the Earth Observation Data Access Gateway project [24], to search and download data, and the software FORCE (Framework for Operational Radiometric Correction for Environmental monitoring) for atmospheric correction, cloud detection, resampling and mosaic creation. Clouds are detected and eliminated, leaving only clear, usable image data. The main inputs include the coordinates of user-defined bounding box, the temporal extent and the desired percentage of cloud cover. The elaborated images, relative to the S-2 bands at 10 m and 20 m native spatial resolution, as shown in Table 1 [25, 26], were resampled at 10 m resolution by SADASADAM [27].

Table 1. S-2 Multispectral bands processed by SADASADAM

Number	Sentinel-2 band number	Band	Center wavelength (nm)	Original spatial resolution [m]
1	2	Blue	490	10
2	3	Green	560	10
3	4	Red	665	10
4	5	Red Edge 1	705	20
5	6	Red Edge 2	740	20
6	7	Red Edge 3	783	20
7	8	Broad Near-Infrared (BNIR)	842	10
8	8a	Near-Infrared (NIR)	865	20
9	11	Short Wave Infrared 1 (SIR1)	1610	20
10	12	Short Wave Infrared 2 (SIR2)	2190	20

3.2 Processing Workflow

The adopted workflow is here presented:

1. Automatic extraction of the pixel values from the multispectral images at the selected five points relating to the measurement nodes of the soil moisture monitoring network (see yellow dots in Fig. 2a), organizing data in a unique dataset considering the vegetation as homogeneous in the study area.
2. Correlation of the reflectance (derived from the ratio of pixel values to a scaling factor of 10.000) with the soil moisture measurements relative to the day of satellite image acquisition. In particular, the multispectral images are referenced to a given time and day, while the ground-based soil moisture data are processed (as described in Sect. 2.1) to obtain daily median values. Four Reflectance – Soil Moisture datasets were thus obtained, one for each of the considered depths (−10 cm, −30 cm, −50 cm and −80 cm).
3. Outlier removal steps:
   a) for each individual multispectral band, an initial scatter plot was created with reflectance values on the x-axis and soil moisture on the y-axis; hence, an initial linear regression was created.

b) The linear regression was shifted up and down by two times the standard deviation of the reflectance, so to define a tolerance range outside of which the data are rejected. The cleaned dataset is therefore obtained (green points in Fig. 4).
c) A further cleaning was applied, defining a tolerance range of amplitude equal to the standard deviation of the previously cleaned dataset, multiplied by a factor of 1.

4. Calibration and validation of the correlations: the Reflectance – Soil Moisture datasets were randomly divided into two datasets. 70% of data was used for the definition of the Reflectance – Soil Moisture relationship calibration, considered as linear (because polynomial regression did not significantly improve the correlation in terms of increasing coefficient of determination R^2), while 30% was used for its validation and for calculation of the statistical parameters RES STD (Residual Standard Deviation) and MAE (Mean Absolute Error). An example of this phase is shown in Fig. 5 in the following section.

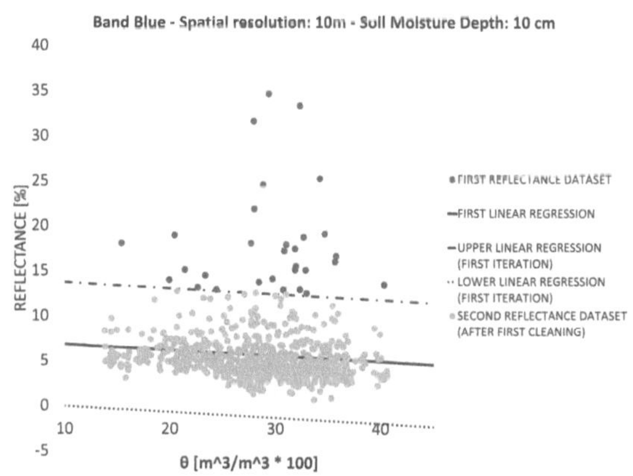

Fig. 4. Application to the blue band of outlier removal phase: First Reflectance – Soil Moisture dataset in blue points, linear regression in continuous red line, upper and lower linear regressions in dashed red lines, second reflectance dataset inside the range in green points (color figure online).

The described workflow was defined with the aim of investigating the correlations between different bands of multispectral images and soil moisture. The multiplicative factors of 2 (first iteration) and 1 (second iteration) used in outlier removal were chosen on the basis of Chebyshev Theorem [28].

4 Results

4.1 Reflectance – Soil Moisture Correlation

The processing workflow was applied to each of the available multispectral bands and to all reference depths. During the analysis, it has been noted that too low soil moisture values (<20% θ) are not always well represented by the Reflectance – Soil Moisture correlations. According to this observation, the results reported in Tables 2, 3, 4, and 5 are related to soil moisture values above 20% θ. The best results in terms of correlation between reflectance and soil moisture are obtained for the Red Edge 2, Red Edge 3, Broad Near Infrared and Near Infrared bands at the reference depth of 10 cm, since R^2 values are higher under these conditions. Moving deeper into the soil, the correlations result weaker, as might be expected (see Tables 2, 3, 4, and 5).

Table 2. Statistical parameters obtained from the calibration (on 70% of the cleaned dataset) and validation (on 30% of the cleaned dataset) analyses of the Reflectance – Soil Moisture correlation for each band at a depth of 10 cm.

DEPTH: 10 cm			
BAND	R^2 (70% dataset)	RES STD (30% dataset) [%]	MAE (30% dataset) [%]
BLUE	0.20	4.88	4.09
GREEN	0.27	4.48	3.85
RED	0.17	4.83	4.12
RED EDGE1	0.23	4.88	4.19
RED EDGE2	**0.47**	**3.85**	**3.12**
RED EDGE3	**0.50**	**3.65**	**2.96**
BNIR	**0.48**	**3.30**	**2.85**
NIR	**0.46**	**3.55**	**3.06**
SIR1	0.20	4.59	3.87
SIR2	0.10	4.92	4.19

Table 3. Statistical parameters obtained from the calibration (on 70% of the cleaned dataset) and validation (on 30% of the cleaned dataset) analyses of the Reflectance – Soil Moisture correlation for each band at a depth of 30 cm.

DEPTH: 30 cm			
BAND	R^2 (70% dataset)	RES STD (30% dataset) [%]	MAE (30% dataset) [%]
BLUE	0.17	4.54	3.60
GREEN	0.16	4.45	3.32
RED	0.16	4.11	3.23
RED EDGE1	0.13	4.60	3.67
RED EDGE2	**0.36**	**4.36**	**3.61**
RED EDGE3	**0.37**	**3.86**	**3.09**
BNIR	**0.36**	**4.47**	**3.61**
NIR	**0.37**	**4.23**	**3.40**
SIR1	0.24	4.16	3.19

(*continued*)

Table 3. (*continued*)

DEPTH: 30 cm			
BAND	R^2 (70% dataset)	RES STD (30% dataset) [%]	MAE (30% dataset) [%]
SIR2	0.13	4.39	3.26

Table 4. Statistical parameters obtained from the calibration (on 70% of the cleaned dataset) and validation (on 30% of the cleaned dataset) analyses of the Reflectance – Soil Moisture correlation for each band at a depth of 50 cm.

DEPTH: 50 cm			
BAND	R^2 (70% dataset)	RES STD (30% dataset) [%]	MAE (30% dataset) [%]
BLUE	0.14	4.65	3.75
GREEN	0.01	5.16	4.23
RED	0.03	4.34	3.55
RED EDGE1	0.01	5.00	6.06
RED EDGE2	**0.13**	**5.07**	**4.46**
RED EDGE3	**0.25**	**5.15**	**4.44**
BNIR	**0.25**	**4.65**	**3.98**
NIR	**0.22**	**4.64**	**4.09**
SIR1	0.01	4.65	3.93
SIR2	0.00	5.46	4.60

Table 5. Statistical parameters obtained from the calibration (on 70% of the cleaned dataset) and validation (on 30% of the cleaned dataset) analyses of the Reflectance – Soil Moisture correlation for each band at a depth of 80 cm.

DEPTH: 80 cm			
BAND	R^2 (70% dataset)	RES STD (30% dataset) [%]	MAE (30% dataset) [%]
BLUE	0.15	4.33	3.53
GREEN	0.12	4.85	3.86
RED	0.15	4.33	3.55
RED EDGE1	0.10	4.37	3.63
RED EDGE2	**0.19**	**4.65**	**3.73**
RED EDGE3	**0.20**	**4.39**	**3.55**
BNIR	**0.23**	**4.16**	**3.36**
NIR	**0.23**	**4.69**	**3.72**

(*continued*)

Table 5. (*continued*)

DEPTH: 80 cm			
BAND	R^2 (70% dataset)	RES STD (30% dataset) [%]	MAE (30% dataset) [%]
SIR1	0.20	4.49	3.64
SIR2	0.12	4.54	3.75

Figure 5 shows the calibration and validation phase for the Red Edge 3 band referred to 10 cm depth. Table 6 reports the linear parameters for the calibration in Fig. 5a, while Table 7 shows the statistical parameters of the validation in Fig. 5b. Moreover, the t-test [29] was applied so to quantify how much the Observed-Estimated Soil Moisture linear regression (green line in Fig. 5b) is distant from the bisector (blue line in Fig. 5b). Table 8 shows the t-test results; note that the t-test for slope ($|t_m|$) and the t-test for intercept ($|t_q|$) are about 6 times the t-value. Even though Red Edge3 band, that is highly correlated with soil moisture (10 cm depth) ($R^2 = 0.5$), the difference between the regression line Observed-Estimated Soil Moisture and the bisector is significant.

The Reflectance – Soil Moisture correlation for Red Edge 3 band (blue line in Fig. 6) is plotted together with the regression lines at the other analyzed depths in Fig. 6. They do not change significantly with increasing depth (Table 9), except for that concerning the 80 cm depth (green line in Fig. 6).

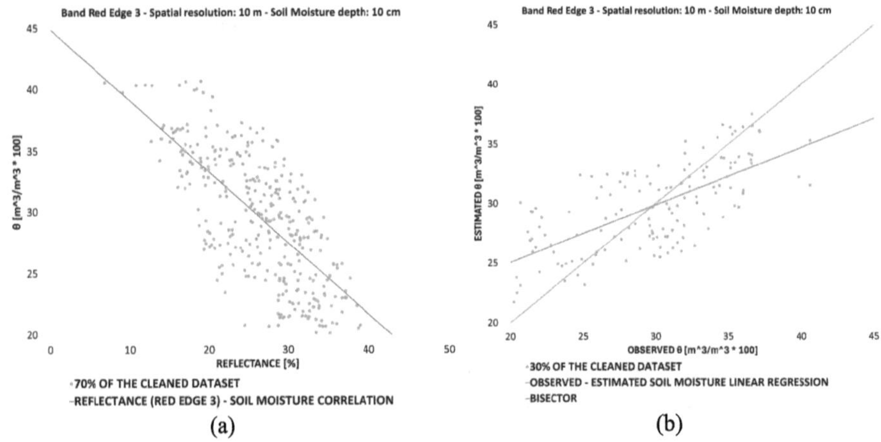

Fig. 5. (a) Reflectance – Soil Moisture (Depth: 10 cm) correlation for Red Edge 3 band: the regression line is in red. (b) Validation of Reflectance – Soil Moisture (Depth: 10 cm) correlation for Red Edge 3 band: the regression line is in green, the bisector of the plan is in blue (color figure online).

Table 6. Reflectance – Soil Moisture (−10 cm) correlation for Red Edge 3 band (Fig. 5a)

Red Edge 3 band (−10 cm)				
Equation: $\theta[\%] = a \cdot REFLECTANCE[\%] + b$				
Dataset	Number of data	a	b	R^2
70% of the cleaned dataset (SM > 20% θ)	337	−0.60	44.87	0.50

Table 7. Validation of Reflectance – Soil Moisture (−10 cm) calibration for Red Edge 3 band (Fig. 5b).

Red Edge 3 band (−10 cm)				
Dataset	Number of data	RES STD	MAE	R^2
30% of the cleaned dataset (SM > 20% θ)	140	3.65	2.96	0.46

Table 8. Regression t-Test (95% confidence level) on Observed-Estimated Soil Moisture linear regression with respect to the Bisector (green and blue lines in Fig. 5b).

Red Edge 3 band (−10 cm)		
$\|t_m\|$	$\|t_q\|$	t
11.6	11.5	1.98

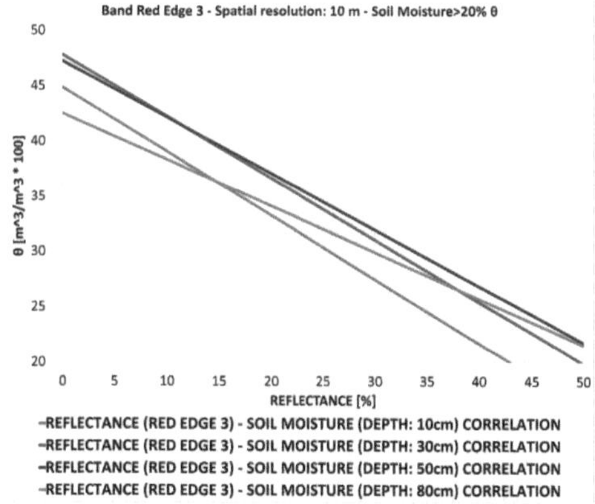

Fig. 6. Reflectance – Soil Moisture correlation for Red Edge 3 band at four analyzed depths.

Table 9. Regression t-Test (95% confidence level) on Pixel Values – Soil Moisture correlations (Red Edge 3 band) referred to 30 cm, 50 cm, 80 cm depth with respect to Reflectance – Soil Moisture correlation (Red Edge 3 band) referred to 10 cm depth

Depth	30 cm	50 cm	80 cm
$\|t_m\|$	0.52	1.29	3.67
$\|t_q\|$	3.01	1.74	1.95
t	1.97		

Spectral signature analysis at different soil moisture levels was performed, relative to 10 m depth soil moisture data. Soil moisture was expressed in terms of relative degree of saturation $S(\%) = {\theta_i - \theta_{min}}/{\theta_{MAX} - \theta_{min}}$, , in order to divide soil moisture value in classes (Class 0: 0% < S < 20%, Class 1: 20% < S < 40%, Class 2: 40% < S < 60%, Class 3: 60% < S < 80%, Class 4: 80% < S < 100%). The general trend confirmed a decrease in reflectance as soil moisture increases, as shown in Fig. 7. The analysis also highlighted the difficulty of representing low levels of soil water content; in fact, class 0 is inconsistent with the trend in particular in the center part of the spectral signature, referred to the four mentioned bands best correlated with soil moisture.

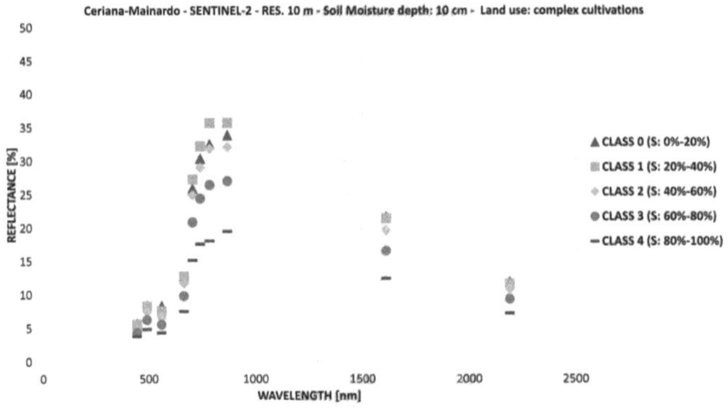

Fig. 7. Spectral signature variation related to soil moisture (depth: 10 cm)

4.2 Soil Moisture Information from Multispectral Images

The analysis of the dependencies between reflectance and soil moisture for the different multispectral bands at the different depths led to the selection of the wavelengths (Red Edge 2, Red Edge 3, Broad Near Infrared, Near Infrared) that correlate best with the variation in soil moisture, and of the reference depth best correlated with the bands (depth: 10 cm). Consequently, the proposed model can be considered valid only for Surface Soil Moisture estimate.

An even stronger Reflectance – Soil Moisture correlation is obtained considering the reflectance resulting from the mean of the four bands mentioned above, excluding soil moisture values below 20% θ. This result is due to the removal of high frequencies determined by the mean value of the four mentioned bands. Calibration and validation of this model are shown in Fig. 8.

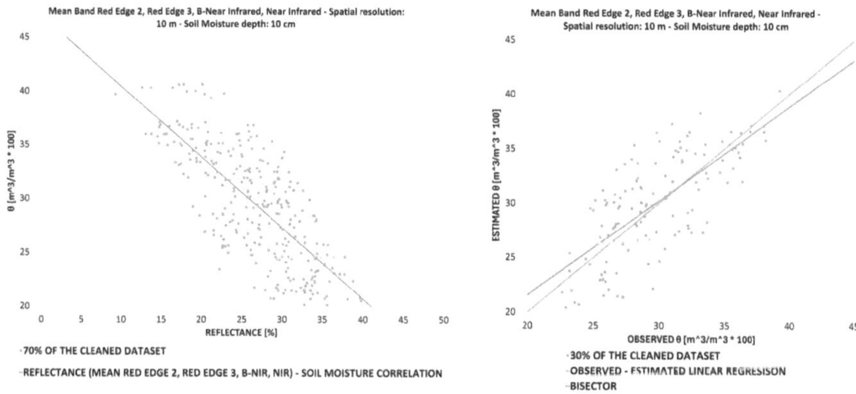

(a) (b)

Fig. 8. (a) Reflectance – Soil Moisture correlation for Mean Band (Red Edge 2, Red Edge 3, Broad Near Infrared, Near Infrared): the regression line is in red. (b) Validation of Reflectance – Soil Moisture dependency for Mean Band (Red Edge 2, Red Edge 3, Broad Near Infrared, Near Infrared): the regression line is in green, the bisector is in blue (color figure online).

The coefficients of the Reflectance – Soil Moisture correlation for Mean Band (Red Edge 2, Red Edge 3, Broad Near Infrared, Near Infrared) are reported in Table 10. RES STD and MAE values, reported in Table 11, are similar to the accuracy of the WaterScout SM100 ground soil moisture sensors (3% θ). t-test results (Table 12) show how well the Observed-Estimated Soil Moisture linear regression approximates the bisector. The present correlation allows the extraction of the SSM information at 10 cm depth relative to complex cultivations land cover, as shown in Fig. 9.

Table 10. Reflectance – Soil Moisture (−10 cm) correlation for Mean Band (Red Edge 2, Red Edge 3, Broad Near Infrared, Near Infrared).

Mean Band (Red Edge 2, Red Edge 3, B-Near Infrared, Near Infrared)				
Equation: $\theta[\%] = a \cdot REFLECTANCE[\%] + b$				
Dataset	Number of data	a	b	R^2
70% of the cleaned dataset	302	−0.7	47.10	0.56

Table 11. Statistical parameters obtained from the validation of Reflectance – Soil Moisture (−10 cm) correlation for Mean Band (Red Edge 2, Red Edge 3, Broad Near Infrared, Near Infrared).

Mean Band (Red Edge 2, Red Edge 3, B-Near Infrared, Near Infrared)				
Dataset	Number of data	RES STD [%]	MAE [%]	R^2
30% of the cleaned dataset	130	3.3	2.1	0.52

Table 12. Regression t-Test (95% confidence level) on Observed-Estimated Soil Moisture linear regression (green line in Fig. 8b) with respect to the Bisector (blue line in Fig. 8b).

Mean Band (Red Edge 2, Red Edge 3, B-Near Infrared, Near Infrared)		
$\|t_m\|$	$\|t_q\|$	t
2.4	2.5	1.98

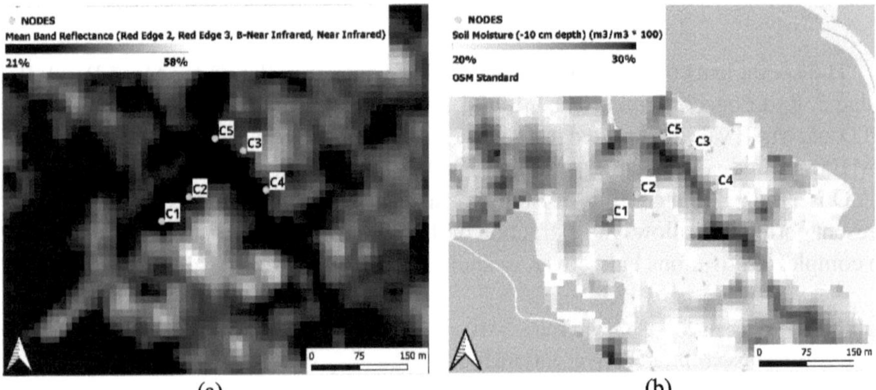

(a) (b)

Fig. 9. (a) Map representing the mean pixel values resulting from Red Edge 2, Red Edge 3, Broad Near Infrared and Near Infrared. (b) Soil moisture map (−10 cm depth, referred to complex cultivation land cover mask) obtained through the correlation in Table 10 and applying the presented workflow.

5 Conclusions

This research investigates the dependency between reflectance of multispectral Sentinel-2 images and volumetric soil water content (θ [m^3/m^3%]) variations over the Ceriana-Mainardo study area at four different depths in the first meter of soil from ground level. The analysis was developed based on the combination of two datasets, one consisting of field measurements (considered as ground truth) of soil moisture performed using a monitoring network with capacitive sensors, the other represented by Sentinel-2 A/B multispectral images, automatically downloaded, cleared of clouds and resampled to a spatial resolution of 10 m using the SAme-Day SAtellite DAta Mosaics (SADASADAM) software. Although the study area is not characterized by bare soil, but by sparsely vegetated surfaces and complex cultivations (consisting mainly of low vegetation, i.e. herbaceous and shrub species), the results of the analysis appear encouraging.

Firstly, the spectral signature obtained at different levels of soil moisture is consistent with the literature [30, 31], which indicates the Near Infrared bands as having the highest reflectance for a vegetated surface (Fig. 7). Moreover, excluding the lowest moisture values (<20% θ), reflectance decreases as soil moisture increases, again confirming literature [32, 33].

Despite the presence of (low) vegetation on the study area, a dependency between reflectance (acquired by multispectral images) and soil moisture is manifest. It can be argued that vegetation, in this case, acts as an indirect indicator of soil moisture. The inverse proportionality between reflectance and soil moisture is confirmed by the results obtained in the correlation analysis (Figs. 5a, 6, and 8a).

The combination of the Red Edge 2, Red Edge 3, Broad Near Infrared and Near Infrared bands in their mean value led to the definition of a sufficiently strong Reflectance – Soil Moisture correlation ($R^2 = 0.56$, RES STD = 3.3% θ, MAE = 2.1% θ). Interestingly, the RES STD and MAE values are similar to the accuracy of the Water-Scout SM100 ground soil moisture sensors (3% θ) [34]. Moreover, results reported in Table 12 suggest that soil moisture values estimated with the model in Table 10 are very close to observed soil moisture, since $|t_m|$ and $|t_q|$ are a little more than one time the t-value (1.2–1.3).

This workflow has been implemented on an area mostly characterized by complex cultivations, but it can be replicated on other land uses, depending on the presence of field soil moisture data, properly installed and calibrated, in the study area for the initial model calibration. Such a procedure provides a method for the automatic SSM estimate on a large scale and with high spatial resolution, providing useful information for engineering but also, for example, agricultural applications.

Acknowledgments. Our due thanks go to Luca Delucchi and the Edmund Mach Foundation (San Michele all'Adige, Trento, Italy) for their essential help during the definition and optimisation phases of the automatic multispectral image download and processing procedure covered by this research. The authors acknowledge the support given by AD-VITAM Partners. A particular acknowledgement goes to the Unione dei Comuni della Valle Argentina e Armea and to the lab technicians of the Department of Civil, Chemical and Environmental Engineering of the University of Genoa.

References

1. Liu, Y.,et al.: Spatiotemporally non-stationary evolution of groundwater levels in Poyang Lake Basin driven by meteorological and hydrological factors. Sci. Total Environ. **950**, 175244 (2024)

2. Liu, B., Brooks, E., Mohamed, A.Z., Kelley, J.: Deep infiltration model to quantify water use efficiency of center-pivot irrigated alfalfa. J. Irrig. Drain Eng. **150**, 04024021 (2024)
3. Passalacqua, R., Bovolenta, R., Federici, B.: An integrated hydrological-geotechnical model in GIS for the analysis and prediction of large-scale landslides triggered by rainfall events. In: Lollino, G., et al. (eds.) Engineering Geology for Society and Territory, vol. 2, pp. 1799–1803. Springer International Publishing, Cham (2015)
4. Lin, R., et al.: Construction and validation of surface soil moisture inversion model based on remote sensing and neural network. Atmosphere **15**, 647 (2024)
5. Tartaglia, M., Pirone, M., Urciuoli, G.: A data-driven approach to assess the role of the groundwater conditions in triggering shallow landslides initiating with frictional failure. Landslides **20**, 1497–1517 (2023)
6. Song, Z., Li, X., Lizárraga, J.J., Zhao, L., Buscarnera, G.: Shallow landslide triggering in unsaturated vegetated slopes: efficient computation of susceptibility maps. Comput. Geosci. **154**, 104826 (2021)
7. Li, M., Sun, H., Zhao, R.: A review of root zone soil moisture estimation methods based on remote sensing. Remote Sens. **15**, 5361 (2023)
8. Babaeian, E., Paheding, S., Siddique, N., Devabhaktuni, V.K., Tuller, M.: Estimation of root zone soil moisture from ground and remotely sensed soil information with multisensor data fusion and automated machine learning. Remote Sens. Environ. **260**, 112434 (2021)
9. Adla, S., Rai, N.K., Karumanchi, S.H., Tripathi, S., Disse, M., Pande, S.: Laboratory calibration and performance evaluation of low-cost capacitive and very low-cost resistive soil moisture sensors. Sensors **20**, 363 (2020)
10. Souza, G., De Faria, B.T., Gomes Alves, R., Lima, F., Aquino, P.T., Soininen, J.-P.: Calibration equation and field test of a capacitive soil moisture sensor. In: Presented at the 2020 IEEE International Workshop on Metrology for Agriculture and Forestry (MetroAgriFor), Trento, Italy, pp. 180–184. IEEE (2020)
11. Kushwaha, Y.K., Panigrahi, R.K., Pandey, A.: Performance analysis of capacitive soil moisture, temperature sensors and their applications at farmer's field. Environ. Monit. Assess. **196**, 793 (2024)
12. Beck, H.E., et al.: Evaluation of 18 satellite- and model-based soil moisture products using in situ measurements from 826 sensors. Hydrol. Earth Syst. Sci. **25**, 17–40 (2021)
13. Plank, S.: Rapid damage assessment by means of multi-temporal SAR – a comprehensive review and outlook to Sentinel-1. Remote Sens. **6**, 4870–4906 (2014)
14. Lei, J., et al.: Prediction of soil organic carbon stock combining Sentinel-1 and Sentinel-2 images in the Zoige Plateau, the northeastern Qinghai-Tibet Plateau. Ecol. Process **13**, 32 (2024)
15. Wang, L., Gao, Y.: Soil moisture retrieval from Sentinel-1 and Sentinel-2 data using ensemble learning over vegetated fields. IEEE J. Sel. Top. Appl. Earth Observ. Remote Sens. **16**, 1802–1814 (2023)
16. Rabiei, S., Jalilvand, E., Tajrishy, M.: A method to estimate surface soil moisture and map the irrigated cropland area using Sentinel-1 and Sentinel-2 data. Sustainability **13**, 11355 (2021)
17. Zhou, T., Geng, Y., Chen, J., Pan, J., Haase, D., Lausch, A.: High-resolution digital mapping of soil organic carbon and soil total nitrogen using DEM derivatives, Sentinel-1 and Sentinel-2 data based on machine learning algorithms. Sci. Total Environ. **729**, 138244 (2020)
18. Land Cover, sc. 1:10.000, Regione Liguria Open Data Geoportal (2019). https://geoportal.regione.liguria.it/catalogo/mappe.html. Accessed 29 January 2025
19. Bovolenta, R., Passalacqua, R., Federici, B., Sguerso, D.: LAMP-LAndslide Monitoring and Predicting for the analysis of landslide susceptibility triggered by rainfall events. In: Landslides and Engineered Slopes. Experience, Theory and Practice, Proceedings of the 12th International Symposium on Landslides, Napoli, Italy, 12–19 June 2016, Volume 1, pp. 517–522. CRC Press, Taylor & Francis Group, London, UK (2016)

20. Bovolenta, R., Iacopino, A., Passalacqua, R., Federici, B.: Field measurements of soil water content at shallow depths for landslide monitoring. Geosciences **10**, 409 (2020)
21. Viaggio, S., Iacopino, A., Bovolenta, R., Federici, B.: Landslide susceptibility assessment: soil moisture monitoring data processed by an automatic procedure in GIS for 3d description of the soil shear strength. Int. Arch. Photogram. Remote Sens. Spatial Inf. Sci. XLVIII-4/W1-2022, 517–523 (2022)
22. MATLAB, Version 9.14 (R2023a). MathWorks, Natick, MA, USA
23. Gitlab Terrasigna Homepage. https://gitlab.terrasigna.com/internal/sadasadam. Accessed 15 August 2024
24. Github Homepage. https://github.com/CS-SI/EODAG. Accessed 15 August 2024
25. Hegazi, E.H., Samak, A.A., Yang, L., Huang, R., Huang, J.: Prediction of soil moisture content from sentinel-2 images using convolutional neural network (CNN). Agronomy **13**, 656 (2023)
26. Manivasagam, V.S., Kaplan, G., Rozenstein, O.: Developing transformation functions for VENμS and Sentinel-2 surface reflectance over Israel. Remote Sens. **11**, 1710 (2019)
27. FORCE Documentation Hompage. https://force-eo.readthedocs.io/en/latest/components/lower-level/level2/param.html#l2-param. Accessed 16 August 2024
28. Chebyshev, P.L.: About mean quantities. Matematicheskii Sbornik **2**, 1–9 (1867)
29. Andrade, J.M., Estévez-Pérez, M.G.: Statistical comparison of the slopes of two regression lines: a tutorial. Anal. Chim. Acta **838**, 1–12 (2014)
30. Bowers, S.A., Hanks, R.J.: Reflection of radiant energy from soils. Soil Sci. **100**(2), 130–138 (1965)
31. Gao, B.-C.: NDWI – a normalized difference water index for remote sensing of vegetation liquid water from space. Remote Sens. Environ. **58**(3), 257–266 (1996)
32. Twomey, S.A., Bohren, C.F., Mergenthaler, J.L.: Reflectance and albedo differences between wet and dry surfaces. Appl. Opt. **25**, 431–437 (1986)
33. Lobell, D.B., Asner, G.P.: Moisture effects on soil reflectance. Soil Sci. Soc. Am. J. **66**, 722–727 (2022)
34. Spectrum Technologies, Inc. Homepage. https://www.specmeters.com/WaterScout-SM100-Soil-Moisture-Sensor-20-Cable. Accessed 16 August 2024

Integrated Geomatics Surveys to Support Hydraulic Studies

Valentina Bonora(✉), Irene Cortesi, Simona Francalanci, Giada Artini, and Lidia Fiorini

Department of Civil and Environmental Engineering, University of Florence, Florence 50139, Italy
{valentina.bonora,irene.cortesi,simona.francalanci,giada.artini, lidia.fiorini}@unifi.it

Abstract. The study and monitoring of river processes have become particularly relevant as climate changes and exceptionally high flood events that ensue make the interactions between sediment transport, water flow interaction, and vegetation more evident and sometimes exacerbated. These characteristics require specific studies, integrating various methods and investigative techniques, and the close collaboration among scientific disciplines. The paper illustrates how 3D data from a geomatic survey can profitably support hydraulic studies by investigating, in particular, the morphology of the banks and the characterisation of the topographical elements that influence their roughness. The results obtained with direct measurements and data extracted from the 3D model on a sample stretch are compared; the study is then extended to an entire bend of the river, thus also considering the generally neglected aspects of curvature.

Keywords: Fluvial environment · Geomatic surveys · River bank roughness · Hydrodynamic models · 3D models · UAV photogrammetry

1 Introduction

River ecosystems are particularly dynamic and represent complex elements of the landscape. They are transitional zones where morphology changes rapidly and is influenced by the presence and type of vegetation, as well as by geological and lithological composition. The dynamics of riverbanks is determined by the complex interactions between hydraulic forcing, sediment transport, and vegetation. The bank retreat process is an essential element in the equilibrium of natural channels as it can lead to loss of land, damage to property and infrastructure, as well as issues related to sediment, nutrient, and contaminant dynamics [1]. The importance of modeling and monitoring fluvial processes is therefore evident, particularly in a scenario characterized by climate change and consequently exceptionally high flood events. These particular characteristics require specific studies and the integration of various methods and investigative techniques, as well as close collaboration among different scientific disciplines. In the

E. Borgogno-Mondino and P. Zamperlin (Eds.): ASITA 2024, CCIS 2463, pp. 20–35, 2025.
https://doi.org/10.1007/978-3-031-91141-5_2

aforementioned context, the synergistic use of heterogeneous data from different fields and formats (such as images, 3D models, GNSS data, etc.) is essential, and a multiscale and multisource approach is advisable. The common georeferencing of all the data considered, both from existing databases and from field surveys, plays a fundamental role by using a common datum [2].

This study illustrates how the contribution of geomatics in fluvial hydraulic research includes various aspects and analyses conducted at different scales. Specifically, in the application to the Ombrone Grossetano River, the focus ranges from territorial aspects related to the dynamics of natural rivers, such as meandering, to the large-scale analyses that investigate in detail a characteristic section of the river, considering its three-dimensional morphology. The first aspect is briefly discussed in the present work, while more attention is focused on developing an automated workflow for the processing of bank parameters, derived from riverbank shape models obtained through digital photogrammetry or laser scanning. The proposed method is compared with manual direct measurement techniques, both in terms of results and time required for data acquisition and processing. In all the contexts considered, the integration of different geomatics techniques is advocated to accelerate processes, improve accuracy, and offer new opportunities for hydraulic studies.

1.1 State of the Art

The emerging digital techniques and technologies provided by Geomatics enable the creation of innovative digital products. This is not limited to the surveying phase but extends to the representation and visualization stages, thus offering a precise and digital description of objects, structures, and territories, while providing robust data analysis and exploration tools. In the last decade, technologies employed in remote sensing have undergone significant improvements. Laser scanners and digital cameras have enhanced the detail and quality of the information, providing high-resolution and high-quality data over increasingly large areas, thanks to the use of drones, aerial platforms, and satellites. In this context, it is orthomosaics, Digital Terrain Models (DTMs), and Digital Surface Models (DSMs), with spatial resolutions that can sometimes reach the centimeter scale, allowing for change detection, thus considering the temporal factor [3] [4].

The Earth's surface is subject to numerous and continuous changes due to a variety of activities performed by natural and anthropogenic agents. Among these, water plays a primary role: it is capable of eroding, transporting, and depositing sediments, thereby modifying the morphology of the terrain [5]. The detection of geomorphological changes using high-resolution remote sensing data is a particularly efficient methodology for monitoring the progression of bank erosion along river courses. For these purposes, the use of aircraft and Unmanned Aerial Systems (UASs) not only allows for the coverage of vast areas in a short time but also enables the collection of high-resolution data under favorable weather conditions, unlike satellites [6]. Finally, it is necessary to consider the number of dimensions to be investigated in studies related to hydraulic bank erosion. The use of pseudo-nadiral images and SfM techniques allows for a 2D or, at most, 2.5D analysis by means of orthomosaics and DEMs. These outputs can be produced quickly and inexpensively and are, in many cases, largely adequate if the aim of monitoring is the planimetric changes in the channel path. On the other hand, however, this significantly limits analyses that intend to consider the three-dimensional morphology of the river, which is considered essential in studies related to riverbanks. Using merely a projection of pseudo-vertical points on a plane (as in the case of 2.5D) may overlook some essential aspects of fluvial erosion [7]. For this reason, this work intends to focus on the 3D component, thus using 3D points models and meshes.

2 Data Collection

The study area was surveyed through two separate data collection campaigns conducted in February and April 2024. In these two surveys, which employed partly different instruments and methodologies, consecutive sections of the Ombrone River (Tuscany, Italy) were acquired (Fig. 1). The key aspect of these data collections lies in the simultaneous execution of geomatics surveys and hydraulic surveys using direct and manual techniques.

2.1 Study Area

The case study analyzed is a sinuous section of the Ombrone Grossetano River near the locality of Camigliano (SI). The reach is characterized by wide meanders, where the high water velocity during flood events makes the design and management of warning and protection measures challenging, increasing its vulnerability. The area is characterized by cohesive banks (i.e., riverbanks composed of compact materials with high resistance to erosion) with significant vegetation cover and a planimetric layout that shows considerable migration. This river section was specifically chosen due to its notable planimetric changes, indicating active bank migration. Particularly, over the last 20 years, the left bank has shifted approximately 150 m eastward, leading to the loss of large portions of arable land. The river sections considered for the conducted surveys are consecutive; both study areas are characterized by high pseudo-vertical banks in the curved sections, resulted from river erosion and bank sliding failures (Fig. 2). During floods, shear stress increases with bank height more rapidly than soil strength, causing the detachment of soil blocks, especially in areas with low cohesion [8]. This process leads to the formation of irregular topographic features, or "bumps", along the riverbank surface (more details in Sect. 3). The banks vary in height from about 2 m to about 5 m. At the time of the survey the water level was low such that it was accessible a strip of land a few metres deep in zone 1 and between 5 m and 30 m in zone 2, thus making it possible to operate not only from above but also in front of the banks. Riparian vegetation is present on the ground at the base of the banks and, particularly in zone 1, on the bank itself. Additionally, the chosen reach is characterized by high banks in the curved sections, resulted from sliding failures of the banks [8].

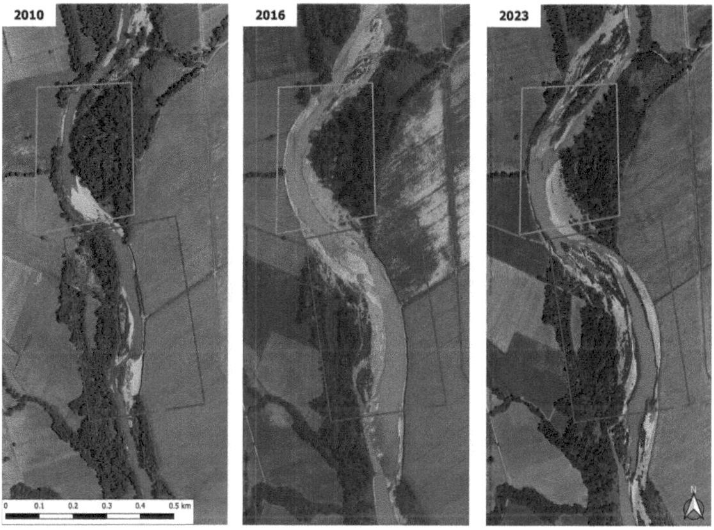

Fig. 1. Evolution of the Ombrone River over 13 years (municipality of Paganico: in the orange box is the study area of February 2024, and in the red box is the study area of April 2024). Maps is from [9] (Color figure online).

2.2 Equipment

The UAS employed comprised an Unmanned Aerial Vehicle (UAV), the DJI Matrice 300 RTK, equipped with the DJI P1 camera. The camera features a full-frame 45 MP CMOS sensor with a 35 mm lens and a 3-axis stabilized gimbal. In both survey campaigns, two types of flights were conducted:

- the first type with the camera oriented nadir, allowing for orthomosaic processing; the flight path has been designed to make strips orthogonal to the direction of the bank, plus some transversal strips to strengthen the photogrammetric block (AGL flight height about 30 m, allowing for a GSD of about 0.5 cm).
- the second type of flight was necessary for acquiring photos of the pseudo-vertical part of the bank. In this case, the flight was conducted with the camera tilted to frame the riverbank; several flight strips were made, and the UAV was operated manually to maintain the distance from the bend bank as constant as possible.

For both surveys, Ground Control Points (GCPs) and Check Points (CPs) were positioned on the ground and on the pseudo-vertical river bank. A topographical control network was defined with a GNSS measurements (by a Trimble R12 receiver); targets not accessible for GNSS measurements, such as those

Fig. 2. View of the right bank in Zone 1 (Survey campaign on February 2024).

located on the bank walls, were determined with a total station (TCR1202 by Leica Geosystems) (Fig. 3).

3 Bank Roughness Assessment

One of the most relevant results carried out through the surveyed 3D data was the estimation of the number and geometry of irregular topographic protrusions, known as "bumps", which form due to the erosion and collapse of the cohesive bank material, as well as the presence of protruding roots and grass clumps [10]. The bumps significantly influence the flow field in the bank region by generating form resistance, which adds to the friction component related to the sediments on the bank surface. The roughness of the bank thus depends on the geometry of the bumps, which determines the distribution of the total shear stress between the form and friction components. This latter component, in turn, determines the rate of bank erosion and consequently the migration of the main channel axis. Specifically, for a given formative discharge, the width of the cross-section is in equilibrium when the friction component of the shear stress on the bank surface corresponds or is below to the critical value associated with the erosion of bank material [11]. Additionally, the shear stresses on the bank and the sediment transport capacity can be influenced by the presence of vegetation, depending on the amount of foliage and the flexibility of the plants during floods [12,13]. An accurate determination of the total and local resistance to flow is essential for an effective prediction of the morphodynamic evolution of river systems [10]. The integration of different geomatics techniques is advocated to accelerate processes, enhance accuracy, and offer new opportunities compared

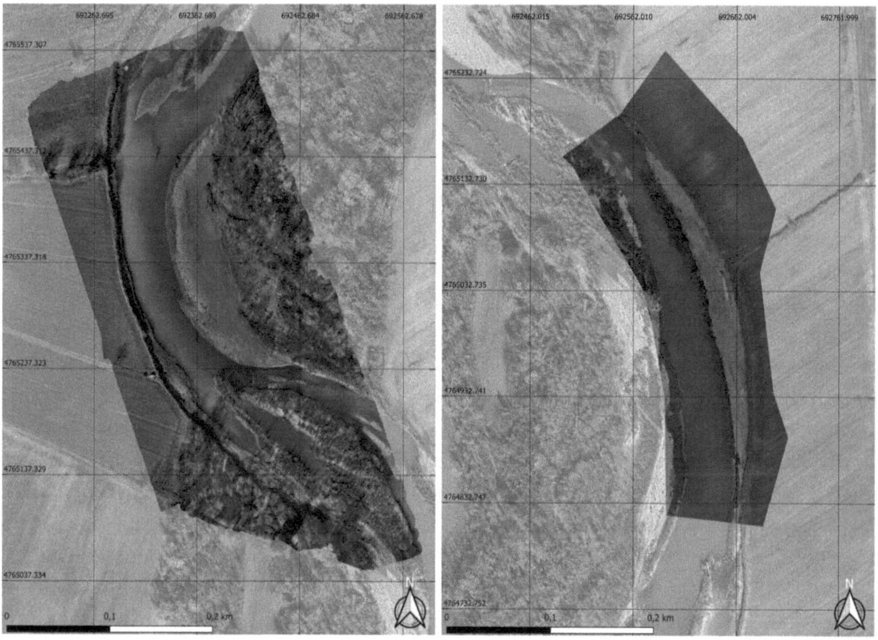

Fig. 3. High-resolution orthomosaics in zone 1 (left) and zone 2 (right).

to traditional direct survey methods used for characterizing riverbank morphology. These conventional methods, as used in [14–16], typically involve stretching a rigid reference of at least ten metres along the bank and measuring, at regular intervals, the deviation of the bank surface from this reference.

3.1 Geometric Parameters for Bumps Modelling

According to [10], most individual topographic elements can be approximated using 2D Gaussian-shaped features. The Gaussian curve provides parameters for modeling natural bump geometry by adjusting the ratio between its streamwise and cross-stream length scales. The parameters include the protrusion height H, the streamwise length scale σ (equivalent to the standard deviation in a Gaussian probability distribution) and the spacing between the crests of the elements, λ (Fig. 4).

In natural banks, the bumps exhibit a wide variety of sizes and shapes, depending on soil cohesion, flow conditions and presence of vegetation. [14] demonstrate that a sequence of bumps with varying sizes and spacing can be represented as a set of uniform, roughness-equivalent Gaussian-shaped topographic elements. The authors also showed that H, σ, and λ can be regularized into a reach-scale average using the 88th percentile:

$$H_{reg} = H_{88}; \quad \sigma_{reg} = \sigma_{88}; \quad \lambda_{88} = 6H_{88} \tag{1}$$

where $H_{reg}, \sigma_{reg}, \lambda_{88}$ are the shape parameters for the equivalent regular sequence, and H_{88}, σ_{88} represent the 88th percentiles of the size distributions for the irregular sequence. The parameters $H_{reg}, \sigma_{reg}, \lambda_{88}$ are frequently employed to evaluate the form drag related to the bumps in studies that assess channel flow resistance and investigate bank erosion.

This study compares the direct measurement method with a workflow that extracts the parameters mentioned above from the 3D metric survey carried out in zone 2, which represents a digital model of the real river. During the second survey campaign, a rigid, 20-meter-long calibrated reference was positioned for the direct measurements, ensuring that it was horizontal using a leveling instrument. The orthogonal distance from the reference to the riverbank was measured every 5 cm using a laser distance meter. This process produced a list of rectangular coordinates, expressed in the reference system shown in orange in Fig. 4. These coordinates must then be transformed into the system highlighted in blue to apply the formulas proposed by Kean and Smith (Eq. 1). This operation is already integrated into the KSGaussfit Matlab code developed by [17], which was employed in this study to analyze the geometry of the bumps, as detailed in the following. Obviously, the curvature of the riverbank is not taken into account for this first test, approximated instead as the chord corresponding to the rigid reference used for the measurements.

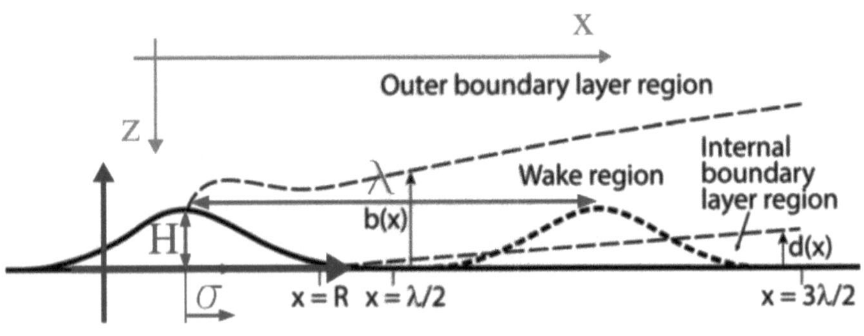

Fig. 4. The coordinates extracted from the surveyed profile are initially expressed in the orange reference system, then transformed into the one highlighted in blue on the image from Kean and Smith [10] (Color figure online) against which their proposed formulas for characterising roughness are expressed. Geometric parameters relevant to model bank roughness are in red: H is the height of the element, σ is the streamwise length of the element and λ is the spacing between the crests of the elements.

3.2 Comparison Between Traditional Measurement Methods and Data from Geomatic 3D Models

The photogrammetric survey enabled the reconstruction of the morphology of the studied riverbank segment with a resolution of about 0.5 cm, exceeding the sampling requirements for estimating the parameters mentioned above. Therefore, scale-dependent effects were disregarded [17,18]. A mesh surface was generated from the point cloud produced by the photogrammetric survey, integrating geometry with photographic texture, and was intersected with a horizontal plane at the same elevation as the one used for measuring the rectangular coordinates through the direct method, allowing the datasets to be comparable (Fig. 5).

Fig. 5. Mesh model of the bank with the profile considered for further elaboration.

First, a test was conducted on the section corresponding to the area where the fixed reference was positioned (Fig. 6). This represents the virtualization of survey operations, which, instead of being performed in the field, were carried out on the 3D model.

The visualization of the rigid reference relative to the profile was done in Rhinoceros [19], using the start and end coordinates of the rod measured in the field with GNSS (Fig. 7). The distances of the segments corresponding to the sampling points were automatically recorded in a text file using an ad hoc developed Python [20] script. The data were then processed with the KSGaussFit Matlab code [17].

Fig. 6. Bumps' direct measurement on the field: rod fixed as a rigid, horizontal reference to the bank (left) and detail of the measuring system (right).

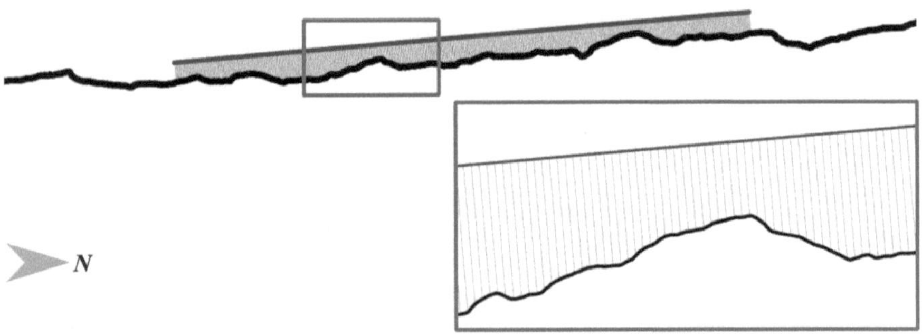

Fig. 7. Profile extracted from the mesh surface and reference corresponding to that used for direct measurements (in red, the rigid reference is 20 m (Color figure online) long). In orange, the distances measured orthogonally every 5 cm.

3.3 Extension of the Method Considering Curvature

The availability of a 3D model of the entire bend, spanning approximately 400 m, prompted the extension of the sampling process to consider the entire cross-section profile. While the area selected for direct measurements did not feature vegetation at the elevation corresponding to the profile under consideration, the situation varies across the entire profile. Thus, sections of the profile corresponding to vegetation were removed and replaced with straight segments. Overall, the removal of vegetation from the profile resulted in a 3% reduction in the data (Table 1).

To optimize subsequent processing, the polyline was resampled by reducing the number of its nodes (Table 1) thanks to the RamerDouglasPeucker algorithm [21], which is widely used for cartographic generalization (Fig. 8).

Table 1. Overview processed profile data on zone 2.

Profile length	418.49 m
Removed sections length (due to vegetation)	12.92 m (3%)
Original profile	66,610 nodes
Resampled profile	2,939 nodes

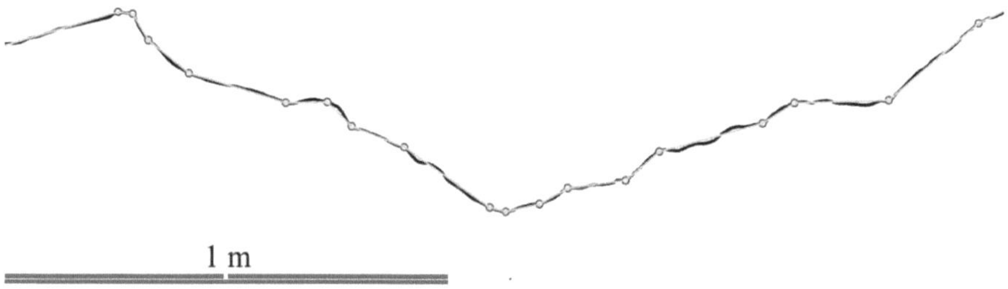

Fig. 8. Detail of the original profile (in black) and the reduced profile (in yellow, with nodes highlighted in red); the maximum deviation between the two polylines is 1 cm (Color figure online).

When studying the profile of the entire bend, the curvature of the watercourse could not, of course, be overlooked. Therefore, a second-degree polynomial was used to interpolate the vertices of the new polyline, and it was assumed as a base curve to "unbent" the bank profile along a straight line. The polynomial radius is much higher than the maximum differences in-depth due to bank roughness, and the target (straight) line-span is equal to the reference (bent) polynomial. Therefore, the geometric transformation does not entail significant scaling along the length, the points from the curve are mapped 1:1 to the straight line, and distances between corresponding vertices remain proportional to their original spacing along the curve (Fig. 9).

Furthermore, the choice of different interpolations for the profile, or various techniques for its development, could yield only slightly different results. As an example, Fig. 10 illustrates the comparison between an interpolating circle and the polynomial described above. Even though the two unbended profiles are slightly rotated concerning each other, their overall lengths correspond, and the topographical deformation paths, albeit with somewhat different deformations in the two cases, allow the bumps to be recognised and characterised equivalently. Further studies in this regard will be developed in the future to quantify the effect of different interpolation criteria and the degree of the curves used.

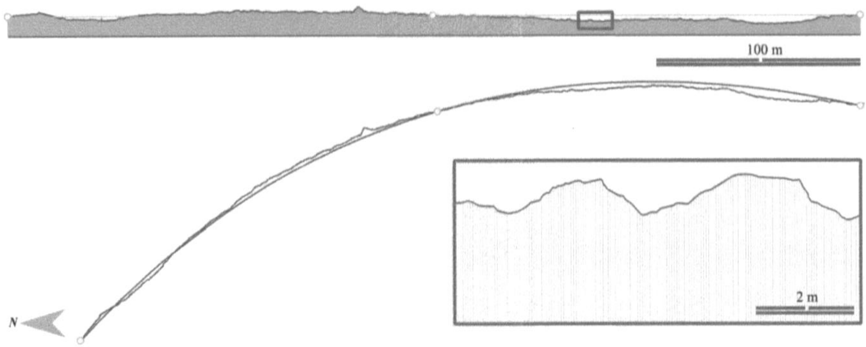

Fig. 9. Resampled section profile (in red) and polynomial interpolating the nodes (in violet), development of the section profile corresponding to the 'unbending' (Color figure online) of the polynomial.

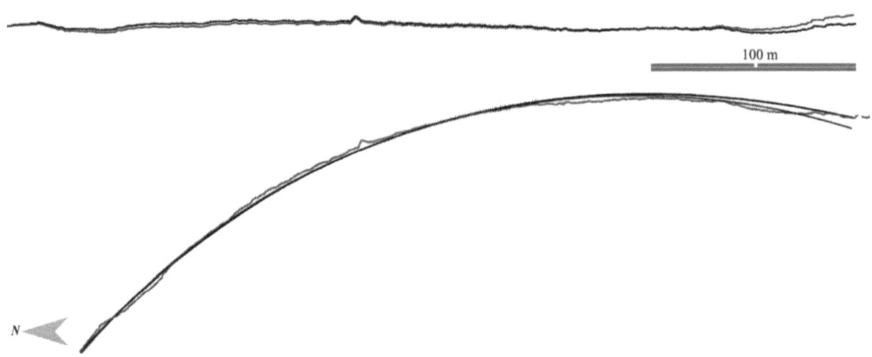

Fig. 10. Comparison of the circumference (in blue) with the polynomial (in violet) interpolating the section profile (in red), and its development. (Color figure online)

3.4 Modelling of Bump Geometry

Similarly to the test conducted on the 20 m rod, rectangular coordinates were automatically extracted in this case, referenced to an X-axis overlapping with the interpolating polynomial and a Z-axis that corresponded, point by point, to the normal direction of the polynomial itself.

To run the KSGaussFit code, it requires a profile data file of two columns, where column 1 is the along-bank distance and column 2 is the distance into the bank from the reference plane. The code involves an interactive definition of the Gaussian curve minima as initial condition for the curve fitting. After the user identified all roughness elements, the code fits Gaussian curve to each "bump" specified by the operator. The protrusion height H, the profile length scale σ, and the spacing λ, are then calculated from each fitted Gaussian bump.

Moreover, the code calculates key metrics for each bump, including the coefficient of determination (R^2) and the root mean squared error (RMSE) for the Gaussian fits. It then cleans the raw statistics by filtering out poor Gaussian fits, such as those with negative or excessively high values. Subsequently, the formulations proposed by [14] (Eq. 1) are applied to the cleaned profiles to regularize the irregular sequences of Gaussian profiles.

The KSGaussFit code was executed using the rectangular coordinates of the profiles obtained from both direct measurements and those extracted from the mesh surface.

Firstly, the 20-m-long profiles, i.e., the one directly measured and the one extracted from the mesh surface at the same location of the direct measurements, were considered (Fig. 7). The two profiles were visually compared, showing good agreement between the directly measured and extracted data (Fig. 11).

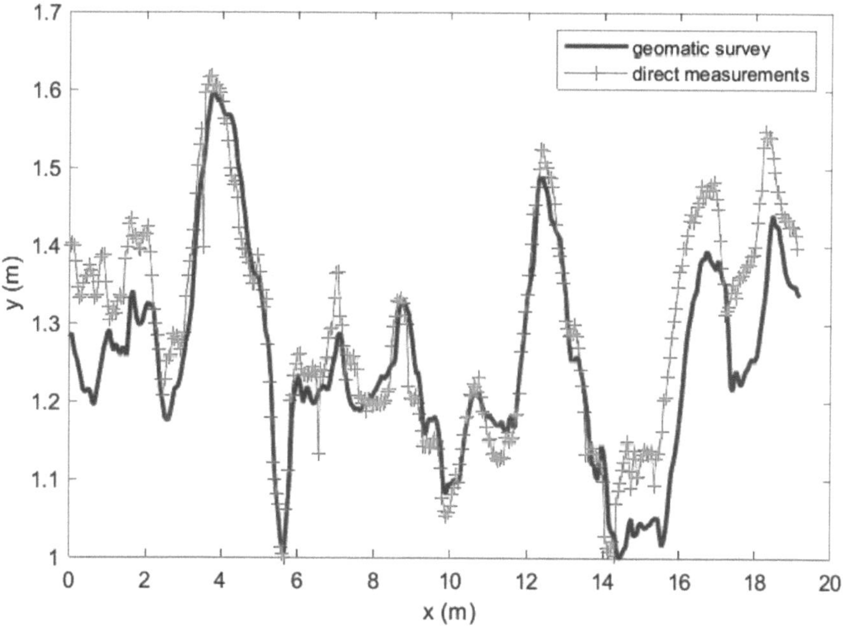

Fig. 11. Comparison between the profile measured directly in the field (in red) and the one extracted from the mesh surface (in blue). (Color figure online)

Each profile was analyzed three times using the KSGaussFit code, varying the selection of minima points and thus the identification of the bumps. Tables 2 and 3 present the results for each run of the code, along with a summary of the analysis, including mean and standard deviation values for both the measured and extracted profiles. Comparing the results, focusing on H_{reg} and σ_{reg} parameters, we observe a notable variability in the obtained values across different attempts. In contrast, the mean values align closely for σ_{reg}, which was

0.17 m for both profiles. However, for H_{reg}, the measured value (9.7 cm) is 2 cm higher than the value obtained from the extracted profiles (7.7 cm). Specifically, the standard deviation for H_{reg} is three times higher in the measured profile than in the extracted one, while for σ_{reg}, the standard deviation of the values obtained from the different attempts is relatively consistent.

Table 2. Summary of Gaussian fit parameters for different profile attempts from the direct measurements survey.

#	H_{reg} (m)	σ_{reg} (m)	λ_{reg} (m)	RMSE	R^2	# Gaussian profiles
1	0.0894	0.1697	0.5363	0.0034	0.7477	34
2	0.0708	0.1527	0.4249	0.0027	0.7610	35
3	0.1329	0.1976	0.7977	0.0030	0.8115	26
Mean	0.0977	0.1733	0.5863	0.0030	0.7734	31.7
St.dev.	0.0319	0.0227	0.1914	0.0004	0.0337	4.93

Table 3. Summary of Gaussian fit parameters for different profile attempts extracted from the digital model.

#	H_{reg} [m]	σ_{reg} [m]	λ_{reg} [m]	RMSE	R^2	# Gaussian profiles
1	0.0923	0.1502	0.5538	0.0020	0.8030	30
2	0.0689	0.1678	0.4131	0.0020	0.8106	34
3	0.0853	0.2018	0.5115	0.0021	0.7604	35
Mean	0.0771	0.1733	0.4928	0.0020	0.7913	33
St.dev.	0.0116	0.0262	0.0722	0.0001	0.0271	2.6

Moreover, it is important to note that the number of detected bumps may impact the final results. To include this aspect in the analysis, a 400-meter-long profile extracted from the mesh surface, referenced to the second-degree polynomial polyline, was used as input for the KSGaussFit code. The results obtained are shown in Table 4. Four different attempts were conducted in this case, yielding a mean H_{reg} value very similar to that obtained from direct measurements (see Table 2). In contrast, the resulting σ_{reg} value is nearly double then that obtained from both the measured and extracted profile analyses.

Thus, the comparison of results obtained from the 20-meter-long profile and the 400-meter-long profile indicates that the length of the profile and thus the number of detected bumps significantly influence the final results, particularly with regard to the σ_{reg} parameter.

Table 4. Summary of Gaussian fit parameters for the 400-m-long profile.

#	H_{reg} (m)	σ_{reg} (m)	λ_{reg} (m)	RMSE	R^2	# Gaussian profiles
1	0.0915	0.2829	0.5488	0.0030	0.7463	515
2	0.0973	0.3391	0.5836	0.0030	0.7260	469
3	0.0891	0.2774	0.5346	0.0028	0.7513	543
4	0.0963	0.3372	0.5776	0.0030	0.7275	468
Mean	0.0935	0.3092	0.5612	0.0030	0.7378	498.7
St.Dev.	0.0039	0.0335	0.0233	0.0001	0.0129	36.7

4 Conclusion and Perspectives

In this work, we discussed in detail the application of an integrated geomatics survey to the characterization of fluvial bank parameters. The accurate estimate of bump geometry is fundamental for predicting the contribution of bank form drag and friction resistance on the flow velocity field, which is one of the main controlling factor in shaping the morphology of river meander. We therefore quantified the error measurements caused by the different survey techniques, and we demonstrated the efficacy and effectiveness of the results obtained with the geomatic survey compared to the direct measurements of bank roughness. We have therefore proposed a method that allows us to go beyond the limits of direct measurement sampling, which is unlikely to cover an extension of more than ten metres and, therefore, depending on the geometric characteristics of the bumps present, may not be statistically significant. Several aspects can be considered in drawing future perspectives of this work. First of all, considering the robustness of the analysis of the bank parameters, it would be useful to define a minimum number of bumps, i.e., a threshold, to ensure a statistically representative series of Gaussian profiles that define the reach-averaged form drag of the bank surface. Establishing this threshold would significantly reduce operator bias, thereby increasing the reliability of the results. Additionally, setting a threshold could streamline the analysis, minimizing the time and effort spent on developing a digital model that spans extensive distances. Another related aspect is the arbitrary selection of minima points, carried out by the user in the KSGaussFit code, which can significantly affect the final results: the selection of minima points is user-sensitive and leads to variability in the analysis of bank roughness elements. Finally, the proposed approach extracts the geometric parameters from a 3D shape model of the entire bank, but for the time being, a constant height section profile is used for modelling. The depth of the protrusions, on the other hand, could decrease from the top to the bank toe, thus requiring the bank to be sampled at different heights, a possibility offered by the availability of a 3D model.

Another aspect that deserves attention is the time and resource effort required for classical survey techniques over the past decades: due to this limitation in the modelling approach proposed by Kean and Smith, the bank roughness is considered time-invariant throughout the erosion process, while instead, it evolves and changes in time. In this direction, new advanced technologies coming from the geomatic field make it possible to record 3D data in an ever faster and more cost-effective manner: in addition to UAS systems, which allow photogrammetric surveys with high productivity, SLAM systems are becoming more widespread, providing resolution and accuracy compatible with those required for this type of study, as well as considerable operational flexibility. Moreover, integrating GNSS RTK receivers also allows georeferencing of the survey, realising the possibility of rapid change detection assessments and allowing for low-budget repetitions of surveys over time and, therefore, detailed change detection analysis.

Acknowledgments. The authors would like to give a special thank to Fabiana Di Ciaccio, Nicola Marchiani, Adele Meucci, and Erica Isabella Parisi who participated in the survey campaigns. Filippo Fiaschi skillfully piloted the UAS for the photogrammetric survey. The instruments are from the Geco Laboratory of the Department of Civil and Environmental Engineering of the University of Florence (headed by Prof. Grazia Tucci). This research fell within the framework of the SECURE project "Safety Equilibrium Conditions for rivers UndeR changing climatEs", funded by the European Union "Next Generation EU" (M4.C2.1.1).

References

1. Nardi, L., Campo, L., Rinaldi, M.: Quantification of riverbank erosion and application in risk analysis. Nat. Hazards **69**, 869–887 (2013)
2. Aminti, P., Bonora, V., Corongiu, M., Mugnai, F., Parisi, E.I., Tucci, G.: Geomatics techniques for the 3d survey of the Arno river to support hydraulic studies. In: IOP Conference Series: Materials Science and Engineering, vol. 949, p. 012104. IOP Publishing (2020)
3. Tarolli, P., Sofia, G., Dalla Fontana, G.: Geomorphic features extraction from high-resolution topography: landslide crowns and bank erosion. Nat. Hazards **61**, 65–83 (2012)
4. Hamshaw, S.D., Engel, T., Rizzo, D.M., O'Neil-Dunne, J., Dewoolkar, M.M.: Application of unmanned aircraft system (UAS) for monitoring bank erosion along river corridors. Geomatics, Natural Hazards and Risk (2019)
5. Pyle, C., Richards, K., Chandler, J.: Digital photogrammetric monitoring of river bank erosion. Photogram. Rec. **15**(89), 753–764 (1997)
6. Aher, S.P., Bairagi, S.I., Deshmukh, P.P., Gaikwad, R.D.: River change detection and bank erosion identification using topographical and remote sensing data. Int. J. Appl. Inf. Syst. **2**(3), 1–7 (2012)
7. Schwanghart, W., Scherler, D.: Bumps in river profiles: uncertainty assessment and smoothing using quantile regression techniques. Earth Surf. Dyn. **5**(4), 821–839 (2017)
8. Zhao, K., et al.: A review on bank retreat: mechanisms, observations, and modeling. Rev. Geophys. **60**(2), e2021RG000761 (2022). https://doi.org/10.1029/2021RG000761
9. Toscana, R.: Geoscopio wms (2024). https://www.regione.toscana.it/-/geoscopio-wms. Accessed 30 Sept 2024

10. Kean, J.W., Smith, J.D.: Form drag in rivers due to small-scale natural topographic features: 1. regular sequences. J. Geophys. Res. Earth Surface **111**(F4), 1–13 (2006)
11. Francalanci, S., Lanzoni, S., Solari, L., Papanicolaou, A.: Equilibrium cross section of river channels with cohesive erodible banks. J. Geophys. Res. Earth Surface **125**(1), e2019JF005286 (2020)
12. Bywater-Reyes, S., Diehl, R.M., Wilcox, A.C., Stella, J.C., Kui, L.: A green new balance: interactions among riparian vegetation plant traits and morphodynamics in alluvial rivers. Earth Surf. Proc. Land. **47**(10), 2410–2436 (2022)
13. Caroppi, G., et al.: Flow and wake characteristics associated with riparian vegetation patches: results from field-scale experiments. Hydrol. Process. **36**(2), e14506 (2022)
14. Kean, J.W., Smith, J.D.: Form drag in rivers due to small-scale natural topographic features: 2. irregular sequences. J. Geophys. Res. Earth Surface **111**(F4), 1–13 (2006)
15. Darby, S., et al.: A physically based model to predict hydraulic erosion of fine-grained riverbanks: the role of form roughness in limiting erosion. J. Geophys. Res. **115**, 1–20 (2010).https://doi.org/10.1029/2010JF001708
16. Nardi, L., Scozzafava, R.A., Darby, S., Rinaldi, M., Solari, L., et al.: Estimation of near-bank shear stresses for modelling bank erosion in a meander bend. In: GEOPHYSICAL RESEARCH ABSTRACTS. vol. 10 (2008)
17. Leyland, J., Darby, S.E., Teruggi, L., Rinaldi, M., Ostuni, D.: A self-limiting bank erosion mechanism? Inferring temporal variations in bank form and skin drag from high resolution topographic data. Earth Surf. Proc. Land. **40**(12), 1600–1615 (2015)
18. Sanner, A., Nöhring, W.G., Thimons, L.A., Jacobs, T.D., Pastewka, L.: Scale-dependent roughness parameters for topography analysis. Appl. Surface Sci. Adv. **7**, 100190 (2022)
19. Associates, R.M..: Rhinoceros 3d (nd). https://www.rhino3d.com/it/. Accessed 23 Sept 2024
20. Foundation, P.S.: Python programming language (nd). https://www.python.org/. Accessed 23 Sept 2024
21. Douglas, D.H., Peucker, T.K.: Algorithms for the reduction of the number of points required to represent a digitized line or its caricature. Cartographica: Int. J. Geogr. Inf. Geovisual. **10**(2), 112–122 (1973)

Mapping Burned Areas with Optical and Sentinel-1 Synthetic Aperture Radar Data

Alessandro Gatti[1](✉), Marco Manzoni[1], Andrea Monti-Guarnieri[1], Giovanna Sona[2], Giovanna Venuti[2], and Daniela Stroppiana[3]

[1] Politecnico di Milano, Dipartimento di Elettronica, Informazione e Bioingegneria (DEIB), Milano, Italy
alessandro.gatti20@gmail.com

[2] Politecnico di Milano, Dipartimento di Ingegneria Civile e Ambientale (DICA), Milano, Italy

[3] Consiglio Nazionale delle Ricerche – Istituto per il Rilevamento Elettromagnetico dell'Ambiente (CNR-IREA), Milano, Italy
stroppiana.d@irea.cnr.it

Abstract. This work focuses on monitoring wildfires using remote sensing and time series change detection of multi-spectral and Synthetic Aperture Radar (SAR) data. Remote sensing can offer detailed information on fire conditions and risks paired with frequent revisit times. Multispectral satellites, like Landsat and Sentinel-2 (S-2), data have been, and still are, widely used in Earth Observation thanks to the wide range of wavelengths and the frequent rate of observation. On the other hand, Sentinel-1 (S-1) SAR data offers the advantage of independence from solar illumination and weather conditions. This work focuses on generating and classifying time series of Landsat and Sentinel-2 data into burned/unburned areas using a random forest (RF) algorithm. Python and Google Earth Engine (GEE) tools were developed to automate the extraction of fire reference perimeters from multi-spectral images and merging the results to form a burned area dataset, while providing support to the user.

S-2 burned area perimeters over the Sahel (Africa) and Amazon (South America) regions were used to assess the sensitivity to burned surfaces of S-1 SAR data pre- and post-fire backscatter in the VV and VH polarizations. Statistical tests and data visualization were used to assess the change in intensity of the backscatter signal (γ^0) after a fire event. The changes in the distribution of γ^0 values were found significant for the majority of the test cases, and more visible in the VH polarization mode. Classification tests were conducted using the S-1 backscatter values and dedicated radar indices to identify the occurrence of fires, considering different time configurations. Longer temporal baselines of S-1 acquisitions were found to produce more accurate results in detection in high fire activity regions. Although S-1 SAR shows promise in wildfire detection, challenges remain in interpreting radar returns. Further research could explore other polarization methods and longer temporal baselines to enhance accuracy in different biomes.

Keywords: Earth Observation · Synthetic Aperture Radar · Copernicus

---

The original version of the chapter has been revised. Correct formula was updated. A correction to this chapter can be found at https://doi.org/10.1007/978-3-031-91141-5_29

E. Borgogno-Mondino and P. Zamperlin (Eds.): ASITA 2024, CCIS 2463, pp. 36–45, 2025.
https://doi.org/10.1007/978-3-031-91141-5_3

1 Introduction

The objective of this work is monitoring wildfires using remote sensing techniques and time series classification of multi-spectral and SAR data. In the context of climate change, a trend regarding the increase in occurrences and intensity of this phenomenon has been observed due to increasing air temperatures and prolonged droughts. This results in larger emission of greenhouse gases (25–35% globally) and other pollutants in the air [1], as well as local losses of vegetation. Remote sensing makes it possible to extract information about pre-, during and post-fire conditions, climate conditions, fuel characteristics and fire risk, as well as fire impacts at both local and large scales (up to global coverage). Thanks to the short revisit time of Copernicus Sentinel missions, this information can be captured at regular intervals. This project makes use of multispectral satellite images (Landsat 5, 8 and Sentinel-2) as well as SAR (Synthetic Aperture Radar) satellite data (Sentinel-1). The advantage of radar over optical measurements lies in the capacity of the radar beams to pass through the atmosphere and obtain images independently from cloud presence and light condition.

This work has been partially developed within the framework of the FireCCI project [2] of the European Space Agency (ESA) with the goal of creating a burned area dataset derived from multi spectral data to validate FireCCI Burned Area (BA) products. To accomplish this, time series of Landsat 5 (L5), Landsat 8 (L8) and Sentinel-2 images are generated and classified into burned/unburned areas with a random forest (RF) algorithm to build the reference data for validating FireCCI BA products. Scripts were coded in Python and Google Earth Engine (GEE) [3] to automize procedures for generating time series and for extracting fire reference perimeters. First, a Python script was created to analyze the metadata of the S-2 and L5, L8 archives to extract the best dates of acquisition of the images suited cloud cover for temporal analysis. Then, a GEE application was developed to extract burned areas perimeters from consecutive pairs of optical images and to combine the results into single maps/datasets. A Random Forest (RF) algorithm was implemented to identify areas burned between two dates (pre-fire and post-fire). The fire reference perimeters generated from multispectral images were used to analyze the signature of S-1 in the areas identified as burned, where the S-1 backscatter was extracted for the VV and VH antenna polarization and categorized by the burned severity. Finally, a change detection algorithm was tested using only S-1 SAR VV and VH backscatter and indices as input information for assessing the performance of S-1 in detecting the areas affected by fires.

The analysis was focused on two study regions located in Africa (Sahel) and South America (Amazonia).

2 Data

Over the two regions of interest in Sahel (Africa) and Amazonia (South America), 100kmx100km tiles were selected across different biomes and fire regimes (low and high amount of area burned). These tiles were part of the validation sites selected for the FireCCI project. The selection of the tiles to be classified to extract fire reference perimeters was carried out with a stratified random sampling approach. For each tile, time series used consist of multispectral optical images from Sentinel-2 and Landsat 5 and 8 (R, G, B, NIR, SWIR1, SWIR2 reflectance bands), with resolution ranging from 10 to 30 m; the SCL (Scene Classification Layer) and QA_PIXEL bands were retained for Sentinel-2 and Landsat, respectively, for identifying cloud pixels. Each tile time series represents a "long unit": series of acquisitions close in time (maximum time interval 16 days) and with low cloud coverage (max 15% for a single image and max 30% total for the long unit). Each pair of successive acquisitions inside a long unit is here denoted as a "short unit" (Fig. 1).

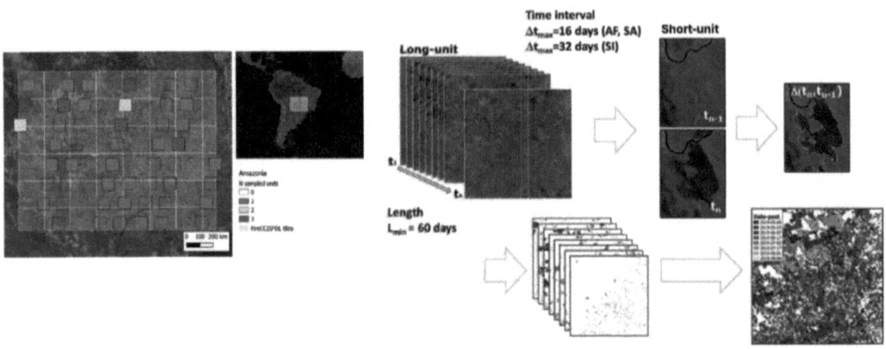

Fig. 1. (Left) sampled tiles over South America. (Right) long units' creation criteria, example of the classified burned area between the pre-date (t_{n-1}) and post-date (t_n) of a short unit and example of a long unit classification (all burned polygons between the first and last images of the unit).

Over the same regions, S-1 SAR GRD (Ground Range Detected) products at C-band 5.405 GHz (cross-polarized vertical transmit-horizontal receive VH, co-polarized vertical transmit-vertical receive VV, *incidence_angle_from_ellipsoid* bands) and 10 m spatial resolution were used. C-band has a wavelength of ~5.5 cm which allows the beam to penetrate the forest canopy, while retaining sensitivity to small vegetation elements. These images, selected at the beginning and end of each short unit time span, were used for analyzing the burned signal and conducting test classifications. Table 1 shows the sites and series selected and processed for this work in the two study regions:

Table 1. Long units tested

ID (pathrow)	Sensing period S-2 (year 2019)	Region	Characteristics
176053 1	09/01 – 09/05	Sahel	Tropical Savanna, high fire activity
176053 2	21/10 – 30/12	Sahel	""
168056	09/01 – 20/03	Sahel	Tropical forest, high fire activity
173051	18/01 – 02/06	Sahel	Tropical savanna, low fire activity
227073	31/07 – 09/10	Amazonia	Tropical rainforest

3 Methods and Results

3.1 The GEE Application and FireCCI Burned Areas Validation

Initially, a Python script was developed to extract the available acquisition dates for the generation of the short and long units of S-2 images to use for the extraction of the burned areas; the Python script reads the image product metadata of the satellite missions (date of images and cloud coverage percentage) to retain only dates that satisfy the conditions on maximum cloud cover and are maximum 16 days apart. The script writes the results to a file that is successively imported into Google Earth Engine for querying the S-2 GEE catalogue of images. In GEE, an application was developed to use the imported image dates for building the S-2 collection for each tile and to classify pixels into burned or unburned with a supervised random forest algorithm applied to pairs of pre- and post-fire images. A graphical user interface was created for better interaction with the user, and pre and post-fire images of each pair are displayed in a false RGB composite to highlight burned surfaces. Users can control the application from the control panel and interact with images in the map panel, where polygons can be drawn to collect training data for the algorithm. At each step a short unit (image pair) is loaded and the application makes available two empty layers for the training to be filled, and it calculates the NDVI (Normalized Difference Vegetation Index), NBR (Normalized Burn Ratio) and NBR2 indices to be used as input features in the classification. MODIS active fires (from the Fire Information for Resource Management System, FIRMS, at 1 km resolution included in the GEE catalog) between the two dates of the short unit can also be loaded to aid the training selection. The workflow that the user commands through the control panel is illustrated in Fig. 2.

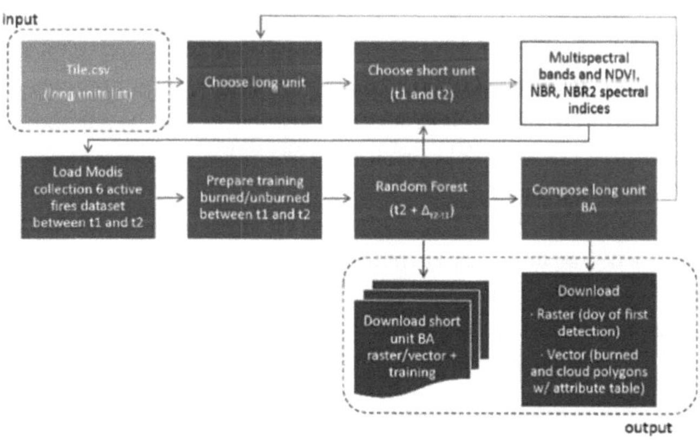

Fig. 2. Workflow of the application.

To keep track, the data used and the results for each step are also displayed in a dedicated console panel above the map.

Within the classification module, a Random Forest algorithm comprising 100 decision trees combined with a thresholding technique for binary classification into burned/unburned areas, is used. Otsu's method of thresholding is applied for optimally separating "probably" burned from "probably" non-burned areas based on the variance of the burned probability sample's histogram. Once classification is performed, the user can choose one of the following alternatives: i) export the results (as shapefiles/GeoTIFF), ii) move to the next short unit, iii) modify the training and re-classify the same short unit, iv) merge and export the merged results (shapefiles/GeoTIFF). A download option for storing the output classification of each short unit, as well as the current cloud cover and the training layers, is made available in the tasks panel (*"Export short BA & training"*). When more than one short unit belonging to the same time series is classified, the user can select *"Export long BA"* to create a synthetic raster map with the classified layers up to the last processed short unit. The exported rasters of burned pixels contain the date of the year (doy) of burned detection, while clouds are represented with a negative value; the vector layer consists of the burned and cloud polygons (with fields: *predate, postdate, category, pathrow, area*). The results will resemble the format of the bottom right image in Fig. 1. Since merging spatial data can be resource-intensive, an ancillary Python script was also developed to help merge the vectorized results of the short unit classifications belonging to the same long unit. The GEE application has been developed for both Sentinel-2 and Landsat 5/8 data processing as part of the validation activities of the FireCCI project; however, in this work only S-2 perimeters limited to 2019 (Table 1) were exploited for the analysis of S-1 backscatter. In summary, five long units burned area maps were produced in this work from the four test tiles, while more than one hundred were generated for the period 1990–2019 and relying also on Landsat imagery using the application developed in this work: these perimeters were exploited for the validation of FireCCI BA products.

3.2 Analysis of S-1 SAR

The S-2 fire perimeters obtained as described above were exploited in GEE to be used as reference for extracting S-1 backscatter; since the classification approach implemented in the GEE application is highly supervised, these burns can be assumed to be highly reliable. The Sentinel-1 SAR GRD product in the GEE catalogue was pre-processed and extracted to obtain C-band γ^0 returns in the areas affected by fires and depicted in S-2 classification. Since the goal was to monitor changes in S-1 backscatter when a fire occurs, S-1 images before and after each fire event were selected (using the available S-1 images closest to S-2 dates, usually separated by a few days). The σ^0 dataset in the Earth Engine Catalogue is provided with thermal noise, radiometric and terrain correction. We further applied Lee filter to reduce the speckle noise and terrain flattening to remove the beam geometry dependence (defined by the incidence angle ϑ parameter that is included as an additional band at 20 km resolution) with a custom-made GEE script, then the resulting backscatter

$$\gamma^0 = \sigma^0/\cos(\vartheta) \tag{1}$$

was primarily affected by the type, geometry, orientation of the target, the surface roughness and moisture content [4].

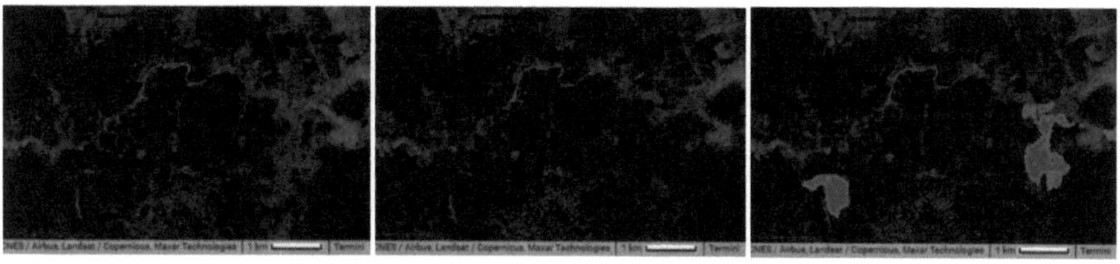

Fig. 3. SAR backscatter detail (VH band) showing pre-fire (left), post-fire (middle) and post-fire overlayed with S-2 burned polygons (right).

From the S-2 reference fire polygons derived from long unit classifications, only polygons larger than 1 ha were retained; for these polygons, mean and standard deviation, as well as percentiles, were extracted for the cross-polarization VH and co-polarization VV S-1 bands for pre and post-fire dates. Moreover, the post-fire dataset was split into burn severity classes obtained from the difference between pre- and post-fire NBR (*deltaNBR*) from S-2 bands [5]. Burned areas generally show a reduction in radar signal backscatter (Fig. 4), this is visualized as a darker area in the cleaned image (Fig. 3).

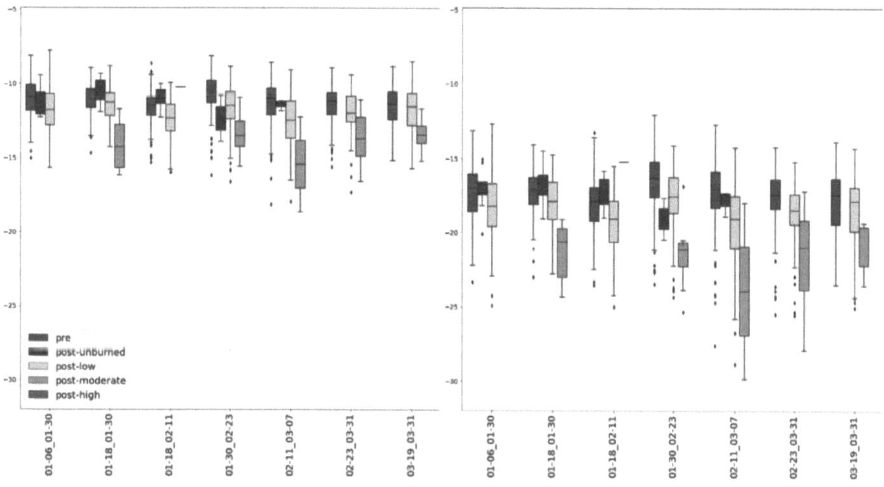

Fig. 4. The distribution of the backscatter (dB) in boxplot for the pre-fire and post-fire signal, for a portion of the short units in a single long unit. VV band (left) and VH band (right), on the same scale.

To test the statistical significance of the difference between burned and unburned γ^0 values, we applied a non-parametric paired Wilcoxon signed-rank test, equivalent to a paired t-test, after confirming that the dataset was not normally distributed [6]. This test was applied for each polarization and for each of the five long units. In nine out of the 10 cases, the difference between burned and unburned signal was statistically significant thus suggesting that S-1 SAR backscatter could be used as input feature to classify burned areas. The analysis stratified by burn severity revealed that the average decrease in S-1 γ^0 power (dB) ($\Delta\gamma^0$) for the VH band was of about 1.5 for low burn severity areas and $\Delta\gamma^0 \sim 3.79$ for moderate severity, while for the VV band -0.59 for low and -1.94 for moderate. Overall results are synthetized in Fig. 5.

long unit	low	moderate	high	unburned	regrowth
176053 - first	1120	148	0	36	0
176053 - second	1350	824	1	107	1
168056	5097	410	0	180	1
173051	75	364	1	2	0
227073	218	322	1	4	0

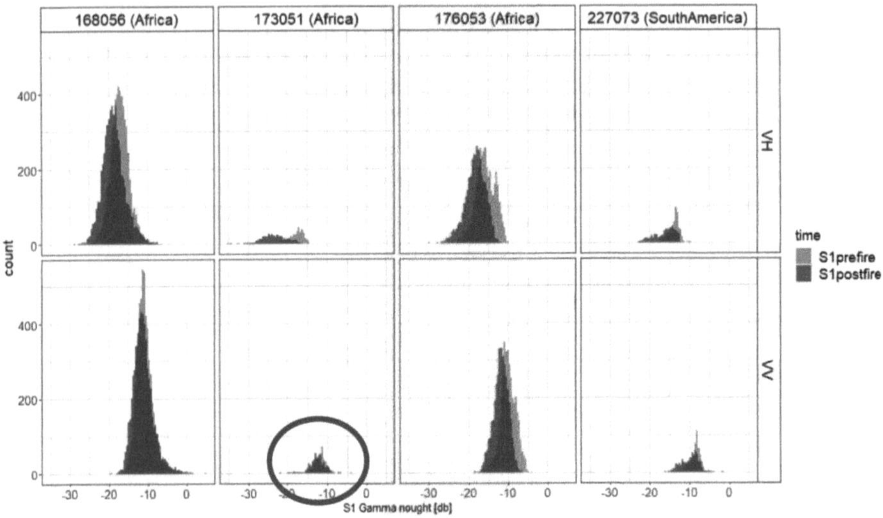

Fig. 5. (Top) Count of burned area polygons analyzed. (Bottom) Total pre and postfire distribution of the S-1 backscatter samples [dB]. Circled the only case of the non-significant population variation.

The classification tests, to verify the ability to identify the burned changes based solely on S-1 SAR backscatter, were executed using Random Forest (RF) algorithm. The post-fire γ^0 as well as the following indices, calculated from the linear values of the backscatter bands, were used as input features to the classification:

- VV and VH Radar Burn Ratio

$$RBR = \frac{\gamma^0_{postfire}}{\gamma^0_{prefire}} \tag{2}$$

- VV and VH Radar Burn Difference

$$RBD = \gamma^0_{postfire} - \gamma^0_{prefire} \tag{3}$$

- Delta Radar Vegetation Index [7]

$$\Delta RVI = \left(\frac{4 \cdot \gamma^0_{VH}}{\gamma^0_{VV} + \gamma^0_{VH}} \right)_{postfire} - \left(\frac{4 \cdot \gamma^0_{VH}}{\gamma^0_{VV} + \gamma^0_{VH}} \right)_{prefire} \tag{4}$$

For unburned surfaces, where conditions typically remain stable, the RBD and ΔRVI indices are expected to follow a normal distribution with zero mean, while fire events skew towards negative values ($\gamma^0{}_{prefire} > \gamma^0{}_{postfire}$). The RBR index is expected to be close to 1 for unburned, and leaning more towards 0 for burned areas. An example of the distribution of these indices across burned regions, after detected fire events, and unburned regions is shown in Fig. 6. The rate of change detected, for both pre- and post-fire backscatter values (Fig. 5.) and the indices to detect burning, are influenced by the terrain type, the polarization and the severity of the fires, which make defining thresholds for separating the distributions a challenging task.

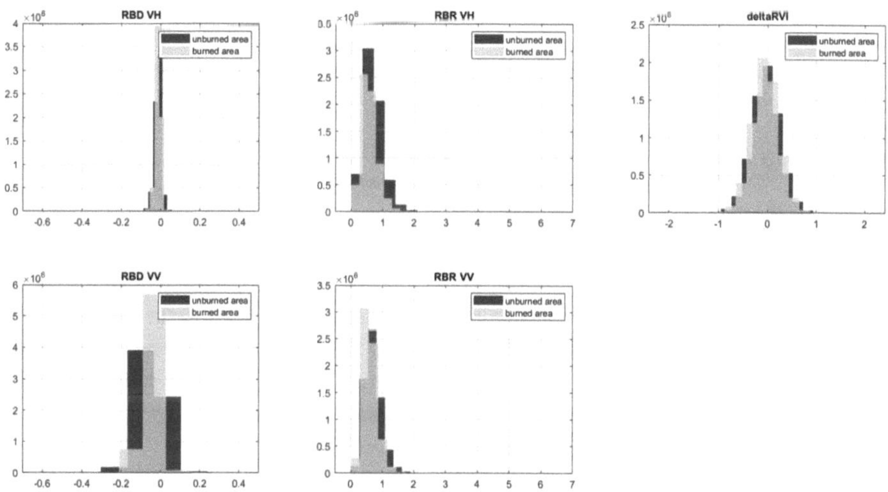

Fig. 6. Histograms of the radar burned indices in burned and unburned areas for a single S-1 pair (moderate and low burn severity).

Validation of the S-1 classifications was carried out with respect to the S-2 derived burned area maps using the confusion matrices. Burned detection was conducted using all S-1 image pairs, mainly formed by 12 days interval, and combining the results into a synthetic long unit map; a procedure similar to the one applied to S-2. The results in terms of accuracy metrics (Table 2) show that SAR can identify burned areas to a certain extent, however, signal noise and other sources of uncertainty (such as drop in backscatter due to soil moisture changes unrelated to fires, like near water flows) need to be addressed.

Table 2. Validation of the burned areas classifications tests performed on SAR

Long unit	Commission	Omission	Dice coefficient
176053 1	0.85	0.74	0.18
176053 2	0.39	0.85	0.24
168056	0.86	0.82	0.16
173051	0.49	0.5	0.5
227073	0.55	0.4	0.51

The ranking of the features in the RF classifier, based on the Gini Index over the RF nodes, showed an overall higher importance for VV values/indices, which are more sensitive to change in soil moisture content and surface roughness after fires compared to the VH counterparts, which in turn are more sensitive to volumetric scattering changes in the vegetation geometry [8]. This result aligns with the lower found importance of ΔRVI, as the sites are mostly characterized by grasslands/low vegetation.

4 Conclusions

In this work, a GEE application and ancillary Py scripts were developed to generate burned area maps from time series of automatically retrieved Sentinel-2 and Landsat satellite images. This work has contributed to the ESA FireCCI project since the application was further used to generate the reference fire perimeters dataset used by CNR IREA for validation of the project's BA products. The GEE application is compatible with Sentinel-2 and Landsat 5 and 8 and offers an interface for easier selection of the input image data and for the training phase; the automation and integration with Python makes this process scalable and reproducible.

Moreover, the analysis of S-1 SAR burned area signals and the test classification into burned/unburned areas conducted in this work represent an important step for assessing the contribution of SAR data to burned area mapping, especially in regions with persistent cloud cover (such as in the case of boreal regions). The SAR results show that omission error can be relevant (OE $>$ 50%) in most of the test cases of this study; S-1 SAR images for the identification of burned areas could be best suited for integration or to fill gaps in the optical data due to climate condition, but further research is still needed to develop efficient SAR-based algorithms. The main challenges lie in the complex nature of the radar returns, making it difficult to interpret the signals. For this reason, an extensive work of data pre-processing in the returns is needed. The main sources of error in fire detection that need to be addressed are not significant backscatter changes, speckle noise, soil moisture variation (especially near water), and the creation of the training.

This topic has potential be studied and expanded more, for example the use of both or either polarization methods and longer temporal baselines could be investigated, addressing different biomes/fire regimes, as well as employing the full complex returns in the context of interferometry. The use of different machine learning algorithms and further calibration with ground truth data could also provide insight in defining threshold values for change detection and developing new fire-specific SAR indices that account for both post-fire changes in vegetation and surface roughness.

Acknowledgments. The authors have no competing interests to declare that are relevant to the content of this article.

References

1. Van der Werf, et al.: Global fire emissions and the contribution of deforestation, savanna, forest, agricultural, and peat fires (1997–2009). Atmos. Chem. Phys. **10**, 11707–11735 (2010), https://doi.org/10.5194/acp-10-11707-2010
2. ESA Climate Office Web Page: https://climate.esa.int/en/projects/fire/
3. Earth Engine Homepage: https://earthengine.google.com/
4. Tanase, M., de la Riva, J., Santoro, M., Perez-Cabello, F., Kasischke, E.: Sensitivity of SAR data to post-fire forest regrowth in Mediterranean and boreal forests (2010). https://geog.umd.edu/sites/geog.umd.edu/files/pubs/Tanase%20RSE%202011.pdf
5. Keeley, J.E.: Fire intensity, fire severity and burn severity: a brief review and suggested usage. Int. J. Wildland Fire **18**(1), 116–126 (2009)
6. Ghasemi, A., Zahediasl, S.: Normality tests for statistical analysis: a guide for non-statisticians. Int. J. Endocrinol. Metab. **10**(2), 486–489 (2012). https://doi.org/10.5812/ijem.3505
7. Hosseini, M., Lim, S.: Burned area detection using Sentinel-1 SAR data: a case study of Kangaroo Island, South Australia. Appl. Geogr. **151**, 102854 (2023).https://doi.org/10.1016/j.apgeog.2022.102854
8. Belenguer-Plomer, M.A., Chuvieco, E., Tanase, M.A.: Temporal decorrelation of C-band backscatter coefficient in Mediterranean burned areas. Remote Sens. **11**, 2661 (2019). https://doi.org/10.3390/rs11222661

InSAR EGMS for Wide-Area Assessment of Extreme Rainfall-Related Modifications of Ground-Deformation Patterns: The Case of Vaia Rainstorm

Rasoul Eskandari(✉) and Marco Scaioni

Department of Architecture, Built Environment and Construction Engineering, Politecnico di Milano, via Ponzio 31, 20133 Milano, Italy
{rasoul.eskandari,marco.scaioni}@polimi.it

Abstract. Extreme rainfalls may have considerable impacts on the dynamics of deformations over an area, besides the catastrophic direct damages by flooding phenomena, etc. This study presents a framework for leveraging Copernicus European Ground Motion Service (EGMS) datasets to conduct a wide-area assessment of changes in spatiotemporal ground-deformation patterns. The analysis focuses on the Vaia storm (which occurred at the end of October 2018) as the key event and examines its impact on the most severely affected regions. The methodology involves trend analysis on segmented time-series and a novel approach for extraction of differential ground-deformation velocity (difference between pre-event and post-event velocities) in terms of quantity and typology (e.g., acceleration, deceleration, stabilization, etc.). The results are analyzed using statistical tools to provide a comprehensive view of the intense event's effects on the deformation patterns across the study area, facilitating the identification of localized zones where the spatial impact patterns are most evident. The results showed the approach can be successfully applied to the EGMS datasets for wide-area assessment of the pattern modifications. Furthermore, the results of the case study showed that modifications due to the Vaia rainstorm in terms of differential velocity contain all the types of acceleration, deceleration, activation, and stabilization, as well as the high magnitudes observed over the area.

Keywords: European Ground Motion Service (EGMS) · Extreme Rainfall · InSAR · Vaia Storm · Wide-Area Assessment

1 Introduction

Extreme climate events, such as rainstorms, cause damage to the built environment and natural landscape. In addition to the visible damage caused by such intense events, extreme precipitation can trigger hidden and potentially devastating processes. Intense rainfall can lead to both rapid and gradual activation, reactivation, and acceleration of landslides [1, 2]. These shifts in land stability pose serious risks to human lives and threaten critical infrastructure, man-made structures, and natural assets, all of which are

E. Borgogno-Mondino and P. Zamperlin (Eds.): ASITA 2024, CCIS 2463, pp. 46–60, 2025.
https://doi.org/10.1007/978-3-031-91141-5_4

vital from social and economic perspectives. As a result, there is an ongoing need for deep assessment and analysis of the impacts of extreme events to inform effective risk management and mitigation strategies.

The Vaia storm, a catastrophic meteorological event, struck Northern and Northern-East Italy and Southern and Southern-West Austria from October 27 to October 29, 2018. Characterized by unprecedented wind gusts exceeding 200 km/h, the storm caused widespread devastation, including tangible damage to hectares of natural landscape and different urban areas being flooded. Municipal reports indicated that roughly 42,500 ha of forest were either destroyed or severely compromised. The storm fell an estimated 8.5 million cubic meters of trees, dramatically reducing vital forest ecosystem services [3, 4]. Notably, regions such as Veneto, Trentino-Alto Adige in Italy, and Carinthia in Austria were severely affected, being located in the Alpine area. Leveraging the fact that the event brought about extreme weather conditions with rainfall exceeding 400 mm in certain areas over three days, it is expected that the heavy and sustained rainfall may destabilize slopes and alter the existing ground-deformation patterns. These intangible consequences of extreme rainfall can be considered as an additive to the existing level of geohazard, jeopardizing natural and anthropogenic assets and human lives.

A practical, modern and efficient remote-sensing tool for this goal is Satellite-borne Synthetic Aperture Radar (SAR) providing global microwave imagery in all-weather all-day conditions. Multi-Temporal Interferometric SAR (MT-InSAR) processing through advanced techniques [5, 6] offers millimeter-accuracy of ground-deformation time-series, with reasonably high temporal and spatial resolution (a few days and a few meters, respectively, depending on the satellite mission). Since the availability of SAR images in 1992, the unique benefits of this technology over traditional methods [7] have garnered widespread attention, for different domains of applications, e.g., land subsidence [8, 9], and landslides [10], wide-area deformation assessment [11], and particularly for rainfall event related deformations [12–14].

The Copernicus European Ground Motion Service (EGMS) is a useful and freely available database of ground-deformation times series over Europe offering different levels of products. The service provides processed European Space Agency (ESA) Sentinel-1 SAR images [15]. The datasets provided by the service have been successfully applied to several case studies in different domains [16–18].

This study is tailored to provide a framework for utilizing EGMS datasets for wide-area assessment of modifications imposed to spatiotemporal ground-deformation patterns. The Vaia storm is considered as an event of interest and the major affected area by this event is the area under study. The approach consists of trend analysis on partial time-series and extraction of quantity and typology of differential velocities. The outcomes of these processing steps can be illustrated by employing statistical tools to gain an overall perspective on the effect of the extreme rainfall over the whole area of interest, and they facilitate the detection of the local areas with the spatial pattern of the impact enforced by the event. The results revealed the potential of EGMS for such wide-area assessment and the successful implementation of the proposed approach.

2 Material

The area influenced by the Vaia Storm is mainly located over the alpine mountainous range, as shown in Fig. 1, which illustrates the spatial distribution of the magnitude of the accumulative rainfall for three days of the event, i.e., 27 to 29 October 2018, accessed from Visual Crossing platform (https://www.visualcrossing.com). As depicted in the figure, the Area of Interest (AoI) is chosen in a way that it covers the portions with the highest magnitudes of accumulated rainfall, to avoid overwhelming time of analyses and unnecessary information.

To analyze the changes that occurred to the spatiotemporal pattern of deformations in the affected area due to the Vaia Storm, the EGMS datasets have been used in this work. The service provides the results of processing and post-processing of MT-InSAR applied to Sentinel-1 images. A pan-European spatial coverage is offered by the service, as well as the temporal coverage of January 2015–December 2021 and January 2018–December 2022 in the first release and second update, respectively. The nominal temporal resolution of the deformation time-series is 6 days, and the spatial resolution depends on the level of product. Three different levels of products are available through the service, which are summarized in Table 1.

In this work, the L3 ORTHO products have been used with 100 m spatial resolution which are the result of down-sampling of Calibrated datapoints to go from the directions of ascending and descending Line-of-Sight (LOS) to the directions of East-West (E-W) and Up-Down (U-D) (interested readers may refer to [19]). In light of the scope of this study, the spatial resolution of 100 m may be a reasonable fit for such wide-area analyses, and this level benefits from the extracted E-W and U-D direction of deformations. The footprint of the EGMS datasets, each patch containing the data points with E-W and U-D deformations, are shown in Fig. 1.

Table 1. Properties of product levels of EGMS datasets

Level	Name of Prod.	Spatial Res.	Direction of Deform.*	Relative Deform.
L1	BASIC	Sentinel-1 Pixels	LOS of: Ascend. And Desc	Yes
L2	CALIBRATED	Sentinel-1 Pixels	LOS of: Ascend. And Desc	No
L3	ORTHO	100 m	Esat-West and Up-Down	No

*LOS: Line of Sight.
*Relative Deformation points at the presence of local reference point.

3 Methodology

Considering the application domain of this wide-area investigation of spatiotemporal deformation pattern changes, the proposed workflow comprises the trend analysis of partial time-series, as well as the extraction of typology and quantity of differential displacement velocities, i.e., the difference between pre-event and post-event velocities. The manner of using the outcome of these processing steps is also thoroughly explained in this section.

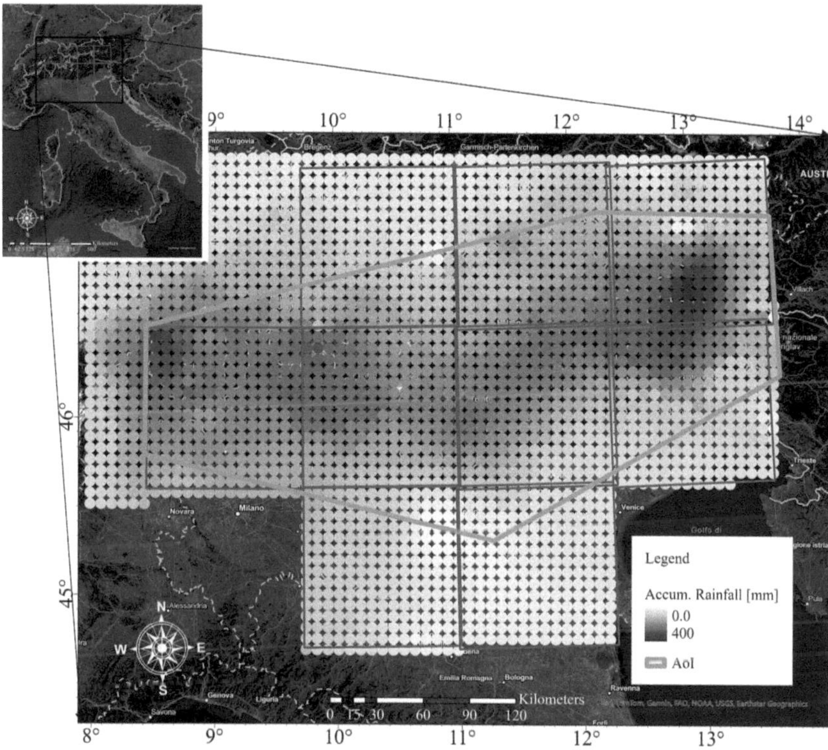

Fig. 1. Area of interest, the spatial distribution of accumulated rainfall from 27 to 29 October 2018, and the footprint of the European Ground Motion Service (EGMS) dataset.

3.1 Partial Time-Series Trend Analysis

Figure 2 (a) and (b) show two time-series of two different points settled in the AoI, for E-W and U-D deformations, respectively. These points have been selected from the areas with a considerable influence of the extreme rainfall, for a more comprehensive understating of how the deformation patterns are modified. The time of the Vaia Storm is considered as the *Turning Time-Point*, since it could be expected that the change in the temporal pattern of deformation occurs after this time-point. The daily precipitation diagram, obtained for a small portion settled in the AoI (related to the Cortina d'Ampezzo area), shows the high intensity of the daily rainfall during the event under investigation, with respect to the usual amount of precipitation in the area. Furthermore, another unusual amount of rain can be seen at the beginning of December 2020, which may cause modifications in temporal deformation patterns.

Hence, the time-series of all the ORTHO EGMS data points have been divided into three time-series, among which the first two periods are the time-series of interest: Pre-Event (05-Jan-2016 to 27-Oct-2018), Post-Event (02-Nov-2018 to 09-Dec-2020). It enables identifying the linear trend (displacement velocity) of the ground-deformation in both phases. Considering the fact that the pre-event and post-event phases contain

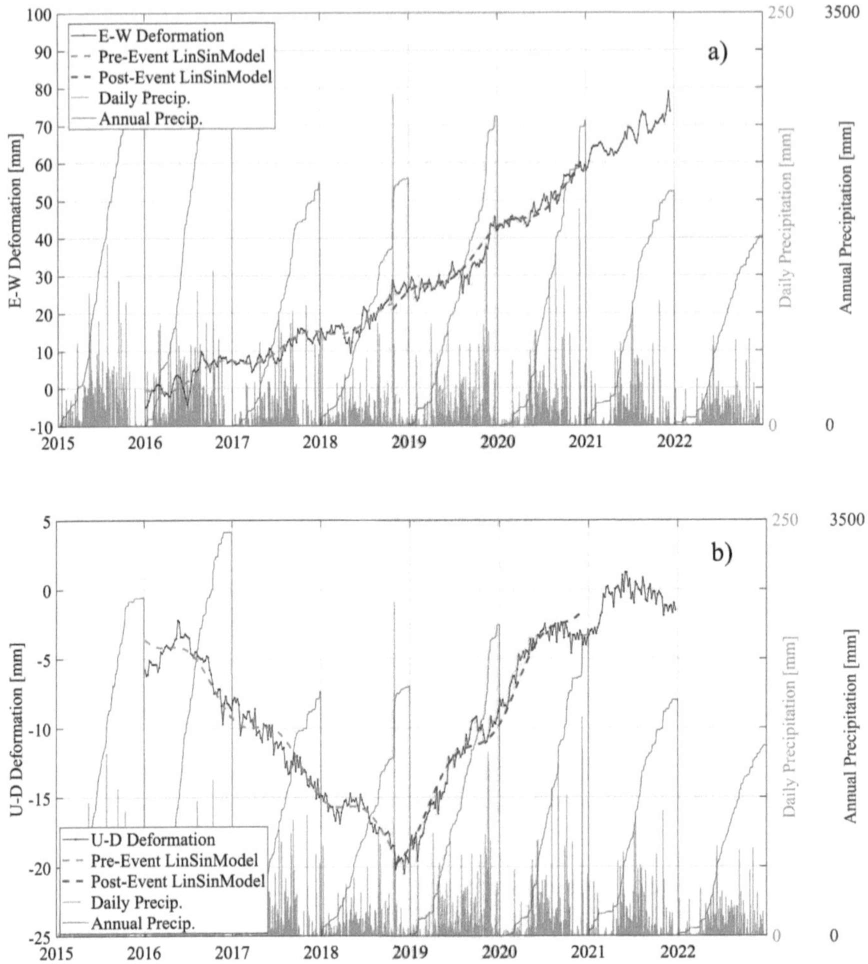

Fig. 2. Temporal distribution of precipitation (related to Cortina d'Ampezzo area) and Deformations time-series: a) East-West direction and b) Up-Down direction, and the fitted models in both pre- and post-event phases.

approx. 2 years - 10 months and 2 years – 2 months of deformation data, respectively, there is enough displacement information in each phase for a reliable trend analysis.

The InSAR technology, with the ability to detect millimetric-accuracy land displacement, is also sensitive to seasonal deformations due to temperature variations. This effect, most of the time, imposes a cyclic sinusoidal deformation which can be seen in the areas affected by the temperature variation. In order to eliminate the effect of this component on the determination of the deformation trend, and also to estimate the deformation velocity, a linear model plus a sinusoidal component is used for trend analysis:

$$D = (c_1 + c_2 t) + (c_3 \cos(2\pi c_4 t)) \quad (1)$$

In Eq. 1, c_1 to c_4 represent the coefficients to be set during least-square fitting. D and t are displacement [mm] and time [year] vectors, respectively. It should be mentioned that Eq. 1 is fitted to both phases of each direction of each data point. The coefficient $c2$ is the linear velocity [mm/y], which will be denoted as v hereafter. Other coefficients are not of interest in this study, however, c3 can be considered as the modelled amplitude of deformation caused by seasonal temperature variations.

After the fitting process, each data point is characterized by v_{Pre}^{E}, v_{Pst}^{E}, v_{Pre}^{U}, and v_{Pst}^{U} representing displacement velocity related to [Pre-event in E-W direction], [Post-event in E-W direction], [Pre-event in U-D direction], and [Post-event in U-D direction], respectively. These values will be used to check the deformation pattern modifications due to the extreme event of the Vaia storm. In Fig. 2, the fitted models are shown for both cases of E-W and U-D time-series with $v_{Pre}^{E} = +7.73[mm/y]$, $v_{Pst}^{E} = +17.38[mm/y]$, $v_{Pre}^{U} = -5.76[mm/y]$, and $v_{Pst}^{U} = 8.82[mm/y]$, as examples.

3.2 Differential Velocity: Quantity and Typology Extraction

Subsequent to the results in the earlier step, here, a mathematical algorithm is offered to obtain the Quantity and Typology of the modifications enforced on ground-deformation patterns. Regarding the InSAR-derived time-series, it should be noted that there are different levels of noise in the time-series which can alter the effectiveness of a proper extraction of the velocity (performed in the preceding step). Although measuring the Root Mean Square Error (RMSE) of the fitting can be a reasonable indicator of the quality of the fitted model, however, a velocity magnitude thresholding is adopted in this study. It was assumed that the points having a displacement velocity magnitude lower than a threshold (T_{Stable}) are considered to be at a stable condition and the velocity (magnitude and sign) is not included in the identification of Differential Velocity (v_{Diff}). . On the contrary, the points presenting a displacement velocity magnitude higher than a threshold (T_{Signif}) are assumed to be characterized by a significant displacement. It should be noted that if both pre- and post-event velocities are lower than T_{Signif}, the typology of the differential velocity is considered to be Stable. In this work, $T_{Stable} = 0.5[mm/y]$ and $T_{Signif} = 2[mm/y]$ are considered. For this threshold setting, no specific operations have been performed, and they are chosen based on a few investigations through the displacement velocities distribution and based on a pragmatical interpretation of the results. However, these values can vary over different case studies for different result interpretations and decision-making.

The sign and magnitude of v_{Diff} is considered to be calculated using

$$v_{Diff,p,dir} = (v_{Pst}^{p,dir} - v_{Pre}^{p,dir}) \times sgn(v_{Pre}^{p,dir}) \quad (2)$$

where p and dir denote the point and the direction of deformation, and $Sgn()$ is the sign function.

The proposed algorithm is as follows:

Algorithm

for each point (p):

  for each direction (dir):

$$if\ |v_{Pre}^{p,dir}| \geq T_{Stable}\ \&\&\ |v_{Pst}^{p,dir}| \geq T_{Signif}$$

$$v_{Diff,\ p,dir}^{Qnt} = \left(v_{Pst}^{p,dir} - v_{Pre}^{p,dir}\right) \times sgn(v_{Pre}^{p,dir})$$

$$if\ v_{Diff,\ p,dir}^{Qnt} > 0$$

$$v_{Diff,\ p,dir}^{Typ} = Acceleration;$$

$$else$$

$$v_{Diff,\ p,dir}^{Typ} = Deceleration;$$

$$if\ |v_{Pre}^{p,dir}| < T_{Stable}\ \&\&\ |v_{Pst}^{p,dir}| \geq T_{Signif}$$

$$v_{Diff,\ p,dir}^{Qnt} = |\ v_{Pst}^{p,dir}\ |;$$

$$v_{Diff,\ p,dir}^{Typ} = Activation;$$

$$if\ |v_{Pre}^{p,dir}| \geq T_{Signif}\ \&\&\ |v_{Pst}^{p,dir}| < T_{Stable}$$

$$v_{Diff,\ p,dir}^{Qnt} = -|\ v_{Pst}^{p,dir}\ |;$$

$$v_{Diff,\ p,dir}^{Typ} = Stabilization;$$

$$else$$

$$v_{Diff,\ p,dir}^{Qnt} = 0;$$

$$v_{Diff,\ p,dir}^{Typ} = Stable;$$

After the implementation of this algorithm, each point is characterized by v_{Diff}^{Qnt} and v_{Diff}^{Typ} which are quantity $\in \mathbb{R}$ and typology $\in$ [Acceleration, Deceleration, Activation, Stabilization, Stable] of the differential velocity. The labels' definition and their relationship with the sign of quantities can be described as follows: i) Accelerations (positive quantities) show that the post-event velocity has increased maintaining the sign of the pre-event velocity; ii) Decelerations (negative quantities) represent that either post-event velocity has decreased maintaining the sign of pre-event velocity, or the post-event velocity has a different sign compared to the pre-event velocity; iii) Activations (positive or negative quantities) shows that the area was stable in pre-event phase and gained significant value of deformation rate in post-event phase; iv) Stabilizations depict an adverse behaviour compared to Activations; v) Stable areas demonstrate stable considerations in both pre- and post-event phases.

3.3 Output Representation

Due to the large number of data points (approx. 1 million) provided by the EGMS L3 ORTHO dataset, in the light of wide-area assessment, the outcome can be used to perform statistical analysis to gain a general overview on the effect of the extreme event and the imposed modifications. Here, a Label Agreement Matrix (labels coming form v_{Diff}^{Typ}) presented to see the density of the points in each pair of E-W and U-D labels (e.g., Acceleration in E-W and Acceleration U-D, or Deceleration in E-W and Stabilization in U-D).

These pairs can be considered as a particular phenomenon derived from the extreme event to the ground-deformation pattern. The points related to each pair can be extracted easily, to check the Spatial Integrity (refer to Sect. 4 for more explanations) and assess the effect on local perspective. This bidirectional investigation of pattern modifications is a more practical approach with respect to the unidirectional approach, since detection of these local areas among the whole dataset is not straightforward. The next section will go into details of the representation of the outcomes of processing steps.

4 Results and Discussions

A number of 978890 data points from the L3 ORTHO EGMS, settled in the AoI, have been processed through the two first steps discussed in Sect. 3. Due to the dense representation of the points in the AoI and to avoid unnecessary information throughout the text, the results for the whole AoI are not presented here, and some examples will be shown when local portions are to be evaluated in this section.

The first observation regarding the spatial distribution of the results in terms of both v_{Diff}^{Qnt} and v_{Diff}^{Typ} was that the situation can be divided into three major groups for each direction of deformation: 1) a great number of points in Stable conditions (and of course, zero value of v_{Diff}^{Qnt}); 2) a scattered representation of points with the same label (small to large variations of v_{Diff}^{Qnt}); ; and 3) different small groups of points close to each other with the same label.

The second group may arise from multiple factors, including noise in InSAR measurements, the selection criteria for velocity thresholding, or localized extreme phenomena. InSAR measurement noise refers to uncertainties and errors introduced by factors such as atmospheric disturbances, decorrelation effects, and processing artefacts, which can ultimately impact velocity estimates. These uncertainties can lead to isolated variations that do not necessarily represent actual ground deformation patterns.

However, the third group exhibits a property referred to as "Spatial Integrity." This term defines the consistency of displacement patterns within a localized region, where clusters of spatially adjacent points with the same label form distinct small groups and reinforce the reliability of observed changes. Spatial Integrity is particularly beneficial for final decision-making, as it strengthens confidence in identifying actual modifications due to the extreme event while mitigating the influence of random noise or isolated anomalies. Recognizing this property is crucial throughout the investigation of the results, as it enhances the interpretability of detected changes.

4.1 Statistics of Wide-Area Assessment

Figure 3 shows the histogram of v_{Diff}^{Qnt} for both E-W and U-D directions of deformation. In the case of E-W, the high values of $+16[mm/y]$ and $-18[mm/y]$ differential velocity have been seen, and in the U-D case, the high values of $+19[mm/y]$ and $-23[mm/y]$ have been observed. However, the dense data representation can be identified approximately in the interval $-5\ to + 5[mm/y]$ of differential velocity. It should be noted that due to the large number of zero values, these values are removed from the histograms to preserve the informativity of the figures. Also, the discontinuities seen in the distributions (around $\pm 2[mm/y]$) are due to the thresholding of the velocity (T_{Signif}).

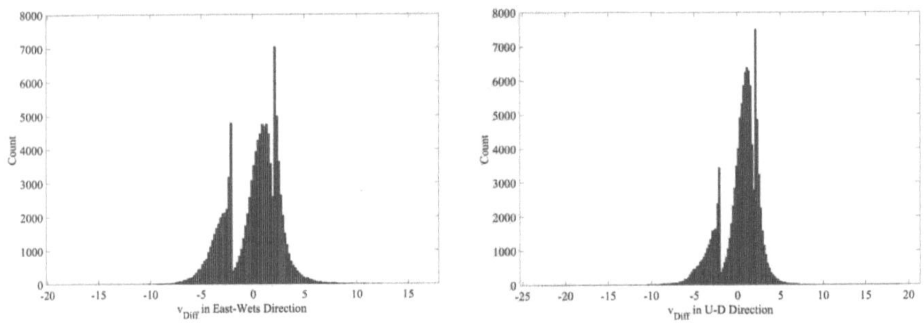

Fig. 3. Histogram of v_{Diff}^{Qnt} in: a) E-W direction and b) U-D direction

A practical approach for assessing such conditions in large scales is to use Label Agreement matrices, to have a comprehensive look at the relationship between the labels in different directions of deformation. Figure 4 shows this matrix which summarizes how many points are characterized by one specific pair of labels. It is evident that numerous points are in a stable condition (both before and after the event) in both E-W and U-D directions. The second important observation is that there are portions which accelerated in only one direction and show stable conditions in another direction: the pair of $Acceleration_{E-W}$ and $Stable_{U-D}$ and the pair of $Acceleration_{U-D}$ and $Stable_{E-W}$.

In general, the matrix can be a useful tool to have a comprehensive understanding of the extreme event's effect on the ground-deformation patterns simultaneously in both directions of deformation. However, a local analysis approach is required to be adopted, in a way that one should choose a pair and look at the spatial distribution of the points in it. Because a portion of the total number of points shown per each pair may present a very sparse distribution without spatial integrity, due to measurement noise or extremely local phenomenon (described at the beginning of Sect. 4). Therefore, in the next part, a closer look at some pairs will be performed to see if there are portions with spatial integrity, enabling a better detection of modifications on the ground-deformation patterns.

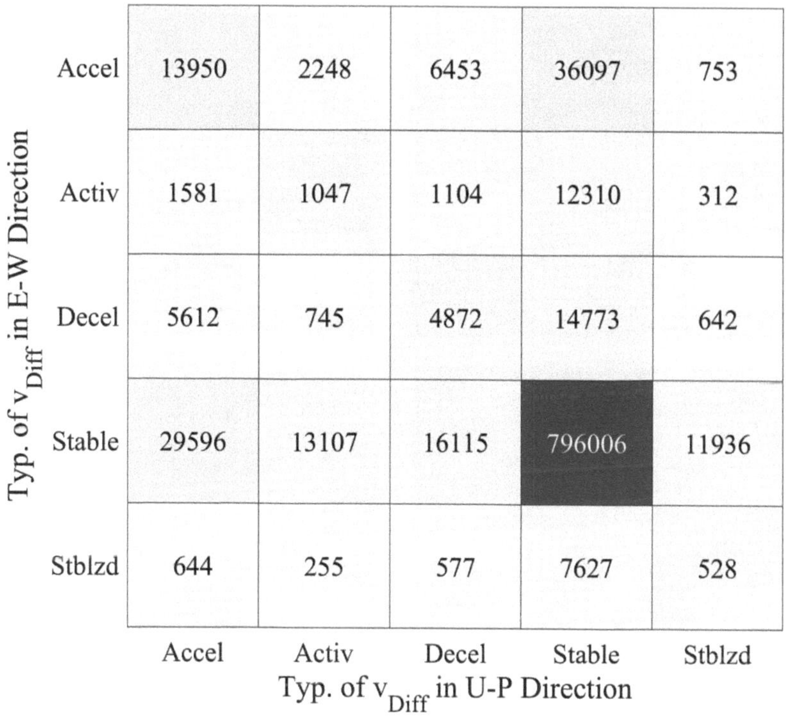

Fig. 4. Label Agreement Matrix for v_{Diff}^{Typ} of E-W and U-D directions (considering 978890 data points).

4.2 Local Cases

After the extraction of the points related to each pair of the Label Agreement Matrix in Subsect. 4.1, it was seen that in all the pairs, there are both groups of points: with and without spatial integrity. However, this pair selection facilitates finding the zones with a group of points with the same pair characteristic, since finding such zones in the whole dataset is not convenient. Here, a few examples are provided to show the spatial pattern modifications in a zone with the same temporal pattern modifications, detected by the group of data points with proper spatial integrity. The examples have been detected fast after the extraction of the points related to each pair and looking for a group of points close to each other forming a proper spatial integrity.

Figure 5 shows the distribution of the pre-event and post-event velocities, as well as the differential velocity quantities. The area is located at the north of Como Lake, Samolaco, Italy. Although the area is nearly stable in terms of deformations in E-W and U-D before the event, a considerable uplift and a slight movement toward the West can be observed over the area. The spatial integrity for the case of U-D differential velocities is significantly visible, however, in the case of E-W differential velocities, a lower level of spatial integrity can be witnessed.

Figure 6 illustrates the differential velocity values for Varna town located in the North-East of Bolzano, Italy. The area is affected by accelerations in both E-W and U-D

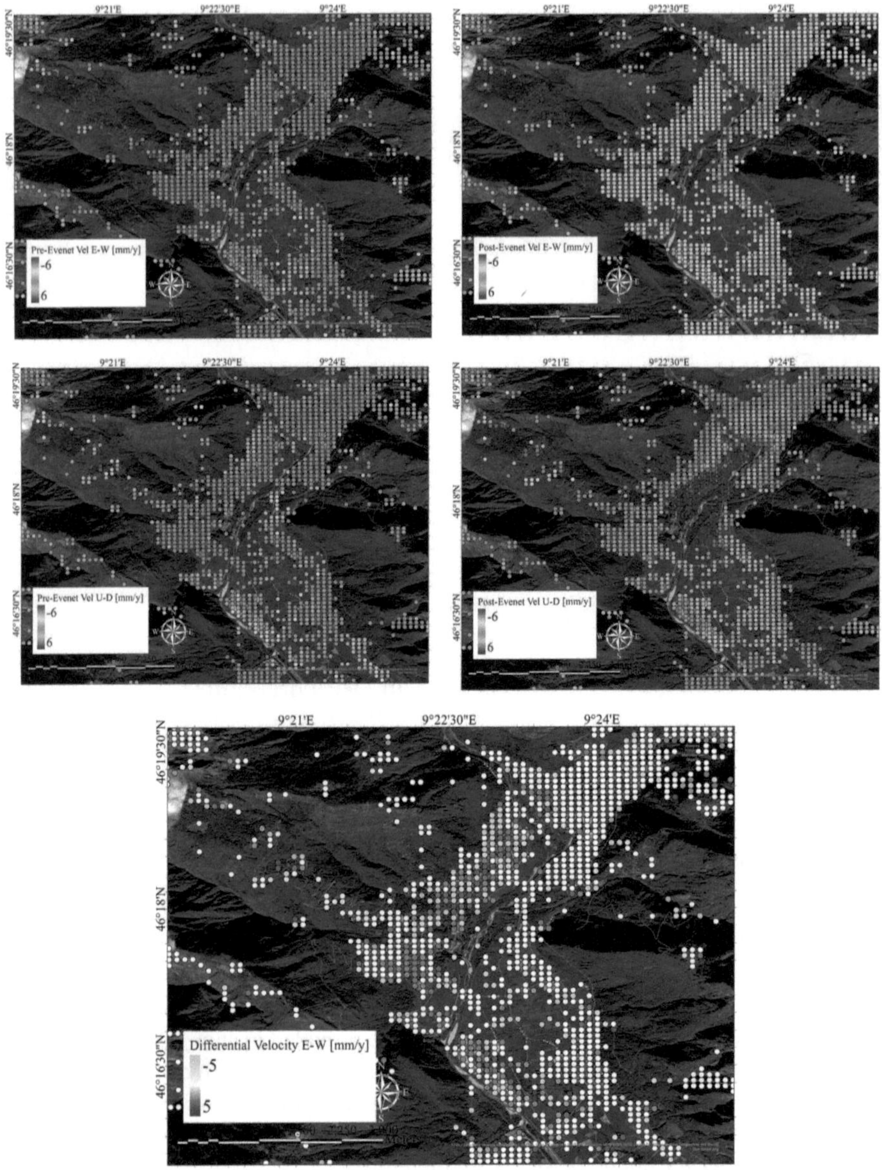

Fig. 5. Pre- and Post-event velocities, and Differential velocities over Samolaco, Italy.

directions of deformation with a reasonable spatial integrity. The uplift (in the vertical direction) and going westbound (in the horizontal direction) accelerated after the event.

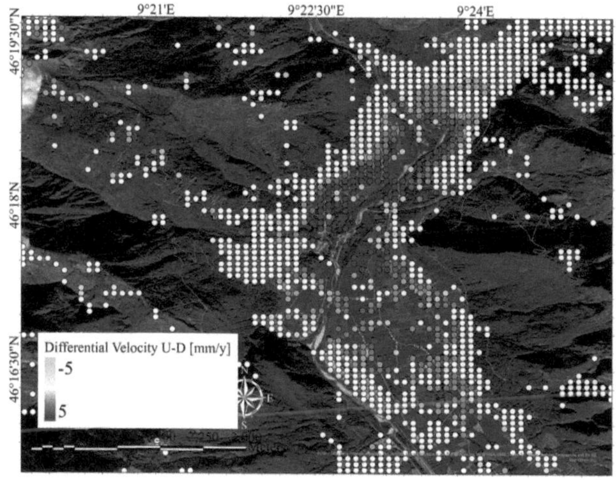

Fig. 5. *(continued)*

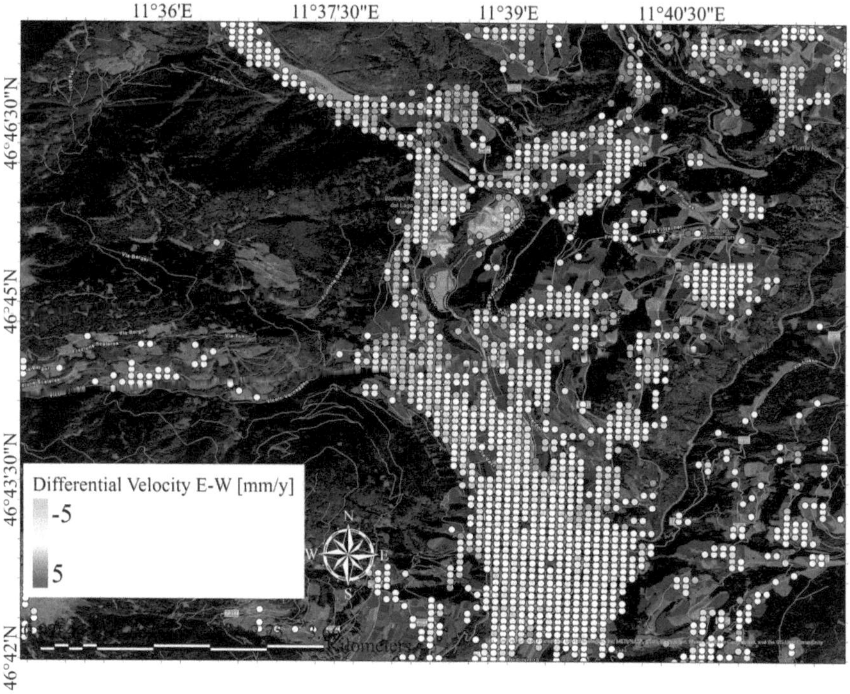

Fig. 6. Differential Velocities: Accelerations in both E-W (above) and U-D (below)

4.3 EGMS Applicability: Potential and Limitations

Based on the use of EGMS for the detection of the Vaia Storm effect on spatiotemporal deformation patterns, it was seen that the datasets are capable of achieving this purpose

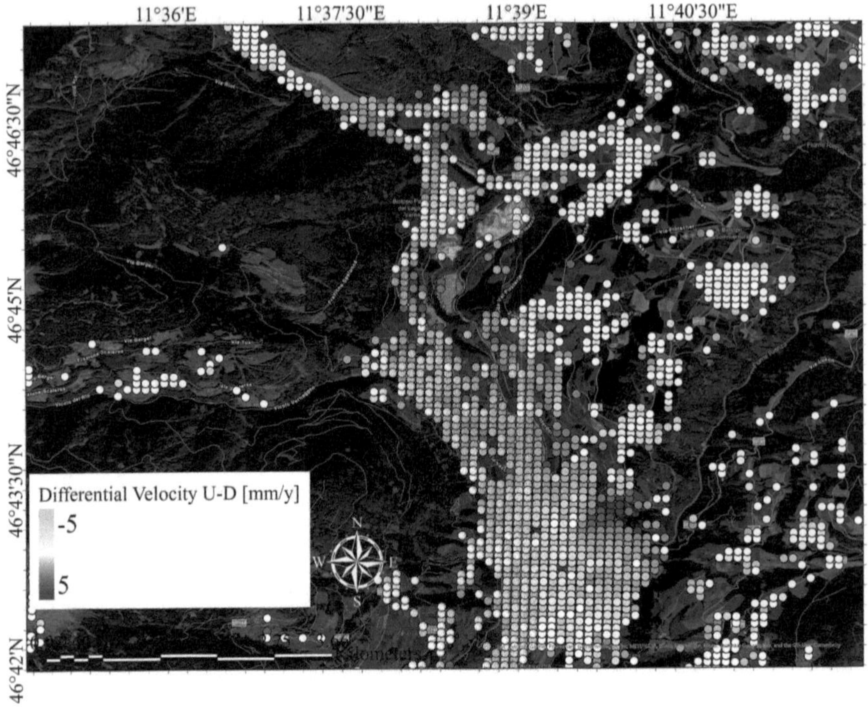

Fig. 6. (*continued*)

for a wide-area assessment (multi-region, in this case). Being free-access, reliable and easy-to-use, the service provides a particular opportunity for different types of time-series analysis to gain basic and advanced information on the dynamics of the ground-deformations all over Europe.

However, the service suffers from InSAR technology-related limitations. InSAR is unable to catch movements in the direction of North-South (N-S) because this type of movement lies mostly along the satellite's trajectory (near-polar orbits) and is largely orthogonal to the LOS direction. Therefore, changes in this direction cause minimal phase shifts in the radar signal, making it difficult to detect north-south deformations effectively. Furthermore, the measurements can be done on sensor-friendly targets and persistent scatterers. As was seen in the local cases, several portions of the ground (mostly densely vegetated areas) were not covered by data points, since the spatial and temporal decorrelations in these zones limit the proper processing of the signals to obtain deformations over time.

5 Conclusions

In this study, a framework is provided to use EGMS data for the detection of changes in spatiotemporal patterns of deformation. The framework contains two steps of processing: trend analysis on partial time-series and extraction of quantity and typology of the differential velocities. The framework has been applied to Vaia Storm and the outcomes have been represented through statistical analysis and localized area assessment. It can be concluded that:

- The framework provides a straightforward workflow for the successful use of EGMS data for the detection of extreme event-related modifications on the ground-deformation patterns.
- The proposed algorithm for the identification of differential velocity and the corresponding outcomes offers a comprehensive overview of the effect of extreme rainfall and facilitates the detection of localized areas with a pattern of deformation modifications.
- The Vaia storm has modified the deformation patterns (in terms of acceleration, deceleration, activation, and stabilization) at several portions of the affected area, with high magnitudes of differential velocity observed.
- EGMS data have proved to be practical and beneficial for wide-area assessment of spatiotemporal displacement pattern modifications.

In this study, a Velocity Thresholding perspective has been adopted during the trend analysis. Future works are needed to improve this approach, and the RMSE values are deemed to be valuable information in this regard. Furthermore, the time of the event (i.e., the expected turning point at the end of October 2018) was known and used throughout the analysis and an informed temporal partitioning of the times series has been carried out. However, novel unsupervised approaches can be developed to detect such turning points (due to different extreme events) towards a higher degree of automation to detect spatiotemporal deformation pattern modifications in a wide-area assessment context.

Acknowledgements. The ground-deformation datasets used in this study have been accessed by the European Ground Motion Service (EGMS) https://egms.land.copernicus.eu/.

Disclosure of Interests. The authors have no competing interests to declare that are relevant to the content of this article.

References

1. Notti, D., Wrzesniak, A., Dematteis, N., Lollino, P., Fazio, N.L., Zucca, F., et al.: A multidisciplinary investigation of deep-seated landslide reactivation triggered by an extreme rainfall event: a case study of the Monesi di Mendatica landslide, Ligurian Alps. Landslides **18**(7), 2341–2365 (2021)
2. Guzzetti, F., Gariano, S.L., Peruccacci, S., Brunetti, M.T., Melillo, M.: Chapter 15 - Rainfall and landslide initiation. In: Rainfall. Elsevier (2022)
3. Motta, R., Ascoli, D., Corona, P., Marchetti, M., Vacchiano, G.: Selvicoltura e schianti da vento. Il caso della "tempesta Vaia" **15**(6), 94–98 (2018)
4. Chirici, G., Giannetti, F., Travaglini, D., Nocentini, S., Francini, S., Amico, G., et al.: Stima dei danni della tempesta "Vaia" alle foreste in Italia **16**(1), 3–9 (2019)
5. Ferretti, A., Fumagalli, A., Novali, F., Prati, C., Rocca, F., Rucci, A.: A new algorithm for processing interferometric data-stacks: SqueeSAR. IEEE Trans. Geosci. Remote Sens. **49**(9), 3460–3470 (2011)

6. Berardino, P., Casu, F., Fornaro, G., Lanari, R., Manunta, M., Manzo, M., et al. (eds.): The SBAS-DInSAR technique as a tool for the observation of active volcanic areas: results and future perspectives. In: 2007 IEEE International Geoscience and Remote Sensing Symposium. IEEE (2007)
7. Scaioni, M., Marsella, M., Crosetto, M., Tornatore, V., Wang, J.: Geodetic and remote-sensing sensors for dam deformation monitoring. Sensors **18**(11) (2018)
8. Raspini, F., Caleca, F., Del Soldato, M., Festa, D., Confuorto, P., Bianchini, S.: Review of satellite radar interferometry for subsidence analysis. Earth Sci. Rev. **235**, 104239 (2022)
9. Eskandari, R., Scaioni, M., (eds.): Retrospective study of vertical ground deformation in Como, Northern Italy: integration of levelling and psi measurements. Int. Arch. Photogramm. Remote Sens. Spatial Inf. Sci. Copernicus Publications (2023)
10. Solari, L., Del Soldato, M., Raspini, F., Barra, A., Bianchini, S., Confuorto, P., et al.: Review of satellite interferometry for landslide detection in Italy **12**(8), 1351 (2020)
11. Wang, Y., Feng, G., Li, Z., Luo, S., Wang, H., Xiong, Z., et al.: A strategy for variable-scale InSAR deformation monitoring in a wide area: a case study in the Turpan–Hami Basin, China. Remote Sens. **14**(15) (2022)
12. Shi, X., Wang, J., Jiang, M., Zhang, S., Wu, Y., Zhong, Y.: Extreme rainfall-related accelerations in landslides in Danba County, Sichuan Province, as detected by InSAR. Int. J. Appl. Earth Obs. Geoinf. **115**, 103109 (2022)
13. Cohen-Waeber, J., Bürgmann, R., Chaussard, E., Giannico, C., Ferretti, A.: Spatiotemporal patterns of precipitation-modulated landslide deformation from independent component analysis of InSAR time series **45**(4), 1878–1887 (2018)
14. Eskandari, R., Scaioni, M.: Spatiotemporal pattern detection of ground deformations induced by extreme rainfall using InSAR EGMS: the case of Cortina d'Ampezzo after Vaia Storm. ISPRS Ann. Photogramm. Remote Sens. Spat. Inf. Sci. (2024)
15. Costantini, M., Minati, F., Trillo, F., Ferretti, A., Passera, E., Rucci, A., et al.: EGMS: europe-wide ground motion monitoring based on full resolution InSAR processing of all Sentinel-1 acquisitions. In: IGARSS 2022 - 2022 IEEE International Geoscience and Remote Sensing Symposium, pp. 5093–5096 (2022)
16. Crosetto, M., Solari, L:. Satellite Interferometry Data Interpretation and Exploitation: Case Studies from the European Ground Motion Service (EGMS). Elsevier, Amsterdam (2023)
17. Crosetto, M., Crippa, B., Mróz, M., Cuevas-González, M., Shahbazi, S.: Applications based on EGMS products: a review. Remote Sens. Appl. Soc. Environ. **37**, 101452 (2025)
18. Eskandari, R., Scaioni, M.: European ground motion service for bridge monitoring: temporal and thermal deformation cross-check using Cosmo-Skymed InSAR. Int. Arch. Photogramm. Remote Sens. Spat. Inf. Sci. **XLVIII-1/W2-2023**, 1235–1241 (2023)
19. Ferretti, A., Passera, E., Capes, R.: Algorithm theoretical basis document. EGMS Documentation (2021)

GIS-Based Assessment of World War I UXO Occurrence Probability Through Military Maps and Aerial Imagery on the Grappa Massif (NE Italy)

Maria Petriccione[1(✉)], Aldino Bondesan[1,2], Francesco Ferrarese[1], Francesca Lucia Gallo[1], Leonardo Mora[1], Chiara Levorato[3], and Simone Busoni[4]

[1] Università degli Studi di Padova, Padova, Italy
[2] University of Stellenbosch, Stellenbosch, South Africa
[3] Adastra Engineering, Padova, Italy
[4] Provincia di Treviso, Treviso, Italy

Abstract. The Grappa Massif served as a critical battlefield during World War I from November 1917 to November 1918, witnessing two defensive battles and one offensive. The extensive military operations, including large-scale offensives and smaller tactical actions, significantly altered the landscape, leading to the construction of an intricate military infrastructure. Despite post-war clearance efforts, the likelihood of encountering unexploded ordnance (UXO) remains high, especially in remote and rugged areas, posing a substantial risk during excavation activities. This study presents the development of a UXO probability map for the Grappa Massif, created within a GIS framework. A series of historical documents, including military maps from World War I preserved at the State Archives of Florence, were collected, georeferenced, and analyzed. Military elements identified in these maps were classified and weighted based on their probability of containing UXO, utilizing the Circular Error Probable (CEP) method. This approach has allowed for the identification of distinct risk zones, providing a crucial tool for preventing accidents during land development and excavation activities.

Keywords: WWI · Military Geography · GIS · UXO Risk Assessment

1 Introduction

The presence of unexploded ordnance (UXO) poses a significant hazard during excavation activities. According to Italian law (as defined in Article 1 of Italian Ministerial Decree No. 82 of May 11, 2015) UXOs are: "explosive devices or their components that, despite being armed or otherwise prepared for detonation, failed to explode due to malfunctions, manufacturing defects, or other causes". These remnants of war continue to present serious risks to the safety of individuals, infrastructure, and ongoing activities in affected areas.

Several operations are known to lead to the discovery of UXOs. Among the most common are excavation works for construction, maintenance of waterways, agricultural

E. Borgogno-Mondino and P. Zamperlin (Eds.): ASITA 2024, CCIS 2463, pp. 61–76, 2025.
https://doi.org/10.1007/978-3-031-91141-5_5

activities involving land movement, hydraulic projects for groundwater management, geological investigations such as coring and drilling, and, in some cases, accidental findings.

In Italy, two main approaches are adopted to address the presence of UXOs prior to beginning construction or excavation in potentially affected areas: the UXO Risk Assessment (it.: *Valutazione di Rischio Bellico, VRB*) and UXO Clearance (It.: *Bonifica Bellica Preventiva, BOB*).

The VRB procedure follows two steps: Historical-documentary UXO Risk Assessment and Instrumental UXO Risk Assessment.

Historical-documentary UXO Risk Assessment (VRB): this process involves conducting a detailed historical and documentary analysis of the site to determine the probability of UXO presence. Historical records, such as maps, military documents, and aerial photographs from the World Wars, are examined to assess whether the area in question was subject to military activities, such as bombings or artillery strikes. The analysis draws from sources including municipal and provincial archives, Carabinieri and Prefecture records, Ministry of Defence archives, the National Aerophotographic Archive (Aerofototeca Nazionale), and, when available, documents from Allied military commands. Additionally, the proximity to roadways, railways, ports, or other strategic infrastructure utilized during the war is considered, along with any previously cleared areas adjacent to the sites under examination. In the initial phase, historical records and documents are reviewed to estimate the likelihood of unexploded ordnance (UXO) presence in a specific area.

Instrumental UXO Risk Assessment: an instrumental investigation is employed when greater precision or additional detail is required, particularly when the documentary analysis identifies areas of concern but lacks the specificity needed for a thorough risk assessment. Instrumental investigations use non-invasive geophysical methods to detect anomalies in the subsurface that might indicate the presence of UXOs. The main techniques employed include magnetic surveys, electromagnetic induction (EMI), and ground-penetrating radar (GPR). Magnetic surveys measure deviations in the Earth's natural magnetic field, which can reveal the presence of ferrous objects, such as bombs or shells. This method is often used for surface-level or shallow detection. Electromagnetic induction involves sending electromagnetic waves into the ground and measuring their response, making it useful for a variety of depths and soil types. GPR, on the other hand, sends radar waves into the ground, which reflect off buried objects, providing detailed images that are especially effective for detecting UXOs at greater depths. Unlike actual UXO Clearance (it.: *Bonifica bellica, BOB*), which involves excavating and removing ordnance, instrumental VRB assessments do not disturb the ground or recover UXOs. They provide a probabilistic evaluation, indicating the likelihood of UXO presence based on the detected anomalies. These assessments help inform whether additional safety measures, such as UXO clearance, are necessary, ensuring the safety of workers and the public during subsequent excavation or construction activities.

The UXO Risk may be faced also with the Preventive UXO Clearance (it.: *Bonifica Bellica Preventiva*). This is a proactive measure that involves specialized companies surveying areas where construction or other land-disturbing activities are planned. They act under a strict military control. The goal is to detect and remove any potential UXO before any work begins to prevent accidents or damage during construction.

When UXO is accidentally discovered, often during excavation, agricultural activities, or other land use the Emergency UXO Clearance (it.: *Bonifica Bellica di Emergenza*) is initiated. Emergency clearance involves the immediate securing of the area and the deployment of specialized military units, such as the Italian Army's bomb disposal teams (it.: *Artificieri EOD*), who neutralize or safely detonate the ordnance. Emergency clearance is a reactive measure that ensures the immediate safety of the population and workers in the area.

1.1 UXO Hazard Maps

Hazard (H) expresses the probability of an event of a certain magnitude occurring in a defined place and time. In the context of UXO risk, it indicates the possibility of encountering unexploded ordnance.

In Italy, particularly in the northeastern regions, the issue of unexploded ordnance remains highly significant, as the area was heavily impacted by both World War I and World War II. In the Veneto region, three key areas that were severely affected during World War I are the Asiago Plateau, the Grappa Massif and the Piave River. The intense warfare that took place on Grappa Massif warrants a thorough evaluation of the residual risk, both concerning the alterations made to the terrain for military purposes and the potential for the discovery of UXO. Despite the passage of a century, the threat posed by these devices remains significant. The long period of dormancy may lead to an underestimation of the associated risks when UXO is discovered during exploration or construction activities, thus increasing the likelihood of accidents. Therefore, it is crucial to adopt a cautious and informed approach during any activity that could potentially disturb these remnants of war.

In this context, a UXO hazard map in the Grappa Massif area has been developed to support risk assessments and ensure safer interventions in the region.

1.2 Geological Overview of Grappa Massif

The Grappa Massif massif is a key segment of the Southern Alpine front, a region of the Alps characterized by southward vergence and the absence of Alpine metamorphism (Castellarin et al. 1992; Dal Piaz et al. 2003). This geological context is heavily influenced by both pre-Alpine Jurassic paleogeography and Alpine-age tectonics, particularly the Bassano-Valdobbiadene line. The geological map of the Grappa Massif showcases Mesozoic formations, with the western sector belonging to the Trento Platform and the eastern sector representing the Belluno Basin. To the north, a major thrust fault elevates a block of the Prealps, while the southern section is relatively less deformed, comprising the so-called "Venetian Molasse."

The Grappa Massif's backbone consists of Mesozoic carbonates, reaching elevations well above 1,000 m. The thickest sedimentary successions here were deposited from the Late Triassic to the Early Jurassic in a shallow marine environment, known as the Trento Platform (Carraro et al. 1989). These deposits are dominated by dolomites from the

Triassic period (Dolomia Principale Formation) and by limestones from the Jurassic (Calcari Grigi Group), frequently dolomitized in this region.

During the Early Jurassic, the Trento Platform was bordered by fault-controlled steep submarine escarpments. The eastern margin, separating the platform from the Belluno Basin, crosses the eastern sector of the Grappa Massif and is represented on the geological map (Bosellini et al. 1981; Carraro et al. 1989). The Mesozoic succession of the Belluno Basin includes thinly stratified limestones interbedded with marls, periodically disrupted by turbidites and submarine landslides that introduced platform-derived oolitic carbonates. This proximity to basin-bounding faults and extensive dolomitization renders the Belluno Basin succession complex and challenging to delineate geologically.

The Grappa Massif transitions sharply to the Treviso plain and Prealpine hills, expressed through the prominent Bassano-Valdobbiadene thrust fault, which lifts the Grappa Massif as a roof block. This structure is especially evident west of Possagno, where it merges into a series of folds that deform the Cretaceous strata.

The area around Possagno is geologically significant due to its continuous, expanded stratigraphic sequence, ranging from the Lower Cretaceous to the Upper Eocene (Fabiani 1915; Bolli 1975). It remains a crucial location for stratigraphic studies because of its proximity to the Belluno Basin, resulting in thicker sediment accumulations than adjacent areas (Agnini et al. 2006; Trevisani et al. 2009).

The southern sector of the map is dominated by elongated hogback ridges formed by moderately deformed, tilted strata dating from the Upper Eocene to the Upper Miocene. These strata include a significant hiatus between the Eocene and Upper Oligocene (Bassi & Nebelsick 2010). The Oligo-Miocene sequence, known as the "Venetian Molasse," represents the infill of a foreland basin initially associated with the Dinaric chain and later with the Southern Alps (Massari et al. 1986; Mellere et al. 2000).

Finally, the stratigraphic sequence in this area spans from the Lower Jurassic to the Miocene, with Quaternary deposits dominating the surface. Extensive dolomitization, linked to both pre-Alpine high-angle faults and the major Alpine-related tectonic structure, the Bassano-Valdobbiadene fault, has affected much of the Jurassic to Cretaceous strata, further complicating the stratigraphy (Ronchi et al. 2012).

1.3 Geomorphology of the Grappa Plateau

The Grappa Plateau is a unique geomorphological unit within the Southern Alps, shaped by a combination of tectonic activity, glaciation, and extensive karst processes. This plateau, primarily composed of carbonate rocks like limestone and dolomite, showcases a complex landscape with deep valleys, steep escarpments, and underground karst systems that are still evolving today.

Glacial Processes

The plateau bears significant traces of Pleistocene glaciations, which played a pivotal role in its current topography. Glaciers descending from Grappa Massif carved deep U-shaped valleys, including the prominent Brenta Valley. These glaciers also deposited moraines and fluvioglacial sediments in lower areas, shaping ridges and terraces still visible today. One of the most significant effects of glacial erosion is found in the formation of cirques near the summit of Monte Grappa, which reflect the retreat of glaciers during the Last

Glacial Maximum (Bondesan & Busoni 2019). The glacial features in the region are particularly prominent in the upper parts of the plateau, where erosion was most intense, creating sharp relief contrasts (Reato 2006).

Karst Processes

Karstification is a dominant geomorphological process on the Grappa Plateau, given the area's carbonate lithology. The plateau's limestone and dolomite bedrock, primarily from the Jurassic and Cretaceous periods, has been subjected to intense chemical weathering, leading to the development of various karst features such as dolines, sinkholes, caves, and subterranean drainage systems (Saccon 2011). The karst landscape is particularly well-developed due to the dissolution of calcium carbonate by slightly acidic water, a process that has been ongoing for millennia (Bondesan & Busoni 2019).

Surface features such as dolines are widespread across the plateau. These depressions, often circular or elliptical, are formed by the collapse of underground voids or the dissolution of surface limestone. The plateau also hosts numerous sinkholes and vertical shafts that penetrate deep into the subsurface, providing access to extensive cave networks, some of which reach impressive depths.

Subterranean karst systems, like the Grotta di Oliero, are essential components of the plateau's geomorphology, indicating significant underground water flow through the fractured rock. Water percolates through the plateau, emerging in springs at lower elevations, such as the notable Fontanazzi di Solagna, which marks the resurgence of underground streams (Reato 2006). These subsurface flows, combined with the absence of surface rivers, underscore the advanced stage of karst development on the plateau (Saccon 2011).

The structural control exerted by faults and fractures in the rock enhances karstification, allowing water to infiltrate deeper into the subsurface. This process has created a network of underground channels that further erode the limestone, expanding caves and conduits over time (Doglioni et al. 1996). The plateau's karst landscape is thus a testament to both past and ongoing geomorphological processes, making it a key region for the study of karst systems in the Southern Alps (Bondesan & Busoni 2019).

1.4 Historical Contest

The extensive military infrastructure still visible today on the Grappa Massif serves as a testament to the significant fortification and entrenchment works carried out during World War I. Although geographically isolated, the area shares many similarities with the Asiago Plateau, enabling the design of an independent defensive system (Cadorna 1921; Caviglia 1934). The Austro-Hungarian offensive, executed in three coordinated phases, placed Mount Grappa at the center of the conflict (Caviglia 1934; Meregalli 2003). However, the limited territorial depth controlled by the Italian forces hindered any possibility of mobile defense, compelling them into static resistance on the highlands. Both the attacking and defending armies were acutely aware of these constraints, which led to intense and protracted battles (Caviglia 1934; Meregalli 2003).

Mount Grappa did not see occupation by the opposing forces until late 1917, following the Italian defeat at Caporetto, when the front was forced to retreat approximately

100 km, stabilizing only on the Grappa Massif and along the Piave River. Nonetheless, the Italian army had begun constructing roads and other logistical infrastructure as early as the end of 1916, in response to the Austro-Hungarian Spring offensive (Cadorna 1921). The difficult-to-defend positions on the Grappa Massif required extensive military and logistical preparations. This included the construction of new roads for trucks and artillery, water-lifting systems, and the installation of secondary railways (Decauville lines) capable of reaching the mountain's base (Caviglia 1934; Meregalli 2003). However, it was the three major battles fought here that truly marked the peak of military activity.

The Halting Battle

The first defensive battle unfolded in two distinct phases: the first from November 14 to 26, 1917, and the second from December 11 to 21, 1917 (Caviglia 1934; Meregalli 2003). On November 14, the Austro-Hungarian forces launched a massive offensive against the newly established Italian defensive lines on the Grappa Massif, deploying a wide array of destructive measures. These included large-caliber artillery, flamethrowers, and poison gas, resulting in an unrelenting assault. The attack was launched simultaneously from the east and west, striking the ridges converging on Cima Grappa. The enemy persisted with repeated and relentless waves of attacks, continuously reinforcing their numbers. On November 26, the Italians successfully reclaimed Col Beretta in the western sector of the massif, marking the conclusion of the first and most grueling phase of the battle, which coincided with the Italian Army's desperate retreat crisis (Caviglia 1934). Following this ordeal, Allied forces, including the French XXXI Corps, arrived in Italy and reinforced the eastern ridge of the Grappa Massif at Monfenera on December 5 (Pozzato & Volpato 2024). After regrouping, the Austro-Hungarians resumed their offensive on December 11, briefly capturing key peaks such as Valderoa and Monte Asolone. Nevertheless, further attacks were repelled, and by December 21, the Austro-Hungarians abandoned any further attempts.

The Battle of June 1918

During the winter, the Italian defenses were significantly reinforced with rock fortifications, trenches, pillboxes, and extensive barbed wire. Among the most notable additions was the famed Vittorio Emanuele III tunnel, carved into the rock beneath the summit of Cima Grappa. This engineering marvel housed powerful cave artillery positions and offensive outlets for counterattacks (Cadorna 1921). The Austro-Hungarians launched their final offensive on June 15, 1918, supported by their 11th Army. In this sector, the Italian artillery was able to deliver a formidable counter-battery barrage, almost simultaneous with the Austro-Hungarian preparatory fire, thereby mitigating much of its destructive potential (Meregalli 2003). Despite initial successes, as the Austro-Hungarian forces exploited dense fog to break through Italian front lines, their advance was swiftly halted. By the following day, June 16, Italian counterattacks had regained all lost ground. The conclusion of the June 1918 battle proved decisive in the broader context of the war against the Austro-Hungarian Empire, which would collapse just four months later (Montanari 2001).

The Final Battle

The task entrusted to the IV Italian Army, operating on the Grappa Massif, was to break through to the north towards Feltre to facilitate the action of the Armies attacking on the plain along the Piave River. The Italian attack began on 24 October 1918, preceded by intense artillery preparations (Caviglia 1934; Meregalli 2003). The first successes were followed by repeated counterattacks that lasted until 28 October: on 29 October the IV Army, also thanks to the successes of the Italian armies on the plain, advanced along the entire front, overwhelming any remaining resistance. 4 November was the date set for the armistice, and by that time the IV Army had already overrun the entire Grappa Massif.

2 Data Sources and Methodologies

2.1 Data Sources

During the 20th century, the two World Wars saw the warring armies engage in the large-scale production of strategic information. This mass of data, critical for the planning and execution of military operations, took various forms. Supreme commands issued directives and daily battle orders through written communications, while detailed topographic maps provided a visual representation of the battlefield, depicting enemy deployments, fortifications, artillery positions, and encampments. The use of aerial photography enabled further analysis of enemy-held territories and facilitated the assessment of bombing raids' impacts. After the conflicts, much of this information was preserved in military and national archives, where it is now accessible for consultation and reproduction for historical research purposes.

For this study, we analyzed a series of 51 maps at a 1:25,000 scale, which detailed the positioning of Italian defenses and military assets (trenches, pathways, artillery, machine guns, etc.) as recorded by Austro-Hungarian cartographic services. These maps are part of a collection titled *Miscellanea di mappe militari della Prima Guerra Mondiale*, housed in the State Archives of Florence and published in Bondesan and Scroccaro (2017). The collection includes both topographic and military maps produced by Italian and Austrian services between 1916 and 1918.

Although all the maps focus on the Grappa Massif, not all of them cover the mountain in its entirety, and they span a chronological range from February to October 1918. To comprehensively represent the entire war front of the Grappa Massif—from the Brenta Valley in the west to the Piave River in the east—we selected eight maps that cover this area in three chronological phases: February-March, May, and August. This selection allowed us to track the updates in military assessments over time (Table 1).

We also analyzed the First World War aerial photos (Table 2) from the "First World War" collection held at the archive of the Ufficio Storico dell'Aeronautica Militare (AUSAM), which is part of the Italian Air Force General Staff 5th Department 'Communication'.

2.2 Digitization and Categorization of Military Elements

The maps were georeferenced using ArcMAP 10.8.1™, achieving a mean least square error of 16 m (equivalent to less than a millimeter on these maps). The military data were

Table 1. The 8 maps digitized and vectorized for GIS analysis.

ASFi Code	Issue date	Map title	Editor	Type of assessment	Scale
R6 15	02/05/1918	Valbrenta	k.u.k 11. Armeekommando. Kriegsvermessung Nr 11 Res. Nr 105/Phm	trenches, artillery, and logistic items	1: 25.000
P 200/12	03/08/1918	Grappa	k.u.k Kriegsvermessung n. 11, Feldpost 511	trenches, artillery, and logistic items	1: 25.000
P 200/14	04/05/1918	Brenta - Tal	k.u.k Kriegsvermessung n. 11, Op. Nr. 23.900/17 Art, Feldpost 511	trenches, artillery, and logistic items	1: 25.000
R5_200	05/22/1918	Brenta-Tal	k.u.k Kriegrsvermessung Nr. 11 Res. Nr 4288/Phm	trenches and artillery	1: 25.000
R5 200/10	05/22/1918	Grappa	k.u.k Kriegrsvermessung Nr. 11 Res. Nr. 288. Phm, Feldpost 511	trenches, artillery, and logistic items	1: 25.000
R5 200/9	07/20/1918	Grappa - Südhälfte	k.u.k Kriegrsvermessung Nr. 11, Feldpost 511	trenches, artillery, and logistic items	1: 25.000
R5 200/3	08/25/1918	Grappa - Südhälfte	k.u.k Kriegrsvermessung Nr. 11	trenches, artillery, and logistic items	1: 25.000
R5 200/4	08/25/1918	Grappa Nordhälfte	k.u.k 11. Armeekommando. Op. Nr. 23900/58 art	trenches, artillery, and logistic items	1: 25.000

digitized on screen into three GIS feature types—points, polylines, and polygons—each accompanied by descriptive information in the attribute table.

The photos were georeferenced in QGIS (version 3.34 LTR); the Thin Plate Spline (TPS) transformation type was used, with Cubic resampling method.

Once maps and aerial images were georeferenced, military elements such as trenches, artillery, and logistic structures were digitized and classified into point, line, and polygon geometries. These were further organized into thematic layers according to their military function:

- **Artillery and weaponry:** including light, medium, and heavy artillery, anti-aircraft guns, and machine gun positions.

Table 2. The 5 photos digitized and vectorized for GIS analysis.

AUSAM Code	Issue date	Photo title	Type of assessment
163/5117	26/12/1917	Monte Grappa (trinceramenti sulla cresta)	forward observation posts. Communication trench and logistic items
172/5157	13/12/1917	Cima del Monte Grappa	trenches, communication trench and Forward observation posts
175/5170	26/12/1917	Trinceramenti e baraccamenti su Monte Grappa	manned trench sections, unmanned trench sections, wire entanglement belts, shelter huts, truck road
228/5210	08/08/1918	Monte Grappa	trenches and logistic items
918/5173	Not present	Ricoveri sulle pendici del Grappa	logistic items

- **Logistics and infrastructure:** such as barracks, observation posts, command stations, and supply depots.
- **Defensive structures:** trenches, wire entanglements, and communication trenches.
- **Communication networks:** roads, mule tracks, narrow-gauge railways (Decauville lines), and cableways.

The maps' original symbology was enhanced by comparing and integrating additional elements from Austrian and Italian legends, resulting in a more comprehensive digital legend with 47 classes for point features, 12 for line features, and 5 for polygon features.

The historical series of 1:25,000 scale maps from the Istituto Geografico Militare Italiano (IGMI) of Florence, held at the Ca' Borin Library of the University of Padua, which covers the Grappa Massif area, was used to map civilian targets (bridges, railways, railway stations and roads). These maps were georeferenced using QGIS, employing a Thin Plate Spline transformation, with a Nearest Neighbor resampling method. Finally, data on war ordnance disposal operations carried out in the study area over the last ten years were acquired from the 5° Reparto Infrastrutture - Ufficio B.C.M. of the Comando Forze Operative Nord of the Italian Army based in Padua, which deals with the disposal of war ordnance. The UXO disposal reports contain information on the location and type of ordnance found. The recovery points were mapped in QGIS, with the information from the reports being entered in the attribute table.

2.3 Spatial Analysis Using GIS

The digitized elements were subjected to various spatial analyses, including visibility analysis and cost analysis, to model battlefield conditions. The visibility analysis, utilizing a Digital Terrain Model (DTM), was used to determine areas visible from key positions in the Italian and Austro-Hungarian frontlines. This allowed for an understanding of how terrain impacted military strategies during the war. Additionally, cost analysis was applied to estimate the resistance of different elements (e.g., trenches, machine gun positions) to enemy advances based on the terrain's slope, visibility, and exposure to artillery fire.

To assess the risk of unexploded ordnance (UXO), buffer zones were created around artillery positions and other sensitive targets using Circular Error Probable (CEP) values. This method allowed for the development of UXO probability maps, helping to identify areas that are at higher risk for UXO discovery.

One of the measures used for the evaluation of bomb risk is the CEP (circular error probable), a measure of a weapon system's precision. It is defined as the radius of a circle around the target within which 50% of the projectiles or munitions will fall in repeated firing (Mackenzie, 1990). A smaller CEP indicates higher precision, meaning the shots are more tightly clustered around the target. (Fig. 1).

For the creation of the probability map, buffer zones were generated in QGIS around sensitive targets, using the CEP values as the radius.

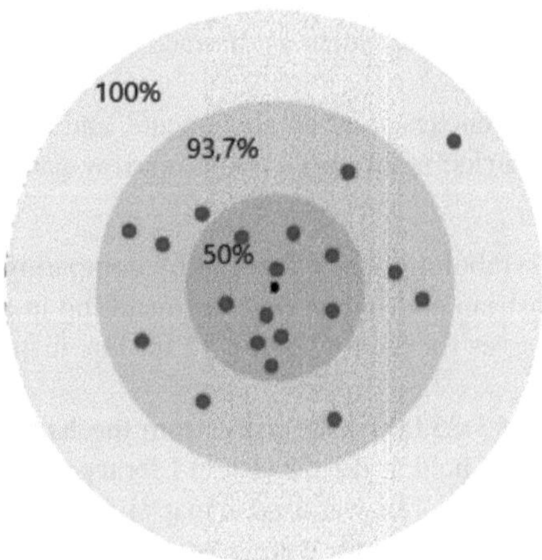

Fig. 1. CEP (circular error probable), a measure of a weapon system's precision.

2.4 Chronological Development of the Frontline

The chronological development of military structures on Monte Grappa was carefully analyzed using maps from different time periods—March, May, and August 1918. This temporal analysis revealed the evolution of the Italian defensive lines, including key battlegrounds such as Monte Asolone and Cima Grappa. For example, in the western Grappa sector, a series of defensive lines—Alba, Bianca, and Clelia—were identified, along with defensive posts (referred to as "rock positions") that were designed to slow down any Austrian advances.

The construction of extensive military infrastructure, particularly in the period following the Battle of Caporetto in late 1917, greatly altered the landscape of Monte Grappa. New roads, including the famous "Cadorna road," as well as cableways and water supply systems, were built to support the movement of troops and artillery. Additionally, large-scale fortifications, including the Vittorio Emanuele III tunnel, were excavated to house artillery and supply depots. These fortifications played a crucial role in both the defensive and offensive operations during 1918, and their locations were carefully digitized to reflect their strategic significance.

2.5 Data Analysis and Statistics

Using GIS, the linear and areal extent of trenches, communication trenches, and wire entanglements were calculated for each map. For example, the total length of trenches digitized from the maps ranges from 50 km in February 1918 to nearly 180 km in August 1918. Similarly, the area of logistical structures, such as supply depots and barracks, was measured, with significant expansions noted as the war progressed. These datasets provide quantitative insights into the scale of military operations on Monte Grappa, further enhancing our understanding of the war landscape.

The methodology employed in this study ensures a detailed and accurate reconstruction of military structures and landscapes, offering valuable data for future studies on war risk and landscape transformation.

3 Results

A first result of the GIS analysis on the military maps was the map of military installations (Fig. 2). This resulted in three series of military installations and arrangements: a late winter one, a spring one and a summer one. It was noted how the installations gradually settled and completed towards an "optimal" form in a military logistical sense for the needs of that type of war. Suffice it to say that on a front of about 25 km, from the Brenta

Canal in the west to the Piave Canal in the east, there will be the development of about 325 km of trenches alone, or 13 km of preparations for every km of front. But to these are also added about 94 km of walkways, almost always dug into the rock. Almost 800 artillery positions, also counting the anti-aircraft ones, which is equivalent to one every 25 m of linear development of the front. The cave positions that the Austro-Hungarians managed to map are 1219, as if to say one every 20 m of front development.

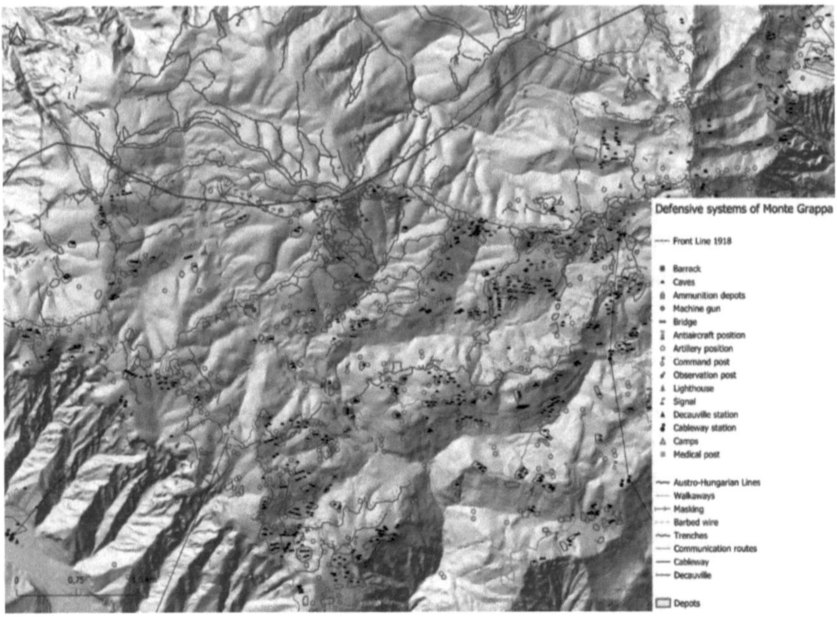

Fig. 2. Map of WWI military installations in the Grappa Massif.

It is possible to understand from these numbers and considering the difficult access to these places how it is of great interest to be able to locate the major concentrations of these elements to draw indications on the danger that still lurks after more than a century. A first index, not exhaustive however, can be the density of installations per unit area (Fig. 3).

This analysis of the Italian side of the front reveals that the most intense points of conflict were inevitably those with the highest levels of both defensive and offensive fortifications, such as Cima Grappa, Monte Tomba, the Colli line, and particularly Monte Asolone, where the concentration of recorded information is at its maximum. It should be noted that reclamation efforts focused on the areas most densely littered with material and subject to frequent bombardment, as well as those that were more easily accessible. Consequently, it is possible that the current risk remains higher in the more inaccessible and less frequently bombarded areas, or in zones less impacted by logistics and preparations.

For the mapped civilian targets and findings (exposed elements), buffer zones were created using a value equal to the Circular Error Probable (CEP). Each buffer was

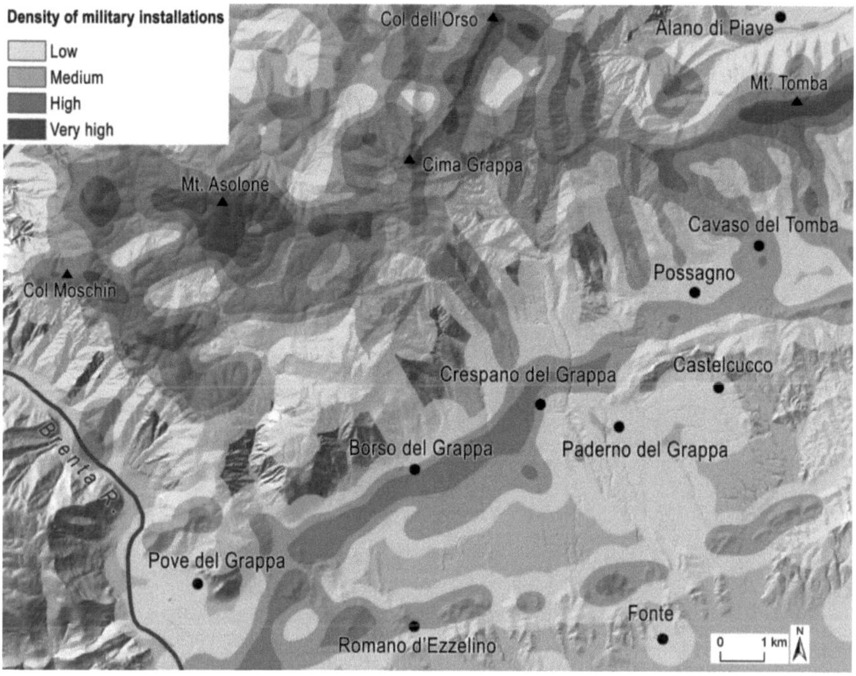

Fig. 3. Map of the density of military installations on the Grappa massif during the last year of the First World War.

assigned a weight —a probability value ranging from 4 to 0.66— based on the type of exposed element and its distance from the target of the bombardment. The resulting overlay of these buffers was classified into a hazard range, with values spanning from 1 (very low) to 10 (extremely high) (Fig. 4).

Areas with a high density of defensive emplacements, located on the highest part of Grappa Massif, are at greater risk of UXO (Unexploded Ordnance) discovery. However, areas further downstream, especially along the old railway (Decauville) and the rear trench lines, are not exempt from danger. These areas are now urbanized, therefore more exposed to UXO risk.

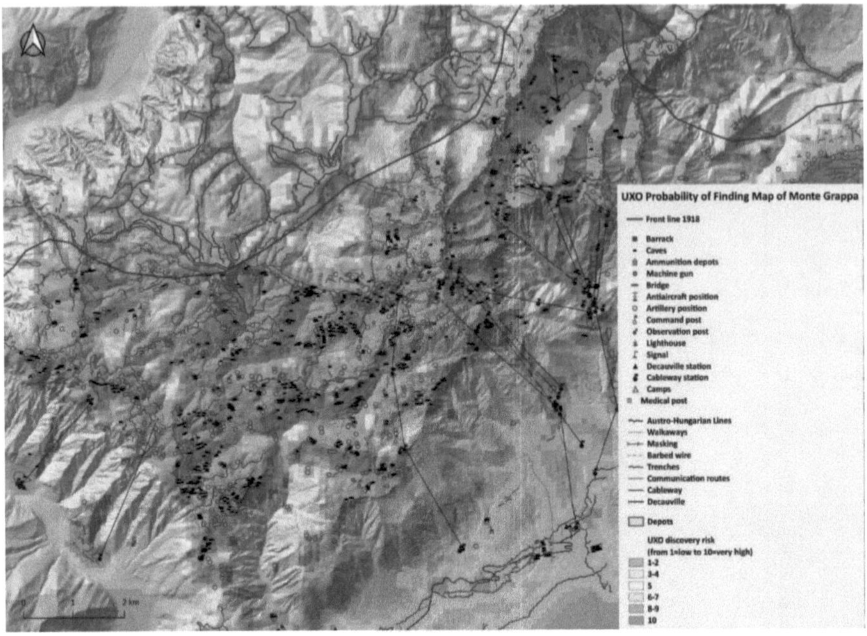

Fig. 4. Map of WWI military installations in the Grappa Massif.

4 Conclusions

This study has successfully integrated a GIS-based analysis of military maps and aerial imagery to evaluate the occurrence probability of unexploded ordnance (UXO) on the Grappa Massif. By leveraging historical data, particularly the maps from the "Miscellanea di Mappe Militari della Prima Guerra Mondiale" (Bondesan and Scroccaro, 2017), and modern geospatial technologies, this research provides a detailed spatial perspective on the military landscape during World War I, with a specific focus on the distribution of fortifications and conflict zones. The Grappa Massif, a key battleground during the war, remains an area of significant historical and environmental concern due to the enduring presence of UXO, particularly in remote or less accessible regions.

The comprehensive georeferencing of the maps and subsequent digitalization of military structures such as trenches, artillery, and logistical installations has revealed the density and distribution of military elements over time. These data allowed for the creation of UXO probability maps, crucial for modern excavation, conservation, and land-use planning activities. Areas with higher concentrations of military installations, such as Monte Asolone and Cima Grappa, were identified as having a higher UXO risk. Despite past efforts to clear UXO, the rugged and less accessible terrain remains hazardous, underscoring the need for continued vigilance in risk assessment and clearance operations.

This research also highlights the critical importance of using historical military records in conjunction with modern GIS tools to assess war-related risks. The application of Circular Error Probable (CEP) buffers around key military targets, has provided valuable insights into the spatial patterns of military activity and the areas most likely to contain unexploded ordnance. These findings contribute to both the historical understanding of the Grappa Massif's wartime significance and to practical applications for reducing UXO-related risks today.

References

Agnini, C., Muttoni, G., Kent, D.V., Rio, D.: Eocene biostratigraphy, magnetic stratigraphy and paleoenvironmental history from the Possagno section (Southern Alps, Italy). Geol. Soc. Am. Bull. **118**(3–4), 425–435 (2006). https://doi.org/10.1130/B25781.1

Bassi, D., Nebelsick, J.H.: Facies analysis and paleoenvironmental interpretation of Eocene ramp deposits (northeastern Italy). Facies **56**, 275–290 (2010). https://doi.org/10.1007/s10347-009-0210-5

Bolli, H.M.: Planktonic foraminifera from the Upper Paleocene and Lower Eocene of the Possagno section (Venetian Alps, Italy). Palaeogeogr. Palaeoclimatol. Palaeoecol. **18**(1), 123–154 (1975). https://doi.org/10.1016/0031-0182(75)90062-6

Bondesan, A., Busoni, S.: I segni del passato geologico: Viaggio tra i geositi della provincia di Treviso. Antiga Edizioni, Crocetta del Montello (Treviso) (2019). ISBN: 978-88-8435-169-2

Bosellini, A., Winterer, E.L., Bosellini, A: Subsidence and sedimentation in the Jurassic "Trento Plateau," Southern Alps, Italy. In: SEPM Special Publication, vol. 32, pp. 213–230 (1981). https://doi.org/10.2110/pec.81.32.0213

Cadorna, L: La guerra alla fronte italiana. F.lli Treves, Milano (1921)

Carraro, F., Dal Piaz, G.V., Martin, S.: Carta Geologica del Massiccio del Grappa. In: Le Alpi dal Mesozoico ai giorni nostri, pp. 51–75. Studi Trentini di Scienze Naturali, Acta Geologica (1989)

Castellarin, A., Vai, G.B., Cantelli, L.: The Alpine evolution of the Southern Alps around the Giudicarie faults: a late cretaceous to early Eocene transfer zone. Tectonophysics **223**(1–2), 77–106 (1992). https://doi.org/10.1016/0040-1951(92)90297-F

Caviglia, E.: Le tre battaglie del Piave. Mondadori, Milano (1934)

Dal Piaz, G.V., Massari, F., Castellarin, A.: Alpine tectonics and the evolution of the southern Alps. J. Geol. Soc. **160**(1), 49–59 (2003). https://doi.org/10.1144/0016-764902-093

Doglioni, C., Grandesso, P., Masetti, D., Pellegrini, G.B., Tracanella, E.: Note illustrative del Foglio 063 Belluno alla scala 1:50,000. Istituto Poligrafico e Zecca dello Stato, Roma (1996)

Giardino, G.: Rievocazioni e riflessioni di guerra. III L'Armata del Grappa. Mondadori, Milano (1930)

Meregalli, C.: Grande Guerra sul Grappa. Von Dellmensingen: "Il monte sacro degli italiani". Tassoti, Bassano del Grappa (2003)

Montanari, M.: Caratteristiche e significato della battaglia del Solstizio. AA.VV.: Al di qua e al di là del Piave. L'ultimo anno della Grande Guerra. Franco Angeli, Milano (2001)

Pozzato, P., Volpato, P.: Guerra sul Piave e sul Monte Grappa. La battaglia di Monte Cornella e la conquista di Quero. Itinera Progetti editore, Bassano del Grappa (2024)

Reato, S.: Geomorfologia dei terrazzi torrentizio-glaciali prewürmiani e würmiani generati dalla valle del Làstego, al confine tra Possagno, Fietta e Paderno del Grappa. De Rerum Natura, Quaderni Del Museo di Storia Naturale e Archeologia di Montebelluna **4**, 17–24 (2006)

Ronchi, A., Martin, S., Carraro, F.: Deformation pattern in the northern sector of the Southern Alps (Grappa-Monte Grappa). Tectonophysics **576–577**, 162–180 (2012). https://doi.org/10.1016/j.tecto.2012.04.018

Saccon, L.: Il paesaggio delle colline dell'Alta Marca trevigiana e l'architettura spontanea della Valsana. In: Esercizi di paesaggio. Regione del Veneto, vol. 4, 91–103 (2011)

Winterer, E.L., Bosellini, A.: Subsidence and sedimentation on Jurassic passive continental margins of Tethys. In: SEPM Special Publication, vol. 32, pp. 201–217 (1981) https://doi.org/10.2110/pec.81.32.0201

Zempolich, W.G.: The drowning succession of a Jurassic platform, northern Italy: a record of supercontinent breakup, eustasy, and carbon flux. J. Sediment. Res. **63**(4) (1993). https://doi.org/10.1306/D4267CFA-2B26-11D7-8648000102C1865D

Unmanned Aerial Vehicles (UAV) in Supporting Firefighters Activities in Extreme Weather Calamities: A Real-Case Application

Onofrio Lorusso(✉), Santo Vazzano, and Francesco Spinella

Italian National Fire and Rescue Service, Department of Firefighters, Public Rescue and Civil Defence, Italian Ministry of Interior, Rome, Italy
{onofrio.lorusso,santo.vazzano,francesco.spinella}@vigilfuoco.it

Abstract. Past years several large storms have caused severe weather emergencies affecting the Italian territory and putting a strain on populations and civil protection systems. On this context, the Italian Fire and Rescue Service (CNVVF), deploys specialized resources to deal with this type of emergency such as search and rescue (SAR) activities in aquatic environment, countering aquatic hazards with rescuers and vehicles, as well as rescue management and strategic scenario characterization preparatory to response planning and resources mobilization. In the following, the focus will be on a key tool in monitoring and planning perspective, i.e. the unmanned aerial vehicles (UAV), commonly referred to as drones. In the first stages of the emergency, the use of drones allows a rapid characterization of the scenario and an initial estimate of the magnitude of the damage caused by the event. Due to their high mobility, ready deployment, and high flexibility of use, drones allow to cover large areas of territory in a short time with a reduced deployment of units. Moreover, their utilization allows for an initial qualitative assessment of the intervention requests, which, aided by the topographic applied to rescue (TAS), units permits to obtain georeferenced information on the scenarios useful to the appropriate dimensioning of the rescuer's response. The article will discuss a specific case of drone monitoring technique utilization in a real calamity after a storm that hit the Lombardy region on July 21–24, 2023. The focus will be precisely on the municipality of Turate, in the province of Como, in the northern part of Lombardy. Eventually, with the support of the acquired images, it will be demonstrated how, through the acquisition of real-time georeferenced images, it is possible to provide a broad picture of the scenario to support the decision-making process of the Incident Command System (ICS). With the help of drone monitoring techniques, rescue services corps such as the CNVVF are able to provide faster and more relevant responses to emergencies that in different ways and at different times affect the community.

Keywords: Calamity · Storm · Firefighters · Rescue Service · Drone · UAV

E. Borgogno-Mondino and P. Zamperlin (Eds.): ASITA 2024, CCIS 2463, pp. 77–85, 2025.
https://doi.org/10.1007/978-3-031-91141-5_6

1 Introduction

In the recent past, the frequency and intensity of extreme weather events have increased globally, largely driven by climate change [1]. As well known, Italy its characterized by its diverse geography and complex climatic patterns. This type of territory is particularly vulnerable to such events, including heavy storms, floods and landslides. The Italian Fire and Rescue Service (CNVVF) [2], in its role as one of the main components of the national civil protection system, in collaboration with the civil protection department [3], plays a critical role in responding to these emergencies. A key element for civil protection response strategies is the optimal integration between the widely adopted common procedures and systems with the most recent and advanced technologies, such as unmanned aerial vehicles (UAV), usually referred to as drones [4, 5]. Currently, the use of drones is an essential tool in emergency management. Due to their ability to provide rapid and real-time data across involved areas, it can be a useful tool, supporting the rescuer's decision-making during the events, not only in emergencies caused by severe weather events, but in all those situations where a rapid scenario assessment is crucial, e.g. in forest firefighting [6] or after earthquakes [7]. The ability to collect and analyze information in a rapid and accurate way, and georeferencing crucial information about affected areas, can dramatically improve the effectiveness of response efforts. This is crucial in the early stages of an emergency, when rapid data collection directly improves situational awareness of the disaster's scale, which is often initially unclear. The CNVVF, utilizing its specialized UAV units and the Topographic Applied to Rescue (TAS) service, employs drone technology to comprehensively assess disaster scenarios. These technologies allow the CNVVF forces to assess damage, identify areas in need of immediate intervention, and allocate resources accordingly. The ability to rapidly assess the scenario, allowed by the timely deployment of CNVVF operators specialized in UAV operation, significantly enhances the efficacy of rescue operations, maximizing the life-saving potential within the intervention.

A first section of the paper will be devoted to a brief description of the scenario where CNVVF commonly serves, and to the capabilities and capacities devoted to rescue operations in aquatic hazards scenarios such as floods, heavy storms, rivers or gorges in flood, or lakes and seas. Consequently, the focus will move on the application of drones in the response to a major weather emergency that affected the Lombardy region of Italy in July 2023. The municipality of Turate in the province of Como was one of the most impacted areas by the storm, and the use of drone technology was pivotal in managing the response and in the cooperation with local authorities and volunteers. By capturing real-time, georeferenced imagery, the CNVVF was able to create a detailed overview of the affected area, facilitating a faster and more targeted response and resource allocation. This case study highlights the benefits of integrating drone technology into emergency response strategies, and illustrates the importance of innovative tools in addressing the increasing challenges posed by extreme weather events.

2 The Italian Fire and Rescue Service in Meteo-Hydro and Hydraulic Risk

Meteo-hydro and hydraulic risks refer to the range of phenomena triggered by adverse weather conditions that result in actual or potential damage caused by water. These hazards include a wide variety of events, such as thunderstorms, high winds, sea storms, fog, snow and ice accumulation, landslides, floods, coastal erosion etc. Each of these phenomena presents unique threats to both human populations and infrastructure, often with minimal warning. The increasing frequency of extreme weather events highlights the critical need for efficient risk management and response strategies. As a consequence, the demand for advanced skills and knowledge among rescue personnel has grown, in order to always ensure a response that meets the needs and expectations of the population. Addressing these extreme events requires ongoing adaptation and the development of specialized skills to manage evolving hydrogeological risks. In this context, the Italian Fire and Rescue Service, with its widespread network of commands, fire stations, and specialized units, provides a multifaceted response to a variety of emergencies. The CNVVF is divided into several branches, including land-based firefighting teams, aerial and nautical units, and specialized rescue divisions such as those trained in aquatic rescue. These units work in coordination during emergencies, ensuring a comprehensive and efficient response. The CNVVF carries out its emergency operations using the Incident Command System (ICS), a widely used management model designed to organize and coordinate responses to complex incidents. Implemented within the CNVVF framework through Note n. 01/2020, the ICS provides a clear structure for managing tasks and actions during emergencies. It helps to manage both the intervention phase and the post-incident analysis, ensuring that resources are efficiently allocated and operations are well coordinated. This system allows the CNVVF to effectively manage large-scale emergencies, where multiple teams and specialized units need to work together. When facing weather-related emergencies, particularly in flood-prone or storm-affected areas, the CNVVF mobilizes a wide range of resources and personnel. The early stages are often critical in saving lives. A rapid deployment with suitable units is therefore essential to enhance the overall effectiveness of a rescue operation. Depending on the emergency scenario, the standard rescue teams trained in aquatic self-protection can be supported by specialized swiftwater and flood rescue units (SFA) (Fig. 1), aquatic rescue units (SA), and rescue divers (SMZ).

One of the key strengths of the Italian Fire and Rescue Service in managing large-scale emergencies is the ability to deploy the so-called "mobile column". This operational framework enables the assembly of rescue teams from multiple commands and multiple regions, in order to maximize response efficiency in the immediate aftermath of an event, providing also the greatest possible support to the affected areas. The composition of these teams, in terms of size, vehicles, and equipment, is tailored to the specific scenario. In water-related emergencies, for example, the mobile column can be equipped with amphibious vehicles, multiple teams of aquatic and flood rescuers, high-capacity water pumping modules, and so on. These units can also be integrated with other units for logistical support, guaranteeing the operational autonomy for the duration of the

Fig. 1. CNVVF aquatic and flood rescue units.

emergency, therefore ensuring a sustained and effective response to the crisis, also providing a supportive presence for the affected population during the delicate phases of the emergency.

3 The Weather Emergency of Turate – July 2023

In July 2023 a powerful storm struck northern Italy, causing significant damage in Piedmont and Lombardy. Characterized by heavy precipitation, high winds, and violent thunderstorms, this extreme meteorological event caused extensive damage across provinces including Varese, Como, Milan and Lecco. Over three days (from July 21 to July 24), heavy rainfall led to localized flooding, downed trees and infrastructure damage, particularly affecting urban and rural areas.

The storm resulted in significant hydrological stress on local rivers and drainage systems, overwhelming existing infrastructure and leading to rapid overflow in low-lying areas. The provinces of Varese and Como recorded some of the highest rainfall levels, with over 150 mm recorded in certain areas within a 24-h period (Fig. 2).

The municipality of Turate, located in the province of Como, was one of the hardest-hit areas, suffering from severe flooding, power outages, and extensive damage to residential and commercial properties.

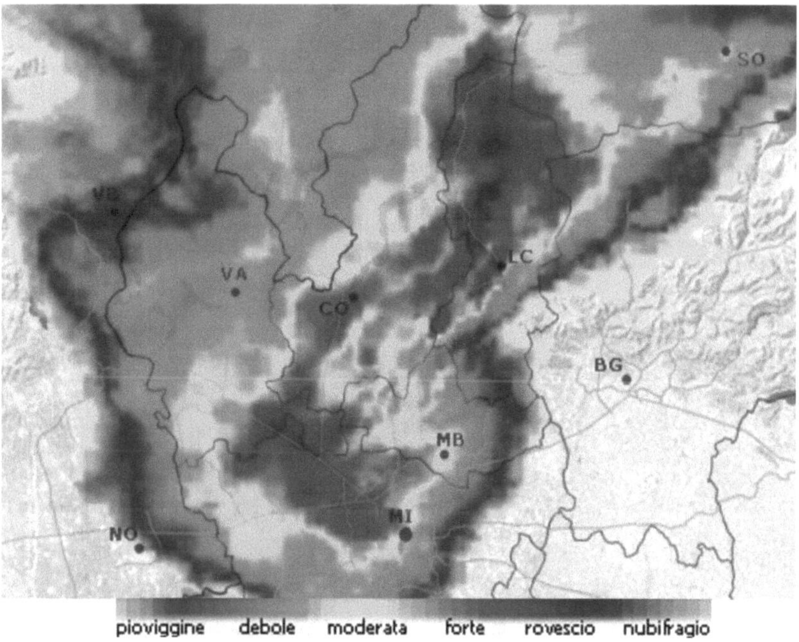

Fig. 2. Climatic event of 23 of July, 4:00 a.m.

The complicated scenario outlined resulted in a high volume of emergency calls to the territorial control rooms, heavily burdening the local response system. Firefighters teams, along with local civil protection volunteers and agencies, activated rescue and recovery operations. The CNVVF was mobilized immediately in response to the weather emergency both with ground-based teams and aerial resources. To address the challenges posed by the storm, UAV units were employed for reconnaissance and damage assessment. This assessment aimed to rapidly estimate the population's service demands, the severity of damage to affected areas, and the potential risks present for the population. In total, hundreds of interventions were carried out by CNVVF personnel, many of which are depicted in Fig. 3, showing the diversity of operations required during the crisis. These interventions mainly consisted of removing fallen trees and branches, securing damaged or uncovered roofs, pumping water from flooded buildings, and providing assistance to individuals affected by the consequences of the severe weather, particularly those with special needs or in critical facilities.

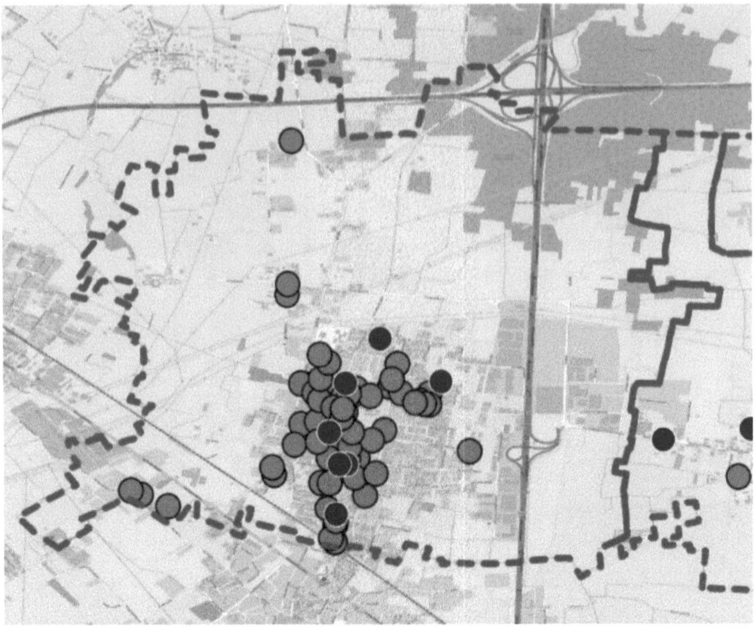

Fig. 3. Turate area with structure damages (orange points) and floods (blue points).

4 The Role of UAV in the Event

The UAV units involved operated over two days, dividing the urban area of Turate into two macro-areas. The surveys conducted, consisting of approximately 1000 images in total, were carried out at altitudes exceeding the standard 120 m above ground level (AGL), ensuring the ability to generate highly detailed orthomosaics. This level of detail significantly surpasses what could be obtained through satellite constellations, such as the European Space Agency's Sentinel-2, NASA's Landsat series, or commercial systems like PlanetScope, which generally require longer revisit times and lower spatial resolution.

The UAV surveys were conducted using a DJI Matrice 300 equipped with a Zenmuse P1 camera, and a DJI Matrice 300 with a DJI H20T camera. The camera orientation for both flights was strictly nadiral at $-90°$ to ensure optimal ground coverage.

Due to the need for rapid data processing and real-time decision-making, no physical ground control points (GCPs) were collected. Instead, the orthomosaic generation relied on an advanced processing workflow within DJI Terra software, leveraging onboard RTK corrections and sensor metadata to approximate GCPs and expedite the georeferencing process. The final orthomosaic achieved a ground sampling distance (GSD) of 1.78 cm/pixel, ensuring high spatial accuracy suitable for emergency response applications.

Due to their ability to quickly cover large areas, drones allowed the CNVVF to create a comprehensive real-time picture of the affected zones, enabling faster decision-making regarding the allocation of resources and prioritization of rescue efforts. The processed outputs from the UAV surveys were invaluable during the rescue planning phase, specifically for identifying the priority of interventions needed for securing roofs and coverings on both residential and industrial buildings. Consequently, these images played a crucial role in managing potential access restrictions to affected properties, ensuring that safety measures could be implemented effectively. Subsequently, the orthomosaics were transmitted via the Municipal Operations Center (COC) to other Civil Protection units and were utilized to facilitate an approximate assessment of the damages, aiding in the overall management of the situation and ensuring that necessary interventions could be promptly identified and executed.

One of the most significant contributions of the drone units during the response to the Turate flooding was the creation of detailed orthophotos of the area in the aftermath of the storm (Fig. 4).

Fig. 4. Raster ortophoto generated by means of CNVVF UAV fleet.

These orthophotos provided a high-definition, georeferenced aerial view of the territory, highlighting the scale of the flooding, the damage to buildings and infrastructure, and the areas where natural barriers have been destroyed. The level of detail allows for swift identification of the most critical situations. In some cases, damage to roofs (Fig. 5a) and photovoltaic systems is clearly visible (Fig. 5b).

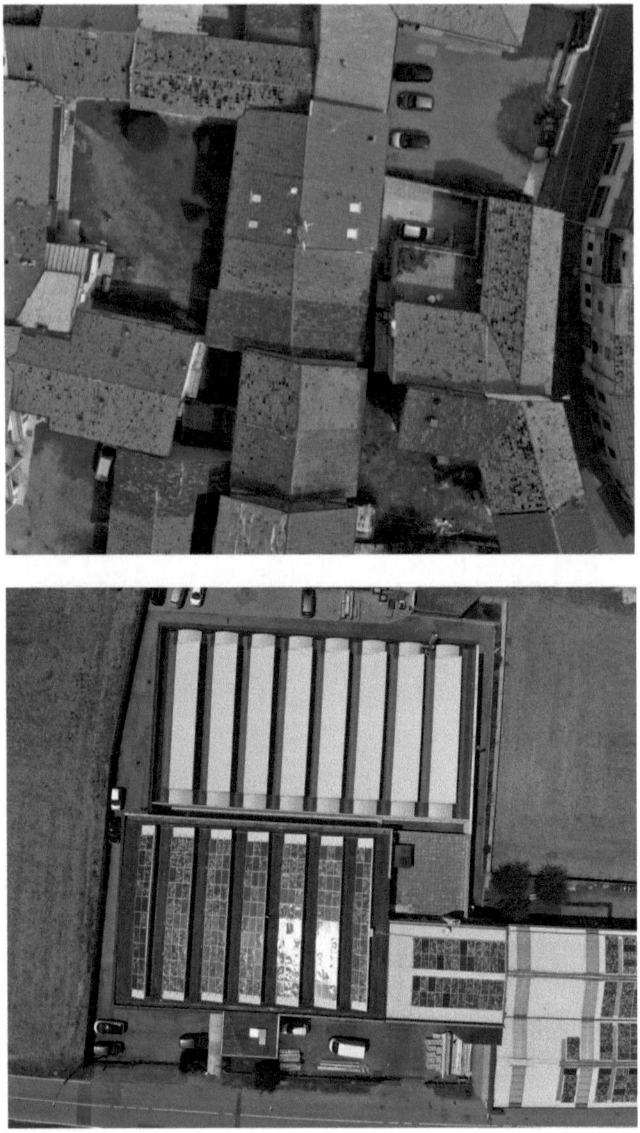

a)

b)

Fig. 5. Close-up detail of hail-damaged buildings. a) residential buildings; b) photovoltaic systems.

This detailed mapping of the affected zones helped CNVVF units to better understand the type and magnitude of damage where needed, and to plan subsequent operations with greater accuracy. Furthermore, the orthophotos were instrumental in coordinating the clean-up and recovery phases, allowing local authorities to prioritize the repair of critical infrastructure such as roads, drainage systems, and electrical grids.

The orthophotos also played a key role in post-event analysis, helping both local authorities and national agencies assess the long-term impact of the event on the environment and urban areas. By using these georeferenced images, the CNVVF could compare pre-event and post-event conditions, providing a clear picture of the changes caused by the storm and enabling the identification of areas that may be more vulnerable to future events. This data will be invaluable in strengthening both immediate response capabilities and long-term resilience planning for the region.

5 Conclusions

The increasing frequency and intensity of extreme weather events, particularly in countries like Italy, present significant challenges to emergency response systems. As demonstrated in the case of the 2023 storm in Lombardy, the use of drones as part of the CNVVF's emergency management toolkit can be a game-changing approach to handling large-scale disasters. By providing real-time, georeferenced imagery and facilitating the rapid assessment of affected areas, drones enhance the ability of rescue services to respond swiftly and effectively. Moreover, the integration of drone technology into emergency response strategies offers several key advantages. These include reducing the time needed to deploy resources, improving the accuracy of situational assessments, and enabling the creation of detailed, data-driven response plans. Drones also minimize the need for personnel to be directly exposed to hazardous environments during the initial stages of a disaster, thus enhancing the safety of rescue operations. In conclusion, as Italy continues to face the growing threat of hydrogeological hazards, the adoption of advanced technologies such as drones is essential for improving the resilience and effectiveness of its emergency response systems. By leveraging these tools, the CNVVF and other civil protection agencies can provide faster, more coordinated responses to the increasing number of weather-related emergencies, ultimately helping to safeguard communities and reduce the impact of these events.

References

1. Clarke, B., Otto, F., Stuart-Smith, R., Harrington, L.: Extreme weather impacts of climate change: an attribution perspective. Environ. Res. Clim. **1**(1), 012001 (2022)
2. Italian Fire Department Homepage. https://www.vigilfuoco.it
3. Italian Civil Protection Department Homepage. https://www.protezionecivile.gov.it
4. Mohd Daud, S.M.S., et al.: Applications of drone in disaster management: a scoping review. Sci. Justice **62**, 30–42 (2022)
5. Feliziani, F., et al.: Progetto di impiego operativo dei Sistemi Aeromobili a Pilotaggio Remoto (SAPR) del CNVVF, Atti VGR 2016, Pisa (2016)
6. Lorusso, O., Vazzano, S.: The Italian National Fire and Rescue Service activity in forest fires: the event in Montegrino Valtravaglia. In: Borgogno Mondino, E., Zamperlin, P. (eds.) Geomatics for Environmental Monitoring: From Data to Services, ASITA 2023. CCIS, vol. 2088, pp. 64–71. Springer, Cham (2024). https://doi.org/10.1007/978-3-031-59925-5_5
7. D'Urso, M.G., Manzari, V., Lucidi, S., Cuzzocrea, F.: Rescue management and assessment of structural damage by UAV in post-seismic emergency. In: ISPRS Annals of the Photogrammetry, Remote Sensing and Spatial Information Sciences, vol. V-5, pp. 61–70 (2020)

Linking the European Ground Motion Service with the Italian Landslide Inventory to Explore the Potential of Satellite Monitoring

Lena Rebecca Zastrow(✉), Gianluigi Di Paola, Carla Iadanza, Francesco Menniti, and Alessandro Trigila

ISPRA – Department of the Geological Survey of Italy, Rome, Italy
lenarebecca.zastrow@isprambiente.it

Abstract. Detecting landslides is of paramount importance for preventing damage to people and historical sites, and for preserving the overall territory. Recently, satellite imagery—specifically Differential Interferometric Synthetic Aperture Radar (DInSAR)—has proven to be an effective solution for detecting and mapping landslides in various contexts. However, the applicability of satellite monitoring for landslide detection at large spatial scales, such as regional or national levels, is still under development. In this ongoing work, we present the EGMS-in-IFFI-dataset, which represents our effort to explore the potential of these techniques. Using a custom-developed Python code, we performed a spatial intersection of the data points provided by the European Ground Motion Service (EGMS) with the geometries of landslide areas stored in the Italian Landslide Inventory (Inventario dei Fenomeni Franosi in Italia - IFFI). We detail the resulting dataset and methodology, accompanied by an exploratory statistical analysis.

Keywords: Landslide Inventory · IFFI · DInSAR · Sentinel-1 · EGMS

1 Introduction

Landslide phenomena represent a concrete threat to life, livelihoods, and the natural environment in various parts of the world [1]. Italy is among the countries most affected by these kinds of phenomena: between 1973 and 2022, landslides caused 1,077 deaths and 1,443 injuries [2]. 1.3 million inhabitants, almost 548,000 families, over 565,000 buildings (3.9% of the total), over 84,000 industries and services, and over 12,500 cultural heritage sites have been estimated to be exposed to landslide risk in Italy [3].

The causes of this fragility can be traced to the geological and geomorphological settings of the Italian territory, which makes it susceptible to slope instability phenomena, sometimes involving entire communities in mountainous and hilly areas. In this context, the localization of landslides and the identification of the types of instability that may affect a study area are crucial. In fact, for the assessment of these areas, the availability of reliable and up-to-date landslide inventories is the key element on which hazard and risk analysis should be based [4].

E. Borgogno-Mondino and P. Zamperlin (Eds.): ASITA 2024, CCIS 2463, pp. 86–101, 2025.
https://doi.org/10.1007/978-3-031-91141-5_7

Traditional methods for studying landslides are essentially based on the visual interpretation of stereoscopic aerial photographs and field surveys, which are sometimes very time-consuming [5]. To make these analyses faster and more cost-effective, the use of satellite images, which are easy to obtain, has become a widely used method for detecting and mapping landslides. Among satellite technologies, Differential Interferometric Synthetic Aperture Radar (DInSAR) has proven to be an ideal solution for detecting and mapping slow moving landslides (movements on the order of a few centimeters per year) [6–8]. DInSAR is an established method used to provide data with broad spatial coverage and to investigate different types of phenomena simultaneously, including those in areas with limited or difficult access [9, 10]. In this sense, the adoption of Multi-Temporal DInSAR (MTInSAR) techniques can be advantageous not only for static mapping of landslide phenomena but also for updating geomorphological and multi-temporal landslide inventory maps, determining landslide activity status and their temporal evolution [5, 11].

Numerous studies have documented the use of interferometric data to monitor and improve the understanding of various surface dynamics [12, 13]. Traditionally, geological hazard mapping has primarily relied on visually inspecting average velocity along the Line of Sight (LoS) or performing critical areas and cluster analysis to detect slow-moving landslides [14]. In Italy, different MTInSAR applications for landslide mapping have been developed, employing diverse approaches and techniques at varying scales of analysis, from basin level [15] to regional scale [16]. The MTInSAR potential for small-scale mapping was first explored at the national level by Confuorto et al. [17].

While satellite imagery has shown great potential in landslide detection, challenges remain, particularly in data processing, accuracy, and the need for validation with ground-truth data. To take a step forward in this direction, in this preliminary work, we present the EGM-in-IFFI-dataset which combine the information on measure points from European Ground Motion Service (EGMS) with those of landslides collected by Italian Landslide Inventory (IFFI). The goal is to create a dataset that can be used to evaluate the potential of satellite monitoring on a national scale. To this aim we collected interferometric data from the EGMS in relation to the IFFI. More specifically, we mapped Measure Points (MPs) inside the IFFI Inventory by means of a custom developed python code, ultimately creating a filtered-small sized dataset. We also perform a statistical explanatory analysis of the data providing first thoughts on its limits and potential in understanding extremely slow and very slow landslides recorded in the national inventory.

The paper is organized as follows. Section 2 presents the source datasets and target parameters. Section 3 details the methodology employed to build the EGMS-in-IFFI-dataset. In Sect. 4 we report our analysis and finally we draw conclusions and give some forwards in Sect. 5.

2 Materials and Methods

In this section, we first provide a detailed description of the sources used to build the EGMS-in-IFFI-dataset, namely EGMS dataset and IFFI Inventory. Then we introduce parameters describing the relation between satellite acquisition (track and incidence angle) and terrain geometry. We also provide an expression for the C-coefficient which simplifies the interpretation of C itself and helps to reduce the dataset dimension.

2.1 Source Data Description

EGMS Dataset. The European Ground Motion Service (EGMS) is part of the Copernicus Land Monitoring Service, designed to deliver high resolution measurements of ground movement across Europe [18]. EGMS data are provided by the Sentinel-1 satellite constellation, part of the European Space Agency's Copernicus Program. The constellation comprises two satellites, Sentinel-1A and Sentinel-1B, moving on the same polar orbit and equipped with Synthetic Aperture Radar (SAR) technology. Satellites capture images in ascending and descending acquisition geometry and operate within the C-band signal, permitting a maximal measurable displacement between two acquisitions limited by to about 14 mm ($^{\lambda}/_{4}$).

The EGMS provides time series of ground deformation for electromagnetically stable measure points (MPs) using multi-temporal interferometric methods. For each MP, descriptors of the dynamics on the overall time period are given, such as the annual mean velocity and temporal coherence computed by linear regression including the seasonality. The temporal coherence, provided as a quality parameter, measures the degree of similarity between radar signals acquired over the same area at different times.

EGMS offers data at three processing levels: at the *basic* level, displacement measurements are referenced to a local point; at the *calibrated* level, GNSS (Global Navigation Satellite System) reference is used for displacement measurements. Both, basic and calibrated have pixel resolution of 5 m $\times$ 20 m. The further elaborated *ortho* data level provides vertical and horizontal displacements on a 100 m $\times$ 100 m grid.

In this paper, to study landslides on a national scale, the calibrated dataset was used, while basic data processing is planned. In total, 815 data packages were selected to cover the study area, each representing a single burst area from the Sentinel-1A or Sentinel-1B satellites. The dataset includes both ascending (417 bursts) and descending (398 bursts) geometries, ensuring comprehensive coverage of the area of slow landslides for the time period between 2015 and 2021. The acquisition time span was 12 days until October 2016, and from October 2016 onwards, it reduced to 6 days.

IFFI Inventory. The Italian Landslide Inventory, also known as IFFI, is a comprehensive database that documents landslides across Italy. It is carried out by ISPRA (Istituto Superiore per la Protezione e la Ricerca Ambientale) and by the Regions and Autonomous Provinces. The IFFI inventory, initiated in 1999, contains detailed records of landslides, their characteristics, and the affected areas, making it a critical resource for understanding landslide hazards and risk management in Italy [19]. The IFFI database includes information on the type of landslides (e.g., falls, flows, slides), triggering factors (such as rainfall or earthquakes), and the geological and morphological conditions of the affected areas. It covers over 634,000 landslides, corresponding to approximately 8.2% of Italy's territory and making it one of the most extensive national landslide databases globally. The inventory is based on field surveys, historical data, and remote sensing techniques. Data from the IFFI inventory can be accessed through the IdroGEO web platform [20], which provides an interactive map and a landslide inventory management system for data entry and approval workflow to maintain the inventory in a distributed and collaborative manner [21].

According to the IFFI data, approximately 28% of Italian landslides are classified as rapid movements—including rockfalls, topples, and rapid debris flows—which are too fast for satellite-based InSAR monitoring. On the other hand, slower-moving landslides, which account for a significant portion of the IFFI inventory, are well-suited to satellite observation. We filtered the IFFI inventory to focus on landslides suitable for slow-motion detection [22]. Specific categories were selected with the intent to include as many relevant landslides as possible: not determined (n.d.), rotational/translational slide, lateral spread, slow earth flow, complex, Deep Seated Ground Slope Deformation (DSGSD), area with numerous shallow landslides. It is important to note that these categories could however include landslides with velocities higher than detectable. In the following, the ensemble of selected landslides is referred to as the Landslide Area of Interest (LS-AOI).

Terrain Geometry. In the framework of using satellite DInSAR data to study landslide activity, one important challenge lies in relating the measured displacement to the actual ground displacement [11].

The measured displacement along the LoS depends on acquisition geometry, defined by the LoS azimuth (ϑ) and incidence angle (φ). For the right-looking Sentinel-1 satellite, the LoS azimuth is derived from the orbit's track angle (χ) as $\vartheta = \chi + 90°$, while the incidence angle represents the deviation between the LoS and the vertical at the measurement point. The terrain geometry is obtained by a Digital Elevation Model (DEM) and is described by aspect (α) and slope (ω).

Perceived Slope. Radar images are subject to distortions depending on the slope of the terrain as perceived by the slant range. To assess this, the perceived slope (ω^*) is defined as the intersection of the plane formed by the steepest slope and the off-nadir direction, and the plane formed by the LoS and nadir direction [23] (Fig. 1).

$$\omega^* = \arctan(\cos(\vartheta - \alpha) \cdot \tan \omega) \tag{1}$$

Two scenarios of hillside exposure to the sensor are distinguished: In the *towards exposure*, where the hillside faces the sensor, LoS azimuth and aspect form an angle greater than 90°, implying $\cos(\vartheta - \alpha) < 0$. While, in the *averse exposure*, where the hillside faces away from the sensor, LoS azimuth and aspect exhibit an angular difference minor than 90° ($\cos(\vartheta - \alpha) > 0$). Consequently, from Eq. (1) it results that the perceived slope has negative values in the towards exposure and positive values in the averse exposure. (see Fig. 1.)

The perceived slope can be used to distinguish the RADAR imaging distortion classes: active layover, foreshortening, good visibility and active shadow (see Table 1) [23–25].

C-coefficient. [26] As landslide movement is driven by gravity, it typically relates to the steepest slope. The C-coefficient permits to evaluate the visibility to the sensor of displacement along the steepest slope, it is defined as the cosine of the angle between the steepest slope direction ($\hat{u}_{stsl}$) and the LoS direction ($\hat{u}_{LoS}$).

$$C = \cos(\sphericalangle(\hat{u}_{stsl}, \hat{u}_{LoS})) = \sin\varphi \cos\omega \cdot (\cos(\vartheta - \alpha)) + \cos\varphi \sin\omega, \tag{2}$$

where $\vartheta = \chi + 90°$, with χ the track angle. α is the aspect and φ and ω are incidence angle and slope respectively. The expression of the C-coefficient in Eq. (2) in terms of the incidence and LoS-azimuth angles is equivalent to the expression in terms of LoS cosines often used in literature (see Appendix A1). The formulation in Eq. (2) is intuitive and has the computational advantage of requiring fewer input variables.

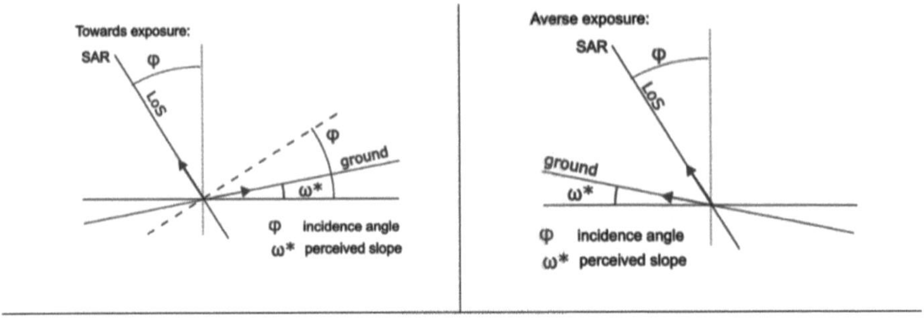

Fig. 1. Satellite acquisition in the section of LoS - nadir plane [23]. The perceived slope determines the RADAR imaging distortion as resumed in Table 1. Direction of positive displacement are indicated by arrows.

Table 1. Schematic representation of the ranges for perceived slope values with different qualitative sensor exposition.

Hillside exposure vs SAR:	Towards		Averse	
Type:	*active layover*	*foreshortening*	*good visibility*	*active shadow*
ω* range	$[-90, -\varphi]$	$(-\varphi, 0)$	$[0, 90-\varphi]$	$(90-\varphi, 90)$

3 Building the EGMS-in-IFFI-Dataset

The EGMS-in-IFFI-dataset stores the average descriptors of MPs (along with a pointer to the original timeseries) from EGMS, as well as the detailed information of the landslide to which they belong, according to their coordinates. The creation of the dataset involves 3 major steps, implemented using Python, by means of the GeoPandas library for geospatial data analysis. This setup allows for efficient handling and manipulation of large geospatial datasets.

After processing the original dataset, occupying about 200 GB of memory, the compressed output is approximately 5 GB in size and compatible with analysis tools in R, Python, and GIS. Figure 2 illustrates the workflow, detailed in the following text.

Step 1: Selection of MPs Within LS-AOI. The EGMS packages covering the national area affected by slow landslides (LS-AOI) are selected using the Sentinel-1 Burst ID map [27]. Then, for each EGMS package, we perform spatial intersection, selecting the MPs whose geographical locations lie within the LS-AOI. In case a MP falls within several landslides, separate records are created. For each MP instance, the landslide-related information is associated from the IFFI Inventory.

The output file contains a list of *MPids*, uniquely identifying each MP, and their corresponding *landslide_IDs*. Since each *MPid* is recorded for every intersecting landslide, the unique entry combines *MPid* and *landslide_ID* and is referred to as *MPinLS*. Table 2 details the associated attributes.

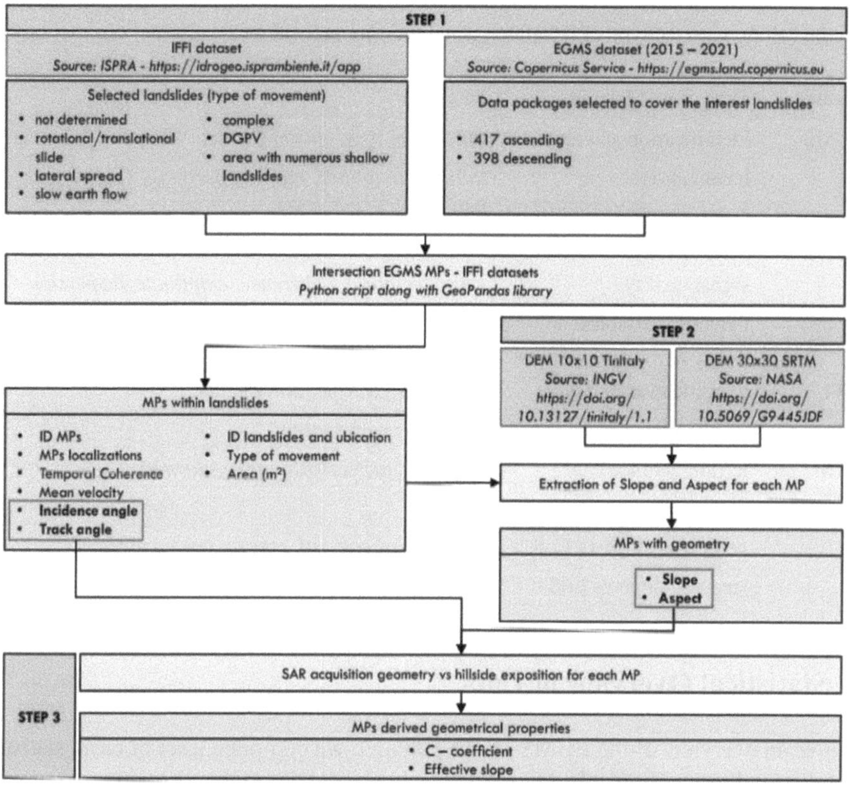

Fig. 2. Flowchart of the elaboration process.

Step 2: Local Terrain Properties Extrapolation. The terrain geometry, specifically the slope and aspect values, are associated to each MP. Two Digital Elevation Models with different resolutions are utilized: the TINITALY DEM with a resolution of 10 m × 10 m provided by National Institute of Geophysics and Volcanology - INGV [28] and the NASA Shuttle Radar Topography Mission (2013) SRTM DEM with a resolution of 30 m × 30 m [29]. Consequently, two different values for each, aspect and slope, are given in the output (*aspect10*, *aspect30* / *slope10*, *slope30*) (see Table 2).

Step 3: Calculation of Geometric Parameters. Perceived slope and C-coefficient (see Sect. 2.1) are computed for each MP using Eq. (1) and Eq. (2), respectively. The computation uses LoS azimuth and incidence angle for satellite geometry, and aspect and slope for terrain geometry. Since aspect and slope are given for either DEM (TINITALY or SRTM), each derived parameter is calculated twice, resulting in pairs of values (e.g., *C10*, *C30*, etc.) for each MP (see Table 2).

Table 2. List of attributes of the EGMS-in-IFFI-dataset. For each attribute the source dataset is specified along with the type of information and the parameter name.

Dataset	Type of information	Parameter
EGMS	identification and class	*MPid, mp_type, cluster_la*
	localization	*latitude, longitude, easting, northing, height, height_wgs, line, pixel*
	acquisition geometry	*incidence, track_angle, orbit_pass, relative_orbit*
	signal quality	*rmse, temporal_coherence, amplitude_dispersion*
	dynamic variables	*mean_velocity, stdev_mean_velocity, acceleration, stdev_acceleration, seasonality, stdev_seasonality*
IFFI	identification and class	*landslide_ID, type_movement*
	localization	*region, province, area*
DEM	terrain geometry	*aspect10, aspect30, slope10, slope30*
Derived variables		
	perceived slope vs LoS	*omega_perceived10, omega_percerceived30*
	steepest slope vs LoS	*C10, C30*

4 Statistical Overview of Data

To give an overview of the EGMS-in-IFFI dataset, we compiled a set of basic statistics useful to understand how this dataset represents landslides at the national level.

The number of detected landslides is represented as a function of MP density and temporal coherence. Specifically, we examine the number of detected landslides, when applying a minimum MP coverage threshold or a minimum value of temporal coherence. Additionally, the distribution of annual mean velocity along the LoS and the stability of derived geometrical parameters across different DEM resolutions are shown.

4.1 Coverage and Quality of Satellite Data in Landslide Areas

MP Coverage over LS-AOI. The total number of landslides within the LS-AOI are 425,003. We detected 4.59 million MPs from the ascending acquisition orbits and 4.63 million MPs from the descending orbits. A total of 102,074 landslides are covered by at least one MP, corresponding to 24% of the total selected landslides. These landslides are referred to as detectable landslides.

In Table 3 the total number and percentage of detectable landslides are shown. The "rotational/translational slides" class constitutes the most numerous class, with nearly 50% of the selected landslides. It further becomes clear that only 24% of the landslides of interest are detectable by satellite data. The DSGSD constitutes the class with the highest percentage of detectability (80%). Indeed, the sparse or absent presence of MPs within landslide areas is understandable when considering land cover; urban areas generally

Table 3. For each LS category of interest and for all LS in LS-AOI is reported the number of landslides in the IFFI inventory and of maximal detectable landslides, i.e. with at least one MP, and the resulting percentage of the detectable landslides.

LS category	Total LS in IFFI	detectable LS	Percentage detectable LS (%)
non determined	30065	5861	19.49
rotational/translational slide	205735	41315	20.08
lateral spread	77	59	76.62
slow earth flow	78091	15092	19.33
complex	56774	20241	35.65
DSGSD	2183	1757	80.49
area with numerous shallow LS	52078	17749	34.08
All categories (LS-AOI)	425003	102074	24.02

exhibit better reflection characteristics, while surfaces covered by vegetation or forest do not provide sufficient scatter points for DInSAR technology [26].

Further, the number of detectable landslides is compared with the number of landslides covered by a minimum of two MPs and those covered by at least one MP in either acquisition geometry (see Fig. 3). The results show that 42% of landslides are detectable only in one acquisition geometry. Indeed, since the ascending and descending acquisition geometries favor different exposures in terms of aspect, a landslide may be clearly visible from one acquisition but either not or partially visible or only partially visible from the other.

To further understand the details of the MP coverage, we introduce the mean density of MPs as the ratio of the total number of MPs within a landslide over the entire area of the landslide. MPs are considered independently from their acquisition geometry (note that the resulting density does not account for irregular coverage in space).

Figure 4 depicts the number of detected landslides as a function of the minimum required MP density. The first density value, corresponding to 0 MPs/sqkm, just represents the scenario with no filter imposed and the corresponding abscissa indicates the total number of detectable landslides. As the MP density increases, the number of detected landslides decreases exponentially. The behavior is illustrated in Fig. 4 with densities ranging from 0 MP/sqkm to 2000 MP/sqkm. The number of detected landslides is reduced to half of the total detectable landslides at approximately 400 MPs/sqkm. This value corresponds to 1 MP per square on a regular grid with 50-m sides.

On the other hand, applying a filter of just 50 MPs/sqkm would retain most of the original data (over 75%). This density roughly corresponds to 1 MP in a square grid with a side length of 140 m.

Figure 5 shows a comparison across different classes, where the number of detected landslides is normalized against the total number of detectable landslides. We observe the same qualitative behavior. Except for "lateral spread", the detected landslides fall below 60% at 400 MP/sqkm. Detected DSGSDs decrease rapidly for densities up to

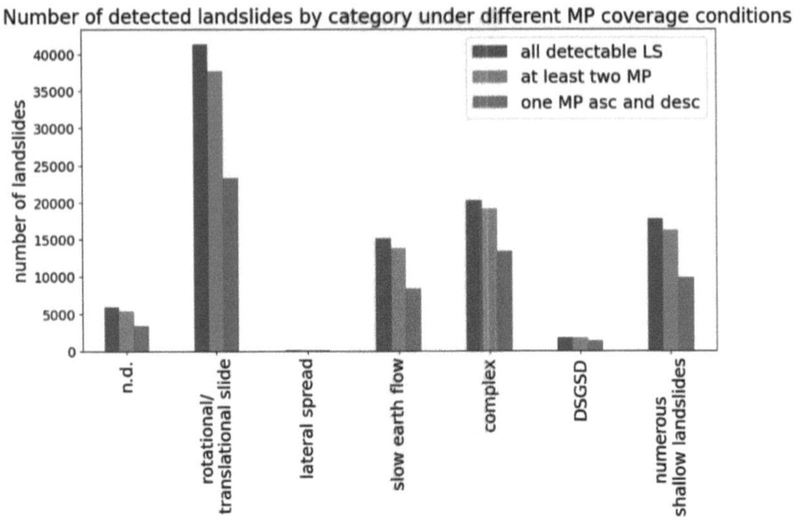

Fig. 3. Number of landslides for each of the selected categories. Blue: all the detectable landslide, orange: landslide covered by at least 2 MP and green: by at least 1 MP in both ascending and descending acquisition geometry.

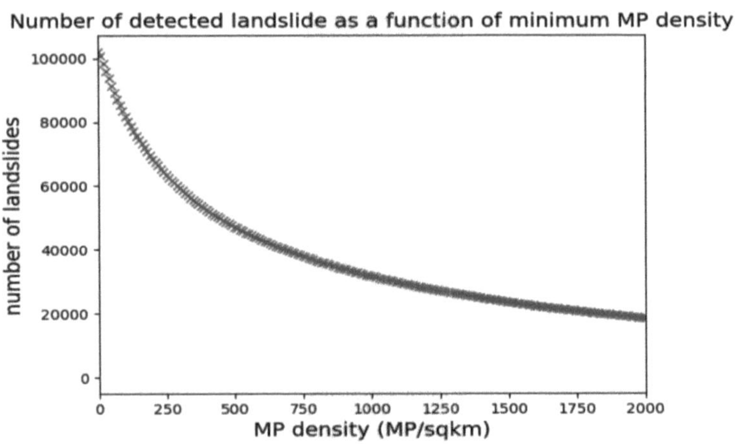

Fig. 4. Total number of detected landslides as a function of minimum required MP density. The MP density is computed as the equivalent homogeneous density of the single landslides.

100 MPs/sqkm, showing that nearly 30% of detectable DSGSDs have low MP coverage (<100 MP/sqkm). Indeed, 77% of the total DSGSD areas in the IFFI Inventory—representing nearly 50% of all DSGSD sites—are located in the Alpine arc, where vegetation and prolonged snow cover can hinder the detection of permanent scatterers [9, 20].

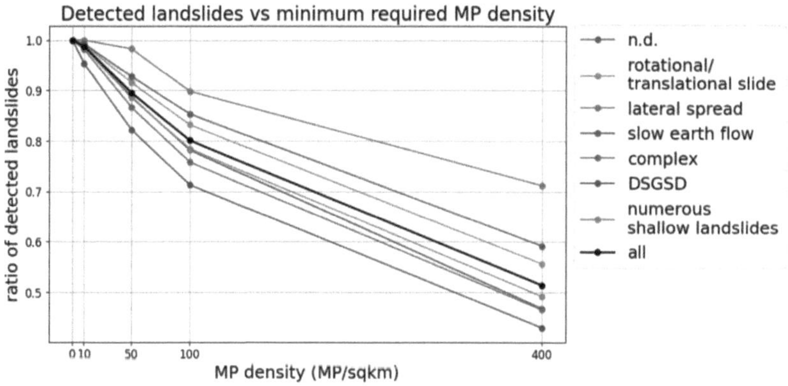

Fig. 5. Number of landslides detected with the constrain of at least 1, 10, 50, 100, 400 MPs/sqkm. Approximately linear decrease in number is observed in all categories for minimum densities up to 100 MPs/sqkm.

Temporal Coherence. Temporal coherence (TC) is a measure of quality of the mean velocity. Our interest is to investigate how, requiring a "good" (TC) impact on the number of detected landslides.

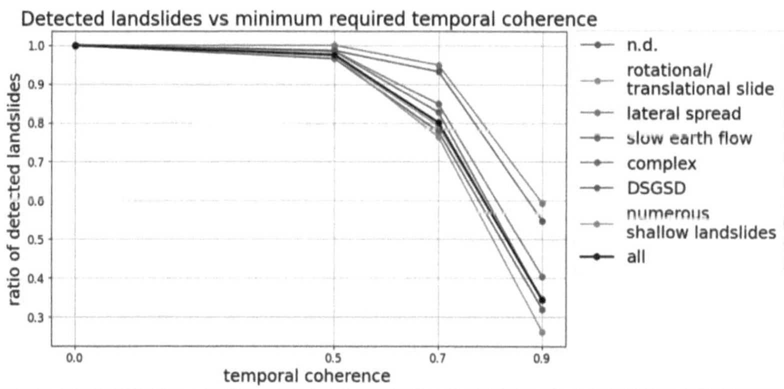

Fig. 6. Number of landslides for each category filtered by temporal coherence threshold.

Figure 6 shows the ratio of detected landslides vs TC for each class, normalized to the number of landslides with at least 1 MP.

We assume that "good" reliability is ensured for temporal coherence values equal to or greater than 0.7 [30]. This constraint leads to a significant reduction in the number of MPs, with only 54% of the MPs in the LS-AOI, while the corresponding number of landslides decreases to about 80% (see Fig. 6, black line). Note that the similar quantitative behavior observed in Fig. 6 suggests an almost uniform distribution of the coherence of the MPs over landslide categories.

The Mean Velocity. Figure 7 illustrates the distribution of mean annual velocity of MPs inside landslides. We observe that most MPs (84%) fall within the velocity range of (−3, 3) mm/year. Dividing this range further, we find that 64% of MPs have an absolute velocity of less than 1.5 mm/year, representing essentially stable points. It is also apparent that the mean velocity is skewed towards negative velocities.

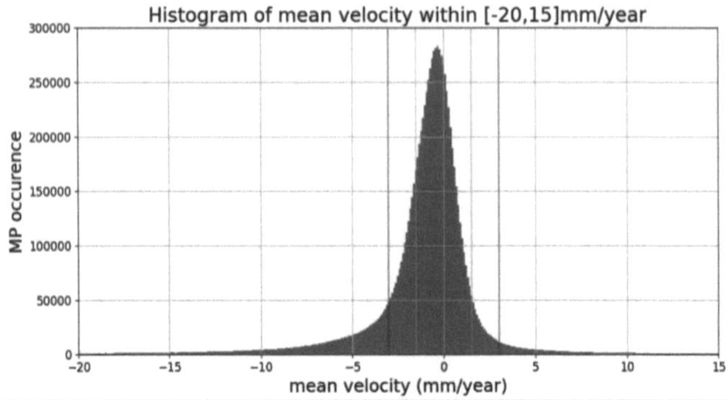

Fig. 7. Histogram of mean velocity with a cutoff interval [−20, 15] mm/year. Red lines correspond to (−3, 3) mm/year, while yellow lines correspond to (−1.5,1.5) mm/year.

Determining whether ground movement indicated by mean velocity reflects actual landslide activity or inactivity requires deeper spatial analysis. This may involve geometric interpretation, clustering within landslide polygons, investigating, in addition to the mean velocity, also accelerations or decelerations of the movement in the time series, or the application of more advanced techniques, such as machine learning.

4.2 Analysis of Derived Geometric Parameters

Due to their use for the interpretation of the mean velocity, it is interesting to evaluate the sensitivity of the geometric parameters to the variation of the underlying used DEM. For each of the two parameters—perceived slope and C-coefficient—we first present the differences in parameter values resulting from various DEM resolutions, followed by an analysis of the distribution in the distortion classes (Table 1). The variability is assessed by calculating the ratio of the absolute difference in histogram areas to the mean area of the histograms:

$$\frac{2 \cdot \sum_{\Delta x}(\mathrm{MP}_{TINITALY} - MP_{SRTM})}{\sum_{\Delta x} \mathrm{MP}_{TINITALY} + \sum_{\Delta x} MP_{SRTM}} \tag{3}$$

Perceived Slope. The variability in this parameter, obtained from DEMs with different resolutions, is estimated at approximately 7.8%, calculated using Eq. (3) on a histogram with 1° intervals ($\Delta x = 1°$). The histogram of the perceived slope is presented in Fig. 8 (left). The coarser SRTM DEM results in an increase in small perceived slope values (around 0°) and a decrease in values greater than approximately 20° in the toward-facing slopes.

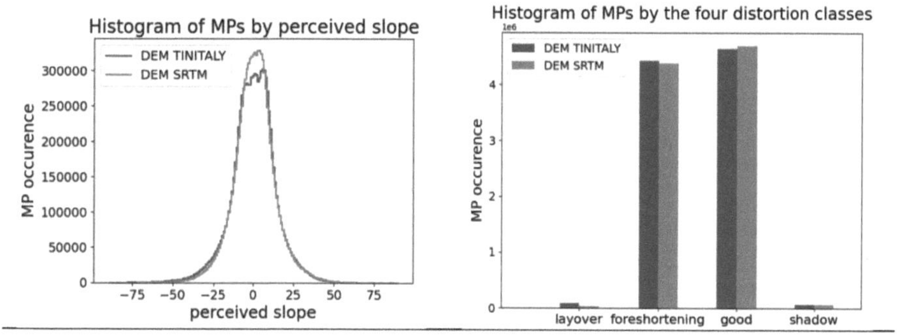

Fig. 8. Left: Histogram of values obtained for all MPinLS. Right: Classification of MPinLS in four RADAR imaging distortion classes.

Additionally, MPs are classified by RADAR imaging distortion classes for both DEMs (see Fig. 8 right). It is shown that a very small portion of MPs falls within the active layover and shadow regions, while most MPs are distributed between the foreshortening region and the region of good visibility. The perceived slope with TINITALY DEM shows a higher number of MPs in the towards exposure, which can be explained by variations of aspect values between the two DEMs.

The C-coefficient. The variability of the coefficient computed from DEM values with different resolutions is calculated using Eq. (8), to be 2.7%. The related histogram with a class interval of 0.1 is shown in Fig. 9 left. For the terrain properties derived from TINITALY DEM, 23% of MPs in our EGMS-in-IFFI dataset have absolute C-coefficient values below 0.2.

As the C-coefficient and the perceived slope furnish two distinct geometric information for each MP, data interpretation involves both [25]. Therefore, to give an overview of their relationship, the histogram of the C-coefficient is shown in Fig. 9 right, with bars color-coded according to distortion classes. It becomes evident that MPs with C values less than 0.2 belong to the towards exposure, mainly in the foreshortening region. For C values between 0.2 and 0.7, MPs are located in both towards and averse exposures and higher C values (>0.7) are found in the region of good visibility.

Interestingly for both these parameters we have found that the sensitivity to DEM resolution is minor than 8%, and in case of the C-coefficient with 2.7% we have a notable stability of values, if further confirmed this would mean that having two DEM may not be necessary.

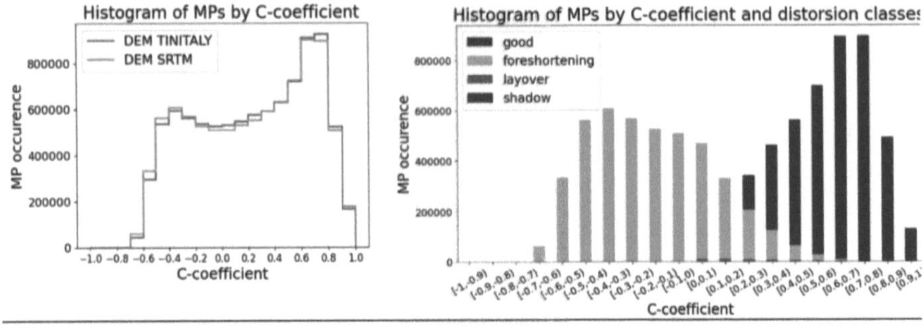

Fig. 9. Left: Histogram of values obtained for all MPinLS. Right: Classification of MPinLS in four RADAR imaging distortion classes.

5 Conclusions

In this work, we present our efforts to create a dataset for evaluating the potential of using satellite data to study slow and extremely slow landslides at the national level. To this end, we have developed the EGMS-in-IFFI-dataset, which stores the average descriptors of measure points from EGMS, along with several information about the landslides to which they are associated, based on their coordinates.

In doing so, we developed a computationally efficient Python code to perform the spatial intersection between measure points from EGMS and polygons from the IFFI Inventory.

Additionally, we conducted some statistics on the dataset to highlight its features, including the landslide coverage by MPs, their temporal coherence, and the distribution of derived geometrical parameters, namely the perceived slope and the C-coefficient.

Overall, we found that the total number of detectable landslides—defined as those for which at least one MP falls within their area—is 102,074, representing 24% of the landslides in the IFFI Inventory for the selected type of movement. The density coverage of MPs decreases exponentially with the number of detectable landslides, with the number of landslides halving at a density of 400 MPs/sqkm, which indicates the need for caution when performing further analyses. Additionally, requiring high temporal coherence significantly reduces the number of detected landslides; setting the temporal coherence threshold to 0.7 excludes 20% of the data. Interestingly, the distribution of mean velocities revealed that 84% of the data is confined to the interval $(-3, +3)$ mm, with a mean value skewed towards negative velocities. The analysis of the geometrical parameters indicated a minimal influence (<8%) of the DEM used, which may require further confirmation.

A comprehensive statistical analysis of the dataset is necessary to fully assess its potential and will be the focus of our future work. Additionally, we plan to reconstruct the dataset using the EGMS basic data. Moreover, given the volume of data, we anticipate using unsupervised machine learning techniques to help distinguish between landslide activity and its various categories.

Disclosure of Interests. The authors have no competing interests to declare that are relevant to the content of this article.

A1 Mathematical Derivation of C-coefficient

The C-coefficient is the cosine between the LoS direction and the steepest slope, with direction defined through the unit vector $\hat{u} = (u_E, u_N, u_{UP})^T$:

$$\hat{u}_{LoS} = \begin{pmatrix} -\sin\vartheta \cdot \sin\varphi \\ -\cos\vartheta \cdot \sin\varphi \\ \cos\varphi \end{pmatrix}, \quad \hat{u}_{stsl} = \begin{pmatrix} -\sin\alpha \cdot \sin\omega \\ -\cos\alpha \cdot \sin\omega \\ \cos\omega \end{pmatrix}, \tag{4}$$

where, (ϑ, φ) are the LoS azimuth and incidenc angle respectively, the LoS azimuth derived from track angle $\chi : \vartheta = \chi + \frac{\pi}{2}$. The steepest slope direction is described by aspect and slope respectively α *and* ω. Notice that, defining the "up" direction for positive displacement, east and north components are pointing in opposite direction with respect to LoS azimuth and aspect.The C-coefficient can be calculated from the unit vectors in Eq. (4) by the scalar product:

$$C = \hat{u}_{LoS} \cdot \hat{u}_{stsl} = \begin{pmatrix} -\sin\vartheta \cdot \sin\varphi \\ -\cos\vartheta \cdot \sin\varphi \\ \cos\varphi \end{pmatrix} \cdot \begin{pmatrix} -\sin\alpha \cdot \sin\omega \\ -\cos\alpha \cdot \sin\omega \\ \cos\omega \end{pmatrix}$$
$$= \sin\varphi \cdot \cos\omega \cdot \cos(\vartheta - \alpha) + \cos\varphi \cdot \sin\omega. \tag{5}$$

In literature the C-coefficient is often given in terms of LoS cosines:

$$C = nlos \cdot \cos\omega \cdot \sin\left(\alpha - \frac{\pi}{2}\right) + elos \cdot \left(-\cos\omega \cdot \cos\left(\alpha - \frac{\pi}{2}\right)\right) + hlos \cdot \sin\omega, \tag{6}$$

where nlos, elos and hlos are respectively the LoS cosines in north, east and nadir direction.

$$\begin{aligned} nlos &= \cos\left(\tfrac{\pi}{2} - \varphi\right) \cdot \cos(\pi - \vartheta) &&= -\sin\varphi \cdot \cos\vartheta \\ elos &= \cos\left(\tfrac{\pi}{2} - \varphi\right) \cdot \cos\left(\tfrac{3\pi}{2} - \vartheta\right) &&= -\sin\varphi \cdot \sin\vartheta \\ hlos &= \cos\varphi && . \end{aligned} \tag{7}$$

The equivalence of the two formulations of C ((5) and (6)) is obtained substituting the LoS cosines from Eq. (7) into Eq. (6):

$$\begin{aligned} C &= [-\sin\varphi\cos\vartheta] \cdot (\cos\omega\cos\alpha) + [\sin\varphi\sin\vartheta] \cdot (\cos\omega\sin\alpha) + \cos\varphi\sin\omega \\ &= \sin\varphi \cdot \cos\omega \cdot \cos(\vartheta - \alpha) + \cos\varphi \cdot \sin\omega \end{aligned} \tag{8}$$

References

1. Geertsema, M., Highland, L., Vaugeouis, L.: Environmental impact of landslides. In: Sassa, K., Canuti, P. (eds.) Landslides – Disaster Risk Reduction, pp. 589–607. Springer, Berlin, Heidelberg (2009). https://doi.org/10.1007/978-3-540-69970-5_31

2. Salvati, P., et al.: Geo-hydrological events and human losses: a gender perspective (No. Plinius18-114). Copernicus Meetings (2024)
3. Trigila, A., Iadanza, C., Lastoria, B., Bussettini, M., Barbano, A.: Dissesto idrogeologico in Italia: pericolosità e indicatori di rischio. Rapporti 356/2021, ISPRA, Roma (2021)
4. Brabb, E.E.: The world landslide problem. Episodes **14**, 52–61 (1991)
5. Guzzetti, F., Mondini, A.C., Cardinali, M., Fiorucci, F., Santangelo, M., Chang, K.T.: Landslide inventory maps: new tools for an old problem. Earth Sci. Rev. **112**(1–2), 42–66 (2012). https://doi.org/10.1016/j.earscirev.2012.02.001
6. Burrows, K., Walters, R.J., Milledge, D., Densmore, A.L.: A systematic exploration of satellite radar coherence methods for rapid landslide detection. Nat. Hazards Earth Syst. Sci. **20**, 3197–3214 (2020). https://doi.org/10.5194/nhess-20-3197-2020
7. Mondini, A.C., Santangelo, M., Rocchetti, M., Rossetto, E., Manconi, A., Monserrat, O.: Sentinel-1 SAR amplitude imagery for rapid landslide detection. Remote Sens. **11**(7), 760 (2019). https://doi.org/10.3390/rs11070760
8. Plank, S., Twele, A., Martinis, S.: Landslide mapping in vegetated areas using change detection based on optical and polarimetric SAR data. Remote Sens. **8**(4), 307 (2016). https://doi.org/10.3390/rs8040307
9. Cignetti, M., et al.: Taking advantage of the ESA G-pod service to study ground deformation processes in high mountain areas: a Valle d'Aosta case study, northern Italy. Remote Sens. **8**(10), 852 (2016). https://doi.org/10.3390/rs8100852
10. Herrera, G., et al.: Multi-sensor advanced DInSAR monitoring of very slow landslides: the Tena Valley case study (Central Spanish Pyrenees). Remote Sens. Environ. **128**, 31–43 (2013). https://doi.org/10.1016/j.rse.2012.09.020
11. Solari, L., et al.: Review of satellite interferometry for landslide detection in Italy. Remote Sens. **12**(8), 1351 (2020). https://doi.org/10.3390/rs12081351
12. Galloway, D.L., Hoffmann, J.: The application of satellite differential SAR interferometry-derived ground displacements in hydrogeology. Hydrogeol. J. **15**, 133–154 (2007)
13. Tomás, R., et al.: Radar interferometry techniques for the study of ground subsidence phenomena: a review of practical issues through cases in Spain. Environ. Earth Sci. **71**, 163–181 (2014)
14. Lu, P., Casagli, N., Catani, F., Tofani, V.: Persistent Scatterers Interferometry Hotspot and Cluster Analysis (PSI-HCA) for detection of extremely slow-moving landslides. Int. J. Remote Sens. **33**(2), 466–489 (2012)
15. Del Ventisette, C., Righini, G., Moretti, S., Casagli, N.: Multitemporal landslides inventory map updating using spaceborne SAR analysis. Int. J. Appl. Earth Obs. Geoinf. **30**, 238–246 (2014)
16. Bonì, R., Bordoni, M., Colombo, A., Lanteri, L., Meisina, C.: Landslide state of activity maps by combining multi-temporal A-DInSAR (LAMBDA). Remote Sens. Environ. **217**, 172–190 (2018). https://doi.org/10.1016/j.rse.2018.08.013
17. Confuorto, P., et al.: Sentinel-1 P-SBAS data for the update of the state of activity of national landslide inventory maps. Landslides **20**(5), 1083–1097 (2023). https://doi.org/10.1007/s10346-022-02024-0
18. EGMS - European Ground Motion Service: Calibrated 2018–2022 (vector), Europe, yearly, October 2023. https://doi.org/10.2909/d92e61be-d6e8-4bc1-aa10-f742bf27bab9
19. Trigila, A., Iadanza, C., Spizzichino, D.: Quality assessment of the Italian Landslide Inventory using GIS processing. Landslides **7**, 455–470 (2010)
20. IdroGeo Homepage. https://idrogeo.isprambiente.it/app/. Accessed 19 Sept 2024
21. Iadanza, C., Trigila, A., Starace, P., Dragoni, A., Biondo, T., Roccisano, M.: IdroGEO: a collaborative web mapping application based on REST API services and open data on landslides and floods in Italy. ISPRS Int. J. Geo Inf. **10**(2), 89 (2021). https://doi.org/10.3390/ijgi10020089

22. Iadanza, C., Cacace, C., Del Conte, S., Spizzichino, D., Cespa, S., Trigila, A.: Cultural heritage, landslide risk and remote sensing in Italy. In: Margottini, C., Canuti, P., Sassa, K. (eds.) Landslide Science and Practice: Volume 6: Risk Assessment, Management and Mitigation, pp. 491–499. Springer, Berlin, Heidelberg (2013). https://doi.org/10.1007/978-3-642-31319-6_65
23. Plank, S., Singer, J., Minet, C., Thuro, K.: Pre-survey suitability evaluation of the differential synthetic aperture radar interferometry method for landslide monitoring. Int. J. Remote Sens. **33**(20), 6623–6637 (2012)
24. Kropatsch, W.G., Strobl, D.: The generation of SAR layover and shadow maps from digital elevation models. IEEE Trans. Geosci. Remote Sens. **28**(1), 98–107 (1990)
25. Colesanti, C., Wasowski, J.: Investigating landslides with space-borne Synthetic Aperture Radar (SAR) interferometry. Eng. Geol. **88**(3–4), 173–199 (2006). https://doi.org/10.1016/j.enggeo.2006.09.013
26. Notti, D., Herrera, G., Bianchini, S., Meisina, C., García-Davalillo, J.C., Zucca, F.: A methodology for improving landslide PSI data analysis. Int. J. Remote Sens. **35**(6), 2186–2214 (2014)
27. Burst ID - Sentinel-1 Burst ID Map, version 20220530, generated by the SAR-MPC service. https://sar-mpc.eu/test-data-sets/. Accessed 30 Sept 2024
28. Tarquini, S., Isola, I., Favalli, M., Battistini, A., Dotta, G.: TINITALY, a digital elevation model of Italy with a 10 meters cell size (Version 1.1). Istituto Nazionale di Geofisica e Vulcanologia (2023). https://doi.org/10.13127/tinitaly/1.1. Accessed 19 Sept 2024
29. NASA: Shuttle Radar Topography Mission (SRTM) Global, Distributed by OpenTopography (2013). https://doi.org/10.5069/G9445JDF. Accessed 19 Sept 2024
30. Solari, L., et al.: A Sentinel-1 based hot-spot analysis: landslide mapping in north-western Italy. Int. J. Remote Sens. **40**(20), 7898–7921 (2019)

Influence of Data Preprocessing and Optimization in Multivariate Statistical Analysis of Landslide Susceptibility

Paola Salmona(✉), Rossella Bovolenta, Bianca Federici, and Ilaria Ferrando

University of Genoa – Department of Civil, Chemical and Environmental Engineering, via Montallegro 1, 16145 Genova, Italy
{paola.salmona,Rossella.Bovolenta,Bianca.Federici}@unige.it, Ilaria.Ferrando@edu.unige.it

Abstract. As part of the PNRR – Extended Partnership RETURN, the research group is developing a procedure for producing landslide susceptibility maps in a GIS (Geographic Information System) environment. The use of the statistical technique of Logistic Regression has proved suitable for the purpose, but the reliability of the resulting models depends greatly on the input data and their preprocessing. To make the proposed procedure effectively usable by land managers, transferable to different areas, and allowing for the comparison of different scenarios, it is necessary to define a minimum standard for the input data, as well as some specifications for their preprocessing. The present work, based on the case study of the Province of Savona (IT), identifies the basic data requirements, and provides instructions for the preparation of spatial datasets (relative to the Italian territory) and for the processing flow for the effective use of Logistic Regression for statistical landslide prediction.

Keywords: Ground instability · Logistic Regression · Geographical Information System

1 Introduction

The Extended Partnership RETURN (Multi-Risk sciEnce for resilienT commUnities undeR a changiNg climate) aims to propose a set of tools to support natural and anthropic risk management. High flexibility and ease of use is required, to transfer methodologies and good practices to the different territory managers and operators [1].

As part of the RETURN Vertical Spoke 2, dedicated to ground instabilities, the authors are engaged in developing a statistically based methodology for elaborating landslide susceptibility maps, indicating the predisposition of hilly and mountainous areas to experience landslides. Starting from the assumption that landslides are more likely to occur in areas with similar characteristics to those where they have already occurred [2], the relationships between present or past landslides and eight predisposing factors have been analyzed through statistical processing in a GIS (Geographic Information System) environment. In this context, a Logistic Regression process relates the

E. Borgogno-Mondino and P. Zamperlin (Eds.): ASITA 2024, CCIS 2463, pp. 102–117, 2025.
https://doi.org/10.1007/978-3-031-91141-5_8

dichotomous variable (i.e., landslide/no landslide) to various factors characterizing an area, assigning each factor a different weight. The result is a probability map, which is subsequently divided into qualitative classes, identifying areas with low, medium, and high susceptibility to landslides.

To meet the goals of the RETURN project and to make Logistic Regression exploitable and widely usable, the authors are carrying out in-depth investigations to identify a "minimum base" of required and available data, accessible on the several existing geographical Open Data providers. The work is therefore carried out along three main streams: to verify the accuracy, completeness, update and relevance of the available datasets; to harmonize the extent of study areas and the working scales on the basis of the available datasets; and to propose specifications for "raw" data preprocessing and optimization. The overall goal is to create a common basis for statistical analysis and to minimize subjective characteristics or gross errors that might be introduced.

2 Statistical Analysis of Landslides Susceptibility in GIS Environment

Statistical analysis in GIS environment is considered effective for analyzing slope instabilities over medium-large areas. It allows to process huge amounts of georeferenced geomorphological, geological, climate and anthropic data, and to provide detailed susceptibility maps, indicating which areas are most susceptible to develop ground instability phenomena, specifically landslides. Among such methods, the use of Logistic Regression is already consolidated and well described in literature [2, 3]. It is mainly used in areas ranging from approximately 100–10,000 km^2 and it takes into consideration several common predisposing factors to landslide instability. Such factors are related to each other and to a sample of actual landslide areas, so to point out the relationships between the single combined factors and the landslide phenomena.

The present work is carried out using the open-source software GRASS GIS [4–6] to perform primary operations such as: classification, vector data geoprocessing (buffer, intersection, feature extraction), data format conversion, raster map algebra, hydrological modeling (using specific tools for basin and hydrological network analysis), data interpolation, statistical analysis.

2.1 Predisposing Factors

The first phase of the work involves identifying the relevant factors for landslide susceptibility. The considered territorial characteristics include morphology, geology, lithology, hydrology, climatic and anthropic aspects. A literature review was then conducted to pinpoint factors that are (1) certainly relevant, (2) describable using open data, and (3) independent from specific situations (e.g., presence of large hydroelectric plants, presence of faults, etc.). Moreover, to ensure that the proposed procedure can be replicated in other areas of Italy with similar characteristics, only open data accessible across the entire Italian territory have been selected.

By cross-referencing the findings from literature review [3] and the currently accessible data at the national level [7] or common to all regions, a dataset has been selected

(Table 1). While morphological and hydrological data are generally available and manageable within GIS applications, land cover, geological and meteorological data are far more heterogeneous in terms of spatial, temporal coverage and associated information, or are available on large scales, leading to significant approximations.

Another important but difficult requirement is the temporal consistency between the various factors, which may vary over time, both with each other and with the observed landslides. Large discrepancies could lead to an incorrect assessment of the factors predisposing the phenomenon under study.

2.2 Present Ground Instability Areas

Predisposing factors has to be related to actual landslides areas to calibrate the regression model. The main reference at the Italian level is the IFFI repository, the Italian Landslide Phenomena Inventory [8], considered as "ground truth". To date (September 2024), 634,790 landslides are reported, divided into twelve types, each associated with an identification code. However, the IFFI spatial coverage is not uniform or consistent across Italian regions. The reported data comes from various sources, have been collected according to heterogeneous criteria, and, even if the IFFI cartography is frequently updated, it does not represent real-time situations [9], which leads to non-negligible inaccuracies for statistical analysis purposes.

The proposed methodology for developing the susceptibility map has been initially applied to rotational/translational slides, slow flows, and fast flows. Successively, the areas with "widespread shallow landslides[1]", "complex landslides[2]" and "undefined landslides", mapped but not described, have been included in the study.

2.3 The Case Study: The Savona Province

The procedure is applied to the province of Savona (Italy), chosen as study area to test and refine the methodology before its adoption on a regional scale. The study area is approximately 1,550 km^2, spanning from the Tyrrhenian Sea to hinterland hills with elevation exceeding 1,000 m, and has an articulated morphology that gives rise to a remarkable variety of environments. It is divided into a coastal part, characterized by many small basins perpendicular to the sea with rather steep slopes, and an inland part, beyond the Tyrrhenian-Padanian border, consisting of the heads of several larger basins tributary to the Po River.

The area is characterized by the prevalence of schistose metamorphic rocks, mainly in the northeastern part and behind the main town. Other relevant formations are ancient seabed carbonate outcrops (the so-called "Pietra di Finale"), giving rise to karst phenomena in the Finale Ligure area, and areas characterized by consolidated clastic rocks, where some erosion phenomena are also evident. Alluvial deposits prevail along the

[1] Areas where multiple shallow landslide events have occurred, but the precise boundary of each landslide is not reported in the repository maps.

[2] Ground movement resulting from the combination of two or more types of landslides. Although a large part of the landslides could be described as complex, many are reported in the IFFI according to the prevailing type of movement.

main watercourses; they form the main plain of Liguria in the proximity of Albenga. The hillsides are mainly covered by forests and natural areas, with a smaller percentage of farmland and scattered settlements. The only flat alluvial area, the provincial capital, and numerous small towns are located on the coast. The climate is typically Mediterranean on the coastal side, while it is more temperate inland.

The whole area is subject to landslide phenomena, above all rotational/translational slides and complex landslides.

Table 1 reports the geodata used to produce the predisposing factors maps. The working scale of 1:100,000, leading to a geometric resolution of 20 m (equal to the cartographic graphical error), was chosen for the study. Hence, the vector maps were converted to raster format with a resolution of 20 m.

It should be noted that the optimal working scale should be determined according to the extent of the study areas, the most appropriate working scale and data availability. Upscaling should be avoided, while satisfactory results could be obtained by downscaling the higher resolution maps.

Table 1. Predisposing factors and data used in the case study.

Predisposing factors	Data	Original data format	Source of data
Elevation	DTM at 5 m resolution	Raster	[10a]
Orientation	DTM processing	Raster	[10a]
Slope	DTM processing	Raster	[10a]
Accumulation	DTM processing	Raster	[10a]
Lithology	Geological map Lithological map at scale 100,000	Vector	[11–13]
Climatic aggressiveness	Cumulative monthly rainfall data	Vector	[14, 15]
Land use and coverage	Land use map at scale 10,000	Vector	[10b]
Distance from transport networks	Regional Technical Cartography at scale 1:5,000	Vector	[10c]

3 Preprocessing of Predisposing Factors Maps

The first preliminary operation is to make sure that the factors considered are not linearly correlated, since in such case the regression reliability would be reduced.

In the case study, Variance Inflation Factor (VIF) analysis was performed [16], to quantify the increase in variance introduced by each factor in the regression model compared with what would occur if all predictors were independent. No significant collinearity emerged, so the factors were considered as independent of each other.

The logistic regression method can be applied on datasets with continuous, ordinal or binomial distribution. However, to allow the comparison between qualitative and quantitative data, all predisposing factors were converted into ordinal data through reclassification and aggregation operations, describing each factor by a discrete number of classes, ordered from 1 to n (n < 10), as described below for the case study analysed.

3.1 Maps Derived by DTM Processing

The Digital Terrain Model (DTM), originally at 5 m resolution [10a], was resampled to 20 m. Subsequently, the elevation values were grouped into 250 m classes, starting with the lowest value in the study area (Fig. 1a). Please note that it may be important to use smaller classes, e.g. every 100 m, in areas with smaller elevation differences.

Then, the following maps were derived from the DTM through deterministic processing, at the same resolution as the DTM, and, because represented by continuous value maps, were grouped into classes, as described below.

Aspect. Aspect values ranges from 0° to 360° with North = 0° and rotating clockwise (Fig. 1b). Because they are uniformly distributed in the study area, four classes were defined: North (from 315° to 360° and then from 0° to 45°), East (from 45° to 135°), South (from 135° to 225°) and West (from 225° to 315°), as shown in Fig. 1b, so that each cardinal direction is at the center of its respective class. For areas with more complex morphology, eight classes may be more appropriate to group orientation values. If some prevailing orientations can be identified in the study area, the conventional division into four or eight classes may not be the most appropriate, but more territory-suitable classification should be made.

Slope. The slope of an area can be expressed in degrees (from 0 to 90°) or as a percentage. In the case study the slope was calculated in degrees, and the values for individual points were grouped into 9 classes (Fig. 1d). Areas with slope under 5° are considered plains and grouped in a single class; areas steeper than 40°, less favorable to soil accumulation, were considered prone to rock landslides, that are not considered in the present study and thus were grouped in one single class. The range between 5° and 40° was divided into equal intervals of 5° each. However, in mountainous areas, it may be useful to add more classes (between 40° and 90°), while in areas where minor differences in slope are more significant, it might be more practical to use percentage values.

Accumulation. The presence of water accumulation or surface runoff is considered an important factor for ground instability, and it can be described through several indexes [17, 18]. Among them, flow accumulation reports the amount of overland flow through each spatial unit of a territory and identifies areas where runoff water is concentrated, also taking into consideration some aspects of the land morphology (valleys, depressions, etc.) The accumulation map is derived from DTM processing and it reports the number of cells draining through for each cell. Accumulation values are usually normalized as log(abs(accumulation_map) + 1). The values reported in the resulting raster map are grouped into 6 classes as reported in Fig. 1c. Values between 0 and 1 indicate a watershed or a ridge, while higher values indicate valleys or other accumulation areas. It should be taken into consideration that, in peri-urban areas or near to infrastructures, water runoff is often altered by the presence of retaining structures that obstruct the natural flow along the slopes, by drainage works, and by soil sealing. In such cases, this parameter should be reconsidered. For example, it might be more relevant to identify situations where there is a convergence of uncovered or tunneled historic streams, retaining walls, and multi-story buildings, and to classify areas based on their proximity to these features.

Range [m]	Class number
0 – 250	1
250 – 500	2
500 – 750	3
750 – 1000	4
1000 – 1250	5
1250 – 1500	6
1500 – 1750	7

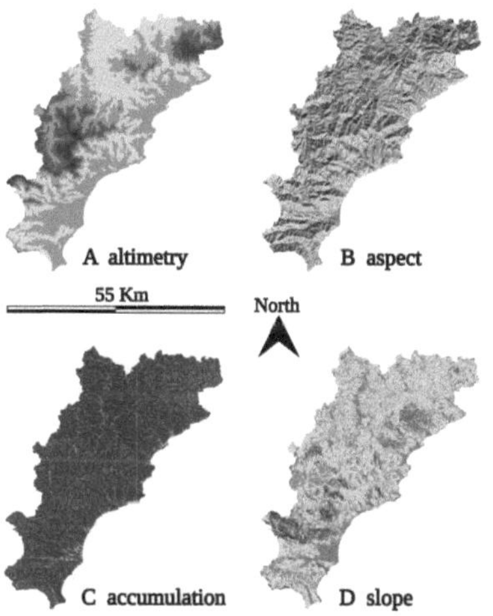

Range [°]	Class number
0 – 45 ∪ 315 – 360	1
45 – 135	2
135 – 225	3
225 – 315	4

Range [-]	Class number
0 – 1	1
1 – 2	2
2 – 3	3
3 – 4	4
4 – 5	5
5 – 6	6

Range [°]	Class number
0 – 5	1
5 – 10	2
10 – 15	3
15 – 20	4
20 – 25	5
25 – 30	6
30 – 35	7
35 – 40	8
40 – 90	9

Fig. 1. Reclassification of DTM-derived maps: a) elevation; b) aspect; c) accumulation; d) slope.

3.2 Maps Derived from Polygonal Vector Data

In the present work, polygonal vector data refer to dataset containing contiguous polygons covering seamlessy the whole study area. Then, the vector maps were converted to raster format with a geometric resolution of 20 m.

Lithology. ISPRA's Geological Map of Italy [11], at scale 1:100,000, is used as a general basis for including bedrock in the analysis. It is the most detailed map available for the entire Italian territory and suitable for use in a GIS environment. To get some basic information, the rock formations have been grouped into five classes (Fig. 2a): class 1 refers to all loose aggregates, regardless of their origin and grain size (from clay deposits to moraine boulders), classes from 2 to 4 group rock formations according to their origin, if they are in compact layers or banks, while class 5 refers to waterbodies. Indeed, to apply the model to smaller areas or areas with peculiar geologic features (i.e. faults, karst phenomena, etc.) or highly prone to the development of landslide, more detailed maps might be desirable. They can be derived from a different classification of the Geological Map of Italy or referring to local geological maps [19], available for a few areas up to scale 1:10,000. Unfortunately, in most cases the latest are not suitable for use in the GIS environment because they are generally images of paper charts, with mashed backgrounds, section lines, and lettering.

Land Use – Land Cover. Land Use maps can vary significantly depending on how reported features are aggregated into classes. At the regional or basin scale, it is advisable to use the land use maps produced by the Regions, which provide a relatively high level of detail, with nominal scale from 1:10,000 to 1:25,000, and then group the different types of use into macro classes. In the case study it has been chosen to group and generalize features from a 1:10,000 land use map in order to keep the correct boundaries of different land uses. It is important to note that the land use map of Liguria Region, as well as those of other Regions, follows a hierarchical classification that echoes the one of the CORINE Land Cover [20] and refers primarily to land use rather than land cover. In these cases, it is advisable to group the features not according to the predetermined hierarchy, but according to the actual land cover (e.g., a chestnut grove according to CORINE is classified as "agricultural area", while it should be classified as "tree vegetation", considering the actual land cover,). In the case study, land-use map features were grouped according to the Land Cover Classification System (LCCS) [21] developed by the Food and Agriculture Organization of the United Nations (FAO) and used to classify ESA maps for 2020–2021 (Fig. 2b). This classification can also be used in those situations where a land-use map at the appropriate scale is not available and needs to be derived from photo interpretation or remote sensing image processing.

Formation	Class number
Deposits	1
Volcanic rocks	2
Metamorphic rocks	3
Sedimentary rocks	4
Other	5

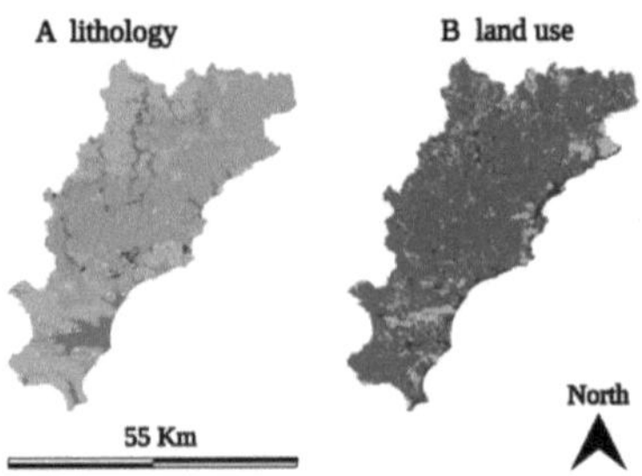

Land cover	Class number
Built-up	1
Crops	2
Tree cover	3
Shrubland	4
Grassland	5
Bare soil / sparse vegetation	6
Water	7
Herbaceous wetland	8

Fig. 2. Reclassification of maps derived from polygonal vector data: a) lithology; b) Land Use.

3.3 Maps Derived from Point and Linear Vector Data

Vector maps consisting of point or linear features scattered throughout the work area can be associated with quantitative data (e.g., rainfall) or qualitative data (e.g., road type, Points of Interest, etc.). In the present work they are used as the base for creating continuous maps through interpolation or geoprocessing, at a geometric resolution of 20 m.

Climate Aggressiveness. Extreme weather events have direct consequences on slope stability. Increased precipitation characterized by significant cumulative precipitation of short duration submits slopes to sudden and significant elevations in soil water content, which reduces soil shear strength as it decreases the apparent cohesion of partially saturated shallow layers of slopes, making them more susceptible to soil instability [22].

On the other hand, rainfall influence is one of the most challenging factors to be included in the model. Rainfall data refer either to the stations where they were recorded (when considering local data) or are reported as continuous maps derived by radar acquisition or meteorological (global, European, or national) modeling, but at a much lower resolution than the data used to describe other predisposing factors. In the first case, data is more reliable, but it is necessary to interpolate the point data to build a continuous map. Such process inevitably leads to approximations that vary depending on the interpolation method used.

Kriging [23] would be the most suitable interpolation method, allowing to understand how the correlation of the rainfall values measured in georeferenced stations vary according to the distance between them (variogram); moreover, the accuracy of the interpolated surface is evaluated. However, it requires the analysis of site specific parameters, assuming a good knowledge of the whole study area and of the principles of kriging itself [25].

Since the objective of the working group is to define a procedure to be applied also by not specialized people, in the case study it was tested even a deterministic and user friendly interpolation method could be suitable for processing rainfall data in order to allow for the inclusion of a climate-related factor in the model. Monthly rainfall measurements since 2002–2022 have been thus interpolated applying the Inverse Distance Weight (IDW) method, which relies solely on the geometric distribution of known points [26]; moreover this technique is able to extrapolate values also outside the perimeter delimited by the stations. A rainfall map was thus interpolated for each month in the considered period. These maps were then used to calculate Climate Aggressiveness, according to the following formula (Arnoldus Index) [27]:

$$AC = \sum_{i=1}^{12} \frac{p_i^2}{P} \quad (1)$$

where p_i is the average rainfall for each month and P is the average annual rainfall.

This index, calculated for significant periods of time (theoretically 30 years, or the longest period for which data are available) provides a general value for the study area. The values reported in the resulting Climate Aggressiveness map for the study area were eventually divided into five classes (Fig. 3a) according to the guidelines provided by the European Commission [28] in 1992: 0–60 (low), 60–90, 90–120, 120–160, over 160 (very high).

A few issues emerged from this procedure. It resulted in 252 monthly accumulated rainfall maps, required to process the monthly average rainfall, the annual average rainfall and finally the Arnoldus Index, with a big effort in terms of RAM and disk space. Actually, it would have been possible to calculate the Climate Aggressiveness for each station beforehand, greatly limiting the number of maps required. However, the stations that recorded complete data for the entire period under consideration are a minority, and this would have reduced the number of points on which to perform the interpolation.

To avoid excessive approximation of interpolated rainfall values in the outer parts of the study area, it would be useful to include in the interpolation process also some rain gauges located outside the area of actual interest. Where this is not feasible (e.g., coastal areas, cross-border areas, etc.), the error is partially compensated by grouping the values into classes. Moreover, close to rain gauges, IDW interpolated rainfall values might be markedly different from the farther ones, leading to a "bumps and holes" effect. This effect, partially mitigated in the calculation of the Arnoldus Index, is further reduced by reclassifying the values.

When working in relatively small territories (less than 100 km^2), the entire study area may fall into a single class. Since constant factors cannot be included in the next phase of multivariate analysis, either Climatic Aggressiveness is not considered, or the single represented class must be subdivided into subclasses.

Finally, it could be useful to calculate, alongside the Arnoldus Index, also a modified version considering cumulative rather than mean values [26], to assess how much rainfall over a limited period deviates from the mean.

$$Cumulative\ AC = \frac{\sum_{j=1}^{n} \sum_{i=1}^{12} \frac{p_i^2}{P_j}}{n} \quad (2)$$

where p_i is the cumulative rainfall for each month for each year considered, P_j is the total rainfall for each year considered, and n is the number of years considered.

Distance from Transportation Infrastructures Network. The transportation infrastructures considered in the case study include vehicular roads (highways, extra-urban and urban thoroughfares, extra-urban and urban roads), railways and their related accessory spaces. For the purposes of this analysis, the focus is not the importance of the infrastructure itself but rather its impact on the morphology of the territory. Bridges, viaducts, and tunnels, which do not directly affect the terrain, have been excluded. In fact, the interaction of bridges and viaducts piers with slopes at regional or basin-scale study is difficult to compute, and tunnels primarily impact the deep bedrock while the considered landslides affect the surface coulters. In those cases where tunnels and viaducts follow one another (e.g., along the highway), site-specific studies in the areas where bridges, viaducts, and tunnels intercept slopes would be needed, but they are beyond the scope of this paper.

To define the area affected by the presence of infrastructure, a number of buffers were considered: 50 m (including the road axis), 100, 150, 200 and more than 200 m from the axis (Fig. 3b), the latter being the distance beyond which the influence of a road is considered negligible [29].

For the analysis of urban and peri-urban areas, it would be advisable to directly use the cartography of road and railway areas and their related service areas (for Liguria and most Italian regions, available as a layer in the Regional Technical Map, CTR), where these infrastructures are represented as polygons with their actual dimensions.

3.4 Landslides Dataset Processing

In the IFFI inventory, each landslide is represented both as a polygon and as a point. The polygon encompasses the entire area affected by the landslide, including both the detachment area and the area where the landslide materials are deposited. The point, on

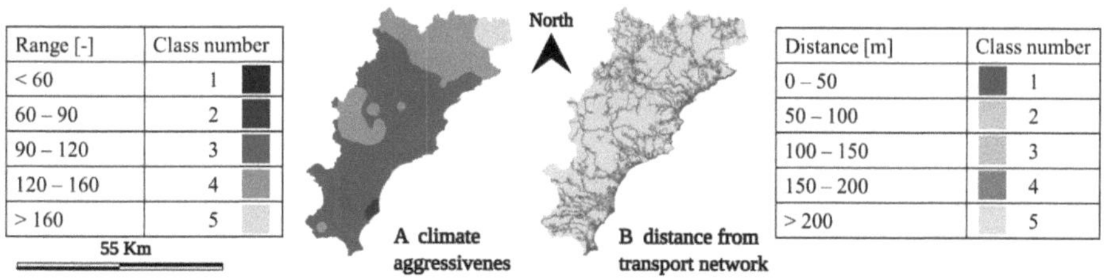

Fig. 3. Reclassification of factors derived from point and linear vector data: a) climate aggressiveness; b) distance from transport network.

the other hand, is located within the polygon at the highest elevation and approximates the location of the detachment point [29].

To apply the multivariate statistical analysis, the entire areas identified as landslides, represented on a raster map with a value of 1, usually constitute the statistical sample from which to extract the characteristics of the predisposing factors previously introduced. Other studies in literature [31] consider many random points in definitely landslide or non-slide locations as a statistical sample. Actually, it is not correct to include deposition areas in the statistical sample because they are characterized by conditions that did not develop landslides but, on the contrary, were altered by a landslide. On the other hand, considering only detachment points as a statistical sample is incorrect because part of the area that actually gave rise to landslides is excluded; moreover the statistical sample is excessively reduced.

Since distinguishing detachment areas from deposition areas would require considerable work, both through photo-interpretation and direct surveys, a good compromise might be to consider, for each landslide reported in the IFFI, only a reduced set of pixels, proportional to the extent of the landslide itself and located within the perimeter immediately downstream of the point of detachment.

Another attention should be paid to analysing the different types of ground instabilities separately, as they are not equally influenced by the different predisposing factors. Since, in some cases (e.g., fast flows), this generates a very small statistical sample compared to the entire study area, work is underway to identify those predisposing factors that would allow different types of instability to be merged and thus to operate on a more meaningful sample.

Finally, it should be pointed out that the need for a correct statistical sample is more relevant in the case of small study areas or in particularly sensitive situations, for example, peri-urban areas or areas characterized by complex morphology. In such cases it is better to devote more time and effort to derive it, in order to get an effectively reliable result.

4 The Statistical Analysis

Statistical analysis initially requires a bivariate statistical analysis of the values of the individual predisposing factors, divided into classes as described in the pre-processing phase, present in the areas inventoried as landslides. Then the multivariate statistical analysis requires the application of logistic regression [32], in order to consider the combination of different factors to estimate the probability of occurrence of the landslide phenomenon in other areas of the territory under study.

4.1 Data Reordering Through Bivariate Statistical Analysis

The number initially assigned to each class of each predisposing factor during the data preparation phase is not necessarily indicative of an increase or decrease in susceptibility to landslides. Instead, statistical analysis requires reordering the classes to exhibit a monotone trend for each factor analyzed. Therefore, through bivariate statistical analysis, the maps of each factor are reclassified, assigning each class an increasing number based on the conditional probability of landslides, calculated as follows:

$$P_{cond} = P(f|k) = \frac{P(f \cap k)}{P(k)} \tag{3}$$

where P(f ∩ k) is the probability that a point is inside a landslide (landslide area/total area), P(k) is the probability that a point belongs to a class (*area* ∈ *k*/total area).

The class with the lowest conditional probability will be numbered as 1, then all others will follow in ascending sequence. If one or more classes have no pixels in a landslide (conditional probability = 0), the value 1 is assigned to that class (or those classes). This step is essential to define the trend of the qualitative data, but, from authors experience, this analysis is also advisable for quantitative data that already has an order, such as altitude or slope.

4.2 Multivariate Statistical Analysis

Considering Landslide Probability = 1 where a landslide has already occurred (Y = 1) and Landslide Probability = 0 where a landslide event is not possible (Y = 0), the probability can be expressed using the logit function defined as:

$$logit(Y) = z = ln\frac{P(Y = 1)}{1 - P(Y = 1)} \tag{4}$$

where P(Y = 1) is the probability that a landslide occurs.

Then the Generalized Linear Logistic Regression model is applied by setting:

$$z = \beta 0 + \beta 1(x1) + \beta 2(x2) + \beta 2(x2) + \ldots + \beta i(xi) \tag{5}$$

where x_1, x_2,..., x_i are the classified and reordered maps of the different predisposing factors, β_0 is the intercept value, β_1, β_2,..., β_i are the weights assigned to the different factors.

This process leads to the creation of a map of expected values for the logit. Through the inverse operation, a map that expresses the probability for each pixel of developing a landslide event (i.e., susceptibility) is generated.

$$\boldsymbol{P(Y_i = 1) = \frac{e^{z_i}}{1 + e^{z_i}}} \tag{6}$$

For each point element or cell in the area used as a statistical sample for training multivariate statistical, the respective logit value is assigned. In the case of a statistical sample consisting of points, the result will be a discontinuous map [5], which is considered not suitable for the analysis in the present study. In the case of a statistical sample in raster format, where 1 identifies the cells in landslide and 0 identifies the cells considered not in landslide, the accuracy of the resulting logit map will be closely related to the precision with which the landslides were perimeter.

4.3 Model Reliability

A preliminary assessment of the model reliability is obtained by calculating the Area Under the ROC (Receiver Operating Characteristic) Curve, named AUC [33]. This method evaluates the accuracy of the landslide susceptibility map, helping to determine whether the considered factors and the used data is adequate. A low AUC value could be due to low quality of input data, to the inclusion of irrelevant or non-independent factors in the model, or to the omission of specific elements that are of particular importance (e.g., erosion conditions, presence of faults, soil type, etc.).

ROC analysis allows to identify the relevant predisposing factors that, for a specific area and a particular type of landslide, lead to the best model. In this regard, the Leave One Out method (Fig. 4) can be used to compare different combinations of factors [34]. The logistic regression model is applied several times to the study area, removing a different predisposing factor each time. When the AUC value, obtained by excluding a specific factor, is higher than that of the general model, it means that the factor worsens the model. Therefore, the model should then be recalculated considering only those factors that improve the model, and possibly re-evaluate the factor combination and decide whether to include other previously omitted factors.

Elev.	Orient.	Slope	Accumul.	Lithol.	Climate	Landuse	Networks
	Orient.	Slope	Accumul.	Lithol.	Climate	Landuse	Networks
Elev.		Slope	Accumul.	Lithol.	Climate	Landuse	Networks
Elev.	Orient.		Accumul.	Lithol.	Climate	Landuse	Networks
Elev.	Orient.	Slope		Lithol.	Climate	Landuse	Networks
Elev.	Orient.	Slope	Accumul.		Climate	Landuse	Networks
Elev.	Orient.	Slope	Accumul.	Lithol.		Landuse	Networks
Elev.	Orient.	Slope	Accumul.	Lithol.	Climate		Networks
Elev.	Orient.	Slope	Accumul.	Lithol.	Climate	Landuse	

Fig. 4. Scheme of the "Leave One Out" method applied to the identification of the relevant predisposing factors.

In the present analysis, the best results were obtained for slow flows, fast flows, and undefined landslides, with AUC > 80% (Fig. 5). In the case of fast flows, it was possible to further improve the model by excluding two factors. Figure 6 shows the best susceptibility map derived for slow flows and fast flows.

Once the set of factors relevant to a study area and a type of landslide has been identified, the analysis can then be extended by introducing other more specific parameters (erosion, presence of faults, etc.) into the model, verifying their relevance.

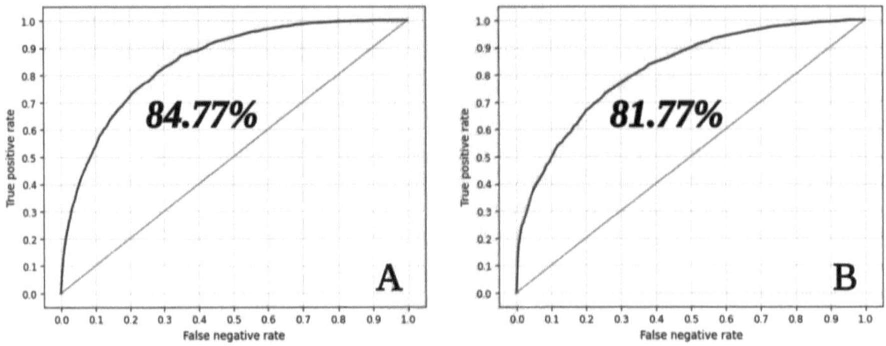

Fig. 5. ROC curve related to slow flows (A; 84,11%) and fast flows (B; 81%).

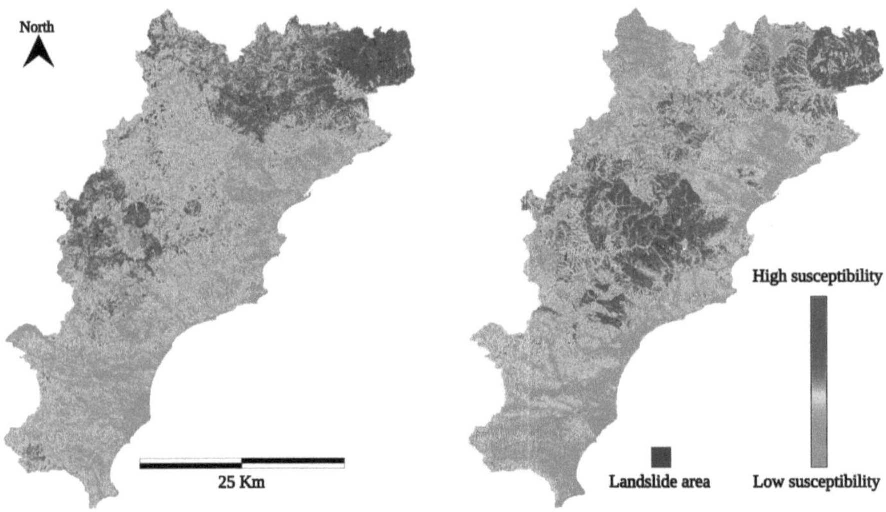

Fig. 6. Slow flows (left) and fast flows (right) susceptibility map. Blue areas (visible zooming in, because they are very small) indicates the landslides areas in the IFFI repository.

5 Final Considerations and Future Developments

The work done so far presents numerous insights to optimize and, above all, makes more usable a methodology that is already recognized as effective for identifying those areas more prone to instability. The suggested procedure allows the reliable calibration of a multivariate statistical model for analysing landslide susceptibility. It has been tested in a case study as part of RETURN project, and it is currently under further development on more different case studies to make it transferable to other areas and scales.

The suggested data optimization procedure is indeed time-consuming, but the preliminary results obtained on Savona Province and on the other areas currently under study seem to indicate its usefulness, in terms of reliability of the resulting models and transferability of the procedure. Some parts of the procedure are being automated through Python scripts, thus reducing complexity and processing time.

The effective validation of the model is currently underway. However, to date, for small sample areas, the model accuracy, tested by using 70% of the areas for calibration and 30% for validation, has been good.

Some final considerations emerge from the authors' experience.

The more homogeneous an area is, the more accurate the model is. For this reason, it is advisable to choose a physical rather than an administrative boundary to avoid including areas with very different characteristics. In the case of small areas (e.g., areas close to infrastructure or settlements), it is still preferable to perform the analysis over a larger territory to work with a statistically significant sample.

The dataset here suggested could be used as a base for localized susceptibility analysis if produced at a higher level of detail by local territorial management agencies (Region Governments, Municipalities, etc.). However, it will always be necessary to check whether data resolution and the reference values of the considered parameters are suitable for the chosen working scale.

The proposed methodology, when applied to high-resolution data, could be particularly useful for highlighting situations of potential instability along the connecting routes between urban areas and small settlements, along infrastructures (e.g., highways, railways, or high-voltage networks), and in peripheral areas where natural and anthropic elements often alternate in a "disorderly" manner. It should also be noted that, in high-resolution analyses, the landslides events reported in the IFFI repository may not constitute a correct statistical sample and should be supported by field surveys or remote sensing techniques to determine the actual areas of detachment.

It is important to note that a susceptibility map provides a geographical indication of a hazard of landslide triggering, but it does not indicate when the event might occur. Therefore, it is preparatory and functional for direct investigation, identifying the most problematic areas where intervention might be prioritized if critical issues are identified.

In the near future, by incorporating climate change projections and other dynamic factors, these models can be continuously updated to reflect new hazard conditions, making them a valuable tool for long-term resilience planning.

Further development being pursued by the authors are the inclusion of other factors such as soil erosion, and changes in vegetation cover over time, using remote sensing data or products.

Acknowledgments. The present work is developed within the RETURN (Multi-Risk sciEnce for resilienT commUnities undeR a chaNging climate) Extended Partnership.

References

1. Fondazione RETURN homepage, https://www.fondazionereturn.it/en/. Accesses 06 September 2024
2. Shano, L., Raghuvanshi, T.K., Meten, M.: Landslide susceptibility evaluation and hazard zonation techniques – a review. Geoenviron. Disast. **7**, 18 (2020)

3. Marzocchi R., Rovegno B., Federici B., Bovolenta R., Berardi R.: Applicazione della regressione logistica per la zonazione della suscettibilità da frana in ambiente GIS. In: BOLLETTINO SIFET n.4 Sezione Scienza (2015)
4. GRASS GIS homepage. https://grass.osgeo.org/. Accessed 06 September 2024
5. GRASS Manual. Raster Data Processing in GRASS GIS. https://grass.osgeo.org/grass84/manuals/rasterintro.html. Accessed 06 September 2024
6. GRASS Manual, Vector Data Processing in GRASS GIS. https://grass.osgeo.org/grass84/manuals/vectorintro.html. Accessed 06 September 2024
7. National Italian Geoportal. https://gn.mase.gov.it/portale/home. Accessed 11 September 2024
8. Trigila A., Iadanza C., Lastoria B., Bussettini M., Barbano A., Dissesto idrogeologico in Italia: pericolosità e indicatori di rischio – Edizione 2021. ISPRA, Rapporti 356/2021 (2021)
9. IFFI – Inventario dei Fenomeni Franosi in Italia. https://beta.idrogeo.isprambiente.it/app/page/inventario-dei-fenomeni-franosi-in-italia-iffi. Accessed 06 September 2024
10. DTM – Modello Digitale del Terreno – Liguria ed. Liguria Region Geoportal (2023). https://geoportal.regione.liguria.it/catalogo/mappe.html
11. Uso del Suolo della Regione Liguria sc. 1:10000 – ed., Liguria Region Geoportal (2024). https://geoportal.regione.liguria.it/catalogo/mappe.html. Accessed 24 September 2024
12. Carta Tecnica Regionale 1:5000 – 2007/2013 – II Edizione 3D/DB Topografico, Liguria Region Geoportal. https://geoportal.regione.liguria.it/catalogo/mappe.html. Accessed 24 September 2024
13. Carta Geologica d'Italia in scala 1:100.000. https://inspiregeoportal.ec.europa.eu/srv/api/records/ispra_rm:Geologia100K_DT. Accessed 29 July 2024
14. Carta Litologica d'Italia in scala 1:100.000. https://inspiregeoportal.ec.europa.eu/srv/ita/catalog.search#/metadata/ispra_rm:Meta_Geo_SV000004_RN. Accessed 24 September 2024
15. Bucci F., et al.: A new digital lithological Map of Italy at 1:100.000 scale (2021). https://doi.org/10.1594/PANGAEA.935673
16. ARPAL – Centro Funzionale Meteoidrologico di Protezione Civile, Atlante climatico della Liguria. https://www.arpal.liguria.it/tematiche/meteo/pubblicazioni-bis/analisi-climatologiche/atlante-climatico-della-liguria.html. Accessed 25 September 2024
17. Consultazione dati meteoclimatici della Regione Liguria. https://ambientepub.regione.liguria.it/SiraQualMeteo/script/PubAccessoDatiMeteo.asp. Accessed 25 September 2024
18. GRASS GIS Manual – Variance Inflation Factor. https://grass.osgeo.org/grass84/manuals/addons/r.vif.html. Accessed 06 September 2024
19. Cheng, C., Yang, Y., Zhong, F., Song, C., Zhen, Y.: An Optimization of statistical index method based on Gaussian process regression and GeoDetector, for higher accurate landslide susceptibility modeling. Appl. Sci. **12**, 10196 (2022). https://doi.org/10.3390/app122010196
20. Meyer, N.K., Schwanghart, W., Korup, O., Romstad, B., Etzelmüller, B.: Estimating the topographic predictability of debris flows. Geomorphology **207**, 114–125 (2014)
21. Carta geologica alla scala 1:50000. https://www.isprambiente.gov.it/it/attivita/suolo-e-territorio/cartografia/carte-geologichee-geotematiche/carta-geologica-alla-scala-1-a-50000. Accessed 24 September 2024
22. CORINE Land Cover. https://land.copernicus.eu/en/products/corine-landcover. Accessed 25 September 2024
23. ESA World Cover. https://esa-worldcover.org/en. Accessed 24 September 2024
24. Gregori, E., Costanza, M., Andrenelli, M.C., Zorn, G.: Assessment and classification of climatic aggressiveness with regard to slope instability phenomena connected to hydrological and morphological processes. J. Hydrol. **329**, 489–499 (2006)
25. Da Silva Charles T., Rocha Lopes T., Nascimento Duarte S., Garcia Nascimento J., De Carvalho Ricardo H., Bicioni Pacheco A.: Estimating average annual rainfall by ordinary kriging and TRMM precipitation products in midwestern Brazil. J. South Am. Earth Sci. **118** (2022)

26. Lucas, M.P., et al.: Optimizing automated kriging to improve spatial interpolation of monthly rainfall over complex terrain. J. Hydrometeorol. Am. Meteorol. Soc. **23**, 567–572 (2022). https://doi.org/10.1175/JHM-D-210171.1
27. GRASS Manual. Inverse Distance Weighting. https://grass.osgeo.org/grass84/manuals/r.surf.idw.html. Accessed 25 September 2024
28. Arnoldus, H.M.J.: An approximation of the rainfall factor in the universal soil loss equation. In: Deboodt, M., Gabriels, D. (eds.) Assessment of Erosion. John Wiley and Sons, Chichester (1980)
29. Dissegna, et al.: Valutazione del rischio di erosione per la Regione Veneto, ARPAV (2017)
30. European Commission: Directorate-General for Environment, Directorate-General for the Information Society and Media and Schneider, G., Corine Soil Erosion Risk and Important Land Resources in the Southern Regions of the European Community – An Assessment to Evaluate and Map the Distribution of Land Quality and Soil Erosion risk. Publications Office (1993)
31. Brenning, A., Schwinn, M., Ruiz-Páez, A.P., Muenchow, J.: Landslide susceptibility near highways is increased by 1 order of magnitude in the Andes of southern Ecuador, Loja Province. Nat. Hazards Earth Syst. Sci. **15**, 45–57 (2015). https://doi.org/10.5194/nhess-1545-2015
32. Iadanza, C., Trigila, A., Starace, P., Dragoni, A., Biondo, T., Roccisano, M.: IdroGEO: a collaborative web mapping application based on REST API services and open data on landslides and floods in Italy. ISPRS Int. J. Geo-Inf. **10**(2), 89 (2021). https://doi.org/10.3390/ijgi10020089
33. Mousavi, S.Z., Kavian, A., Soleimani, K., Mousavi, S.R., Shirzadi, A.: GIS-based spatial prediction of landslide susceptibility using logistic regression model. Geomat. Nat. Hazards Risk **2**(1), 33–50 (2011). https://doi.org/10.1080/19475705.2010.532975
34. Sun, X., Chen, J., Bao, Y., Han, X., Zhan, J., Peng, W.: Landslide susceptibility mapping using logistic regression analysis along the Jinsha River and its tributaries close to Derong and Deqin County, Southwestern China. Int. J. Geo-Inf. **7**, 438 (2018). https://doi.org/10.3390/ijgi7110438
35. Fawcett, T.: An introduction to ROC analysis, 2006. Pattern Recogn. Lett. **27**, 861–874 (2006)
36. Rob Hyndman, R., Athanasopoulos, G.: Forecasting: Principles and Practice, 3rd ed. OTexts (2021). https://otexts.com/fpp3/

Mapping the Threat: Using a Geospatial Lens on Malakand Division, Pakistan, to Gain Early Insights into Antimicrobial Resistance (AMR)

Rizwan Shahid[1], Muhammad Tariq Yousafzai[2], Muhammad Shafique[3], Imran Khan[4], Yi Chen[5], Stefania Bertazzon[1](✉), and Zul Kamal[2,5]

[1] University of Calgary, Calgary, AB T2N 1N4, Canada
bertazzs@ucalgary.ca
[2] Department of Pharmacy, Shaheed Benazir Bhutto University, Sheringal, Pakistan
[3] Department of Pharmaceutical Sciences, Shaqra University, Shaqra 11961, Saudi Arabia
[4] Canadian Hub for Applied and Social Research (CHASR), University of Saskatchewan, Saskatoon, Canada
[5] Chongqing University of Chinese Medicine, Bishan District, Chongqing 402760, China

Abstract. The misuse and over-prescription of antibiotics have contributed to the growing global threat of antimicrobial resistance (AMR), which undermines the efficacy of many antibiotics, including amoxicillin. AMR poses serious risks, such as increased mortality, prolonged hospital stays, and significant burdens on healthcare systems. In this study, we conducted a spatial analysis of amoxicillin resistance across 28 administrative units (Tehsils) of the Malakand region of Pakistan, a mountainous area in the Himalayan foothills where over 90% of the population resides in rural areas with limited access to healthcare. Hotspot analysis and Local Indicators of Spatial Autocorrelation (LISA) were used to identify local clusters of amoxicillin resistance. The central Tehsils of Wari, Lal Qilla, and Kabal were identified as significant hotspots and clusters of resistance. Linear regression explored associations of amoxicillin resistance with potential contributing factors at the regional level. Further, Geographically Weighted Regression (GWR) indicated which of the Tehsils exhibited significant risk factors for amoxicillin resistance. Significant contributors to amoxicillin resistance were rural population portion and illiteracy rates (aged 10 years and above). The GWR analysis provided detailed insight into the geographic variation of these risk factors, highlighting specific Tehsils where interventions may be most needed. Our findings underscore the importance of spatial analysis in identifying geographic inequalities in amoxicillin resistance. These results can aid policymakers and healthcare planners in targeting high-risk areas for further investigation and evidence-based interventions to mitigate the growing AMR threat.

Keywords: AMR · Amoxicillin · Hotspot · LISA · GWR · Malakand (Pakistan)

E. Borgogno-Mondino and P. Zamperlin (Eds.): ASITA 2024, CCIS 2463, pp. 118–130, 2025.
https://doi.org/10.1007/978-3-031-91141-5_9

1 Introduction

According to the World Health Organization (WHO), AMR is among the top global public health threats responsible for millions of direct or indirect death [1]. In 2019, an estimated 4.95 million deaths worldwide were linked to bacterial infections resistant to antimicrobial treatments, with 1.27 million of these deaths directly attributed to (AMR) [2]. Prescription and over prescription of antibiotics exhibit specific geospatial patterns, associated with local health systems and physician training. Overall, higher prescription rates are generally observed in less developed countries. However, the potential AMR resulting from high use of antibiotics is not confined to the regions where prescriptions are high: people travel, visit relatives and friends, and even carry their own prescriptions on their journeys. For example, in major Canadian cities, higher rates of antibiotics have been measured in the portions of the sewage corresponding to neighbourhood of recent immigration, particularly from less developed countries. Therefore, antibiotic over use and AMR raises rapidly from local to global scale [3]. Currently, Pakistan ranks as the third-largest consumer of antibiotics among low- to middle-income countries, following India and China. Between 2000 and 2015, antibiotic consumption in Pakistan increased by 65%, rising from 0.8 to 1.3 billion defined daily doses [4], posing a significant healthcare challenge due to the growing threat of AMR; the WHO has already identified Pakistan as one of the top five countries with the highest neonatal mortality caused by resistant bacteria [5]. In the Malakand region, located in the province of Khyber Pakhtunkhwa (KPK), Pakistan, primary healthcare practices often face significant challenges, including accessibility issues, health literacy, shortages of certified medical professionals, and varying standards of care.

1.1 Standard Medical Practice and Quackery in Pakistan

Public sector hospitals, rural health centers (RHCs), basic health units (BHUs), and private clinics serve the majority of the population in Pakistan. Doctors with MBBS degrees (Bachelor of Medicine, Bachelor of Surgery) are the certified practitioners in these settings. However, the quality and availability of care can vary greatly depending on the region. In more remote and underserved areas of northern KPK, there are reports of non-certified practitioners, often referred to as "quacks", providing healthcare [6]. These practitioners may lack formal medical education, yet it is common practice for them to prescribe medications, including antibiotics. The over-prescription or misuse of antibiotics is a known issue in Pakistan, partly due to a lack of regulation and enforcement in rural areas [7]. The government has launched initiatives to curb quackery, but enforcement in rural areas remains weak. Many patients in northern KPK rely on these providers due to proximity, lower costs, and immediate availability compared to public health services, which are often under-resourced and understaffed.

Despite government attempts, quackery remains a serious issue in rural areas of Pakistan, including northern KPK. Not only do quacks often practice despite their lack of legal qualifications, sometimes they can be even more influential than certified doctors due to their local connections [6]. This practice is prevalent in areas where access to certified healthcare professionals is limited, pushing locals towards unqualified practitioners. These quacks commonly prescribe antibiotics and other treatments without proper medical knowledge, leading to harmful outcomes, including antibiotic resistance and even preventable deaths [8]. For instance, a report from Dawn [7] highlights that over 600,000 quacks operate across the country, providing healthcare to those in underserved areas, which exacerbates health risks due to improper medical practices. Moreover, quacks often serve as the first point of contact for many people, particularly in remote rural areas, leading to complications when patients eventually require care from certified doctors. Similarly, The Express Tribune describes cases where quacks in rural areas mismanage critical health situations, further stressing the need for stronger regulations and better access to legitimate healthcare services [9]. The persistence of quackery, especially in remote areas, reflects the severe shortage of qualified medical professionals and the lack of enforcement of anti-quackery laws. Efforts to tackle this issue, such as public health campaigns and stricter government action, are often advocated but face major challenges in implementation due to the socio-economic conditions of these regions [6].

Non-certified practitioners and sometimes even certified professionals might over-prescribe antibiotics due to a lack of diagnostic facilities, patient demand, or low awareness of AMR. This practice contributes to the growing problem of AMR in the region and nationwide [10]. Key factors contributing to this crisis, beyond the misuse of antibiotics and over-prescription by non-certified practitioners, are self medication and lack of stringent regulations on antibiotic sales [11]. In northern KPK, especially in rural areas, unregulated use of antibiotics by non-certified healthcare providers, pharmacists, and even self-prescription by patients is rampant. Due to limited access to qualified doctors, many patients turn to local pharmacies or uncertified practitioners who often prescribe antibiotics for conditions that do not require them. This is a primary driver of antibiotic resistance in the region [12].

Pakistan is part of the Global Antimicrobial Resistance Surveillance System (GLASS), and reports from various regions, including KPK, indicate a high prevalence of resistant strains of bacteria such as Escherichia coli, Staphylococcus aureus, and Klebsiella pneumonia [13]. According to a study published in Journal of Population Therapeutics and Clinical Pharmacology, Pakistan has reported alarmingly high rates of resistance to commonly used antibiotics, including penicillins, fluoroquinolones, and cephalosporins [14]. Efforts to combat AMR include the National Action Plan for Antimicrobial Resistance 2017–2022 by Pakistan's Ministry of National Health Services, which aims to promote rational use of antibiotics, improve infection control practices, and strengthen surveillance for AMR [15]. However, enforcement and implementation of these measures, especially in northern KPK, have been slow due to infrastructural challenges and a lack of awareness among both healthcare providers and the public. A study conducted by the National Institute of Health (NIH) and Aga Khan University in KPK found high levels of resistance to first-line antibiotics such as ampicillin, co-trimoxazole, and ciprofloxacin. It also highlighted a lack of awareness regarding AMR among healthcare workers in rural areas [10–16]. The AMR situation in KPK poses a significant public health risk, as it complicates the treatment of common infections and increases the burden on an already strained healthcare system. Without urgent action to regulate antibiotic use, increased AMR surveillance and educate both healthcare providers and the public, the spread of resistant bacteria will likely worsen.

1.2 Accessibility to Primary Care

The Malakand region in KPK is mountainous, with many remote villages that are hard to access (see Figs. 1 and 2). This creates significant barriers to healthcare access, particularly in winter or during harsh weather conditions. Public healthcare infrastructure, such as its BHU and RHCs, exists but is often under-resourced [17]. These facilities may be understaffed, lack essential medicines, or have limited diagnostic capabilities. Private healthcare is more readily available in urban centers, but it can be expensive for rural populations. The shortage of trained healthcare professionals in remote mountainous region is inherently linked to local geographical, structural, and socioeconomic conditions: many doctors prefer to practice in urban centers or abroad owing to better facilities, pay, social environment, and career opportunities. The healthcare workforce in rural areas is often supplemented by health care workers like "lady health workers" (LHWs) who provide basic maternal and child healthcare services but are not fully trained physicians [18]. The network of primary healthcare facilities like BHUs is widespread but often ineffective due to poor management, lack of equipment, and limited staffing. As a result, people often rely on secondary or tertiary care hospitals located in larger towns or cities, making primary care access inadequate in remote areas. In summary, while certified doctors do operate in the Malakand region, the presence of non-certified practitioners and the lack of robust healthcare infrastructure pose challenges to standard medical practice. The overuse of antibiotics, along with accessibility barriers, contributes to significant public health risks in the region.

2 Study Area and Methods

2.1 Study Area

Figures 1 and 2 present an overview of the study area, detailing its location, topography, populated places, healthcare facilities, and administrative units (Tehsils). In Pakistan, administrative divisions include Districts, i.e., larger units encompassing multiple Sub-Districts, i.e., Tehsils, which serve for local administration and development planning. The study area comprises 8 Districts and 28 Tehsils, with an estimated population of approximately 9 million according to the Pakistan Bureau of Statistics [19]. All analyses presented in this study were performed at the Tehsil level.

The Malakand region is characterized by rugged and mountainous terrain, forming part of the western Himalayan foothills, which include high mountains (up to 7,700 m) and steep valleys. The area experiences cold winters with heavy snowfall and abundant rainfall in the monsoon season. The harsh winter conditions, coupled with heavy rains and frequent landslides, contribute to poor accessibility to healthcare services, particularly in the winter months. Notably, nearly 90% of the population resides in rural and remote areas, which exacerbates challenges in accessing basic needs and healthcare services.

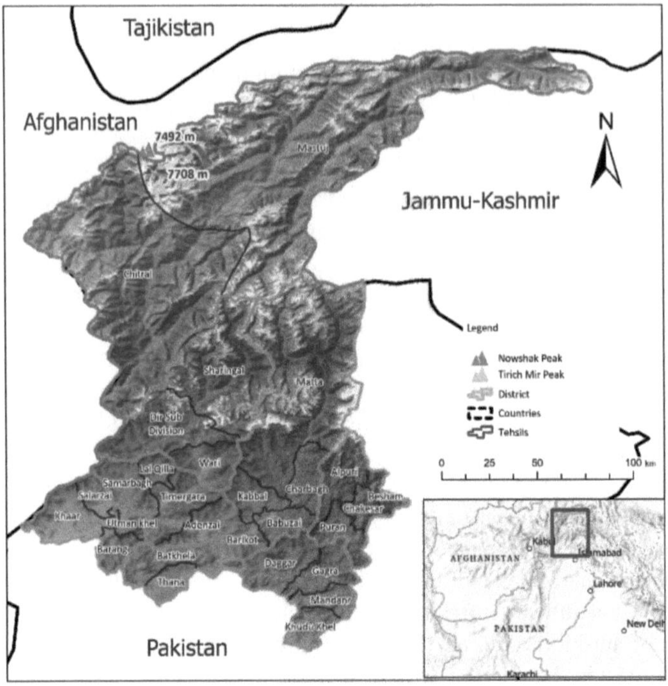

Fig. 1. Study area: location (left) and place names

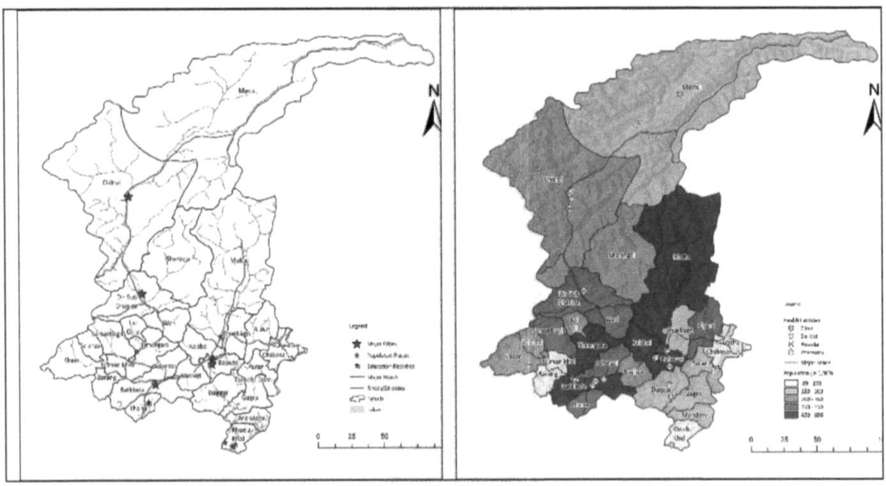

Fig. 2. Study area: facilities (left), and population (right)

2.2 Study Design and Data

This study utilizes data from a retrospective analysis conducted at the Saidu Group of Teaching Hospitals (SGTH), between January and March 2021. SGTH, a tertiary care facility, is a key healthcare provider to the Malakand District. A total of 508 patient case histories were collected with the authorization of the hospital's medical superintendent and chief pharmacist, in accordance with established ethical protocols and procedures. Informed consent was obtained from all participants prior to data collection.

The study population included patients who were admitted to the hospital for more than one day and were on antibiotic therapy for a minimum of three days. Culture sensitivity tests were performed to assess amoxicillin antimicrobial resistance. The amoxicillin resistant population was estimated using the total Tehsil population by determining the proportion of resistant cases within the total sample. In addition, demographic data, including male, female, illiterate population, functional disabilities, urban and rural population for 2023 at the Tehsil level was obtained from the Pakistan Bureau of Statistics [19], providing the necessary population context for the spatial analysis.

2.3 Geospatial Analytical Methods

To assess the presence of spatial autocorrelation in the distribution of the amoxicillin resistant population, Global Moran's I [20] was employed. However, the Global Moran's I statistic does not provide insight into localized patterns, leaving potential spatial autocorrelation at finer geographic levels, such as the Tehsil level, unexplored. To address this, Local Indicators of Spatial Autocorrelation (LISA) [21] were applied to identify local spatial autocorrelation patterns. Getis-Ord Gi* hotspot analysis [22] was used to detect and quantify spatial clustering, identifying both the location and magnitude of statistically significant hotspots.

The analysis of the amoxicillin resistant population and demographic variables was conducted using correlation and cross-correlation at the entire study area level. After identification and exclusion of highly cross-correlated variables, linear regression was employed to explore the associations of resistant population with potential contributing factors across the entire study area. However, linear regression assesses these associations regionally, offering no insights on local (Tehsil level) significance of factors.

To amend this limitation, Geographically Weighted Regression (GWR) was applied. GWR extends traditional linear regression by estimating local parameters [23], thereby estimating local models for each Tehsil. This approach enables a more in-depth understanding of how demographic variables might impact amoxicillin resistance at a localized scale, highlighting variations in significance across different Tehsils.

3 Results

Of the 508 samples collected through 28 Tehsils, 379 were found amoxicillin resistant (74.6%), and 82 sensitive (16.1%), totaling 461, i.e., 90.1% of the sample (Fig. 3). Hotspot analysis and local Moran's I (Fig. 4) identified clustering of amoxicillin resistance in the central portion of the study area.

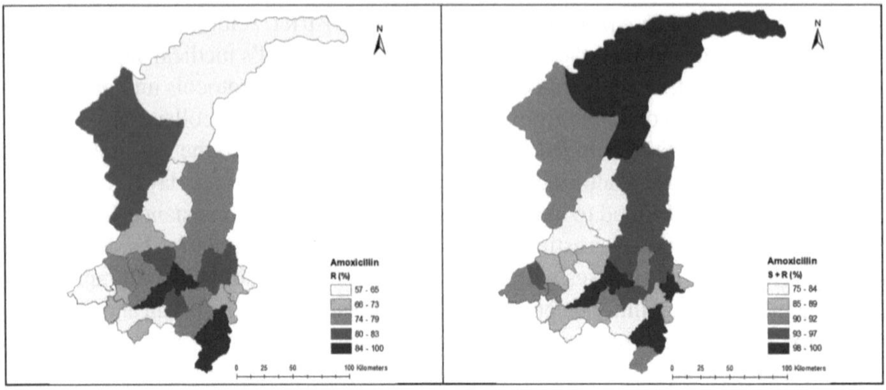

Fig. 3. Amoxicillin resistance (left) and sensitivity (right) across Malakan tehsils

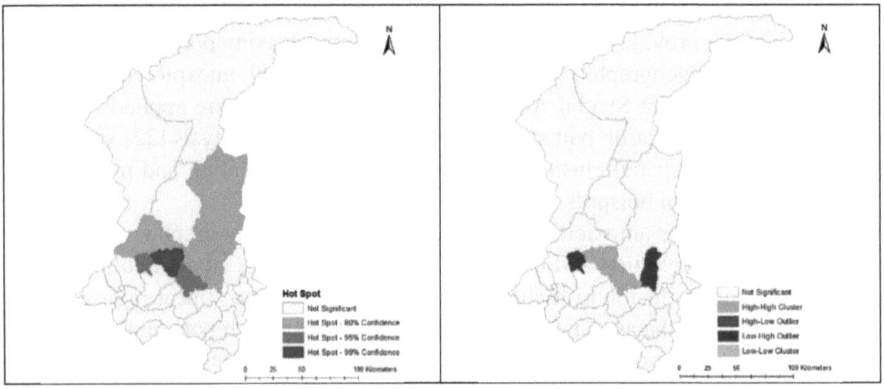

Fig. 4. clustering of amoxicillin resistance analyzed by hotspot and local Moran's I

Amoxicillin resistant population (dependent variable) was tested for Global Moran's I (Table 1). Linear regression residuals were also tested for spatial autocorrelation. Both analysis indicated that spatial autocorrelation was not significant in the dependent variable or in the linear model residuals (Table 1).

Table 1. Global spatial autocorrelation in linear model's dependant variable and residuals

	Moran's I	Z-score	p-value
Resistant Population	0.01	1.29	0.20
Linear Model Residuals	−0.01	0.64	0.52

Table 2 summarizes the linear and GWR regressions. GWR local coefficients are shown in Fig. 5, with t values presented in the insets.

Table 2. Table 2.Linear and GWR regression result summaries

Linear regression: variables			
	Coeff.	Std err.	t-val
Intercept	-1.83e+04	2.38e+04	-0.77
Rural population	0.57	0.07	8.28
Illiteracy >10 yrs	0.91	0.26	3.49

Regression Summaries		
	Linear	***GWR***
Sample	28	
Neighb.	18	
R^2	0.88	0.96
Adj. R^2	0.87	0.93
Std error	5.53e+04	
Sigma		4.06e+04

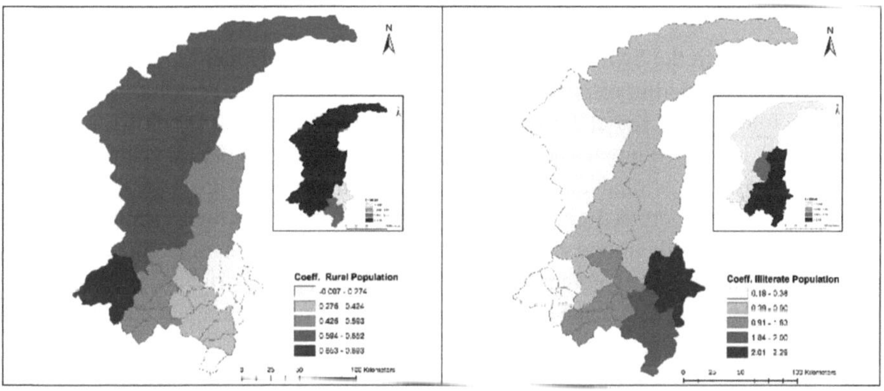

Fig. 5. GWR local coefficients for rural (left) and illiterate (right) population

Figure 6 illustrates the spatial distributions of rural population and illiteracy rate, i.e., contributing factors associated with amoxicillin resistance.

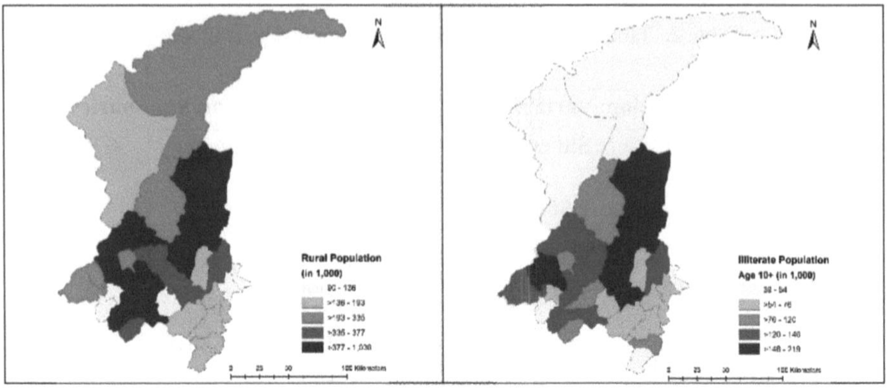

Fig. 6. Spatial distribution of rural and illiterate (right) population

4 Discussion

The Kabal Tehsil in the Swat District and the Wari Tehsil in Upper Dir exhibit clusters (high-high) of amoxicillin resistance. Further, the Wari Tehsil also exhibits a has hotpot at 99% CI, followed by Kabal Tehsil and Lal Qilla Tehsil in Lower Dir, with hotspots at 95% CI. Swat is a well-known tourist destination that attracted 449,000 visitors in 2023, including 4,000 international tourists from 108 different countries [24]. AMR prevalence in the area can be dangerous for international visitors as well as for their country of origin, owing to the higher likelihood of contracting bacterial infections and spreading them upon their return. Moreover, enhancing primary health care infrastructure and services in the region could help attract even more visitors each year, contributing to both Pakistan's tourism industry and overall national revenue.

As shown in Table 3 (which summarizes UNICEF data), the Upper Dir district, where the Wari Tehsil is located, with a high-high cluster and 99% CI hotspot, features the lowest percentage of women with media exposure (only 3.6%) in the region, with one of the highest percentages of *E. coli* risk in drinking water (as high as 92%), and the highest percentage of premature births (as high as 95%) [25].

The low media exposure of women (3.6% vs. 39.7% in men) suggests gender differences in access to education and resources, rather than simply isolation or infrastructure deficiencies. While such differences can be understood in the context of traditional rural societies, it is just in such contexts that poor literacy and education of women can have major impacts. Indeed, in these contexts women attend to cooking and raising children: a poor understanding of infection risk from drinking water is a prime example.

Table 3. Major social and development indicators in the region (UNICEF)

District	Internet access	Women	Men	Pre mature birth	Early childhood development	Basic drinking water access	E. coli risk in drinking water	Global multidimen poverty
		Media exposure (newspaper, tv, radio)						
Bajaur agency	3.5	11.3	40.7	2.2	59.7	81.5	76.3	74.7
Buner	19.4	11.1	56.1	2.4	38	78.8	70	44.7
Chitral	6.2	41.5	64.3	3.6	56.2	84.1	83.6	30.3
Lower Dir	26.3	12.9	62.6	1.5	66.3	87.4	76.7	34.8
Malakand protected area	9.9	39	55.7	15	65.2	97.7	56.6	29.7
Shangla	8.1	9.5	19.7	42	23.6	69	100	75
Swat	33.3	22.5	59.1	6.3	52.8	83.8	65.5	45
Upper Dir	11.7	3.6	39.7	95.2	40.1	82.3	92	67.9
	%	%	%	%	Score	%	%	Index

Data Source: UNICEF Multiple Indicator Survey Dec 2021.

Indeed, our study identified rurality and illiteracy as significant risk factors associated with amoxicillin resistance. As illustrated in the insets of Fig. 5, the local coefficient of rurality is highest and most significant (inset) in the north and west portions of the region, while the coefficient of illiteracy and its significant exhibit almost opposite pattern, with the highest values in the southeast. Interestingly, clusters and hotspots are found in areas that lie at the intersections of these two portions.

Based on our regressions, rurality and illiteracy are significant risk factors for amoxicillin resistance. However, as depicted in Fig. 6, the prevalence of high rates of rurality and illiteracy extend well beyond the areas of high and significant GWR coefficients. In particular, large portions of the center-west and some in the center-east exhibit high values of both risk factors (a total of 8 Tehsils). Even though our results are preliminary, and are subject to limitations, they are important in highlighting high-risk areas that do not currently exhibit clusters or hotspots, nor significant GWR coefficients, but do feature high levels of significant risk factors; hence, they may be the first to be exposed to amoxicillin resistance in the future.

AMR is a global concern [1], with similar challenges observed in northern Pakistan and other remote regions. Northern Canada [26, 27] is another remote region, facing similar, yet distinct challenges. Both areas face healthcare access limitations, remote living conditions, and frequent antibiotic use, which can drive the development of AMR. In northern Canada, higher rates of infectious diseases, lead to increased antibiotic usage, particularly in Indigenous communities [28], contributing to resistance. Like northern KPK, the remoteness of these regions exacerbates healthcare delivery issues, resulting in incomplete treatments and inconsistent antibiotic use. Limited localized AMR surveillance in both regions underscores the need for more comprehensive data and targeted interventions to mitigate this growing public health threat.

The concept of remoteness takes a whole other dimension in Europe; nonetheless, AMR is an emerging concern in this continent as well. Among European countries, Italy has exhibits one of the highest AMR rates, primarily due to high antibiotic consumption and sometimes inadequate infection control measures. Hospitalized patients are especially vulnerable, and the COVID-19 pandemic has worsened the situation. Increased use of antibiotics to treat secondary infections has contributed to rising resistance rates [29, 30].

4.1 Strengths and Limitations

Low income or developing countries tend to exhibit the highest AMR rates; yet, they also tend to suffer from serious AMR data gaps [31]. Current socioeconomic and social indicators data are not available at Tehsil level. We used the best available demographic data to perform spatial analysis. More data are needed to refine the analysis and suggest appropriate interventions. In shear numerical terms, the sample size for amoxicillin resistance is also low, compared to the total population of the area; however, these numbers should also be evaluated in the context of poorly accessible, high-mountain regions, and low income countries, where any data gathering poses serious challenges.

To the best of our knowledge, this is the first study to explore AMR rates in KPK at Tehsil level. It is also the first geospatial analysis examining the spatial distribution of amoxicillin resistance and identifying clustering and hotspots. Hotspot and cluster analysis identified areas of high amoxicillin resistance. Further, linear and GWR regression identified factors significantly associated with amoxicillin resistance, and GWR pointed to local associations, i.e., areas of high local significance. Based on these results, Tehsils comprised in these high-significance areas, rather than the entire region, should be targeted for interventions that would have a lower cost than global or regional interventions. Moreover, the study of the spatial pattern of risk factors identified additional Tehsils at high risk of increased amoxicillin resistance. While intervention in these Tehsils has lower priority, localized preventative measures aimed at reducing the risk factors locally would be most effective and cost-effective.

5 Conclusion

The spatial analysis of amoxicillin resistance in the northern areas of KPK, Pakistan, highlights significant geographic disparities in AMR. This region, characterized by its rugged, mountainous terrain and harsh climatic conditions, poses substantial challenges in healthcare accessibility, especially for the 90% of the population residing in remote and rural areas. With Pakistan ranked as the third-largest consumer of antibiotics, this study highlights the critical role that overuse, quack medical practices, and accessibility issues play in driving AMR. Through LISA and hotspot analysis, distinct tehsil clusters of amoxicillin resistance were identified, with further exploration using linear regression and GWR revealing rural population density and illiteracy as key contributing factors.

These findings suggest that AMR is linked to demographic variables, emphasizing the need for targeted interventions. While this analysis provides important insights, the availability of more detailed demographic and healthcare data is crucial for refining these findings and developing effective, evidence-based interventions. Policymakers and healthcare planners should consider prioritizing these vulnerable Tehsils, addressing the underlying causes of AMR through targeted healthcare improvements, public health education, and stricter antibiotic regulation to mitigate this growing threat in northern KPK.

References

1. WHO. Antimicrobial Resistance, https://www.who.int/news-room/fact-sheets/detail/antimicrobial-resistance. Accessed 02 September 2024
2. Murray, C.J., et al.: Global burden of bacterial antimicrobial resistance in 2019: a systematic analysis. Lancet **399**, 629–655 (2022)
3. Parkins, M., Lee, J., Xiang, K., et al.: Longitudinal Monitoring of Sewershed Resistomes in Socioeconomically Diverse Urban Neighbourhoods, PREPRINT (Version 1) (2024). https://doi.org/10.21203/rs.3.rs-4202677/v1
4. Klein, E.Y., Van Boeckel, T.P., Martinez, E.M., Pant, S., Gandra, S., Levin, S.A., et al.: Global increase and geographic convergence in antibiotic consumption between 2000 and 2015. Proc. Natl. Acad. Sci. U.S.A. **115**, E3463–E3470 (2018)
5. Laxminarayan, R., et al.: Access to effective antimicrobials: a worldwide challenge. Lancet (London, England) **387**, 168–75 (2016)
6. Khalid, S., Khan, M.Z., Atif, M., Farooqui, M., Kakar, Z., Faheem, M.: Assessment & prevalence of malpractice of quacks: survey of district Dera Ismail Khan, Khyber Pakhtoon Khwa Pakistan. Siazga Res. J. **2**(1), 73–77 (2023)
7. Health: The Lure of Quacks. https://www.dawn.com/news/1443342. Accessed 06 September 2024
8. Khan, R., Mustafa, M.A.: An empirical research study on deluging quackery outlets across Sindh, Pakistan and propositions to deal with confounding factors of rising quackery. J. Pak. Med. Assoc. **73**(1), 135–138 (2023)
9. Chronicles of Quackery: When Real Doctors are Outshone. The Express Tribune. https://tribune.com.pk/story/640157/chronicles-of-quackery-when-real-doctors-are-outshone. Accessed 02 September 2024
10. Bilal, H., Khan, M.N., Rehman, T., et al.: Antibiotic resistance in Pakistan: a systematic review of past decade. BMC Infect. Dis. **21**, 244 (2021)
11. Waseem, H., Ali, J., Sarwar, F., et al.: Assessment of knowledge and attitude trends towards antimicrobial resistance (AMR) among the community members, pharmacists/pharmacy owners and physicians in district Sialkot, Pakistan. Antimicrob. Resist. Infect. Control **8**, 1–7 (2019)
12. Saleem, Z., Hassali, M.A., Hashmi, F.K.: Pakistan's national action plan for antimicrobial resistance: translating ideas into reality. Lancet Infect. Dis. **18**, 1066–1067 (2018)
13. WHO, Global Antimicrobial Resistance and Use Surveillance System (GLASS). https://www.who.int/initiatives/glass. Accessed 22 August 2024
14. Antimicrobial resistance trends in wound pathogens: a study at a tertiary care hospital in Peshawar, Pakistan, J. Popul. Ther. Clin. Pharmacol. **31**(6), 528–537 (2024)
15. Antimicrobial Resistance, National Action Plan, Pakistan. https://www.nih.org.pk/wp-content/uploads/2018/08/AMR-National-Action-Plan-Pakistan.pdf. Accessed 25 August 2024

16. Fuller, W., Kapona, O., Aboderin, A.O., et al.: Education and awareness on antimicrobial resistance in the WHO African region: a systematic review. Antibiotics (Basel) **12**(11), 1613 (2023)
17. Zafar, S., Malik, A.M.: The role of BHUs and RHCs in rural health. Pak. J. Public Health **4**(1), 15–20 (2014)
18. Shaikh, B.T., Hatcher, J.: Health seeking behaviour and health service utilization in Pakistan: challenging the policy makers. J. Public Health **27**(1), 49–54 (2005)
19. Pakistan Bureau of Statistics. https://www.pbs.gov.pk/. Accessed 20 August 2024
20. Getis, A.: A history of the concept of spatial autocorrelation: a geographer's perspective. Geogr. Anal. **40**(3), 297–309 (2008)
21. Anselin, L.: Local indicators of spatial association-LISA. Geogr. Anal. (1995)
22. Liu, X., et al.: Geospatial patterns of comorbidity prevalence among people with osteoar-thritis in Alberta Canada. BMC Public Health **20**(1), 1551 (2020)
23. Fotheringham, A.S., Brunsdon, C., Charlton, M.: Geographically Weighted Regression: The Analysis of Spatially Varying Relationships. Wiley, West Sussex (2002)
24. Swat Valley Tourism: A Rising Global Attraction in 2023. https://pakistanwise.com/02/01/2024/swat-global-attraction-tourists-in-2023. Accessed 05 September 2024
25. UNICEF Multiple Indicator Survey Dec 202. https://mics.unicef.org/country-profiles/pakistan/4146. Accessed 07 August 2024
26. CARSS. Canadian Antimicrobial Resistance Surveillance System, 2023 executive summary and link to the Pan-Canadian Action Plan on Antimicrobial Resistance. https://www.canada.ca/en/public-health/services/publications/drugs-health-products/canadian-antimicrobial-resistance-surveillance-system-report-2022.html. Accessed 02 September 2024
27. Saatchi, A., Yoo, J.-W., Schwartz, K.L., et al.: Quantifying the gap between expected and actual rates of antibiotic prescribing in British Columbia, Canada. Antibiotics **10**, 1428 (2021)
28. Jeong, D., Nguyen, H.N.T., Tyndall, M., et al.: Antibiotic use among twelve Canadian First Nations communities: a retrospective chart review of skin and soft tissue infections. BMC Infect. Dis. **20**, 118 (2020)
29. Montalti, M., et al.: Antimicrobial resistance (AMR) in Italy over the past five years: a systematic review. Biologics **2**, 151–164 (2022)
30. Cerini, P., et al.: Trends in antibiotic resistance of nosocomial and community-acquired infections in Italy. Antibiotics **12**, 651 (2023)
31. Murray, C.J.L., et al.: Global burden of bacterial antimicrobial resistance in 2019: a systematic analysis. Lancet **399**(10325), 629–655 (2022)

A Preliminary Geospatial Analysis of Out-of-Hospital Cardiac Arrests in Lombardy

Roberto Primi[1,2,3], Khashayar Yazdanparast[5], Sara Bendotti[1,2], Alessia Currao[1,2], Enrico Baldi[1,2,4], Stefania Bertazzon[5(✉)], and Simone Savastano[1,2]

[1] Division of Cardiology, Fondazione IRCCS Policlinico San Matteo, Pavia, Italy
[2] Resuscitation Science Research Team (RESTART), Fondazione IRCCS Policlinico San Matteo, Pavia, Italy
[3] Department of Public Health, Experimental and Forensic Medicine, University of Pavia, Pavia, Italy
[4] Department of Molecular Medicine, Section of Cardiology, University of Pavia, Pavia, Italy
[5] University of Calgary, Calgary, AB T2N 1N4, Canada
bertazzs@ucalgary.ca

Abstract. Out-of-hospital cardiac arrest (OHCA) is a leading cause of death worldwide. This study presents a preliminary geospatial analysis of OHCA in some provinces of Lombardy (Italy), over the 2015–2023 period. Geospatial analysis can identify areas at high risk of OHCA, highlighting clusters, referred to as "hot-spots" where the occurrence of OHCA is significantly higher than in neighbouring areas or those areas with an increasing number of OHCA during time. This study represents the first spatial distribution of out-of-hospital cardiac arrest (OHCA) in Italy and particularly in the Lombardy region. Our geospatial analysis highlighted a heterogenous distribution of OHCA through the region. A multiscale approach, using global and local analysis from regional to provincial level, highlighted substantial local differences. These differences may be associated with physical features, such as mountains vs. lowland, socioeconomic aspects, such as urban patterns, population density, and rurality, as well as with environmental factors, such as air pollution. We are aware of the limitations of our study and of the importance to refine the territorial grid depending on the purpose. Our results, albeit preliminary, could provide insights for future research in OHCA spatial analysis.

Keywords: Out of hospital cardiac arrest · Lombardy · Space-time clustering

1 Introduction

Out-of-hospital cardiac arrest (OHCA) is one of the leading causes of death worldwide and is characterised by a sudden loss of cardiac function, leading to a cessation of blood flow to vital organs with overall survival rates remaining low despite advances in emergency management and resuscitation techniques. The factors influencing survival after OHCA are well established but there remains considerable variations in incidence and outcome among and within countries [1]. Moreover the chances of survival, indeed,

E. Borgogno-Mondino and P. Zamperlin (Eds.): ASITA 2024, CCIS 2463, pp. 131–145, 2025.
https://doi.org/10.1007/978-3-031-91141-5_10

decrease rapidly without immediate intervention, making prompt access to the Emergency Medical Services (EMS) and the availability of automated external defibrillators (AEDs) crucial [2].

Spatial analysis, that is as "the process of examining the locations, attributes, patterns, and relationships of features in spatial data" [3], can provide valuable tools to understand OHCA occurrence patterns and optimize emergency response [4]. Several papers concerning spatial analysis of OHCA have been published over the last decade, spreading across the world from USA to Australia [5–11], but no information regarding Italian context is available.

With this study we present a preliminary geospatial analysis of OHCA in some provinces of Lombardy region, over the 2015–2023 period. The aim of mapping and spatial analysis is to identify areas at high risk of OHCA, highlighting clusters, referred to as "hot-spots" where the occurrence of OHCA is significantly higher than in neighbouring areas or those areas with an increasing number of OHCA during time.

Once these areas have been identified we can a) delve into how several social, demographics factors correlate with the incidence and outcomes of OHCA, as well as environmental ones, b) optimize emergency response by evaluating the distribution and accessibility of AEDs c) develop predictive models of high-risk areas by integrating various geospatial, demographic and environmental factors.

2 Methods

2.1 Study Population and Territory

Out-of-Hospital Cardiac Arrest registry of the Lombardy region, named "Lombardia CARe" is a population-based registry that enrolls all the patients who experienced a cardiac arrest outside the hospital (OHCA). Patient enrolment started in the province of Pavia in 2015. Data collection was subsequently extended to the provinces of Lodi, Cremona and Mantua in 2019, Varese in 2020 and Brescia and Como in 2021 and all cardiac arrest events are geo-located with latitude and longitude coordinates.

The territory covered by LombardiaCARe encompassed an area of 15,126 km^2, with a population of 4.271.330 million inhabitants. The subdivision of this territory and population across provinces (as of 31st December 2023) is illustrated in Table 1.

2.2 Spatial Analyses, Aggregations, and Scales

Spatial analyses were conducted at different scales: at the case level, i.e., considering the location of each OHCA, and at the municipality (i.e., 'comune') scale, i.e., aggregating OHCA occurrences based on municipal border. At this level, OHCAs were further standardized, i.e., divided by the population (ISTAT, 2023) of each municipality, and multiplied by 100,000. The resulting variable is called SOHCA, which stands for "Standardized OHCA". The reference population data, inhabitants on 31 December 2023, were retrieved from Italian National Institute of Statistics (ISTAT) server.

Both at the case level and SOHCA levels, the spatial patterns of OHCA and SOHCA were visualized and analyzed using Moran's I, Getis G, hotspot analysis on data aggregated for the entire period. Spatiotemporal trends were analyzed using space-time cubes

Table 1. Summary data on the territory and population covered by LombardiaCARe

Provinces	Land area, km^2	Comuni	Population*	OHCA cases
Brescia	4,786	205	1,262,271	2,805
Como	1,279	147	598,604	1,425
Cremona	1,770	113	353,537	1,596
Lodi	783	60	229,628	1,019
Mantua	2,341	64	407,051	2,048
Pavia	2,969	185	539,239	5,797
Varese	1,198	136	881,000	3,194
LombardiaCARe	15,126	910	4,271,330	17,884

*(ISTAT 31/12/2023).

and time series analysis. These analyses were performed at the regional scale, i.e., conducting a single analysis on the entire dataset, comprised of seven provinces; they were further repeated for each of the provinces where data were available.

2.3 Methodology Description

Moran's I spatial autocorrelation index [12] is calculated on a spatial data series, with attribute x measured on a set of point locations i. As an index of self-similarity of attributes over short distances, it compares the value of the attribute x at location i with the value of the attribute at location j. The index calculation relies on a spatial weight matrix [13], which specifies which locations are deemed contiguous. Moran's I is defined in the interval $[\ 1 \leq I \leq 1]$. Values in the interval $[0 < I \leq 1]$ indicate positive spatial autocorrelation, i.e., clustering of similar values (e.g., low values near low values); in the interval $[-1 \leq I < 0]$ they indicate negative spatial autocorrelation, i.e., a dispersed pattern (e.g., low values near high values); whereas null I values indicate lack of spatial autocorrelation, i.e., spatial randomness. Moran's I index is assessed by a Z test under null hypothesis of independent spatial distribution of the variable [14].

In this study, Moran's I is calculated both on the case variable and on the SOHCA. However, specific spatial weights matrices are computed in each case, as the case variable consists of approximately 18,000 spatial data points, whereas the aggregated standardized variable consists of approximately 900 data points, i.e., the total number of municipalities in the seven Lombard provinces considered. As well, specific spatial weights matrices are computed for each variable in each province.

Local clustering is assessed by local indicators of spatial association (LISA)[13], which include local Moran's I, and are defined like global indices, but computed, typically, at each spatial sample points. Global and local indices are related mathematically [13]. Among LISAs, the local version of Getis and Ord's G* index [10], i.e., Gi*, examines the location, intensity, and statistical significance of local spatial clusters. In this study, it examines the clustering of high or low values of OHCA and SOHCA (respectively). The statistical significance of the statistic is assessed under null hypothesis of spatial randomness of the spatial data series [11], i.e., in this study, OHCA and SOHCA, respectively, at the analytical scales considered, i.e., regional and provincial.

Similar to Moran's I, Getis G relies on a spatial weights matrix. Likewise, specific matrices were used for each variable and analytical scale. Based on Gi* values, hotspot analysis assesses the intensity and significance of spatial clusters, using Z scores and associated p-values. Local spatial patterns are assessed with respect to neighboring values as well as to the global (i.e., regional or provincial) spatial pattern [15].

Space-time cubes were created using Esri's ArcGIS 10.3 space-time analysis tools to investigate temporal patterns in OHCA occurrences. The tool aggregates the point data into a multidimensional file based on defined spatial and temporal intervals. This tool allowed for extending the clustering analysis to a dynamic space-time, rather than static spatial clusters. Hence, space-time cubes detected significant clusters, trends, and temporal shifts in OHCA occurrences over time [16–19].

3 Results

3.1 Case Level (OHCA) Analysis

Spatial descriptive analyses for the whole LombardiaCARe, conducted using global Moran's I and Getis G, indicate significant spatial clustering. Local analysis is illustrated in Fig. 1, which shows a plot of Gi* values produced with R (left) and a map of hotspots, estimated from Gi* values produced with ArcGIS (right). These analyses are conducted on individual OHCA cases occurred over the entire study area and period.

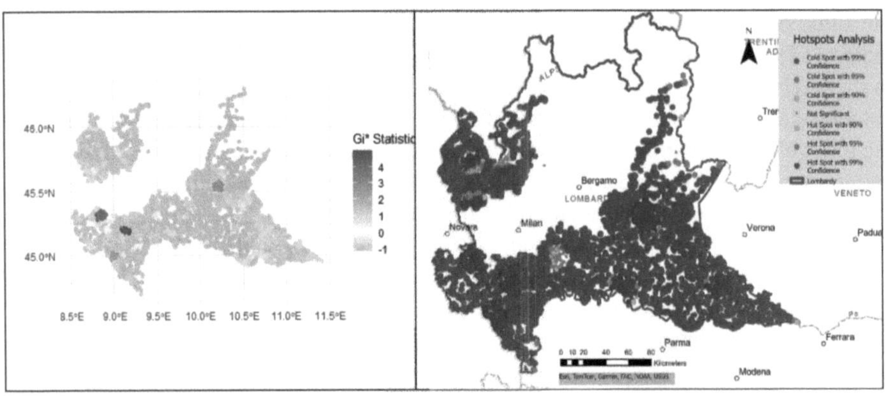

Fig. 1. spatial clustering of OHCA occurrences: Getis Gi* (left) and hotspots (right)

A spatiotemporal analysis of cluster evolution (Fig. 2), conducted using the ArcGIS "Create Space Time Cube By Aggregating Points" geoprocessing tool, shows the location and temporal trend of significant local clusters. OHCA occurrences are low for the majority of the region (blue), with a few locations exhibiting high but stable OHCA occurrences over time (green), and several locations exhibiting high and increasing OHCA occurrences over time (red).

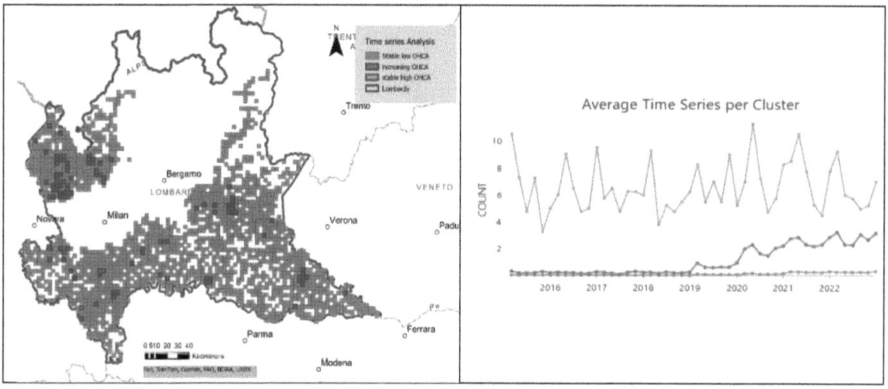

Fig. 2. Spatiotemporal clusters of OHCA occurrences (left) and time series trend (right)

3.2 Population Standardized (SOHCA)

Individual OHCA occurrences over the LombardiaCARe area were aggregated at the municipal (i.e., *comune*) level (Fig. 3, left), and further standardized by population, i.e., SOHCA (Fig. 3, right).

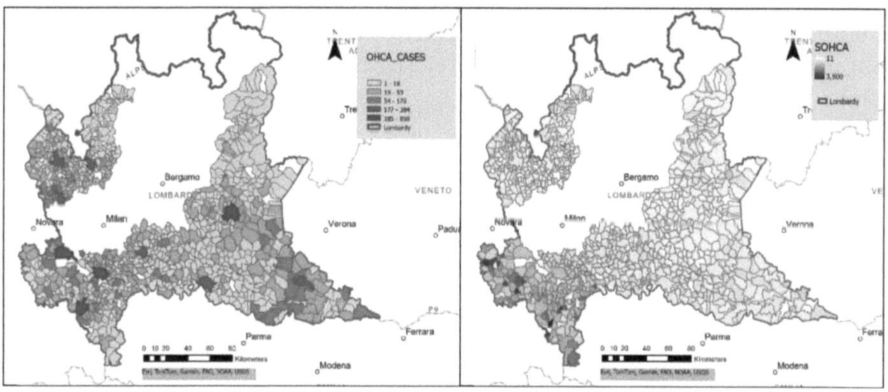

Fig. 3. Spatial pattern of municipal level OHCA (left) vs. SOHCA (right)

Figure 4, which shows a plot of Gi* values (left) and a map of hotspots, estimated from Gi* values (right). These analyses are conducted on SOHCA cases, aggregated at the municipal level, over the entire study area and time period. At this level, global Moran's I was significant (p value = 0.04), while Getis G was not (p value = 0.29).

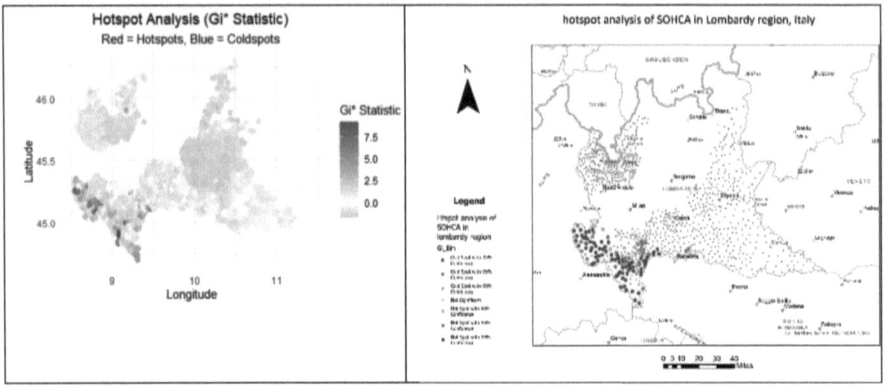

Fig. 4. spatial clustering of SOHCA occurrences: Getis Gi* (left) and hotspots (right)

3.3 Provincial Level SOHCA Analysis

The SOHCA analysis was conducted for each province in the LombardiaCARe area, for the respective period of their participation in the initiative. Table 2 summarizes, Moran's I and Getis G global indices at the provincial level. Both indices are significant in Brescia, Como, and Pavia, while only Moran's I is significant in Lodi and Varese. Figure 5 illustrates the location of provinces within the region. The following Figs. 6, 7, 8, 9, 10, 11, and 12 illustrate: the province within Lombardy (a1), the cluster time series (a2), the spatial pattern of SOHCA (b), local clustering (hotspots) (c), and spatiotemporal cubes (d).

Fig. 5. Overview of the provinces of the region Lombardy and their location

Table 2. Global Moran's I and Getis G on SOHCA at the provincial level

		Brescia	Como	Cremona	Lodi	Mantua	Pavia	Varese
SOHCA		222.22	238.05	451.44	443.76	503.13	1,075.03	362.54
Global Moran I	I	0.29	0.19	0.03	0.31	–0.12	0.23	–0.17
	p(z)	0.00*	0.01*	0.68	0.00*	0.33	0.00*	0.04*
Global Getis G	G	0.01	0.01	0.01	0.02	0.02	0.01	0.01
	p(z)	0.00*	0.01*	0.40	0.07	0.90	0.01*	0.86

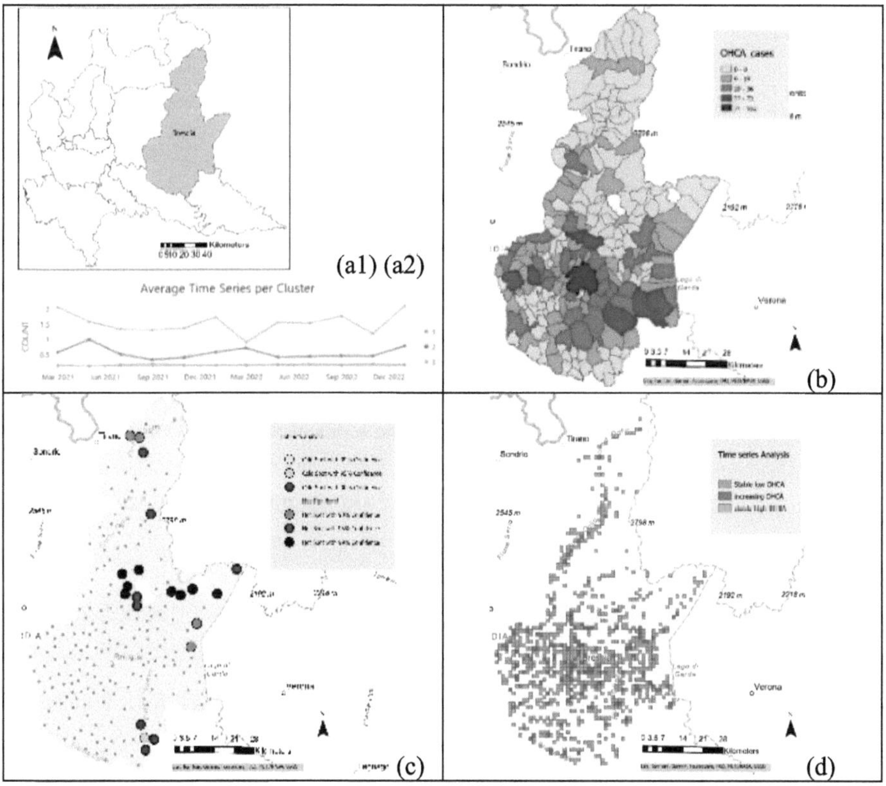

Fig. 6. Distribution, hotspots, spacetime cube, time series of SOHCA – Brescia province

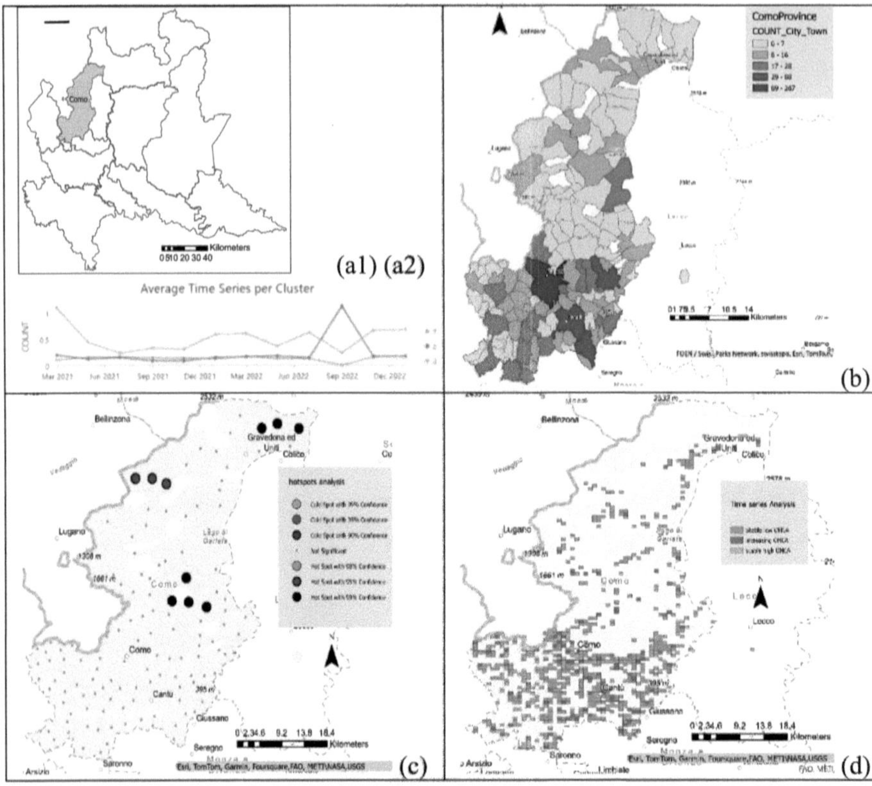

Fig. 7. Distribution, hotspots, spacetime cube, time series of SOHCA – Como province

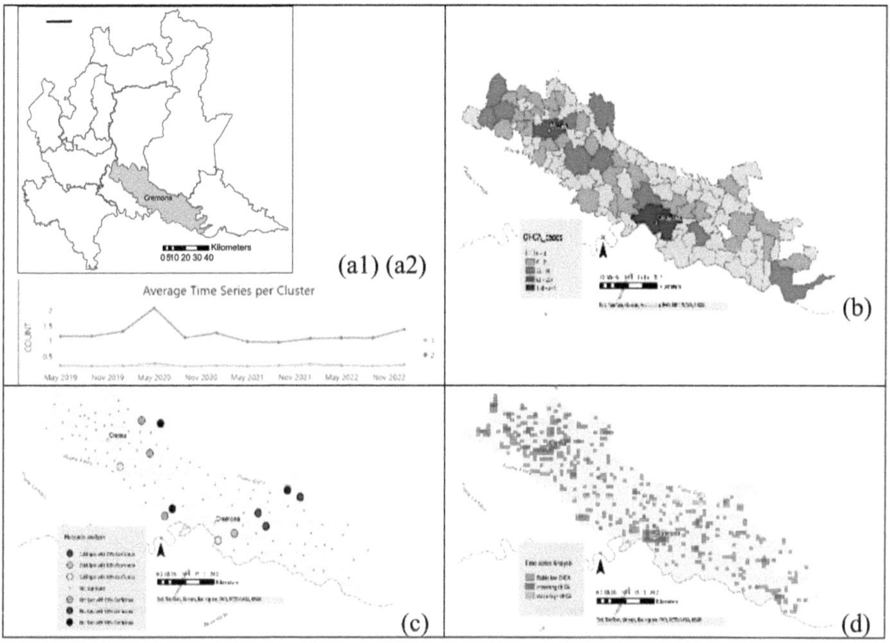

Fig. 8. Distribution, hotspots, spacetime cube, time series of SOHCA – Cremona province

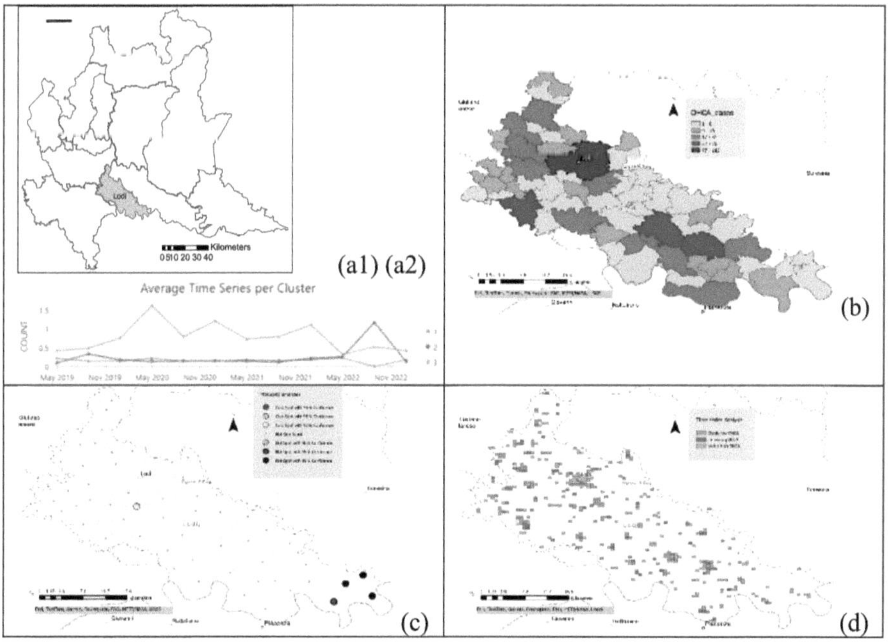

Fig. 9. Distribution, hotspots, spacetime cube, time series of SOHCA – Lodi province

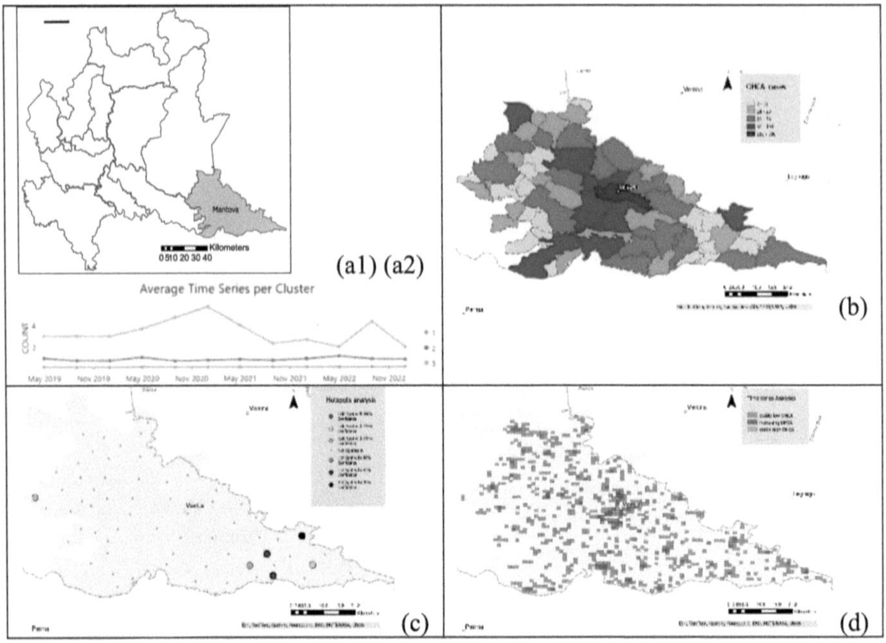

Fig. 10. Distribution, hotspots, spacetime cube, time series of SOHCA-Mantua province

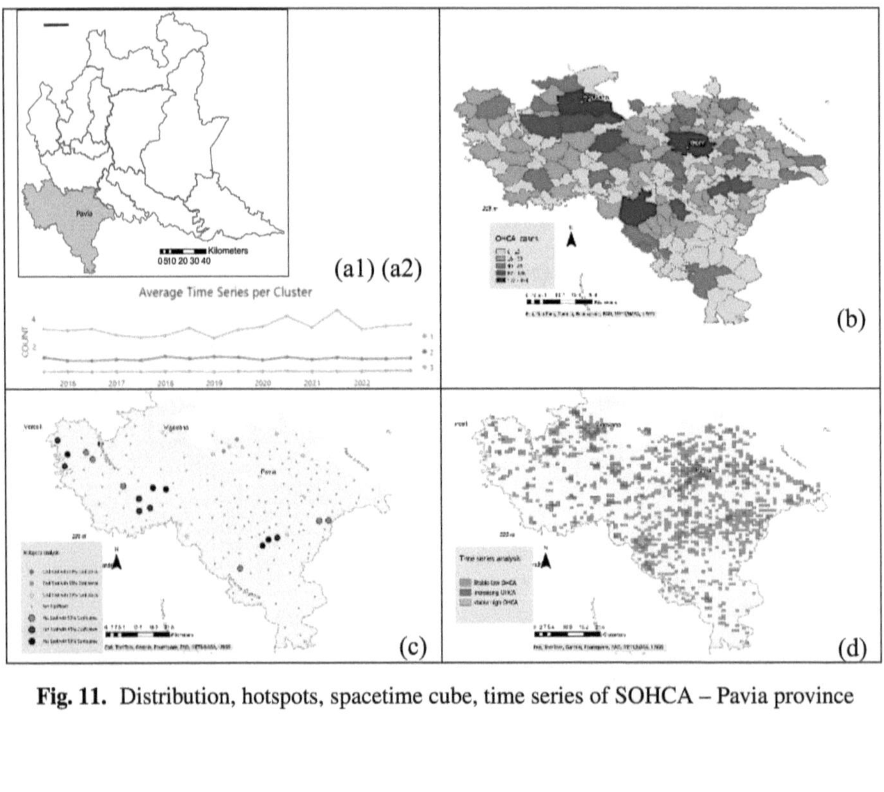

Fig. 11. Distribution, hotspots, spacetime cube, time series of SOHCA – Pavia province

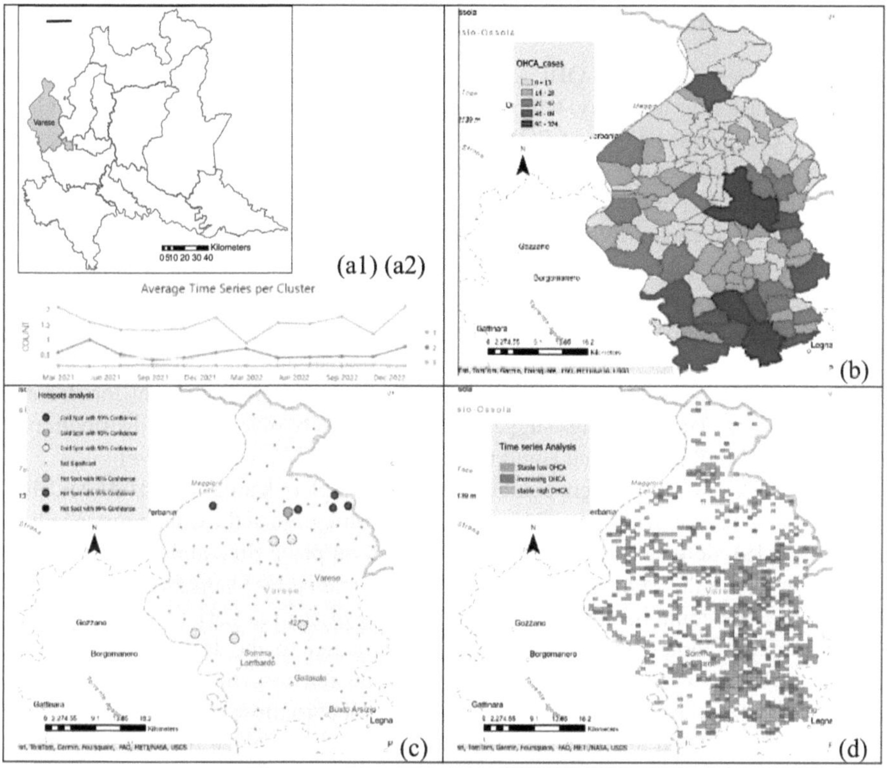

Fig. 12. Distribution, hotspots, spacetime cube, time series of SOHCA – Varese province

4 Discussion

4.1 Case Level Analysis

These preliminary results show that OHCA cases have a strong tendency to concentrate in specific areas (as shown by Moran's I). This behaviour is confirmed locally by significant Getis-Ord-Gi* statistics, suggesting the presence of local hot- and cold-spots.

From the space-time cube analysis, it is evident that certain areas exhibit a consistent pattern of high OHCA events over time, but some areas show emerging clusters where the number of OHCA cases is increasing over time (provinces of Varese, Como and Brescia). In an earlier study, Gentile [20] clarified the link between cardiac arrest and air pollution in the southern part of Lombardy. This suggests a possible influence of air pollution also in the northern part of the region that encompasses the above provinces.

The location and temporal dynamics of these clusters merit attention in further studies, considering climate pattern and industrial emissions. This analysis considered only the location and time of OCHA occurrence; hence, it does not consider the susceptible population. The different spatial pattern between standardized vs. non-standardized variable is emphasized in Fig. 3. However, the standardization is based on residence location, not on OHCA location.

4.2 Population Standardized (SOHCA) and Provinces

With population-standardized OHCA data (i.e., SOHCA), the global analysis showed a less strong clustering tendency, with a significant Moran's I and non-significant Getis G. Indeed, the spatial pattern of SOHCA (Fig. 4) exhibits a more homogeneous pattern than municipally-aggregated OHCA, with a generally higher SOHCA cases in the southwestern portion of the region. Further analyses shall refine the data to consider the length of time that each province participated in the LombardiaCARe initiative. In this preliminary study, space-time analyses provide insights into the temporal trend.

At the province scale clustering pattern varies: Brescia, Lodi, Como and Pavia showed significant global clustering, as evidenced by positive Moran's I values. On the contrary, the province of Varese showed a negative and significant Moran's I, indicating spatial dispersion rather than clustering. As well, Getis G was significant for Brescia, Como, and Pavia. These findings suggest the heterogeneity in the spatial distribution of OHCA across Lombardy, which could target interventions at the local level.

It has been known in different contexts that these "high risk area" could be associated with low socio-economical status [21]. Also the response time of the Emergency Medical Services (EMS), defined as the difference between on place time and call time, could be different within the same region as indeed demonstrated by Svensson [22] as well as OHCA outcomes could be influenced by the rurality of an area [23].

In Lombardy, emergency management is entrusted to the Regional Emergency Agency (AREU), which covers the entire regional territory through the Territorial Agencies (AAT), whose boundaries are almost identical to those of the provinces.

The more localized analysis, i.e., local indicators within each province also show varying degrees of clustering. At this level, clusters emerge that were not visible at the regional scale. Importantly, the LombardiaCARe area is not spatially continuous, which may have affected analyses at that level.

Brescia. At this scale, hotspots emerge in the northern part of the province, in contrast with coldspots in the southern part; however, the space-time analysis suggests emerging clusters in the central part. The relatively short time series suggest a variable temporal pattern. Brescia is the most populous province in LombardiaCARe, whereas Varese is the most densely populated.

Como. Similar to Brescia, hotspots lie in the north, in contrast with a higher density of OHCA in the south. The space-time cube also shows emerging clusters in the center, with a peach in the time series in 2022. Both Como and Brescia encompass mountainous areas in the north, that likely impact population density, rurality, and accessibility.

Cremona. This flatter, more homogeneous province shows a mixture of hot- and cold-spots, confirming the lower global clustering. The time series 2020 peak may be associated with the early stages of the COVID pandemic, that hit the region hard.

Lodi. Few hotspots are visible in the southeast, with some emerging in the OHCA denser north. Like Como, the time series shows a peak in 2022.

Mantua. Similar to Cremona and Lodi, few hot- and cold-spots lie only in the southeastern corner, with some emerging in the center, despite a fairly flat time series.

Pavia. Unlike other provinces, clusters tend to lie in the most OHCA dense areas, especially in the north, though with alternating hot- and cold-spots. The time series (green and red) suggest a steady, or slowly growing pattern.

Varese. Like Brescia and Como, the spatial distribution shows higher OHCA in the low-lying south, with hotspots in the mountainous north. Few, large temporally stable clusters are surrounded by several smaller emerging ones. Like for Cremona, the 2020 peak may be associated with the COVID pandemic.

Provinces are a territorial level of a strictly administrative nature and within them there are often significant spatial differences in the population characteristics. Experimenting with a finer territorial grid could be more appropriate and functional. For example, ISTAT's Local Labour System could provide the geographical framework to correlate the socio-demographic characteristics of the population and the incidence of OHCA in a given area as well as heath districts could help in finalizing the analyses to political-managerial indications.

5 Conclusion

This study represents the first spatial distribution of out-of-hospital cardiac arrest (OHCA) in Italy and particularly in the Lombardy region.

Our geospatial analysis highlighted a heterogenous distribution of OHCA through the region. A multiscale analysis, from regional to provincial level, both globally and locally, highlighted substantial local differences. Though the results are preliminary, these differences may be associated with physical features, such as mountains vs. lowland, socioeconomic aspects, such as urban patterns, population density, and rurality, as well as with environmental factors, such as air pollution.

We are aware of the limitations of our study. One is that not all the tools used are free and this could reduce the replicability of the proposed method.

Another limitation is that LombardiaCARe has not a whole regional coverage yet.

Our results, albeit preliminar, provide the basis for future research aimed at identifying environmental, demographic, and socioeconomic factors able to influence the risk of OHCA resulting in a more effective allocation of resources where they are most needed. Once validated, these predictive models can serve other regions without comprehensive OHCA registries to predict OHCA incidence in their territory.

Authors' Contribution. R.P.: Conceptualization, data curation, writing original draft; K.Y.: methodology, software, formal analysis; Sa.B.: Data curation; A.C.: Data curation; E.B.: Data curation; St.B.: Conceptualization, methodology, supervision; S.S.: writing review and editing, Supervision, project administration.

References

1. Gräsner, J.-T., et al.: European Resuscitation Council Guidelines 2021: epidemiology of cardiac arrest in Europe. Resuscitation **161**, 61–79 (2021). https://doi.org/10.1016/j.resuscitation.2021.02.007
2. Liu, C.H., et al.: Strategies on locations of public access defibrillator: a systematic review. Am. J. Emerg. Med. **47**, 52–57 (2021). https://doi.org/10.1016/j.ajem.2021.02.033
3. ESRI – GIS Dictionary (n.d.). https://support.esri.com/en-us/gis-dictionary/search?q=spatial+analysis

4. Auricchio, A., et al.: Spatio-temporal prediction model of out-of-hospital cardiac arrest: designation of medical priorities and estimation of human resources requirement. PLoS ONE **15**, e0238067 (2020). https://doi.org/10.1371/journal.pone.0238067
5. Sasson, C., et al.: Identifying high-risk geographic areas for cardiac arrest using three methods for cluster analysis. Acad. Emerg. Med. **19**, 139–146 (2012). https://doi.org/10.1111/j.1553-2712.2011.01284.x
6. Ong, M.E.H., et al.: Geographic factors are associated with increased risk for out-of hospital cardiac arrests and provision of bystander cardio-pulmonary resuscitation in Singapore. Resuscitation **85**, 1153–1160 (2014). https://doi.org/10.1016/j.resuscitation.2014.06.006
7. Uber, A., Sadler, R.C., Chassee, T., Reynolds, J.C.: Bystander cardiopulmonary resuscitation is clustered and associated with neighborhood socioeconomic characteristics: a geospatial analysis of Kent County, Michigan. Acad. Emerg. Med. **24**, 930–939 (2017). https://doi.org/10.1111/acem.13222
8. Masterson, S., Teljeur, C., Cullinan, J., Murphy, A.W., Deasy, C., Vellinga, A.: Out-of-hospital cardiac arrest in the home: can area characteristics identify at-risk communities in the Republic of Ireland? Int. J. Health Geogr. **17**, 6 (2018). https://doi.org/10.1186/s12942-018-0126-z
9. Stassen, W., Theron, E., Slingsby, T., Wylie, C.: Out-of-hospital cardiac arrests in the city of Cape Town metropole of the Western Cape province of South Africa: a spatio-temporal analysis. Cardiovasc. J. Afr. **33**, 260–266 (2022). https://doi.org/10.5830/CVJA-2022-019
10. Lengen, G., et al.: Spatial dependence of non-traumatic out-of-hospital cardiac arrest in a Swiss region: a retrospective analysis. Resusc. Plus **19**, 100713 (2024). https://doi.org/10.1016/j.resplu.2024.100713
11. Doan, T., et al.: Identifying areas of Australia with high out-of-hospital cardiac arrest incidence and low bystander cardiopulmonary resuscitation rates: a retrospective, observational study. PLoS ONE **19**, 1–19 (2024). https://doi.org/10.1371/journal.pone.0301176
12. Luc, A.: Spatial Econometrics: Methods and Models (1988)
13. Luc, A.: An Introduction to Spatial Autocorrelation Analysis with GeoDa (2003)
14. Li, H., Calder, C.A., Cressie, N.: Beyond Moran's I: testing for spatial dependence based on the spatial autoregressive model. Geogr. Anal. **39**, 357–375 (2007). https://doi.org/10.1111/j.1538-4632.2007.00708.x
15. O'Sullivan, D., Unwin, D.J.: Local statistics. In: Geographical Information Analysis, pp. 215–38. Wiley (2010). https://doi.org/10.1002/9780470549094.ch8
16. Peuquet, D.J.: It's about time: a conceptual framework for the representation of temporal dynamics in geographic information systems. Ann. Assoc. Am. Geogr. **84**, 441–461 (1994)
17. Cheng, T., Adepeju, M.: Detecting emerging space-time crime patterns by prospective STSS. In: Proceedings of the 12th International Conference on Geocomputation (2013)
18. Create Space Time Cube By Aggregating Points (Space Time Pattern Mining) – ArcGIS Pro|Documentation (n.d.)
19. Time Series Clustering (Space Time Pattern Mining) – ArcGIS Pro|Documentation (n.d.)
20. Gentile, F.R., et al.: Out-of-hospital cardiac arrest and ambient air pollution: a dose-effect relationship and an association with OHCA incidence. PLoS ONE **16**, e0256526 (2021). https://doi.org/10.1371/journal.pone.0256526
21. Jonsson, M., et al.: Relationship between socioeconomic status and incidence of out-of-hospital cardiac arrest is dependent on age. J. Epidemiol. Community Health **74**, 726–731 (2020). https://doi.org/10.1136/jech-2019-213296
22. Svensson, A., Nilsson, B., Lantz, E., Bremer, A., Årestedt, K., Israelsson, J.: Response times in rural areas for emergency medical services, fire and rescue services and voluntary first responders during out-of-hospital cardiac arrests. Resusc. Plus **17**, 100548 (2024). https://doi.org/10.1016/j.resplu.2023.100548

23. Smith, A., Ball, S., Stewart, K., Finn, J.: The reality of rurality: understanding the impact of remoteness on out-of-hospital cardiac arrest in Western Australia – a retrospective cohort study. Aust. J. Rural Health 1–14 (2024). https://doi.org/10.1111/ajr.13184

On the Use of a Hydrogeomorphic Flood Modelling Framework for Building-Scale Assessment of NATCAT Impacts at Large Scale: The GEOSAFE Case Study in Italy

Nardi Fernando[1,2,3](✉), Annis Antonio[3,4], Bonamente Marco[5], and Pasetti Nicola[6]

[1] University of Rome Tor Vergata, Department of Civil Engineering and Computer Science, Rome, Italy
fernando.nardi@uniroma2.eu
[2] IDRAN Engineering and Technology Srl, Rome, Italy
[3] GRIDDIT Srl, Rome, Italy
antonio.annis@unipd.it
[4] University of Padua, Department of Civil, Architectural and Environmental Engineering, Padua, Italy
[5] Urby et Orbit Srl, Rome, Italy
mbonamente@urbyetorbit.it
[6] National Association of Insurance Companies (ANIA), Rome, Italy
nicola.pasetti@ania.it

Abstract. Climate extremes pose major threats, and changing climate, hydrological, and socio-cultural factors present decision-makers with complex challenges for disaster mitigation. The insurance sector, heavily impacted by natural catastrophes (NATCAT), faces rising economic losses alongside new opportunities. NATCAT models—datasets and analytical tools for evaluating risk and economic vulnerability—now require high-resolution simulations to support detailed assessments of natural disasters. In Italy, mandatory NATCAT insurance regulations are prompting the industry to adopt advanced geospatial intelligence for hazard, risk, and exposure data. This work showcases a collaboration among scientific, geospatial, and insurance professionals, resulting in a new NATCAT solution. By integrating the validated GFPLAIN flood model with building-scale data from URBY ET ORBIT in the REBIT solution by GRIDDIT startup, we provide Italy's first high-resolution models of flood-induced economic losses at the cadastral-building scale. These models contribute to the GEOSAFE service developed by ANIA SAFE for flooding NATCAT assessments of Italian insurance companies.

Keywords: Geospatial data · Natural Disasters · NATCAT · Floods · GFPLAIN · Insurance · Property protection

1 Introduction

The increasing impacts of hydro-metro climate extremes constitute one of the major threats to humanity. Climate, hydrological and socio-cultural change provide overall uncertain changing conditions posing serious issues for decision makers to understand

E. Borgogno-Mondino and P. Zamperlin (Eds.): ASITA 2024, CCIS 2463, pp. 146–157, 2025.
https://doi.org/10.1007/978-3-031-91141-5_11

and manage the critical actions for mitigating nuisance effects of natural disasters. Climate change and natural disasters are impacting and engaging several economic sectors that are called to take actions [1–3].

The insurance business is one of the major player, and impacted sector, with NATCAT, namely NATural CATastrophes, that are driving increasing economic losses as well as providing unique opportunities for the insurance industry. NATCAT models are defined as the set of data, numerical models and analytical tools for simulating the biophysical, social and economic processes in order to evaluate economic exposure and vulnerability of human assets at risk. The NATCAT insurance business is requesting scientific and professional CAT modellers to provide distributed granular high resolution simulations of natural disaster dynamics and impacts [4–6]. In Italy the insurance sector is now entering a very critical phase with novel national regulations requesting companies to have mandatory NATCAT insurance coverage [7].

As a result, Italy following major EU and global countries, are pushing the insurance industry to gather, process and use novel geospatial intelligence systems to derive distributed parametric data of NATCAT hazard, risk and exposure.

This work presents the result of synergy of scientific, geospatial and insurance industry professional and companies integrating academic and business know how and models for a novel NATCAT solution for the industry business. This work implements a validated geomorphic model of flood prone areas (GFPLAIN) [8], integrated into the REBIT solution by GRIDDIT [29], coupled with building-scale cadastral data by URBY ET ORBIT company [9] for producing the first country scale high resolution data models of flooding economic losses impacting Italy. The presented data and models were used in the developing of the flooding NATCAT module of the GEOSAFE data service developed by the National Association of Insurance Companies (ANIA) [10].

This paper is structured as follows. In Sect. 2 data and methods are presented focusing on scientific and applied research specification of the GFPLAIN large scale floodplain and flood damage economic quantification, the REBIT solution integrated in synergy with technology by Urby et Orbit for cadastral asset data identification and mapping of flood risk and associated economic damages. Then, in Sect. 3 a focus section is dedicated to the GEOSAFE geo-portal interface and data model with specific focus on the novel Italy-scale flood depth-damage model allowing the distributed quantification of maximum economic damages associated to reference flood scenarios derived using the REBIT solution. Section 3 also include sample applications of the proposed methodology and solutions showing functionalities and performances of the presented solution integrating geomorphometric, hydro-climatic and cadastral data and models for high resolution building-scale assessment of NATCAT insurance-related economic losses of floods in Italy. Last section provides concluding remarks with insights, ongoing work for updates and improvements as well as the sharing of some limitations of this work.

2 Data and Methods

The backbone of the scientific methodology is associated to the GFPLAIN dataset and model, a widely geomorphic floodplain zoning algorithm and geospatial open dataset. Based on the original theoretical framework of the floodplain width scaling research from

2006 [11], GFPLAIN was recently engineered into a novel programming framework, developed using latest more accurate high resolution digital topographic data, applied and validated [12] and now is being implemented in several uses cases and applications.

2.1 GFPLAIN Dataset and Algorithm

The GFPLAIN algorithm is a geomorphic approach to delineating global floodplains, emphasizing high-resolution data and topographic processing to map areas prone to flooding. The methodology primarily relies on a Digital Elevation Model (DEM) and a simplified hydro-modelling routine built around a three-step procedure that identifies flood-prone areas based on geomorphological features rather than hydro-dynamics.

The first step involves processing the DEM data to ensure the elevation model is suitable for floodplain mapping. DEM conditioning corrects inconsistencies, such as depressions and unnatural slopes, which could impact floodplain identification. This is accomplished through hydrological conditioning techniques like "pit filling," which removes anomalies by adjusting elevation values to allow for more consistent representation of flood water flows. The conditioned DEM is then hydrologically corrected to produce a smooth model that represents natural terrain variations and flow paths.

After preprocessing, the GFPLAIN algorithm applies a set of geomorphological rules to delineate floodplain areas based on land surface characteristics. The algorithm identifies areas with low elevations relative to nearby river channels and evaluates slope gradients to determine flood susceptibility. Areas that are both low-lying and have gradual slopes are classified as floodplains, as these characteristics are typically associated with flood-prone regions. Third and final step is implemented to assess maximum floodplain flow depths. A novel routine is implemented to assign to each floodplain cell the maximum flood depth considering the flood hazard zoning, DEM and GFPLAIN hydro-terrain analysis as input variables.

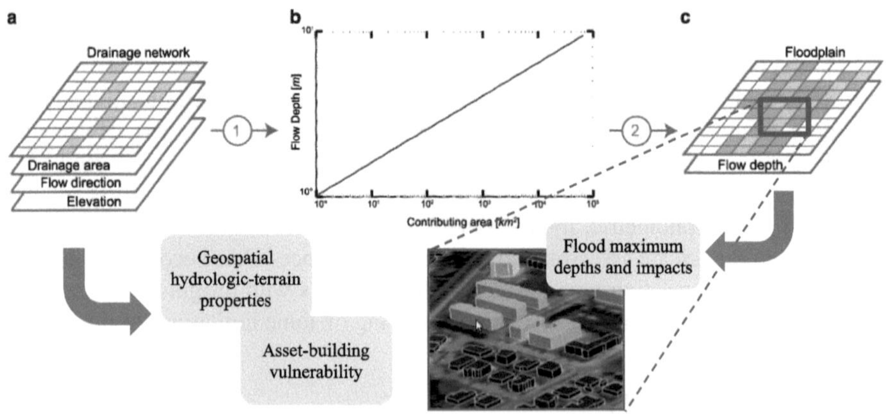

Fig. 1. Three main steps of the procedure are depicted. (a) DTM analysis for flow direction, drainage area and network identification from elevation data. (b) Scaling laws implemented for associating a floodplain flow depth to the contributing area of each drainage network grid cell. (c) GFPLAIN250m gridded layer is derived by flagging as a floodplain those cells whose elevations are lower than corresponding drainage network flow levels. This figure was adapted from [8].

2.2 GFPLAN Algorithm Specifications and Validation

The GFPLAIN algorithm integrates terrain analysis techniques to extract the stream network from a digital terrain model (DTM) of the Earth. Each cell in the drainage network is assigned a maximum potential channel flow depth (h) based on the power law in Eq. (1), where the contributing area (A) serves as a scaling parameter. This equation represents an adapted version of the Leopold scaling law, establishing the proportionality between the potential energy governing floodplain formation and the morphometric parameter A of the river basin.

$$h \propto A^b \tag{1}$$

The GFPLAIN algorithm produces a gridded floodplain layer by identifying low-lying cells along river corridors. The floodplain extent is determined by selecting cells that drain into a given channel and have absolute elevations lower than the corresponding maximum absolute channel flow level H, defined as

$$H = z + h \tag{2}$$

where z is the channel cell elevation derived from the DTM and expressed in meters above sea level and h is the GFPLAIN floodplain flow depth, as estimated using Eq. (1). To analyze variations in floodplain flow levels across different spatial scales, the dimensionless exponent b is used, ensuring a consistent floodplain zoning approach. The Italy INGV TinItaly dataset (10 m resolution) and the SRTM (Shuttle Radar Topography Mission, 30 m resolution), are processed to delineate floodplains for river basins with a contributing area greater than 1000 km^2. The composed model resolution, equivalent to 10 m at the equator aligns with the spatial scale of other country-scale datasets used in earth, environmental, social, and behavioral science applications to represent fluvial corridor processes and features.

The GFPLAIN algorithm was calibrated and validates considering standard flood hazard zoning as a reference. Extensive research work was carried out to understand the sensitivity of parameters, the influence of varying geographic and climatic regimes as well as the impact of source DEM in terms of optimal resolution and accuracy. While pursuing global scale assessment of flood delineations across scales, significant efforts were developed using international dataset and collaboration to test the consistency and validity of the GFPLAIN model and provide solid validation confirming the performances of the dataset and modelling approach [12–15]. The GFPLAIN model is widely used by the scientific and professional community of flood expert worldwide demonstrating to provide consistent and solid floodplain delineations across scales [16–29] (Fig. 2).

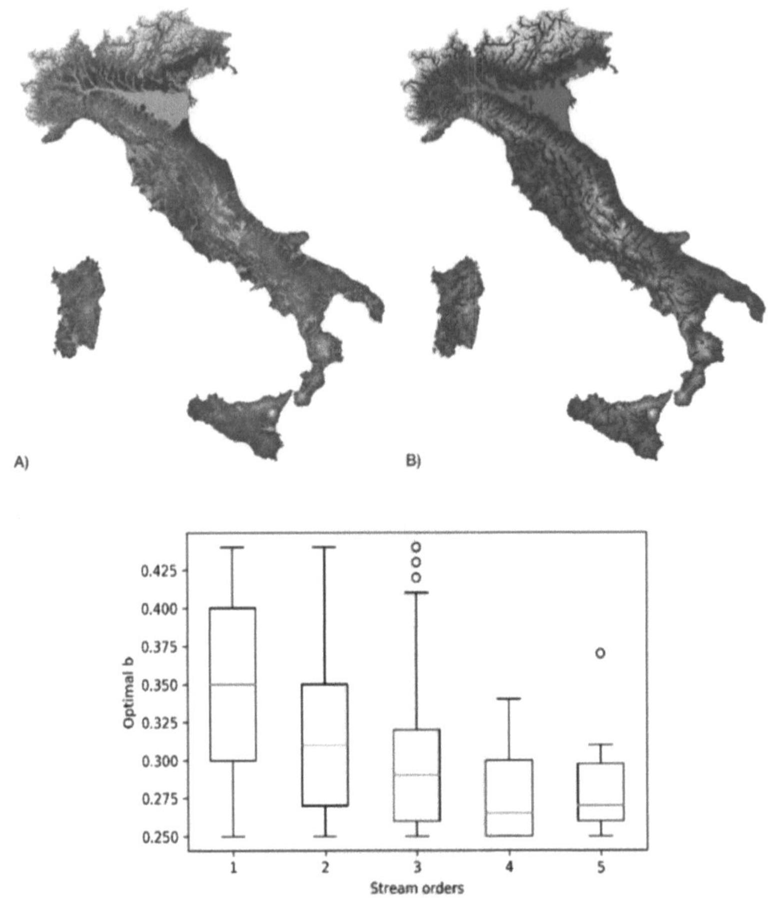

Fig. 2. The standard flood hazard map (PAI) produced by river basin authorities (A) and the GFPLAIN floodplain zoning (B) are compared at the national scale for the Italy case study. In the bottom box plot the optimal b parameter of the floodplain flow depth scaling law (see Eq. (1)) where the optimality is associated to the value of b that best match the GFPLAIN extension with the standard flood hazard PAI zoning.

2.3 From GFPLAIN to REBIT Analytics for Flood Economic Damage Assessment

The GFPLAIN algorithm is used in conjunction with a consolidated flood depth-damage function to provide maximum potential damage estimations at the national scale. The flood damage is estimated following the methodology suggested by the Joint Research Center (JRC) of the European Commission [31]. This methodology involves applying damage curves based on water depths and land use; the curves are calibrated and validated for different areas worldwide. The land use dataset adopted is the Corine Land Cover (CLC) from 2018, provided by ISPRA, which offers detail down to the fourth level. In this study, the original categories of Transport and Road Infrastructure were combined into a single category, as this distinction is not specified in the CLC database. For the dataset of asynchronous maximum water depths associated with the three hazard levels within the PAI zones, a methodology was used based on the application of the GFPLAIN algorithm [8, 11]. The algorithm used a combined DEM using the Italy INGV TinItaly dataset (10 m resolution) and the SRTM (Shuttle Radar Topography Mission) DTM, produced by the National Aeronautics and Space Administration (NASA) and provided by the United States Geological Survey (USGS), with a resolution of 1 arc-second, equivalent to 28 m when reprojected with the same WGS84 datum and Universal Transverse Mercator 33 North projection (UTM33N) for the entire Italian territory. Vertical accuracy of the flow depths is around ± 1 m. The PAI zones associated with the three hazard scenarios P1, P2, and P3 are provided by the National Environmental Information System Network (SINANET) of ISPRA.

The REBIT solution employs GFPLAIN flood depth estimation model in conjunction with the JRC flood damage model and the building scale characterization of building exposed and vulnerable assets (see next section for details). Results of the floodplain flow depth geo-service is represented in Fig. 1 that provides flood hazard data associated to maximum floodplain flow depths for predefined recurrence intervals (i.e. return times). Flood hazard is combined with exposure and vulnerability in the REBIT solution by GRIDDIT [30] to provide a comprehensive flood risk data model including damage functions converting risk into potential maximum economic damages of assets at inundation risk (Fig. 3).

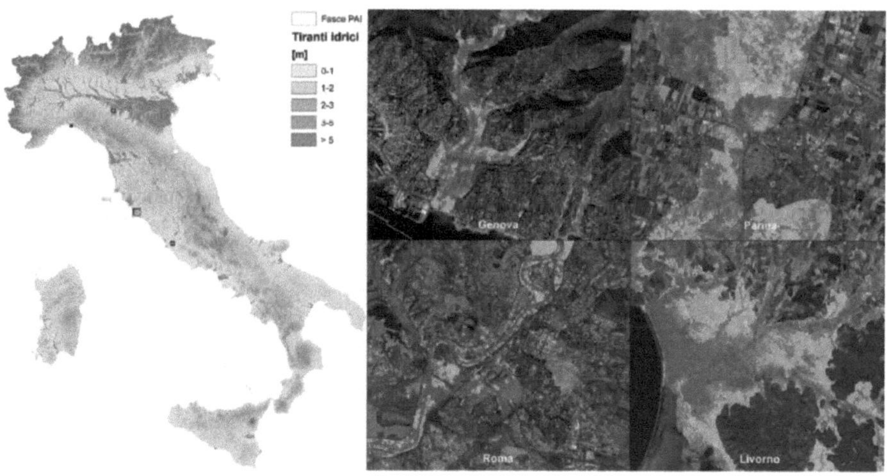

Fig. 3. Application of the GFPLAIN geomorphic flood-prone area delineation model of the REBIT solution by GRIDDIT: Italy scale and some insets showing flood impact maps for major flood-prone cities in Italy (Genova, Parma, Rome and Livorno).

The REBIT data and model for flood risk and economic losses estimation is combined with the high resolution accurate cadastral dataset developed by URBY ET ORBIT [9]. The combined flood-cadastral dataset represents a powerful tool for the NATCAT insurance industry in order to define categories and indices of risk exposure and maximum flood economic losses as a function of the cadastral building types and further socio-economic, demographic and structural geospatial specifications. The presented solution provide further information on the economic and social value and exposure of areas at flood risk from building-local scale to large scale assessments that are needed for insurance risk perils in both the underwriting and the claims management. The presented solution was developed and transferred into the GEOSAFE NATCAT web application by ANIA [10] serving the Italian insurance industries for developing distributed NATCAT hazard and risk indexing and reporting (Fig. 4).

Fig. 4. The integration of the REBIT flood hazard, exposure and economic damages due to floods with the cadastral data model and dashboard by URBY ET ORBIT.

3 The Case Study of the GEOSAFE NATCAT Geo-Model

GEOSAFE is an innovative service developed by ANIA SAFE to support businesses in evaluating and managing risks associated with natural catastrophes (NATCAT). The portal offers a Geographic Information System (GIS) that provides detailed insights into various hazards, including seismic, hydraulic, hydrogeological, climatic, and agricultural risks. Users can access tools for analyzing risk exposure, generating technical reports, and integrating client portfolio data to assess potential vulnerabilities. By leveraging high-resolution geospatial data and advanced analytical capabilities, GEOSAFE aids companies in making informed decisions regarding insurance contracts and risk mitigation strategies.

3.1 GEOSAFE Flood Hazard, Risk and Economic Damage Assessment

The GEOSAFE platform offers comprehensive risk assessments for hydro-meteo hazards, integrating incremental advancements from basic hazard maps to detailed risk evaluations. Initially, it utilizes reference PAI zoning flood hazard maps from ISPRA's PAI services. The platform then incorporates a proprietary "Water Depth" model supported by the REBIT technology to estimate flood depths and hydrodynamic impacts at specific geolocations. Additionally, it factors in asset vulnerability, considering characteristics like building floor, area, type, construction year, and conservation status, providing a refined, location-specific risk profile. Ongoing enhancements integrate climate change impacts, supported by research institutions and various universities.

GEOSAFE's economic damage model for hydraulic risks involves a systematic process: First, it calculates water depth based on terrain morphology across three hazard scenarios, determining flood depth relative to hydrological network proximity and estimating impact force. This depth information, combined with land use and building data, enables the calculation of economic damage estimates. The model applies OMI-AdE maps [32] and JRC tables for damage assessments, focusing primarily on building structures and their susceptibility to flood conditions (Fig. 5).

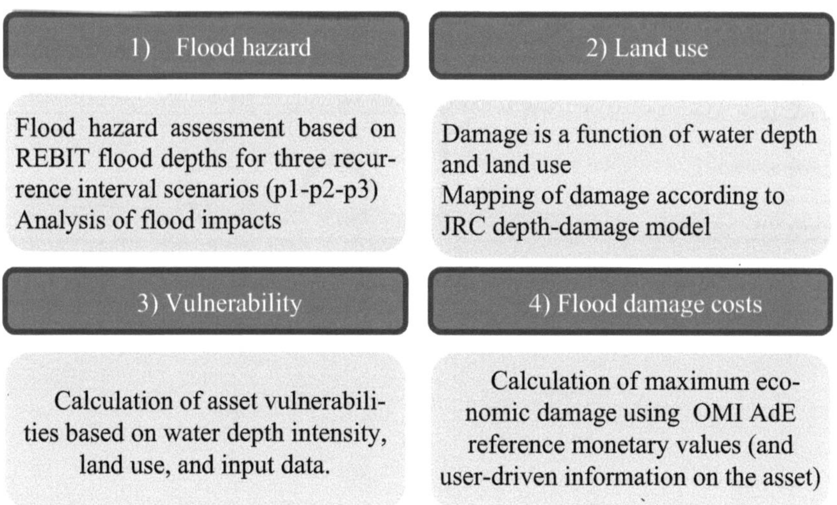

Fig. 5. The GEOSAFE flood hazard, risk and economic damage assessment framework and workflow

3.2 GEOSAFE Reporting and NATCAT Assessment

The NATCAT flood reporting module in the GEOSAFE platform is designed to provide insurers with precise flood risk and damage assessments. It integrates multiple data layers and analyses to evaluate the flood risk, offering insights into water depth levels, asset vulnerability, and potential economic impact (Figs. 6 and 7).

The reporting is characterized by the following major information and indicators:

- Flood Risk Analysis: The platform first calculates water depth based on terrain morphology across three defined hazard scenarios (low, medium, and high associated to P1, P2 and P3 that is generally related to very rare 300–500 years, rare 100–200 years and frequent 30–50 years return time). It considers each area's proximity to the river network and calculates the potential flood impact force;
- Asset Vulnerability and Flood Damage Estimation: The module then evaluates asset vulnerabilities based on water depth intensity, land use, and other relevant building data (e.g., construction year, building type). Damage is estimated using OMI-AdE maps and JRC-developed tables, with a focus on building structures. This allows insurers to access granular flood risk data, enabling them to manage risks effectively and develop informed insurance solutions.

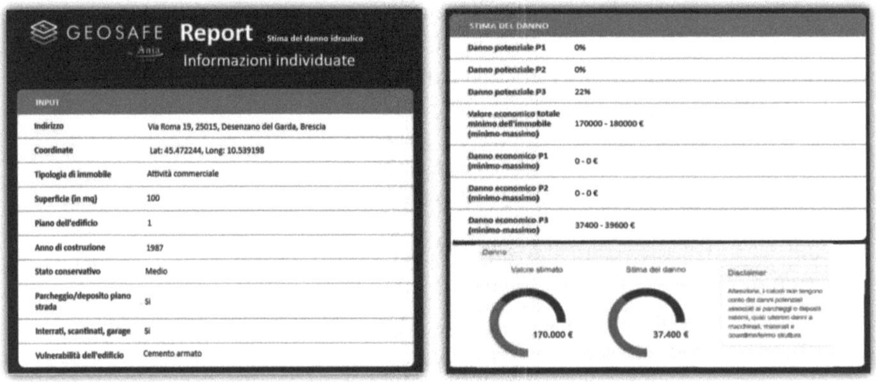

Fig. 6. The GEOSAFE flood hazard, risk and economic damage assessment reporting: a sample realization of the reporting tool

Fig. 7. The GEOSAFE NATCAT reporting framework that applies science-driven hazard, vulnerability and risk assessment for providing accurate information to assess threats and economic damages to Italian assets exposed to natural disasters.

4 Conclusive Remarks

This work underscores the growing importance of precise, high-resolution flood risk assessments within the insurance sector, particularly in response to increasing natural catastrophe (NATCAT) events. Through the integration of the GFPLAIN flood model and advanced geospatial intelligence of the REBIT solution, GEOSAFE enables the insurance industry to navigate and manage flood risks effectively. The platform's capacity to assess vulnerabilities and estimate damages at a granular level provides actionable insights for underwriting and risk mitigation. High-resolution asset data is essential for accurately estimating vulnerability and economic damages, as detailed information on building characteristics and land use directly impacts risk assessments.

As the frequency and intensity of hydro-meteorological hazards rise, tools like GEOSAFE will be crucial for bridging the gap between scientific models and practical applications, supporting both industry needs and societal resilience efforts. Continued advancements and collaborations will enhance GEOSAFE's predictive accuracy and extend its applicability across diverse climate scenarios, strengthening its role in shaping future insurance solutions and disaster preparedness strategies.

Major limitations of this work are linked to the complexity of representing flood physics hydrodynamics at the country scale. While the GFPLAIN model is validated to provide consistent floodplain delineations and maximum levels of simulated flood surfaces, the lack of bridge, culverts, urban features into the modelling determine a known limitation of the presented solution. Uncertainty in hydrologic forcing and climate change driven varying conditions are also not represented in the available scenarios. Nonetheless, these limitations represent, at the same time, the ongoing work by authors and organizations that are working for improvements of the dataset, models and scenarios.

Acknowledgments. This research was the result of a joint effort of researchers and company professionals of co-authors' organizations with specific regard to University of Rome Tor Vergata DICII Department, ANIA SAFE, IDRAN, GRIDDIT and URBY ET ORBIT companies. This paper was funded by the "Multi-risk science for resilient communities under a changing climate (RETURN)", codice progetto PE00000005, CUP B83C22004820002, with specific regard to the project "Climate Risk Policy Nexus: Breaking disciplinary-sector barriers to Transition towards Community-based Multi-sector Multi-Risk Policies promoting a Nexus Transdisciplinary approach balancing cultural, economic jurisdictional and ethics trade-offs", CUP B83C22004820002.

Disclosure of Interests. The authors have no competing interests to declare that are relevant to the content of this article.

References

1. IPCC. Climate Change 2022: Impacts, Adaptation, and Vulnerability. Contribution of Working Group II to the Sixth Assessment Report of the Intergovernmental Panel on Climate Change. Cambridge University Press (2022). https://doi.org/10.1017/9781009325844
2. Field, C.B., Barros, V.R., Stocker, T.F., Qin, D.: Managing the Risks of Extreme Events and Disasters to Advance Climate Change Adaptation: Special Report of the Intergovernmental Panel on Climate Change. Cambridge University Press (2012). https://doi.org/10.1017/CBO9781139177245
3. Cutter, S.L., Boruff, B.J., Shirley, W.L.: Social vulnerability to environmental hazards. Soc. Sci. Q. **84**(2), 242–261 (2003). https://doi.org/10.1111/1540-6237.8402002
4. Swiss Re Institute. Natural Catastrophes in Times of Economic Disruption: The Road to Resilience. Swiss Re (2023). https://www.swissre.com/institute/research/research-in-focus/natcat-economic-disruption.html
5. Kunreuther, H., Michel-Kerjan, E., Pauly, M.V.: Insuring against catastrophes. In: The Foundations of Insurance Economics, pp. 434–460. Springer (2009). https://doi.org/10.1007/978-1-4615-5207-7_13
6. Jongman, B., Ward, P.J., Aerts, J.C.: Global exposure to river and coastal flooding: long term trends and changes. Glob. Environ. Chang. **22**(4), 823–835 (2012). https://doi.org/10.1016/j.gloenvcha.2012.07.004
7. Ministero delle Imprese e del Made in Italy (MIMIT). Presentato alle categorie produttive il decreto sull'obbligo assicurativo per le imprese contro rischi catastrofali (2024). https://www.mimit.gov.it/it/notizie-stampa/mimit-rischi-catastrofali-presentato-alle-categorie-produttive-il-decreto-sullobbligo-assicurativo-per-le-imprese
8. Nardi, F., Annis, A., Di Baldassarre, G., Vivoni, E.R., Grimaldi, S.: GFPLAIN250m, a global high-resolution dataset of Earth's floodplains. Sci. Data **6**(1), 1–6 (2019)
9. Urby et Orbit (2024). https://www.urbyetorbit.it/. Accessed 09 November 2024
10. ANIA Geosafe (2024). https://www.geosafe.ania.it/. Accessed 09 November 2024
11. Nardi, F., Vivoni, E.R., Grimaldi, S.: Investigating a floodplain scaling relation using a hydrogeomorphic delineation method. Water Resour. Res. **42**, W09409 (2006)
12. Annis, A., Nardi, F., Morrison, R.R., Castelli, F.: Investigating hydrogeomorphic floodplain mapping performance with varying DTM resolution and stream order. Hydrol. Sci. J. **64**(5), 525–538 (2019)
13. Annis, A., Nardi, F., Morrison, R.R., Grantham, T.E.: On the influence of river basin morphology and climate on hydrogeomorphic floodplain delineations. Adv. Water Resour. **159**, 104078 (2018)

14. Annis, A., Nardi, F., Castelli, F.: Simultaneous assimilation of water levels from river gauges and satellite flood maps for near-real-time flood mapping. Hydrol. Earth Syst. Sci. **26**(4), 1019–1041 (2022)
15. Di Baldassarre, G., Nardi, F., Annis, A., Odongo, V., Rusca, M., Grimaldi, S.: Brief communication: comparing hydrological and hydrogeomorphic paradigms for global flood hazard mapping. Nat. Hazard. **20**(5), 1415–1419 (2020)
16. Rajib, A., et al.: The changing face of floodplains in the Mississippi River Basin detected by a 60-year land use change dataset. Sci. Data **8**(1), 271 (2021)
17. Ignacio, J.A.F., Cruz, G.T., Nardi, F., Henry, S.: Assessing the effectiveness of a social vulnerability index in predicting heterogeneity in the impacts of natural hazards: case study of the Tropical Storm Washi flood in the Philippines. In: Vienna Yearbook of Population Research, pp. 91–129 (2015)
18. Annis, A., Nardi, F.: GFPLAIN and multi-source data assimilation modeling: conceptualization of a flood forecasting framework supported by hydrogeomorphic floodplain rapid mapping. Hydrology **8**(4), 143 (2021)
19. Lindersson, S., Brandimarte, L., Mård, J., Di Baldassarre, G.: Global riverine flood risk – how do hydrogeomorphic floodplain maps compare to flood hazard maps? Nat. Hazard. **21**(10), 2921–2948 (2021)
20. Rajib, A., et al.: Human alterations of the global floodplains 1992–2019. Sci. Data **10**(1), 499 (2023)
21. Pérez-Murillo, G., McIntyre, N., Cohen, R.C., Prakash, M.: Evaluating the applicability of a terrain-based floodplain delineation tool for a broad-scale assessment of flood exposure of tailings deposits. EGUsphere **2022**, 1–41 (2022)
22. Wohl, E., Knox, R.L.: A first-order approximation of floodplain soil organic carbon stocks in a river network: the South Platte River, Colorado, USA as a case study. Sci. Total. Environ. **852**, 158507 (2022)
23. Knox, R.L., Morrison, R.R., Wohl, E.E.: A river ran through it: floodplains as America's newest relict landform. Sci. Adv. **8**(25), eabo1082 (2022)
24. Kemper, J.T., et al.: Estimating Catchment-Scale Sediment Storage in a Large River Basin, Colorado River. River Research and Applications, USA (2024)
25. Knox, R.L., Morrison, R.R., Wohl, E.E.: Identification of artificial levees in the contiguous United States. Water Resour. Res. **58**(4), e2021WR031308 (2022)
26. Richardson, C.A., Beighley, R.E.: Optimizing height above nearest drainage parameters to enable rapid flood mapping in North Carolina. Front. Water **5**, 1296434 (2024)
27. Scheel, K., Morrison, R.R., Annis, A., Nardi, F.: Understanding the large-scale Influence of levees on floodplain connectivity using a hydrogeomorphic approach. J. Am. Water Resour. Assoc. **55**(2), 413–429 (2019)
28. Peña, F., Nardi, F., Melesse, A., Obeysekera, J.: Assessing geomorphic floodplain models for large scale coarse resolution 2D flood modelling in data scarce regions. Geomorphology **389**, 107841 (2021)
29. Morrison, R.R., Bray, E., Nardi, F., Annis, A., Dong, Q.: Spatial relationships of levees and wetland systems within floodplains of the Wabash Basin, USA. J. Am. Water Resour. Assoc. **54**(4), 934–948 (2018)
30. GRIDDIT Web Page. https://griddit.space/the-rebit-solution/. Accessed 09 November 2024
31. Huizinga, J., De Moel, H., Szewczyk, W.: Global Flood Depth-Damage Functions: Methodology and the Database with Guidelines. EUR 28552 EN, Publications Office of the European Union, Luxembourg (2017). ISBN: 978-92-79-67781-6. https://doi.org/10.2760/16510
32. OMI Cadastral Maps. https://www1.agenziaentrate.gov.it/servizi/geopoi_omi/index.php. Accessed 09 November 2024

Urban Systems: Structures, Cities, and Infrastructure

Snap4City Digital Twin Meeting European CityVerse Action

Pierfrancesco Bellini[1(✉)], Enrico Collini[1], Marco Fanfani[1], Luciano A. Ipsaro Palesi[1], Paolo Nesi[1], Gianni Pantaleo[1], and Paola Zamperlin[2]

[1] DISIT Lab, DINFO University of Florence, Florence, Italy
{pierfrancesco.bellini,enrico.collini,marco.fanfani, lucianoalessandro.ipsaropalesi,paolo.nesi, gianni.pantaleo}@unifi.it

[2] Deptartment of SAGAS, University of Florence, Florence, Italy
paola.zamperlin@unifi.it

Abstract. The CityVerse initiative, part of the European Commission's Digital Decade Policy Program 2030, aims to promote shared investments in digital infrastructure and knowledge to support the development of digital twins across Europe, contributing to the EU's digital transformation goals. This paper examines how the Snap4City Digital Twin solution, created by the DISIT Lab at the University of Florence, aligns with CityVerse requirements.

Snap4City offers tools to build digital 3D models of buildings or cities, enabling simulations, predictions, and strategic urban planning. It is a FIWARE-certified, OASC, and EOSC platform, adhering to MIMs Plus standards. Conformant with DS4SSCC blueprint and LDTs Toolbox, Snap4City provides innovative, interoperable solutions for managing Living Digital Twins, facilitating the simulation of real-world scenarios and integration into smart city ecosystems. Key features of Snap4City include its open-source, interoperable platform, comprehensive IoT integration, support for Sustainable Development Goals (SDGs), and training resources. These aspects make it a valuable contributor to the CityVerse initiative by advancing sustainability, Digital Twin technology, and open-source collaboration.

Overall, Snap4City's versatile platform aligns with the European Commission's objectives for CityVerse, positioning it as a crucial tool in fostering digital transformation and supporting smart, sustainable urban development across Europe.

Keywords: Digital Twin · Snap4City · 3D model · CityVerse

E. Borgogno-Mondino and P. Zamperlin (Eds.): ASITA 2024, CCIS 2463, pp. 161–174, 2025.
https://doi.org/10.1007/978-3-031-91141-5_12

1 Introduction

1.1 European Actions and Initiatives

The DS4SSCC Blueprint

The DS4SSCC Blueprint, part of the European Data Space for Smart Communities (DS4SSCC-DEP) initiative[1], is a comprehensive framework designed to develop a unified, secure, and scalable data space for smart and sustainable cities and communities across Europe. Co-funded by the Digital Europe program, this initiative brings together municipalities, private organizations, and academic institutions to promote the European Green Deal and Sustainable Development Goals. It focuses on advancing innovative data sharing and governance practices to drive sustainable urban development.

It consists of:

i) Multi-Stakeholder Governance Scheme: Establishes core principles, defines roles and responsibilities, and sets governance structures and legal frameworks to ensure secure and reliable data transactions within the data space ecosystem.
ii) Technical Blueprint: Provides a catalog of specifications and a reference architecture model for building the necessary technical infrastructure. It promotes data sharing and trust among stakeholders by recommending standards, technologies, and clear governance mechanisms.
iii) Roadmap and Action Plan: Outlines a strategic approach to developing a pan-European data space for smart communities, focusing on middleware service solutions to enable data sharing and management. This phase also involves refining the blueprint based on insights from local pilot projects.

The DS4SSCC-DEP initiative highlights the importance of data as a vital societal asset, aiming to develop a territorial, place-based data space that spans multiple domains and supports governance across various societal levels. It strives to establish a data space managed by public data holders, integrated with broader data ecosystems and the Smart Middleware Platform.

The initiative will be validated and refined through 10–12 cross-sector data pilots across different EU communities. By leveraging high-value datasets and combining data from various domains, this approach aims to enhance sustainability, reduce infrastructure investments, and promote innovation and ecosystem alignment.

The CityVerse action

The CityVerse action, introduced by the European Commission within the framework of the "Local Digital Twin & CityVerse EDIC" (European Digital Infrastructure Consortium)[2], forms a key component of the Commission's Digital Decade Policy Program

---

[1] *European data space for smart communities* (DS4SSCC-DEP): https://www.ds4sscc.eu/; https://inventory.ds4sscc.eu/; https://eurocities.eu/latest/data-collaboration-to-enable-the-eu-green-deal/; https://eurocities.eu/projects/data-space-for-smart-and-sustainable-cities-and-communities-ds4sscc/; https://finestcentre.eu/project/ds4sscc-dep/.

[2] https://digital-strategy.ec.europa.eu/en/policies/edic; https://living-in.eu/news/ldt-citiverse-edic-fact.

2030. This initiative seeks to promote collaborative investments in knowledge and funding across Europe, with the goal of advancing digital infrastructure and technological capabilities.

In partnership with five member states, the European Commission has launched this action to facilitate the development and scaling of digital twins and associated technologies throughout the continent. By doing so, the initiative aims to contribute significantly to the broader objectives of the EU's digital transformation strategy for 2030, ensuring that European cities and communities can harness the potential of advanced digital solutions to drive innovation, efficiency, and sustainability.

Minimal Interoperability Mechanisms (MIMs)
The Minimal Interoperability Mechanisms (MIMs)[3] (current v6.0) contain technical specifications developed under the Living-in.EU initiative to promote interoperability across European cities and communities.

MIMs has the key goal to enable "good-enough" interoperability between different digital systems and platforms across cities and communities, focusing on providing essential, minimal capabilities that allow data to be shared, used, and re-used efficiently across various systems, ensuring seamless integration without requiring full standardization.

By defining common requirements and guidelines, MIMs aim at facilitating cities to overcome technical barriers, enabling them to develop scalable, interoperable solutions that work with existing infrastructures. This approach prevents vendor lock-in, fosters innovation, and supports the development of smart cities by ensuring that diverse systems can communicate and collaborate effectively. Ultimately, MIMs aim to create a flexible, standardized foundation for data exchange, driving local digital transformation and contributing to broader goals of sustainability, efficiency, and innovation across Europe. The role of MIMs is essential in supporting various aspects of smart cities, including context information management, personal data management, geospatial information, and more.

The MIMs Plus v6.0 technical document introduces a new structure and method to improve the adaptability and implementation of MIMs, integrating lessons from ongoing projects and collaborations with global standards organizations. The framework includes guidance on architecture, compliance, and suggested mechanisms, ensuring cities can build on a reliable, future-proof foundation. Overall, MIMs Plus v6.0 aims to create a standardized yet flexible environment, supporting local digital transformation while aligning with broader European strategies for data-driven innovation and smart, sustainable urban development.

[3] *MIMs Plus Living-in.EU Technical Specifications*: https://living-in.eu/sites/default/files/files/approved-mims-plus_li.eu_v6.0.docx_1.pdf.

2 Snap4City Digital Twin Solution

2.1 Snap4City's Brief Description

Snap4City is a framework developed by the DISIT Lab of the University of Florence, Italy, aimed at facilitating the rapid implementation of decision support systems and smart applications for cities, industries, and developers[4]. Snap4City is an officially certificated FIWARE platform and of EOSC.

The LDTs Toolbox offers a comprehensive suite of methodologies and tools designed for the creation and management of Living Digital Twins in urban environments. Snap4City enhances the capabilities of the LDTs Toolbox with its advanced analytics, simulation, and visualization technologies, fostering the development of dynamic and interactive digital twins. These digital twins enable the simulation of real-world scenarios, support informed decision-making, and facilitate strategic urban planning and management. Moreover, they seamlessly integrate with the broader smart city ecosystem, contributing to a cohesive and intelligent urban infrastructure.

Snap4City's platform adheres to a wide range of interoperability standards and protocols, ensuring seamless compatibility and integration with diverse IoT solutions, including FIWARE. As a Gold Member of FIWARE and an officially recognized FIWARE platform, Snap4City complies with FIWARE protocols, such as NGSI (Next Generation Service Interface), which facilitates robust interaction with various IoT connections, applications, and dashboards [1]. Beyond FIWARE, the platform supports multiple other protocols, including JSON, MQTT, Lightweight M2M, LoraWAN, OPC, SigFOX, and more, enabling versatile data integration and communication[5]. Designed for flexibility, Snap4City allows direct connections to data sources and endpoints, either via brokers or through external services. It can interface with third-party IoT brokers across any protocol or API, ensuring a comprehensive and adaptable approach to IoT data management and integration.

Snap4City's architecture and features are designed to enhance its adaptability and integration capabilities. It supports edge and fog computing, allowing for direct connections with Snap4City microservices, whether deployed on the cloud or installed locally. The platform also provides dedicated APIs for various functions, including authentication and authorization, to ensure secure and efficient integration with existing city infrastructure and data sources. This flexible architecture enables Snap4City to interact seamlessly with a wide range of systems, fostering robust and scalable smart city solutions.

Overall, Snap4City offers a comprehensive solution for smart city development, leveraging its flexibility, open-source framework, and compatibility with FIWARE and other standards to facilitate the creation of living labs and innovative urban solutions. Its digital twin capabilities provide interactive dashboards, data models, processing applications, and AI-driven analytics, all of which are essential for developing intelligent, sustainable city applications. These features empower cities to build sentient urban environments, enhancing operational efficiency and fostering smarter, more adaptive urban management (see Fig. 1).

[4] https://www.snap4solutions.org/.

[5] https://www.snap4city.org/65.

Fig. 1. Snap4City Global Digital Twin of Florence. In this visualization, some valuable buildings are included at high resolution, others are obtained by extrusion with the roof pitches oriented as per LIDAR data. In the background, cylinders represent environmental data, and moving arrows on the ring roads represent traffic flows. Much more information can be displayed, such as origin-destination matrices, dynamic routes based on user choices, underline heatmaps, etc.

2.2 Snap4City and DS4SSCC

Snap4City, with its advanced smart city management capabilities and digital twin technologies, aligns closely with the objectives set forth by the DS4SSCC initiative. Its indirect involvement with DS4SSCC stems from its status as an official FIWARE and OASC platform, enabling Snap4City to support numerous shared objectives. These include:

Interoperable Data Spaces: Snap4City's platform, grounded in open standards, is designed to facilitate the development of interoperable data spaces for smart cities. This capability aligns with DS4SSCC's objective of creating a secure and unified marketplace for data, which encourages the development of innovative products and services[6] [2].
Sustainability and Innovation: the DS4SSCC initiative seeks to assist cities in their transition to climate neutrality through enhanced data sharing across multiple sectors. Snap4City's suite of tools for monitoring and managing energy consumption, mobility, and environmental data can deliver valuable, actionable insights, empowering cities to progress towards their sustainability objectives. This capability aligns with the DS4SSCC's vision of utilizing data-driven innovation to support environmental and climate goals[7].
Governance and Technical Infrastructure: the DS4SSCC blueprint outlines a comprehensive governance scheme and technical infrastructure recommendations. Snap4City's framework, which facilitates the integration and analysis of diverse data types via its IoT applications and analytics platforms, aligns well with these guidelines. Its robust and flexible architecture could serve as a reference model or be directly implemented

6 https://www.snap4city.org/283.
7 https://www.snap4city.org/776.

within DS4SSCC's proposed governance and technical structure, supporting efficient data management and interoperability.
Pilot Projects and Innovation: the DS4SSCC initiative intends to validate and refine its data space through a series of pilot projects across EU communities. Snap4City's extensive experience in deploying smart city solutions and digital twin technologies in multiple cities positions it as a valuable resource for these pilots. Its technical expertise and proven methodologies could offer critical insights and support, helping to ensure the success and scalability of the DS4SSCC pilot projects[8].
Middleware Services for Data Sharing: the DS4SSCC initiative emphasizes the development of middleware service solutions to streamline data sharing and management across various sectors. This focus aligns closely with Snap4City's capabilities in enabling seamless data integration and interoperability across different smart city domains and services. Through its federation of cities initiative, Snap4City facilitates collaborative data ecosystems, enhancing the ability of cities to share and utilize data effectively[9].

Leveraging Snap4City's expertise and technological capabilities can significantly enhance smart city initiatives in their efforts to develop a federated, innovative data space that drives the sustainable and digital transformation of cities and communities across Europe. Collaboration between such initiatives and platforms will play a critical role in accelerating the realization of the EU's Green Deal objectives, as well as the broader vision set forth for Europe's Digital Decade.

2.3 Snap4City and CityVerse

CityVerse aims to create a digital counterpart of buildings and cities, continuously synchronized with their physical counterparts, to enable comprehensive analysis, simulations, and what-if scenarios. This concept aligns perfectly with the capabilities provided by Snap4City Digital Twin[10].

Snap4City offers a comprehensive suite of tools and technologies that serve as a robust foundation for developing smart city solutions compatible with CityVerse. Its platform adheres to MIMs Plus standards and integrates the DS4SSCC blueprint along with the LDTs Toolbox, ensuring seamless interoperability and advanced functionality. This integration fosters the creation of innovative, scalable, and impactful smart city projects, driving forward the vision of connected, intelligent urban environments (Table 1).

Snap4City plays a vital role in advancing the CityVerse initiative by utilizing its extensive suite of tools and services tailored for smart cities and digital twin technologies. Through its robust platform, Snap4City facilitates the creation of dynamic digital counterparts of urban environments, enabling seamless integration, real-time analysis, and advanced simulations. This contribution supports the development of intelligent, interconnected urban ecosystems, aligned with the CityVerse vision. Key contributions of Snap4City to the CityVerse initiative include, but are not limited to:

8 FinEst Centre for Smart Cities: https://finestcentre.eu/; https://www.snap4city.org/4.
9 Further details on this federation model can be found at https://www.snap4city.org/673.
10 https://digitaltwin.snap4city.org/.

Open-source and Interoperable Platform: Snap4City is a fully open-source FIWARE platform, ensuring compatibility and interoperability with other smart city solutions across Europe. This open-source nature supports seamless integration with diverse systems, enabling cities to build cohesive, interconnected urban environments. This aligns perfectly with CityVerse's objective of promoting shared digital infrastructures and services, facilitating collaboration, and fostering the development of unified, scalable smart city ecosystems across the continent[11].
Comprehensive IoT Integration: the platform provides a comprehensive suite of IoT microservices, which simplifies the integration of diverse data sources and IoT devices. This capability is essential for the development of digital twins and plays a pivotal role in creating the interconnected digital ecosystem that CityVerse envisions. By streamlining data integration, Snap4City enables seamless connectivity between systems, fostering a more cohesive and intelligent urban infrastructure[12].
Support for Sustainable Development Goals (SDGs): Snap4City offers solutions that directly support several United Nations Sustainable Development Goals (SDGs), including smart agriculture, health monitoring, energy consumption management, and smart city infrastructure. These contributions align closely with CityVerse's objective of driving sustainable and inclusive digital transformation. By addressing key areas such as efficient resource management, improved healthcare, and sustainable urban development, Snap4City plays a crucial role in promoting a smarter, more sustainable future in line with global sustainability goals (See Footnote 7).
Digital Twin Technology: Snap4City's digital twin solutions provide highly interactive and secure management of multidomain data, making them essential for both smart city initiatives and Industry 4.0 applications. These solutions include advanced features such as 3D city modeling, data analytics, and IoT applications, which enable comprehensive simulations and detailed insights into urban environments. By offering these capabilities, Snap4City can significantly empower the CityVerse initiative, facilitating the development of interconnected, data-driven ecosystems that enhance urban planning, management, and sustainability (See Footnote 10).
Training and Development Support: Snap4City offers an extensive array of documentation, guides, and training materials to support the development of smart city solutions. This educational component helps enhance the skills of individuals and organizations engaged in the CityVerse initiative, fostering innovation and facilitating knowledge sharing across the European digital ecosystem. By empowering users with the necessary expertise, Snap4City promotes the effective implementation of smart city projects, driving forward the goals of interconnected and sustainable urban development[13].

Overall, Snap4City's versatile platform, combined with its strong alignment with the goals of sustainable development, digital twin technology, and open-source interoperability, positions it as a key contributor to the European Commission's CityVerse initiative. Its comprehensive suite of tools and technologies supports the creation of interconnected, sustainable urban environments, making Snap4City an essential partner in advancing the digital transformation of cities across Europe.

[11] https://www.snap4city.org/drupal/node/559.
[12] https://www.snap4city.org/drupal/node/944.
[13] https://www.snap4city.org/944.

Table 1. Compliance of Snap4City with MIMs Requirements.

MIM	Subject	Name	Status	Snap4City
MIM1	Context	OASC MIM1: Context Information Management	Governance	Fully compliant, NGSI V2 and LD
MIM2	Data Models	OASC MIM2: Shared Data Models	Governance	Fully compliant. Devices can be directly deployed using Smart Data Models, custom data models, and Snap4City IoT Device Models Reference ontologies are available. By default, it is provided with Km4City ontology based on several standard vocabularies (SAREF, OTN, SSN, FOAF, etc.). Other ontologies can be added to the Knowledge Base
MIM3	Contracts	OASC MIM3: Ecosystem Transactions Management	Capability	Secure by design, GDPR compliant, passed PENtest, Vulnerability test, etc. And devices and transactions can be tracked by Blockchain
MIM4	Trust	OASC MIM4: Personal Data Management	Capability	Secure by design, GDPR compliant. Personal and public data can be managed
MIM5	Transparency	OASC MIM5: Fair Artificial Intelligence	Capability	Possibility to develop ML/AI/XAI including Explainability modules that are GDPR compliant. Able to enforce verification to be fair, and replicable, etc. according to AI-Act, etc.
MIM6	Security	OASC MIM6: Security management	Work item	Snap4City is secure by design, is GDPR compliant, passed PENtest, Vulnerability test, etc

(*continued*)

Table 1. (*continued*)

MIM	Subject	Name	Status	Snap4City
MIM7	Places	OASC MIM7: Geospatial information management	Capability	Ability to manage 2D and 3D data at local and global scales integrated. It accepts multiple formats and protocols for delivering 2D/3D elements, for example, OCG, WFS, WMS, etc., and entities in NGSI
MIM8	Indicators	OASC MIM8: Ecosystem indicator management	Work item	Several indicators already available: 15 Min City Index, SUMP/PUMS, SUMI, SDG, etc.
MIM9	Analytics	OASC MIM9: Data Analytics Management	Work item	Full support for Data Analytic Management. DA processes include statistics, ML, AI, XAI, operating research, simulations, etc., and can be developed in Python, RStudio, or other languages, exploiting MLOps, NVIDIA boards, or other accelerators, and containers
MIM10	Resources	OASC MIM10: Resource Impact Assessment	Work item	Full support for monitoring resource consumption and performing impact assessment

3 Snap4City Digital Twin Implementations

In literature, three main layers of a Smart City Digital Twin (SCDT) were defined [3]: the first layer integrates diverse data types, creating the City Information Model (CIM); the second layer focuses on core functionalities, communications, and analytics, supported by an IoT/IoE platform to handle large datasets; the third layer manages visualization and distribution through 3D engines and web applications. Key design and development requirements for SCDTs, classified according to their main characteristics in data, interactivity, and interoperability, were outlined in [4]. Accurate, available data is crucial for effective SCDT representation, requiring interoperability in data formats, software, and system compatibility. Free licenses are preferred to enhance accessibility and avoid proprietary lock-in [5, 6].

The design and development of Snap4City have continuously addressed the practical needs of urban planners and decision-makers, providing tools to simulate accurately the potential impact of urban planning changes. This includes modeling 3D structures in real-world contexts and assessing how adjustments to road networks affect traffic, the impact of new buildings on pollution, solar shading effects, microclimatic shifts, and more.

With regard to Local Digital Twins (LDTs), which differ from global twins in the extent of the digitally reproduced area, existing applications range from urban scale (smart city) to industrial facilities (Industry 4.0 applications). It is challenging to determine the exact number of Snap4City installations worldwide, as the platform is open source and can be freely downloaded and installed on private premises. Therefore, assessments can only be made for registered installations, it can be observed that the Snap4City platform is implemented in numerous smart cities and regions across Europe in cities like Antwerp, Santiago de Compostela, Valencia, Pont-du-Gard-Occitanie, Dubrovnik, Mostar, and Western Greece as well as across Italy, including Florence, Pisa, Livorno, Prato, Lonato del Garda, Modena, Merano, and Cuneo. Its largest deployment serves as a multi-tenant platform for advanced IoT/IoE applications, supporting 20 organizations, 40 cities, and thousands of operators and developers.

Existing Smart City Digital Twin (SCDT) solutions are limited, handling only a few data types, lacking interoperability, and omitting analytics for simulations and what-if analyses. The proposed framework addresses these gaps by leveraging the Snap4City platform, offering an interactive, 3D web-based interface to simulate and analyze urban environments, meeting the needs of urban planners and decision-makers. Key components include a high-performance 3D data model engine (FusionLayer) for efficient browser-based access, specialized functionalities like what-if analysis, real-time traffic visualization, heatmaps, BIM management, and interactive road graphs. Additionally, a comprehensive set of requirements for SCDTs – Field Interoperability, Data and Computing for Representation, and Distribution and Interaction – has been outlined to formalize urban designers' core needs. A thorough State-of-the-art review assesses leading SCDT solutions, evaluating their alignment with these identified requirements.

Snap4City's architecture, as shown in Fig. 2, emphasizes Field Interoperability and data processing to support the collection and exchange of data from diverse sources, pushing data toward brokers, gateways, and services. It is compatible with numerous protocols and formats[14], facilitating the federation of smart cities.

Snap4City ingests real-time and event-driven data streams using IoT brokers, which are indexed and shadow-stored in an OpenSearch cluster, making them accessible to various consumer processes. Internal brokers utilize Orion Broker NGSI, supporting smart data models, with data retrievable in push or event-driven modes. Node-RED flows facilitate interoperability with external services like GIS, ITS, TV cam services, CKAN, BIM servers, and social media, with dedicated libraries and microservices for data transformation. Data is stored across multiple systems: a Virtuoso RDF store for Km4City ontology, an OpenSearch cluster for real-time and time-series data, and the Snap4City GeoServer for georeferenced data, supporting analysis of pollutants, temperature, energy, traffic, and population density.

The Km4City ontology [7] represents road networks with entities for Roads, RoadElements, Lanes, and Restrictions, based on OpenStreetMap (OSM) data. Sensors,

[14] For the complete list: https://www.snap4city.org/65.

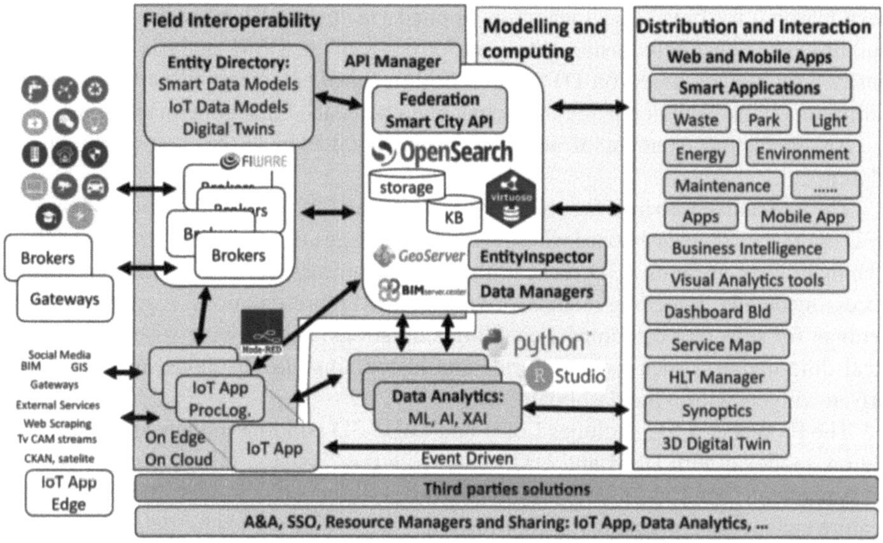

Fig. 2. Overview of the Snap4City architecture.

including traffic, weather, and air quality, as well as devices for monitoring shared vehicles, bike racks, parking, and people counting [8], are integrated using FIWARE Smart Data Models and Snap4City IoT Device Models. Points of Interest (POIs) are categorized as Service entities across 20+ categories, with over 500 subcategories, covering areas such as accommodation, culture, emergency services, finance, and commerce.

Building 3D models are stored using a tiled structure with a hierarchical Z/X/Y folder format, similar to GIS applications like OSM, where Z is a fixed zoom level, and X and Y are tile coordinates. This approach enables fast loading in a browser's interactive interface. The city map is divided into distinct tiles, with each building uniquely linked to a tile based on its ground-level centroid. Although grouped in tiles, each building is individually represented to allow for specific selection and substitution functionalities [9].

Snap4City's IoT platform supports fast, reliable data acquisition and retrieval through dedicated queries and APIs, enabling data visualization on the digital twin interface and fulfilling interoperability requirements. Key challenges in developing an SCDT include meeting Data and Computing for Representation (operative processes to obtain heatmaps and generative processes for the construction of the 3D models), as well as Distribution and Interaction requirements (dynamic 3D representations).

The 3D Map construction process in Snap4City involves gathering multiple data inputs, processed and stored on the platform. Inputs include street-level and aerial RGB images for roof and façade textures, building shapes from OSM or land registry data for geographic localization, building heights and DSM (digital surface model) data for 3D structure modeling, and DTM (digital terrain model) data to set accurate terrain elevation. High-Value Buildings (HVBs) are modeled through manual design or computer vision techniques like Structure from Motion. Roof and façade textures are extracted using deep learning for precise segmentation, applied via custom Blender plugins. Ordinary buildings are constructed using extrusion for flat-roofs or DSM analysis for 3D-roofs, positioning models based on DTM data. Additional 3D elements like trees and street furniture are incorporated using municipal and open data, enhancing map detail[15].

An interesting example of an urban-scale digital twin is the case of the city of Florence[16].

The interactive web interface of the Florence Smart City Digital Twin on Snap4City is a 3D multi-data map dashboard where users can manage analytic or real-time data layers. The main view presents a 3D scene with controls for interacting with building models, accessing details, switching models, or viewing BIM representations. A gear icon opens settings for selecting orthomaps, enabling animations, and viewing road information. Real-time updates, such as time series and histograms, are displayed through event-driven widgets within the dashboard.

The Florence SCDT includes LoD1 and LoD3 3D building models and terrain elevation, modeled with DSM and DTM data from the "Sistema Informativo Territoriale ed Ambientale" of Tuscany[17], based on high-resolution LIDAR data. Building models feature enhanced roof textures from orthomaps, with RGB photos for detail. The SCDT displays POIs, IoT sensors, bus stops, and parking as PINs on the map, semantically categorized with specific icons via Snap4City's knowledge base. In addition to historical data, the interface shows city traffic data in 3D columns, heatmaps of pollutants and climate variables, and animated traffic densities for visual clarity. The road graph provides street information directly from the knowledge base. The system enables users to perform routing simulations and analyses, with controls for running what-if scenarios integrated directly into the web interface.

4 Conclusion

Current scientific and political debates [10, 11] focus on several key issues regarding digital twins. First, questions arise about the expected accuracy of digital twin representations, which depends on data quality, spatial coverage, and update frequency. Further considerations include computational and energy requirements, as well as the potential of digital twins to enhance complex urban management [12]. While 3D virtual models may integrate real-time processes like traffic or energy use, their relevance is often limited to short timeframes and specific city sections [6].

This work aimed to highlight how the proposed solution, Snap4City, can respond to the technical and functional requirements and the purposes that the EU action CityVerse aims to achieve.

In Snap4City, Local Digital Twins (LDTs) and the CityVerse contribute to sustainable urban planning and Green Deal goals by enabling advanced data integration, real-time monitoring, and interactive simulations. LDTs support environmental monitoring, resource management, and energy efficiency, allowing cities to track air and water quality, optimize waste and energy use, and reduce emissions. The platform's simulation

[15] Code is available on the DISIT GitHub.

[16] For updates and demos, see: https://digitaltwin.snap4city.org/.

[17] https://www.regione.toscana.it/-/il-portale-del-governo-del-territorio.

tools aid in traffic optimization, disaster response, and heatwave management, helping urban planners make informed decisions. Citizen engagement is facilitated through participatory planning platforms and interactive VR experiences, fostering community involvement and awareness of sustainability practices. Additionally, Snap4City CityVerse provides 3D urban models for immersive visualization, enabling collaboration among stakeholders and virtual public spaces that promote sustainable lifestyle choices. Through data-driven decision-making, resource optimization, and community involvement, Snap4City's LDTs and CityVerse help create greener, more resilient, and inclusive urban environments.

Snap4City is actively implementing data spaces, Local Digital Twins (LDTs), and Cityverse solutions across various use cases to improve urban living, sustainability, and city management[18]. As an integrated urban data hub, Snap4City consolidates data from multiple sources (e.g., transport, environment, social media), supporting policy-making and smart mobility. LDTs enable predictive maintenance for infrastructure, energy optimization in buildings, and urban planning simulations, while the CityVerse offers virtual tours, collaborative urban design, and disaster response simulations to engage citizens and stakeholders.

Snap4City has also deployed smart city control rooms for real-time city monitoring, optimized transportation, air quality management, energy efficiency, and waste collection, enhancing service reliability and sustainability. These use cases demonstrate how Snap4City's technologies are transforming cities into smart, connected, and resilient environments aligned with Green Deal goals.

CityVerse also promotes citizen engagement through interactive platforms, encouraging transparency and community involvement in decision-making. It strengthens public safety with surveillance integration, emergency simulations, and real-time analytics, enhancing emergency response and disaster management. Additionally, it reinforces health monitoring and virtual healthcare supporting proactive health management, particularly for vulnerable populations, as well as enriching community activities, fostering social cohesion and preserving local heritage [13].

In summary, Snap4City in a CityVerse perspective, can create a collaborative environment for sustainable urban growth, efficient public services, and enriched quality of life, making it a transformative tool for modern cities.

References

1. Bauer, M., Cirillo, F., Fürst, J., Solmaz, G., Kovacs, E.: Urban digital twins – a FIWARE-based model. Automatisierungstechnik **69**(12), 1106–1115 (2021)
2. Bellini, P., Bilotta, S., Collini, E., Fanfani, M., Nesi, P.: Data sources and models for integrated mobility and transport solutions. Sensors **24**(2), 441 (2024). https://doi.org/10.3390/s24020441
3. Ketzler, B., Naserentin, V., Latino, F., Zangelidis, C., Thuvander, L., Logg, A.: Digital twins for cities: a state of the art review. Built Environ. **46**(4), 547–573 (2020)

[18] See Snap4Altair, https://www.snap4city.org/815, Snap4ISPRA, https://www.snap4city.org/970, Snap4Cuneo, https://www.snap4city.org/975, Snap4Merano, https://www.snap4city.org/968, and more.

4. Adreani, L., Bellini, P., Fanfani, M., Nesi, P., Pantaleo, G.: Design and develop of a smart city digital twin with 3D representation and user interface for what-if analysis. In: Gervasi, O., et al. Computational Science and Its Applications – ICCSA 2023 Workshops. ICCSA (2023). Lecture Notes in Computer Science, vol. 14111. Springer, Cham. https://doi.org/10.1007/978-3-031-37126-4_34
5. Lei, B., Janssen, P., Stoter, J., Biljecki, F.: Challenges of urban digital twins: a systematic review and a Delphi expert survey. Autom. Construct. **147**, 104716 (2023)
6. Lei, B., Stouffs, R., Biljecki, F.: Assessing and benchmarking 3D city models. Int. J. Geogr. Inf. Sci. **37**, 788–809 (2023)
7. Badii, C., Bellini, P., Cenni, D., Difino, A., Nesi, P., Paolucci, M.: Analysis and assessment of a knowledge based smart city architecture providing service APIs. Future Gener. Comput. Syst. **75**, 14–29 (2017)
8. Collini, E., Palesi, L.A.I., Nesi, P., Pantaleo, G., Zhao, W.: Flexible thermal camera solution for Smart city people detection and counting. Multimed. Tools Appl. **83**, 20457–20485 (2024). https://doi.org/10.1007/s11042-023-16374-x
9. Adreani, L., Bellini, P., Fanfani, M., Nesi, P., Pantaleo, G.: Smart city digital twin framework for real-time multi-data integration and wide public distribution. IEEE Access **12**, 76277–76303 (2024). https://doi.org/10.1109/ACCESS.2024.3406795
10. Batty, M.: The Computable City, Histories, Technologies, Stories, Predictions. MIT Press (2024)
11. Batty, M.: Digital twins in city planning. Nat. Comput. Sci. **4**, 192–199 (2024). https://doi.org/10.1038/s43588-024-00606-7
12. Grieves, M., Vickers, J.: Digital Twin: mitigating unpredictable, undesirable emergent behavior in complex systems. In: Kahlen, J., Flumerfelt, S., Alves, A. (eds.) Transdisciplinary Perspectives on Complex Systems. Springer, Cham (2017). https://doi.org/10.1007/978-3-319-38756-7_4
13. Garau, C., Nesi, P., Zamperlin, P.: Beyond the limits of the city: strategies to regenerate fragile territories. In: Morar, C., Berman, L., Erdal, S., Niemets, L. (eds.) Achieving Sustainability in Ukraine through Military Brownfields Redevelopment. NATOARW 2023. NATO Science for Peace and Security Series C: Environmental Security. Springer, Dordrecht (2024). https://doi.org/10.1007/978-94-024-2278-8_19

Groupware Planning Support Tools. The SIMS Approach

Mario Tartaglia[1], Andrea Fiduccia[2(✉)], Ilaria Lopresti[1], and Lorenzo Vannacci[1]

[1] FS Research Centre, Ferrovie dello Stato Italiane Spa, Stazione Santa Maria Novella Binario 2, 50123 Florence, Italy

[2] FS Research Centre, Decision Support Models, Ferrovie dello Stato Italiane Spa, Piazza della Croce Rossa 1, 00161 Rome, Italy

a.fiduccia@fsitaliane.it

Abstract. Even today, many econometric and transport mathematical models are of the "desktop" type. Using such models in a corporate context generates the risk of presenting inconsistent results across various divisions of the company. Two typical causes of such inconsistencies are the use of different versions of the input datasets or different updates of the processing algorithms due to update deployment policies.

The remedy to these problems is the creation of "centralized" models that can be used via intranet/internet using information systems that guarantee the availability of a unique and easy to update database of input data, the consistency of the algorithms, the segregation of the outputs but also the possibility of sharing the same outputs with other analysts. For each analysis performed, the system will guarantee the relationship between input data, version of the algorithms and output also through metadata.

The Ferrovie dello Stato Italiane Group has created through FS Research Center of FS Holding two planning support models:

- an Economic Impact Assessment model based on a more comprehensive Input-Output approach [1]
- a multimodal model for the simulation of medium and long distance mobility [2].

"*The Italian Ferrovie dello Stato Group has adopted and continues its roadmap for the implementation of a Strategic Information Monitoring System (SIMS) aimed at supporting the strategic decision-making processes of the Holding Company FSI and the other FS Group companies and at "the collection, storing and processing of official Group data according to the "Process of Supply and Management of Official Data of the FS Italiane Group*" [3].

The Data Warehouse of SIMS and its application and presentation layers based on the Geo-Business Intelligence paradigm [4] guarantees the segregation of data and representations (WebGIS and Geo-BI apps) by profiling of users.

SIMS is, therefore, the perfect container for enterprise-level distribution of the two aforementioned models in a groupware and collaborative environment. This paper presents the first results of this implementation.

E. Borgogno-Mondino and P. Zamperlin (Eds.): ASITA 2024, CCIS 2463, pp. 175–188, 2025.
https://doi.org/10.1007/978-3-031-91141-5_13

Keywords: Transportation Planning · Economic Impact Analysis · Geo-Business Intelligence

1 Introduction

The FS Italiane Group has created the SIMS information system with the aim of establishing a platform for the analysis of alphanumeric and geospatial data on mobility and the social, economic, territorial, technological and environmental systems that interact with it.

SIMS also constitutes the repository of official and certified corporate data of the FS Group integrated with data from systems external to the Group, fed by official and accredited sources. The method of feeding such data into the SIMS is based, where possible, on automatic data-ingesting flows from the corporate or Group systems on which such data originate and are managed.

SIMS is managed by the FS Research Centre (FSR) organizational structure of the holding company Ferrovie dello Stato Italiane SpA.

Users, appropriately authorized and profiled, access the analysis functions of the SIMS platform by the SharePoint SIMS portal, which therefore represents the main tool for interacting with the system, made available to both end users and those responsible for creating content. All data ingesting procedures are managed through the use of specific ETL workflows (automatic and semi-automatic) while the contents displayed in the portal are created with the aid of COTS software (GIS, WebGIS, BI and GeoBI).

The users of the SIMS system are profiled. They have access in consultation (and processing, where permitted) only to data for which they are authorized according to the policies of the data owners/data providers.

In SIMS the data warehouse manages the temporal extension of the data through the mechanisms of historicization and versioning.

The term "historicization" of data means the presence within the database of the temporal component of the data using the "tuple timestamping" approach [5].

The SIMS manages the corrections over time of a specific dataset using the versioning mechanism: the corrected dataset replaces the one of the previous supply. The various versions are not deleted, but "labeled" to be retrieved in case of need.

A detailed description of SIMS and of its technological architecture can be found in [3].

2 The Economic Impact Assessment Model

The Economic Impact Assessment (E.I.A.) is a methodology aimed at measuring the potential of an investment, a new business, a company or an organization to contribute directly and indirectly to the economic development of a given socioeconomic and territorial system.

In 2021, the FS Italiane Group adopted a first version of this methodology coordinated by FS Holding and shared by the other companies of the Group, with the aim of measuring and analyzing the economic and employment impacts of recurring activities (for the

Group and for individual companies) and investments (in railway or road infrastructure, or even in other areas of expertise of the Group).

The Economic Impact Analysis model developed is based on a more comprehensive Input-Output approach, i.e. including the use of the Supply and Use Tables (SUTs). Such an approach enables the appraisal process to take into account the entire productive structure of the economy. Input-Output models are usually demand driven models based on various hypothesis, like fixed prices, homogeneous production and supply unconstrained.

The SUT-based model is commodity driven. It is mainly composed by two ex-ante causal relations. The first one, is a technical relationship based on the Leontief Production Function determining the intermediate demand for products by sectors by fixed coefficients. The second, is a trade pattern determining the spatial area where intermediate and final demand will be satisfied through sectoral output. The final demand expressed as "products" is redirected to sectors by market shares (e.g.: Agriculture produces 3% of all Electric Power). Finally, for a change in final demand, the commodity driven model solution is based on the Leontevian inverse that is the matrix of multipliers.[1]

Going into more detail, a consistent time series of national SUTs, at current basic prices were estimated. Consistency refers to the European ESA2010 accounting methodology and Nace Rev.2 Statistical classification of economic activities. Since 1995 the Italian National Institute of Statistics (ISTAT) has released yearly SUTs but some methodological and classificatory changes have occurred. In 2013, "*the new system of national account ESA2010 was introduced (replacing the previous ESA95) and a new classification: in 2007, the Nace Rev.2, replaced the previous Nace Rev 1.1. Moreover, the ESA2010 was updated in 2019. The previous considerations show the need to make the national SUTs, released under various accounting systems and classifications, consistent with the last ESA2010 and Nace Rev.2 to perform consistent impact assessment. These reconstructed time series include rebalancing the SUTs, released under previous systems and classification, using the available information from national accounts and administrative sources*" [1]. Once rebalanced and reconstructed, the SUTs were e used in the impact model.

The first release of the FS Italiane Group' EIA Model was applied to the analysis of investments in the Italian High-Speed Railway (HSR) system. The study was performed by a team of researchers of Ferrovie dello Stato Italiane SpA, Rete Ferroviaria Italiana and IRPET coordinated by FS Research Centre [1].

The aim of such an application was to assess the impact of investments in High Speed Rail on the Italian economy sector by sector using a symmetric input-output model.

For this assessment, the research team needed a map that links goods and services included in investments to the sectors that supply them. For this purpose, the supply tables provided by Istat from 1995 to 2018 [6,7] were used. The supply tables provide information on the goods and services produced by a given economy and the sectors that produce them. HSR investments were related to four types of goods and services: the construction of structures (mainly i. construction works and ii. Processed metal products); the supply of iii. Electrical equipment; the supply of design services (iv.

[1] The EIA model follows a different approach for the simulation of the impact of FS Holding Profit and Loss Account, namely the Hypothetical Extraction Method [8].

Engineering services). These goods and services were mapped into the product categories (CPA) related to NACE rev. 1 and rev. 2 classifications, then linked to the product/sector groups referred to the Global Inter-Country Input-Output Tables (ICIO) produced by the OECD, the Organization for Economic Co-operation and Development [9]. The same mapping between sectors from NACE rev. 1 and rev. 2 and ICIO industries was also carried out for sectors in the Istat supply and usage tables 1995–2018.

A market share matrix was then constructed from the supply tables to identify which sectors of the Italian economy were producing these goods and services in the period under consideration. The supply tables were also used to estimate trade and transport margins, and net taxes related to the supply of goods and services related to the construction of high-speed railway structures. Finally, the research team used the Use matrices to estimate the propensity to import each of the goods and services under consideration in the period 1995–2018.

Based on this information, the value chain was identified to estimate the investment shocks that have impacted the Italian economy.

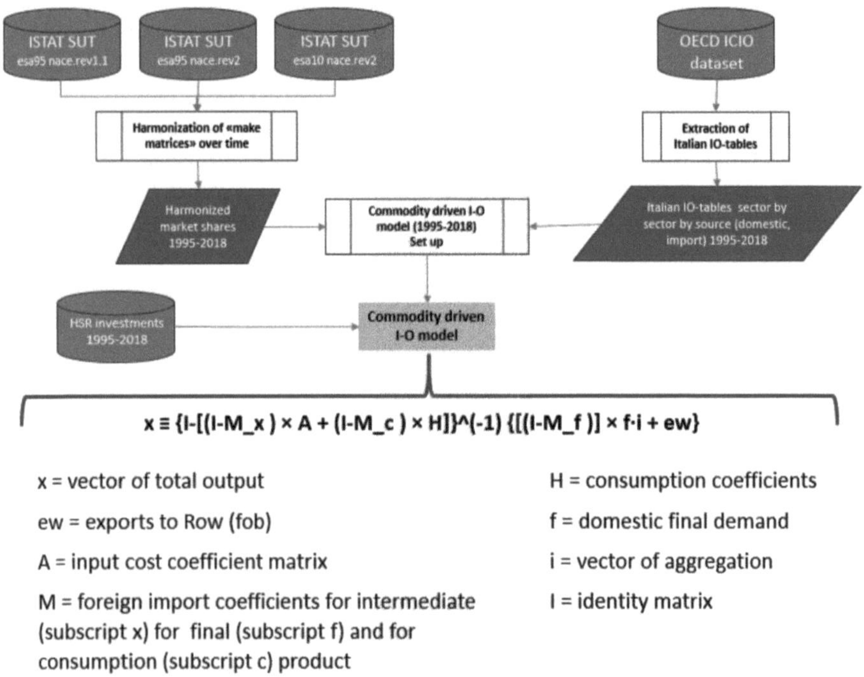

Fig. 1. EIA Model with partial endogenization of household consumption. Methodology and data applied to the analysis of investments in the Italian HSR system.

Given the investment in the four types of goods and services described above for each year, imported goods and services were excluded. Once the share of these items produced by the Italian economy were estimated, the research team estimated net taxes and trade and transport margins (which was attributed to the trade and transport sectors).

The flow of goods and services net of imports, taxes and trade and transport margins was finally mapped into sectoral shocks using market share matrices.

After the sectoral shocks were reconstructed, the sector-by-sector symmetric input-output model was run to estimate the impact of HSR investment in terms of output, value added and employment. A schematic representation of the methodological framework used is shown in Fig. 1.

For a detailed description of the FS Italiane Group' EIA Model applied to the analysis of investments in the Italian HSR system see [1].

The first release of the EIA model - developed by IRPET for FS Research Centre in 2021 – and the following release of the improved EIA model were in the form of scripts in the statistical analysis software R fed by Excel sheets containing the input data and performing some calculations. The distribution of the EIA "desktop" model to users highlighted a series of problems, the most relevant of which were:

- the difficulty in distributing updates of both the application and the input "foundation" datasets;
- the possibility of alteration by users of parameters contained in the Excel files with consequent loss of consistency of results of the same simulation;
- dislike by ICT for desktop solutions that imply potential cybersecurity risks;
- the impossibility or at least the difficulty of sharing the simulations in the user population.

To solve these problems, FS Research Centre decided to implement the model as a new feature offered by SIMS.

The SIMS Portal offers the EIA Model through its web interface while the calculations are performed by an application server in the backend. The input "foundation" datasets are stored in the SIMS data warehouse and systematically updated using ETL procedures with versioning and historicization logic. User profiling and data segregation allow users to access their draft or executed simulations and to run new ones.

Each simulation is described by a metadata that contains the following information:

- Simulation Title, indicating the name of the simulation created.
- Type, referring to the type of simulation, which can be one of the following:

  – Profit and Loss Account;
  – Investment of the Profit and Loss Account;
  – Infrastructure Investment;
  – Final Demand (other than Investment).

- Base Year, represents the reference year chosen by the user when creating the simulation and from which he will start for inserting the amounts relating to the selected number of years. The current range of possible values based on what is established by IRPET is (2018->2030).
- Created By, which indicates the user who created the simulation.
- Modified By, which indicates the user who made the last change to the simulation.
- Last Modified, indicating the date on which the last change to the simulation was made.

- Status, relating to the processing step in which the simulation is located, which may be one of the following:
  - Executed, if the simulation following processing has been sent to the calculation engine and therefore ready to display the results;
  - Draft, if the simulation has only been saved by the user but not sent to the calculation engine;
  - Error, if the simulation has been sent to the calculation engine but the operation was not successful.
- Validated, which affirms or denies the validation status.

The workflow requires the users to choose the type of simulation, fill in the metadata, configure specific parameters through the interface, and then save the draft or execute. To date, the output is only tabular.

The user can manage his/her simulation performed according to the following Actions:

- Validate, if you decide to publish the simulation, i.e. to make it visible to all SIMS users enabled for the EIA model.
- Duplicate, if the user decides to duplicate the simulation by taking the input data and other details of the selected simulation.
- Export, if you decide to export the simulation results in xls format outside of SIMS. This action will allow you to receive the export in xls format of both the input and output data of the simulation, contextual to the status of the simulation itself. That is, if a simulation is in Draft status, the export will only contain the input data of the simulation, whereas if the simulation has been performed (Performed, Validated) both the inputs and the outputs can be exported.
- Edit, if you decide to make changes to the input data.
- Delete, to completely delete the simulation, except for validated simulations.

SIMS, therefore, allows each user to also benefit from simulations carried out by other users who explicitly consent to sharing by defining the simulation as "validated".

When accessing the EIA Model in SIMS through its profiled interface, users find both their simulations – in the state in which they saved them – and the simulations "validated" by other users.

3 The Multimodal Model for the Simulation of Medium and Long Distance Mobility

The "FS Research Centre" of the Italian State Railways [10], and ISFORT have implemented a four-stage partial rate multimodal passenger model [11] for the estimation of medium and long-distance (MLP) trips generated by Italian residents, integrated with calculation modules for the updating of exogenous variables of forecast scenarios deriving from ongoing trends of change in the territorial demographic and occupational structure (Fig. 2). The MLP demand model, calibrated with data from the year 2019, assumed as the last pre-pandemic stable equilibrium state, implemented in 2021, was born downstream of the preparatory development of a generation model for the estimation of local daily passenger demand based on the specification of 20 regional passenger mobility models.

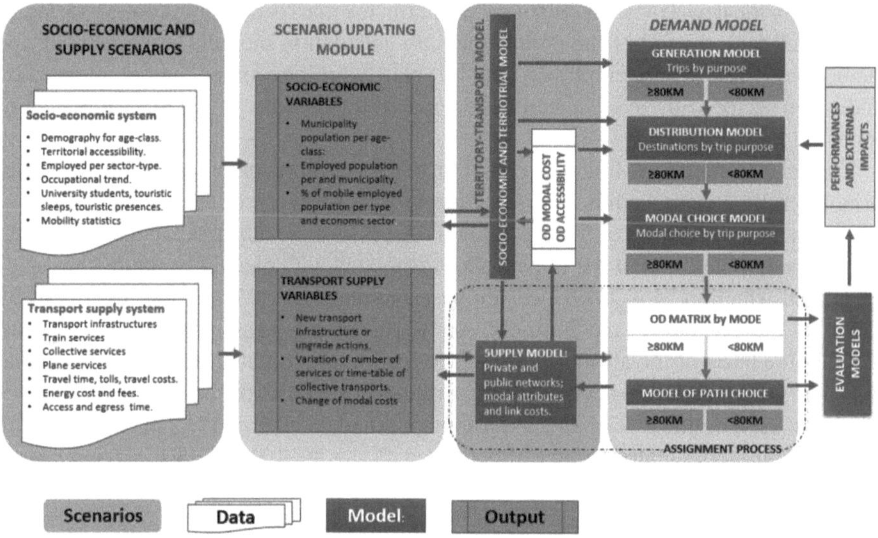

Fig. 2. Medium and Long-distance four-stage partial rate multimodal Passenger (MLP) model.

For the specification, calibration and validation of the multimodal offer and demand sub-models, multiple information sources have been integrated: the microdata of the Observatory on mobility styles and behaviors Audimob, with which ISFORT has been providing the country with a snapshot of the mobility of Italians since 2010 [12, 13] the data on transport demand and offer of the FS Group (Trenitalia, RFI, ANAS); the offer of railway services of NTV and Trenord, and the extra-urban bus services of Flixbus; the official open statistics released by ISTAT, MIUR, Eurostat, Banca d'Italia, ACI; and the mobility statistics extracted from a national sample of mobile telephony Big data and Float Car Data (FCD). The data used offer a homogeneous standard for the national territorial representation, furthermore a periodic release plan of the data selected for calibration allows to program, with respect to past experiences, a continuous maintenance of the models, an essential condition for the strongly applicative needs to which the developed models must respond.

The preliminary phase of model construction consisted of analysis and organization of a rich national georeferenced database, to support the development of the different components of the model, in the identification of the radius of 80 km as the prevalent area of local Italian mobility, overcoming the implicit administrative definition adopted by the national model SIMPT2 [14], and in the subdivision into 911 homogeneous internal zones of the national territory. The model calibrated for the 2019 presents a functional structure with a "four-stages partial rates" with a disaggregated modeling of demand by age group and professional condition of the user which favors a more rigorous control of the coherence of the outputs simulated by the model. Since it is not possible to assume the hypothesis of stationarity of the 2019 demand, due to the pandemic shock, in consideration of the hypotheses of evolution of the epidemiological scenario deriving from the analysis of the risk factors, a Tx date is estimated for the start of a new equilibrium phase "New Normal", and in relation to the macroeconomic impacts expected for the new Transport-Territory Scenario, the macroeconomic context variables are updated with the aid of the complementary calculation modules implemented: the population by age group, employed people, smart-working workers and employees by production sector with an advancement compared to the state of the art of this type of model [11].

The MLP Generation Model, as a function of the exogenous socioeconomic territorial variables, estimates the number of trips disaggregated by type of user generated by the individual areas by reason of the trip, and on the basis of the attributes of the generating and attracting poles, and of the impedances associated with each OD relationship.

The Distribution Model produces the demand matrices of MLP passenger trips by reason of the trip (work and business, study, private business, tourism and leisure). Then, on the basis of the attributes of the service levels estimated with the Multimodal Transport Offer Model by reason, having evaluated the costs of the modal alternatives referred to the individual OD pairs, as an application of the national modal choice model, the passenger modal matrices are estimated.

Finally, the Assignment Procedures, whose outputs feed the production of system impact indicators, simulate the choices of the routes on the daily offer of railway services, distinguishing the users of High Speed (AV) services from those of Intercity and Regional (IC&R), and after the transformation into vehicles the choices of users on the road network. Integrating local passenger vehicle equivalents and freight demand into the private MLP matrix allows for the impact of congestion on users' travel choices to be taken into account.

The database of the territorial socioeconomic system, of the demand for passenger mobility and of the multimodal system of national transport offer, organized on municipal administrative territorial unit, ensures a wide flexibility for the remodulation of the zoning of the demand model in relation to the need for the territorial analysis objectives. When possible, the same time reference was ensured for the acquired data sets (month of October and weekday Wednesday 2019); furthermore, all historical data, for example those of Commuting 2011 [15] and employees by sector ATECO 2017 [16], were traced back to the administrative classification in force on 31 December 2019. The coherence, significance and any limitations of the data adopted to interpret the modeled phenomenon were also assessed. For example the data driven approach of correcting the road OD matrices estimated with the flows of the ANAS monitoring sections, was not implemented as they do not allow to distinguish the MLP traffic component from the local one. The availability of periodic releases of all data used for the calibration and specification of the model represents a further strength for the maintenance and future updating of the model.

The historical series of the "Audimob" survey was found to be fundamental for the model, which with 16,000 interviews represents the only source of annual investigation of the passenger mobility behaviors of Italians with regional significance [13, 17].

From the national sample of elementary data Float Car Data of VEM Solutions (FCD) from the Mobile Data Network by Vodafone Analytics, referring to the entire month of October 2019, the inter-zonal car OD matrices and the overall passenger OD were extracted respectively.

The exogenous territorial variables provide a snapshot of the settlement structure of Italy. The main sources used are: ISTAT, MIUR [18, 19] and the Cohesion Agency for municipal accessibility classes [20]. The most numerous statistics are still from ISTAT: Commuting [15, 21 , 22], Multipurpose on Commuting [23], Presence of accommodation business [24], Travel and Holidays [25], integrated by those of the Bank of Italy survey on International Tourist Demand [26], and on airport traffic from Eurostat [27] and ENAC [28]. The FS Group provided: the daily demand for station-to-station flows of passengers transported by the Trenitalia company in October 2019, broken down by type of service and train, allowing for segmentation of the demand by time slot; and the TGM average daily traffic of the month of October, monitored by the subsidiary company ANAS [29] (2,472 control points of the national road network, distinguished by private and commercial vehicles and direction of travel). These mobility data were not used to calibrate or correct the estimates of the models, but for a validation of the model to integrate the tests on the calibration coefficients.

The 20 regional modal matrices of the local demand estimated in a previous research by FS Research Centre and ISFORT complete the picture of passenger demand [30].

The **geographical zoning** of the national territory has identified 911 homogeneous traffic zones of which 23 coincide with sub-areas of the metropolitan municipalities of Rome, Milan, Turin, Naples, Genoa and Venice; 148 with single municipalities and 740 with the aggregation of contiguous municipalities. For the areas with very low population density the zones identify the reference Local Labour System [21]. The hierarchical structure of the zones is expressed by an indicator that varies from 0 to 10 obtained as a synthesis of the values of the socio-economic and transport attributes of the municipalities that make up the zone.

The **multimodal offer model** has been implemented to calculate the performance of transport infrastructures and services such as time and cost. The road offer model includes two different geographical scales. The local one [31] - extremely detailed - and the national one based on the road supply model of the entire main extra-urban national network developed by the ANAS company, controlled by the FS Group, complete with the attributes useful for characterizing the flow functions [32]. The graph of the national railway network of the FS Group, complete with functional characteristics [33], has been integrated with the arcs of the regional railway networks extracted from a national open graph [34]. For air services, the distances as the crow flies for all the airport OD pairs referred to the 29 airports operating in the month of October 2019 were calculated [27], the average tariffs from the analysis of a sample of air lines and routes, the overall access times in the airport nodes to the air services. The database of the railway service offer has been structured in General Transit Feed Specification (GTFS) format, and includes the weekday high-speed (HSR), Intercity and regional (IC&R) railway services extracted from the winter timetable in force in October 2019 of Trenitalia, NTV and Trenord. The offer of bus services has been obtained from the open GTFS data of FlixBus [35].

For the defined territorial model, the offer model allows to estimate the cost matrix (911×911) for the modes: car, plane, bus and railway (HSR, IC&R). The generalized inter-zonal costs have been calculated [36] by homogenizing the relative tariff costs in consideration of an average hourly value of time (VOT) for the reason of the trip from literature [37].

The forecasting phase of exogenous scenarios for the updating of exogenous variables is a prelude to the application of the demand model in future scenarios. The calculation module of exogenous variables, integrated and linked with the national generation model, is composed of three submodules:

- Updating module of exogenous demographic variables:
- Updating module of variables of active workers (employed, students) and employees.
- Updating module of exogenous variables of smart workers.

The parameters of the MLP **generation model** were estimated with the microdata of the Audimob survey cumulated over three years (2017–2019).

The model disaggregated by homogeneous groups of user required the specification of per capita indices for four travel reasons (work/business; study; personal business; leisure; and vacation and other together).

The formulation of the local mobility generation model is similar to that of the MLP generation model, differing in the class of reasons that generate daily local trips (work, study, family management, leisure, other and return home), and in the introduction of the active mobile population among the rates for homogeneous socio-demographic profile.

The functional formulation adopted for the medium and long-distance national **distribution model** is of the gravitational type based on Newton's theory, and calibrated with the aid of OD extracted from telephone data. The cost attribute Cod used in the model summarizes the average inter-zonal travel time by road as the sum of the average travel time between zones, estimated through the road graph of the supply model and the egress time, and the access time to the connecting arcs of the centroids of the traffic zones to the road graph as a function of the settlement structure of the individual zone. The 911×911 matrix of distances in km was also calculated to exclude from the distribution algorithm couples with an inter-zonal distance of less than 80 km. Four distribution models were specified, in each of which the zonal attractiveness d was assessed with attributes differentiated by travel reason. For each medium and long-distance travel motivation, a territorial model of attractiveness of the entire national territory was built, which allowed us to define, in relation to the distribution in classes of values of the specific attributes listed above, a national attractiveness hierarchy structured in 5 decreasing levels (S, A, B, C and D). The highest hierarchy S identifies the poles with attractive capacity for medium and long-distance macro-regional and supranational travel. The national distribution model was calibrated with the aid of the OD matrix of total daily movements above 80 km extracted from mobile phone data, which summarizes the hierarchical structure of the relationships woven in the territory [2].

The **Modal Choice Model** estimates the probability p[m/ods] that a user travels from zone or to zone d for reason s using mode m considering expressions of random utility [38] which are simplified functions of attributes of the level of service and socio-economics of the travel reason. The model used for the modal choice of MLP passengers is of the Multinomial Logit type, on which there is a rich and numerous national and international literature bibliography especially in the urban context, less rich that of the MLP [11, 39].

The assignment of demand matrices on the supply models represents the last step of the four-stage modeling. The (average) flow on the path that connects an OD pair is obtained by the product of the corresponding demand flow and the probability of choosing the path. The assignment model estimates with the help of the Visum software, the distribution of demand among the alternative paths offered by the network model for each OD pair, according to the perception that users have of the costs on the individual alternative paths [2]. The approach adopted was the probabilistic equilibrium approach. In order to consider the contribution of local demand on the national road network, the spatial consolidation of the 20 inter-municipal regional matrices estimated starting from the outputs of the local demand generation model with the regional distribution and modal choice models was carried out [30].

For a detailed description of the FS Italiane Group' Medium and Long-distance four-stage partial rate multimodal Passenger (MLP) model see [2].

The MLP Model was created by ISFORT for FS Research Centre in the form of Excel sheets that contain input data and perform calculations and calculation procedures in the VISUM software.

This has posed the problems already seen in the case of the EIA Model also for the use of the MLP Model by analysts of FS Italiane SpA and of the companies of the Group.

Therefore FS Research Centre has started the porting of the MLP Model in SIMS excluding, for now, the Assignment Model. The Assignment Model will be managed externally to the SIMS system, using the Visum software that will be manually fed with the outputs produced by the processing of the modal choice stage, made available through a specific download action of the results in a compatible format, implemented on the SIMS Portal - Sharepoint side. This data will then be transferred to the standard work area/folder configured in Visum.

As for the EIA Model, the SIMS Portal offers the MLP Model through its web interface while the calculations are performed by an application server in the backend. The input datasets are stored in the SIMS data warehouse and systematically updated through ETL procedures with versioning and historicization logics. User profiling and data segregation allow users to access their draft or executed simulations and to carry out new ones.

The workflow is a step-by-step process that follows the Four-Stage Transport Model, where the outputs produced by the calculation engine for a stage are the inputs that will be used to obtain the outputs of the next stage. Changing the inputs of a stage invalidates the processing of the stages following the current one and produces different outputs.

The successful completion of a previous stage unlocks the possibility of processing the next stage.

For each successfully completed processing, a set of outputs are generated (tabular reports, GeoBI, WebGIS) linked to the unique key of the simulation.

The concept of "scenario" is central to the design approach followed. The articulation of the model provides, in addition to the sequence in the four steps, also the user/system interaction and the capability of use of intermediate products produced. Just as its use is foreseen for specialized processing of stand-alone software (e.g. Visum).

The sharing of simulations between users is enabled, as for the EIA Model, using the logic of "Validation"/publication of scenarios.

The solution created has a high degree of flexibility: analysts, during the execution of the processing workflow, can modify their simulation from one stage to another of the model. This can be done by acting on the input variables (generation stage) or by selecting different scenarios/datasets in terms of O/D matrices, zone classification, pre-coded and system-available offers.

Each element of the workflow is metadata-tagged. Some elements require the metadata to be populated by analysts, for other elements the metadata is populated automatically by the system.

4 Conclusions

Given the availability of two important models, the Environmental Impact Analysis Model and the Long and Medium Distance Transport Model, in a multi-user environment, with a web interface, with the guarantee of consistency and rapid updating of the datasets and with the possibility of sharing the results of the simulations, SIMS has gone from a simple, albeit important, tool for sharing documents, data and contents of the GeoBI and WebGIS type, to a tool capable of inducing a virtuous circle in the analysis and planning activities at enterprise level in the Ferrovie dello Stato Italiane Group.

This capacity of SIMS is in a phase of further evolution.

In fact, SIMS was chosen by MOST National Center for Sustainable Mobility, one of the five National Research Centers activated by the PNRR in the MUR mission 4.2, as the system in which to develop the IT platform of the Model4Italy Flagship Project aimed at offering models for urban traffic planning to the entire Italian Public Administration.

From a technological point of view, the producers of specialized software for transport planning are evolving their platforms towards the full cloud paradigm, and, consequently, the MLP Model can be entirely incorporated into the SIMS Platform As A Service architecture, avoiding the delicate phases of exporting and importing data between systems and the use of desktop applications.

References

1. Tartaglia, M., Cerullo, M., Ferraresi, T., Paniccià, R., Radicioni, M., Cieri, E.: Evaluation of the Economic Effects of High-Speed Rail on the Italian Economy Through a Broader Input–Output Model Approach. In: Pagliara, F. (eds) Socioeconomic Impacts of High-Speed Rail Systems. IW-HSR 2022. Springer Proceedings in Business and Economics. Springer, Cham (2023). https://doi.org/10.1007/978-3-031-26340-8_2
2. Tartaglia M.,et al.: A multimodal model for the simulation of medium and long-distance mobility of people in Italy. Ingegneria Ferroviaria n. 3\2023 (2023)
3. Tartaglia, M., Fiduccia, A.: Geo-business intelligence and spatial data warehousing: a railway company case study. In: Borgogno-Mondino, E., Zamperlin, P. (eds) Geomatics for Green and Digital Transition. ASITA 2022. Communications in Computer and Information Science, vol 1651. Springer, Cham (2022). https://doi.org/10.1007/978-3-031-17439-1_10

4. Julio, Y.F.H., Bernal, W.N.: Capítulo 14. Business intelligence using geo-location and computational intelligence: a systematic literature review. In: Canabal, J.D., Munoz Herdandez, H., Franco, D.P., Castillo Osorio, B. (eds.) Retos del sector Empresarial en el Proceso de Convergencia al marco normativo contable y de aseguramiento de la informacion financiera, Universidad del Sinu, Ediciones Unisinú, 193, ISBN: 978–958–8553–53–5 (2018)
5. Atay, C.: An attribute or tuple timestamping in bitemporal relational databases. Turkish J. Electr. Eng. Comput. Sci. **24**. 4305–4321. https://doi.org/10.3906/elk-1403-39 (2016)
6. ISTAT: Annual National Accounts. Years 1995 – 2018 https://www.istat.it/it/ar-chivio/233518 and https://www.istat.it/en/archivio/233525 (English version) (2019) retrieved on 1st November, 2022
7. ISTAT: i.Stat Datawarehouse. Gross Domestic Product and main components http://dati.istat.it/?lang=en&SubSessionId=f34c402a-8d5e-46fc-9ae8-596fb4432544, (2022) retrieved on 1st November, 2022
8. Dietzenbacher, E., van Burken, B., Kondo, Y.: Hypothetical extractions from a global perspective. Econom. Syst. Res., Taylor & Francis J. **31**(4), 505–519 (Oct 2019)
9. OECD: OECD Inter-Country Input-Output Database, http://oe.cd/icio. (2021) retrieved on 1st November, 2022
10. Tartaglia, M., Cerullo, M.: Gruppo Ferrovie dello Stato Italiane. In: Ministero delle Infrastrutture e della Mobilità Sostenibili, Conto Nazionale delle Infrastrutture e della Mobilità Sostenibili, pp. 131–146. Istituto Poligrafico e Zecca dello Stato, Roma ISBN 978–88–901545–8–4 (2021)
11. Cascetta E.: Modelli per i sistemi di trasporto. Teoria e applicazioni. Utet Università, EAN 9788860080127 (2006)
12. Carminucci C., Chindemi, Procopio M., Saccà V.: 18° Rapporto sulla mobilità degli italiani. Governare le transizioni per una ripresa sostenibile (2021) https://www.ISFORT.it/wp-content/uploads/2020/12/RapportoMobilita2020.pdf. Accessed June 2022
13. Eurostat: Mobility data for thirteen Member States with different characteristics. Novembre (2021). Passenger mobility statistics - Statistics Explained (europa.eu) (2021) Accessed June 2021
14. MIT: Linee Guida per la valutazione degli investimenti in opere pubbliche nei settori di competenza del Ministero delle Infrastrutture e dei Trasporti D.Lgs. 228/2011. 1 giugno 2017 (2017)
15. ISTAT: Indagine Censuaria e Matrici intercomunali pendolari per motivo, mezzo, orario di partenza e durata dello spostamento. Matrici di Contiguità, Distanza e Pendolarismo 1991, 2001, 2011 (2021) https://www.ISTAT.it/it/archivio/157423 Accessed June 2021
16. ISTAT: Registro Statistico delle Unità Locali (ASIA UL) per comune: Imprese - Struttura -- Unità locali. http://dati.ISTAT.it/ Accessed June 2022
17. ARMOOGUM J., et al.: Survey harmonisation with New technologies improvement (SHANTI). Cost Action TU0804 RECHERCHES © Les collections de l'INRETS Avril 2014 ISBN 978–2–85782–704–7 (2014)
18. https://www.cost.eu/publication/survey-harmonisation-with-new-technologies-improvement-shanti/ Accessed June 2022
19. MIUR: Iscritti Istituzioni Scolastiche https://dati.istruzione.it/opendata/opendata Accessed June 2021
20. MIUR: Iscritti universitari residenti italiani e stranieri http://ustat.MIUR.it/opendata Accessed June 2021
21. Agenzia per la Coesione territoriale: Strategia Nazionale delle Aree Interne (SNAI) (2020) https://www.agenziacoesione. gov.it/strategia-nazionale-aree-interne/ Accessed June 2021
22. ISTAT: I Sistemi Locali del Lavoro 2011 (2021) https://www.ISTAT.it/it/informazioni-territoriali-ecartografiche/sistemi-locali-del-lavoro Accessed June 2021

23. ISTAT: Gli spostamenti per motivi di studio o lavoro secondo il Censimento permanente della popolazione, 13 maggio 2021 (2021) https://www.ISTAT.it/it/files//2021/05/Censimento_spostamenti_pendolari.pdf. Accessed: June 2022
24. ISTAT: Indagine campionaria Multiscopo Aspetti della vita quotidiana, Sezione Servizi. Spostamenti abituali per andare a lavoro e studio http://dati.ISTAT.it/. Accessed June 2021
25. ISTAT: Indagine censuaria del Movimento dei clienti negli esercizi ricettivi. In Servizi, Turismo, Movimenti http://dati.ISTAT.it/ Last access: June, 2021
26. Banca d'Italia: Indagine sul turismo internazionale condotta dal 1996 (2022) https://www.bancaditalia.it/pubblicazioni/indagine-turismo-internazionale/index.html?dotcache=refresh. Accessed June 2022
27. Eurostat: Statistiche del traffico passeggeri aeroportuale (2022) https://ec.europa.eu/eurostat/statisticsexplained/index.php?title=Air_passenger_transport_-_monthly_statistics. Accessed June 2022
28. ENAC: Statistiche di traffico passeggeri aeroportuale (2022) Last access: June, 2022
29. ANAS Gruppo FS: Osservatorio del traffico (2022) https://www.stradeanas.it/it/le-strade/osservatorio-del-traffico/dati-traffico-medio-giornaliero-annuale. Accessed June 2021
30. ISFORT: Modello di generazione e distribuzione Audimob (sviluppato in collaborazione con Ferrovie dello stato Italiane) (2020) https://www.ISFORT.it/progetti/modello-di-generazione-audimob/. Access: June 2022
31. OpenStreetMap: http://download.geofabrik.de/. Accessed June 2022
32. Ricci S.: Tecnica ed Economia dei trasporti. Hoepli. ISBN: 9788820345945 (2011)
33. Rete Ferroviaria Italiana: Prospetto Informativo della Rete 2019. Edizione maggio 2019 (2019)
34. Centro interregionale http://www.centrointerregionale-gis.it/DBPrior/DBPrior1.html. Accessed June 2021
35. FlixBus GTFS: OpenMobilityData (transitfeeds.com). Accessed June 2022
36. Trenitalia: I costi medi delle tariffe unitarie medie per OD (stazione-stazione) applicate da Trenitalia (2021)https://www.trenitalia.com/it/informazioni/condizioni_generaliditrasporto.html. Accessed June 2022
37. Cherchi E.: Derivazione del valore del tempo (VOT) utilizzando dati misti RP/SP con funzioni di utilità non lineari. Editore Università della Calabria (1999)
38. Ben Akiva M., Lerman S.: Discrete Choice analysis. Theory and application Travel demand. The Massachusetts Institute of technology, ISBN 0–262–02217–6 (1985)
39. Moeckel R., Fussell R., Donnelly R.: Mode choice modeling for long-distance travel (2015) https://www.researchgate.net/publication/272546582_Mode_choice_modeling_for_long-distance_travel. Accessed June 2022

Ecosystem Services Assessment Through GeoAI Applications for Driving Urban Planning Processes

Carolina Salvo(✉) and Alessandro Vitale

Department of Civil Engineering, University of Calabria, Calabria, Italy
{carolina.salvo,alessandro.vitale}@unical.it

Abstract. Assessing ecosystem services (ESs) and exploring the balance between supply and demand is critical for driving urban planning decision-making processes and promoting sustainable land use management, ecological protection, and inhabitants' well-being.

However, integrating and assessing multisource data into spatial planning is challenging due to urban ecosystems' complexity.

This study introduces an innovative methodological approach that connects the power of GeoAI, remote sensing techniques, and Geographic Information Systems to measure and map mismatches between the demand and supply of ESs, providing a new perspective on urban planning.

In developing a Google Earth Engine cloud computing platform, a Random Forrest (RF) classifier is employed to process and automatically classify multispectral satellite images and interpret complex Land Use Land Cover (LULC) patterns. This enables an accurate mapping of ESs supply-demand mismatch. The RF classifier accuracy was rigorously measured by comparing the model predictions with those derived from the visual interpretation of high-resolution Google Earth images. Overall Accuracy (OA) and the Kappa coefficient were the accuracy metrics.

The results of our study reveal a significant spatial mismatch between ES demand and supply across different land use types, shedding light on urban areas where ESs are either over-utilized or under-provided. This enlightening information can guide future urban planning decisions.

Following a performance-based approach, this study demonstrates significant utility in aiding policymakers and urban planners in making informed decisions for enhancing urban sustainability.

Keywords: Urban Ecosystem Services · GeoAI · Urban Planning

1 Introduction

Today, environmental issues in urban areas have been widely recognized as closely related to socioeconomic factors and issues. Urban planning activities are expected to address the complexities of urban transformations while improving inhabitants' quality of life. Within this context, ecosystem services (ESs), which denote the benefits humans

E. Borgogno-Mondino and P. Zamperlin (Eds.): ASITA 2024, CCIS 2463, pp. 189–206, 2025.
https://doi.org/10.1007/978-3-031-91141-5_14

derive from ecosystems, including the natural processes and functions of the environment, represent a suitable framework for understanding and addressing the relationship between urban changes and transformations' environmental, social, and economic aspects. Indeed, rapid transformations driven by urbanization and deforestation lead to significant Land Use Land Cover (LULC) changes directly affecting ESs [1]. These ESs, including runoff mitigation, air purification, climate regulation, and recreation, are crucial for maintaining environmental balance and ensuring human well-being in urban areas. Evaluating LULC changes and understanding their impact on ESs provision becomes increasingly essential to inform sustainable land-use planning and improve environmental conservation.

While foundational, traditional methods for assessing ESs often fail to address urban transformations' dynamic and complex nature. Conventional approaches frequently rely on static datasets, field surveys, or the use of predefined models such as InVEST (Integrated Valuation of Ecosystem Services and Trade-offs) or ARIES (Artificial Intelligence for Ecosystem Services), which represent limited temporal resolutions and manual or semi-automated analyses, which can be time-consuming and resource intensive. These methods struggle to capture fine-grained spatial and temporal variations in ES supply and demand, limiting their ability to inform timely and adaptive urban planning strategies. Moreover, the increasing availability of geospatial data, especially from satellite imagery, has outpaced the capacity of traditional methodologies to process and analyze such vast and complex datasets effectively.

In recent years, research and technological advancements in Geomatics have created new opportunities for efficient mapping and analyzing LULC changes at various spatial and temporal scales, which can contribute to assessing and mapping the impact of such changes on ESs provision. Geomatics technologies, such as remote sensing, Geographic Information Systems (GIS), and spatial modeling, allow for collecting and processing vast amounts of geospatial data [2]. However, the complexity of LULC and ESs mapping requires more sophisticated analytical methods, which can be addressed by integrating Geospatial Artificial Intelligence (GeoAI) [3–5].

GeoAI represents a significant advancement in ES assessment by addressing the limitations of traditional methods. By integrating artificial intelligence algorithms, GeoAI enables the automation of processes such as satellite image classification, change detection, and predictive modeling, drastically reducing the time and effort required for analysis. Furthermore, GeoAI techniques are essential to identify and interpret complex spatial and temporal patterns within large geospatial datasets. These provide more accurate and granular insights into the relationship between LULC changes and ES supply and demand. Employing machine learning models, GeoAI can manage high-dimensional data and adapt to the inherent variability of urban environments, offering robust solutions for mapping ESs across diverse landscapes.

Remote sensing imagery is the most widely used technique for mapping LULC and ESs over time [6]. The leading world space agency programs, such as Landsat, Sentinel-2, and MODIS, provide RGB, Multispectral (MSI), and Hyperspectral (HSI) satellite images, generating a large amount of data [7, 8]. GeoAI techniques, thanks to the combination of advanced spatial models and AI algorithms, allow data management, enabling the automation of satellite image classification, change detection, and predictive modeling, offering powerful tools for assessing the impacts of LULC on ESs.

Cloud computing resources facilitate this task by employing advanced machine-learning algorithms. For example, Google Earth Engine [9] is a cloud-based platform for geospatial analysis [10] that is open-access and free for research, education, and non-profit purposes. Access to the platform requires only a simple online application and a Google user account. Earth Engine features a JavaScript code editor and provides access to a vast collection of imagery (including nearly the entire Landsat archive and related surface reflectance products), which can be directly retrieved for testing and developing algorithms interactively, with real-time result previews. The platform also offers a variety of pixel-based supervised and unsupervised classifiers, including machine learning algorithms, for mapping applications.

These resources represent valuable support for improving the ESs mapping and assessment, consenting to a better understanding of the impact of urban interventions and consequent changes on ESs supply and the demand for ESs related to socioeconomic and structural conditions [11]. It enhances the quality of urban planning processes [12] by coordinating the relationship between humans and nature from a functional and performance-based perspective [13].

This paper aims to investigate the ESs framework supporting performance-based urban planning and regeneration by analyzing ESs supply-demand mismatch through innovative GeoAI techniques. Specifically, the authors accurately assessed regulating and cultural ESs supply-demand mismatch at the municipal scale on the Upper North Thyrrenian area (Calabria, Italy) utilizing a Google Earth Engine cloud computing platform based on a Random Forrest (RF) classifier to process and automatically classify multispectral satellite images and interpret complex data patterns. The novelty of this study lies in integrating cloud computing capabilities with GeoAI to automate the classification of multispectral satellite images and detect LULC changes while further utilizing QGIS for post-processing and visualization. This unique combination allows a seamless transition from automated analysis to practical spatial decision-making, enhancing the usability of results in urban-scale ES evaluation. The integration with QGIS also supports advanced spatial querying and scenario modeling, refining and visualizing GeoAI outputs, and, as a consequence, ensuring that the results are actionable and accessible for practical applications, offering a comprehensive framework for assessing and addressing ES supply-demand mismatches in urban environments.

The study is structured as follows. The second section describes the study area and the ESs analyzed, while the third section defines the methods employed. The results are presented in the fourth section and discussed in the fifth section, while the sixth section concludes the research.

2 Study Area and Ecosystem Services Selection

The proposed methodology is tested on the Upper Tyrrhenian Coast Area of the Calabria region (Fig. 1), which comprises 14 municipalities: Aieta (1), Belvedere Marittimo (2), Bonifati (3), Buonvincino (4), Diamante (5), Grisolia (6), Maierà (7), Praia a Mare (8), San Nicola Arcella (9), Sangineto (10), Santa Domenica Talao (11), Santa Maria del Cedro (12), Scalea (13), and Tortora (14).

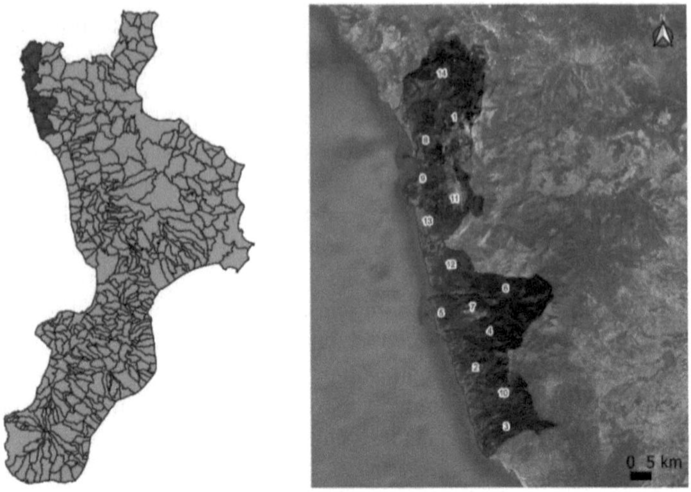

Fig. 1. Study area.

According to the Regional Territorial Framework with landscape value (so-called QTRP) of Calabria, the Upper Tyrrhenian Coast Area is one of the Territorial Landscape Unit belonging to the Regional Territorial Landscape Area 1 "Tirreno Cosentino", which spans from Bonifati to Tortora and represents the physical boundary between the Calabria and Basilicata regions. This territorial system is characterized by small to medium-sized urban centers with a high touristic vocation. The most important are Praia a Mare, Scalea, and Diamante, as they contribute to delivering uses and functions to the other urban centers distributed around them. Access to the Upper Tyrrhenian Coast Area is guaranteed through longitudinal axes, represented by highway A2, SS18, and the railway Praia a Mare – Reggio Calabria.

The Upper Tyrrhenian Coast Area has a total surface of 424.94 sqkm and a population of 55,131 inhabitants, distributed across the municipalities as represented in Table 1.

Within this work, the authors referred to regulating and cultural ESs as they impact more urban areas and need to be controlled through proper planning actions within general and sectorial urban plans. Specifically, they are runoff mitigation, air purification (PM10), urban temperature regulation, and recreation.

The interest in assessing ESs for such a territorial context is related to the fact that more emphasis should be placed on ESs, as almost all the Municipal Structural Plans (so-called PSC), only adopted, both adopted and approved or in the process of being drawn up, such as, for example, Bonifati, Sangineto, and Scalea, aim at protecting ESs but do not indicate how they can be integrated into municipal planning.

Table 1. Main information about the study area.

ID	Popoluation (inhab.)	Area (sqkm)	Population density (inhab./sqkm)	Elevation (m)
1	740	47.93	15	524
2	9,067	36.60	247	150
3	2,570	33.37	77	425
4	1,995	30.36	66	400
5	5,019	11.88	422	25
6	2,171	51.31	42	465
7	1,123	17.64	64	360
8	6,367	23.32	273	5
9	1,973	11.39	173	110
10	1,221	27.24	45	275
11	1,131	35.84	32	304
12	5,093	18.22	280	110
13	11,427	22.09	517	25
14	5,974	57.73	103	300

3 Methodological Approach

The methodology applied within this study is represented in Fig. 2.

3.1 Ecosystem Services Supply, Demand, and Related Mismatch Assessment

Water management ES is often calculated through hydrological modeling. However, since this work aims to analyze runoff mitigation concerning LULC in a specific municipality area, a runoff mitigation spatial method based on LULC is used. Specifically, we measured the runoff mitigation capacity of a single municipality by applying the method proposed by [14] as the product of the total precipitation times, a coefficient of water infiltration based on LULC. As within a municipality, there are multiple LULC, we calculated the weighted average of water infiltration. The higher the value of runoff mitigation, the higher the permeability characterizes the municipality, and the better the municipality's performance in runoff mitigation.

The demand for runoff mitigation was calculated by considering the total population living in the municipality and the built-up area falling into high and very high hydraulic risk areas. We integrated these two dimensions using a simple linear combination method [15]. Before aggregating them, both were re-scaled on a range from 0 to 1 using the min-max standardization procedure. The higher the value, the higher the demand for runoff mitigation.

Supply values of air purification per municipality were obtained by considering different vegetation types' capacity to remove PM10. Specifically, we considered the

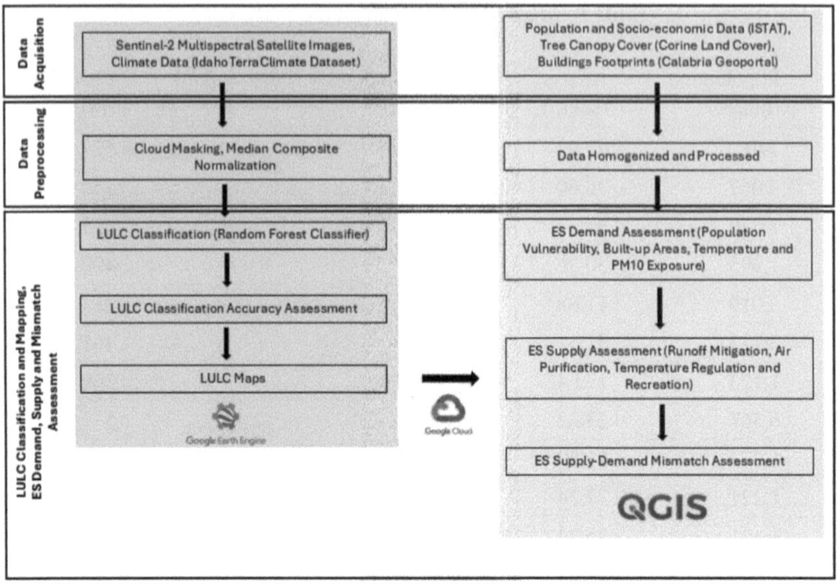

Fig. 2. Methodological framework.

tree cover and grass and shrub areas. This analysis did not include the agricultural area as its capacity to supply PM10 removal is limited to some periods during the year. The PM10 removal rates considered for tree cover and grass and shrubs refer to the values estimated by [16] for ESs assessment in the city of Trento, which considers that tree cover contributes to air quality regulation around three times more than grass and shrubs as also highlighted by other scholars [17]. The supply values of air purification are estimated for each municipality and then normalized.

The demand for air purification (PM10) generally refers to existing normative values or measured PM10 concentrations in the case study. However, this latter data is not always available due to the absence of monitoring campaigns or data sharing. For these reasons, the demand for air purification within this study was estimated based on vulnerable populations exposed to air pollution, which is assumed to be composed of the elderly (over 74 years old) and young people (under 14 years old). The percentage of vulnerable people is assessed for each municipality and then normalized.

The supply of urban temperature regulation ecosystem service was estimated following [18]. Specifically, we considered the supply of urban temperature regulation delivered by trees through the evapotranspiration process and the shading effect using the tree canopy cover percentage as a proxy measure of these services. Data on tree shade areas was assessed for each municipality and then normalized.

The demand for the ES urban temperature regulation was estimated by combining two factors: i) the maximum temperature of each municipality during 2024 and (ii) the vulnerable people living in the municipality evaluated for the case of air purification ES demand. The two factors were assessed, normalized, and then combined linearly.

The supply of recreation ES for each municipality was assessed by considering the quantity, quality, and accessibility of urban green areas. Specifically, for each municipality, we evaluated the quantity (sqm) of urban green areas and the number of buildings served by those green spaces in a service area obtained from a buffer zone with a radius of 300 m. The two factors, namely the quantity and accessibility of urban green spaces available at the municipality level, were assessed, normalized, and combined linearly.

The demand for recreation ES was evaluated considering the vulnerability of the population living in each municipality. The degree of vulnerability of the population living in each municipality is assessed by considering the following factors: (i) rate of highly educated (i.e., Bachelor) residents among the total population (-); (ii) rate of employed people aged between 15 and 64 years old (-); (iii) rate of foreign resident minors over the total population (+); (iv) rate of families with one or six and more components (+). The factors were assessed, normalized considering the effect of each variable shown in brackets, and combined linearly.

The supply and demand of ecosystem services were compared by evaluating and mapping the Supply-Demand Mismatch (SDM), which consents to identify the areas with ecosystem service provision deficit or surplus. The SDM for the i-th ES has been calculated as follows:

$$SDMi = Si - Di \tag{1}$$

Si and *Di* refer to the normalized Supply and Demand values for the i-th ES. The *SDM* provides an immediate interpretation of surplus (*SDM* > *0*), balance (*SDM* ≅ *0*), and deficit (*SDM* < *0*) in ES provision. Therefore, the theoretical lower and upper limits of *SDM* are -1 (extreme deficit) and 1 (extreme surplus). Moreover, based on *SDM* scores, we classified each municipality according to its ES balance, applying the criteria reported in Table 2 [19].

Table 2. ESs supply-demand mismatch ranking based on SDM values.

SDM interval	Ranking
$-1 \leq \text{SDM} < -0.5$	High deficit
$-0.5 \leq \text{SDM} < -0.15$	Moderate deficit
$-0.15 \leq \text{SDM} \leq -0.15$	Balance
$0.15 < \text{SDM} \leq 0.5$	Moderate surplus
$0.50 < \text{SDM} \leq 1$	High surplus

3.2 Data Description, Acquisition, and Processing

Sentinel-2 multispectral satellite images were used to derive the 2024 LULC map of the study area. The Sentinel-2 (S2) satellites are equipped with the MSI multispectral optical sensor, which captures 13 spectral bands across the visible, near-infrared, and short-wave infrared regions, with spatial resolutions as fine as 10 m and a revisit interval of 5 days. Compared to other free satellite imagery (e.g., Landsat), S2 offers three additional bands in the red-edge part of the spectrum, recognized for their significance in identifying vegetation types and monitoring vegetation health. This study utilized level-2A (L2A) processed data from the Google Earth Engine (GEE) catalog. L2A products are derived from L1C after applying atmospheric correction algorithms, resulting in bottom-of-atmosphere reflectance.

For the S2 L2A data, all images from April 2024 to May 2024 were utilized, considering the higher cloud coverage observed during the remaining periods of the year.

In the study area zones where clouds and cirrus were present, they were masked using the QA60 band [20]. Using the cloud distribution probability score of the images, we selected those with less than 10% cloud coverage. A median composite method was then applied to merge the collection into a single image, producing an annual cloud-free image dataset for 2024.

Remotely sensed data were processed using the Google Earth Engine (GEE) cloud computing platform [21]. The GEE platform guarantees direct access to many datasets, such as Sentinel-2, avoiding complex downloading and storing operations. It also allows large-scale image processing, which usually requires high computational power.

Starting from the multispectral satellite images of the study area for 2024, the LULC mapping was conducted using an image classification operation, categorizing and labeling groups of pixels in different classes. Improved outcomes with these techniques depend on factors such as class complexity, the amount of training data, the type and number of input features, and the chosen classification method [22]. RF is among the most effective and widely used solutions for classification tasks.

RF supervised machine learning algorithm constructs multiple decision trees on different subsamples of the dataset and employs averaging to enhance predictive accuracy while mitigating overfitting [23]. RF has demonstrated robustness to reference data errors of up to 15%, performs well with small sample sizes and high-dimensional feature spaces, and offers relatively quick execution compared to other classification techniques [24, 25].

In this study, RF classification was conducted using the Google Earth Engine (GEE) platform. To maintain a balance between operational efficiency and the accuracy of results, this study set the number of decision trees in the random forest to 100, based on iterative testing.

From the multispectral satellite image classification operations, six LULC types, detailed in Table 3, characterize the investigation area of this study.

Table 3. LULC classification framework and its associated descriptions.

LULC Type	Abbreviation	Description
Grassland - Shrubland	Grass - Shrub	Areas covered by natural grasslands and vegetation dominated by woody shrubs and small trees
Agricultural	Cult	Cultivated areas refer to land used for growing crops, including fields and plantations, often managed through human agricultural practices
Tree Cover	Trees	Regions dominated by trees with a continuous canopy, typically including forests and wooded lands
Built-Up	Built-up	Buildings and other human-made structures
Permanent water bodies	Water	Surfaces covered by water as rivers, lakes, and basins
Bareland	Bare	Regions with minimal or absent vegetation, such as exposed soil, sand, or rock

The collection of training and validation samples was conducted through visual interpretation of high-resolution Google Earth images, a widely used method in the literature [26, 27].

The training and validation datasets were selected independently to ensure more accurate validation. For the training stage, 1119 reference elements were selected, while for the validation stage, 414.

After the training and validation stages, the accuracy assessment is a crucial final step in image classification. It quantitatively evaluates how accurately pixels (or segments) are assigned to their correct LULC classes. Essentially, accuracy reflects the level of agreement between the generated maps and reference maps. For this study, the accuracy measures employed were Overall Accuracy (OA), the Kappa coefficient, and the confusion matrix [28]. OA represents the likelihood of correctly classifying a randomly chosen location on the map. The Kappa coefficient ranges from -1 to 1, where 0 indicates classification like random assignment, negative values suggest worse-than-random classification and values near 1 indicate highly accurate classification. The confusion matrix summarises the relationship between ground truth and predicted classes and forms the basis for calculating all the above metrics. The diagonal elements of the matrix represent correct predictions, while off-diagonal elements highlight misclassifications.

The tree shade area was assessed by intersecting data from LULC derivation and data from Corine Land Cover on tree canopy cover, which is available for 2018.

Data on population was retrieved from the Italian Institute of Statistics and is available for 2024.

Data on precipitation was retrieved from the report on environmental themes available for the Calabria region. It was assumed to be equal for all the analyzed areas, as no further data for each municipality was available. The percentage of water infiltration is derived from [14], while data on maximum temperature at the urban scale is obtained from the Idaho TerraClimate Dataset. This dataset is a comprehensive, high-resolution (4 km) global climate dataset, specifically by the University of Idaho, and provides monthly climate and climatic water balance data spanning from 1958 to the present.

Data on the urban green areas' location and building footprints came from multispectral image processing and the Calabria region geoportal. Other specific data on urban green areas were obtained by analyzing Google Earth and Google Street View.

4 Results

Before assessing the ESs supply-demand mismatch, the authors classified the 2024 multispectral satellite images for the LULC mapping of the study area, achieving an Overall Accuracy (OA) of 0.80 and a Kappa coefficient of 0.75. These metrics indicate good agreement between the predicted and reference data, with the Kappa coefficient suggesting substantial agreement beyond chance.

As shown in Table 4, the confusion matrix reveals the classification performance for each LULC class. The matrix highlights high classification accuracy for certain classes, such as "Trees," which shows a high number of correctly classified instances (108) compared to relatively few misclassifications, and class "Bare," with 61 correctly classified instances. However, some confusion is evident. For instance, class "Cult" is often misclassified as class "Trees" or class "Grass-Shrub," with 35 and 2 misclassified instances, respectively. Similarly, the class "Grass-Shrub" is occasionally confused with "Trees" and "Bare," indicating challenges in distinguishing between vegetation types with overlapping spectral characteristics. Class "Built-up" shows relatively lower misclassification rates, but some instances are incorrectly classified as "Grass-Shrub" or "Bare." The confusion between class "Water" and class "Bare" is minimal, reflecting the distinct spectral signatures of these classes.

Table 4. LULC Validation Confusion Matrix for 2024.

ID	Grass-Shrub	Cult	Trees	Built-up	Water	Bare
Grass-Shrub	54	1	5	1	0	4
Cult	2	61	35	0	0	1
Trees	1	18	108	0	0	0
Built-up	2	0	0	25	0	2
Water	0	0	0	0	23	1
Bare	4	2	1	1	1	61

As shown in Table 5, which refers to LULC prediction, the areas characterized by a higher built-up density are in the coastal municipalities to the east of the study area. These municipalities are characterized by a strong tourist demand and, therefore, a higher level of built-up areas. The municipalities with the greater built surface are Scalea (517.81 ha), Belvedere Marittimo (342.91 ha), and Praia a Mare (283.80 ha).

In the central part of the study area, located between the coast to the East and the mountainous reliefs to the West, agricultural zones are concentrated and characterized by valuable crops, such as cedars in Santa Maria del Cedro. The municipalities with the most significant extension of agricultural areas are Belvedere Marittimo (1206.92 ha), Grisolia (1008.06 ha), and Tortora (990.89 ha).

Corresponding with the mountainous reliefs, the predominant land covers are Tree Cover, Grasslands, Shrublands, and Barelands. The municipalities with these predominant LULC are Aieta, Grisolia, and Tortora.

Instead, the Permanent Water Bodies LULC class is characterized by rivers and streams, which are more concentrated in the municipalities of Tortora (17,46 ha) and Scalea (13,88 ha).

Table 5. Predicted study area LULC for 2024.

ID	Area (ha)	Grass-Shrub (ha)	Cultiv. (ha)	Trees (ha)	Built-up (ha)	Water (ha)	Bareland (ha)
1	4792.81	1557.10	774.98	1,508.98	99.70	5.35	846.70
2	3660.25	320.05	1,206.92	1,588.11	342.91	2.56	199.70
3	3337.21	175.53	860.00	2,039.41	147.23	0.50	114.54
4	3035.66	382.92	771.15	1,626.98	87.62	5.48	161.51
5	1188.47	104.73	436.60	300.55	242.73	6.30	97.56
6	5131.44	520.08	1,008.06	2,697.04	121.97	2.97	781.32
7	1764.42	223.16	457.21	993.10	35.93	0.08	54.94
8	2332.32	699.03	371.31	479.91	283.80	7.98	490.29
9	1138.95	294.97	309.02	277.12	152.13	2.40	103.31
10	2723.93	197.04	736.27	1,638.36	81.46	1,39	69.41
11	3584.09	896.45	836,86	1,457.24	74.31	9.92	309.31
12	1821.63	181.24	753.66	545.02	231.15	5.70	104.86
13	2209.27	316.45	649.79	447.33	517.81	13.88	264.01
14	5773.36	1,439.53	990.89	2,304.52	277.79	17.46	743.17

Meanwhile, the authors gathered all data from different sources, applied the methods described in the previous Section, and subsequently obtained the results shown in Fig. 3.

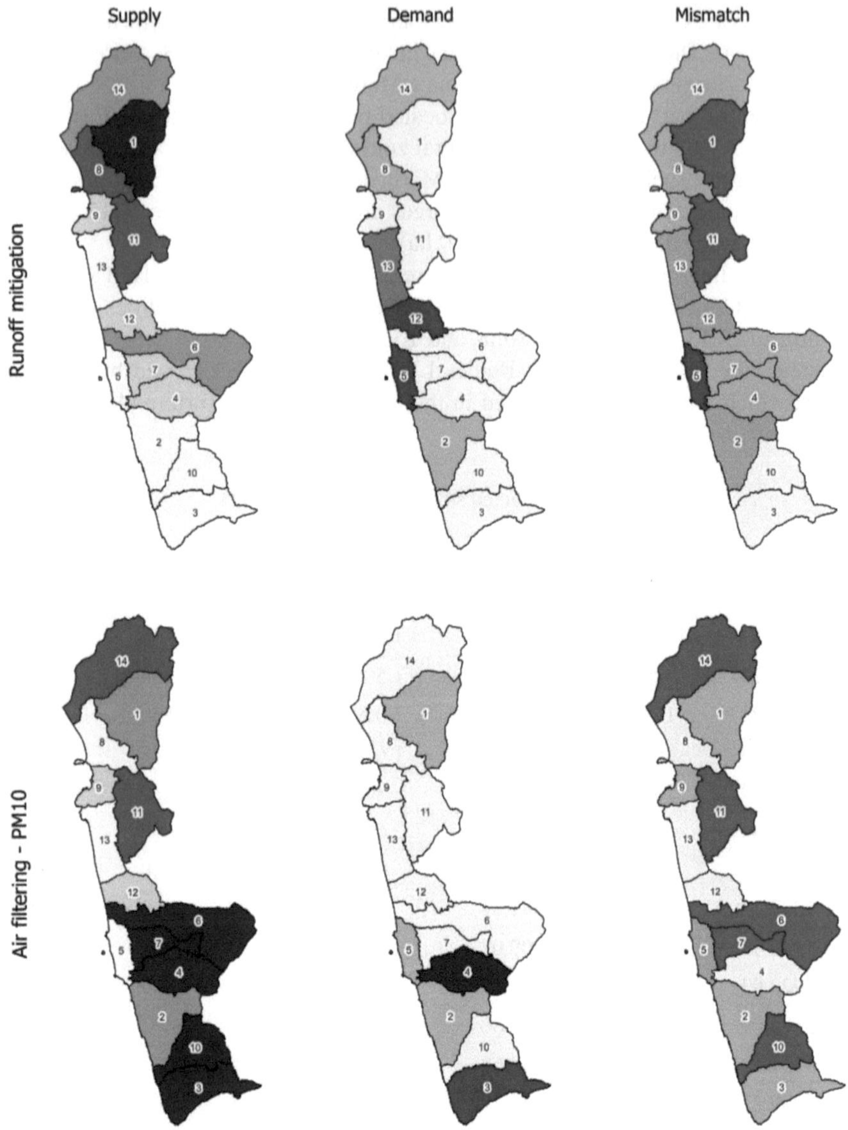

Fig. 3. ES supply, demand and their mismatch assessment.

Fig. 3. (*continued*)

For runoff mitigation, the supply showed the highest values in Aieta (1), Praia a Mare (8), and Santa Domenica Talao (11), while the lowest values characterize Belvedere Marittimo (2), Bonifati (3), Diamante (5), Sangineto (10), and Scalea (13). Medium values are related to Grisolia (6), and Tortora (14). The demand for runoff mitigation, assessed considering the population living in each municipality and the built-up area exposed to high and very high hydraulic risk areas, is high for Diamante (5), and Santa Maria del Cedro (12), while it is medium in Scalea (13). Most of the municipalities present a low demand for runoff mitigation. Therefore, looking at the mismatch for runoff mitigation, it emerges that a high deficit characterizes Diamante (5), while Aieta (1) and Santa Domenica Talao (11) present a high surplus. A balanced supply-demand mismatch relates to Belvedere Marittimo (2), Santa Maria del Cedro (12), and Scalea (13).

For air filtering (PM10), most of the municipalities present the highest supply values. These include Bonifati (3), Buonvicino (4), Grisolia (6), Maierà (7), and Sangineto (10). Diamante (5), Praia a Mare (8), and San Nicola Arcella (9) show the lowest values of air filtering supply.

Medium values characterize Belvedere Marittimo (2) and Aieta (1). Regarding air filtering demand, which is evaluated as the vulnerable population in each municipality, Buonvicino (4) is characterized by a very high air filtering demand. At the same time, Bonifati (3) has a high level of demand. Aieta (1), Belvedere Marittimo (2), and Diamante (5) present low levels of air filtering demand, whereas the other municipalities have a very low level of air filtering demand. The supply-demand mismatch for air filtering ES is characterized by a high surplus in Maierà (7), Grisolia (6), Sangineto (10), Santa Domenica Talao (11), and Tortora (14), while Diamante (5) is in moderate deficit. A balanced supply-demand mismatch characterizes Buonvicino (4), Praia a Mare (8), Scalea (13), and Santa Maria del Cedro (12). None of the analyzed municipalities present a high deficit.

Concerning urban temperature regulation, Bonifati (3), Buonvicino (4), and Grisolia (6) present the highest supply values. Diamante (5), Praia a Mare (8), San Nicola Arcella (9), and Scalea (13) depict very low urban temperature regulation supply levels. At the same time, Aieta (1) and Belvedere Marittimo (2) show a medium supply level of urban temperature regulation. The lowest values of urban temperature supply are available in Diamante (5), Praia a Mare (8), San Nicola Arcella (9), and Scalea (13). The demand for urban temperature regulation is medium in almost all municipalities. Bonifati (3) is characterized by a high demand for urban temperature regulation, while Grisolia (6) and Maierà (7) depict a low supply level. Hence, the mismatch between urban temperature regulation supply and demand is in high surplus for Grisolia (6), balance for Aieta (1), Belvedere Marittimo (2), and Santa Domenica Talao (11), and high deficit for Scalea (13).

Regarding recreation ES, supply values are very high in none of the analyzed municipalities. Only Praia a Mare (8) presents a high level of recreation ES supply, while Diamante (5), Grisolia (6), and Scalea (13) present a medium level of recreation supply. Tortora presents a low level of recreation supply, while all the other municipalities depict a very low level. The demand for recreation ES is high in Scalea (13) and low for Belvedere Marittimo (2), Diamante (5), and Praia a Mare (8). All the other municipalities have a medium level of demand for recreation ES. Therefore, analyzing the mismatch between supply and demand recreation ES, it emerges that it is in surplus for Diamante (5) and Praia a Mare (8), and balanced for Grisolia (6) and Scalea (13). Moreover, while Aieta (1), Maierà (7), and Santa Domenica Talao (11) present a high deficit in recreation provision, all the other municipalities show a deficit.

5 Discussion

The results show the spatial distribution of ESs supply and demand and their mismatch at the municipality level by employing an innovative approach based on integrating remote sensing, geospatial analysis, and artificial intelligence. The paper presents how the ESs supply and demand and their mismatch substantially vary across the municipalities and the different urban areas that compose the analyzed study area. Such analysis consents to managing such complex data and showing the location of ESs mismatches at the urban scale, giving information about ESs deficit areas to urban planners and spatial decision-makers.

The results show that the analyzed case study presents a good supply-demand mismatch for runoff mitigation and air filtering (PM10), a medium situation in urban temperature regulation, and a worse situation in recreation ES provision. Specifically, for air filtering (PM10), as natural forests and grassland have an important role in contributing to PM10 filtering, most municipalities have a surplus in the supply-demand mismatch for such ES. For runoff mitigation, the municipalities with a worse supply-demand mismatch situation are the most urbanized, such as Scalea Diamante Belvedere Sangineto and Bonifati. On the other hand, the supply of air purification is higher, whereas the rate of urbanization is lower, and the rate of vegetation is higher. Regarding urban temperature regulation, the results align with the other results available in the scientific literature, for which the shading effect significantly improves urban temperature regulation. In the case of recreation ES, the supply is relatively low because of the lack of green spaces in urban areas, which, considering the high demand for these spaces, determines a very high deficit in this ES provision.

In such analysis, using GeoAI, through integrating multispectral satellite imagery and RF classification, proved highly effective for generating and mapping LULC data and consenting ES supply-demand mismatch estimation. The application of the RF classifier, known for its robustness and flexibility in handling complex datasets, played a crucial role in achieving accurate LULC classification, which is essential for ESs assessment. By employing the Google Earth Engine (GEE) cloud computing platform, the computational process allowed for efficient handling of satellite imagery, which was essential given the scope of data covering multiple years and regions.

The classification results showed a high level of accuracy, as evidenced by an OA of 0.80 and a Kappa coefficient (K) of 0.75. These metrics indicate a strong agreement between the classification outputs and the reference data, suggesting that the RF model, in combination with the GEE platform, is well-suited for large-scale LULC mapping tasks. The overall accuracy of 0.80 reflects the system's ability to classify most land cover types correctly. At the same time, the Kappa coefficient, which accounts for the possibility of random agreement, further confirms the classification's reliability.

The confusion matrix revealed detailed insights into the classification performance. High classification accuracy was achieved for classes such as "Trees" (108 correctly classified instances out of 127) and "Bare" (61 correctly classified instances out of 70), reflecting the robustness of the RF model in distinguishing these land cover types. However, moderate misclassifications were observed between "Cult" (35 misclassified as "Trees") and "Grass-Shrub" (5 misclassified as "Trees" and 4 as "Bare"), indicating some challenges in differentiating vegetation types with overlapping spectral characteristics. "Built-up" areas showed good classification accuracy with minimal misclassifications (25 correctly classified instances), reinforcing the reliability of the mapping outputs for urbanized regions.

Considering these numerical results, this paper proposed and tested an innovative methodological approach, which employs innovative techniques and spatial modeling analysis for measuring and mapping the mismatch between supply and demand of specific regulating and cultural ESs. The innovative element of the proposed approach addresses the complexity of such an analysis by suggesting a possible approach and method to support the decision-making process in enhancing the scientific and practical knowledge on integrating ESs in urban planning processes. From a geomatic perspective, the proposed methodology addresses innovative GeoAI technologies, remote sensing, and GIS techniques, which are the most suitable for determining information about territorial systems from satellite imageries and complex and intricate databases. From an urban planning perspective, the paper proposes a methodology for supporting urban planners and policymakers in better understanding ESs and integrating them into urban planning practice.

Despite the different innovative characteristics of the proposed research, it certainly has some limitations, which can be overcome with further research developments. Specifically, it could be interesting to analyze other ESs, such as supporting and provisioning ESs, for such a territorial scale. This could be of great interest for addressing regional planning more properly in maintaining and enhancing ESs and integrating ES concepts at such a scale. Moreover, it could be interesting to consider also coastal ESs through which, in conjunction with those analyzed within this study, could simultaneously protect the environment and the territory, promote sustainable forms of tourism and agricultural activities, and ensure the liveability of urban dwellers – both residents and visitors. Considering this latter aspect, the research would be extended by integrating different aspects of coastal areas and other coastal ESs to define a comprehensive decision support system capable of integrating ES into planning decisions in coastal areas to enhance coastal protection. Moreover, the proposed analysis will be further developed by assessing ESs supply-demand mismatch at a finer scale to have an appropriate quantification of ESs supply-demand mismatch and, therefore, drive urban regeneration interventions.

6 Conclusion

This paper provides an innovative approach based on geospatial analysis, remote sensing, and artificial intelligence to assess mismatches in regulating and cultural ESs. It uses a performance-based approach to drive urban planning and decision-making processes.

The approach has been revealed to be appropriate for assessing such ESs, improving human well-being, and ensuring sustainability in urban areas.

The analysis of the proposed case study revealed that the mismatch between ES supply and demand is in deficit more for cultural ES than regulation ESs, suggesting that further protection and restoration of urban green infrastructure is needed to improve urban dwellers' quality of life in terms of the quantity and quality of urban green areas available in the urban environment. Results showed that the highest share of municipalities need to increase the supply of recreation ES.

Urban planners and policymakers should consider such considerations and employ all the possibilities that such a method could offer to increase the multiple benefits of urban green infrastructures in urban areas.

References

1. Salvo, C., Vitale, A.: Spatiotemporal dynamics of urban growth and greening goals towards sustainable development. In: International Conference on Innovation in Urban and Regional Planning, pp. 183–195. Springer, Cham (2023). https://doi.org/10.1007/978-3-031-54096-7_17
2. Pierdicca, R., Paolanti, M.: GeoAI: A review of artificial intelligence approaches for the interpretation of complex geomatics data. Geoscientific Instrumentation, Methods and Data Systems Discussions, 1–35 (2022). https://doi.org/10.5194/gi-11-195-2022
3. Francini, M., Salvo, C., Vitale, A.: Combining deep learning and multi-source GIS methods to analyze urban and greening changes, Sensors **23**(8) (3805), (2023). https://doi.org/10.3390/s23083805
4. Vitale, A., Salvo, C.: Monitoring and forecasting land cover dynamics using remote sensing and geospatial technology. In: Italian Conference on Geomatics and Geospatial Technologies, pp. 126–140. Springer, Cham (2023). https://doi.org/10.1007/978-3-031-59925-5_10
5. Vitale, A., Salvo, C., Lamonaca, F.: A novel geospatial methodology for measuring and mapping spatiotemporal built-up dynamics based on Google Earth Engine and unsupervised K-means clustering of multispectral satellite imagery. In: 2024 IEEE International Workshop on Metrology for Living Environment (MetroLivEnv), pp. 57–62. IEEE (2024). https://doi.org/10.1109/MetroLivEnv60384.2024.10615674
6. Noi Phan, T., Kuch, V., Lehnert, L.W.: Land cover classification using Google Earth Engine and random forest classifier—the role of image composition. Remote Sens. **12**, 2411 (2020). https://doi.org/10.3390/rs12152411
7. Khachoo, Y.H., Cutugno, M., Robustelli, U., Pugliano, G.: Machine learning for quantification of land transitions in Italy between 2000 and 2018 and prediction for 2050. In: 2022 IEEE International Workshop on Metrology for the Sea; Learning to Measure Sea Health Parameters (MetroSea), pp. 225–230. IEEE (2022). https://doi.org/10.1109/MetroSea55331.2022.9950871
8. Khachoo, Y.H., Cutugno, M., Robustelli, U., Pugliano, G.: Unveiling the dynamics of thermal characteristics related to LULC changes via ANN. Sensors **23**(15), 7013 (2023). https://doi.org/10.3390/s23157013
9. Google Earth Engine. https://earthengine.google.com/. Accessed 13 Sept 2024
10. Gorelick, N., Hancher, M., Dixon, M., Ilyushchenko, S., Thau, D., Moore, R.: Google earth engine: planetary-scale geospatial analysis for everyone. Remote Sens. Environ. **202**, 18–27 (2017). https://doi.org/10.1016/j.rse.2017.06.031
11. Haase, D., Haase, A., Rink, D.: Conceptualizing the nexus between urban shrinkage and ecosystem services. Landsc. Urban Plan. **132**, 159–169 (2014). https://doi.org/10.1016/j.landurbplan.2014.09.003

12. Geneletti, D., Cortinovis, C., Zardo, L., Esmail, B.A.: Planning for ecosystem services in cities. Springer, Cham (2020). https://doi.org/10.1007/978-3-030-20024-4
13. Scorza, F., Corrado, S., Muzzillo, V.: GeoAI approach for analyzing territorial specialization in ecosystem services provisioning. In: Gervasi, O. et al. (eds.) Computational Science and its Applications – ICCSA 2023 Workshops, Lecture Notes in Computer Science, vol. 14106, pp. 1–12. Springer, Cham (2023). https://doi.org/10.1007/978-3-031-37111-0_45
14. Pauleit, S., Duhme, F.: Assessing the environmental performance of land cover types for urban planning. Landsc. Urban Plan. **52**(1), 1–20 (2000). https://doi.org/10.1016/S0169-2046(00)00109-2
15. The Organisation for Economic Co-operation and Development (OECD): Annual Report 2008. OECD, https://www.oecd.org/newsroom/40556222.pdf, last accessed 2023/05/13
16. Geneletti, D., Cortinovis, C., Zardo, L., Esmail, B.A.: Planning for ecosystem services in cities. In: Planning for Ecosystem Services in Cities, pp. 1–16. Springer, Cham (2020). https://doi.org/10.1007/978-3-030-20024-4_1
17. McPhearson, T., et al.: Advancing urban ecology toward a science of cities. Bioscience **66**(3), 198–212 (2016). https://doi.org/10.1093/biosci/biw002
18. Baró, F., Haase, D., Gómez-Baggethun, E., Frantzeskaki, N.: Mismatches between ecosystem services supply and demand in urban areas: a quantitative assessment in five European cities. Ecol. Indic. **55**, 146–158 (2015). https://doi.org/10.1016/j.ecolind.2015.03.013
19. Fusaro, L., Nardella, L., Manes, F., Sebastiani, A., Fares, S.: Supply and demand mismatch analysis to improve regulating ecosystem services in Mediterranean urban areas: insights from four Italian municipalities. Ecol. Indic. **155**, 110928 (2023). https://doi.org/10.1016/j.ecolind.2023.110928
20. Weigand, M., Staab, J., Wurm, M., Taubenböck, H.: Spatial and semantic effects of LUCAS samples on fully automated land use/land cover classification in high-resolution Sentinel-2 data. Int. J. Appl. Earth Obs. Geoinf. **88**, 102065 (2020). https://doi.org/10.1016/j.jag.2020.102065
21. Mutanga, O., Kumar, L.: Google earth engine applications. Remote Sens. **11**, 591 (2019). https://doi.org/10.3390/rs11050591
22. Amini, S., Saber, M., Rabiei-Dastjerdi, H., Homayouni, S.: Urban land use and land cover change analysis using random forest classification of Landsat time series. Remote Sens. **14**(11), 2654 (2022). https://doi.org/10.3390/rs14112654
23. Breiman, L.: Random forests. Mach. Learn. **45**, 5–32 (2001). https://doi.org/10.1023/A:1010933404324
24. Belgiu, M., Dragu, L.: Random forest in remote sensing: A review of applications and future directions. ISPRS J. Photogramm. Remote Sens. **114**, 24–31 (2016). https://doi.org/10.1016/j.isprsjprs.2016.01.011
25. Inglada, J., Vincent, A., Arias, M., Tardy, B., Morin, D., Rodes, I.: Operational high-resolution land cover map production at the country scale using satellite image time series. Remote Sens. **9**, 95 (2017). https://doi.org/10.3390/rs9010095
26. Hansen, M.C., Roy, D.P., Lindquist, E., Adusei, B., Justice, C.O., Altstatt, A.: A method for integrating MODIS and Landsat data for systematic monitoring of forest cover and change in the Congo Basin. Remote Sens. Environ. **112**, 2495–2513 (2008). https://doi.org/10.1016/j.rse.2007.11.012
27. Rabiei-Dastjerdi, H., Amini, S., McArdle, G., Homayouni, S.: City-region or city? That is the question: Modelling sprawl in Isfahan using geospatial data and technology. GeoJournal 1–21 (2022). https://doi.org/10.1007/s10708-021-10554-8
28. Liu, C., Frazier, P., Kumar, L.: Comparative assessment of the measures of thematic classification accuracy. Remote Sens. Environ. **107**, 606–616 (2007). https://doi.org/10.1016/j.rse.2006.10.010

Benefits of Low-Cost GIS-Based Tools for Evaluating Ecosystem Services of Urban Green Spaces

Nicholas Fiorentini(✉) and Massimo Rovai

Department of Civil and Industrial Engineering (DICI), The University of Pisa, Largo Lucio Lazzarino 1, 56122 Pisa, Italy
nicholas.fiorentini@ing.unipi.it

Abstract. Integrating urban green spaces is essential for sustainable city planning, providing numerous ecosystem services that enhance urban resilience and quality of life. This study examines the benefits of using low-cost GIS-based tools for evaluating ecosystem services of public and private green areas within urban environments. Specifically, we developed four indicators using QGIS software, leveraging its open-source capabilities and easily accessible data from local authorities and industry professionals. Centimetric high-resolution multispectral orthoimages (4 bands: RGB and Near Infrared, NIR) were utilized to calculate the Normalized Difference Vegetation Index (NDVI). The study area, comprising 50 hectares on the outskirts of Lucca, Italy, was divided into 1-hectare grid cells for detailed analysis. Using NDVI data, we defined the following indicators: 1) Permeable Area (PA), which addresses the capacity of green spaces to manage adverse climatic events like floods, thus correlating directly with urban resilience and recovery functions; 2) Pollutant Removal (PR), which assesses the green areas' efficiency in mitigating urban emissions predominantly from traffic, industrial activities, and residential heating/cooling systems; 3) Heat Island Mitigation (HIM), which evaluates the role of green cover in reducing urban heat islands, particularly in areas with limited arboreal coverage; and 4) Public/Private Green Area Ratio (P-GAR) which explores the nature and distribution of ecosystem services provided by urban green spaces. These indicators, derived from the combined use of NDVI and Land Use/Land Cover data, demonstrate that low-cost GIS tools can facilitate reliable and robust environmental assessments. The results underscore the potential for these tools to aid managers and professionals in conducting comprehensive studies within urbanized areas, thereby informing sustainable urban planning and environmental management strategies.

Keywords: GIS-based tools · Ecosystem Services · Sustainable Urban Planning · Urban Green Spaces · Normalized Difference Vegetation Index (NDVI)

E. Borgogno-Mondino and P. Zamperlin (Eds.): ASITA 2024, CCIS 2463, pp. 207–223, 2025.
https://doi.org/10.1007/978-3-031-91141-5_15

1 Introduction and Motivation

Urban green areas are vital components of sustainable cities, playing a critical role in enhancing environmental quality, public health, and overall urban resilience [1]. These areas, which include parks, gardens, street trees, and other vegetated spaces, offer a wide range of ecosystem services. They contribute to air and water purification [2], climate regulation [3, 4], noise reduction [5], and provide recreational and aesthetic benefits. Furthermore, green spaces foster biodiversity by serving as habitats for various species, thus maintaining ecological balance within urban environments [6].

In the face of accelerating climate change, cities are increasingly adopting Nature-based Solutions (NbS) to address urban challenges [7]. NbS involve the sustainable management and use of nature to tackle socio-environmental issues, promoting biodiversity and improving human well-being [8]. Urban green spaces, as part of NbS, enhance the resilience of cities by mitigating the impacts of climate change, such as extreme heat [9], flooding, and pollution [10]. For instance, green spaces can absorb excess rainwater, reducing the risk of flooding, and provide cooling effects to counteract urban heat islands [11, 12].

Despite their numerous benefits, the planning and management of urban green areas present significant challenges that require careful consideration and strategic approaches. Urban planners must navigate the complexities of balancing competing land uses, such as residential, commercial, and industrial development, with the need to preserve and expand green spaces [13]. As cities grow and densify, green areas are often at risk of being fragmented or reduced, compromising their ability to deliver essential ecosystem services [14]. Fragmentation can lead to isolated green patches that are less effective in supporting biodiversity, regulating climate, or providing recreational spaces [15]. Additionally, the spatial distribution of green areas often varies across different neighbourhoods, leading to inequitable access to these vital resources. Disparities in green space availability can exacerbate social inequalities, with marginalized communities frequently having less access to the environmental and health benefits that green areas provide [16].

Moreover, the effectiveness of green spaces in delivering ecosystem services is not solely dependent on their existence but also on their size, distribution, and connectivity within the urban fabric [12, 17]. Larger, well-connected green areas can support more diverse ecosystems, provide better climate regulation, and offer more significant recreational opportunities. In contrast, small, isolated patches may struggle to deliver the same level of benefits. Connectivity between green spaces is particularly important for maintaining ecological corridors that allow for species movement and genetic exchange, thereby sustaining urban biodiversity [18, 19]. Therefore, ensuring that green areas are adequately sized, strategically distributed, and connected is crucial for maximizing their ecological and social functions.

Given these challenges, urban planners and environmental managers require reliable and detailed information to make informed decisions about the design, implementation, and management of green spaces. Accurate data on the current state of urban green areas, including their vegetation density, species composition, and spatial configuration, is essential for assessing their capacity to provide ecosystem services. This information must be timely and precise, as urban environments are dynamic and subject to rapid changes. However, traditional methods of data acquisition, such as field surveys [20], although accurate and detailed, can be prohibitively expensive and time-consuming, often limiting their use in ongoing urban planning processes.

Consequently, there is an increasing demand for low-cost, yet effective, tools that can deliver the necessary insights without the associated financial and temporal burdens. Geographic Information Systems (GIS) offer a powerful solution, enabling the collection, analysis, and visualization of spatial data, which is critical for the effective planning and management of cities and related green areas [21].

With GIS, planners can integrate various types of spatial data, such as land use, vegetation cover, and topography, to create comprehensive models of urban ecosystems, especially in the current "era of data", where spatial and temporal information, even accurate, are available to land managing bodies. This allows for a more precise understanding of how green spaces function within the urban environment and how they can be optimized to enhance sustainability and resilience of the city.

Furthermore, the use of open-source GIS platforms significantly reduces costs by eliminating the need for expensive proprietary software. These platforms are not only free to use but also supported by a large community of developers and users, who continually improve the software and expand its capabilities. By leveraging these tools, urban planners and researchers can conduct sophisticated spatial analyses, all within a cost-effective and accessible framework. This technology allows for broader participation in urban planning processes, ensuring that even cities and communities with limited resources can benefit from advanced spatial analysis and data-driven decision-making.

With these aspects in mind, the present study aims to propose an operating methodology for evaluating ecosystem services provided by urban green areas using low-cost GIS-based tools. In the framework of the present research, it is worth noting that the term "*low-cost*" refers to an approach that minimizes financial barriers by using open-source GIS, freely available datasets, and limited computational resources. While open-source GIS themselves are free, the term "low-cost" encompasses the broader affordability and accessibility of the methodology for urban planners and researchers with limited budgets.

By focusing on a real case study in the outskirts of the city of Lucca, Central Italy, the study demonstrates how high-resolution multispectral ortho-images (freely available in the whole Region for academic purposes), and the computation of the NDVI can be utilized to derive four key indicators that inform urban green space planning and management. These indicators, computed in QGIS software, include Permeable Area (PA), Pollutant Removal (PR), Heat Island Mitigation (HIM), Public/Private Green Area Ratio (P-GAR). Furthermore, a 1-hectare grid-based approach allows for a structured spatial analysis of urban vegetation, enabling comparative assessments across different urban settings. This methodological framework is scalable and adaptable, making it a valuable tool for urban planners, policymakers, and researchers aiming to enhance urban resilience and sustainability.

Chapter 2 describes the proposed methodology, spanning from data collection to the derivation of the four GIS-based indicators. Chapter 3 outlines the leading findings, emphasizing strengths of the proposed solution. Finally, Chapter 4 wraps up the present study with some concluding remarks.

2 Methodology and Data Collection

2.1 Overview and Data Sources

The methodology for evaluating ecosystem services of urban green areas involves processing high-resolution multispectral ortho-images within a GIS environment (such as QGIS, https://qgis.org/, as in this research) to derive the four GIS-based indicators. This chapter outlines the data sources, processing techniques, and analytical methods used to compute indicators of urban ecosystem services.

The primary data source for this study is high-resolution multispectral ortho-images provided by the Tuscany Region; such images have a Ground Sampling Distance (GSD) of 20 cm x 20 cm and include four spectral bands: Red, Green, Blue (RGB), and Near-Infrared (NIR). The high spatial and spectral resolution of these images allows for detailed analysis of vegetation cover and condition at a sub-meter scale. In addition to the ortho-images, land use and land cover (LULC) data were obtained from Tuscany Region through the open-data regional Geoscope, a web-GIS platform incorporating morphologic, hydro-geomorphologic, social, orographic, and topographic data (https://www502.regione.toscana.it/geoscopio/cartoteca.html). LULC data provides information on the types of land use and the distribution of different land cover classes within the study area. In the framework of the present research, LULC data is essential for interpreting the orthoimages and determining which green areas belong to the public spaces and which ones to the private spaces.

2.2 Study Area

The study area is located on the outskirts of Lucca, Italy, covering 50 hectares. To facilitate detailed analysis, the area was divided into a grid of 1-hectare cells. This grid-based approach enables a systematic assessment of the spatial variation in ecosystem services across the study area, allowing to compute the GIS-based indicators within each cell of the grid.

2.3 NDVI Calculation and Derivation of Indicators

The four GIS-based indicators developed within the present research rely on the Normalized Difference Vegetation Index (NDVI) parameter. NDVI is a widely used vegetation index in remote sensing and GIS applications [22–24]. It utilizes the reflectance of light

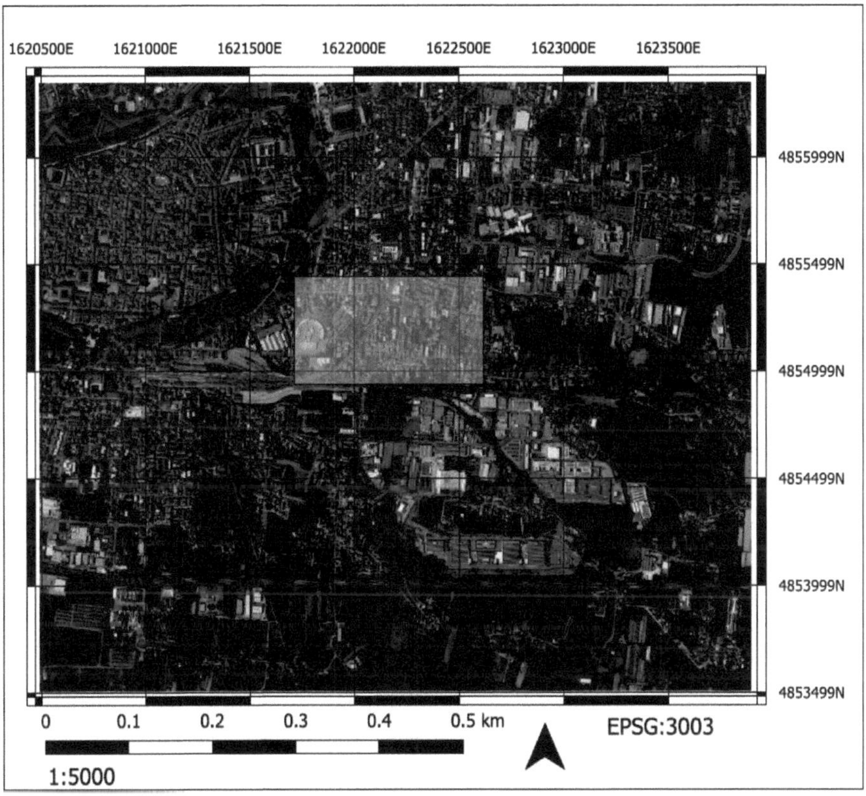

(a)

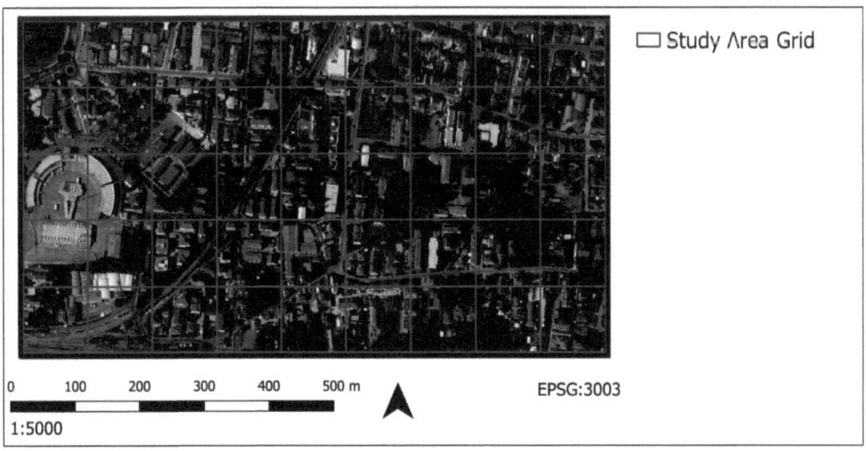

(b)

Fig. 1. Study area: (a) Extension of a high-definition orthoimage with the City of Lucca, Tuscany Region, Italy, on the top-left side of the orthoimage. The red rectangle represents the investigated study area; (b) investigated study area extended for 50 hectares and a overlapping grid (with solid blue lines)

in the RED and NIR wavelengths to assess vegetation health and density. NDVI can be computed using Eq. (1):

$$NDVI = \frac{NIR - RED}{NIR + RED} \tag{1}$$

NDVI values range from -1 to 1, where higher values indicate denser and healthier vegetation, while lower values correspond to sparse vegetation or poor vegetation health. This index is commonly applied to monitor vegetation growth, detect changes over time, and analyze land cover.

Using the NDVI values and LULC data, four GIS-based indicators have been developed to assess the ecosystem services provided by urban private and public green areas. They have been defined as follows:

1. *Permeable Area Indicator*: The PA Indicator measures the proportion of the study area covered by vegetation that can absorb rainwater and mitigate flooding. It is calculated by identifying areas with NDVI values above a certain threshold, indicating vegetated surfaces, as in Eq. 2:

$$PA = \frac{Area\,with\,NDVI > threshold_{PA}}{Total\,Area} \cdot 100 \tag{2}$$

where *Area* refers to the area of 1 hectare of each cell of the grid (indeed, the PA is computed for each cell), and $threshold_{PA}$ is equal to 0.35

2. *Pollutant Removal Indicator*: The PR indicator estimates the capacity of green areas to remove pollutants from the air. It is based on the relationship between vegetation density (indicated by NDVI) and pollutant removal efficiency, as in Eq. 3:

$$PR = \frac{Area\,with\,NDVI > threshold_{PR}}{Total\,Area} \cdot 100 \tag{3}$$

where *Area* refers to the area of 1 hectare of each cell of the grid (indeed, the PA is computed for each cell), and $threshold_{PR}$ is equal to 0.6.

3. *Heat Island Mitigation Indicator*: The HIM Indicator evaluates the potential of green areas to reduce urban heat island effects. The indicator is calculated as in Eq. 4:

$$HIM = \frac{\frac{Perimeter\,of\,tree\,species}{Area\,of\,tree\,species}}{100 - Permeable\,Areas} \tag{4}$$

where areas and perimeters of *tree species* are identified with NDVI greater than 0.6, and *Permeable Areas* are those areas with NDVI greater than 0.35. We considered the ratio between perimeter and area of tree species since a high ratio reflects an area with a well-distributed and spread vegetation cover (high perimeter), while a low ratio reflects an area with a clustered vegetation cover. In the denominator of Eq. 4 we considered the complement of the percentage of Permeable Areas (i.e., the factor $100 - Permeable\,Areas$), in order to obtain high HIM in the case in which the extension of green spaces within the analyzed cell is high. On the contrary, if the vegetation is also well spread but its extension is limited, the calculation $100 - Permeable\,Areas$ will be high and, therefore, a low HIM will result.

4. *Public/Private Green Area Ratio Indicator*: The P-GAR indicator assesses the distribution of green areas between public and private ownership and, therefore, provides information on the different contribution that private owners and public bodies make in furnishing ecosystem services, in order to implement more effective policies. It has been used LULC data to classify public and private green areas and calculates the ratio as in Eq. 5:

$$P - GAR = \frac{areas\ of\ public\ green\ spaces}{areas\ of\ private\ green\ spaces} \cdot 100 \quad (5)$$

where *public* and *private* areas are identified by the LULC data, and *greenspaces* are those with NDVI greater than 0.6. A P-GAR indicator value greater than 100 indicates a prevalence of public green spaces and, vice versa, if the value is less than 100, indicates a prevalence of private green spaces.

3 Results and Discussion

3.1 NDVI Computation

The NDVI analysis of the study area (Fig. 2), encompassing 50 hectares on the outskirts of Lucca, Italy, revealed significant spatial variability in vegetation density and distribution.

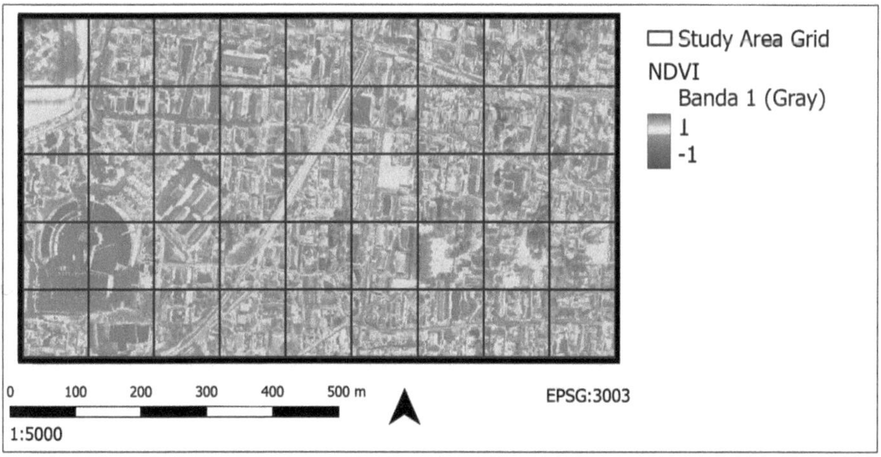

Fig. 2. Computation of NDVI within the Study Area.

High NDVI values, close to 1, were observed in regions with dense vegetation, such as parks and large green spaces, indicating healthy and vigorous plant life. Conversely, NDVI values near 0 were recorded in urbanized areas with little to no vegetation, such as roads, buildings, and other impervious surfaces. Importantly, the study area did not register NDVI values indicative of water bodies (close to -1).

4 GIS-Based Indicators

As stated in chapter 2, the PA indicator was defined using a threshold NDVI value of 0.35, as determined by in-situ surveys. This threshold effectively differentiated vegetated areas capable of absorbing rainwater from non-permeable surfaces. The results, visualized in Fig. 3, show the spatial distribution of permeable areas within the study grid.

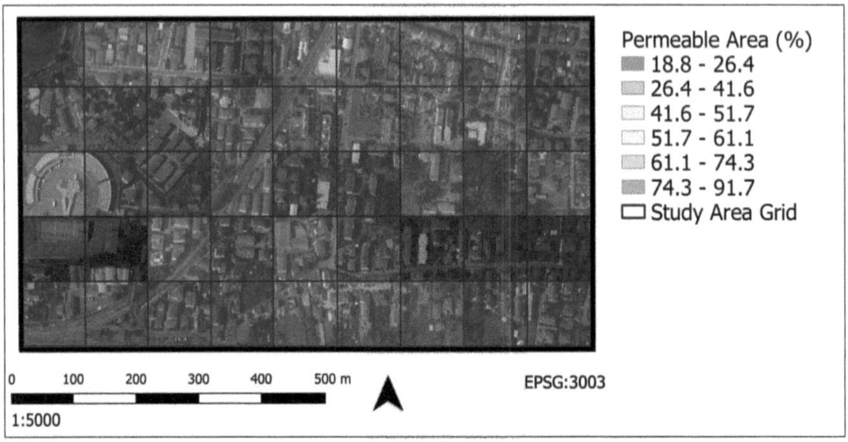

Fig. 3. Permeable Area indicator.

It is possible to observe green spaces, i.e., those regions corresponding to areas with NDVI values above 0.35, indicating significant vegetation cover capable of water infiltration, and urbanized areas, i.e., those spaces with NDVI values below 0.35, predominantly corresponding to non-permeable surfaces such as asphalt, buildings, and cemented urban environment.

Generally speaking, the analysis identified that the average PA of the study area is 56.4%, suggesting that the whole study area has a moderate capacity to manage stormwater and mitigate flood risks. Also, it can be observed that the east part of the study areas has a higher PR respect to the west one. Although in both cases there are mainly residential areas, the eastern part shows a greater capacity for water permeability in case of rain (greater presence of private gardens, greater presence of public parks, etc.). Further descriptive statistics are provided at the end of the present subsection in Table 1.

The PR indicator was determined using a higher NDVI threshold of 0.6, targeting areas with dense vegetation known for their effectiveness in air pollutant removal. Figure 4 illustrates the distribution of these high NDVI zones.

This indicator provides valuable insights into the green areas' efficiency in mitigating urban emissions, particularly those from traffic, industrial activities, and residential heating/cooling systems. By understanding pollutant removal capabilities, urban planners and environmental professionals can make informed decisions to enhance air quality and promote sustainable urban development.

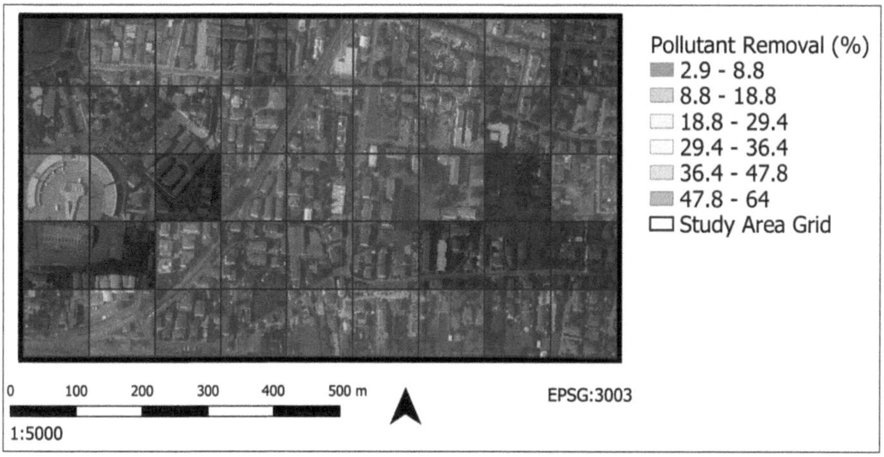

Fig. 4. Pollutant Removal indicator.

It is possible to observe both dense vegetated spaces, i.e., those areas with NDVI values above 0.6, indicating dense vegetation with high pollutant removal capacity, and, conversely, less vegetated spaces, i.e., those areas with NDVI values below 0.6, which are less effective in removing air pollutants.

Approximately the average PR of the study area is 32.1%, highlighting a moderate potential of these green spaces to contribute to urban air quality improvement. Similar to what is observed in Fig. 3, the study area shows substantial differences between the east and west zones. In the former, the highest PR values are recorded, up to about 65%, while in the latter, the lowest (within the cells containing the city squares), whose PR value is around 3%. This clear distinction of PR would suggest that there may be a different air quality within the study area; additional data and in-depth analysis could validate this hypothesis. Further descriptive statistics are provided at the end of the present subsection in Table 1.

The HIM indicator allows for assessing the spread and distribution of green spaces, which are critical for mitigating urban heat islands. The results are presented in Fig. 5.

As HIM has been defined in Eq. 4, the areas with a high HIM represent spaces with a high perimeter-to-area ratio and, concurrently, extensive vegetation cover; such high values indicate widely spread vegetation that can effectively dissipate heat islands. Conversely, areas with a low HIM represent areas with a low perimeter-to-area ratio or with low vegetation cover extension, where vegetation is more clustered and less effective in spreading the cooling effect.

The average HIM for the study area was found to be 0.017, suggesting that the green spaces, while present within the study area, are not adequate and satisfactory to face heat islands. These areas could benefit from more strategic spatial distribution to maximize HIM. Figure 5 shows that higher HIM values are located next to the public green spaces (considering also Fig. 6 below), despite their limited presence within the study area compared to private ones; this aspect indicates that public green spaces are essential in urban areas to mitigate heat islands, since their shape are specifically designed to

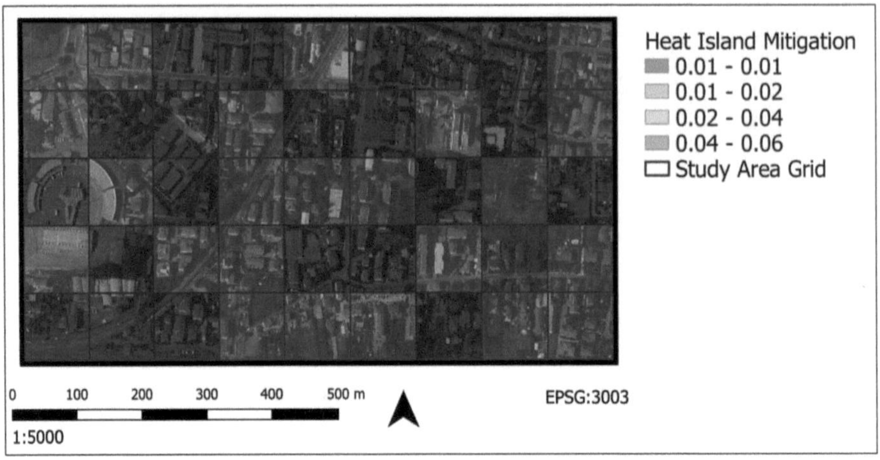

Fig. 5. Heat Island Mitigation indicator.

address also this issue. Public green areas are often larger, more widely distributed, and contain a greater diversity of large, healthy tree species, making them more effective in cooling the urban environment. Further descriptive statistics are provided at the end of the present subsection in Table 1.

Finally, the P-GAR indicator assessed the distribution of green spaces between public and private ownership. Public green areas spaces are publicly accessible, such as parks and recreational areas, whereas private ones are vegetated areas within private properties, including residential gardens and commercial green spaces. This analysis is crucial for understanding the accessibility and equitable distribution of urban green spaces within the urban environment of a city. Figure 6 illustrates the P-GAR indicator within the study grid.

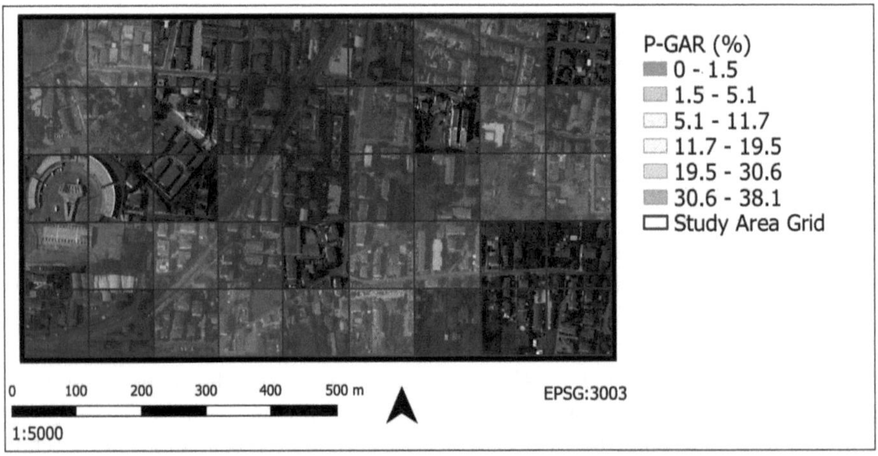

Fig. 6. Public/Private Green Area Ratio indicator.

The study found an average public to private green area ratio of 7.83% (excluding areas with no presence of public green spaces), indicating a heavy predominance of private green spaces. In the framework of the present study area, there is a significant lack of accessibility and equitable distribution of urban green spaces; only small portions of the study area have direct access to public green spaces. Furthermore, within the 1-hectare cells, there are areas that do not have public green spaces, emphasizing this criticality (Fig. 7). It is worth noting that private green areas contribute significantly to the ecosystem services related to permeability and pollutant removal. Nonetheless, as observed, private green spaces are not suitable to address heat islands.

Further descriptive statistics of P-GAR are provided in Table 1 below, along with those of PA, PR, and HIM indicators; it shows the descriptive statistics, reporting the mean, standard deviation, minimum and maximum values, the median, and the mode.

Table 1. Descriptive statistics of GIS-based indicators*

	PA	PR	HIM	P-GAR
Mean	56.4	32.1	0.017	7.83
St. Deviation	15.4	14.3	0.095	9.5
Median	56.4	32.7	0.020	3.3
Mode	67.8	42.3	0.01	0.02
Minimum	18.8	2.9	0.01	0
Maximum	91.7	64.0	0.06	38.1

* unit of measure of PA, PR, P-GAR is percentage [%], whereas HIM is unitless.

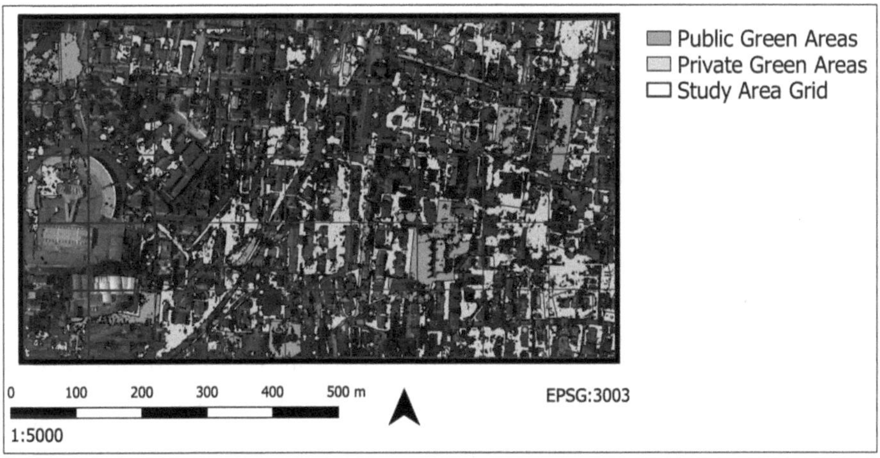

Fig. 7. Public and Private Green Areas

Table 1 provides further useful insights for comprehensively assessing an urban space. For instance, the PA indicator, with a mean of 56.4%, indicates that just over half of the study area consists of permeable surfaces, crucial for stormwater management. The standard deviation of 15.4% suggests a moderate variation in permeability across the area, while the median (56.4%) matches the mean, reflecting a fairly uniform distribution of permeable surfaces. Notably, the mode is higher (67.8%), pointing to the presence of multiple zones with relatively high permeability.

As for the PR indicator, the mean value of 32.1% indicates that nearly a third of the study area has dense vegetation with strong potential for air pollutant removal. The standard deviation of 14.3% shows some variability in the pollutant removal capacity, and the mode of 42.3% suggests that areas with substantial pollutant removal potential are not rare, though there are also zones with much lower capacity, as indicated by the minimum value of 2.9%.

The HIM indicator, with a mean value of 0.017, highlights the overall modest effectiveness of the green spaces in the study area for mitigating urban heat islands. The high standard deviation of 0.095 suggests considerable variability in this capacity, with some areas performing much better than others (i.e., there is an overdispersion of the HIM around the mean). The mode of 0.01 indicates that many areas have minimal heat island mitigation capacity, reflecting the fragmented or clustered nature of vegetation in most of the study area.

Finally, the P-GAR indicator has a mean of 7.83%, clearly pointing to a significant predominance of private green spaces. The high standard deviation of 9.5% and the wide range between the minimum (0%) and maximum (38.1%) values reveal substantial variability in the distribution of public versus private green areas across the study site. The low median value of 3.3% and mode of 0.02% further emphasize the limited presence of public green spaces, underscoring the challenge of ensuring broad community access to green areas.

Table 1 further underscore the diverse conditions within the study area and highlight the importance of tailored urban planning strategies to enhance ecosystem services, particularly in enhancing permeability, improving air quality, mitigating heat islands, and ensuring equitable access to green spaces.

Considering the outcomes of the present analysis, we suggest urban planners to focus on increasing the proportion of permeable surfaces within cities to improve stormwater management and reduce flood risks. This can be achieved through the creation of more green spaces and the implementation of green infrastructure, such as green roofs and permeable pavements. Moreover, to enhance air quality, efforts should be made to increase the density of urban vegetation. This includes planting more trees and maintaining existing green spaces to ensure they remain healthy and effective in pollutant removal. In this sense, for example, the public could provide specific incentives to encourage the involvement of private properties in the creation and management of green areas. Furthermore, the spatial distribution of green spaces should be strategically planned to maximize their cooling effects and mitigate urban heat islands. Large, well-distributed public green spaces with diverse tree species are particularly effective in this regard. Finally, while private green areas contribute significantly to urban ecosystem services, public green spaces are essential for ensuring equitable access to greenery and providing communal benefits. Policies should encourage the development and maintenance of both public and private green areas.

4.1 Future Developments

This study demonstrates the effectiveness of low-cost GIS-based tools for evaluating ecosystem services in urban green spaces. However, further research is needed to enhance the proposed methodology. One key improvement is the development of a WebGIS application, which could provide urban planners, policymakers, and researchers with a more accessible and interactive platform [25–27]. While the present study focused on a standalone GIS-based approach to ensure ease of implementation without additional infrastructure, integrating WebGIS would allow for real-time visualization, data sharing, and broader accessibility. Future work should explore the feasibility of developing a WebGIS platform using free and open-source software (FOSS) to maximize user-friendliness and reach a wider audience [28–31].

Additionally, as discussed previously, this study used a 1-hectare grid-based approach to compute and analyze ecosystem service indicators. While this grid size provided a structured framework for analysis, it should be also important to investigate how different grid cell sizes and shapes may influence results [32–34]. The finer spatial resolution of orthoimages could allow for more localized assessments, while coarser grid sizes might provide a broader perspective suitable for regional planning.

Furthermore, validation of findings with in-situ measurements is a crucial step to improving accuracy. While NDVI-based assessments are widely accepted, incorporating ground-truth data could refine the reliability of indicators.

Moreover, integrating temporal data analysis could offer insights into long-term trends in urban green space dynamics. A time-series approach could help identify seasonal variations of the developed indicators, long-term vegetation health trends (identified by NDVI variations [35, 36]), and the effectiveness of urban greening policies over time.

Finally, another crucial aspect for future research is the economic valuation of green spaces, with the aim of supporting Cost-Benefit Analyses (CBA) with specific consideration of ecosystem services [37–39]. Accordingly, public institutions and local managing bodies could leverage this methodology to quantify the economic value of transforming urban areas into green spaces through regeneration projects [40], ensuring that investments in NbS are data-driven and aligned with strategic urban planning objectives.

5 Conclusions

This study presented a comprehensive methodology for evaluating the ecosystem services provided by urban green areas using low-cost GIS-based tools. By leveraging high-resolution multispectral ortho-images and open-source software (QGIS), we developed four key indicators—Permeable Area, Pollutant Removal, Heat Island Mitigation, and Public/Private Green Area Ratio—aimed at assessing the ecological contributions of urban greenery.

Outcomes from our analysis of the 50-hectare study area on the outskirts of Lucca, Italy, highlights the significant potential of using low-cost GIS-based tools to assess and enhance the ecosystem services provided by urban green areas. By offering reliable and detailed insights into vegetation distribution and its ecological functions, the methodology supports informed decision-making and promotes sustainable urban development.

As cities continue to grow and face the challenges of climate change, the integration of such tools into urban planning practices is crucial for creating resilient and liveable urban environments.

Acknowledgments. The authors sincerely thank Tuscany Region for providing ortho-images of the study area (Fig. 1a) free of charge and LULC information.

Author Contribution. Nicholas Fiorentini: Conceptualization, Data Curation, Formal Analysis, Investigation, Methodology, Resources, Software, Validation, Visualization, Writing – Original Draft, Writing – Review & Editing. Massimo Rovai: Conceptualization, Funding Acquisition, Methodology, Project Administration, Resources, Supervision, Validation, Writing – Review & Editing.

Disclosure of Interests. The authors have no competing interests to declare that are relevant to the content of this article.

References

1. Jabbar, M., Yusoff, M.M., Shafie, A.: Assessing the role of urban green spaces for human well-being: a systematic review (2022). https://doi.org/10.1007/s10708-021-10474-7
2. Russo, A., Cirella, G.T.: Urban ecosystem services: advancements in urban green. Development (2023). https://doi.org/10.3390/land12030522
3. Baró, F., Chaparro, L., Gómez-Baggethun, E., Langemeyer, J., Nowak, D.J., Terradas, J.: Contribution of ecosystem services to air quality and climate change mitigation policies: The case of urban forests in Barcelona, Spain. Ambio. **43**, (2014). https://doi.org/10.1007/s13280-014-0507-x
4. Kumar, A., Ekka, P., Upreti, M., Shilky, Saikia, P.: Urban green spaces for environmental sustainability and climate resilience. In: The Palgrave Handbook of Socio-ecological Resilience in the Face of Climate Change (2023). https://doi.org/10.1007/978-981-99-2206-2_23
5. Wickramathilaka, N., Ujang, U., Azri, S., Choon, T.L.: Influence of urban green spaces on road traffic noise levels: - a review. In: International Archives of the Photogrammetry, Remote Sensing and Spatial Information Sciences - ISPRS Archives (2022). https://doi.org/10.5194/isprs-archives-XLVIII-4-W3-2022-195-2022
6. Blessing Aibhamen, E.: Urban green spaces and their impact on environmental health: a global review. World Journal of Advanced Research and Reviews. **21**, (2024). https://doi.org/10.30574/wjarr.2024.21.2.0518
7. Sturiale, L., Scuderi, A., Timpanaro, G.: Citizens' perception of the role of urban nature-based solutions and green infrastructures towards climate change in Italy. Front Environ Sci. **11** (2023). https://doi.org/10.3389/fenvs.2023.1105446
8. Salmond, J.A., et al.: Health and climate related ecosystem services provided by street trees in the urban environment (2016). https://doi.org/10.1186/s12940-016-0103-6

9. Marando, F., Salvatori, E., Sebastiani, A., Fusaro, L., Manes, F.: Regulating ecosystem services and green infrastructure: assessment of urban heat island effect mitigation in the municipality of Rome. Italy. Ecol Modell. **392**, 92–102 (2019). https://doi.org/10.1016/j.ecolmodel.2018.11.011
10. Pamukcu-Albers, P., Ugolini, F., La Rosa, D., Grădinaru, S.R., Azevedo, J.C., Wu, J.: Building green infrastructure to enhance urban resilience to climate change and pandemics (2021). https://doi.org/10.1007/s10980-021-01212-y
11. Nyelele, C., Kroll, C.N., Nowak, D.J.: Present and future ecosystem services of trees in the Bronx. NY. Urban For Urban Green. **42**, 10–20 (2019). https://doi.org/10.1016/j.ufug.2019.04.018
12. Song, P., Kim, G., Mayer, A., He, R., Tian, G.: Assessing the ecosystem services of various types of urban green spaces based on I-Tree Eco. Sustainability (Switzerland). 12, (2020). https://doi.org/10.3390/su12041630
13. Moilanen, A., et al.: Balancing alternative land uses in conservation prioritization. Ecological Applications. 21, (2011). https://doi.org/10.1890/10-1865.1
14. Pezzagno, M., Frigione, B.M., Ferreira, C.S.S.: Reading urban green morphology to enhance urban resilience: a case study of six southern European cities. Sustainability (Switzerland). 13, (2021). https://doi.org/10.3390/su13169163
15. Misiune, I., Kazys, J.: Accessibility to and fragmentation of urban green infrastructure: importance for adaptation to climate change. In: Human-Nature Interactions (2022). https://doi.org/10.1007/978-3-031-01980-7_19
16. Wen, M., Zhang, X., Harris, C.D., Holt, J.B., Croft, J.B.: Spatial disparities in the distribution of parks and green spaces in the USA. Annals of Behavioral Medicine. **45** (2013). https://doi.org/10.1007/s12160-012-9426-x
17. Alexandre Castanho, R., et al.: Assessing ecosystem services delivered by public green spaces in major european cities. In: Landscape Architecture - Processes and Practices Towards Sustainable Development (2021). https://doi.org/10.5772/intechopen.91415
18. Salviano, I.R., Gardon, F.R., dos Santos, R.F.: Ecological corridors and landscape planning: a model to select priority areas for connectivity maintenance. Landsc Ecol. **36** (2021). https://doi.org/10.1007/s10980-021-01305-8
19. Lovell, S.T., Taylor, J.R.: Supplying urban ecosystem services through multifunctional green infrastructure in the United States. Landsc Ecol. **28**, (2013). https://doi.org/10.1007/s10980-013-9912-y
20. Aleixo, C., et al.: Urban Green Connectivity Assessment: a comparative study of datasets in European Cities. Remote Sens (Basel). **16**, (2024). https://doi.org/10.3390/rs16050771
21. Pouya, S., Aghlmand, M.: Evaluation of urban green space per capita with new remote sensing and geographic information system techniques and the importance of urban green space during the COVID-19 pandemic. Environ Monit Assess. **194** (2022). https://doi.org/10.1007/s10661-022-10298-z
22. Fiorentini, N., Bacco, M., Ferrari, A., Rovai, M., Brunori, G.: Remote sensing and machine learning for riparian vegetation detection and classification. In: 2023 IEEE International Workshop on Metrology for Agriculture and Forestry, MetroAgriFor 2023 - Proceedings. pp. 369–374. Institute of Electrical and Electronics Engineers Inc. (2023). https://doi.org/10.1109/MetroAgriFor58484.2023.10424205
23. Zhao, Z., Dai, E.: Vegetation cover dynamics and its constraint effect on ecosystem services on the Qinghai-Tibet Plateau under ecological restoration projects. J Environ Manage. **356** (2024). https://doi.org/10.1016/j.jenvman.2024.120535
24. Spahr, K.M., Bell, C.D., McCray, J.E., Hogue, T.S.: Greening up stormwater infrastructure: Measuring vegetation to establish context and promote cobenefits in a diverse set of US cities. Urban For Urban Green. 48, (2020). https://doi.org/10.1016/j.ufug.2019.126548

25. Mathiyalagan, V., Grunwald, S., Reddy, K.R., Bloom, S.A.: A WebGIS and geodatabase for Florida's wetlands. Comput Electron Agric. **47** (2005). https://doi.org/10.1016/j.compag.2004.08.003
26. Mallinis, G., et al.: A national scale web mapping platform for mainstreaming ecosystem services in Greece. Ecol Inform. **78**, (2023). https://doi.org/10.1016/j.ecoinf.2023.102349
27. Polderman, A., Vurunić, S., Houbé, N., Bender, O., Haller, A.: WebGIS for communicating alpine ecosystem services: Stakeholder engagement in Slovenian protected areas. Eco Mont. **12**, (2020). https://doi.org/10.1553/eco.mont-12-1s55
28. Brovelli, M.A., Minghini, M., Giori, G., Beretta, M.: Web Geoservices and Ancient Cadastral Maps: The Web C.A.R.T.E. Project. Transactions in GIS. **16**, (2012). https://doi.org/10.1111/j.1467-9671.2012.01311.x
29. Bachri, S., et al.: FOSS (Free Open Source Software) Integration to Implement WebGIS-Based Information System of Kelud Volcano. In: IOP Conference Series: Earth and Environmental Science (2022). https://doi.org/10.1088/1755-1315/1066/1/012010
30. Akbari, M., Peikar, S.R.H.: Evaluation of free/open source software using OSMM model case study: WebGIS and Spatial Database. Adv. Comput. Sci.: An Int. J. **3** (2014)
31. Belcore, E., Angeli, S., Colucci, E., Musci, M.A., Aicardi, I.: Precision agriculture workflow, from data collection to data management using FOSS tools: An application in Northern Italy vineyard. ISPRS Int J Geoinf. **10** (2021). https://doi.org/10.3390/ijgi10040236
32. Zhou, L., et al.: Multiscale perspective research on the evolution characteristics of the ecosystem services supply-demand relationship in the chongqing section of the three gorges reservoir area. Ecol. Indic. **142**, (2022). https://doi.org/10.1016/j.ecolind.2022.109227
33. Vidal, D.G., Fernandes, C.O., Viterbo, L.M.F., Vilaça, H., Barros, N., Maia, R.L.: Combining an evaluation grid application to assess ecosystem services of urban green spaces and a socioeconomic spatial analysis. Int. J. Sustain. Develop. World Ecol. **28**, (2021). https://doi.org/10.1080/13504509.2020.1808108
34. Zhou, X., Ma, M., Chen, Q., Qi, W., Gao, Y., Cui, J.: Uneven distribution of ecosystem services along the yarlung zangbo river basin in Tibet reveals the quest for multi-target policies of rural development in less-favored areas. Land (Basel). 11, (2022). https://doi.org/10.3390/land11111961
35. Krishnaswamy, J., Bawa, K.S., Ganeshaiah, K.N., Kiran, M.C.: Quantifying and mapping biodiversity and ecosystem services: utility of a multi-season NDVI based Mahalanobis distance surrogate. Remote Sens Environ. **113**, (2009). https://doi.org/10.1016/j.rse.2008.12.011
36. Xi, H., Cui, W., Cai, L., Chen, M., Xu, C.: Spatiotemporal evolution characteristics of ecosystem service values based on NDVI changes in island cities. IEEE Access. **9**, (2021). https://doi.org/10.1109/ACCESS.2021.3051244
37. Saarikoski, H., et al.: Multi-criteria decision analysis and cost-benefit analysis: comparing alternative frameworks for integrated valuation of ecosystem services. Ecosyst Serv. **22**, (2016). https://doi.org/10.1016/j.ecoser.2016.10.014
38. Li, M., Liu, S., Wang, F., Liu, H., Liu, Y., Wang, Q.: Cost-benefit analysis of ecological restoration based on land use scenario simulation and ecosystem service on the Qinghai-Tibet Plateau. Glob Ecol. Conserv. **34** (2022). https://doi.org/10.1016/j.gecco.2022.e02006

39. Cao, S., Yu, Z., Zhang, J., Feng, F., Xu, D., Mu, X.: Cost–benefit analysis of ecosystem services in China. Ecol Eng. **125**, (2018). https://doi.org/10.1016/j.ecoleng.2018.10.022
40. Fiorentini, N., Mariotti, D., Rovai, M.: Defining risk curves in feasibility analyses of urban regeneration projects with Monte Carlo method. Valori e Valutazioni. **2024**, 149–170 (2024). https://doi.org/10.48264/VVSIEV-20243609

Dynamics Between Population Distribution and Location of Services: The Case Study of Desio Town, Italy

Manuel Garramone(✉) and Marco Scaioni

Department of Architecture, Built Environment and Construction Engineering, Politecnico di Milano, Via Ponzio 31, 20133 Milano, Italy
{manuel.garramone,marco.scaioni}@polimi.it

Abstract. As global concerns about public health and environmental sustainability increase, urban planners and decision-makers are developing new policies to encourage both active and public transportation habits. Alternatives to private car transport provide important benefits, such as reducing carbon emissions and traffic congestion and enhancing physical fitness and mental well-being. Under this premise, during the last few years, the '15-Minute City' concept has evolved around the urban configuration that distributes functions to optimise people's time travel related to basic activities. Building on the idea of chrono-urbanism, this city model provides that the fundamental functions of living (e.g., employment, education, healthcare, entertainment, and commerce) are concentrated within a radius of 15 min on foot or by bicycle, integrating the dimensions of density, proximity, diversity, and digitalisation. Starting from a bibliometric analysis about the research topic, this study proposes an approach to analyse the dynamics between population distribution and services location in Desio, north of Italy. The authors conducted studies on georeferenced population and network analysis to frame the current state and to use it as a basis for planning new actions.

Keywords: 15-Minute City · Geospatial Data · Human Mobility · Network Analysis · Population Distribution

1 Introduction

Urban planning has recently witnessed a paradigm shift towards more sustainable and human-centred models [1]. Among the most prominent concepts is the '15-Minute city', which proposes that essential services – such as healthcare, education, work, leisure, and retail – should be accessible within a 15-min walk/bike ride from every resident's home [2]. This idea responds to the growing need for cities to address issues such as congestion, pollution, and time poverty.

The '15-Minute city' model promotes localised living, reducing car dependence, cutting greenhouse gas emissions, and fostering vibrant communities where people can interact more easily [3]. Moreover, this model encourages mixed-use urban development, where residential, commercial, and public spaces are mixed-up together to enhance

E. Borgogno-Mondino and P. Zamperlin (Eds.): ASITA 2024, CCIS 2463, pp. 224–233, 2025.
https://doi.org/10.1007/978-3-031-91141-5_16

quality of life. In this way, the '15-Minute city' supports environmental sustainability and social equity, offering everyone access to urban services, regardless of the individual socioeconomic status [4].

Alongside the concept of the '15-Minute city,' 'chrono-urbanism' introduces a temporal dimension to urban planning. "Chrono-urbanism" focuses on how time is distributed and experienced in urban spaces [5]. It seeks to optimise the city's rhythm by addressing temporal inequalities and ensuring that urban environments align better with their residents' daily schedules and needs [6].

Both the '15-Minute city' and 'chrono-urbanism' share a common goal: to make urban life more efficient, equitable, and enjoyable [7]. These frameworks challenge traditional urban planning paradigms that prioritise vehicular traffic and economic output over human well-being. By rethinking spatial and temporal dynamics, cities may become more resilient, adaptable, and sustainable in the face of global challenges such as climate change, economic inequality, and public health crises [8].

Starting from a bibliometric analysis focused on the research topic, this study proposes an approach to analyze the dynamics between population distribution and services location in the town of Desio, north of Italy. The authors conducted studies on georeferenced population and network analysis to frame the current state and to use it as a basis for planning new actions.

2 Bibliometric Analysis

A literature overview was accomplished to analyze publications about '15-Minute city' and 'Chrono Urbanism' concepts. It allows to comprehend the dynamics of the specific knowledge domain as well as to identifying trends, gaps and future development.

2.1 Method

As a first step, specific keywords related to the research topic were used to query the Scopus database. The research was conducted in August 2024. Figure 1 shows the research process, starting from the search code to the filtering phases (by subject area, publication stage, language, document type, and completeness of bibliometric data).

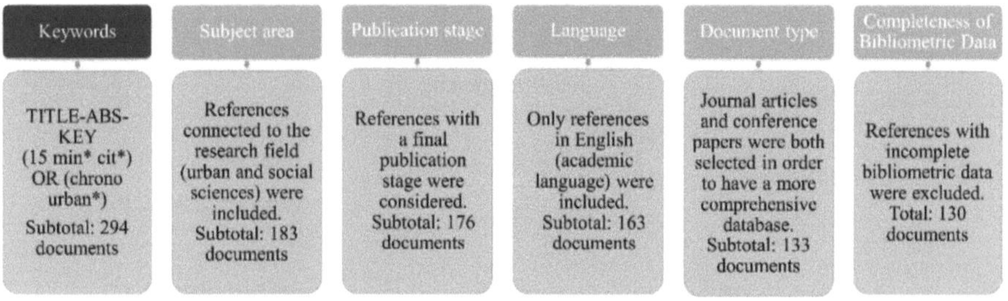

Fig. 1. Research process for the literature overview.

The bibliometric analysis was carried out using the web-based data analysis framework Biblioshiny for Bibliometrix [9] and the visualisation software VOSviewier, version 1.6.16 [10].

2.2 Results

The final selection of 130 documents was published by 414 authors, who provided a total of 473 keywords.

The publication timespan (2015:2024) highlights that the research topic is scientifically analysed over a few years. The annual production shows a consistently growing trend in the last five years, with a significant increase in the number of publications from 2021 and a peak in 2023, when 41 references were published. The annual growth rate of 153.04% (excluding the current year, which has not finished yet) confirms the growing interest in this topic.

2.2.1 Words Analysis

Before starting with the analysis, similar keywords have been checked out and aggregated to improve the method (e.g., '15-Minute city' includes '15-Minute city,' '15-Minute cities,' '15 Minute cities,' etc.). The main keyword used in the search query (i.e., '15-Minute City') ranked on the top as expected, followed by 'accessibility' and 'sustainability'. In addition, the presence of 'walkability,' 'proximity,' and 'mobility' indicates that there is a great attention to these themes into the 'urban planning' and 'public space' domain. A special mention must go to 'Covid-19', which has represented a source of great reflection and debate about population distribution and urban management.

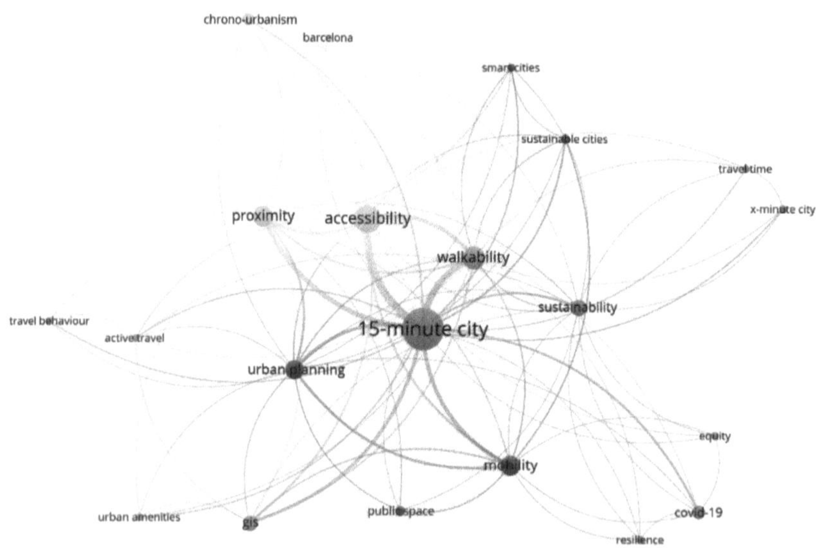

Fig. 2. Keywords co-occurrence network (conceptual network).

To complete the keywords' analysis, a co-occurrence network was implemented to highlight connections and elements about the concept of '15-Minute city.'

The network was generated by conducting density-based spatial clustering using the full counting method [11]. The minimum frequency of keyword occurrences was set at three, and a network with four clusters was created (see Fig. 2). This layout visually illustrates the connections between keywords, emphasising which terms are more frequent and how strongly they are linked within the dataset.

The most relevant cluster (red) rotates around the core concept of '15-Minute city,' which presents a strong connection with 'sustainability' and 'Covid-19,' highlighting the need for new urban post-pandemic scenarios. The second cluster (green), led by 'GIS,' is more related to walkability and travel behaviour, while the third cluster (blue) led by 'urban planning' is more focused on city efficiency ('smart,' 'sustainable cities' and 'mobility'). The last cluster (yellow) concerns the concepts of 'accessibility' and 'proximity.'

3 The Case Study

The '15-Minute city' concept was tested on the town of Desio (see Fig. 3), in the Italian region of Lombardy. It has an extension of approx. 14 km^2 and a total population of a little more than 40 thousand people.

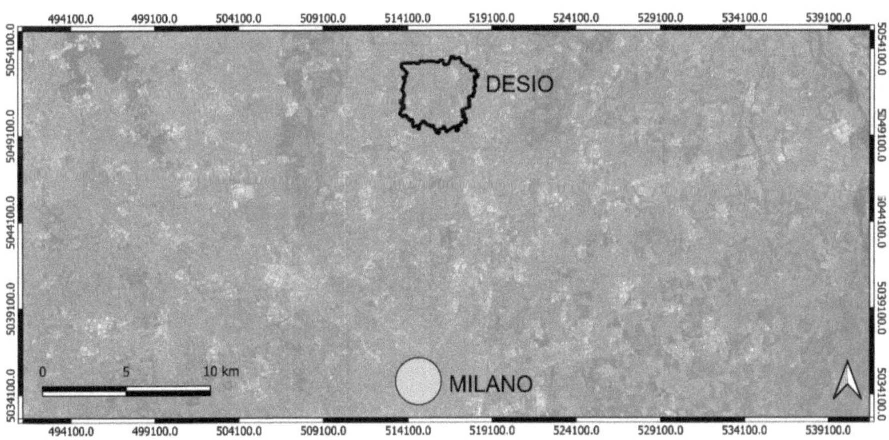

Fig. 3. Location of the study area, Desio, with respect to the capital of Lombardy, Milano (background map from Google®).

The open-source desktop GIS software QGIS, version 3.34 [12], was used to carry out the analysis.

3.1 Quantitative Data and Demographic Characteristics of the Population

Population analysis provides an essential overview for understanding the composition and structure of a society. The study was conducted based on a set of data and information regarding the population of the municipality of desio, aimed at providing a detailed demographic and spatial analysis. The initial data, some of which required preliminary processing, were sourced and organised as follows:

- *population extraction from the Municipal Registry*: the primary source of data was the population register [13], which was queried on June 30, 2023. This dataset included demographic information such as the date of birth and residential address of each individual, specified by street name and house identifier;
- *georeferenced mapping of house identifier*: to achieve spatial precision in the analysis, house numbers were georeferenced and stored in a SHP file (Shapefile format) that contained point elements representing each address. This step allowed for the accurate spatial mapping of the population, facilitating analyses related to population density, spatial distribution, and proximity to various public services and infrastructures; and

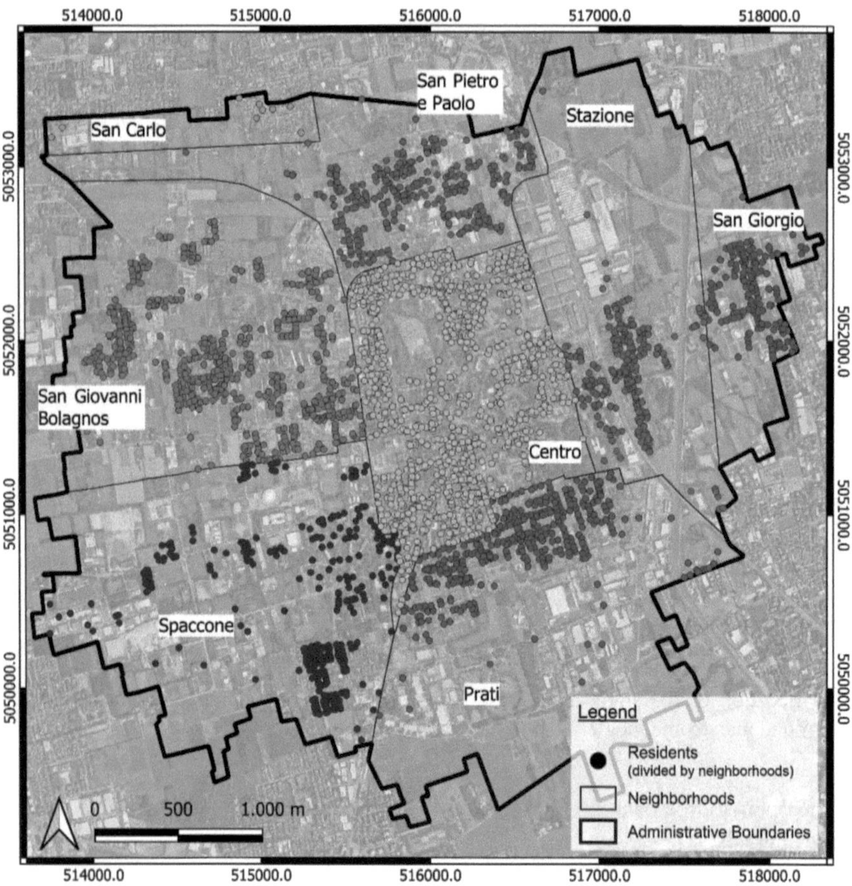

Fig. 4. Distribution of the resident population in the town of Desio. (CRS: EPSG 7791 – RDN2008 / UTM zone 32N - background map from Google®).

- *age group classification based on ISTAT* [14] *criteria*: the population was categorised into age groups according to the classification used by ISTAT (Italian National Institute of Statistics) for its official demographic analyses [15]. The age groups ranged from early childhood (up to 5 years) to the elderly population (over 75 years). Intermediate classes between these extremes spanned over consecutive five years. These categories allow for targeted analyses of specific age cohorts, including insights into the needs of various population segments, such as children, working-age adults, and elder people.

Starting from the Municipal Registry data and the georeferenced house numbers, each resident was georeferenced based on their home address. This operation required intervention to complete the mapping of house numbers, as approximately 25% of the population was not associated with a geographic location. The main reasons for this incompleteness were: lack of mapping of the house number, non-uniqueness of street names, and incompleteness of the street directory.

In order to georeference the entire population, preliminary steps were taken to resolve these issues. In particular, a point was inserted to represent missing house numbers, located at a central position relative to the street's geometry. This solution allowed for mapping the entire population, except for ten people, some of whom were classified as homeless (see Fig. 4).

Table 1 shows the results: 'Centro' and 'San Giovanni Bolagnos' are the most populated neighbourhoods, followed by 'Prati' and 'Spaccone'. The other four neighbourhoods have less than 10% of the population each.

Table 1. Residents in the town of Desio divided by neighbourhood.

	Residents	
Neighborhood	[n]	[%]
Centro	13274	31.50
Prati	5050	11.98
San Carlo	422	1.00
San Giorgio	1943	4.61
San Giovanni Bolagnos	9366	22.22
San Pietro e Paolo	3897	9.25
Spaccone	4878	11.57
Stazione	3313	7.86
Total	42143	100.00

Thanks to this georeferencing process, population density maps were created based on both the current age groups and the projected age groups over the next 10 years. Figure 5 shows the heatmap of the resident population (age 10 – 14) and related services (secondary schools).

Table 2 highlights that four of eight neighbourhoods are covered by secondary schools ('scuole secondarie di primo grado'): about 42% of total students (age 10–14) live in a neighbourhood without secondary school.

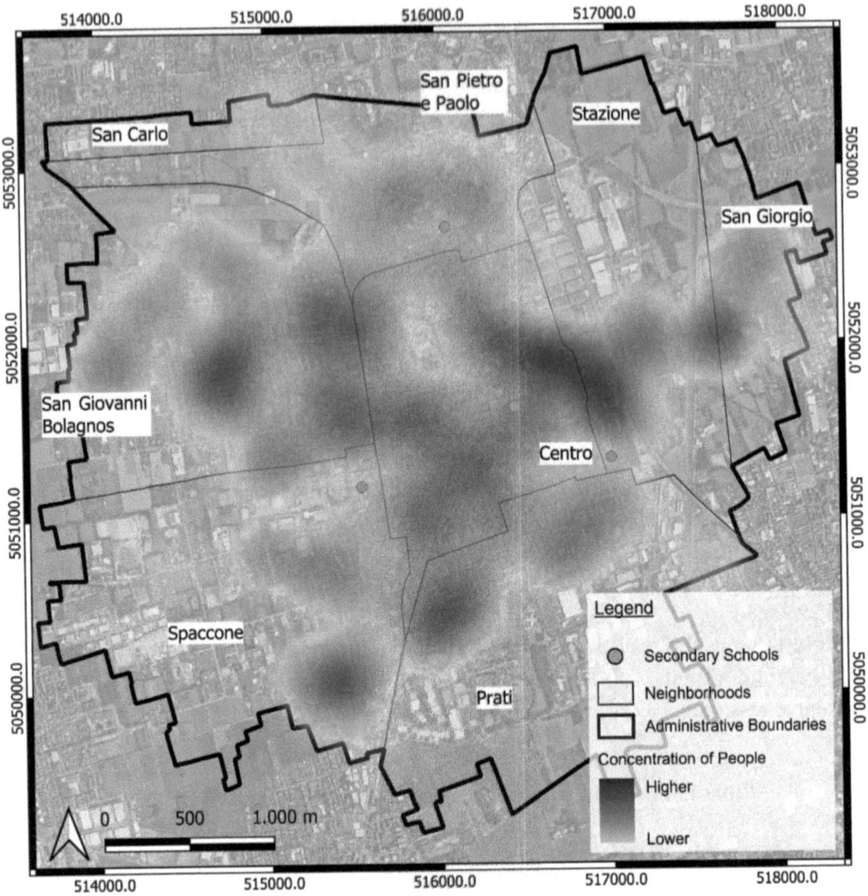

Fig. 5. Heatmap of the resident population (age 10–14) in relation to the secondary schools. (CRS: EPSG 7791 – RDN2008 / UTM zone 32N - (background map from Google®).

Table 2. Table 2.Number of students (age 10–14) related to secondary schools.

	Students (age 10-14)		Schools	
Neighborhood	[n]	[%]	[n]	[%]
Centro	601	29.12	1	25.00
Prati	261	12.65	0	0.00
San Carlo	15	0.73	0	0.00
San Giorgio	96	4.65	0	0.00
San Giovanni Bolagnos	502	24.32	0	0.00
San Pietro e Paolo	163	7.90	1	25.00
Spaccone	238	11.53	1	25.00
Stazione	188	9.11	1	25.00
Total	2064	100.00	4	100.00

3.2 Network Analysis

Starting from the georeferencing of residents, a series of analyses were conducted to assess the accessibility of services located within a 15-min walking distance.

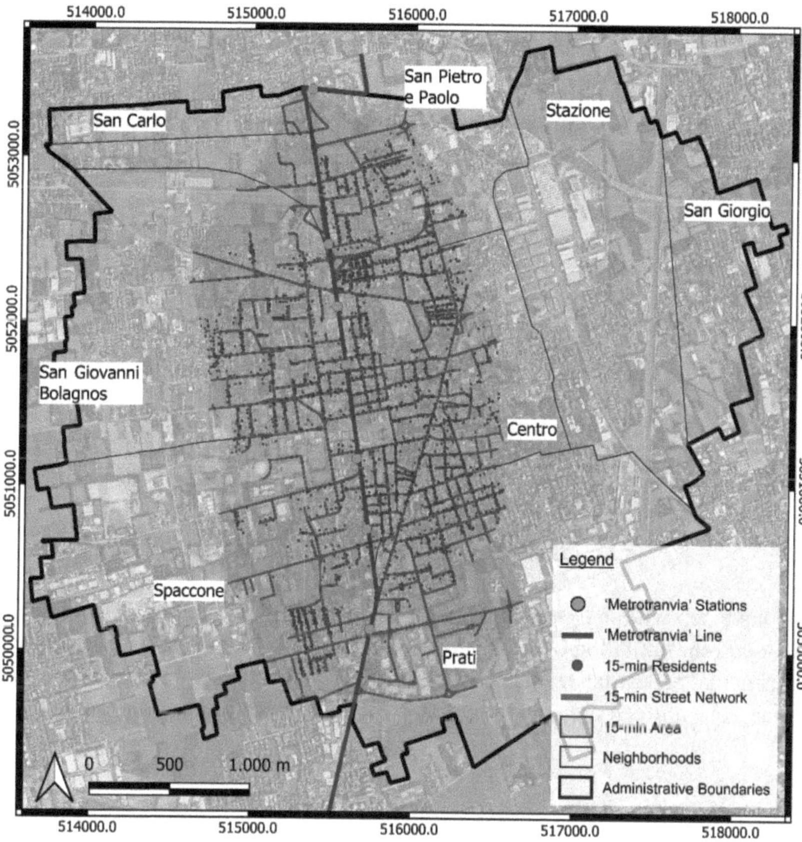

Fig. 6. Network analysis: analysis of 15-min walking distance from the new 'Metrotranvia' stations. (CRS: EPSG 7791 – RDN2008 / UTM zone 32N - background map from Google®).

A distance of 1 km was chosen as the equivalent of this time-lapse, based on an average walking speed of 4 km/h - a pace that individuals across various age groups may comfortably maintain within the considered distance. The street network spans a total length of 160.3 km. However, after excluding the statal road 'SS36' (also known as 'Valassina'), which crosses the eastern part of the municipality and serves as a high-speed arterial route, the total effective road network was reduced to 143.9 km. This refined network better represents the walkable areas accessible to residents without being hindered by major highways that are unsuitable for pedestrian traffic.

The points of interest (public transport nodes) selected for this analysis were:

- the 'metrotranvia' (light rail) stations, under construction at the moment of writing: the area of influence covers 53.7% of the street network and 66.1% of the total population (see Fig. 6);
- the railway station: the area of influence covers 29.1% of the street network and 20.2% of the total population; and
- for road transport, as an example, the bus stops of line Z250: the area of influence covers 56.2% of the street network and includes 73.1% of the total population.

Table 3 shows that the 'Metrotranvia' location favours accessibility for the population residing along the north-south axis, while the external areas are disadvantaged due to the higher distance.

Table 3. Table 3.Number of residents related to the 'Metrotranvia' stations.

	Residents		Residents 15-min	
Neighborhood	[n]	[%]	[n]	[%tot]
Centro	13274	31.50	10880	81.96
Prati	5050	11.98	2711	53.68
San Carlo	422	1.00	13	3.08
San Giorgio	1943	4.61	0	0.00
San Giovanni Bolagnos	9366	22.22	6323	67.51
San Pietro e Paolo	3897	9.25	2972	76.26
Spaccone	4878	11.57	4602	94.34
Stazione	3313	7.86	0	0.00
Total	42143	100.00	27501	65.26

The next step will be to assess routes type and quality within the 15-min influence radius. A current limitation of this analysis is the updating of the street network graph, considering that pedestrian traffic can include routes not accessible to cars (for example, pedestrian zones, green areas, and parks), which are therefore not represented in this layer.

4 Conclusions

This research aims to propose an approach to analyse the dynamics between population distribution and services location in the Municipality of Desio. As a first step, the knowledge base was organised: population data (address and age) was georeferenced within the municipality and boundaries, and some services (schools, hospital, local public transport, etc.) were identified. Then, a network analysis (15-min walking distance) was carried out considering the population divided by neighbourhood and the new light rail (*Metrotranvia*) that will cross the municipality from north to south, far as Milan. As a result, the possibility of identifying inequalities in the spatial distribution of services can support evidence-based policy recommendations to promote improvement strategies. This study demonstrates the potential of integrating geospatial data, statistics, and population distribution as key aspects of urban planning, environmental management, and public health.

Acknowledgments. The authors want to thank the Municipality of Desio, Lombardy Geoportal and ISTAT for the data; QGIS Association for the open-source software it provides.

References

1. Pozoukidou, G., Chatziyiannaki, Z.: 15-Minute City: Decomposing the New Urban Planning Eutopia. Sustain. **13**,928 (2021). https://doi.org/10.3390/SU13020928
2. Moreno, C., Allam, Z., Chabaud, D., Gall, C., Pratlong, F.: Introducing the "15-Minute City": sustainability, resilience and place identity in future post-pandemic cities. Smart Cities ***4*** 93–111 (2021). https://doi.org/10.3390/SMARTCITIES4010006
3. Giuffrida, N., Mölter, A., Pilla, F., Carroll, P., Ottomanelli, M.: On the equity of the x-minute city from the perspective of walkability. Transp. Eng. **16**, (2024) https://doi.org/10.1016/j.treng.2024.100244
4. Logan, T.M., Hobbs, M.H., Conrow, L.C., Reid, N.L., Young, R.A., Anderson, M.J.: The x-minute city: measuring the 10, 15, 20-minute city and an evaluation of its use for sustainable urban design. Cities **131**, 103924 (2022). https://doi.org/10.1016/J.CITIES.2022.103924
5. Liu, D., Kwan, M.P., Wang, L., Kan, Z., Wang, J., Huang, J.: Development of a chrono-urbanism status composite index under the 5/10/15-minute city concept using social media big data. Tijdschr. voor Econ. en Soc. Geogr. **115**, 554–570 (2024). https://doi.org/10.1111/TESG.12613
6. Willberg, E., Fink, C., Toivonen, T.: The 15-minute city for all? – measuring individual and temporal variations in walking accessibility. J. Transp. Geogr. **106**, 103521 (2023). https://doi.org/10.1016/J.JTRANGEO.2022.103521
7. Rojas-Rueda, D., Norberciak, M., Morales-Zamora, E.: Advancing health equity through 15-min cities and chrono-urbanism. J. Urban Health **101**, 483–496 (2024). https://doi.org/10.1007/S11524-024-00850-2
8. Khavarian-Garmsir, A.R., Sharifi, A., Sadeghi, A.: The 15-minute city: urban planning and design efforts toward creating sustainable neighborhoods. Cities **132**, 104101 (2023). https://doi.org/10.1016/J.CITIES.2022.104101
9. Aria, M., Cuccurullo, C.: Bibliometrix: an R-tool for comprehensive science mapping analysis. J. Informetr. **11**, 959–975 (2017). https://doi.org/10.1016/J.JOI.2017.08.007
10. van Eck, N.J., Waltman, L.: Software survey: VOSviewer, a computer program for bibliometric mapping. Scientometrics **84**, 523–538 (2010). https://doi.org/10.1007/S11192-009-0146-3/FIGURES/7
11. Kriegel, H.P.; Kröger, P.; Sander, J.; Zimek, A. Density-based clustering. *Wiley Interdiscip. Rev. Data Min. Knowl. Discov.* **2011**, *1*, 231–240, https://doi.org/10.1002/WIDM.30
12. QGIS Association QGIS 3.34 Available online: https://qgis.org/
13. Municipality of Desio, 2024. Municipal Registry, Desio, Italy (2024)
14. ISTAT Istituto Nazionale di Statistica Available online: https://www.istat.it/
15. ISTAT Indicatori demografici Available online: http://dati.istat.it/Index.aspx?DataSetCode=DCIS_INDDEMOG1

Urban Heat Islands in Palermo: Land Surface Temperature Analysis of a Mediterranean Coastal City

Luca Balsamo[1,2], Carlo Zanetti[3], Salvatore E. Pappalardo[4(✉)], and Massimo De Marchi[5]

[1] Department of Earth and Sea Sciences (DISTEM), University of Palermo, Palermo, Italy
[2] Department of Civil, Construction and Environmental Engineering (DICEA), Sapienza – University of Rome, Rome, Italy
[3] Human Rights Centre, University of Padua, Padua, Italy
[4] Master GIScience, ICEA Department, University of Padua, Padua, Italy
salvatore.pappalardo@unipd.it
[5] Jean Monnet Center of Excellence on Just Fossil Fuel Transition, ICEA Department, University of Padua, Padua, Italy

Abstract. The effects of climate change are becoming increasingly evident worldwide, with one of the most notable being the rise in the frequency of extreme weather events, such as intense heat waves. These phenomena tend to be more pronounced in densely urbanized areas [1] disproportionately affecting vulnerable populations. This study focuses on Palermo, a coastal city in Sicily (southern Italy), surrounded by mountains and home to over 600,000 inhabitants. Palermo is highly urbanized, making it particularly susceptible to urban heat island effects. In this work, we employ remote sensing techniques to assess Land Surface Temperature (LST) in order to visualize the temperature distribution across the urban area. This approach allows us to identify the parts of the city where temperatures are highest, considering factors such as altitude, proximity to the coast, and Local Climate Zones, classified based on the type of urban fabric or vegetation present.

Keywords: Remote sensing · Urban Heat Island · Land Surface Temperature · Palermo

1 Introduction

Climate-related events and news are increasingly becoming part of everyday life on a global scale. It is evident that the world, in its interconnected state, faces an exceptional challenge that will require equally exceptional efforts. Extreme weather events, particularly those related to temperature and precipitation, are becoming more frequent and intense [2, 3]. According to the Intergovernmental Panel on Climate Change (IPCC), it is now virtually certain (99–100% probability) that phenomena such as heatwaves (HWs) will increase in frequency, duration, and intensity in many regions of the planet, largely driven by human activities [4].

E. Borgogno-Mondino and P. Zamperlin (Eds.): ASITA 2024, CCIS 2463, pp. 234–248, 2025.
https://doi.org/10.1007/978-3-031-91141-5_17

Urban areas, characterized by high levels of concretization, population density, infrastructure, economic activity, and industrial clusters, have been observed to experience more intense HWs. These conditions can lead to the formation of Urban Heat Islands (UHIs), localized zones within urban environments where temperatures are higher than those of surrounding urban and, especially, rural areas [5]. The urgency of mitigating and preventing this phenomenon becomes clear when considering that cities, although occupying only about 3% of the Earth's surface, are home to more than 50% of the global population. Moreover, due to the variety of activities that take place in cities, they are responsible for more than 70% of global greenhouse gas emissions and consume about 75% of global resources [6].

The social impact of such events must also be emphasized. Public administrations sometimes pay less attention to the needs of suburban districts, and UHIs can disproportionately affect the most vulnerable segments of the population, who have less capacity to respond to extreme heatwaves. Given that excessive heat can increase the risk of cardiovascular and respiratory diseases, it is easy to see how this phenomenon can become an issue of climate injustice.

In this work, remote sensing techniques were employed to initiate a scientific and social assessment of the impact that these extreme climate events may have on a large, densely populated city like Palermo. The choice of Palermo as a case study is motivated by its status as a Mediterranean coastal city, making it a climate hotspot. This study represents a first step toward a multidisciplinary characterization that could, in some way, support administrative decisions. In fact, the study of UHIs has recently gained prominence in several cities, where local governments and citizens have begun to explore solutions such as increasing tree cover, implementing reflective pavements, and adding fountains to mitigate the heat [7].

The summer of 2023 saw record-breaking temperatures globally, and Palermo experienced one of its hottest weeks on record. Due to the Libeccio wind descending from the surrounding mountains (Foehn effect), the already warm air from the North African anticyclone brought extremely high temperatures to the city. On July 24, the meteorological station at Palermo's Astronomical Observatory recorded its highest temperature since it began operations in 1865: 44.6 °C, with values exceeding 40 °C continuously since 8:00 a.m. Moreover, maximum temperatures remained above 40 °C for the previous three days, above 36 °C the week before, and over 32 °C since July 7 [8]. This extreme heatwave was the main cause of a series of fires that ravaged the Palermo province on the night of July 24 and throughout July 25, destroying over 14,500 hectares of land, including some suburban areas of the city, resulting in at least three deaths and the evacuation of hundreds of families. This underscores the urgent need to investigate the city's relationship with extreme heat events in order to implement protective measures for residents' well-being.

2 Study Area

For this study, we selected Palermo, a coastal city in southern Italy facing the Tyrrhenian Sea to the north and northwest (Fig. 1). As the capital of Sicily, Palermo has over 600,000 inhabitants, making it the fifth largest city in Italy. It covers an area of approximately

160 km^2, predominantly flat (the Plain of Palermo), and is surrounded by the Palermo Mountains, a segment of the Sicilian mountain range with peaks exceeding 1,000 m. Of the rivers that once flowed through the city, only the Oreto River, a 22 km-long torrential stream, remains unburied.

In the northern part of the city, two natural landmarks stand out: Monte Pellegrino, a 606-m-high promontory, and the "Parco della Favorita," an urban park that extends for over 4 km^2 at the base of Monte Pellegrino, forming an Oriented Nature Reserve. This reserve acts as a natural barrier between the urban area of Palermo and the seaside village of Mondello, which, along with Sferracavallo, represents the northernmost part of the city.

According to the Köppen-Geiger climate classification, Palermo falls under the Csa category, indicative of a Mediterranean climate with hot summers. Data from the Sicilian Agrometeorological Information Service (SIAS) show that between 2002 and 2022, the city recorded an average annual air temperature of 18.9 °C, with an average summer temperature of 26.2 °C and a winter average of 12.4 °C. Annual precipitation during this period averaged 740 mm [10].

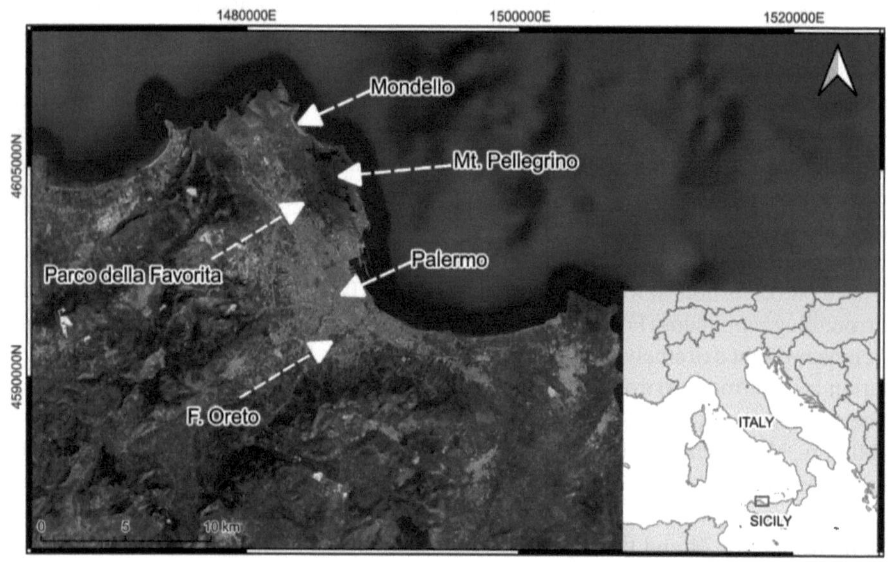

Fig. 1. Localisation of Palermo from Google Earth Satellite Image. Reference system: EPSG 3857 – WGS84/Pseudo Mercator.

3 Materials and Methods

3.1 Data

All data and software used in this study are fully open access and open source.

The initial phase of the research involved a thorough investigation of meteorological data from the databases of the National Institute of Astrophysics (INAF, astropa.inaf.it), which manages the city's astronomical observatory, and primarily from the SIAS database (sias.regione.sicilia.it). Based on this meteorological data, we selected satellite images for analysis by choosing from those available, depending on the satellite platform's passage over the area of interest.

For the analysis of temperature behaviour, data from two major land use and land cover projects were utilized. The first dataset comes from the CORINE project (land.copernicus.eu/en/products/corine-land-cover), part of the European Commission's and European Space Agency's (ESA) Copernicus initiative. Updated every six years, CORINE consists of 44 thematic classes. The version used in this study (2018) was derived from Sentinel-2 satellite data and has a resolution of 100 m. The second dataset used was the Local Climate Zone (LCZ, wudapt.org/lcz) classification scheme, developed by Stewart and Oke [9], which includes 17 zones primarily classified based on surface structure properties and surface types.

A Digital Terrain Model (DTM) with a 2-m resolution, provided by the Region's Territorial Information System (SITR, sitr.regione.sicilia.it), was employed to assess temperature variations with altitude.

For satellite imagery, data from the Landsat 8 and 9 satellites (Collection 2 Level 1 data) were selected. These satellites are equipped with the Operational Land Imager (OLI) and the Thermal Infrared Sensor (TIRS), and have been capturing images since February 2013. Their products, with an approximate North-South dimension of 170 km and East-West of 183 km, consist of 11 spectral bands, and acquisitions occur every 8 days. In this study, Bands 4 (RED) and 5 (Near-Infrared), captured with OLI at a spatial resolution of 30 m, and spectral Band 10 in the thermal infrared range, acquired with TIRS at a resolution of 100 m, were used. These data were downloaded from the USGS Earth Explorer platform (earthexplorer.usgs.gov).

Satellite imagery was processed using QGIS v.3.34.4 (qgis.org), and the products were cropped according to two distinct approaches depending on the analysis performed. Specifically, the LST (Land Surface Temperature) calculation was conducted on a circular buffer with a 25 km radius, cantered on the municipality of Palermo, to focus on identifying the most affected neighbourhoods. Additionally, a 6 km buffer along the northern Sicilian coast was used to compare the city's urban areas with rural zones.

3.2 Land Surface Temperature Computation

To calculate the Land Surface Temperature (LST), we followed the approach outlined in [11], computing the reflectance at the top of the atmosphere for bands 4 and 5. This was done using the formula provided in the *Landsat 8 Data Users Handbook* [12]:

$$TOA\ Reflectance = \frac{(Band * 0.00002) - 0.1}{0.889286} \quad (1)$$

Following the Landsat guidelines, we used band 10 to derive the formula for calculating the Brightness Temperature at the top of the atmosphere, which represents the intensity of electromagnetic energy emitted from Earth's surface and detected by the satellite:

$$TOA\ Brightness\ Temperature = \frac{1321.0789}{ln\left(\left(\frac{774.8853}{(Band*0.000342)+0.1}\right)+1\right)} - 273.15 \quad (2)$$

The Normalized Difference Vegetation Index (NDVI) was calculated using the previously computed reflectance at the top of the atmosphere (TOA_Refl) for bands 4 and 5 [13]:

$$NDVI = (TOA\_Refl5 - TOA\_Refl4)/(TOA\_Refl5 -- TOA\_Refl4 \quad (3)$$

The NDVI is widely used to classify areas as vegetated or non-vegetated based on the ratio of near-infrared (NIR) to red (RED) reflectance values. Positive values close to + 1 indicate dense leaf cover, while values near −1 are indicative of water bodies.

An estimate of the Proportion of Vegetation (PV) was calculated using the following formula [14]:

$$PV = \left(\frac{(NDVI - 0.2)}{(0.8 - 0.2)}\right)^2 \quad (4)$$

PV is defined as the ratio of the vertical projection of the vegetated area (including leaves, stems, and branches) to the total area considered vegetated [15]. Following this, an estimate of the emissivity of the Earth's surface was calculated [16]:

$$Emissivity = (0.004 * PV) + 0.986 \quad (5)$$

Using the TOA Brightness Temperature (BT) and the emissivity calculated with the formulas above, we were able to derive the Land Surface Temperature (LST) [17]:

$$Land\ Surface\ Temperature = \frac{BT}{1 + \left(\left(\frac{10.895*BT}{14388}\right) * ln(emissivity)\right)} \quad (6)$$

3.3 Comparison with Rural Areas

The aim was to calculate an average LST of rural areas in northern Sicily for comparison with urban areas. The mean LST in rural areas was calculated from a 6 km buffer extending inland along the northern Sicilian coast. Since the images from the three examined dates were obtained from two different scenes, the buffers for July 9 and August 2 did not correspond to the westernmost buffer for July 24. Within these buffers, areas categorized in the CORINE database as belonging to Level 1 classes 2 (Utilized Agricultural Areas) and 3 (Wooded Areas and Semi-Natural Environments) were taken into account. Areas classified as artificial surfaces (Class 1), wetlands (Class 4), and water bodies (Class 5) were subsequently excluded.

To ensure the validity of the temperature measurements, inaccessibility poles for these rural polygons were identified, representing the points furthest from the boundaries with other non-rural classes. Only those polygons with a pole at least 300 m away from contact with another class were selected. This approach guaranteed that temperature measurements were taken in rural and/or heavily vegetated areas, sufficiently distanced from anthropogenic influences that could affect LST readings. Finally, the average temperature of the selected points was calculated for each date.

3.4 Elaborations on Distance from the Coast, Altitude and Local Climate Zone

For subsequent processing, a single raster was created by averaging the LST values from the three dates. This approach aimed to reduce noise in the recorded data and mitigate errors caused by outliers. From this raster, average LSTs were calculated for various distance buffers from the coast. Specifically, 44 strips, each 250 m wide, were generated starting from a 12 km stretch of coastline extending from the port area of Palermo toward the city's southern coast. This covered the entire urban area up to the surrounding mountains, with a total distance from the coast of 11 km. Using the geoprocessing tool "Zonal Statistics," an average LST was assigned to each buffer based on the temperature raster.

To assess LST behaviour in relation to altitude, the 2 m resolution Digital Terrain Model (DTM) of the Sicilian Region was cropped over Palermo and the surrounding mountains, then reclassified into 20 altitude classes of 50 m using GRASS tools, covering altitudes up to 1000 m above sea level. The "Dissolve" tool was used to aggregate all polygons belonging to the same altitude class. Again, using "Zonal Statistics," an average LST was attributed to each polygon in every class.

4 Results and Discussion

4.1 Meteorological Data Analyses

A collection and analysis of meteorological data from the SIAS database was conducted. This data is freely available upon request after registration. Among the values observed for July and August, two in particular warrant attention. First, we compared the daily average temperature data (derived from hourly measurements) from two different stations (Fig. 2): the station in Palermo (locality Uditore) and the one in Caronia (ME), locality Buzza (shown in Fig. 3). Although both stations are situated at an altitude of 50 m, the former is located in a highly urbanized area, while the latter is set in a purely rural context. The average temperature in Palermo was 28.09 °C, whereas in Caronia it was 24.57 °C, revealing a difference of over 3.5 °C.

The second noteworthy data point is the minimum temperature recorded in Palermo during these two months. Out of a total of 62 nights, the minimum temperature fell below 20 °C on only two occasions, resulting in 60 'tropical nights' [18]. As illustrated in all three graphs in Fig. 2, despite the similar altitudes and comparable distances from the coast, temperatures recorded at the two stations are consistently higher in Palermo. This clearly underscores the significant influence of the urban fabric on temperature distribution.

4.2 LST and Land Cover

Using the methodology described in paragraph 3.3, we were able to extract points and calculate an average LST value for rural areas classified under Corine Land Cover classes 2 and 3, situated at least 300 m away from urbanized zones. Specifically, the average LST in non-anthropic areas on July 9, 2023, was 33.42 °C. On July 24, the average rose to 36.6 °C, before dropping to 26.12 °C in the third case study on August 2. From these

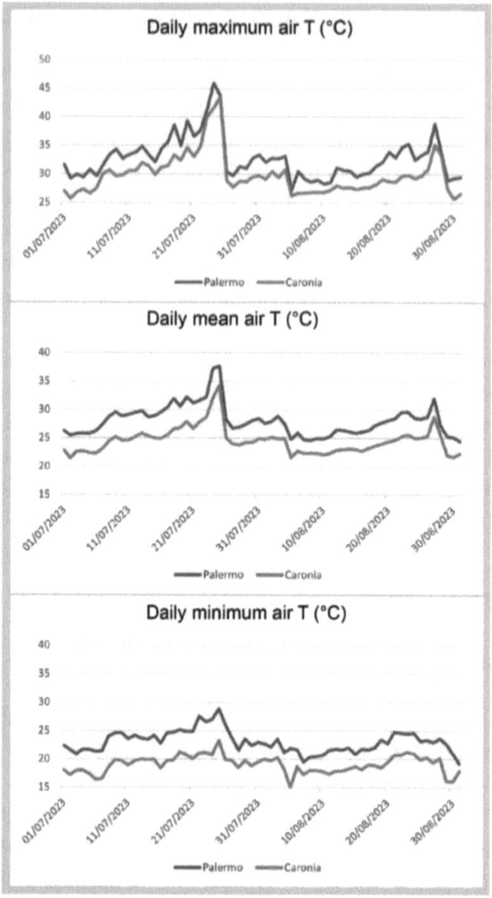

Fig. 2. Measurements of the maximum, mean and minimum temperatures recorded in Palermo and Caronia in the months of July and August 2023. The location of the two stations is shown in Fig. 3.

values, maps were generated to represent the deviation of measured temperatures from the rural area averages (Fig. 3).

The observation of these maps clearly shows that heavily urbanized areas, such as the city of Palermo and its neighbouring municipalities, experienced significantly higher temperatures compared to rural areas. In the first two cases, temperature peaks were observed to be up to 7 °C above the rural average, while in the third case, the peak reached an impressive 13 °C. Conversely, the easternmost areas shown in Fig. 2, corresponding to the mountainous regions of the Madonie and Nebrodi, which are minimally urbanized and have dense vegetation cover, recorded LST values significantly below the rural average, with some peaks as much as 13 °C cooler than the rural average.

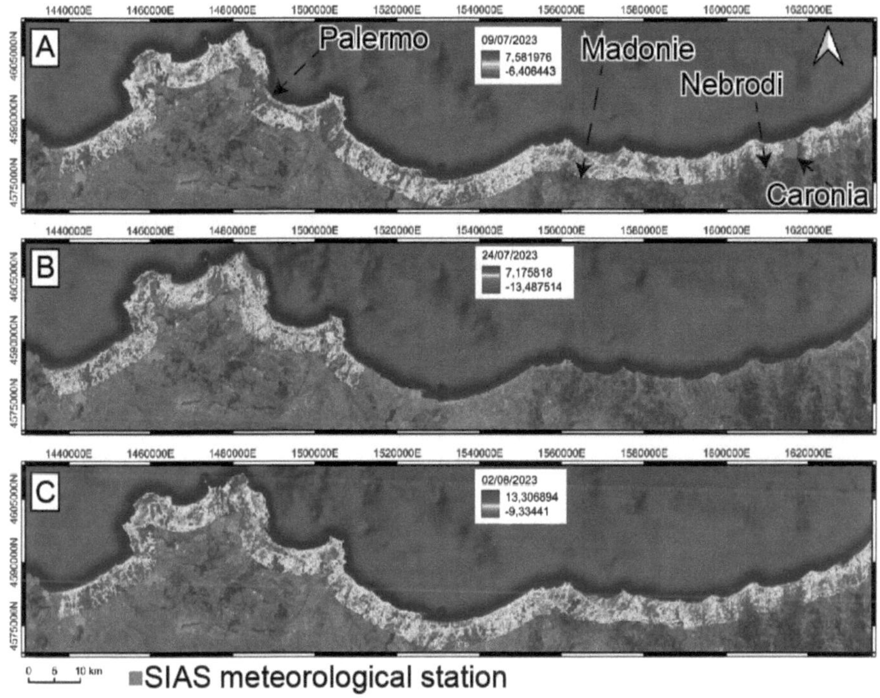

Fig. 3. Differences in °C of the LST compared to the mean value calculated on rural areas (classes 2 and 3 of Corine) at least 300 m from urbanised areas. Inset A: 09/07/2023 value. Inset B: 24/07/2023 value. Inset C: 02/08/2023 value. The green square indicates the location of SIAS stations.

4.3 Distribution of Green Areas

Using the methodology described in Sect. 3.3, with a focus on the city of Palermo and its surrounding areas, an NDVI index map was generated to visualize the distribution of green spaces (Fig. 4). In inset A, the NDVI distribution is shown within a 25 km radius, cantered on the centroid of the municipality of Palermo. The map highlights the extensive vegetated areas covering the mountains surrounding the city. However, it is also evident that no area within the surveyed region has an NDVI value exceeding 0.5, indicating the absence of densely forested regions.

Similarly, the NDVI values drop sharply in the urban areas of the city. Inset B shows a zoomed-in view of the city, highlighting only areas with an index higher than 0.2. At this scale, there is a widespread lack of large green spaces, with the exception of a few small urban parks, particularly in the neighbourhoods of the historic centre (highlighted by the dashed white circle).

4.4 LST and Distance from the Coast

From the LST values calculated for the three study days, a raster was created to represent their point-by-point average. This approach helped reduce the impact of potential outliers

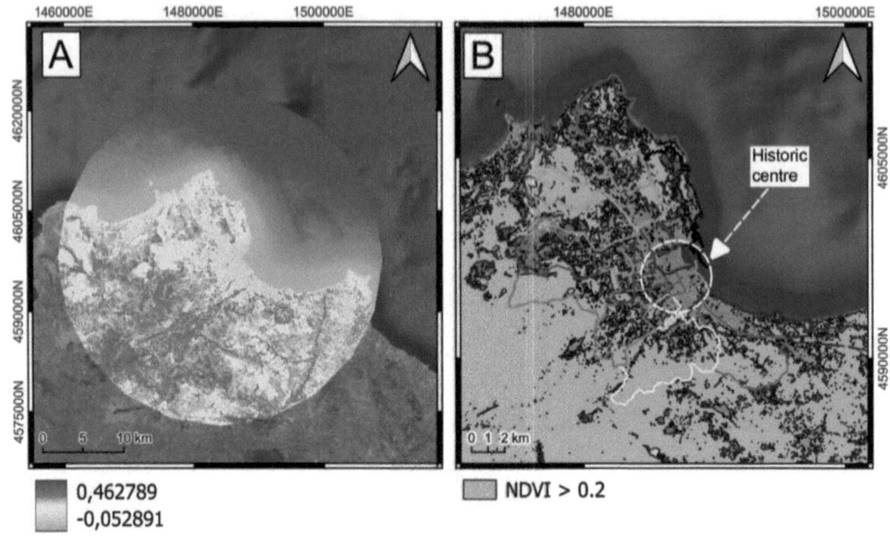

Fig. 4. Inset A) Distribution of the NDVI index in the 25 km buffer over Palermo. Inset B) Areas with NDVI index above 0.2 in the urban area of Palermo.

that could affect the analysis. To assess the influence of distance from the coastline on LST values, the average value was calculated in 250-m increments moving inland (Fig. 5). It is clear that the areas closest to the sea benefit from the lowest recorded temperatures. However, between 1,000 and 2,000 m from the coast, the most urbanized areas in the city centre show the highest temperature values. The average LST decreases again to below 34 °C at around 6,000 m from the coast, where it rises above 34.5 °C before dropping again. In Fig. 6, a third-degree polynomial trend line illustrates the LST pattern. From the graph, we can infer that the coastline's influence on temperature diminishes after approximately 1 km, at which point the characteristics of the urban fabric—explored in more detail in Sect. 4.6—take over. The peak in temperatures observed between 5.9 and 7 km from the coast, where temperatures rise nearly to the levels seen in the city centre, will be investigated in future studies. Beyond this peak, as the analysis approaches the hills surrounding the urban area, the temperature decreases to levels similar to those recorded just a few hundred meters from the coast.

4.5 LST and Elevation

The evaluation of the LST trend with altitude was made possible by reclassifying the 2-m resolution DTM of the Sicilian Region into 50-m altitude classes (Fig. 7). The average LST remains constant up to an altitude of 300 m, after which it begins to decrease, reaching 29.2 °C at 1,000 m compared to nearly 34 °C recorded in the Palermo Plain. Specifically, the temperature drops by about 1.5 °C between 600 and 800 m, and by almost 2 °C between 800 and 1,000 m (Fig. 8). However, it is important to note that this trend appears to be strongly influenced by the urban fabric. In fact, the most densely

Fig. 5. Average LST by distance from the coastline in 250 m wide buffers.

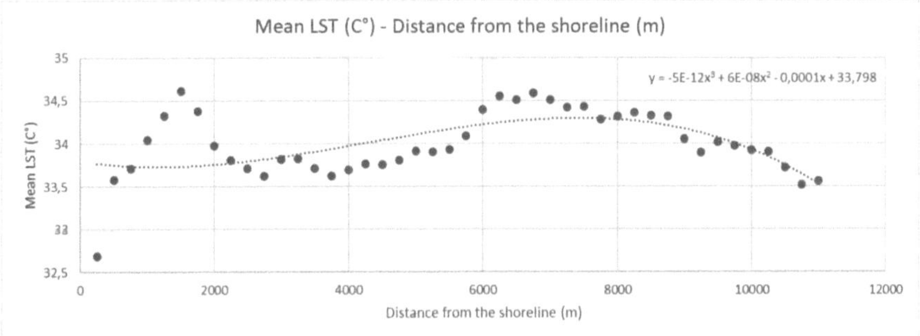

Fig. 6. Graph with third-degree polynomial trend line representing the LST trend with distance in metres from the coastline.

urbanized areas with extensive concrete structures and dense residential and industrial development are located within the first 500 m of altitude.

4.6 Analysis of the LST in Local Climate Zones

Finally, the relationship between the registered LSTs and the distinct Local Climate Zones (LCZs) in the study area was evaluated (Fig. 9) according to the classification by Stewart & Oke [9]. These zones are distinguished based on building types and land coverage. In particular, factors such as building height, proximity, and the presence of vegetation or bare soil are considered. The urban area of Palermo is divided mainly into two LCZ classes. The first is the "Compact midrise," characterized by a dense mix of medium-height buildings (3–9 floors), few trees, and predominantly cemented or paved surfaces. The second class, which makes up most of the southern part of the city, is

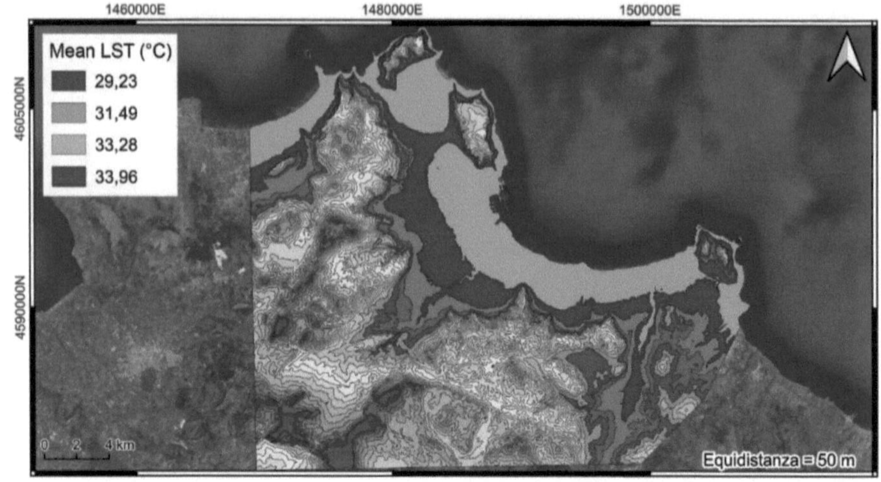

Fig. 7. Average LST based on altitude bands with 50 m equidistance.

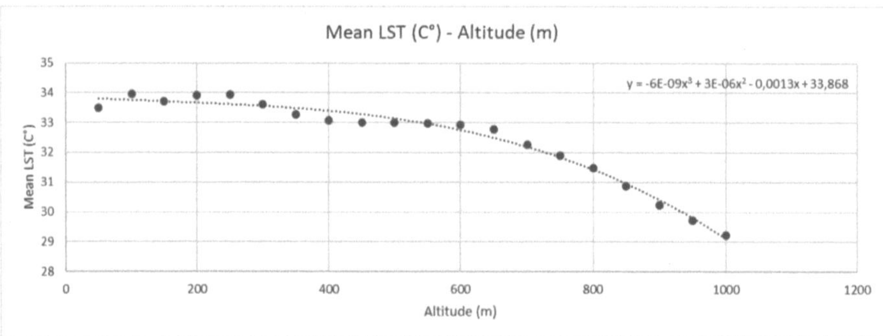

Fig. 8. Graph with third-degree polynomial trend line representing the LST trend with altitude.

the "Large low-rise" zone, mainly consisting of sparsely placed low-rise buildings (1–3 floors) with limited trees and primarily concrete or asphalt pavements.

The remaining part of the Palermo Plain is mostly classified as "Open low-rise," featuring a low-density arrangement of 1–3 floor buildings but with significant portions of permeable surfaces, such as low vegetation and scattered trees. The surrounding mountainous areas alternate between dense tree cover and regions primarily consisting of small-to-medium-sized shrubs.

To explore the LST variations across different LCZs, a mean LST was assigned to the polygons representing each LCZ in the study area. Additionally, each LCZ polygon was assigned an average altitude using the 2-m resolution DTM of the Sicilian Region. The results of these calculations are displayed in the trend lines in Fig. 10.

Not surprisingly, there is a general trend of decreasing temperatures as altitude increases in most LCZs, while the heavily urbanized areas show an increase in temperature with altitude. This trend may be related to the proximity to the coast, as the most urbanized areas are located within the first 500 m from the coastline. Naturally, the lower-altitude areas closest to the sea benefit from the cooling effect of the sea, as demonstrated in Figs. 5 and 6. However, as one moves farther from the coast, even as the altitude increases, temperatures tend to rise in these urban areas, indicating that the urban heat effect is stronger than the minor topographic elevation in the Palermo Plain.

The box-plot in Fig. 11 summarizes the average LSTs recorded across different LCZs, highlighting their varying temperature distributions. In urban areas, as building heights and density decrease, so do temperatures. In vegetated areas, a denser and taller vegetation cover corresponds to lower average LSTs. After accounting for variables such as altitude and proximity to the coast, it becomes evident that the average LST in the "Compact midrise" class is about 5 °C higher than in the "Dense tree" class.

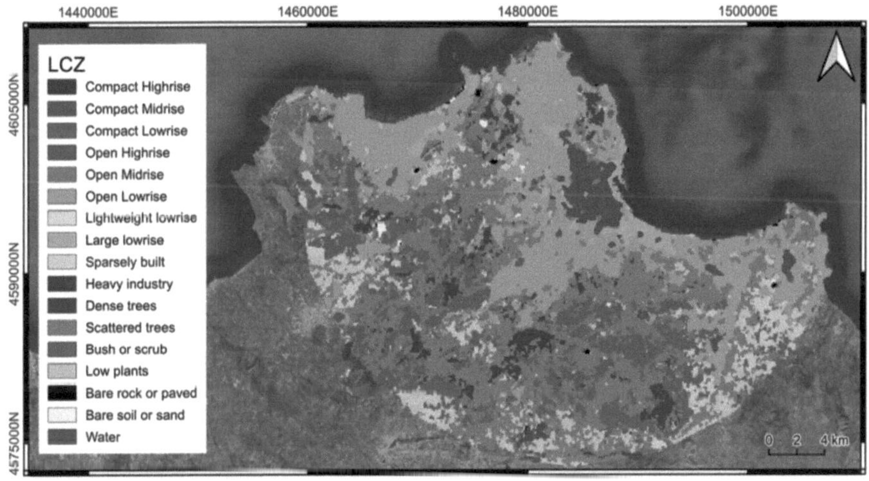

Fig. 9. Classification according to the Land Climate Zones of Palermo and surrounding areas. The legend shows all 17 LCZs including those not in the survey area.

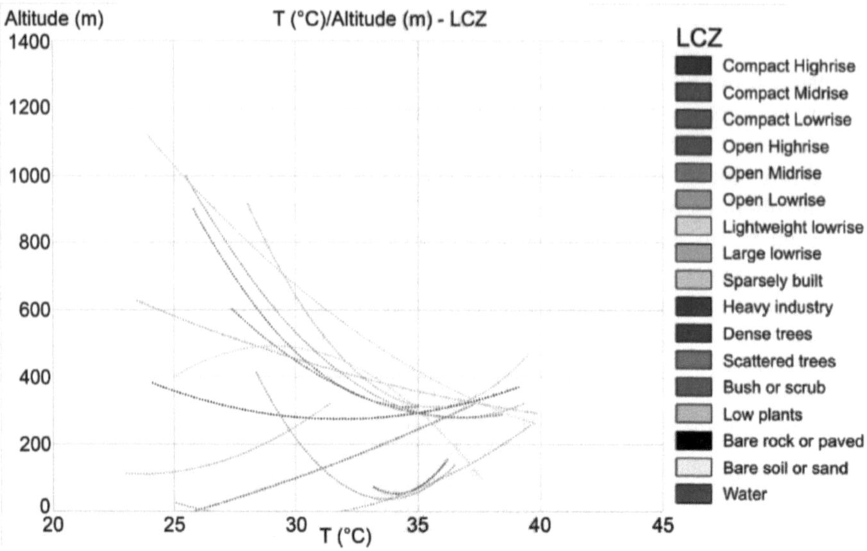

Fig. 10. Scatter-plots with polynomial trend lines of second degree relating the mean LST and the altitude of the different LCZs polygons.

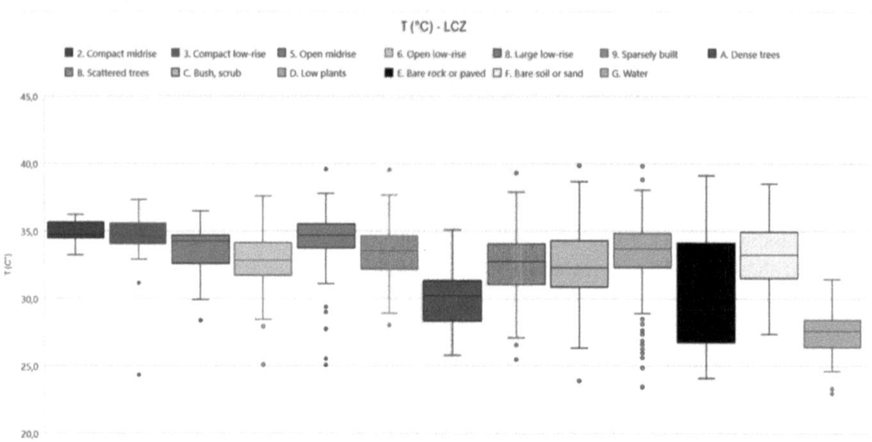

Fig. 11. Box-plot of the LST recorded in the different LCZs in the study area.

5 Conclusions

The results obtained from this study provide significant insights into the temperature dynamics in the Palermo area. These findings can be used to inform the development of urban planning strategies aimed at mitigating the effects of intense heat events, which are increasingly affecting urban areas. One of the key findings was the limited presence of green spaces across the central and high-density neighbourhoods of the city and the result in high LST values.

The analysis of the LST trend with respect to distance from the coast revealed that the cooling effect of proximity to the sea diminishes within the first kilometre. Beyond this point, the influence of the urban fabric becomes more dominant, particularly in the historic city centre, characterized by densely packed medium-height buildings and extensive concrete or asphalt surfaces.

Regarding altitude's influence on temperature values, it is noteworthy that there is no pronounced effect within the first 300 m of elevation. However, the cooling trend becomes much more pronounced at higher altitudes. The study also confirmed the overwhelming impact of the urban environment on temperature variations. The comparison of temperature trends across Local Climate Zones (LCZs) clearly demonstrated that temperature is strongly correlated with the density and height of buildings as well as the presence of vegetation. Specifically, an increase in building density and height leads to higher temperatures, while a larger vegetated area corresponds to a cooling effect of approximately 5 °C.

This work serves as a foundation for future studies that could include a social analysis of the city, exploring the impacts of urban heat islands by socioeconomic status. Such analyses could help identify areas where urgent climate justice interventions are needed.

References

1. Pappalardo, S.E., Zanetti, C., Todeschi, V.: Mapping urban heat islands and heat-related risk during heat waves from a climate justice perspective: A case study in the municipality of Padua (Italy) for inclusive adaptation policies. Landsc. Urban Plan. **238**, 104831 (2023)
2. Easterling, D.R., Evans, J.L., Groisman, P.Ya., Karl, T.R., Kunkel, K.E., Ambenje, P.: Observed variability and trends in extreme climate events: a brief review. Bull. American Metereol. Society **81**(3), https://doi.org/10.1175/1520-0477(2000)081_0417_OVATIE_2.3.CO_2 (2000)
3. Gualtieri, A.E., Sundby, A.: Heat waves are hitting around the globe. Scientists say climate change is making them more frequent, CBS News. www.cbsnews.com/news/heat-wave-climate-change-getting-more-frequent/. Accessed 5 Jan 2023
4. IPCC: Climate Change 2021: The Physical Science Basis. Contribution of Working Group I to the Sixth Assessment Report of the Intergovernmental Panel on Climate Change Masson-Delmotte, V., et al., (eds.). Cambridge University Press, Cambridge, United Kingdom and New York, NY, USA, 2391 p. 10https://doi.org/10.1017/9781009157896. (2021)
5. Oke T. R.: City size and the urban heat island, Atmospheric Environment (1967), Volume 7, Issue 8, 769–779, (1973)
6. Yensukho, P., Sugsaisakon, S., Kittipongvises, S.: City-wide greenhouse gas emissions of communities nearby the world heritage site of Ayutthaya. Thailand, Scientific Reports **12**(1), 1–11 (2022)
7. Morales-Gonzales, J.I., Verichev, K., Carpio, M.: Efficiency assessment for the urban heat island mitigation measures in a city with an oceanic climate during the summer period: Case of Valdivia. Chile. Urban Climate **55**, 101897 (2024)
8. Redazione media INAF (Istituto Nazionale di Astrofisica): Palermo, 47 gradi all'Osservatorio Inaf: è record. (24/07/2023)
9. Stewart, I.D., Oke T.R.: Local climate zones for urban temperature studies. Bull. American Meteorol. Society **93**, 12, 1879–1900 (2012). https://doi.org/10.1175/BAMS-D-11-00019.1

10. Pumo, D., Alongi, F., Cannarozzo, M., Noto, L.V.: Climate adaptive urban measures in Mediterranean areas: Thermal effectiveness of an advanced multilayer green roof installed in Palermo (Italy). Build. Environ. **243**, 110731 (2023)
11. Todeschi, V., Pappalardo, S.E., Zanetti, C., Peroni, F., De Marchi, M.: Climate justice in the city: mapping heat-related risk for climate change mitigation of the urban and peri-urban area of Padua (Italy). ISPRS Int. J. Geo Inf. **11**(9), 490 (2022)
12. U.S. Geological Survey: Landsat 8 (L8) Data Users Handbook, Version 5.0. (2019)
13. Yuan, F., Bau: Comparison of impervious surface area and normalized difference vegetation index as indicators of surface urban heat island effects in Landsat imagery. Remote Sens. Environ. **106**(3), 375–386 (2007)
14. Jeevalakshim,i D., Narayama Reddy, S., Manikiam, B.: Land surface temperature retrieval from LANDSAT data using emissivity estimation. Int. J. Appl. Eng. Res. **12**, 20, 9679–9687 (2017)
15. Deardorff, J.W.: Efficient prediction of ground surface temperature and moisture, with inclusion of a layer of vegetation, J. Geophys. Res. – Oceans **83**(C4), 1889–1903 (1978)
16. Anandabadu, D., Purushothaman, B.M., Babu Suresh S.: Estimation of land surface temperature using LANDSAT 8 Data. Int. J. Adv. Res., Ideas Innov. Technol. **4**(2) (2018)
17. Stathopoulou, M., Cartalis, C.: Daytime urban heat islands from Landsat ETM+ and Corine land cover data: An application to major cities in Greece. Sol. Energy **81**(3), 358–368 (2018)
18. Skarbit, N., Gal, T.: Projection of intra-urban modification of night-time climate indices during the 21st century, Hungarian Geographical Bulletin, **65**(2), 181–193 (2016) https://doi.org/10.15201/hungeobull.65.2.8

Mapping Out the Territorial Dynamics: The Geography of Recycling and Reuse of Secondary Raw Materials in Industrial Zones

Francesca Sinatra(✉) and Giuseppe Borruso

University of Trieste, Alfonso Valerio 4/1 Street, Trieste, Italy
francesca.sinatra@phd.units.it, giuseppe.borruso@deams.units.it

Abstract. This paper is aimed at studying the possibilities of implementing circular economical processes and industrial symbiosis in industrial areas, rooting this procedure into the theoretical framework of location theories and applying GIS and spatial analytical techniques. The location model of production activities provided in the standard location theory by Alfred Weber in 1909, can be extended, where the production site also serves as the source of secondary raw materials. The purpose of this paper stems from previous research that examined the concepts of Circular Economy (CE) and Industrial Symbiosis (IS) in relation to the organization of industrial areas. Such concepts are implemented to create a more resilient economic and production system, with the aim of promoting the minimization of waste production and the efficient use of resources. Territorial dynamics have a significant impact in implementing CE processes for recovering and reusing waste, taking into account the qualities and characteristics of secondary raw materials. The methodology is based on a previous project, "MEISAR - Materials for sustainable construction and infrastructure: recycled aggregates", which focused on recycled aggregates and waste materials as second-source materials for sustainable construction and infrastructure. The model, initially implemented for the case study of the demolition and reconstruction of the Football Stadium of the city of Cagliari, is hereby applied and tested to a different context, as that of the industrial area of Trieste, proximal to port facilities, adopting a multi-scalar approach.

In this approach it is crucial to take into account the existing spatial constraints during cluster analysis, where the distance between the plants and the place where secondary raw materials are utilized could not exceed 30 km.

In light of this background, this paper aims to apply this methodology to a wider context. The scope is to take into account a specific sector, in this case the construction and demolition's sectors, with the aim of applying the methodology employed in the MEISAR project in the industrial and port area of Trieste, considering the points that can be reached within 30 km around a given site that could be subjected to demolition and reconstruction interventions, identifying those actors involved. The case study will concentrate on Trieste's industrial area, which is strategically located due to its geographical location near the borders of Slovenia, Austria and Croatia, and the proximity between the city and the port, considered a crucial hub in international trade.

E. Borgogno-Mondino and P. Zamperlin (Eds.): ASITA 2024, CCIS 2463, pp. 249–261, 2025.
https://doi.org/10.1007/978-3-031-91141-5_18

1 Introduction

In the past few decades, the importance of the relationship between economic activities, environment, and well-being has significantly grown [11]. The global increase in natural resource consumption and waste production is causing negative effects on the ecosystem and risks for companies due to the rise in raw material costs [12].

The attention given to sustainable phenomena and the subsequent application of new distribution models on the territory is what distinguishes industrial contexts today. Consequently, territorialization processes for production activities are designed to maximize efficiency in the use of natural resources, along with a plan to reduce environmental impacts. The rise of links between industrial areas leads to the strengthening of industrial clusters, where activities are interconnected through the use of synergies and resource and skill sharing [1].

In recent years, a circular economy concept has emerged, which involves the regeneration and reuse of materials to their maximum usefulness, creating a closed- loop economy aimed at the transformation of waste generated by production activities into new secondary raw materials [1–3].

Industrial symbiosis strategies are a concept that involves integration and cooperation between enterprises from various sectors in order to achieve optimal resource use, waste reduction, and overall efficiency. As a result, circular economy and industrial symbiosis are key concepts in the promotion of new processes in localizing production activities. So, in this context, it is necessary to reorganize the production system from a linear model to a circular one, which would improve both local production and the competitiveness of the territory, and consequently, enhance the well-being of communities.

To hypothesize how IS activities and good CE practice could be implemented in industrial contexts, the first step involved creating a georeferenced database for the circular activities and using geographic information systems for their representation, visualization, and analysis.

The focus of the research is on the industrial area of Trieste, which is strategically positioned due to its proximity to foreign countries like Austria, Slovenia, and Croatia, and logistically because it is an essential hub for international trade [9, 10].

The paper's aims to assess the potential effects of industrial symbiosis and circular economy strategies can aid in the development and reorganization of industrial areas and assess their potential effects in this context.

The aim of the research is to combine the use of databases on the activities present in the industrial zone of Trieste and, through the analysis of a real case study in the construction and demolition sector, to assess the applicability of the extended Weber model with GIS tools. In addition, it is intended to examine the material flows existing in the industrial zone of Trieste, verifying the presence of circular economy dynamics. Furthermore, geographic information tools used in the construction of a database are crucial for capturing essential information for timely analysis and optimal georeferencing. From this perspective, it is clear how these tools can be crucial not only in identifying the parties and stakeholders involved but also in understanding possible strategies for industrial localization in a circular optic.

The paper is organized as follows: paragraph 2 The Study Area; 3 Materials and Methods.; sub-paragraph 3.1 Data; subparagraph 3.2 Methods; 4 Result and Discussion; 5 Conclusions.

2 The Study Area

The chosen research area is the industrial zone of Trieste, situated in Friuli Venezia Giulia. It is in particular the limited area centred on the Co.SELAG, the consortium covering the industrial area in Trieste province, which includes part of the municipalities of Trieste (in green on the map), Muggia (in red) and San Dorligo della Valle – Dolina (in blue) (Fig. 1). A wider area, partly corresponding to the Province of Trieste in its extension, as presented in the map, has been considered as well for a wider range scale of analysis. The map highlights the boundaries of the consortium to emphasize the impact of the industrial area on different municipalities. As a public economic entity, linked to the Port Authority of Trieste, the consortium's goal is to create new jobs and enhance economic growth in its area, while also fostering technological growth and the competitiveness of local businesses [13, 14]. Furthermore, the consortium prioritizes environmental challenges and develops projects that are financed by both Friuli Venezia Giulia Region and the European Union.

This study area was chosen due to the proximity of the industrial zone to the port and urban areas. Indeed, studies, models, and representations of this proximity can be made, as this area represents a favorable environment for implementing processes for reusing waste generated by companies present within the territory, and therefore, the possibility of reusing them on site as secondary raw materials. The study area was therefore chosen both as a target for hypothesizing the local emergence of industrial symbiosis' processes, and for implementing, at a wider range, circular economical ones, involving activities not strictly related to the boundaries of the consortium itself.

3 Materials and Methods

3.1 Data

The development of this research starts from the construction of a geographic database, developed in collaboration with the consortium that led in previous work to the mapping of companies (mainly manufacturing) within the consortium district, obtaining a spatial idea of their location and distribution. (Fig. 2) [15]. This database was the first one to be realized and considered, particularly for focusing the attention on some specific activity to be considered as a case study for the industrial symbiosis. A second database was then realized to go more in depth into the analysis and for considering economic activities to be potentially involved in circular economical processes, not strictly located within the consortium's boundaries.

Specifically, the database developed in collaboration with Co.SELAG, involves mapping of settled activities (Fig. 1) and the areas, within the consortium's boundaries, interesting for testing the case study of circular economy. This database's development has enabled us to consider the various activities carried out in the region, even considering

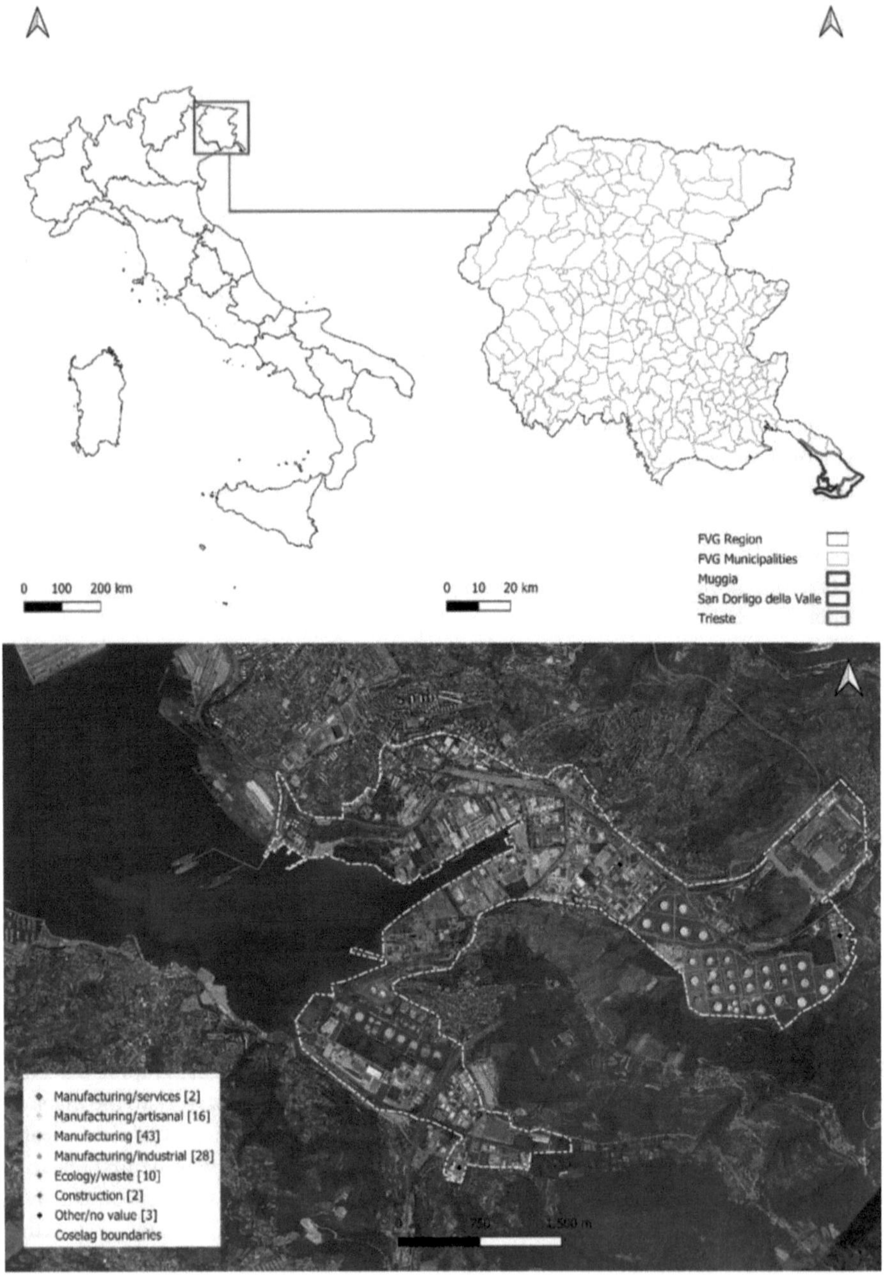

Fig. 1. Activities carried out on Co.SELAG territory (Sinatra F, 2024) [8]

the potential application of circular economy and industrial symbiosis strategies. Indeed, the mapping shows potential companies that can produce by-products and implement good practices in the circular economy (Table 1). This work has led to the identification of:

- Industrial symbiosis activity: identification of a liquor producer company that uses only the outer part of lemons for its own production, resulting in waste. The consortium was successful in identifying companies that might require these production wastes through ad hoc interviews and transferring these by- products to other companies.
- Circular economy strategies: an interesting case has been identified in the construction sector, where a plant that measures around 26,000 square meters is being demolished, which could lead to a potential flow of material into and out of treatment plants [15].

Table 1. Sample of Co.SELAG database

Company ID	*Address*	*Sector*	*ATECO code*	*Size*	*Activity*	*N° of employees*
1	*Via Pietra Ferrata*	*Ecology/waste*	*38.32.3 - Recovery and penetration for recycling of municipal solid waste, industrial waste, and biomass*	*Small*	*storage, processing by volume adjustment, the treatment of special waste, sorting, shredding and volumetric conditioning of special waste similar to urban*	*24*
2	*Strada delle saline*	*Manufacturing*	*10.37 - Manufacture of pasta, couscous, and similar farinaceous products*	*Big*	*Pasta pruduction*	*173*
3	*Via Flavia*	*Manufacturing*	*10.83.01 - Processing of coffe*	*Big*	*Activities related to coffee production*	*659*

To deepen the research, it was decided to focus on the demolition and construction field to examine the flows of second-generation raw materials in and out of the area mentioned above. Thus, different data were employed in the analysis. It was therefore essential to realize a second database containing the georeferenced data regarding the activities relevant for the circular economy study (Table 1).

Table 2. Data used for the construction of the database

Dataset	Open Data	Data Source
Quarries	✔	*Friuli Venezia Giulia Region*
Batching plants	✔	*Yellow Pages*
Recovery plants	✔	*Friuli Venezia Giulia Region*
Landfills	✔	*Friuli Venezia Giulia Region*
Areas to be redeveloped	✔	*Friuli Venezia Giulia Region*

The data in Table 2 was scrutinized and narrowed down based on the research requirements, excluding useless information. Thus, only installations that could be advantageous for providing materials for demolition or construction are considered.

This database was instrumental in the demolition/construction analysis, according to the extended Weber model and the application of GIS tools.

Subsequently, these data were processed and cross-referenced, in order to develop an ex novo database related to the different types of facilities and actors considered relevant to the operations of raw material procurement, demolition, waste delivery, waste treatment, and secondary raw material realization. The databases considered were taken to be managed and processed in GIS environment (QGIS) and visualization and sharing platforms (Google MyMaps) [8].

Furthermore, the industrial plan of the industrial zone of Trieste was also analysed, which provides for the redevelopment of some areas/buildings belonging to the consortium today and in the coming years (Figs. 2, 3):

- The recovery of abandoned areas: the Noghere area and the former Ferriera of Servola;
- Building of Caboto street: former headquarters of the Consortium, destined for demolition as the recovery of these spaces has been interrupted due to the assessment of criticality of the structural elements of the property;
- During 2024, the Consortium completes the railway connection in the direction of former Italcementi [8].

Fig. 2. Areas to be recovered (Personal elaboration, 2024)

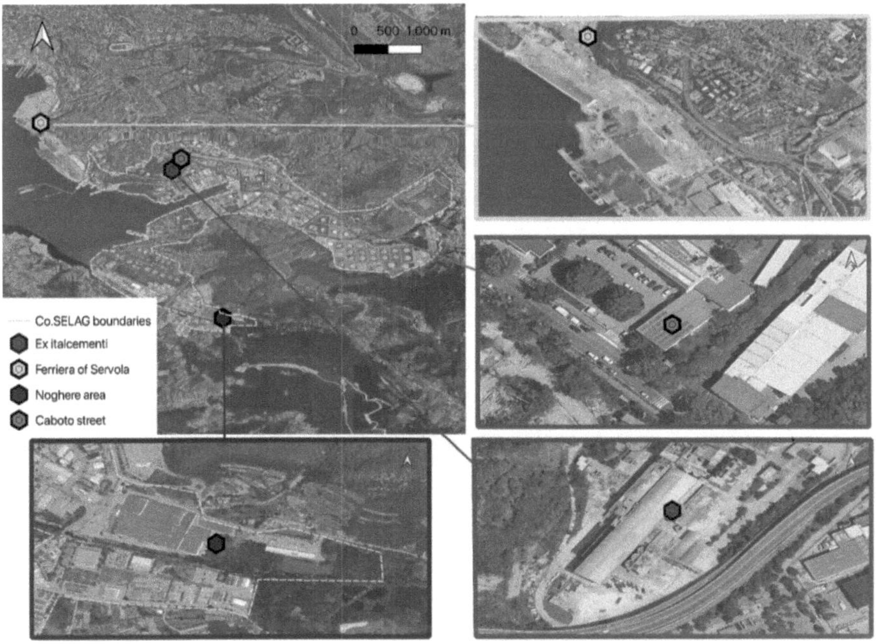

Fig. 3. Areas to be recovered zoom (Personal elaboration, 2024)

3.2 Methods

The methodology was built upon a previous project, titled 'MEISAR - Sustainable building materials and infrastructure: recycled aggregates', which was originally developed for a case study of demolition and reconstruction, and used waste materials as secondary raw materials, applied to the Football Stadium of Cagliari (Sardinia island, Italy) [5]. The logic behind the model was to extend Weber's industrial localization model, in which the place of production also becomes the origin of a secondary raw material [7].

Weber's classical model [7] analyses industrial location, explaining how companies decide on and choose the most optimal location in order to minimise transport, labour and agglomeration costs. In fact, according to this model, industries locate close to raw materials when transporting them is expensive, and close to markets when the cost of transporting the final product is high.

In the extended model it is essential to consider the spatial constraint in cluster analysis, where the distance between the plants and the place where the raw materials are used must not exceed 30 km. The rationale is to minimize transportation costs related to materials energy and products extended to recycled waste in the dual nature of waste and potential secondary raw materials.

Thus, the production facility could be situated in proximity to the waste generation site. Minimizing location and costs during the transformation process into second-grade raw materials requires a high level of flexibility in the construction of mobile plants. To quantify waste and its resulting percentage in a circular production process, it is necessary to use the classical Weber model. Weber's extended model is therefore essential for considering new waste generation sites and for encouraging the development of new opportunities given the proximity of the different activities.

The extension of the Weber model into circular optics focuses on considering second-hand raw materials as location variables, seeking to reduce transport costs and environmental impacts. Consequently, it is necessary to optimize the positioning of plants but also pay attention to minimizing waste and optimizing the reuse of materials, aiming to close the production cycle to increase the sustainability of the industrial zone.

Within the MEISAR project authors have expanded the classical Weber theory to incorporate concrete production. It is characterized by the presence of two types of materials:

- raw materials from quarries;
- secondary materials, resulting from recycling.

The model's circularity occurs when waste is fed back into circulation. The authors identified multiple scenarios during this project, which analyzed the demolition and reconstruction of the stadium in Cagliari (Fig. 4):

- Scenario 1, the production is located in the proximity of the quarry; the concrete plant instead located near the resources and no recycling of waste from demolition is foreseen.
- Scenario 2, the market M is also considered as resource origin (R2), in addition to quarries (R1). The concrete plant (F) is located close to the raw materials, although R2 becomes important for the extraction of raw and secondary materials. In this scenario, it is also assumed that raw and secondary materials are transported to the processing

site (F), located in R1. In this case, however, since these still need processing, it is assumed that the raw materials 'second' from the extraction site to the processing site (F), still located at R1, and simultaneously to the M market.

- Scenario 3, the market M is also considered as resource origin (R2), in addition to quarries (R1). Here the place of production (F) is in proximity to the market (M) and secondary raw materials (R2).
- Scenario 4, the market M is also considered as the source of resources (R2), in addition to the quarries (R1). This case is defined by the authors as a case à la Weber, because the concrete plant could be located in an intermediate position where the raw material cost function can be optimized [4–6].

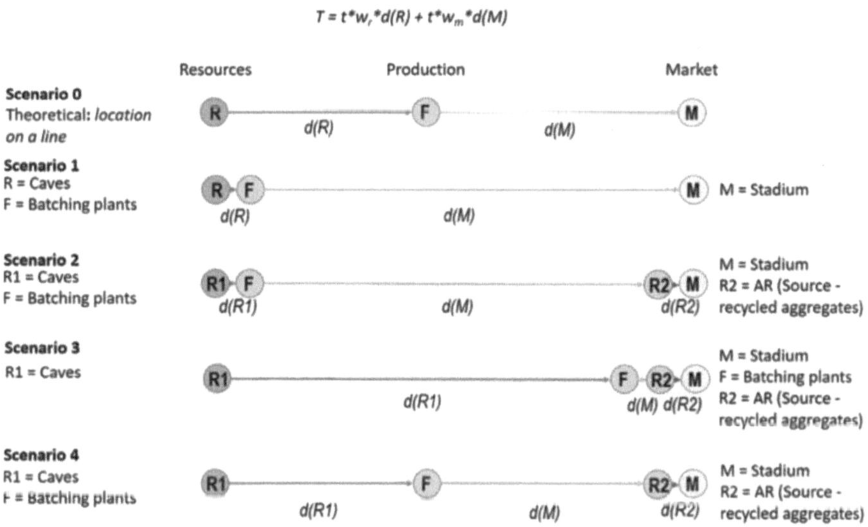

Fig. 4. Weberian localization model of batching plant in circular economy: Cagliari stadium case study (Balletto et al. 2019) [10–12]

This methodology has been applied within an industrial context with the objective of conducting proximity assessments, highlighted in the area of the port of Trieste.

All this was done in a framework where the GIS and spatial analysis part was crucial for the development of the research project. In fact, the GIS environment was used for collection, organization and selection of the data, consequently leading to the construction of the MEISAR Map. Furthermore, Google MyMaps has been used as a useful and practical tool that supports both the display of collected data and the research team's work.

The framework developed on QGIS has not only provided a precise scheme of the activities carried out in the industrial zone, but it has also identified the boundaries of Co.SELAG, Port system authority and all the stakeholders involved. Furthermore, it reveals useful for the identification of the target and for the realization of isochron maps. The isochron is the space of distance that can be traveled in a certain amount of time or distance using a predefined method of transport. They are important for visualizing and analyzing distances, taking into account the maximum distance of 30 km, in order to identify the plants reachable from the selected points.

4 Results and Discussion

The MEISAR project's methodology can be utilized to construct a map that is connected to Weber's theory in a circular perspective and can be a useful tool for sharing data. A mapping has taken place to pinpoint the batching plants, quarries, recovery plants, and landfills that are present in Friuli Venezia Giulia's territory (Fig. 5).

Fig. 5. MEISAR map FVG (Personal elaboration, 2024)

To get a more comprehensive perspective, we used Travel Time [16], a QGIS tool that enables the creation of isograms that allow for spatial analysis of data and assist in understanding and visualizing the relationships between places based on distance to reach them. In fact, thanks to this tool, a map of isochrones was developed. This map outlining and representing the area within 30 km from the consortium's redevelopment points allows the identification of inert recovery plants, quarries, and batching plants in the area. (Fig. 6).

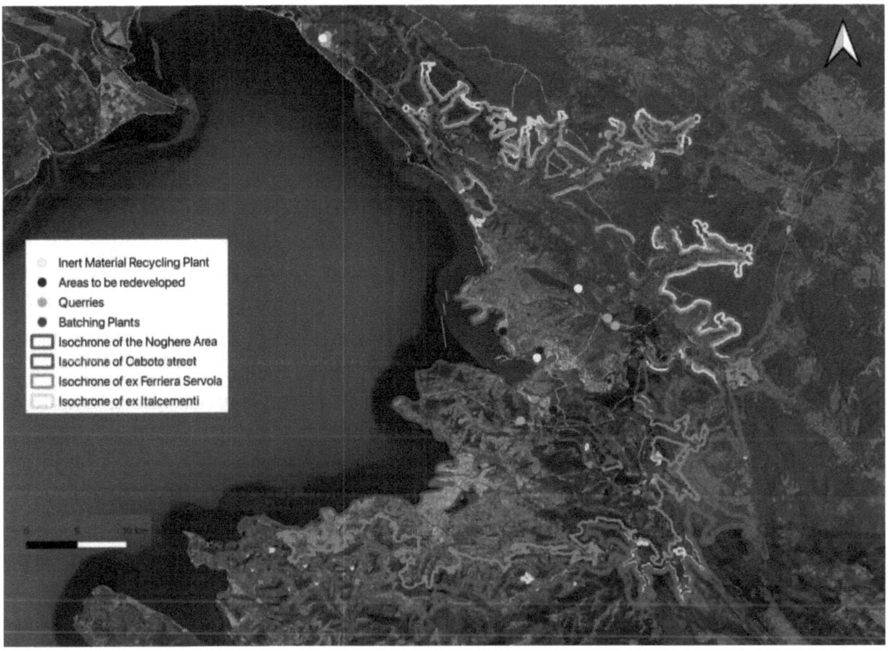

Fig. 6. Isochrone Map (Personal elaboration, 2024)

Taking into consideration the 30 km radius for the construction of the isochrone map and analysing the data processed within the MEISAR map of Friuli Venezia Giulia, it emerged that a significant percentage of the plants are located within our study area. Specifically, of the installations present in the region (401), approximately 6% are located in Trieste (23). Referring to the isochrones constructed during the analysis, 16 plants are included, i.e. 4% of the regional total (Table 3).

Table 3. Data used for the construction of the database

Location	Quarries	Batching Plants	Recovery Plants	Landfills	Total
Trieste	*10*	*2*	*3*	*8*	*23*
Friuli Venezia Giulia	*68*	*18*	*64*	*251*	*401*
Pants within the Isochrones	*7*	*2*	*2*	*8*	*23*

In addition, focusing on the Trieste area, it was found that almost 70% of the installations in Trieste fall within the radius we considered. This highlights a strong concentration of such facilities within our case study and confirms the attractiveness of the area under analysis.

5 Conclusion

Based on the analysis, it can be concluded that the industrial zone of Trieste can represent an interesting laboratory where Industrial Symbiosis and Circular Economy processes can be experimented. The combination of its geographical position, logistics, structural, and economic factors can enhance the development of a given region. The research carried on so far represents a first step in a wider analytical and operational proposal for implementing circularity in the economic production process, fostering industrial symbiosis in an industrial area. The case study analyzed, as that of the Trieste industrial area, appears promising in applying a model previously implemented, as an evolution of the Weber's model of industrial location applied to the concept of industrial symbiosis. The novelty of the approach lies in the application of the extended model to an industrial area, where, therefore, the potential for implementing innovative processes starting from existing activities can be set. The study so far presented was in fact aimed at setting up the workflow for implementing working and operational cases of industrial symbiosis. For this reason, the research presented was based on a similar research dealing with demolition and reconstruction in the construction sector, given an already available literature and best practices. A more in depth analysis will be needed to complete the database of companies and the activities they carry on, in order to observe their potential in terms of setting up industrial symbiotical processes at local level. The evolution of the research needs also to implement the theoretical aspects and model a more detailed and refined evolution of the industrial location theory model to include, in a renovated way, the possible local spatial interactions to be implemented in a circular economical process.

Acknowledgments. This publication was produced while attending PhD programme in Circular Economy at the University of Trieste, Cycle XXXVIII, with the support of a scholarship financed by the Ministerial Decree no. 351 of 9th April 2022, based on the NRRP - funded by the European Union - NextGenerationEU - Mission 4 "Education and Research", Component 1 "Enhancement of the offer of educational services: from nurseries to universities" - Investment 4.1 "Extension of the number of research doctorates and innovative doctorates for public administration and cultural heritage". Conceptualization, methodology, formal analysis, materials and resources, data curation and validation: all authors. In particular: Sinatra wrote Sects. 1, 2, 3 and 4; Borruso wrote the abstract and section 5.

Disclosure of Interests. The Authors Have no Competing Interests to Declare that Are Relevant to the Content of This Article

References

1. Lloyd, P.E., Dicken, P.: Location in space. A theoretical approach to economic geography (1977)
2. BruntlandCommission:Ourcommonfuture, https://sustainabledevelopment.un.org/content/documents/5987our-common-future.pdf. Accessed 10 Sept 2024
3. World Economic Forum, https://www.weforum.org/agenda/2024/03/sustainable-resource-consumption-urgent-un/#:~:text=Global%20natural%20resource%20consumption%20is,according%20to%20the%20United%20Nations. Accessed 25 Sept 2024

4. Geisendorf, S., Pietrulla, F.: The circular economy and circular economic concepts - a literature analysis and redefinition. Thunderbird Int. Business Rev. **60**(5), 771–782 (2018)
5. Savi, P.:Industria4.0Economiacircolare:possibiliconvergenzeeimplicazioniterritoriali. Società di Studi Geografici, **19**, 697 (2021)
6. Co.SELAGHomepage. https://www.coselag.it/,lastaccessed2024/09/04
7. Piano Industriale 2024 -2026 https://www.coselag.it/media/files/A00412/attachment/03_-_Piano_industriale_2024–2026_def-signed.pdf. Accessed 18 Sept 2024
8. Sinatra, F.,Borruso, G., Primiceri, S.: integrating territorialization, circular economy, and industrial symbiosis: leveraging gis for enhanced efficiency in industrial zones. In: Computational Science and Its Applications-ICCSA 2024: 24th International Conference, Part III, pp. 369–383, Hanoi (2024)
9. Piano Industriale 2024 -2026 https://www.coselag.it/media/files/A00412/attachment/03_-_Piano_industriale_2024-2026_def-signed.pdf. Accessed 18 Sept 2024
10. Balletto, G., Borruso, G., Mei, G.: Location theory and circular economy. Demolition, constructions and spatial organization of firms-an applied model to Sardinia Region. The case study of the New Cagliari Stadium. In: Computational Science and Its Applications- ICCSA 2019: 19th International Conference, Part III 19, pp. 535–550, Saint Petersburg (2019)
11. Balletto, G., Borruso, G., Mei, G., Milesi, A.: Economia circolare, gestione dei rifiuti da costruzione e demolizione e produzione di Aggregati Riciclati. Il progetto MEISAR-Un'applicazione alla Sardegna. Bollettino dell'Associazione Italiana di Cartografia (2020)
12. Balletto, G., Borruso, G., Mei, G., Milesi, A.: Strategic circular economy in construction: Case study in Sardinia, Italy. Journal of Urban Planning and Development, 147(4), (2021)
13. Weber,A.:Uberdenstandortderindustrien,Tubingen.EnglishtranslationbyCJFriedrich (1929) Theory of the Location of Industries. (1909)
14. Mappe temporali o "isocrone", https://cesaregerbino.wordpress.com/2012/01/23/mappe-temporali-o-isocrone/ Accessed 30 Sept 2024
15. TravelTimeHomepage. https://traveltime.com/,lastaccessed2024/09/20

A Comparison of Algorithms for the Spatial Clustering of Technological Assets

Magurno Davide[1], Lugli Andrea[1](✉), Bologna Fabio[1], Seravalli Alessandro[1], Battistini Alessandro[2], and Seraceni Matteo[2]

[1] Sis.Ter Srl SB, Via Emilia 69, Imola, BO, Italy
a.lugli@sis-ter.it
[2] Hera Luce Srl, Via Spinelli 60, Cesena, FC, Italy

Abstract. We compared in a GIS environment three algorithms for the spatial clustering of electrical panels, to optimize maintenance team routes and schedule their activities across quarters. The considered algorithms are the constrained K-means, an application of the traveling salesman problem and a third one which, despite being specifically developed, turned out to be less effective. This latter approach involves the discretization of the bounding polygon containing the panels using a vector grid, the subsequent identification of the cells on which the panels lie, and finally the aggregation into groups through statistical evaluations of the row and column coordinates of the grid cells. The processed samples consist of sets of panels in seven Italian cities, characterized by different sample sizes, distributions and densities. The algorithms' effectiveness was established as the capability to get good clustering results in all the considered situations. The evaluation was conducted using both qualitative and quantitative methods. Qualitatively, clusters were inspected visually. Quantitatively, we calculated intra-cluster and inter-cluster distances, compactness and separation indices such as the Dunn's and the Silhouette indices. The constrained K-means turned out to be the algorithm more suitable to our needs and so it has been implemented in a WebGIS application used as a decision support system by the electrical utility company Hera Luce srl[1] in Italy. A further enhancement involves using distances over a real road network instead of Euclidean ones, but this assumes the availability of an updated network, which is not always granted.

1 Introduction

The aim of this clustering is to optimize the maintenance activities of the electrical panels located in the Italian municipalities managed by the multi utility company Hera Luce srlhttps://www.heraluce.it. In normal conditions, maintenance is required to be performed once a year for each panel, excluding extraordinary activities. The maintainers are supposed to reach a panel, execute a check-up and operate any necessary operation, then move to the next one and repeat the operations for several panels a day, distributing the activities over the year in four quarters. Panels to be visited in a quarter should be grouped in a logical way so that they are close together, for two main reasons: the time spent in traveling from panel to panel should be as short as possible to maximize the

E. Borgogno-Mondino and P. Zamperlin (Eds.): ASITA 2024, CCIS 2463, pp. 262–291, 2025.
https://doi.org/10.1007/978-3-031-91141-5_19

maintenance activities; maintenance executed per area ensures a better efficiency of the system avoiding cascade failures on close panels. The same activities, and the necessity of clustering, are also required for other assets such as poles and lamps. The clustered assets are displayed in a WebGIS application called CityLight®, developed by Sis.Ter srl SB[1]. This platform functions as a management tool, providing features for planning and monitoring periodic maintenance.

To tackle this problem we compared the results of clustering obtained using three different approaches, namely the constrained K-means, the traveling salesman problem algorithm and a GIS approach specifically developed by us. Since the back-end of the CityLight® web application is written in PHP programming language, the dialogue between the front-end requests and the back-end responses has to be synchronous, avoiding as much as possible delays, otherwise the user cannot perform other operations while waiting for a response. This is the main reason why we chose to evaluate only algorithms whose implementation in PHP, Python or SQL language is not too complex so as to keep their execution as fast as possible. Also, the algorithm should be globally efficient for different sizes and shapes of the municipality and of the panels' envelope, both for large metropolitan areas and small rural towns, avoiding to differentiate the approaches in the code of the application.

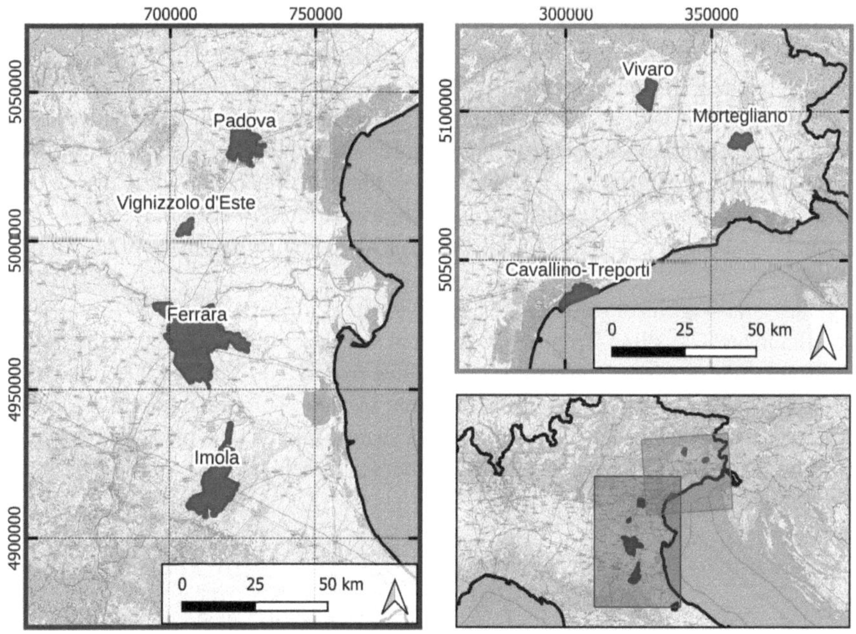

Fig. 1. Area of interest, located in Northern Italy. The considered municipalities are represented in red. Orange and blue bordered panels zoom the insights of the bottom left small-scale panel. The map with the orange frame is georeferenced in WGS84 UTM33 coordinates (EPSG 32633) while the other two maps are georeferenced in WGS84 UTM32 coordinates (EPSG 32632).

[1] https://www.sis-ter.com.

We compared indices relying on the intra-cluster and inter-cluster distances, namely the Dunn's and the Silhouette ones, to quantitatively evaluate the clustering performances. In general, the most challenging problem to manage is the kind of distance to consider, either Euclidean or calculated over a real road network. The distance metric can indeed significantly influence the obtained results and their evaluation, particularly in suburban and rural areas, where the road network density is lower.

2 Case Study Area

The case study area is located in Northern Italy and it is made up of seven out of 250 municipalities served by Hera Luce srl. We selected these municipalities among the others considering variations of the following factors:

- a shape index built on the planimetric distribution of the panels
- the number of panels
- the panels density
- urban/countryside context

The shape index has been calculated starting from the envelope of the panels of each municipality and by dividing the length of its East-West length side by the North-South one. Thus, when the shape index is larger than one we have rectangular envelopes oriented in the East-West direction, when it is one we have square envelopes, when it is smaller than one we have rectangular envelopes oriented in the North-South direction.

The panels density has been calculated as the number of panels divided by the envelope area, expressed in square kilometers. In line with the activities of CityLight®, when the number of panels is very low (i.e. less than 15) it is better not to divide them, thus all the maintenance is executed during a single quarter. However, the cases of Vivaro (11 panels) and Mortegliano (14 panels) are considered to accomplish a more complete analysis.

Vivaro and Vighizzolo d'Este are small towns with less than 2,000 inhabitants, Mortegliano and Cavallino-Treporti are medium size cities of 5,000-15,000 inhabitants, while Imola, Ferrara and Padova are large cities from 70,000 to 200,000 inhabitants. By considering the combination of the different factors, each municipality has its own characteristics; for instance, Vivaro and Imola share similar shape index and density of panels, but have very different sizes and numbers of panels.

We also took into account the statistical behavior of the panels of each municipality. The following Fig. 2 shows the dispersion of the planimetric positions of the panels around the center of the distribution, accounting the distances as Euclidean ones and assuming the spatial distribution of the panels as Gaussian. To note that the ratio between the length of the semi-axes of the ellipse, along with their orientation, reflects the shape index.

From this point forward, all the maps of the municipalities of Padova, Ferrara, Imola and Vighizzolo d'Este are georeferenced in WGS84 UTM32 coordinates (EPSG 32632), while the maps of the municipalities of Cavallino-Treporti, Mortegliano and Vivaro are georeferenced in WGS84 UTM33 coordinates (EPSG 32633).

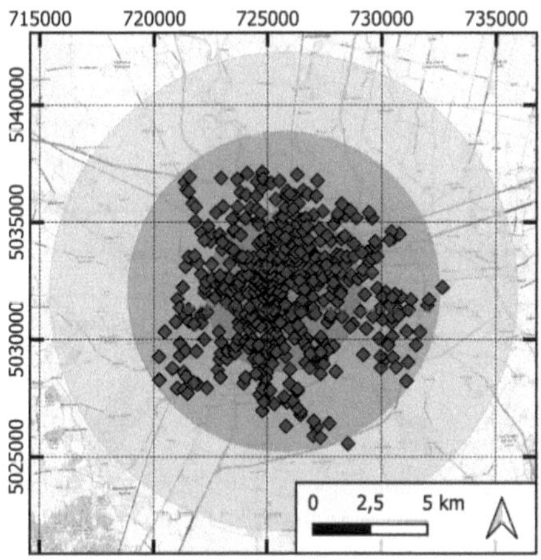

Padova (PD)

The distribution of the panels is compact and almost circular, with no clear separation into distinct groups of panels. The panels are located within 2σ from the center of the distribution and can be grouped in several equivalent ways.

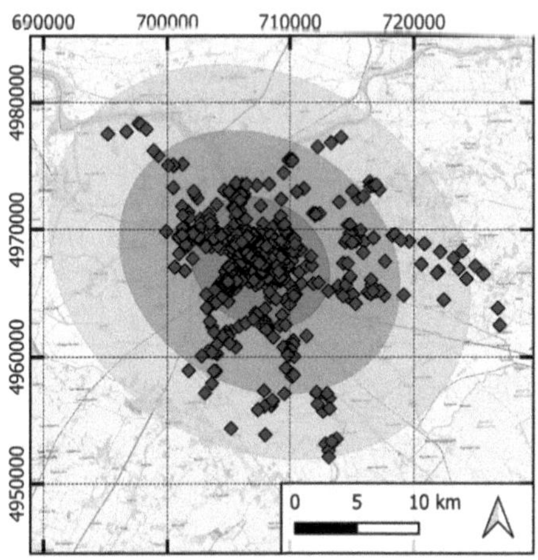

Ferrara (FE)

Most of the panels are located at the center of the distribution, but radial branches are evident along the main roads, reaching over 3σ from the center. These branches can be intuitively interpreted as separated groups of panels for an ideal clustering.

Fig. 2. Planimetric distribution of the panels for all the investigated municipalities. The concentric ellipses are related to 1, 2 and 3 standard deviations (σ) of the panels positions with respect to the center.

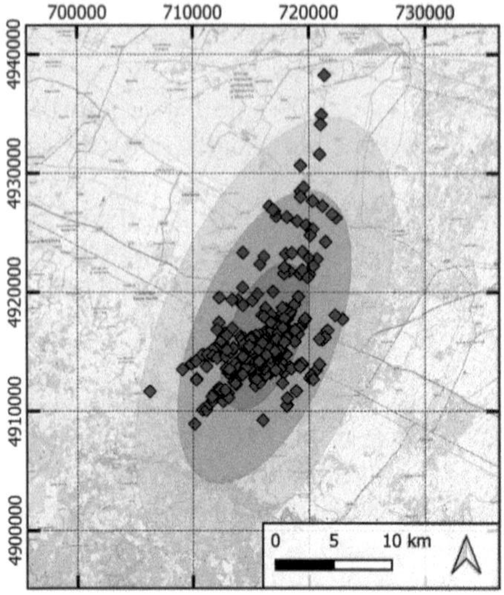

Imola (BO)
Extremely unbalanced in the north-south direction, it shows a long tail of panels northward, over 3σ from the center of the distribution, which are expected to be grouped together by the clustering algorithms. The center itself is anyway very rich in panels.

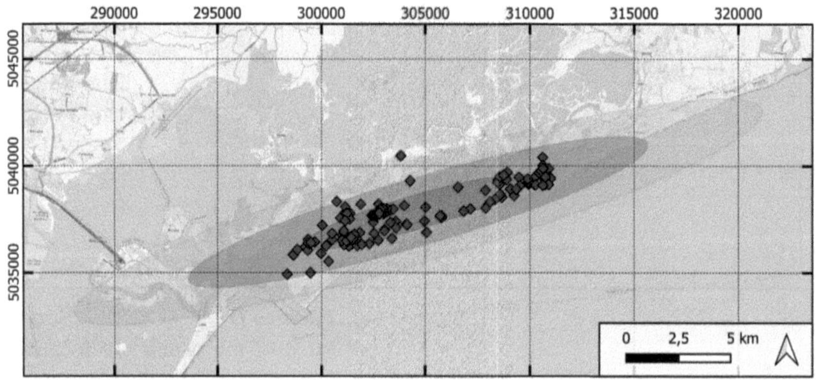

Cavallino - Treporti (VE)
With an evident East-West elongation, this municipality extends over a number of islands separated by canals in the Venetian lagoon. Clustering of panels could be affected by the lack of connections between the islands. The distribution is still compact and mostly within 2σ from the center.

Fig. 2. (*continued*)

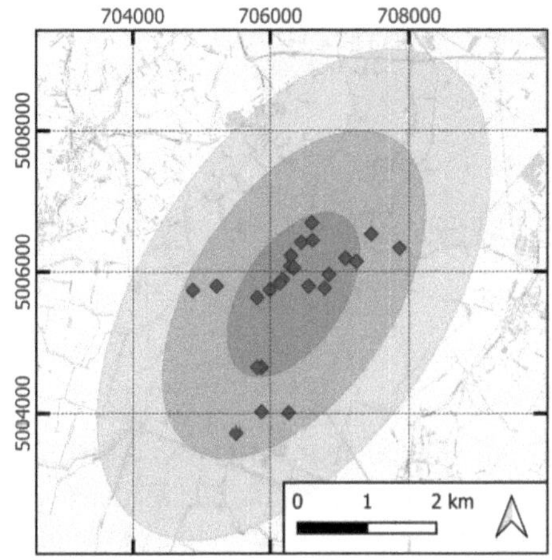

Vighizzolo d'Este (PD)

Despite the limited number of panels it is possible to identify two main groups: the first is close to the center of the distribution and almost horizontal; the second is southward, still within 2σ, causing a north-south extension of the envelope.

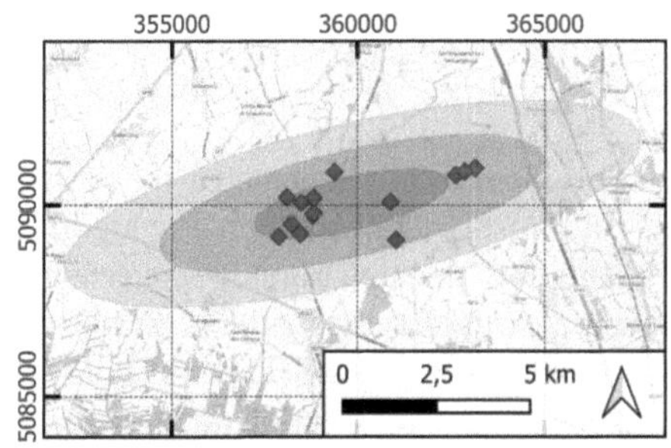

Mortegliano (UD)

The small amount of panels makes it difficult to identify clear groups, even if the extension of the envelope in the East-West direction eases the job. The panels are concentrated within 2σ from the center.

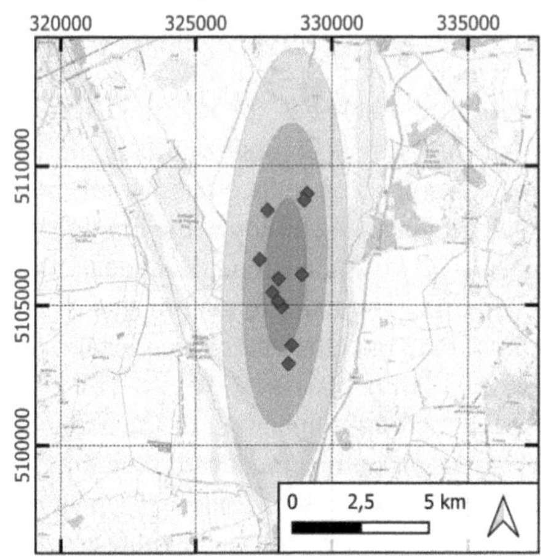

Vivaro (PN)

Similar to the case of Mortegliano, it shows few panels within 2σ from the center of the distribution and without clear groups, but with a North-South extension of the envelope.

Fig. 2. (*continued*)

Considering municipalities with such diverse characteristics makes the sample, though small, statistically representative and, consequently, provides the analysis with a certain degree of reliability, once the proper distribution is identified, as discussed more in detail in paragraph 5.4.

3 Methods

We tested three clustering approaches and a variant of the last one, namely:

- Traveling Salesman Problem (TSP)
- a GIS algorithm created ad hoc (AHG)
- Euclidean K-Means (KME)
- K-Means over a road network graph (KMG)

As for the metrics considered by the algorithms, TSP, AHG and KME rely on Euclidean distances, while KMG distances are calculated over the real road network. In the trials the panels have been divided into four clusters corresponding to the quarters in which the maintenance is planned through the year.

3.1 Traveling Salesman Problem (TSP)

This approach refers to the traveling salesman problem, as implemented in the PgRouting extension of the PostgreSQL dbms, relying on Boost Graph Library[2]. The algorithm is initialized at a specified starting point (or a randomly selected point if no starting point is provided). It then follows a greedy approach, iteratively visiting the nearest unvisited panel until all panels are covered. This problem is classified as NPHard, meaning that no known polynomial-time algorithm can guarantee an optimal solution for large instances [1]. To address this, a heuristic method based on the Nearest Neighbour (NN) algorithm is employed to construct an initial route [2]. Afterward, optimization techniques are applied to refine the solution and reduce the total travel distance. Specifically, after generating the initial route with the NN heuristic, pgRouting enhances the solution using local optimization methods, such as the 2-opt algorithm. This technique works by iteratively swapping two edges in the route to remove crossings and reduce the overall distance, leading to a more efficient route [3]. More specifically, we employed the Euclidean TSP variant, which uses the coordinates of points in a two-dimensional Euclidean plane as input, rather than a predefined connectivity matrix. The main feature of this algorithm is that in solving the path it does not pass more than once from the same location.

To process the data we wrote two SQL scripts. The first script solves the TSP problem and then divides the panels into four almost equal groups depending on the connectivity order and starting from the number of panels present in the considered municipality.

When the number of panels is very small, like in the case of Vivaro (11 panels), the groups consist of only two or three panels. The second script traces the route connecting the panels, in the defined order, and it is intended mostly for validation and visual inspection of the obtained results.

We performed several trials, both specifying the starting/ending points by considering the shape index (e.g., for a low shape index, the starting point was set at the northern

[2] https://www.boost.org/doc/libs/1_86_0/libs/graph/doc/metric_tsp_approx.html Last visited: 2024/09/20

panel and the ending point at the southern panel) or without defining them. In this latter case, the starting "seed" point is chosen randomly by the algorithm itself. As for the web-application, this approach is implementable on the database side, where it can be scheduled to run nightly so to have the results ready to be queried by the back-end the subsequent morning. Even considering all the municipalities, execution time and computational load remain low, allowing also a real-time on-demand processing.

Attempts to use the TSP as a clustering approach had previously been made [4] but without considering its relations with the shape index of the study area and the compactness and separation of the obtained clusters.

3.2 Ad Hoc GIS Gridding (AHG)

Seeking the faster approach in terms of computational time, we also developed an ad hoc algorithm, to be executed as a Python script called by the PHP back-end. We conceived it in ESRI ArcGIS Pro but it can also be tested in other GIS environments, such as QGIS. The following is a brief description of the main steps, referred to a single municipality for clarity, which are also shown in the graphic schema in Fig. 3:

1. determination of the envelope of the panels, intended as the smallest rectangle (bounding box) aligned with the coordinate axes that fully contains all the panels;
2. creation of a vectorial grid sharing the same extent of the envelope. As for the spacing, we consider square cells of 200 m side;
3. spatial join to link the panels to the grid, to obtain the number of panels inside each cell, stored in a field named "join count";
4. to reduce time in calculations, we consider only the cells that have at least a panel inside;
5. we add a new field named "cluster" both to the grid and to the panels shapefiles (or tables if data are stored in a spatial database);
6. in a *while* cycle a cursor loops all the cells of the grid updating a variable named "counter" with the sum of the values of the "join count" field until it reaches a quarter of the total number of panels;
7. when the above condition is satisfied, we update the "cluster" field in the grid shapefile with a progressive number, which identifies the cluster;
8. the loop cycle continues on the other quarters, filling the last one with all the remaining panels;
9. finally all the not empty cells of the grid have the "cluster" field valued; 10. With a spatial join we assign the cluster number from the grid to the panels.

To note that the loop direction (e.g. along the rows or the columns of the grid) at point 6 is controlled by the shape index of the envelope of the panels. When the shape index is larger than one (corresponding to an envelope elongated in the East-West direction) or equal to one, the grid is looped along rows. While the shape index is instead smaller than one, the table corresponding to the grid is transposed and it is looped by columns. It is important to note that the logic behind the partitioning of the panels into groups, as described in steps 7 and 8, is conceptually similar to the Traveling Salesman Problem (TSP), where the list of panels, ordered by their connectivity, is divided into quarters. As regards the execution time, once optimized this approach is indeed fast.

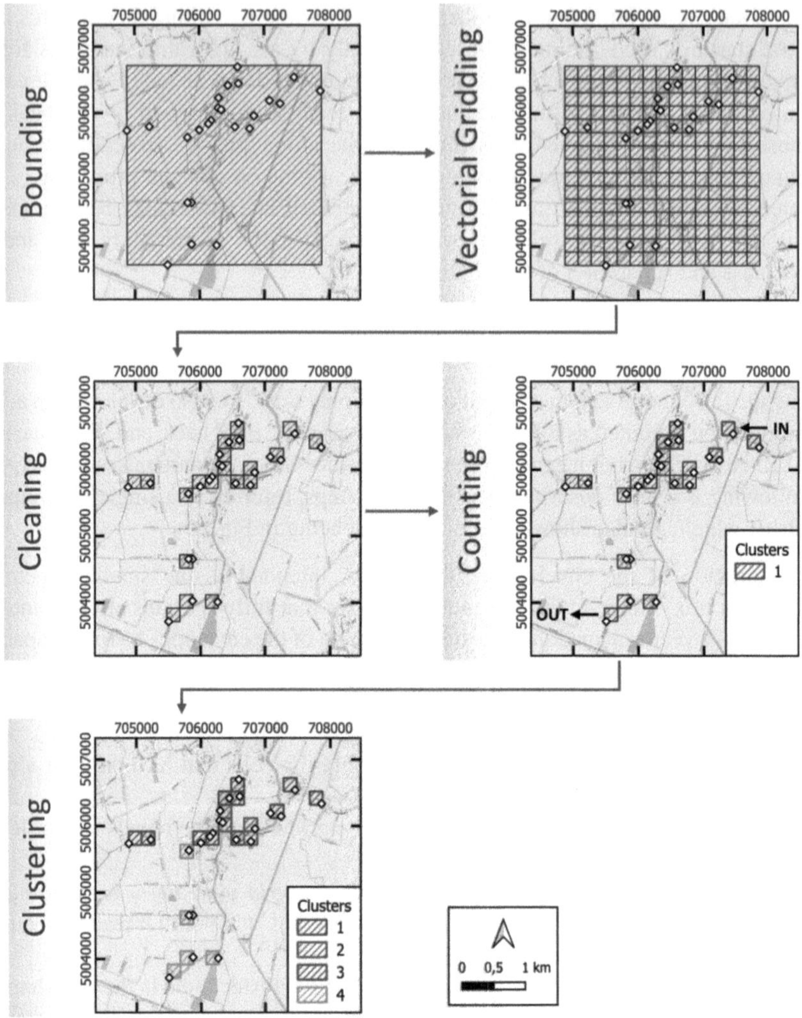

Fig. 3. Schematization of the AHG procedure, for the case of Vighizzolo d'Este.

3.3 Euclidean K-means (KME)

K-means clustering [5] is a common method to partition objects, thanks to its simple implementation. It consists in an unsupervised algorithm where the number n of clusters is fixed as initial condition. Given n centroids randomly chosen within the Euclidean space of the elements to be classified, the process proceeds iteratively in two steps:

1. each element is assigned to a cluster according to the closest centroid
2. new centroids are computed as the Euclidean mean coordinates among the elements assigned to the cluster

The process runs until convergence, fixing the clusters.

The disadvantages can be identified in a large number of iterations for large amounts of data and in a dependence on the initial centroids assignment in case of significant symmetries.

Despite the fact that the number of clusters is fixed from the beginning, their size is not and, depending on the distribution of the elements, it could end with just a single large cluster and *n-1* very small ones, that is not the goal of our analysis. Therefore, we applied a constrained K-means algorithm[3] based on [6] where the number of elements per cluster can be limited to an upper and/or lower limit; we fixed the maximum number of panels for each quarter as

$$\frac{p}{4} + 0.1 \cdot \frac{p}{4}$$

where p is the total amount of panels, ensuring a uniform workload distribution over the year.

3.4 K-means Over Road Network Graph (KMG)

Differently from an ideal Euclidean world, computing the shortest path between two points should take into account the real available road network, so should the K-means algorithm since the accuracy of using Euclidean distances rapidly declines with increasing the complexity of the network [7]. The impact of considering real road distances could be relevant in many fields, even if only few studies used it to estimate optimal location for hydrogen stations [8], supply chain nodes [9], or logistic hubs [10], and no one tried to evaluate its weight in scheduling a maintenance plan.

In a GIS environment distances between two points can be calculated basically in two ways: Euclidean distance and the so-called Manhattan distance, which is measured over a grid-like path. In a Manhattan metric (also known as "taxicab" metric) the points are assumed to be located on a regular square grid and distance between points is measured as a "rectilinear" distance (i.e. the sum of the absolute values of the differences of their corresponding components) along the lines of the grid [11]. While in Euclidean metric the shortest path corresponds to the straight line joining the two points, here it is usually calculated through Dijkstra's algorithm [12] (or its variations, such as A* [13]) as a result of a shortest path tree [14]. Better approximating a road network, of course it is the Manhattan distance that describes in a likely way the reality, especially in urban areas. Nevertheless, with the exception of many US cities, roads in Europe and in Italy form anything but a regular grid. Therefore, a more consistent approach is required to account for the fact that two geographically close urban elements could be far apart in terms of road segments connecting each other, especially when rivers or hills fragment the road network. We decided to compute the actual road distances by downloading the road network from OpenStreetMap[4] (OSM) and considering a 2 km buffer around the city limits; this ensures that roads connecting the most external boroughs are not truncated, especially in hilly areas. Then, we cleaned it to simplify the graph (Fig. 4) and to reduce the computation time by:

3 K-means-constrained 0.7.3 - PyPI.Available at https://pypi.org/ Last visited 2024/09/13

4 http://download.geofabrik.de/europe/italy.html Last visited: 2024/09/13.

- removing the road categories (OSM definition) bridleway, cycleway, footway, path, pedestrian, service, steps, track, which are useless for our maintenance purposes
- removing the dead-end streets, if no panels are there
- removing closed loop street elements with no panels along the path, since they won't be traveled
- ignoring two-levels crossroads, which are usually only relevant along the highway path outside the city center
- ignoring the distinction between one-way and two-ways road

Despite the last point could be controversial, especially considering that most of the Italian city centers are structured with many one-way streets, we want here to maintain the computation time as short as possible for the largest cities. Moreover, the areas where we expect the highest effectiveness for this approach are those outside the city center, where the network is sparse and it is unusual to find one-way streets.

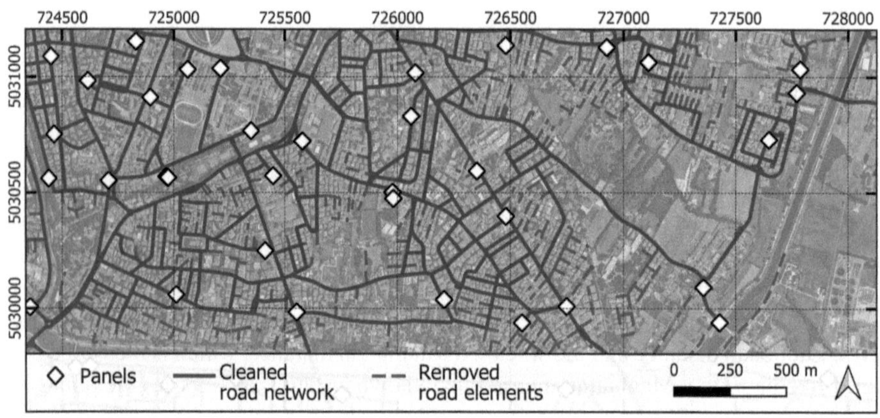

Fig. 4. Details of the city center of Padova. Dead-end streets and closed loops (orange dashed lines) are removed from the road network if no panels are detected (white diamonds).

We modified the constrained K-means algorithm so that road intersections are nodes of the undirected graph; target panels for this study are also considered as nodes. Road segments between two intersections are considered as arches of known length. The distance between each panel and every other grid node is computed through Dijkstra's algorithm as the shortest path along the network. Then, we randomly selected four starting nodes, one for each quarter, and the algorithm solves the minimum cost flow problem to associate panels to centroids. The process is repeated iteratively until convergence, by considering as new centroids the nodes with the minimum total distance from the panels of the same cluster along the road network.

The time required for the minimum cost flow solutions increases dramatically with the size of the city and the complexity of the graph. In our case study, the small town of Vivaro only has 11 panels and 427 road segments, running in less than a third of a second. On the other hand, Ferrara has 780 panels to connect through 10919 road segments; once cleaned by removing useless segments as explained above, Ferrara's network can be halved to 5379 segments, still requiring about two hours to complete. Nevertheless, by assuming that the road network is fixed over time, it is possible to compute the cost matrix in the background with Dijkstra's algorithm, then the routing optimization for cluster separation is performed in almost real time within the CityLight® web application.

A possible alternative to speed up the computation of the cost matrix could be the A* algorithm [13], which is essentially an evolution of Dijkstra's. This algorithm applies heuristics to estimate the direction to explore when searching for the shortest path between two points, thus limiting the number of connections to verify based on an initial estimate of the origin-to-destination distance (e.g. by computing Euclidean distance). However, A* is optimized to find the minimum path between a single couple of points, whereas Dijkstra's allows the computation of the entire matrix in only one run, being more suitable for our purpose. Other solutions, like Johnson's [15], BellmanFord's [16] or Floyd-Warshall's [17] algorithms have different advantages for some kind of graph, which is not our case, and are less efficient overall, so they are also excluded in favour of Dijkstra.

4 Analysis

The comparison between the tested approaches has been evaluated both qualitatively and quantitatively, considering clustering indices like the Dunn's and the Silhouette ones. We also considered the total length of the path, computed over the road network, necessary to connect all the panels inside each cluster, even when these clusters were obtained from approaches relying on Euclidean metric, since in the real world maintenance teams move on the road network. For the qualitative evaluation, we assessed the clustering results with respect to natural features (e.g. rivers) and anthropogenic features (e.g. major roads) that characterize the areas of interest.

4.1 Dunn's Index

Among the several indices available to evaluate the effectiveness of different clustering approaches, Dunn's index [18] is both readable and simple to calculate. It is defined as the ratio between the minimum inter-cluster distance and the maximum intra-cluster distance:

$$min_j \neq id_(i,j)$$

$$Dunn's = min_{1in}\left(\frac{}{maxk \in idk}\right)$$

where the inter-cluster distance $d_{(i,j)}$ is computed as that between the centroids of the clusters i and j, and the intra-cluster distance d_k is computed between two elements of the same cluster. Dunn's index is the minimum value computed for all the clusters. To note that the index is always positive, with a minimum value of zero corresponding to two coincident centroids. The higher the index, the more the clusters are compact and well separated with respect to each other. On the contrary, low index values mean close/overlapping clusters or poorly defined ones.

A key strength of this approach is its versatility with respect to the kind of metric to be considered in distance calculation: it can be an Euclidean distance, a Manhattan one or even a distance calculated over a road network [19][20]. We computed the Dunn's index (Table 2) for the clusters obtained with the four techniques described in Section 3 by considering two variants: distances are computed in an Euclidean space for TSP, AHG, and KME, since Euclidean distances are used to cluster them, whereas they are computed over the road network for KMG because of the different clustering technique. However, since the panels' maintainers will move on the road network, we also evaluate the first three approaches by computing the Dunn's index on graph distances, which is also shown in Table 2 (last three columns, suffixed with -G as Graph). Fig. 5, top panel, shows the index as a function of the number of panels, for different techniques. The highest values are always obtained for a low number of panels, when it is easier to create well separated groups compared with the short overall distances, then the index decreases with increasing the number of panels since the clusters' separation becomes smaller with respect to their size. KME always produces higher index values, however, when evaluating the clustering effectiveness in relation to the road network, KMG shows better or comparable results than KME-G.

No peculiar trends are observed, instead, when comparing the Dunn's index with the municipality's shape index (Fig. 5, bottom panel).

Table 1. Morphology and characteristics of the case study municipalities.

municipality	shape index	municipality area [km^2]	envelope area panels [km^2]		density (in thousands) [# / km^2]
Vivaro	0.258	37,628	9,694	11	1.1
Imola	0.567	204,948	486,481	325	0.7
Vighizzolo d'Este	1.001	17,078	8,888	24	2.7
Padova	1.075	92,984	143,838	490	3.4
Ferrara	1.209	405,408	834,852	780	0.9
Cavallino-Treporti	1.927	45,080	78,297	145	1.9
Mortegliano	2.322	29,999	11,149	14	1.3

Table 2. Dunn's index for different clustering techniques. Indices in columns suffixed with -G are computed by considering distances over the road network instead of euclidean ones.

municipality	TSP	AHG	KME	KMG	TSP-G	AHG-G	KME-G
Vivaro	0.45	0.73	1.15	0.94	0.29	0.83	0.68
Mortegliano	0.40	0.23	0.75	0.44	0.35	0.18	0.57

(continued)

Table 2. (*continued*)

municipality	TSP	AHG	KME	KMG	TSP-G	AHG-G	KME-G
Vighizzolo d'Este	0.53	0.43	0.74	0.23	0.01	0.00	0.22
Cavallino-Treporti	0.37	0.37	0.52	0.39	0.02	0.09	0.19
Imola	0.12	0.12	0.33	0.13	0.07	0.08	0.14
Padova	0.05	0.13	0.36	0.29	0.09	0.12	0.27
Ferrara	0.16	0.06	0.26	0.15	0.07	0.05	0.10

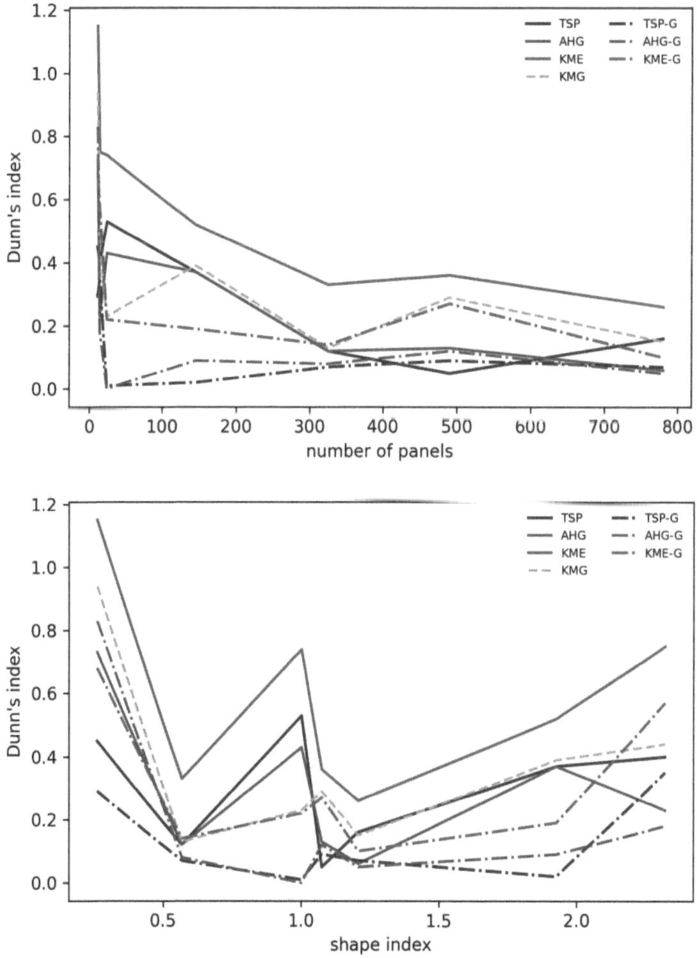

Fig. 5. Dunn's index as a function of the number of panels (top panel) and shape index (bottom panel). Solid lines show approaches based on Euclidean distances, also evaluated on Euclidean distances. The yellow dashed line shows the pure road network approach KMG. Dashdot lines show the same results of the corresponding solid lines (color coded) but evaluated over road network distances.

4.2 Silhouette Index

Another common internal metric to evaluate the effectiveness of clustering results is the Silhouette index [21], which measures the consistency of element assignment to a cluster rather than the identification of the cluster as a whole. Define

$$a_k = \frac{\sum_{k\prime \in i \rightarrow} \rightarrow d(k, k\prime)}{p_i - 1}$$

where $d_{k,k'}$ is the distance between two of the p_i elements of the cluster i, then being a_k the average distance of element k to all the other elements in the same cluster. Define

$$b_k = min_j \cdot \frac{\sum_{w \notin i} d(k, w)}{p_j}.$$

where $d_{(k,w)}$ is the distance between the element k of cluster i and any element w of a different cluster j, then being b_k the minimum average distance of element k to all the other clusters. The silhouette value of element k is defined as

$$s_k = \frac{b_k \; - \; a_k}{max(a_k, b_k)}$$

that is by definition a value in the range $-1 \leq s \leq 1$, where 1 indicates that k is close to its cluster neighbors and far from the other clusters, while –1 indicates that it is probably badly matched. Values around zero are of uncertain significance. The average Silhouette value for cluster i is defined as the average for all its elements

$$s_i = \frac{\sum_k \in i \rightarrow sk}{p_i}.$$

Finally, the Silhouette index for the clustering process is the average value of all the clusters means

$$Silhouette\ index = \frac{\sum i \rightarrow si.}{n}$$

where n is the number of clusters.

As for the Dunn's index, also the Silhouette index can be computed in an Euclidean space or by considering distances over a road network. Once again, we computed it (Table 3) for the clusters obtained with the four techniques described in Section 3 by considering the two variants: TSP, AHG, and KME are evaluated with Euclidean distances, while KMG is computed over a road graph, which is also used to re-evaluate the first three approaches in a real world situation (last three columns of Table 3, suffixed with -G as Graph).

Figure 6, top panel, shows the index as a function of the number of panels, for different techniques. The highest values are always obtained for a low number of panels, when it is easier to associate panels to specific groups, then the index decreases with increasing the number of panels since the panels' separation becomes smaller with respect to the cluster size. KME and KMG produce higher index values, however, when evaluating the clustering effectiveness over the road network, KMG shows better results than KME-G, with a single exception for the city of Padova (490 panels) due to its peculiar shape (see discussion in Section 5.3).

Nevertheless, no clear trends are observed for the Silhouette index as a function of the municipality's shape index (Fig. 6, bottom panel).

Table 3. Silhouette index for different clustering techniques. Indices in columns suffixed with G are computed by considering distances over the road network instead of Euclidean ones.

municipality	TSP	AHG	KME	KMG	TSP-G	AHG-G	KME-G
Vivaro	0.24	0.38	0.50	0.47	0.21	0.38	0.45
Mortegliano	0.29	0.08	0.46	0.35	0.25	0.06	0.36
Vighizzolo d'Este	0.23	0.19	0.39	0.33	-0.01	0.01	0.16
Cavallino-Treporti	0.22	0.22	0.36	0.40	0.16	0.18	0.26
Imola	0.04	0.07	0.19	0.17	0.06	0.05	0.12
Padova	0.11	0.15	0.33	0.28	0.11	0.14	0.30
Ferrara	0.01	0.03	0.15	0.19	0.01	0.00	0.11

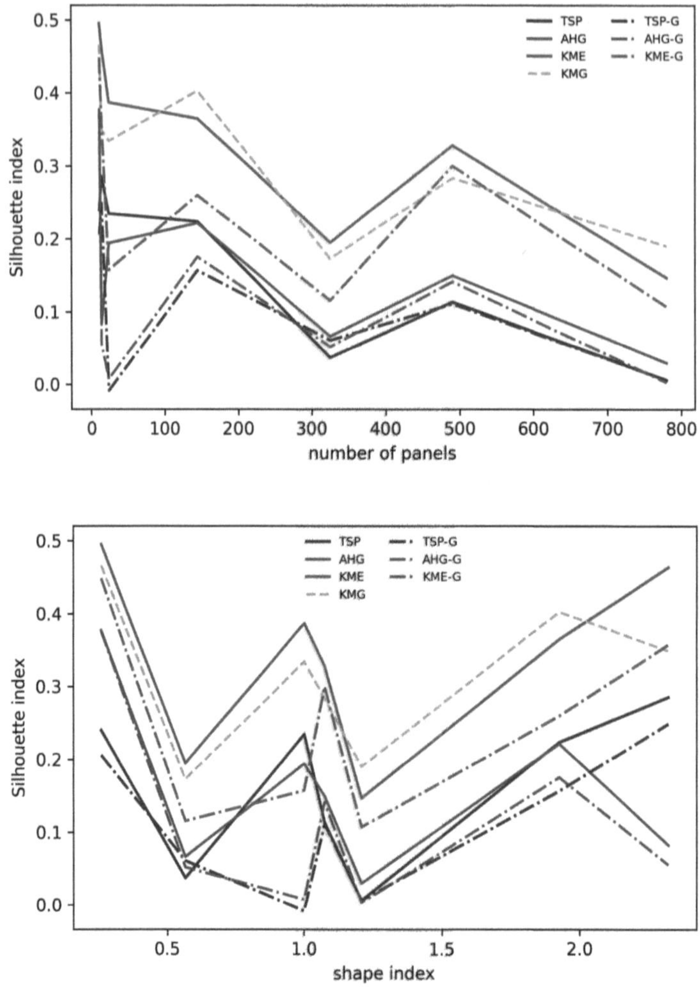

Fig. 6. Silhouette's index as a function of the number of panels (top panel) and shape index (bottom panel). Solid lines show approaches based on Euclidean distances, also evaluated on Euclidean distances. The yellow dashed line shows the pure road network approach KMG. Dashdot lines show the same results of the corresponding solid lines (color coded) but evaluated over road network distances.

4.3 Quantitative Assessment of the Clustering Indices

To quantitatively assess which clustering approach is the most appropriate to our data, we compared the statistical features of Dunn's and Silhouette indices of the obtained clusters. Given that we are considering only seven values, we cannot assume their distribution as Gaussian, also because of their skewness with respect to the arithmetic average (Table 4). Therefore, we chose to consider the Skew-t distribution [22], which is a generalization of the Student's t-distribution that also introduces positive and negative skewness into the model. The Skew-t distribution demonstrates a good likelihood function, which represents the probability of the observed index values occurring if they were truly generated by the selected distribution [23].

We also considered other distributions suitable for modeling small amounts of skewed data, but for various reasons, we concluded that none of them was appropriate. For instance, the Gamma distribution is suitable to model small amounts of skewed data but it results to be biased in case of negative skewness [24]. As a matter of fact, while the Dunn's index presents a negative skewness only in the case of the TSP approach, about a half of the Silhouette skewness values are negative, making the Gamma distribution unsuitable. As for the Beta distribution, it is more appropriate for modeling data constrained within the 0-1 range, which does not apply to the Dunn's index.

Table 4. Skewnesses of the Dunn's and Silhouette indices values, calculated for the clusters obtained with the seven approaches, along with the logarithms of the likelihood functions assuming a Skew-t distribution. Note that the skewness is calculated with respect to the arithmetic mean, so it is not the t-skewness.

approach	skewness	log-likelihood	skewness	log-likelihood
TSP	-0.159	3.3	−0.36	6.8
AHG	0.855	2.9	0.80	7.3
KME	0.703	0.7	−0.35	6.2
KMG	1.362	2.6	−0.03	7.1
TSP-G	0.854	7.6	0.09	8.0
AHG-G	1.881	5.2	1.15	7.6
KME-G	0.823	3.5	0.28	6.7

4.4 Graph Connectivity

The selected case studies represent cities between 900 and 210,000 inhabitants, thus with a completely different size and development of their road network. This means that all the evaluations concerning the clustering of panels over the graph are strongly dependent on its connectivity level. The road networks ranges from 27 kilometers for the town of Vighizzolo d'Este (reduced to 14 kilometers once the graph is cleaned from the useless – for our goals – segments) to 1087 kilometers for the city of Ferrara (936 km cleaned), which are usually referred to as the cost of the network. Also, the number of nodes and links in the network are proportionally different, with Vighizzolo d'Este which is about 2% the size of Ferrara. Nevertheless, the connectivity level within the perimeter of the different municipalities could be somehow scaled but similar, thus, we evaluated it through a series of indices [25]:

- Network density: total cost of the network compared to the surface of the municipality. The higher the index, the denser the network, but roads could lack inter-connections.
- Eta index: average length of the links. The lower the index, the higher the complexity of the network.

- Beta index: average number of links per node. The higher the index, the higher the number of routing options available at each crossroad.
- Alpha index: ratio between the number of existing cycles (closed loops along the road network) and the maximum number of possible cycles. The higher the index, the higher the number of alternative routings between the same origin/destination couples.

By combining them into a comprehensive Connectivity index, computed as the average of the four normalized components (see details in Table 5), it is clear that Padova owns the most complex and dense road network, where many options are available to connect different nodes with short paths. On the contrary, Vighizzolo d'Este owns the least complex network due to its reduced size, followed by Cavallino-Treporti which is conditioned by its own morphology being extended over different islands connected by bridges.

Table 5. Road network connectivity parameters.

municipality road cleaned nodes links network index municipality road cleaned nodes links network Eta Beta Alpha Conn network road density index index [km] [m/km^2]

Vivaro	46	30	153	196	0.8	153.46	1.28	0.15	0.66
Mortegliano	64	30	228	294	1.0	100.80	1.29	0.15	0.59
Vighizzolo d'Este	27	14	131	148	0.8	95.91	1.13	0.07	0.45
Cavallino-Treporti	152	101	909	1092	2.2	92.42	1.20	0.10	0.54
Imola	574	515	2243	2964	2.5	173.83	1.32	0.16	0.76
Padova	955	802	5147	7196	8.6	111.47	1.40	0.20	0.91
Ferrara	1087	936	5377	7088	2.3	132.04	1.32	0.16	0.69

4.5 Shortest Routing Costs

As the maintenance of the panels requires that a number of them are visited by the maintainer in the same day, it is interesting to evaluate the effort, in terms of traveled kilometers, that is necessary to reach the panels along a continuous path, once separated into clusters with the aforementioned approaches. This means that we have once again to solve a traveling salesman problem on clustered panels. Differently from the TSP approach described in Section 3, which was intended to be fast and relied on Euclidean distances, in this case it was applied over the real road network, that is, we considered the shortest path computed with Dijkstra's algorithm as the distance between two panels. We defined a panels connection matrix as input for the pgRouting pgr_tsp algorithm for each cluster, then we summed the costs of visiting all the panels which are reported in Table 6.

Table 6. Sum of the shortest path routes computed with a TSP algorithm within each cluster, for different clustering techniques. Values are in kilometers.

municipality	KMG	KMG-G	TSP-G	AHG-G
Vivaro	7.0	7.1	9.0	9.0
Mortegliano	8.0	8.4	7.8	12.4
Vighizzolo d'Este	14.3	15.0	18.1	16.6
Cavallino-Treporti	75.2	85.6	90.7	94.4
Imola	266.1	274.8	272.9	289.3
Padova	299.7	302.6	320.0	311.2
Ferrara	485.3	480.8	513.1	529.4
Total	1,155.6	1,174.2	1,233.4	1,262.4

5 Results

The results of the analysis show how the different approaches change in effectiveness according to the method itself, to the size of the city, and to the way of calculating distances. The approaches have been evaluated only in terms of obtained results and not with respect to their computational load or execution time, as these aspects are not deemed relevant to the scope of this paper.

5.1 Tsp

The best results have been obtained defining the extremes, that were chosen considering the shape index of the envelope of the panels, in case of:

- a low value (<1) of the index we chose as extremes those panels respectively with the lower and higher Northern coordinates
- a values equal or very close to one, corresponding to a nearly square envelope, it's the same to consider a direction or another
- at high value (>1) the extremes correspond to the panels respectively with the lower and higher Eastern coordinates

Figure 7 refers to the results obtained in clustering the panels of Ferrara, with and without defining the extremes. In both cases the four groups are clearly defined, however, from a practical point of view problems arise where their bounding boxes overlap each other. In other words, the panels of one group result to be mixed among the other ones, which is not the optimum for operation planning. This situation is particularly evident in the city center but occurs also in the suburbs (Fig. 8).

As a consequence, this leads to a poor Dunn's index, especially in complex situations like medium to large cities. Results are better in small towns, like Mortegliano and Vivaro (Fig. 9), once the two extrema have been fixed according to the shape index.

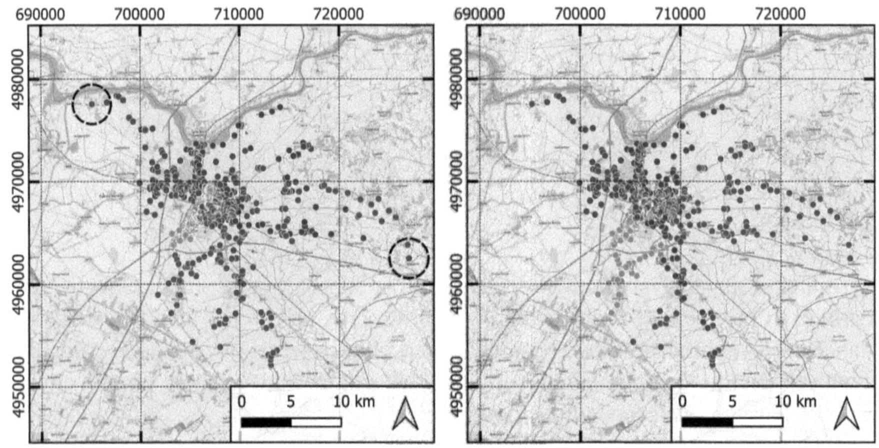

Fig. 7. TSP applied to Ferrara's panels, with (left panel) and without (right panel) fixing the first and last panel in input, which are highlighted by black circles in the first panel.

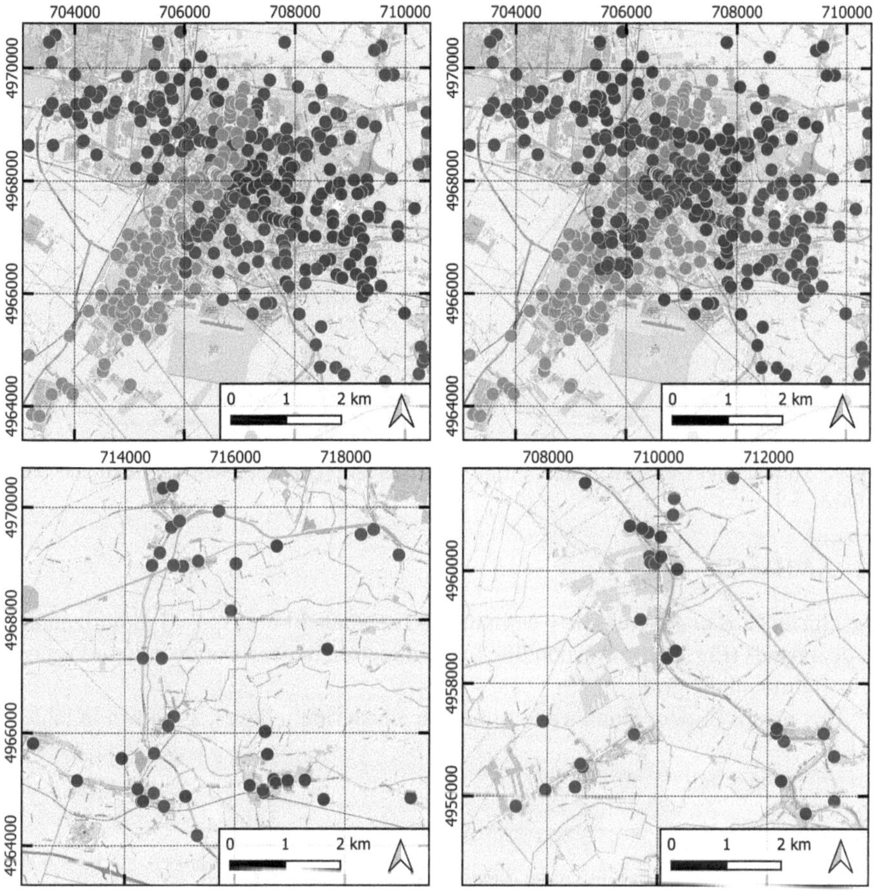

Fig. 8. Zooming of the mixing up of the panels belonging to different groups (Ferrara, TSP approach). In the top row the city center, in the bottom one the suburbs towards the countryside. Different areas are shown for the suburbs to better highlight the issue of clusters' permeation. In both rows, the left panel shows the processing with defined extreme points, the right one without them.

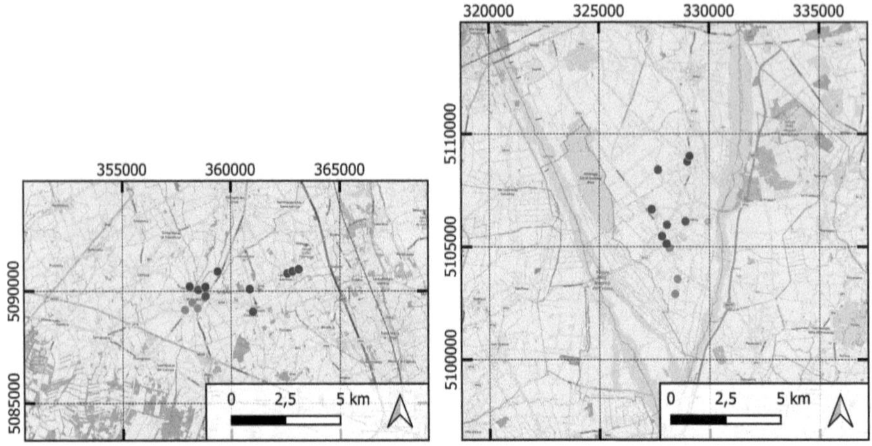

Fig. 9. Mortegliano (left panel) and Vivaro (right panel), TSP approach with extreme points defined.

5.2 Ad Hoc GIS

The clusters are in general fairly compact and separated but disposed in horizontal or vertical bands (Fig. 10), corresponding to the direction (by rows or by columns) chosen to loop through the grid.

This results in poor Dunn's and Silhouette clustering indexes, as shown in tables 2 and 3.

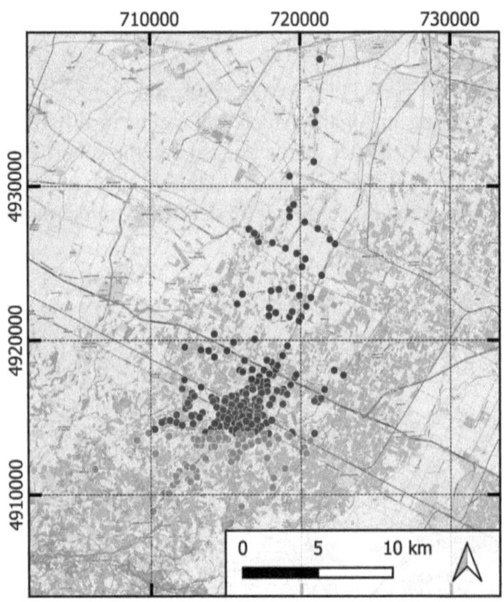

Fig. 10. Spatial clustering of the panels in the municipality of Imola obtained with the AHG approach.

Moreover, especially in small datasets like Vighizzolo, the horizontal/vertical alignment of the clusters could result in apparently illogical results, with some panels not being grouped according to their Euclidean proximity (Fig. 11).

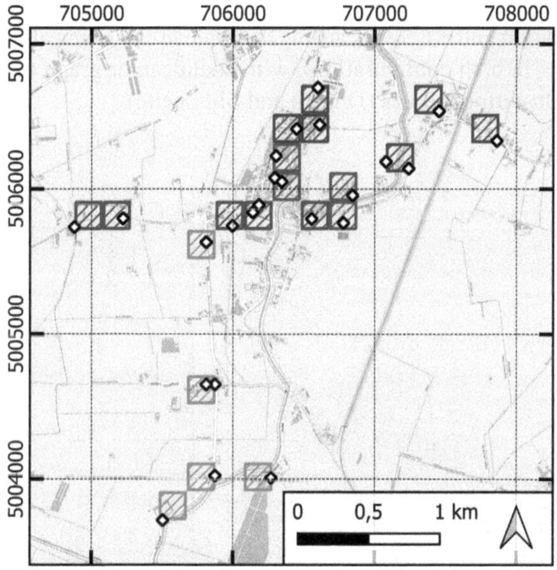

Fig. 11. Spatial clustering of the panels in the municipality of Vighizzolo using the AHG approach. The dashed squares correspond to the cells of the vector fishnet considered as a basis for the clustering, with their colors indicating different clusters.

5.3 K-means

The highest impact of such an approach is evident wherever there are complex areas which are connected to the main network by just a single node. Cavallino-Treporti (Fig. 12) is a perfect example of this configuration, being a small city closed between the sea and the Venetian lagoon, extended in the South West - North East direction (shape index = 1.927) and diffused over four main islands, connected one to each other by a single chain of bridges. When considering Euclidean distances, the two northern panels in the 4th island (Fig. 13, top) are geometrically closer to the central part of the city and are classified in the blue cluster, whose other panels are located in the 3rd and 1st islands, while the orange cluster is split between all the islands and the red one has just one panel in the 2nd island and all the others in the 1st. On the other hand, when considering graph distances, the two northern panels are classified in the orange cluster (Fig.12, bottom), consisting of all the panels located in the 4th, 3rd and 2nd islands, plus a few panels of the 1st island close to the connecting bridge. The other clusters have all the panels located in the same 1st island. This means that in the former case the maintainers are forced to travel over longer distances and to cross bottlenecks (the bridges) during three out of four quarters without practical benefits; in the latter case only a quarter requires to manage panels over different islands, traveling shorter distances and easing the maintenance.

Differently from the case of Cavallino-Treporti, more homogeneous cities show less significant differences between the two approaches. This is the case of the largest cities in our sample, such as Ferrara and Padova. In particular, Padova is a perfect example of a round shaped, well connected, internally homogeneous city. The motorway rings embracing the urban area and the dense network in the city center make the links between all the panels very short and efficient, causing the k-mean clustering algorithm to produce very similar results in both configurations, with euclidean or graph distances (Fig. 14), even in terms of clustering indices (Dunn's and Silhouette).

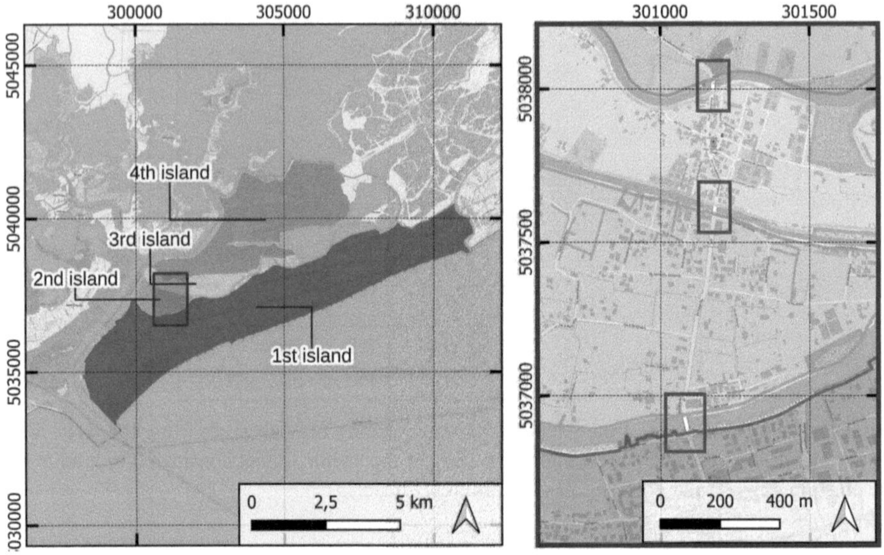

Fig. 12. The municipality of Cavallino-Treporti develops over four different islands (left panel), connected to each other by a single bridge (detail of the blue insight in the right panel, the bridges are framed in red).

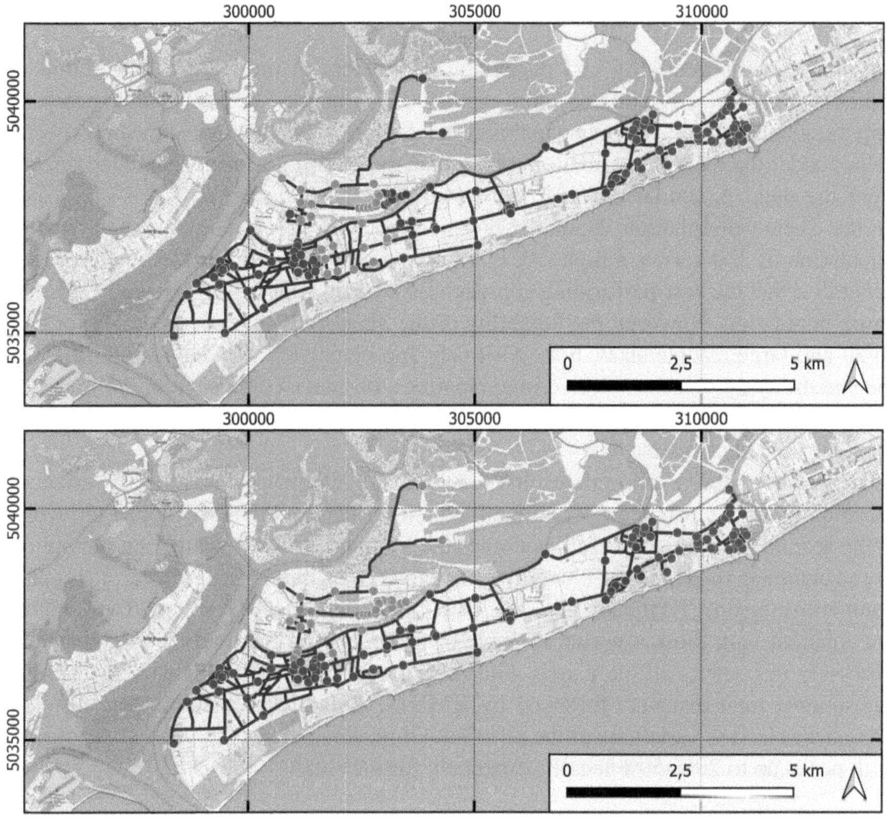

Fig. 13. K-means clustering results based on Euclidean distances (top) or on graph distances (bottom) for the municipality of Cavallino-Treporti. Dots' colors identify different clusters

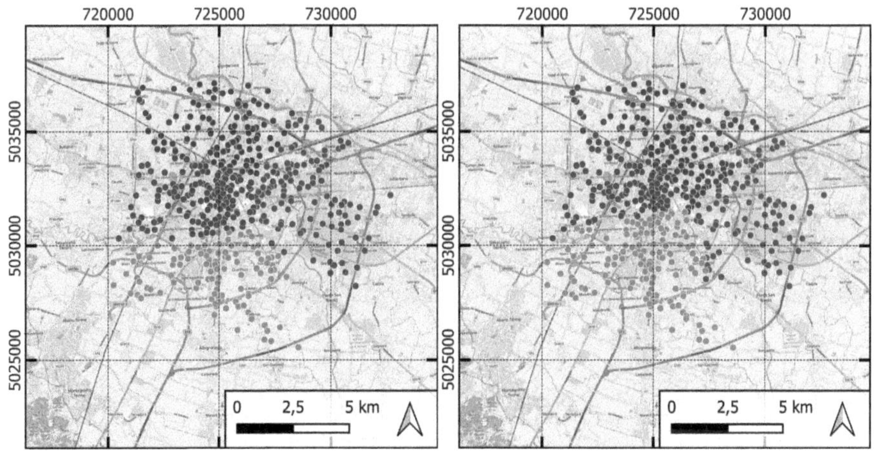

Fig. 14. K-means clustering results based on Euclidean distances (left) or on graph distances (right) for the municipality of Padova. Dots' colors identify different clusters.

5.4 Quantitative Assessment of the Best Performing Approach

We analyzed the centrality and dispersion parameters of the Dunn's and Silhouette indices of the obtained results, assuming a Skew-t distribution (Table 7). In this regard, it's important to clarify that the mean in this context refers to the theoretical mean (expected value) under the Skew-t distribution, rather than the arithmetic mean calculated directly from the data. A similar consideration applies to the variance, which is also based on the Skew-t distribution. Naturally, considering only seven municipalities out of a population of 250 carries a high risk of extrapolation, making it harder to confidently generalize that the best-performing approach for the sample will perform well across the entire population. However, the flexibility of the Skew-t distribution - suitable for both small and large sample sizes, both positively and negatively skewed - combined with the variability among the selected municipalities, provides confidence in the statistical robustness of our inference. That said, a larger sample would be ideal for achieving stronger statistical power.

KME shows the best overall results, with high indices mean values and low variances, meaning that the clusters are well identified. Nevertheless, the KMG approach, which is the second best option overall, becomes the best choice when evaluating the indices over a complete road network (-G suffixes in Table 7). As the KME-G clustering remains competitive against KMG, we can state that TSP-G and AHG-G are not. These results are coherent with those reported in Table 6, which expose the total traveled distances necessary to connect all the panels with the shortest path. Once again, KMG ensures the shortest total distance, followed by KME-G, TSP-G and AHG-G. The different approaches lead to variations of the retrieved kilometers between 2% and 10%, overall, with peaks up to 20%-50% locally, especially for the smallest towns.

Table 7. Centrality and dispersion parameters of the Dunn's and Silhouette indices of the tested approaches, assuming a Skew-t distribution. Two cases (TSP-G and AHG-G) show infinite variance because of the properties of the Skew-t distribution on the observed data.

approach	Dunn		Silhouette	
	mean	variance	mean	variance
TSP	0.290	0.033	0.156	0.012
AHG	0.300	0.057	0.166	0.011
KME	0.610	0.070	0.340	0.015
KMG	0.384	0.367	0.309	0.011
TSP-G	0.177	∞	0.112	0.009
AHG-G	0.220	∞	0.130	0.082
KME-G	0.336	0.032	0.258	0.012

6 Conclusions

The three approaches and one variant we tested for clustering electrical panels in urban areas have both advantages and disadvantages. Both TSP and AHG are easy to implement and require a low computational effort, however, they produce low quality clusters according to the value of Dunn's and Silhouette indices, which are used to quantitatively evaluate the clustering effectiveness. On the contrary, KME is easy to implement, fast to run, and also produces satisfactory clusters, with good values of the clustering indices. KMG is defined on a different metric, relying on real distances over a road network, which requires a higher effort to input the algorithm and to run a solution, nevertheless producing good results which are of the same order of KME. When evaluating each algorithm with the same metric used for the clustering, i.e. using a Euclidean metric for KME and a road network metric for KMG, KME produces the best results overall, confirming its popularity for clustering problems. However, since our case studies must be evaluated in a real world context, where the maintainers move on a road network from panel to panel, we also evaluated the different Euclidean approaches with a road distance metric. Under this condition, KMG provides the best results overall, both in terms of clustering effectiveness, expressed by the clustering indices, and in terms of minimization of the path connecting all the panels within the different quarters. The cluster/path optimization obtained by KMG is of the order of 2% overall with respect to KME-G, with peaks up to 14% in the case of peculiar road configurations as it is for Cavallino-Treporti, which is spread over different islands. In case the cities are more homogeneous, as in the case of Padova, whose road network is highly structured and dense, differences in the optimal path between KMG and KMEG are limited to less than 1%. Higher differences are observed for the other two approaches, TSP-G and AHG-G, up to 50%.

The tests demonstrated that the clustering results are not influenced by the shape index of the envelope enclosing the panels, making the approach applicable to any type of municipality. Nevertheless, an inverse dependence of the clustering indices on the number of panels is observed, mainly due to the higher complexity of the city centers which make it more difficult to separate the panels into four quarters of equal size. As a future research direction, we are considering the definition of the optimal path within the road network for each cluster, while accounting for the fact that maintenance teams return to the depot at the end of each workday. Additionally, we aim to incorporate other travel costs into our model beyond simple distance, such as one-way streets, average traffic congestion, frequency of intersections and traffic lights. Finally, a highly interesting research perspective would be to also consider travel time as impedance and explore its connection to travel costs.

Acknowledgements. We would like to thank Prof. Maurizio Barbarella for his insightful discussions and constructive feedback, Dr. Alessandra Masala for assisting us with the proofreading and draft revision.

References

1. Cormen, T.H., Leiserson, C.E., Rivest R.L., Stein, C.: Introduction to Algorithms, 3rd Edition. MIT Press (2009)
2. Applegate, D.L., Bixby, R.E., Chvatál, V., Cook, W.J.: The Traveling Salesman Problem: A Computational Study. Princeton University Press (2006)
3. Johnson, D.S., Lyle, A. M.: The Traveling Salesman Problem: A Case Study in Local Optimization (2008)
4. Bruggeman C.M., Liu W., Mitchell M., You E.: Creating Clusters: An Analysis of Traveling Salesman as a Clustering Mechanism (2010), https://www.math.cmu.edu/~af1p/Teaching/OR2/Projects/P12/2010FinalProject.pdf (accessed 2024/09/01)
5. MacQueen, J.: Some methods for classification and analysis of multivariate observations. In: Proceedings of the Fifth Berkeley Symposium on Mathematical Statistics and Probability, Volume 1: Statistics, pp. 281–297, University of California Press (1967)
6. Bradley, P.S., Bennett K.P., Demiriz, A.: Constrained K-means clustering. Technical report, MSR-TR-2000–65, Microsoft Research (2000)
7. Tatit, P., Adhinugraha, K., Taniar, D.: Navigating the maps: Euclidean vs. road network distances in spatial queries. Algorithms **17**, 29 (2024)
8. Kuby, M., Lines, L., Schultz, R., Xie, Z., Kim, J.G., Lim, S.: Optimization of hydrogen stations in Florida using the flow-refueling location model. Int. J. Hydrogen Energy **34**(15), 6045–6064 (2009)
9. Bozkaya, B., Yanik, S., Balcisoy, S.: A GIS-based optimization framework for competitive multi-facility location-routing problem. Netw. Spat. Econ. **10**, 297–320 (2010)
10. Rahman, M.A., Basheer, M.A., Khalid, Z., Tahir, M., Uppal, M.: Logistics Hub Location Optimization: A K-Means and P-Median Model Hybrid Approach Using Road Network Distances. arXiv:2308.11038v2 (2024)
11. Boots, B.: Voronoi (Thiessen) polygons, Concepts and techniques in modern geography 45. Geo Books Norwich, UK (1986)
12. Dijkstra, E.: W: A note on two problems in connection with graphs. Numer. Math. **1**, 269–271 (1959)
13. Hart, P.E., Nilsson, N.J., Raphael, B.: A formal basis for the heuristic determination of minimum cost paths. IEEE Transactions on Systems Science and Cybernetics **4**(20), 100–107 (1968)
14. Hart, P.E.: The condensed nearest neighbor rule. Inst. Electr. Electron. Eng. Transact. Information Theory **14**, 515–516 (1968)
15. Johnson, D.B.: Efficient algorithms for shortest paths in sparse networks. J. ACM (JACM) **24**(1), 1–13 (1977)
16. Bellman, R.: On a routing problem. Q. Appl. Math. **16**(1), 87–90 (1958)
17. Floyd, R.W.: Algorithm 97: shortest path. Commun. ACM **5**(6), 345 (1962)
18. Dunn, J.C.: A fuzzy relative of the ISODATA process and its use in detecting compact well-separated clusters. J. Cybernet. **3**(3), 32–57 (1973)
19. Ding, Y., Xu, J.: RN-Cluster: a novel density-based clustering approach for road network partition. In: Li, B., Yue, L., Tao, C., Han, X., Calvanese, D., Amagasa, T. (eds) Web and Big Data. APWeb-WAIM 2022. LNCS, vol. 13423. Springer (2023)
20. Cheng, T., Anbaroglu, B.: Spatio-temporal clustering of road network data. In: Wang, F.L., Deng, H., Gao, Y., Lei, J. (eds) Artificial Intelligence and Computational Intelligence. AICI 2010. Lecture Notes in Computer Science, vol 6319. Springer (2010)
21. Rousseeuw, P.J.: Silhouettes: a graphical aid to the interpretation and validation of cluster analysis. Comput. Appl. Math. **20**, 53–65 (1987)

22. Theodossiou, P.: Financial data and the skewed generalized t distribution. Manage. Sci. **44** (12–part–1), 1650–1661 (1998)
23. Walpole, RE., Myers, R. H., Myers, S.L., Ye, K.E.: Probability and Statistics for Engineers and Scientists, Pearson Education (2011)
24. Casella, G., Berger, R.L.: Statistical Inference. Thomson Learning (2002)
25. Rodrigue, J.-P.: The Geography of Transport Systems. 6th edn. Routledge (2024)

Accessibility Evaluation in Cortina D'Ampezzo: Use of Advanced Geomatics Technologies for Inclusive Design

Caterina Balletti(✉), Fabio Martinello, Mattia Menardi, and Valeria Tatano

Università Iuav di Venezia, Venice, Italy
{balletti,valeria.tatano}@iuav.it

Abstract. The paper presents the first results of a research project started in 2023 focused on studying routes accessibility in the city of Cortina d'Ampezzo and developing an urban orientation tool. This tool aims to help people understand the organization of spaces and choose routes that best meet their needs and mobility capabilities.

Cortina d'Ampezzo faces significant challenges in terms of inclusive accessibility, particularly considering the upcoming 2026 Winter Olympic Games. Architectural barriers and topographical features limit access for people with reduced mobility. This situation requires a concerted effort from authorities, communities, and businesses to create a more inclusive environment. Even more important, it necessitates detailed mapping to highlight obstacles, elevation changes, and pavement types, enabling individuals to identify the best routes for their needs. Today Mobile Mapping Systems, particularly SLAM technology, integrated with well-known urban and territorial surveying methods (photogrammetry, topography, GNSS), plays a significant role in 3D mapping, supporting inclusive accessibility strategy. The result, currently being completed, is a webGIS that will provide users with a useful navigator for planning their movements in the urban center of Cortina. In particular, the application will have to process and make available information regarding the level of usability of routes, urban elevation differences and other types of obstacles present, as well as information regarding the accessibility of buildings of public interest and of major cultural/sports relevance.

Keyword: Urban accessibility · Urban surveying · Mapping

1 Introduction

Inclusive accessibility on an urban scale is a fundamental requirement that both small and large cities must guarantee, as it ensures that people with disabilities have the right to an independent life. This importance was internationally recognized in 2006 by the ONU Convention, which advocates for the "full and equal enjoyment of all human rights and fundamental freedoms" [1].

Being able to move with ease and safety in urban spaces, living outdoors, and leaving home with the confidence of maintaining the same autonomy as within familiar,

E. Borgogno-Mondino and P. Zamperlin (Eds.): ASITA 2024, CCIS 2463, pp. 292–304, 2025.
https://doi.org/10.1007/978-3-031-91141-5_20

disability-specific environments are crucial for the quality of life of people with physical disabilities. This accessibility is also a significant factor in the usability of urban spaces for everyone [2, 3].

In historic cities and tourist destinations, the theme of accessibility broadens its scope to include providing effective responses for stakeholders, residents, and tourists. This effort is part of the sustainability path of local development, which is now an essential component of every intervention program (Goal 11 of the ONU Sustainable Development Agenda).

In this context, the research conducted by Iuav University of Venice focuses on identifying and studying accessible routes in the city of Cortina d'Ampezzo. The aim is to define an urban orientation tool that not only helps individuals understand the organization of spaces and choose the most suitable routes based on their needs and mobility, but also assists local government in designing inclusive urban planning.

Today, the center of Cortina has a number of critical issues, some due to the natural morphology of the place with frequent changes in elevation, and others related to an inadequate pedestrian viability due to the lack of sidewalks and, recently, the presence of construction sites (Fig. 1). The research, which was interdisciplinary in nature, combined the specific skills of surveying with those of inclusive design and was divided into two phases, made possible through two separate grants.

The first phase, initiated through an agreement with the CortinaSenzaConfini[1] association, involved mapping the city to assess its urban accessibility. This includes evaluating the accessibility of hotel facilities, with the goal of creating a comprehensive information database in preparation for the Milan-Cortina 2026 Winter Olympics and Paralympics. The second part, which is still ongoing, was made possible through a research grant awarded under the POR Veneto FSE+ 2021–2027, through which the mapping will be completed and a dedicated webpage created to allow for consultation of the collected data.

The project aims to address the lack of information regarding accessibility using the latest geomatics technologies. The support of these methods for urban and territorial monitoring aligns with the transversal driver DT2 – Green and Circular Transition of the Smart Specialization Strategy – S3 of the Veneto Region. This initiative potentially links the economy, environment, and society through the themes of mobility and transversal inclusion, always prioritizing the centrality of the person. The project's aims are consistent with numerous objectives within the Regional Strategy for Sustainable Development (SRSvS), particularly those in Strategy 3: For the well-being of communities and people, which addresses overcoming accessibility issues of infrastructures and services for community use, thus encouraging the permanence of communities in the territory. Strategy 4: For an attractive territory, focuses on the regeneration of cities, ensuring accessibility, and enhancing the sustainability of connections through efficient networks and mobility plans that eliminate architectural barriers.

The data collected, appropriately structured in a GIS environment, will populate a freely accessible WebGIS platform. This platform will allow interested users to identify and propose routes favorable to people with reduced mobility.

[1] CortinaSenzaConfini is a nonprofit association, website: https://www.cortinasenzaconfini.org/ (last accessed September 10, 2024).

Although mobile and/or web applications on accessibility already exist in the world, the one presented in this paper seems to have a greater level of detail, both in terms of the elements mapped and the audience it is aimed at, than those currently available. Indeed, after reviewing the state of the art[2], it can be concluded that most existing applications typically provide information only on the accessibility of points of interest (POIs), parking spaces, or temporary obstacles. As a result, their use is generally limited to individuals in wheelchairs (both electric and manual), with or without a companion. In an era where information is readily available through apps, the project presented here aims to serve as a valuable tool for everyone—regardless of disability—making it easier to navigate the city and offering a more comprehensive view of urban accessibility in Cortina.

Fig. 1. Urban obstacles.

2 Materials and Methods

2.1 The Accessibility Survey Today

The first phase of the research had the operational goal of developing a series of forms to survey the most important activities and services, as well as studying existing resources in the Municipality of Cortina d'Ampezzo that cater to the needs of people with reduced mobility (such as those with motor disabilities, the elderly, or children in strollers) and others with temporary movement difficulties. To achieve this, in collaboration with CortinaSenzaConfini and Confcommercio Belluno, a questionnaire was created and distributed to the owners and managers of various commercial establishments (bars, restaurants, shops) and hotels in the center of Cortina, the project's test area (with around 150 responses received). Data collection was conducted on-site, with responses recorded and managed using Esri's ArcGIS Survey123 application [4]. This dynamic form generator not only accelerates data collection but also visualizes and analyzes map-based information, helping to better understand the locations and reasons behind certain

[2] As examples, see the site of the accessible Dolomites: https://www.visitdolomites.com/page1/dolomiti-accessibili/; and the accessible tourism portal of: https://friuliveneziagiuliapertutti.it/it/ or the australian site https://www.cityofsydney.nsw.gov.au/lists-maps-inventories/accessibility-map-city-centre (last accessed September 10, 2024).

events. In addition to the questionnaire data, a series of images were taken to document the current state of access. The collected data was then uploaded directly into the GIS environment (ArcGIS Pro) [5], where the project is being developed (Figs. 2 and 3).

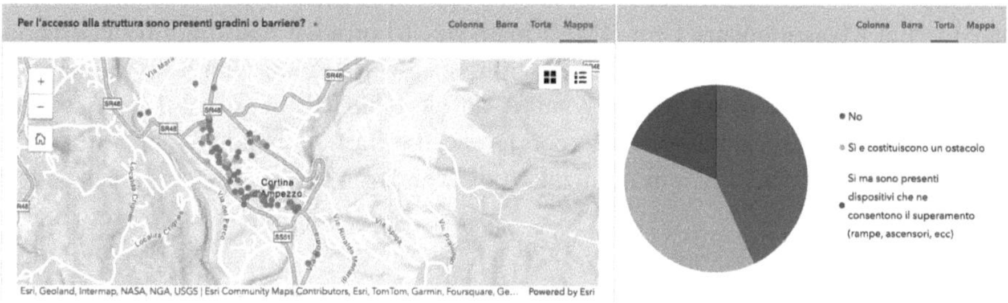

Fig. 2. Surveying the activities and services accessibility (answers to the question of whether there are barriers to entry)

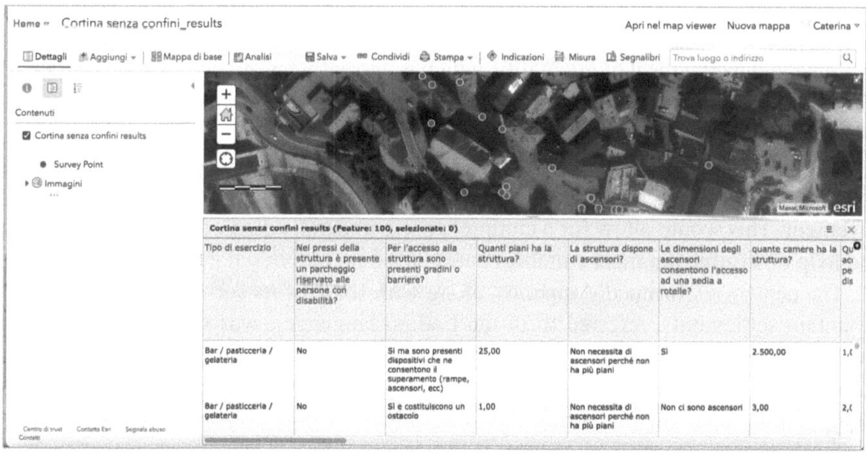

Fig. 3. Surveying the activities and services accessibility (some fields of the questionnaire).

In the second part of the research, the urban survey of Cortina is being carried out using the latest geomatic techniques that can better document these contexts. The available sensors range from RGB and multispectral cameras in both terrestrial and aerial photogrammetry to terrestrial laser scanners (TLS), aerial LiDAR (Laser Imaging Detection and Ranging), and mobile mapping systems (MMS) based on SLAM (Simultaneous Localization And Mapping) algorithms capable of simultaneously mapping the environment and locating within the generated 3D map [6, 7]. Given the different ways of acquiring and returning three-dimensional urban data, terrestrial laser scanners embedded in MMS seem to be the most suitable solution to solve the critical issues that the configurations of historic centers possess. These systems, precisely because of their ease of use, speed of acquisition, and lower cost, have assumed an important role in comparing these sensors with other established approaches [8–11].

These systems integrate and synchronize mapping sensors, such as Light Detection And Range (LiDAR) scanner and spherical or hemispherical cameras, as well as navigation/positioning sensors, such as Global Navigation Satellite System (GNSS) receiver and Inertial Measurements Unit (IMU) platform, to provide real-time 3D geospatial point clouds obtained from automatic scan-to-scan registration with an accuracy of a few centimeters. One of the main advantages of portable MMSs is that they enable the collection of a significant amount of georeferenced information quickly and efficiently, enabling the rapid and efficient digitization of even large urban areas and inaccessible locations.

2.2 The Urbany Survey

The center of Cortina d'Ampezzo has a typical mountain landscape, with sloped pathways that are often navigated by stairs or inclined ramps with varying degrees of slope. These routes are made even more challenging by the presence of ice during the winter months. Architectural barriers, therefore, are a distinct feature of the area, and over the years, they have not been systematically addressed. Some barriers can be mitigated by selecting alternative routes, while others require permanent solutions that should be implemented by the local municipality, which is currently tasked with preparing a PEBA (Plan for the Elimination of Architectural Barriers). However, this plan has not yet been enacted.

To identify existing barriers, it is necessary to go beyond topographical features and create large-scale maps that highlight obstacles, elevation changes, and types of pavement. This would allow for a comprehensive understanding of all the critical issues and help determine the most suitable routes based on individual needs.

The center of Cortina d'Ampezzo, along with some of its surrounding *villas* (small mountain settlements, referred to in the Ladino language), was selected as the initial study area for the survey and mapping process. The main objective was to develop an operational methodology that could be easily expanded and adapted to other areas facing similar challenges. During the initial phase of data collection, which included basic cartography (numerical format, DTM, orthophoto), it became clear that the only available map for the project was the regional map at a 1:5000 scale (CTRN, 2004). Unfortunately, there are no municipal maps at a larger scale, which would have been more suitable for detailed mapping or for planning interventions. Lidar data, with a 1-m resolution, was also obtained from the Ministry of the Environment's Geoportal to create a digital elevation model. This model is crucial for identifying elevation differences and slopes in urban and natural routes, though it is insufficient for pinpointing pavements and steps within the town center.

To provide an accurate mapping of the accessibility of public paths in Cortina, both traditional (GNSS, photogrammetry, lidar) and innovative tools are employed, including data acquisition via SLAM, mainly in the streets of the town center, and optical UAV, particularly along nature trails. The measurement campaign in the urban center with SLAM technology aims to provide more detailed cartography, indicating pavements, steps, and changes in altitude—information which are not present in the 1:5000 scale

CTRN. The instrumentation adopted is the Stonex one (Figs. 4 and 5) with a rotating head capable of generating 360° × 270° coverage of the point cloud. Three 5MP cameras cover a field of view of 200° horizontal and 100° vertical, synchronously obtaining texture information and producing full-color point clouds and panoramic images [12].

Fig. 4. SLAM urban survey: acquisition.

Fig. 5. SLAM point cloud of Cortina d'Ampezzo center.

The system provides a relative accuracy of 6 mm according to the manufacturer's standards; however, this precision can decrease depending on how effectively the SLAM algorithm performs. The characteristics of the scanned environment, the absence of loop closures (in fact 19 data sets were acquired, corresponding to 19 close paths along the main pedestrian and car streets) on the trajectory and the procedures inaccuracy in acquisition phase can significantly affect the data reconstruction. To ensure the accuracy of data collection the STONEX® X120GO SLAM Laser Scanner devices has to remain stable and avoid any sudden movements, and to prevent any obstruction from pedestrians or vehicles in front of the device during the initialization. This is applicable to all MMS devices [13].

A survey using GNSS technology in RTK mode was also carried out to obtain useful points to reconstruct more closely the trajectory followed by the SLAM instrumentation. In fact, the surveyed points were used during the SLAM survey as stationing points for the instrument. This mode offered by the instrumentation used, which provides for stationing on points of known coordinates, is particularly effective when, as in the case of the survey carried out, the control points are defined in the same reference system in which the GNSS receiver of the SLAM operates. The expediency of relying on the same correction provider and in the same acquisition period thus avoids possible problems caused by different configurations of reference constellations.

Since the survey was made for a detailed urban scale considering the identification of possible obstacles (1:200), the precision on the GCPs is ±4 cm. In the SLAM data processing phase, the odometry was recalculated according to a non-rigid adjustment.

2.3 Dataset Processing and Results

An assessment based on the actual features present in an urban area can help define a set of routes that can be classified as accessible. The automatic identification and classification of sidewalks and other urban elements from MMS point clouds is a topic that has been explored by various researchers, albeit with different approaches [14–17]. The core idea is to identify elements like curbs, then differentiate the sidewalk from the street, either using the surveyed curb or based on variations in elevation between the features. However, these methods are not easily applicable to historic cities, especially in mountainous regions [18, 19], where the arrangement of elements is often non-standard, such as sidewalks and streets being at the same elevation (without curbs). Additionally, there are sometimes unconventional solutions and unique spatial arrangements designed to address physical constraints imposed by the environment. In such cases, identifying pedestrian paths becomes a challenging task, often requiring manual intervention, which could be addressed through alternative strategies.

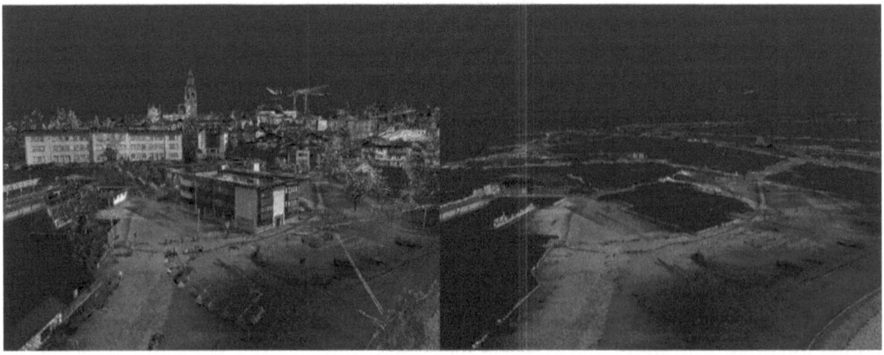

Fig. 6. SLAM point cloud: terrain classification.

Given the large amount of data acquired, cloud classification (Fig. 6) was useful in facilitating cartographic restitution and path identification (graphs). The survey conducted provided an opportunity to evaluate some classification algorithms that are implemented in some commercial software. The approaches offered by these softwares are largely automated and intuitive and, as such, represent a useful alternative to more technical approaches that require specialized knowledge or additional software. To evaluate the results that can be obtained, part of the surveyed route along Corso Italia was also acquired with Leica RTC 360 terrestrial laser scanner. The data obtained are clearly different. The SLAM acquisition is much faster than the static laser scanner and is larger in the acquisition area, but noisier in the data collected. As a first classification test, we used Autodesk's new terrain-related Recap Pro algorithm [20].

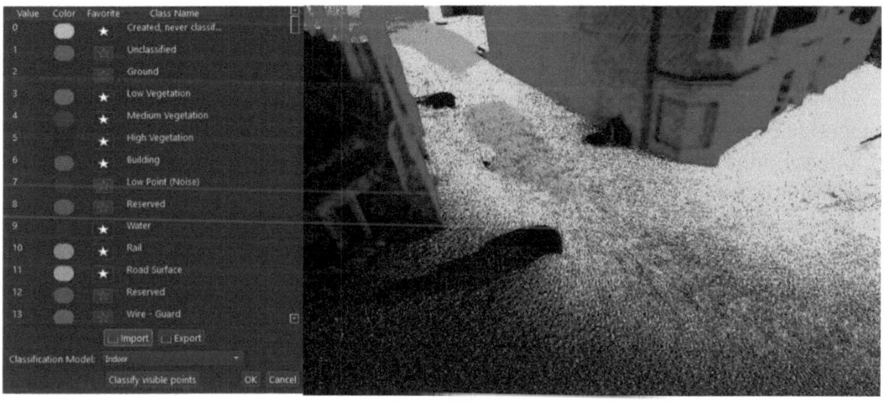

Fig. 7. Leica Cyclone Register 360 classification.

The software offers the possibility to set a grid for terrain processing and give a window size of the processing so that elements such as buildings, which would otherwise be classified as terrain, are included within it. Both point clouds have been classified into "terrain" and "other," but is how the ground attachment of buildings is not well recognized, retaining part of the facades and making digitization of the neighboring areas complex.

As a second test, we used the Leica Cyclone Register 360 [21] classification algorithm for both clouds (Fig. 7). The latter gives the possibility to classify up to 256 elements, but for the purpose of the research project only terrain was considered. This algorithm is more robust and needs greater workstation characteristics. The results of the two classifications are two point clouds that are much cleaner in both noise removal and cleanliness of the ground attachment of buildings, making digitization easier and more intuitive. According to the algorithm, the classification should have also subdivided the ground type, going to assign different RGB values depending on its material composition (cobblestones, asphalt, etc.). The latter diversification turns out to be incorrect, probably because the textural changes do not correspond to actual elevation changes but identify and diversify pedestrian paths from vehicular paths. The last classification test was carried out through the Agisoft Metashape [22] providing a suite of point cloud classification tools that facilitate the production of DTMs from a subset of points in a model [23]. These include four options to classify points at varying levels of automation. First, a nearly fully automated classification (Classify Points) is available, applying machine learning techniques to sort points into standard classes. Users have the option to select which classes will be used and a confidence parameter for point classification (i.e.: as confirmed in [23], at 0.00 confidence, this tool will classify every point in a scene based on Agisoft's proprietary classification algorithm). This tool is the simplest to use, requiring only a single parameter input. A second, mostly automated tool (Classify Ground Points) asks the user to set three geometric parameters, which help differentiate terrain points from other features based on the angle and slope relative to neighboring points. This tool involves an iterative process in which the user manually adjusts the parameters and re-runs the tool to achieve an optimal result. The third tool provided by Agisoft, Select Points by Color, ranks points based on their color values, allowing the user to set a tolerance range. It can be used to select and classify points into different categories, one at a time. The final tool, Assign Class, is entirely manual, allowing users to select and categorize points individually. Creating a Digital Terrain Model (DTM) from a subset of a dense point cloud in Agisoft Metashape is straightforward and requires only the selection of relevant point classes during DEM production.

When comparing different software, it becomes apparent that a cleaner, denser point cloud, such as that produced by the static laser scanner RTC 360, leads to better results when using the same parameters.

As for the three software programs and their various algorithms, though not always clearly described or specified in li, it's evident that Recap Pro is the least flexible and performs the weakest. It has only recently introduced classification features in its latest updates. In contrast, Metashape and Cyclone offer more robust management and classification capabilities, allowing users to handle and categorize data into multiple classes with greater flexibility. These tools also generate less noisy data, which makes the results easier to read and interpret.

The WebGIS Navigator

The project, which is nearing its final stages, is developing a webGIS application designed to offer users an easy-to-use navigation tool for planning their movements within the heart of Cortina. The application will specifically provide data on the accessibility of routes, changes in urban elevations, and potential obstacles, along with information on the accessibility of public buildings and those of notable cultural or sports significance.

The system development unfolds in two key stages: first, a map of pedestrian routes is generated from the data obtained through SLAM surveys, with a focus on elevation variations (see Figs. 8 and 9); second, the webGIS platform is built, placing significant importance on a user-friendly interface and clear graphic design, in alignment with the guidelines provided by the Agenzia per l'Italia Digitale (AGID).

Drawing on insights from a previous interactive mapping project in Venice [24] and considering the features offered by contemporary web platforms, which typically offer descriptions of locations, it was decided to create a tool designed to assist users in selecting point-to-point routes within the urban landscape. This tool will leverage the public pedestrian network and consider various physical obstacles. After identifying the starting and ending points, the navigator will propose possible routes, highlighting elements such as the slope, presence of steps or ramps, and pavement variations, allowing users to choose the best route based on their specific needs.

Fig. 8. The graph of the pedestrian routes.

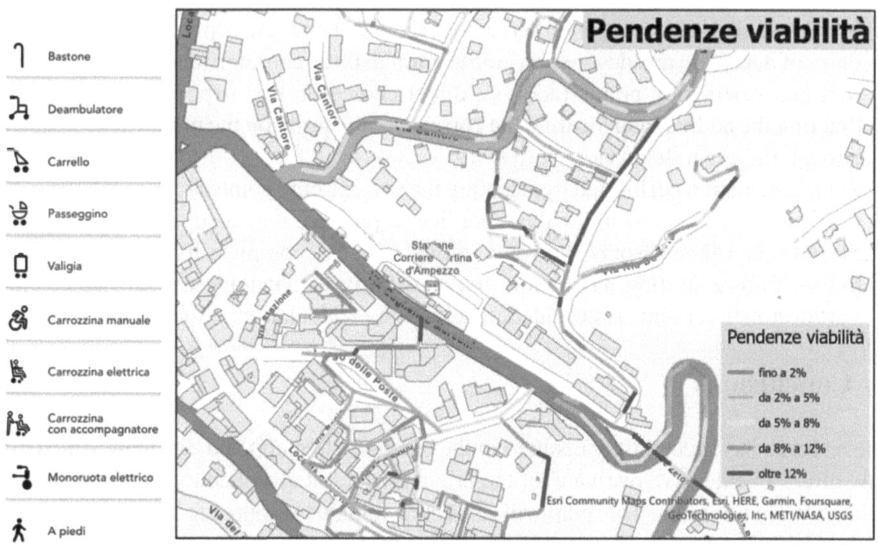

Fig. 9. Final display of slopes.

The main software components of the project are: a network analysis service and a geocode service (managed through ArcGIS Server 10.6.1), a webGIS application (to be built with Web AppBuilder for ArcGIS). For the creation of the network analysis service, a special multimodal network dataset was constructed by integrating the pedestrian path graph. A graph is defined in general terms as the data structure of linear type (polyline) that records the pattern (network) of possible paths within a given area. The graph of the public pedestrian thoroughfare was created from scratch, as a digital product with the necessary geometric characteristics was not available.

It was created in the ArcGis Pro environment, using the SLAM survey restitution as the cartographic basis. In digitizing the graph, special attention was paid to the construction of intersections and crossing lines of larger spaces. At the end of the construction, through a spatial join operation followed by the necessary checks and corrections, road codes and corresponding toponyms were assigned to the graph arcs. Next, the graph was processed by considering data on the elevation of the walking surface, the accessibility profile, and the presence of obstacles. The procedure of attributing the elevation data to the arcs of the graph was rather complex, involving the sequential use of some tools (spatial join, dissolve, select by attributes, feature to line, planarize, simplify) and an external toolbox transect.tbx. As a result of these elaborations, the initial pedestrian path graph was divided into segments, of varying lengths of not less than 30 cm, to each of which was assigned the corresponding footfall elevation, rounded according to a criterion of aggregating the elevation values into intervals of five centimeters and assigning the calculated elevation the minimum value of the interval to which it belongs.

Basically, the functional structure of the webGIS application will be defined as follows:

- Setting of parameters useful for route finding and, in particular, the choice of user profile among several possible alternatives, the use or non-use of public transportation.
- Entry of departure and destination points through three common modes for both route start and destination points (address, direct choice on the map, place of interest). Entering the address and locating the corresponding point on the map will be handled through the geocode service.
- Route calculation performed by selecting the two extreme points of the route, the software prompts the network analysis service to produce the calculation of the shortest route and then display the route, along with the complete list of directions to follow. Before starting navigation, the possibility of changing one or both of the start/destination points is provided, resulting in recalculation of the route.

3 Conclusions

The research has successfully resulted in the creation of an updated city map, which not only offers an extensive overview of the urban layout but also identifies key challenges within the environment. This map will serve as a valuable resource for the local government as it embarks on drafting the PEBA. The urban survey, conducted using advanced technologies, especially SLAM, plays a pivotal role in the production of large-scale urban maps. These maps are not only vital for spatial planning but also crucial for guiding actions aimed at enhancing the accessibility of urban areas.

The goal is to make all collected survey data publicly available, encouraging collaboration among various parties involved. This collaboration will foster a coordinated effort to accelerate the development of an inclusive and comprehensive map. It will empower local authorities to make informed decisions about urban planning and accessibility improvements, while also facilitating more effective communication with the public. By offering detailed, up-to-date information, the map will equip residents and visitors with the knowledge they need to navigate Cortina in an accessible and inclusive way.

Through this approach, scientific research aligns with Public Engagement goals, positioning the work not only as an academic achievement but also as a tool for cultural advancement and societal progress. The intention is to share the research for a broader social purpose, leveraging the university's expertise to promote an inclusive culture. This initiative highlights the academic community's responsibility in fostering a culture of inclusion, ultimately improving both the city's environment and the quality of life for its inhabitants.

Acknowledgments. This study was funded by POR Veneto FSE+ 2021–2027 (grant number 2).

Disclosure of Interests. The authors have no competing interests to declare that are relevant to the content of this article. Menardi M. and Martinello F. has received research grants from Regione Veneto POR FSE+ 2021–2027.

References

1. NU: Convenzione delle Nazioni Unite del 13 dicembre 2006 sui diritti delle persone con disabilità, ratificata in Italia con Legge n.18/2009 (2006)
2. Baratta A.F.L., Conti, C., Tatano, V.: Manifesto lessicale per l'accessibilità ambientale. 50 parole per progettare l'inclusione. Anteferma, Conegliano (TV) (2023)
3. Tatano, V.: Atlante dell'accessibilità urbana a Venezia. Anteferma, Conegliano (TV), (2018)
4. Esri ArcGis Survey 123 Homepage. https://survey123.arcgis.com/. Accessed 29 Sept 2024
5. Esri ArcgisPro Homepage. https://www.esri.com/it-it/arcgis/products/arcgis-pro/overview. Accessed 29 Sept 2024
6. Elhashash, M., Albanwan, H., Qin, R.: A review of mobile mapping systems: from sensors to applications. Sensors. **22**(11), 4262 (2022)
7. Rodríguez-Gonzálvez, P., et al.: Mobile LiDAR system: new possibilities for the documentation and dissemination of large cultural heritage sites. Remote Sens. **9**(3), 189 (2017)
8. Conti, A., Pagliaricci, G., Bonora, V., Tucci, G.: A comparison between terrestrial laser scanning and hand-held mobile mapping for the documentation of built heritage. Int. Arch. Photogramm. Remote Sens. Spatial Inf. Sci. **XLVIII-2/W4-2024**, 141–147 (2024)
9. Chiabrando F., et al.: 3D documentation towards heritage conservation: a rapid mapping approach applied to Bahrain Forts. Int. Arch. Photogramm. Remote Sens. Spatial Inf. Sci. **XLIII-B2-2022**, 769–776 (2022)
10. Maset E., Cucchiaro S., Cazorzi F., Crosilla F., Fusiello A., Beinat A.: Investigating the performance of a handheld mobile mapping system in different outdoor scenarios. Int. Arch. Photogramm. Remote Sens. Spatial Inf. Sci. **XLIII-B1-2021**, 103–1 09 (2021)
11. Li, S., Li, G., Wang, L., Qin, Y.: SLAM integrated mobile mapping system in complex urban environments. ISPRS J. Photogramm. Remote Sens.Photogramm. Remote Sens. **166**, 316–332 (2020)
12. Martino, A., Breggion, E., Balletti, C., Guerra, F., Renghini, G., Centanni, P.: Digitization approaches for urban cultural heritage: last generation mms within venice outdoor scenarios. Int. Arch. Photogramm. Remote Sens. Spatial Inf. Sci. **XLVIII-1/W1-2023**, 265–272 (2023)

13. Tanduo, B., Teppati Losè L., Chiabrando F.: Documentation of complex environments in cultural heritage sites. A slam-based survey in the Castello del Valentino basement. Int. Arch. Photogramm. Remote Sens. Spatial inf. Sci. **XLVIII-1/W1-2023**, 489–496 (2023)
14. Serna, A., Marcotegui, B.: Urban accessibility diagnosis from mobile laser scanning data. ISPRS J. Photogramm. Remote Sens. **84**, 23–32(2013)
15. Balado, J., Díaz-Vilarino, L., Arias, P., Gonzalez-Jorge, H.: Automatic classification of urban ground elements from mobile laser scanning data. Autom. Constr.. Constr. **86**, 226–239 (2018)
16. Treccani D., Fernández A., Díaz-Vilariño L., Adami A.: Automating the inventory of the navigable space for pedestrians on historical sites: towards accurate path planning. Int. J. Appl. Earth Observ. Geoinf. **122** (2023)
17. Franzini, M., Casella, V., Niglio, O.: Leica BLK2GO point cloud classification with machine learning algorithms: the case study of Sant'Eusebio's crypt in Pavia (Italy). Int. Arch. Photogramm. Remote Sens. Spatial Inf. Sci. **XLVIII-M-2-2023**, 593–600 (2023)
18. Treccani, D., D´ıaz-Vilarino, L., Adami, A.: Side-walk detection and pavement characterisation in historic urban environments from point clouds: preliminary results. Int. Arch. Photogramm. Remote Sens. Spatial Inf. Sci. **XLIIIB4-2021**, 243–249 (2021)
19. Treccani, D., Díaz-Vilariño, L., and Adami, A.: Accessible path finding for historic urban environments: feature extraction and vectorization from point clouds. In Int. Arch. Photogramm. Remote Sens. Spatial Inf. Sci. **XLVI-2/W1-2022**, 497–504 (2022)
20. Autodesk Recap Pro Homepage. https://www.autodesk.com/it/products/recap/overview?term=1-YEAR&tab=subscription. Accessed 29 Sept 2024
21. Leica Cyclone REGISTER 360 Homepage. https://leica-geosystems.com/it-it/products/laser-scanners/software/leica-cyclone/leica-cyclone-register-360. Accessed 29 Sept 2024
22. Agisoft Metashape Homepage. https://agisoft.com. Accessed 29 Sept 2024
23. Howland, M.D., Tamberino, A., Liritzis, I., Levy, T.E.: Digital deforestation: comparing automated approaches to the production of digital terrain models (DTMs) in Agisoft Metashape. Quaternary **5**(1), 5 (2022)
24. Tatano, V., Revellini, R., Mazzanti, M.: Accessible Venice: an interactive urban mobility map. TECHNE J. Technol. Archit. Environ. **19**, 153–161 (2020)

Composite Index to Evaluate Urban Settlements Efficiency. An Application to the Territorial Context of Baronissi Municipality

Federica Cicalese(✉), Michele Grimaldi, and Isidoro Fasolino

University of Salerno, Via Giovanni Paolo II, 132, Fisciano, SA, Italy
{fcicalese,migrimaldi,i.fasolino}@unisa.it

Abstract. The growing ecological awareness in recent years has led to the widespread adoption of various protocols that allow for the certification of the sustainability of a building or a district. However, comprehensive tools for the multidimensional evaluation of urban planning projects on an urban scale are not yet available. The paper goal is to provide the urban planning process with tools for designing livable and inclusive settlements, in line with sustainable development goals. The focus is on the urban settlement, which can be identified as a neighborhood or an urban area that is the subject of a neighborhood plan, in an attempt to lead the debate to an operational scale and to reflect on the contents of the plan on a detailed scale. This paper proposes a novel Urban Settlements Efficiency Evaluation Methodology which includes a multicriteria solution TOPSIS (Technique for Order Preference by Similarity to Ideal Solution) based to rank a set of settlements according to their efficiency level. The model uses a system of indicators specifically built from a broad survey of scientific articles and international experience. More than fifteen quantitative and qualitative criteria are proposed as the basis for evaluation. This methodology led us to the definition and calculation of the composite settlement efficiency index (I_{SE}).

Keywords: Urban sustainability · Multi-criteria analysis · TOPSIS method

1 Introduction

The physical and functional organization of settlements is called upon to deal with paradigms, principles and disciplinary criteria such as: contrast to land use, urban compactness, density and multifunctionality, adaptation to climate change. The 2030 Agenda for Sustainable Development promotes an integrated approach to achieving sustainability goals at a global level and defines Goal 11 [1], concerning the creation of sustainable cities and communities. This objective aims to make urban areas inclusive, safe, resilient and sustainable, through actions aimed at reducing pollution, sustainable management of resources and improving the quality of urban life. In support of these strategies, the National Recovery and Resilience Plan (PNRR), with Missions 2 and 5, promotes the ecological transition and the improvement of the quality of life in cities, paying particular attention to urban regeneration and the improvement of infrastructure to promote fair and sustainable territorial development.

E. Borgogno-Mondino and P. Zamperlin (Eds.): ASITA 2024, CCIS 2463, pp. 305–321, 2025.
https://doi.org/10.1007/978-3-031-91141-5_21

In the context of urban development, there is a need to incorporate these objectives into the decision-making process [2]. In fact, there is currently no concrete and applicable tool that planners can use to obtain empirical and measurable results on how to achieve these goals. In several countries—both in Europe and in Asia, as well as in other emerging countries—the approach to urban planning is evolving in line with these principles, orienting the development of new settlements towards the design of eco-neighborhoods or eco-cities [3–8], as it seems to represent the most comprehensive and holistic integration of sustainable urban principles. However, these experiences often remain isolated, lack a standardized procedure, and are therefore difficult to replicate in different contexts [9]. It should also be considered that traditional urban planning and management methods are becoming increasingly inadequate in addressing contemporary challenges. As cities evolve, new approaches that incorporate computerized techniques and interactive planning tools are essential. The urban context must be digitally modelled and supported by reliable, up-to-date spatial data. Since most relevant urban planning data is spatially related, the role of spatial information sciences, particularly geomatics, is fundamental to any forward-looking urban design and planning process [10].

This article proposes an Urban Settlements Efficiency Evaluation Methodology, designed as a tool to support planners in assessing the efficiency of different design choices in the context of neighborhood planning. The efficiency of a settlement is a concept that operates in a framework of the effectiveness of the planning system. The use of the term "efficiency" rather than "effectiveness" highlights the critical role that resources play. "Efficiency" refers to the ability to achieve a system of objectives with the minimum expenditure of resources, thereby maximizing the instrumental value of the approach, its productive capacity, and its overall performance [11]. In a setting marked by structural scarcity of resources of all kinds, the relationship between available resources and the objectives to be achieved takes on exceptional importance. Indeed, general settlement inefficiency reflects the outcome of a complex interplay between weaknesses in urban planning, social dynamics, the often unintended consequences of sectoral policies, and the market forces that often intersect with these factors [11]. The methodology relies on a set of indicators specifically developed through an extensive review of scientific literature and international experiences. Identifying indicators for the urban environment is crucial to monitor urban trends and manage the measurement and evaluation of the contribution of each component to the overall functioning of the settlement, in a controlled manner. Therefore, in the face of an established awareness dictated by the agenda and the resources planned to achieve the objectives of sustainable development, the need emerges to introduce decision support mechanisms that effectively allow the urban transformation to be evaluated on an urban scale starting from the elements of the project that can effectively contribute to the achievement of sustainability, hereinafter referred to as "devices".

The assessment is conducted with reference to three types of capital: *natural*, which includes ecosystems, biodiversity, and environmental matrices essential for preserving natural resources; *artificial*, which derives from the transformation of natural capital (e.g., houses, roads, bridges); and *social*, which encompasses the wealth of knowledge and interactions within settled communities [2, 12–18].

The evaluation of urban projects and the identification of indicators represent a challenge both technically and scientifically [19–21] due to the complexity of the topic, which involves multiple data types and criteria. To address the multicriteria decision-making problem (MCDM), the Order of Preference by Similarity to the Ideal Solution (TOPSIS) technique is applied (Sect. 2). Section 3 proposes sixteen quantitative and qualitative criteria to assess settlement efficiency. The proposed methodology outputs a composite index, the Settlement Efficiency Index (I_{SE}), which provides a multicriteria framework for classifying settlements based on their efficiency level. Section 4 presents an application to ten different intervention areas in southern Italy.

2 Materials and Methods

Most real-world situations have a lot of dependencies, and when it comes to analyzing a decision, several elements come into play. These challenges often present contradictory criteria and multiple solutions [22]. To address these complexities, multi-criteria decision-making methodologies (MCDM) are the most suitable for designing or selecting the best option from a finite set of alternatives. One of the main characteristics of the MCDM is its scalability, which allows it to be applied to a wide range of problems, from individual to complex decision-making, while managing uncertainty and providing accurate analyses [22].

A wide range of MCDM methods have been largely explored in the scientific literature. Generally, these methods can be categorized into two main types [23, 24]: multi-objective methods, which address decision-making problems with solutions belonging to a continuous space, trying to determine the ideal compromise solution through mathematical models; multi-attribute methods, where the optimal solution is determined within a discrete set of alternatives, applying discrete mathematics to a predefined group of possible solutions, providing effective decision support in numerous practical situations.

In summary, the fundamental steps of a multi-criteria analysis include identifying alternatives and evaluation criteria to assess the consequences of each alternative.

The activities carried out in this phase are common to all MCDM methods and provide the necessary information to determine which specific method should be applied [25, 26].

After that, the process moves on to the choice and application of an MCDM method. To ensure its suitability for the given problem, the method should not be chosen before the decision problem has been properly structured [25]. This step includes: estimating the weights assigned to each criterion; measuring the characteristics of each alternative in relation to the criteria; normalizing the measurements to a comparable scale; and calculating synthetic values. The key differences between MCDM methods become evident at this stage.

Finally, in the last stage, the higher the overall score, the more preferable the alternative will be [26]. The results obtained should be further examined through a sensitivity analysis, which is useful for addressing "what-if" questions that decision-makers might have [27].

To tackle the problem at hand, rating systems are often the most effective way to assess the objectivity of sustainable urban projects and policies [28, 29]. Therefore, the focus is on methods that exploit cardinal information, as these are more widely adopted than others. Among these methods, the choice fell on the TOPSIS method [30] because the analysis of the investigated phenomenon relies on indicators that require a comparative approach due to the lack of threshold values. Additionally, compared to other multi-criteria decision-making methods, it offers a simple, user-friendly and easily programmable program [26]. Moreover, the number of steps remains the same regardless of the number of attributes considered. Furthermore, this method stands out for its effectiveness in identifying the alternative that has the least distance from the ideal solution, making it particularly useful in complex and multidimensional decision-making contexts.

3 TOPSIS Method

The method is based on the assumption that the selected alternative should be the one closest to an ideal alternative, which represents the best possible option. For this reason, it is referred to as the positive ideal or simply the ideal alternative. Conversely, the worst possible option is called the negative ideal or anti-ideal alternative, as it is positioned at the greatest distance from the ideal. Therefore, the ultimate goal of the TOPSIS method (see Fig. 1) is to define the two virtual solutions (ideal and anti-ideal) and to measure the relative distance of each real alternative from them.

The starting point is the definition of the decision matrix D, which includes the set of alternatives along with their respective values, as well as the criteria, and their associated weights.

The second step involves the normalization of the decision matrix. Since the criteria in matrix D typically have different units of measurement, normalization is necessary to ensure comparability. This is carried out by determining each element r_{ij} of the normalized matrix R, as shown below:

$$v_{ij} = \frac{r_{ij}}{\sqrt{\sum_{i=1}^{m} r_{ij}^2}} \tag{1}$$

After normalizing the matrix, each value is weighted according to the weight of its corresponding criterion. This results in the determination of the ideal and anti-ideal solutions. The ideal solution is determined by considering, for each criterion, the best performance offered by the alternatives at stake. The anti-ideal solution is obtained, on the other hand, by combining the worst performance of the alternatives with respect to each criterion. By "best" performance we mean the maximum value offered by the alternatives, if we are referring to a benefit criterion, the minimum, if we are referring to a cost criterion. Conversely, it applies to the definition of "worst performance". Once the ideal and anti-ideal solutions are determined, the distances from these solutions are calculated using the following formulas:

$$\overline{d_i^+} = [\textstyle\sum_i (\overline{v}_{ij} - \overline{A_j^*})^2]^{\frac{1}{2}} \tag{2}$$

$$\overline{d_i^-} = [\textstyle\sum_i (\overline{v}_{ij} - \overline{A_j^*})^2]^{\frac{1}{2}} \tag{3}$$

Each of the n (real) alternatives Ai and two (virtual) alternatives can be understood as a point in an m-dimensional space (where m is the number of criteria) where the generic j-th axis measures the normalised, weighted performance (of the type v_{ij}) of the considered alternative with respect to the criterion C_j. The proximity relative to the solution is then calculated using the formula:

$$\overline{RS_i} = \frac{\overline{d_i^-}}{d_i^+ + d_i^-} \tag{4}$$

and to define the ranking of the alternatives. The ranking is done according to the value of relative proximity *RSi* in a descending order: the higher the value of the proximity coefficient of an alternative, the lower its rank. Thus, the alternative with *RSi* closest to 1 is considered the most suitable alternative for the decision problem.

4 Methodology

The proposed methodology consists of 3 macro-phases (see Fig. 1).

Macrophase 1 – Identification of devices. This phase focuses on identifying project elements that can effectively contribute to achieving high performance from natural, artificial and social perspectives.

1a) Analysis of Eco-neighborhoods: this step involves the study of international best practices in urban neighborhoods regeneration to identify devices that can contribute to the efficiency of urban settlements;
1b) Analysis of the Certification Protocols: this step allows, through a comparison with the certification protocols on an urban scale, the identification of the indicator to be considered for the measurement of the devices identified in phase 1a);
1c) Qualitative evaluation of benefits: a literature review identifies the potential benefits these devices can bring to natural, social, and artificial capital in urban transformation projects. A total of 28 benefits are identified.

Macrophase 1 provides a set of 16 indicators that uniquely measure the performance of the identified devices.

Macrophase 2 – Construction of the performance scale using the TOPSIS method.

2a) Selection of sample: this step involves selecting intervention areas for the simulation of a neighborhood plan based on the provisions of the *Norme Tecniche d'Attuazione* (NTA), the technical implementation rules of the Municipal Urban Plans;
2b) Definition of weights: the weights for each criterion are determined through the construction of a frequency matrix (16 × 28), where the rows represent the devices and the columns correspond to the benefits identified in phase 1c).
2c) Polarity definition: this fundamental step defines which indicators must be maximized and which must be minimized to obtain the best performance.

Macrophase 3 – Construction of project scenarios.

To assess the robustness of the methodology, a sensitivity analysis was carried out, in order to identify which devices are most sensitive to achieving sustainability.

3a) Reapplication of the TOPSIS Method: the TOPSIS method is reapplied, considering the size of the settlements, resulting in a normalised ranking.
3b) Elaboration of three simulations: in this phase, the values of the indicators of some devices are increased in the various case studies to evaluate their impact.

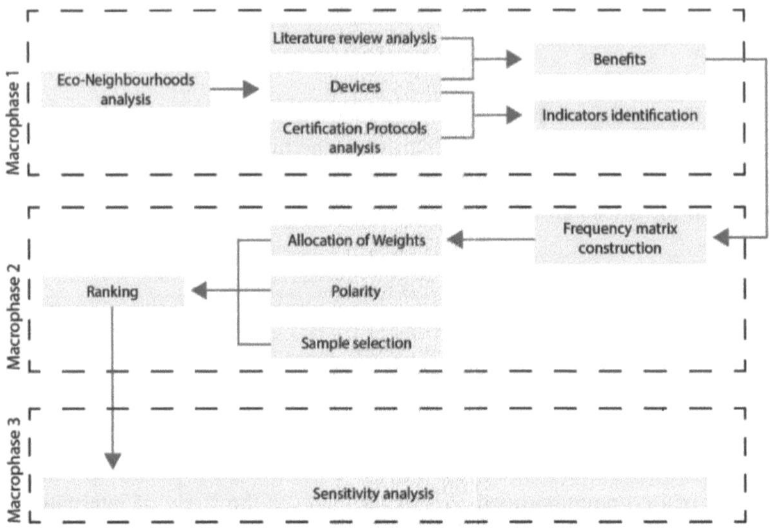

Fig. 1. Methodological flowchart. Subdivision into the three macro-phases.

4.1 *Macrophase 1* - Devices Identification

Through a preliminary analysis of international experiences in urban regeneration [5, 7, 9, 31], an attempt was made to compile a repertoire of experiences and best practices. This collection aims to serve as a solid foundation for identifying key elements to consider when drafting a neighborhood plan, as well as tools to improve the efficiency of urban settlements. This sample of interventions [9] has enabled the identification of innovative and sustainable design solutions. These solutions are valuable for evaluating the quality and impact of urban transformations. They help identify various devices (see Table 1) that can effectively address environmental challenges, as well as the new forms of living and mobility that urban planners currently face.

Subsequently, we proceeded with the identification of the indicators to be used in the evaluation phase. This phase represents a complex and delicate operation. Beyond environmental aspects, indicators from other dimensions of sustainable development such as urban morphological parameters (functional diversity, density, urban and landscape quality, etc.), social measures (social diversity, welfare, etc.), and economic measures (financial feasibility, overall cost, control of land, economic dynamics, etc.) are either absent or insufficiently representative. This finding highlights the lack of strong reference points for evaluating certain key components, as well as the need for further progress

Table 1. The 16 devices considered, with description, formulas and units of measurement.

No	Device	Description	Indicator	Unit of measure
1	Mirrors of water	Percentage of bodies of water (S_{H_2O}) with respect to the total area (S_t)	$R_{H_2O} = \frac{S_{H_2O}}{S_t}100$	$\frac{m^2}{m^2}$
2	Permeable surfaces	Percentage of permeable or filtering area (S_p) with respect to the total area (S_t)	$R_p = \frac{S_p}{S_t}100$	$\frac{m^2}{m^2}$
3	Ecological habitat	Percentage ratio between the planted area (S_{au}) with native shrubby tree species and the external surface (S_e)	$R_{EH} = \frac{S_{au}}{S_e}100$	$\frac{m^2}{m^2}$
4	Urban gardens	Incidence of areas destined for urban gardens (S_{ug}) with respect to the number of settleable inhabitants (N_{inhab})	$I_{UG} = \frac{S_{ug}}{N_{inhab}}100$	$\frac{m^2}{inhab}$
5	Ecological micro-corridors	Percentage of connected green areas (S_{vc}) compared to the total area of green areas (S_{vt})	$R_{vc} = \frac{S_{vc}}{S_{vt}}$	$\frac{m^2}{m^2}$
6	Tree density	Number of tall trees (N_{alb}) to be planted per m^2 of reference area (S_t)	$I_{alb} = \frac{N_{alb}}{S_t}100$	$\frac{alb}{m^2}$
7	Cycle paths	Ratio between the weighted length of the different types of cycle paths (m_{eqCP}) and the number of inhabitants (N_{inhab})	$I_{pc} = \frac{m_{eqCP}}{(100)N_{inhab}}$	$\frac{m}{100\ inhab}$
8	Pedestrian spaces	Percentage of streets and pedestrian spaces (S_{sp}) in relation to the total area of streets and roads (S_v)	$R_{sp} = \frac{S_{sp}}{S_v}100$	m^2/m^2

(*continued*)

Table 1. *(continued)*

No	Device	Description	Indicator	Unit of measure
9	Photovoltaic	Percentage of areas used for photovoltaics (S_{fot}) compared to the total area (S_t)	$R_{fot} = \frac{S_{fot}}{S_t}100$	m^2/m^2
10	District heating	Annual energy consumption produced by the centralized system (district heating or district cooling) compared to the total annual energy consumption	$EP_T = \frac{EP_T}{EP_{gl}}100$	$\frac{kWh/m^3}{kWh/m^3}$
11	Urban compactness	Indicator that allows to evaluate settlement dispersion	$CU = \frac{\sum_{i=1}^{n} p_i d_i^2}{\sum_{i=1}^{n} p_i}$	$\frac{m^5}{m^3}$
12	Sustainable urban drainage system	Quantity of surfaces equipped with drainage devices (S_D) compared to the total urbanized area (S_t)	$S_D = \frac{\sum S_D}{S_t}100$	m^2/m^2
13	Green roofs	Ratio between the surface area of green roofs $\left(S_{gr}\right)$ and 50% of the covered area (S_c)	$R_{gr} = \frac{S_{gr}}{50\%S_c}100$	m^2/m^2
14	Multifunctional square	Presence of a square that satisfies multiple needs: meeting place, market point, square for events, square for emergency management	P_{pol} Presence/Absence	n
15	Functional mixité	Application of the Entropy index [37]	$ENT = \frac{-\left[\sum_{j=1}^{k} P^j ln\left(P^j\right)\right]}{ln(k)}$	[-]
16	Social mixité	Application of the Gini heterogeneity index [38]	$I_G = 1 - f_i^2$	[-]

[8, 32]. Therefore, in order to have reference values, existing urban-scale certification protocols, such as ITACA-SU, GBC-Q, LEED-ND, BREEAM-C, and DGNB-UD [33–36] were analyzed. For each protocol, indicators were identified and associated with the

previously identified devices. These indicators (see Tab. 1) are of different kinds: qualitative or quantitative, and are capable of capturing information about environmental, social, and economic conditions in urban areas.

The identification of the benefits produced by the different devices in the urban design of urban settlements is an essential component of understanding the impact of these devices on the different components of sustainability, in economic, social and environmental terms. A literature analysis was carried out to identify them, which led to a final set of 28 benefits (see Table 2). Below are some examples concerning the devices: cycle paths, pedestrian spaces, urban compactness and tree density.

Studies have shown that the introduction of cycle paths and pedestrian spaces reduces traffic congestion and improves road safety, as well as encouraging sustainable modes of transport [39]. They also contribute to the reduction of motorized traffic, thus improving urban livability [40]. Therefore, the following benefits have been associated with these devices: IUM, RTC, PCT, and RS.

Urban compactness, on the other hand, favors the reduction of the use of resources, such as land consumption and energy demand, also improving the quality of life through greater accessibility to services [41]. It follows that the benefits considered are: RRC, QL, and IUM. Finally, a higher density of trees in urban areas contributes to the reduction of outdoor temperatures (ETC), oxygen production and CO2 storage (OP); it promotes natural urban water drainage (UWD) and contributes to acoustic and visual insulation and shading, improving urban comfort (UC), thus making cities more livable [42].

Table 2. List of 28 identified benefits.

No	Benefits		No	Benefits	
1	RPE	Reduction of pollutant emissions	15	BP	Biodiversity protection
2	RRC	Reduction of resource consumption	16	EE	Energy efficiency
3	WR	Waste reduction	17	EVR	Increase in the economic value of real estate
4	RIS	Reduction of impermeable surfaces	18	SA	Social aggregation
5	CR	Cost reduction (management)	19	ED	Economic development
6	PU	Public use	20	BR	Brownfield redevelopment
7	ETC	External temperature control	21	IUM	Improvement of urban mobility
8	NL	Natural lighting	22	RHL	Reducing heat loss
9	WCR	Water collection and reuse	23	RER	Reduction of entrepreneurial risk
10	UWD	Urban water drainage	24	RTC	Reduced traffic congestion
11	RS	Road safety	25	PSV	Parking for sustainable vehicles

(continued)

Table 2. (*continued*)

No	Benefits		No	Benefits	
12	HS	Housing security	26	PCT	Pedestrian/cycling travel
13	UC	Urban comfort	27	OP	Oxygen Production-Carbon Storage
14	FRP	Flood risk prevention	28	QL	Greater quality of living

4.2 *Macrophase 2* - Definition of the Evaluation Structure to Construct the Performance Scale on the Selected Sample

Macrophase 2 saw the application of the TOPSIS method to a selected sample of case studies. A 10x16 matrix was constructed, with case studies as rows and indicators as columns. To apply the method, it was necessary to define the weights to be associated with each indicator. The assigned weights were obtained from the benefits identified in step 1(c). In particular, a frequency matrix (16x28) was built, in which the rows are made up of the devices and the columns of the benefits. If the i-th device produces the j-th benefit then the cell aij is assigned a value of 1, otherwise, is assigned a value of zero. By summing all the values in the i-th row and then dividing by the total weight, we obtain the frequency of the i-th device. Subsequently, the indicators were polarized, a fundamental step to balance often conflicting objectives and optimize overall performance, especially in complex urban decision-making contexts. In this specific case, only the indicator related to urban compactness was inverted, as it is inversely proportional: an increase in urban compactness corresponds to greater urban sprawl, a phenomenon that contrasts with the goal of sustainable densification and resource optimization. By applying the TOPSIS method, the output of this macro-phase is a ranking of the composite efficiency indices (I_{SE}) for each case study.

4.3 *Macrophase 3* – Construction of Project Scenarios

To test the robustness of the method, an analytical approach based on simulations was adopted. In the context of urban regeneration, simulations are used to predict the effects of different design configurations and interventions on urban areas.

This method is an essential tool, as it allows us to model hypothetical scenarios by evaluating the effects produced by different strategies on urban settlement. Through this process we are able to identify which devices have a more or less significant impact on achieving settlement sustainability.

Although we do not yet fully understand the effects of each identified device and despite the lack of structured data, simulations provide us with a solid basis for making informed predictions and guiding future decisions.

First, all indicators were normalized, to take into account the size of each settlement. Based on the normalized ranking—referred to as Simulation 0, which does not include any indicator increases—three additional simulations were defined, each of which predicts a different increase in the indicators associated with various devices. The output of each simulation is expressed as a ranking.

The three simulations (see Table 3) were designed to test different combinations of devices, such as permeable surfaces, tree densities, green roofs, urban gardens, remote heating systems and photovoltaic systems, all of which are considered relevant for improving environmental sustainability and urban resilience. Each simulation involves an increase in specific indicators, allowing us to observe how these variations affect the final ranking of the case studies.

Table 3. Simulations performed with the detail of the increased indicators

Simulation No	Application object and purpose	Increased indicators
0	-	-
1	All case studies	Permeable Surfaces, Tree Density and Green Roofs
2	All case studies	Urban gardens, ecological habitats and micro-corridors
3	All case studies	District heating, Photovoltaic system, Sustainable urban drainage system

5 Application

The application was carried out on a sample of 10 urban settlements subject to neighborhood planning located in the Campania Region, in Southern Italy. For the selection, the municipalities belonging to the territorial context of the municipality of Baronissi were chosen (see Fig. 2). The selection supports the exploration of the effectiveness of urban regeneration interventions in different local contexts within the same area.

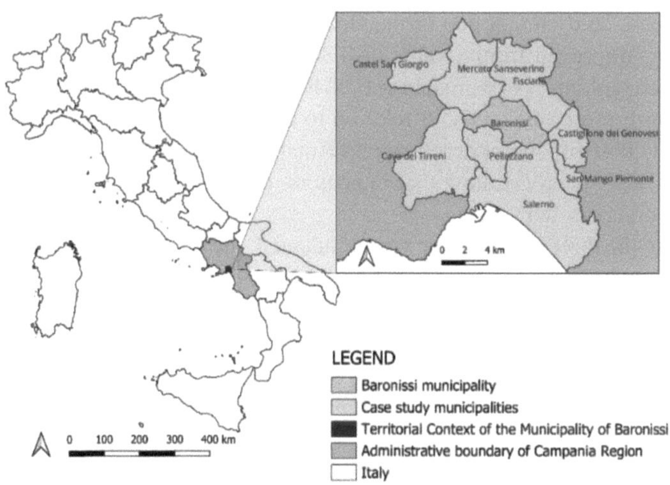

Fig. 2. Territorial framework with the indication of Baronissi municipality (in dark yellow), and the case study municipalities (in light yellow).

For each of the 10 case studies, the 16 indicators defined in Macrophase 1 were measured. These values serve as input for the application of the TOPSIS method to obtain the final ranking. The method was then reapplied, taking into account the size of each settlement, resulting in a normalized ranking (see Table 4).

Table 4. Ranking obtained through the application of the TOPSIS method. *Ranking 0*: Performance scale derived from the 10 draft neighborhood plans, developed according to the NTAs; *Normalised ranking*: Performance scale obtained by dividing all the indicators by the corresponding territorial surface.

S_t [m^2]	Sample No	Ranking 0	Normalized ranking	% variation
59821	Case study n.1	0,473945961	0,394326363	−17%
227696	Case study n.2	0,438145311	0,275913185	−37%
40688	Case study n.3	0,301811259	0,344070201	14%
90168,78	Case study n.4	0,318752473	0,162445596	−49%
41458,55	Case study n.5	0,337159945	0,363263788	8%
53382	Case study n.6	0,442383277	0,396919636	−10%
27000	Case study n.7	0,368743519	0,543605754	47%
41436	Case study n.8	0,370932154	0,393943233	6%
72246	Case study n.9	0,423041055	0,313182883	−26%
46542,96	Case study n.10	0,451873098	0,441679824	−2%

From the results shown in Table 4, it can be concluded that case study no. 2 (i.e., the one with the largest territorial surface) initially had a relatively high value in the ranking 0 (0.4381), but then experienced a drastic reduction in the normalized ranking (−37%, to 0.2759). This suggests that, despite the high absolute values of the indicators, when they are related to the territorial dimension, their relative efficiency drops significantly. In contrast, case study no. 3, one of the smallest case studies with a territorial surface of 40,688 m^2, improved from a value of 0.3018 in the ranking 0 to a higher value in the normalized ranking (+14%, reaching 0.3440). This indicates that smaller settlements tend to perform more efficiently in relation to their territorial surface. Similarly, case study no. 7 (27,000 m^2) shows excellent performance. Its value in the normalized ranking increased by 47%, demonstrating that indicators related to quality per unit area tend to favour more compact settlements.

After that, the three simulations were conducted, the results of which can be viewed in Fig. 3.

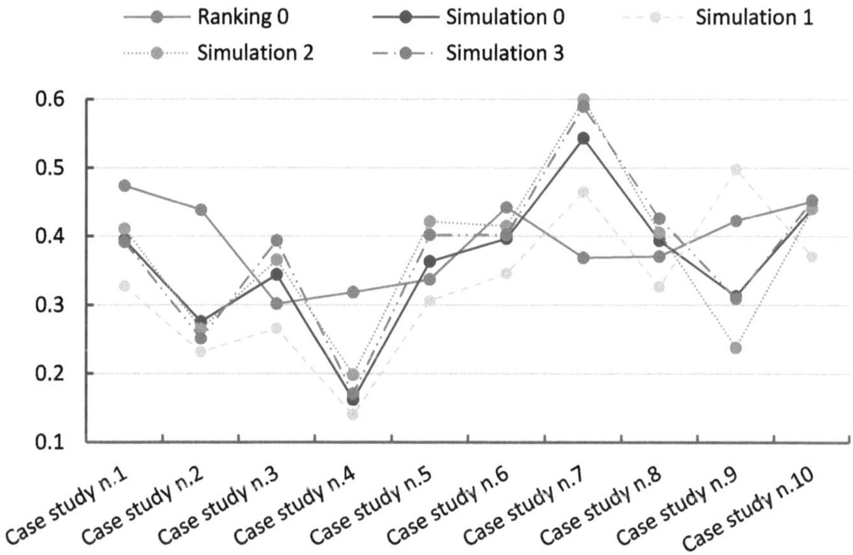

Fig. 3. Comparison of rankings obtained through the TOPSIS method across different simulations. The graph illustrates the ranking variations for each case study, highlighting differences between the initial ranking (Ranking 0) and the results from Simulations 0, 1, 2, and 3.

The graph illustrates the trend of ranking values obtained for each case study across the various simulations. By analyzing the percentage changes of the individual simulations compared to Simulation 0 (normalized ranking), it is evident that case study no.2 consistently experiences negative changes, indicating poor adaptability to the proposed interventions. Case study no. 9 stands out as an outlier, with a substantial increase in Simulation 1, followed by a decrease in the subsequent simulations. This suggests sensitivity to changes in the indicators. Case study no. 4 is the only one to show clear improvements in all simulations, indicating that the improved indicators were particularly effective in this case. In summary, the results reveal a mixed impact of the indicator increases. Some case studies benefit significantly, while others remain stable or even show slight deterioration. These findings suggest that, in general, the case studies vary in their capacity to absorb interventions.

6 Conclusions

The main objective of this research is the development of an operational tool that can be concretely applied based on the available data and usable by planners in drafting neighborhood plans. This tool relies on simulations that make it possible to control, in an ex-ante phase, the effectiveness of design choices, identified by the model, allowing the planner to make informed decisions to improve the efficiency and sustainability of urban settlements.

The methodology developed, while not claiming to be definitive, offers a framework that can be further verified and refined, thus promoting the development of more sustainable urban settlements. The hierarchical structure of the model, with a composite index

[43] that includes indicators for each of the selected 'capitals' and devices, allows the project to be examined in detail and to intervene on specific aspects where necessary. This ensures more precise control over the design factors that contribute to sustainability. A key feature of this methodology is the ability to construct a performance scale across a sample of urban settlements and evaluate the sensitivity of each design intervention. This approach supports the pursuit of objectivity in sustainability assessments, ensuring that urban planning decisions are based on empirical evidence rather than subjective judgment. However, given that the results are contingent upon the analyzed sample, the current validation remains relative.

The results suggest that the interventions tested in simulations might be more or less suitable for certain contexts. It was also noted that the size of the urban settlement plays a significant role. Case studies with a larger territorial surface respond better to interventions requiring physical space (such as green roofs or permeable surfaces). These insights reinforce the idea that ecological and technological interventions yield different outcomes depending on the scale and type of urban settlement.

As future developments, the research aims to expand the sample size to improve the robustness of findings and enhance the model's applicability. Furthermore, an essential next step involves integrating the model into a GIS-BIM environment [10, 44–47]. This integration will facilitate spatial analysis, improve data management, and enhance visualization capabilities, providing urban planners with a more sophisticated decision-making tool.

Acknowledgments. This study was funded by the municipality of Baronissi (Salerno, Southern Italy) under grant number (Prot. 93882 –REP 269/2023) in accordance with the Agreement between DiCiv and municipality of Baronissi for "studies and research to support the formation of the Municipal Urban Plan". Michele Grimaldi and Isidoro Fasolino are the project scientific responsibles and Federica Cicalese is a member of the research group.

Disclosure of Interests. The authors have no competing interests to declare that are relevant to the content of this article.

References

1. UN-Habitat: Urbanization and development: emerging futures. UN-Habitat, Nairobi, Kenya (2016)
2. Schetke, S., Haase, D., Kötter, T.: Towards sustainable settlement growth: a new multi-criteria assessment for implementing environmental targets into strategic urban planning. Environ. Impact Assess. Rev. **32**, 195–210 (2012). https://doi.org/10.1016/j.eiar.2011.08.008
3. Andersson, E.: Urban Landscapes and Sustainable Cities. E&S. 11, art34 (2006). https://doi.org/10.5751/ES-01639-110134
4. Holden, M.: Urban indicators and the integrative ideals of cities. Cities **23**, 170–183 (2006). https://doi.org/10.1016/j.cities.2006.03.001
5. Wang, R., Zhou, T., Hu, D., Li, F., Liu, J.: Cultivating eco-sustainability: social–economic–natural complex ecosystem case studies in China. Ecol. Complex. **8**, 273–283 (2011). https://doi.org/10.1016/j.ecocom.2011.03.003

6. Li, L., Shen, C., Wu, A.C., Li, X.: Propensity score-based sensitivity analysis method for uncontrolled confounding. Am. J. Epidemiol. **174**, 345–353 (2011). https://doi.org/10.1093/aje/kwr096
7. Joss, S.: Eco-cities and Sustainable Urbanism. In: International Encyclopedia of the Social & Behavioral Sciences, pp. 829–837. Elsevier (2015). https://doi.org/10.1016/B978-0-08-097086-8.74010-4
8. Chastenet, C.A., et al.: The French eco-neighbourhood evaluation model: contributions to sustainable city making and to the evolution of urban practices. J. Environ. Manage. **176**, 69–78 (2016). https://doi.org/10.1016/j.jenvman.2016.03.036
9. Cicalese, F.: Insediamenti e adattamento. Aspetti chiave nelle esperienze internazionali. Territorio della Ricerca su Insediamenti e Ambiente. Rivista internazionale di cultura urbanistica, pp. 127–142 Paginazione (2023). https://doi.org/10.6093/2281-4574/10601
10. Li, D., Shan, J., Shao, Z., Zhou, X., Yao, Y.: Geomatics for smart cities - concept, key techniques, and applications. Geo-spat. Inf. Sci. **16**, 13–24 (2013). https://doi.org/10.1080/10095020.2013.772803
11. Fasolino, I., Grimaldi, M.: The urban planning efficiency of settlements. Techniques and actions. ARCHIVIO DI STUDI URBANI E REGIONALI, 5–10 (2020). https://doi.org/10.3280/ASUR2020-127-S1001
12. Bott, L.-M., Ankel, L., Braun, B.: Adaptive neighborhoods: the interrelation of urban form, social capital, and responses to coastal hazards in Jakarta. Geoforum **106**, 202–213 (2019). https://doi.org/10.1016/j.geoforum.2019.08.016
13. Fang, K., Zhang, Q., Yu, H., Wang, Y., Dong, L., Shi, L.: Sustainability of the use of natural capital in a city: measuring the size and depth of urban ecological and water footprints. Sci. Total. Environ. **631–632**, 476–484 (2018). https://doi.org/10.1016/j.scitotenv.2018.02.299
14. Olewiler, N.: Environmental sustainability for urban areas: the role of natural capital indicators. Cities **23**, 184–195 (2006). https://doi.org/10.1016/j.cities.2006.03.006
15. Wentink, C., Vaandrager, L., Van Dam, R., Hassink, J., Salverda, I.: Exploring the role of social capital in urban citizens' initiatives in The Netherlands. Gac. Sanit. **32**, 539–546 (2018). https://doi.org/10.1016/j.gaceta.2017.05.011
16. Cicalese, F., Fasolino, I.: A multidimensional assessment model of settlement efficiency at the urban scale. In: Marucci, A., Zullo, F., Fiorini, L., Saganeiti, L. (eds.) Innovation in Urban and Regional Planning, pp. 251–262. Springer, Cham (2024). https://doi.org/10.1007/978-3-031-54118-6_24
17. Singh, R.K., Murty, H.R., Gupta, S.K., Dikshit, A.K.: An overview of sustainability assessment methodologies. Ecol. Ind. **15**, 281–299 (2012). https://doi.org/10.1016/j.ecolind.2011.01.007
18. Fasolino, I., Coppola, F., Grimaldi, M.: A model for urban planning control of the settlement efficiency. A case study. In: Archivio di studi urbani e regionali, pp. 181–210. FrancoAngeli, Milano, Italy (2020)
19. Boulanger, P.-M., Bréchet, T.: Models for policy-making in sustainable development: the state of the art and perspectives for research. Ecol. Econ. **55**, 337–350 (2005). https://doi.org/10.1016/j.ecolecon.2005.07.033
20. Smyth, R.L., Watzin, M.C., Manning, R.E.: Defining acceptable levels for ecological indicators: an approach for considering social values. Environ. Manage. **39**, 301–315 (2007). https://doi.org/10.1007/s00267-005-0282-3
21. Macchiaroli, M., Dolores, L., De Mare, G.: Design the water tariff structure: application and assessment of a model to balance sustainability. Cost Recovery Wise Use Water **15**, 1309 (2023). https://doi.org/10.3390/w15071309
22. Chaube, S., et al.: An overview of multi-criteria decision analysis and the applications of AHP and TOPSIS methods. Int. J. Math. Eng. Manag. Sci. **9**, 581–615 (2024). https://doi.org/10.33889/IJMEMS.2024.9.3.030

23. Zimmermann, H.-J., Gutsche, L.: Multi-Criteria Analyse. Springer, Heidelberg (1991). https://doi.org/10.1007/978-3-642-58198-4
24. Voogd, H.: Multicriteria Evaluation for Urban and Regional Planning. Pion, London (1983)
25. Roy, B.: Multicriteria Methodology for Decision Aiding. Springer US, Boston (1996). https://doi.org/10.1007/978-1-4757-2500-1
26. Sitorus, F., Cilliers, J.J., Brito-Parada, P.R.: Multi-criteria decision making for the choice problem in mining and mineral processing: applications and trends. Exp. Syst. Appl. **121**, 393–417 (2019). https://doi.org/10.1016/j.eswa.2018.12.001
27. Keeney, R.L.: Feature article—decision analysis: an overview. Oper. Res. **30**, 803–838 (1982). https://doi.org/10.1287/opre.30.5.803
28. Gerundo, R., Marra, A., Grimaldi, M.: A preliminary model for promoting energy communities in urban planning. In: Calabrò, F., Della Spina, L., Piñeira Mantiñán, M.J. (eds.) New Metropolitan Perspectives, pp. 2833–2840. Springer, Cham (2022). https://doi.org/10.1007/978-3-031-06825-6_270
29. Gerundo, R., Marra, A.: Paesaggi a rischio di periferizzazione. Un quadro metodologico per la valutazione del rischio a supporto delle strategie di pianificazione regionale. Sustainable Mediterranean Construction, pp. 73–79 (2021)
30. Hwang, C.-L., Yoon, K.: Multiple Attribute Decision Making. Springer, Heidelberg (1981). https://doi.org/10.1007/978-3-642-48318-9
31. Holman, N.: Incorporating local sustainability indicators into structures of local governance: a review of the literature. Local Environ. **14**, 365–375 (2009). https://doi.org/10.1080/13549830902783043
32. Macchiaroli, M., Dolores, L., Nicodemo, L., De Mare, G.: Energy efficiency in the management of the integrated water service. A case study on the white certificates incentive system. In: Gervasi, O., et al. (eds.) Computational Science and Its Applications, ICCSA 2021, pp. 202–217. Springer, Cham (2021). https://doi.org/10.1007/978-3-030-87010-2_14
33. BRE, Building Research Establishment: BREEAM communities. Technical Manual- SD202 (2012)
34. GBCI, Green Building Council Italia: Sistema di verifica GBC QUARTIERI. Per progettare, realizzare e riqualificare aree e quartieri sostenibili. Edizione 2015. Rovereto (2015)
35. DGNB Criteria Set Districts, Version 2020 (2020)
36. LEED v4 for NEIGHBORHOOD DEVELOPMENT (2018)
37. Zhuo, Y., Zheng, H., Wu, C., Xu, Z., Li, G., Yu, Z.: Compatibility mix degree index: a novel measure to characterize urban land use mix pattern. Comput. Environ. Urban Syst. **75**, 49–60 (2019). https://doi.org/10.1016/j.compenvurbsys.2019.01.005
38. Gini, C.: Measurement of inequality of incomes. Econ. J. **31**, 124 (1921). https://doi.org/10.2307/2223319
39. Gehl, J.: Cities for People. Island Press, Washington, DC (2010)
40. Newman, P., Kenworthy, J.R.: Sustainability and Cities: Overcoming Automobile Dependence. Island Press, Washington, D.C. (1999)
41. Burton, E., Jenks, M., Williams, K. (eds.): The Compact City. Routledge (2003). https://doi.org/10.4324/9780203362372
42. McPherson, E.G., et al.: No title found. Urban Ecosystems. **1**, 49–61 (1997). https://doi.org/10.1023/A:1014350822458
43. OECD, European Union, Joint Research Centre - European Commission: Handbook on Constructing Composite Indicators: Methodology and User Guide. OECD (2008). https://doi.org/10.1787/9789264043466-en
44. Shen, L., Kyllo, J., Guo, X.: An integrated model based on a hierarchical indices system for monitoring and evaluating urban sustainability. Sustainability. **5**, 524–559 (2013). https://doi.org/10.3390/su5020524

45. Ahmad, T., Thaheem, M.J.: Developing a residential building-related social sustainability assessment framework and its implications for BIM. Sustain. Cities Soc. **28**, 1–15 (2017). https://doi.org/10.1016/j.scs.2016.08.002
46. Malczewski, J.: GIS and Multicriteria Decision Analysis. Wiley, New York (1999)
47. Tao, W.: Interdisciplinary urban GIS for smart cities: advancements and opportunities. Geo-spat. Inf. Sci. **16**, 25–34 (2013). https://doi.org/10.1080/10095020.2013.774108

Investigating the Safety of Green Areas in Naples Through the Analysis of Environmental Risk and Crime Risk

Silvana D'Ambrosio[1](✉), Eleonora Giovene di Girasole[2], Ferdinando Maria Musto[3], and Alessandro Sgobbo[1]

[1] DiARC - Department of Architecture, University of Naples Federico II, Naples, Italy
{silvana.dambrosio,alessandro.sgobbo}@unina.it
[2] Construction Technologies Institute (ITC), National Research Council of Italy (CNR), Naples, Italy
e.giovenedigirasole@itc.cnr.it
[3] Centro LUPT, University of Naples Federico II, Naples, Italy
ferdinandomaria.musto@unina.it

Abstract. The paper presents the first results of ongoing studies under the National Research Project 2022 "Security Town through Urban Planning" (SeTUP), which aims to develop a risk mapping model in green areas to highlight the spatial component and guide urban planning decisions. The paper focuses on top-down and bottom-up analysis of some parks in Naples. On the one hand, the analysis involves the multiple aspects of urban morphology associated with the four types of green areas identified by the City of Naples: gardens/parks, historic parks, neighborhood parks, and urban parks, integrating the visions of regeneration of some neighborhoods in Naples identified in the preliminary drafting of the PUC (Municipal Urban Plan).

The paper shows the first results of the project with the analysis on the top-down real security associated with environmental risk (natural hazards) and crime dropped on the green areas and parks of Naples in order to select the case studies on which to carry out the bottom-up perceptual survey.

Keywords: Environmental Risk · Criminal Risk · Park Safety

1 Introduction

A city can be considered well-functioning and sustainable when there is the possibility of enjoying safe streets and public spaces (Jacobs, 1969; Dewberry, 2003; Cozens, 2007; INU, 2013). At the same time, the issue of urban crime is closely connected to the shape of the city and the way it functions (Hillier & Sahbaz, 2005, p. 456). No city can truly be called sustainable if its citizens fear for their personal safety and the security of their belongings (Du Plessis, 2000).

E. Borgogno-Mondino and P. Zamperlin (Eds.): ASITA 2024, CCIS 2463, pp. 322–337, 2025.
https://doi.org/10.1007/978-3-031-91141-5_22

Numerous studies and field experiences have demonstrated that when citizens demand greater security, they are not referring just to criminal behavior but to a large range of factors that contribute to the perception of an unsafe urban environment, including uneasiness and fear. The perception of insecurity can affect city life as well as the functionality and attractiveness of certain urban areas. When people feel threatened, they modify their lifestyles and, consequently, the way they use the city daily.

The perception of risks is contradictory: it ranges from the classic fear for physical safety due to potential criminal acts to increased sensitivity toward natural hazards, exacerbated in recent years by significant climate change. "Crime risk" does not have a single definition in scientific literature; rather, it varies depending on the study context. In this article, crime risk is analyzed through the paradigm of territorial risk, considering it as a constructed anthropogenic risk, defined as the probability that a criminal event—characterized by a spatial dimension—occurs in a vulnerable context, causing damage to people or property due to human behavior.

The issue of security and crime risk gained prominence in the second half of the twentieth century, beginning with studies from the Chicago School. These early works examined how human behavior was influenced by the physical and social environment of cities, using crime mapping techniques. In the 1970s, the Brantinghams, with their Crime Pattern Theory, explored the characteristics of urban fabric and the criminal opportunities it provided. Simultaneously, Oscar Newman, through the Defensible Space Theory, identified urban areas more vulnerable to crime and suggested that urban planners design spaces capable of preventing deviant behaviors. The Broken Windows Theory (1982), formulated by Wilson and Kelling, posited that urban neglect and deterioration could lead to increased crime and, consequently, the marginalization of an area (Bianchini, Sicurella, 2012).

In 1971, C. Ray Jeffery introduced the CPTED (Crime Prevention Through Environmental Design) theory, which analyzed how environmental design could influence criminal behavior. The perception of crime risk is often fueled not only by actual crimes but also by social fear. Even when crime rates decrease, the demand for security may remain unchanged (Chiesi, 2004). This phenomenon is linked to incivility—violations of social norms that regulate coexistence in public spaces and care for the territory. Signs of disorder, such as graffiti and litter, may be perceived as a threat to security and social order (Skogan, 1990; Wilson & Kelling, 1982). Such signs are considered indicators of a potential threat, contributing to the persistent fear of crime (Sampson & Raudenbush, 1999). Given the relationship between crime, the physical environment, and the perception of security, achieving safe conditions requires integrating various approaches to obtain effective and lasting results.

Crime risk is determined by three factors: crime hazard (Pc), crime vulnerability (Vc), and crime exposure (Ec), linked by the fundamental risk equation: Rc = Pc x Vc x Ec. Crime hazard describes the probability that a spatially-based criminal event will occur in a given area, with a certain intensity, within a specific time frame. Crime vulnerability represents the ability of urban space—considering its physical and functional characteristics—to either discourage or facilitate the occurrence of a particular spatially-based crime. Crime exposure describes the elements (people, monuments, or sites of particular interest) that are exposed to risk from the occurrence of a criminal event in a given area.

On the other hand, humans have always faced dangers of natural origin (volcanic eruptions, earthquakes, tsunamis, floods, droughts, landslides, etc.). In recent years, the effects of these events have increasingly been catastrophic, often amplified—or even induced—by various human interventions in the environment. Environmental risk is defined as the product of three parameters according to the equation R = P * V * E, where P represents the hazard—the probability that a given event (which may cause negative effects on humans and/or the environment) will occur with a certain intensity in a given area within a specific time frame; V indicates vulnerability, or the susceptibility of an exposed asset to damage from a specific disastrous event; and E refers to exposure, meaning the total value of at-risk elements within the exposed area (ISPRA, 2011).

Environmental hazards can arise from natural causes, such as earthquakes, tsunamis, volcanic eruptions, and extreme weather events; from the combination of environmental and human factors, such as erosion, landslides, river flooding, and heavy rainfall-induced flooding; or from purely human activities, such as wildfires, nuclear accidents, and pollution of water, air, and soil.

Another recognized risk factor linked to human impact, which strongly influences the performance of the built environment by introducing new vulnerabilities (Chiesa, 2017; Santamouris, 2014; Matteoli & Pagani, 2010), is the Urban Heat Island (UHI). This phenomenon, caused by urbanization, involves modifications to the surface and atmosphere that generally lead to changes in the urban climate, making it warmer than surrounding areas (Voogt, 2003; Coseo et al., 2014). The Urban Heat Island effect describes a characteristic of urban areas where night-time temperatures are higher than in the surrounding landscape (Santamouris, 2013). Elevated urban air temperatures result from interconnected factors associated with changes to the natural surface due to urbanization, as well as heat and pollution released by human activities in urban environments (Morris & Simmonds, 2000). The Urban Heat Island effect is associated with city development and urban expansion (Taleb et al., 2013) and has a direct impact on energy efficiency, the environment, and ultimately, human comfort and health.

Finally, what makes a city unsafe is not only the actual risk of being a victim of predatory crimes but also the perception of insecurity in certain spaces, which is linked to urban decay and social distress. The demand for security is thus tied to multiple factors that influence and alter the perception of urban spaces, making them appear unsafe. The quality of a space cannot be assessed in an objective and uniform manner; subjective and perceptual aspects must also be considered (Dessi, Astolfi, 2020). It is crucial to take into account the perceptions, emotions, and opinions of the local community when evaluating spaces. Top-down analyses alone are not sufficient (Bonnes, Uzzell, Carrus, Kelay, 2007).

In particular, it is necessary to introduce a risk-based model in the study of security conditions, allowing for the identification and assessment of critical issues in a given spatial context and the definition of appropriate risk mitigation actions proper to that context, as well as systematic actions to adapt spaces to safety criteria defined based on the simulation of risk scenarios that urban planning choices may generate (Fasolino, Coppola, Grimaldi, 2018).

This paper is part of the research project SeTUP—Security through Urban Planning, which won the PRIN 2022 PNRR grant. The project focuses on urban security as a fundamental aspect of city policies aimed at designing and managing sustainable cities and communities, as recommended by the Sustainable Development Goals (SDGs) of the United Nations' 2030 Agenda. The research, in accordance with CPTED principles, investigates the real and perceived security of selected green areas in Naples, carrying out a top-down analysis of their context based on quantitative data, considering environmental risk, related to hazard and territorial vulnerability factors (Pinna, 2002), and crime risk, directly linked to anthropogenic components (Coppola, 2021) also with a bottom-up qualitative investigation using the study perceived risk through questionnaires and participatory mapping.

The ultimate goal of the research is to propose a crime risk mapping model applicable to any territorial context. This model will help construct knowledge frameworks simulating different crime risk scenarios, effectively identifying critical areas and developing appropriate intervention strategies. The paper presents the project's initial results, analysing top-down real security risk, related to environmental hazards (natural risk) and crime across Naples' parks and green spaces to select case studies for bottom-up perceptual investigations.

2 Materials and Methods

The research originates from a study conducted by the University of Fisciano within the Department of Engineering (Coppola, Fasolino, Grimaldi, 2021), which developed a comprehensive model for crime risk mapping through the construction of a composite index with a spatial dimension. This model integrates three types of information corresponding to the three main approaches to security—situational, social, and environmental—translating them into crime risk maps. This process started with the composite index and led to the definition of the crime risk map through an overlay of risk matrices. The second phase focused on assessing the robustness of the composite index model by conducting a sensitivity analysis, examining the uncertainties associated with the spatial indicators on which the index depends.

Considering that the analyses must be conducted in relation to the specific intervention context, the paper develops a methodology for constructing both the Environmental Risk Map and the Crime Risk Map to investigate the real top-down security associated with environmental risks (natural hazards) and crime, applied to the green areas and parks of Naples.

To construct the Environmental Risk Map, specific risks associated with the analysed territories were investigated, including:

- Seismic risk
- Hydrogeological risk
- Volcanic risk
- Urban heat island effect

Using open-source data processed by national, regional, and municipal institutions regarding territorial vulnerability, risk maps were developed. Additionally, the study examined the guidelines outlined in Civil Protection Plans to verify whether parks or green areas had been designated as waiting areas, assembly points, or shelters due to their suitability for accommodating people, essential services, food stations, medical facilities, parking, and emergency vehicles in the event of seismic or volcanic emergencies.

Specifically, for the analysis of the urban heat island effect, data from the Horizon 2020 CLARITY project[1] (Integrated Climate Adaptation Service Tools for Improving Resilience Measure Efficiency) were used. This project highlights how urban morphology influences microclimatic conditions and maps urban heatwave scenarios.

These data were processed and analysed using GIS software, providing a spatially referenced representation applied to the green areas and parks under investigation. This approach enables a visualisation of the relationship between these spaces and the assessed risks.

Similarly, in constructing the Crime Risk Map, understanding crime risk conditions—based on reported crimes across different city districts—was a fundamental prerequisite. The map was compiled using available data on reported offences within a given timeframe, as provided by police headquarters and prefectures upon official request. In cases where such data were unavailable, it was possible to create georeferenced maps (using QGIS, My Maps, or Google Earth) based on alternative datasets, allowing for a targeted analysis of criminal phenomena, their classification, and their spatial distribution. If official data were not accessible, other databases, such as Minecrime[2], could be utilised.

In this context, the Mapping Overlay technique emerges as an appropriate and effective method for thematic layering, aimed at producing synthesis maps. Mapping Overlay is widely employed in spatial planning and territorial governance. In the 1960s, landscape architect Ian L. McHarg developed an overlay mapping technique that involved identifying various values (historical, hydrological, scenic, recreational, residential, wildlife, forestry, and institutional) within a given area and creating thematic maps for each. McHarg's map layering approach allows for measuring, mapping, monitoring, and modelling territories.

Natural factor maps—such as bedrock geology, soil composition, slope, and vegetation—are overlaid to identify areas where specific factor combinations occur. This process can be carried out manually by superimposing thematic maps or digitally using Geographic Information Systems (GIS). Digital tools such as CAD and GIS are widely used for creating these overlaid maps.

This technique provides a clear and simultaneous representation of natural risks affecting a given area, offering a synthesised spatial reading. In Italy, this method is referred to as "sovrapposizione di carte" (map overlay), allowing for the superimposition

[1] (https://clarity-h2020.eu/)

[2] (https://www.minecrime.it/)

of thematic maps to generate a summary map related to risk analysis. This method will be employed in the second phase of the research to investigate and overlay different types of risk—not only environmental risks but also those related to crime. Therefore, it is possible to refer to risk maps (Treu, 2009), which allow for both comparative analysis and the simultaneous localization of various risks associated with crime and environmental hazards.

2.1 Study Area

Throughout its history, the city of Naples coexisted with environmental risks, which have intensified in recent years due to human intervention. Naples represents one of the most pronounced cases of this phenomenon, given its high level of urbanisation and anthropisation. The geological characteristics of Naples play a crucial role in understanding the primary natural hazards affecting the municipal territory. Its morphology is shaped by the volcanic nature of the landscape, with the city nestled between the Somma-Vesuvius tectonic high to the east and the vast (25,000 km^2) caldera of the Phlegraean Fields to the west (Calcaterra, 2023). However, natural shaping forces—climate and the sea—have profoundly modified the Neapolitan landscape, attenuating its morphology while still leaving the city exposed to persistent environmental risks.

From a geomorphological perspective, volcanic activity contributes to the formation of the city's orographic structures, whose reliefs are particularly fragile. Their slopes are incised by valleys of varying depths, carved by ephemeral watercourses that extend beneath the city. This geological fragility makes densely populated areas particularly vulnerable during extreme rainfall events, which can trigger landslides and associated environmental hazards. As a result, Naples' specific geographical location and geological history give rise to three primary risk categories: hydrogeological, seismic, and volcanic.

At the same time, Naples is also affected by crime and urban decay. According to statistics from the inter-agency database of the Department of Public Security of the Ministry of the Interior for 2023, Naples ranks 12th in the national "crime trend" ranking, based on the number of reported offences (43%) recorded by law enforcement and forwarded to the judiciary. The majority of criminal incidents are linked to organised crime, while petty crime—particularly theft and counterfeiting—also plays a significant role, often involving minors.

In this context, territorial and environmental security becomes a central issue, both in terms of governance policies and in understanding how people can live safely despite continuous exposure to various risks.

This paper focuses on integrating these risk analyses within Naples' green space system by conducting an inventory and classification of the city's parks. In recent years, Naples' green infrastructure has undergone significant revitalisation, driven by urban planning initiatives aimed at sustainable development. The Municipality of Naples has carried out a comprehensive survey of the city's green areas, categorising them based on location, size, and intrinsic characteristics. For the most significant parks, detailed maps have been produced, indicating pathways, refreshment points, playgrounds, and sports facilities. This classification distinguishes green areas into four main categories:

- Gardens or small parks are green areas ranging from 500 to 5,000 m^2, featuring herbaceous and arboreal vegetation, intended for walking, resting, recreation, and entertainment;
- Neighbourhood parks, covering between 5,000 and 50,000 m^2, are located within 1,000 m of residential areas, and including spaces for relaxation, refreshment, play, sports, and events;
- Urban parks, exceeding 50,000 m^2, are situated within or near urbanised areas, characterised by extensive vegetation and equipped spaces for recreational and sports activities;
- Historic parks or gardens, ranging from 4,000 to 1,300,000 m^2, contain vegetation of significant landscape value and often incorporating villas or buildings of historical and artistic importance.

The municipal survey identified 53 green areas, categorised as 11 gardens or small parks, 30 neighbourhood parks, 4 urban parks, and 6 historic parks or gardens. Subsequently, the SeTUP research group expanded the study, identifying additional green areas, bringing the total to 73 sites: 19 gardens or small parks, 41 neighbourhood parks, 4 urban parks, and 9 historic parks or gardens (Fig. 1).

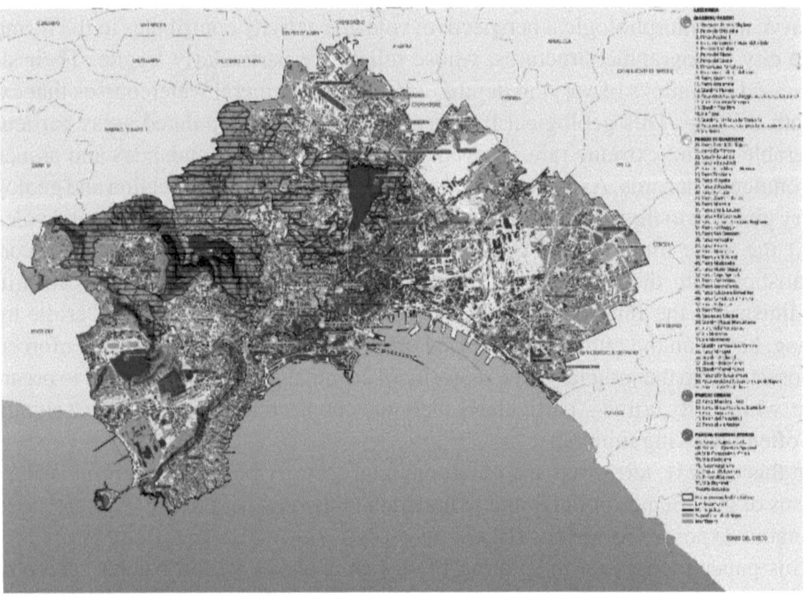

Fig. 1. Naples' parks and green areas. Elaboration by authors.

3 Results

3.1 Environmental Risk Map

The risk analyses, previously described, were conducted at the municipal scale across the territory of Naples, with particular attention to the green areas and parks considered in the census.

The first investigation focused on the development of the Environmental Risk Map, for which the natural hazards related to hydrogeological, volcanic, and seismic vulnerabilities-the biggest threats for the city—were studied. A thematic map was produced for each of these risks.

Hydrogeological risk is associated with phenomena such as landslides, soil erosion, slope failures and flooding problems which typically occur in hillside areas that are particularly vulnerable from a morphological and lithological perspective. The landslide and flood risk maps for the Municipality of Naples highlight the areas most exposed to hydrogeological instability. These maps, produced by the Southern Apennines River Basin District Authority, were developed based on geomorphological studies and serve as essential tools for risk prevention and management.

The parks located in areas of highest risk include: Terme di Agnano, Parco Virgiliano, Mausoleo Schilizzi, Parco dei Camaldoli, Villa Floridiana, Villa Cellamare, the gardens of the Certosa di San Martino, Parco dei Quartieri Spagnoli, Giardino Trinità delle Monache, Parco Viviani, Parco dei Ventaglieri, Parco Minopoli, Parco di Viale del Poggio, and Parco di Capodimonte (Fig. 2).

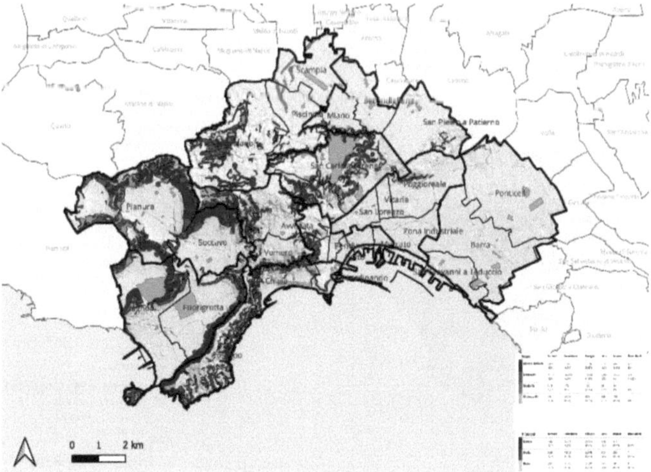

Fig. 2. Map of hydrogeological risk. Authors' elaboration

Another major concern for the territory of Naples is the volcanic risk posed by the Campi Flegrei. This is a vast volcanic area located in the west of Naples, consisting of an active caldera that spans approximately 13 km in diameter, with numerous peripheral eruptive centres. Given the volcano's hazardous nature, a continuous monitoring system is in place, managed by the Vesuvius Observatory and the National Institute of Geophysics and Volcanology (INGV).

Authorities have developed an evacuation plan for the risk areas, which are divided into two alert zones:

- Red zone that includes the areas closest to the caldera, such as Pozzuoli and parts of Bacoli and Quarto. In the event of an imminent eruption warning, these areas would be the first to be evacuated;
- Yellow zone related to areas that could be affected by ash and gas fallout, including some districts of Naples[3].

The parks located within the red zone include: Parco Camaldoli a Pianura, Parco Attainese, Parco Anaconda, Parco Costantino, Parco Anco Marzio, Terme di Agnano, Mostra d'Oltremare, Parco dei Camaldoli, Parco su Via Nerva, Parco Robinson, Parco Totò, Parco del Casale, Mausoleo Schilizzi, Parco Virgiliano, Parco Vergiliano, Villa Comunale Chiaia, Villa Pignatelli, Parco Agricolo Buglione, and Giardini Piazza Mercadante.

The remaining parks fall within the yellow zone, except for Parco Fratelli De Filippo, Parco De Simone, and Palavesuvio, which are outside these designated risk zones (Fig. 3).

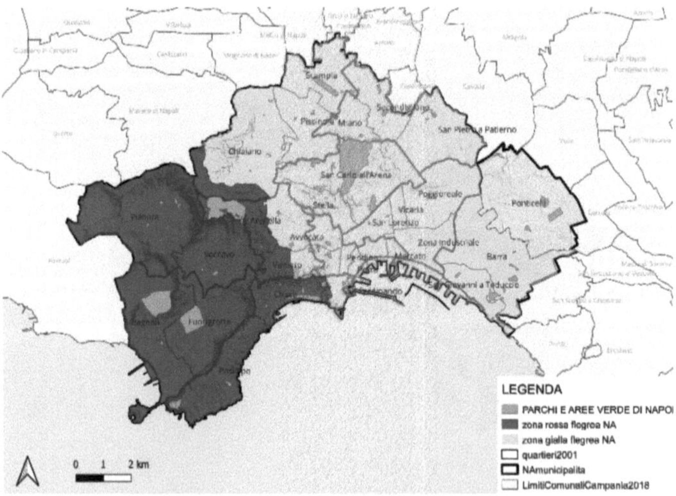

Fig. 3. Map of the volcanic risk of the Campi Flegrei. Authors' elaboration

[3] These areas have been delineated in accordance with Regional Council Resolution No. 669 of 23/12/2014 (Red Zone Campi Flegrei) and Regional Council Resolution No. 175 of 03/04/2015 (Yellow Zone Campi Flegrei).

Another volcanic hazard is associated with Mount Vesuvio, which, despite being in a state of quiescence since 1944, is considered an active and highly dangerous volcano located just a few kilometres from Naples. It poses a risk not only to the densely populated eastern districts of the city but also to the surrounding municipalities. Through continuous monitoring and emergency planning, the authorities aim to minimise the associated risks. The portion of Naples' territory classified as a Yellow Zone includes the districts of Ponticelli, Barra, and San Giovanni a Teduccio, which are exposed to volcanic ash and lapilli fallout. However, only parts of these districts, specifically in the easternmost areas, are designated as a Red Zone[4].

The parks located in the Red Zone include: Parco delle Repubbliche Marinare, Parco Villa Salvetti, and part of Parco Villa Letizia. Meanwhile, those within the Yellow Zone include Parco dei Fratelli De Filippo, Parco Troisi, Parco De Simone, Palavesuvio, Parco Teodosia, Parco via Mastellone, and Parco del Forte di Vigliena (Fig. 4).

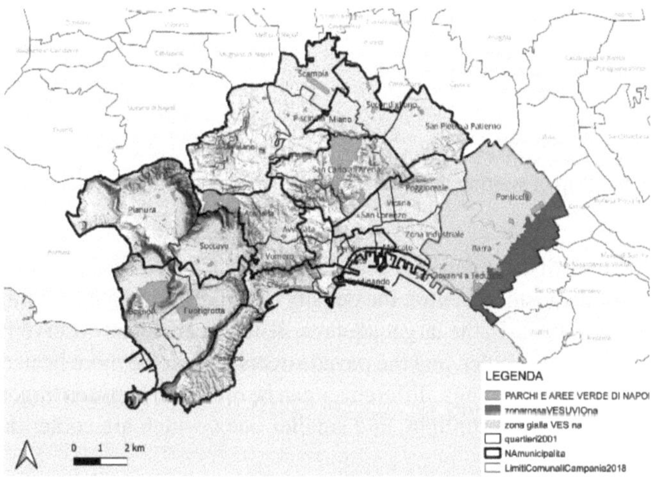

Fig. 4. Map of the volcanic risk of Vesuvio. Authors' elaboration.

In addition, an analysis of the Civil Protection Plan was conducted regarding volcanic and seismic risks, which revealed the presence of 134 emergency areas—assembly, waiting, and reception—some of which coincide with portions of the parks and green areas identified. Specifically, for seismic risk, the analysis showed that the parks selected as waiting areas include: Parco Fratelli De Filippo, Parco De Simone, Parco Villa Letizia, Parco Troisi, Parco Barbato, Parco di Capodimonte, Parco San Gennaro, Parco Quartieri Spagnoli, Villa Comunale Chiaia, Parco Agricolo Buglione, Parco Mascagna, Parco Emilia Laudati, Parco di Scampia, Viale della Residenza, Parco Mario Musella, Parco Marianella, Parco Cupa Spinella, Parco Villa Capriccio, Parco dei Camaldoli,

[4] This delimitation was carried out in accordance with Regional Council Resolution No. 250 of 26/07/2013 (Red Zone Vesuvius) and Regional Council Resolution No. 29 of 09/02/2015 (Yellow Zone Vesuvius). The data considered for volcanic risk assessments are updated as of 2024.

Parco Costantino, Parco Anaconda, Parco Attainese, Parco Camaldoli in Pianura, Parco Falcone e Borsellino, and Mostra d'Oltremare. (Fig. 5).

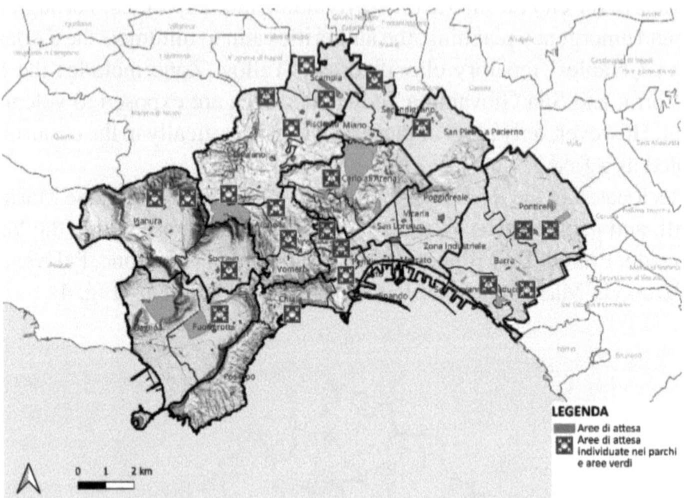

Fig. 5. Map of waiting areas related to seismic risk. Authors' elaboration.

Finally, the study of the urban heat island from the CLARITY project (Fig. 6) revealed that in the area of the historic centre, the density of buildings creates shading conditions that reduce thermal stress. In the larger squares, differences can be observed between the greener areas, which are cooler, and the paved streets, which are more heated. Within the courtyards of historical buildings, differences can be observed between larger courtyards, which are exposed to more sunlight, and smaller ones, which are cooler due to greater

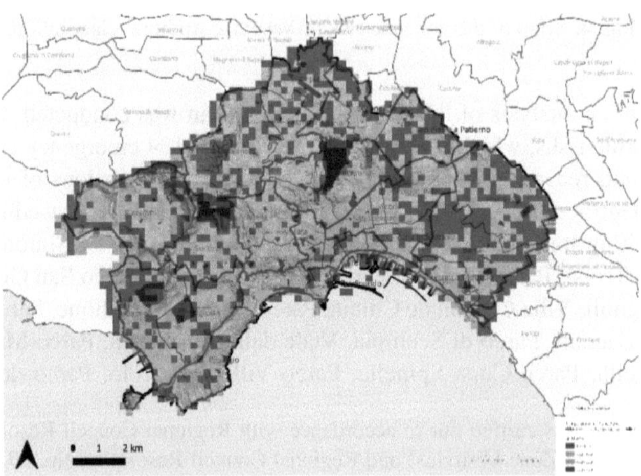

Fig. 6. Map of the Urban Heat Island. CLARITY Project.

shading throughout the day. The presence of green areas and trees is a significant factor in reducing thermal stress in the larger courtyards. In the areas of Rione Traiano and Ponticelli, the greater distances between buildings and the reduced presence of trees cause high overheating, which is mitigated, especially in the case of Ponticelli, by the large green areas found in some city blocks.

3.2 Crime Risk Map

The second investigation in this first part of the research focused, also, on the creation of the Crime Risk Map. For the city of Naples, despite requesting data from the relevant authorities on criminal activities, it was not possible to obtain the information. Therefore, the MineCrime platform was used, developed by the Mine Crime Startup. This software collects and analyses data on urban crime, both criminal and administrative, allowing for a geographical visualisation of the information. Through the platform, users can access an interactive map that displays the most significant crimes and urban degradation incidents of the past year, divided by categories (thefts, violence, fires, fraud, etc.).

For the city of Naples, during the period from 28 August 2023 to 28 August 2024, there were 62 reports of urban degradation, with the highest concentration in the areas of San Lorenzo (11) and Vomero (10). There were 48 reports of fires, particularly in Piazza Municipio (7). A total of 160 incidents of violence were recorded, with the highest concentration in San Lorenzo (49) and Avvocata-Montecalvario (32). There were 213 reports of threats, primarily in San Lorenzo (24) and the San Ferdinando district (13). There were 85 reported incidents of accidents, mostly in San Lorenzo (21) and Chiaia (13). Additionally, 113 thefts were recorded, particularly around Piazza Garibaldi (20), near the Naples Central Station. There were 88 cases of homicide, 71 drug dealing incidents, mainly in Scampia (19), 60 robberies, particularly around Piazza Garibaldi (16), 10 fraud cases, 3 cases of counterfeiting, 8 extortions, and 2 incidents of usury. The data reveals that the most prevalent types of criminality are threats and violence, with a high concentration of crime in the districts of San Lorenzo and Piazza Garibaldi.

To provide a more immediate summary, the areas with more crime are: the historic centre, including the Garibaldi station area and the San Lorenzo district; the eastern outskirts, with particular focus on San Giovanni and Ponticelli; the western outskirts, including Fuorigrotta and Bagnoli; and the northern areas, such as Scampia and Secondigliano (Fig. 7).

In relation to parks, the following locations are found in the historic centre: Giardini del Molosiglio, Giardini di Castel Nuovo, Villa Cellamare, Villa Comunale di Chiaia, Villa Pignatelli, Parco della Floridiana, Parco Viviani, Parco dei Ventaglieri, Parco dei Quartieri Spagnoli, Parco Mascagna, Giardini di Piazza Mercadante, Giardini della Certosa di San Martino, Giardini Trinità delle Monache, Parco Minopoli, Giardini del Palazzo Reale, Giardino Storico di S. Maria della Fede, Giardino Storico Re Ladislao, Orto Botanico, and Parco San Gennaro. In the western outskirts, there are the Mostra d'Oltremare, Parco Robinson, and Parco Totò. In the eastern outskirts, the following parks are located: Palavesuvio, Parco Fratelli de Filippo, Parco de Simone, Parco Via Volpicella, Parco Via Mastellone, Villa Letizia, Parco Villa Salvetti, Parco delle Repubbliche Marinare, Parco Troisi, Giardini del Forte di Vigliena, and Parco di Pazzigno. For Scampia and Secondigliano, the parks include Parco di Scampia, Parco di Via Marrazzo, Viale della Resistenza, Parco di Via Monterosa, Parco Emilia Laudati, Parco delle Galassie, Area Verde Giovanni Fiorentino, and Parco su Via Roma.

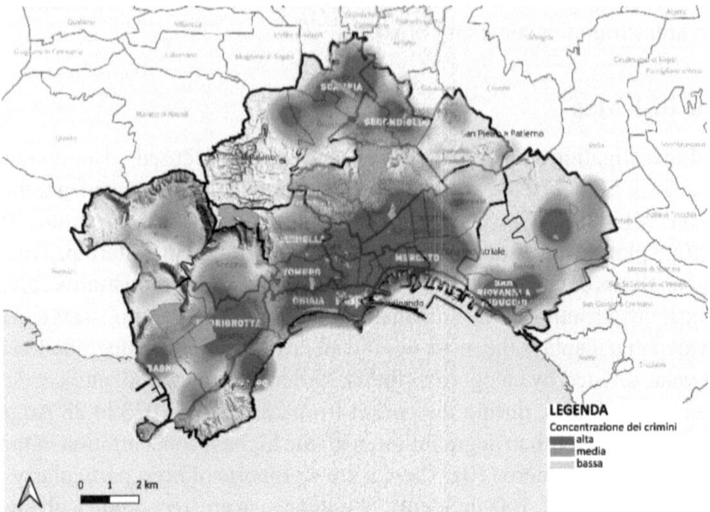

Fig. 7. Crime Risk Map. MINECRIME data processed by the authors.

4 Conclusions

The quality of the environment is increasingly regarded as a fundamental factor in enhancing quality of life, making it a vital resource (Leone, 2006). However, this quality can be compromised in the Neapolitan territory due to its exposure to "natural" risks such as volcanic activity and bradyseism in the Campi Flegrei and Vesuvius areas, as well as its general vulnerability to hydrogeological risks, alongside the various challenges related to both organised crime and petty crime, which make Naples one of the fifteen Italian cities with the highest rates of reported crime, particularly theft.

Through an integrated methodological approach that combines quantitative analysis of environmental and criminal risks, a detailed outline of the vulnerabilities present in urban green spaces has been established. The integration of georeferenced spatial data and GIS tools has allowed for the development of a dynamic analysis system, useful for the continuous monitoring of security conditions.

Following the creation of thematic maps detailing the different risk factors, both natural (hydrogeological, seismic, volcanic, and urban heat island effects) and anthropogenic (crime risks), the mapping overlay technique will be applied to integrate and layer the various informational levels within a single multilayered cartographic system. This approach will provide a detailed, multidimensional spatial representation of the phenomena analysed, enabling a synergistic and comprehensive assessment of the risks studied. This technique will facilitate the simultaneous reading of the Neapolitan territory, identifying critical areas where multiple risk factors converge spatially, thus highlighting regions with heightened territorial vulnerabilities. The AutoCAD tool has been used to create this thematic map overlay.

This final analysis will serve as the basis for selecting the most pertinent sites for further attention, chosen also in relation to their specific context, in order to investigate their distinct characteristics and how these may vary across different neighbourhoods.

Particular attention is given to the selection of the district or context in which the parks are located. According to Jane Jacobs' theories (1969), urban parks can fulfil a positive role if situated within a lively urban context. A park located in an area characterised by functional, architectural, and social mixité fosters interaction among residents, helps prevent degradation and abandonment, and contributes to the vitality of the area. Conversely, if located in an area devoid of urban functions, the park may be less attractive, less visited, and therefore less secure. Selecting parks situated in different contexts allows for a more in-depth analysis, illustrating how a park is experienced across various neighbourhoods.

Simultaneously, it was considered important to evaluate the presence of ongoing or planned plans, programmes, and projects that are central to public policies, particularly concerning the green spaces and parks under study. This will help guide revitalisation actions capable of improving not only the individual sites but also the surrounding areas. In this way, dynamic monitoring will be implemented, comparing the current scenario with the future one following the changes made, to assess whether these actions have led to improvements in both real and perceived safety.

Subsequently, qualitative investigations will be conducted in the selected parks, focusing on the perception of insecurity, as this influences the vitality and attractiveness of specific urban areas. This highlights the need for a multidimensional approach to security, one that considers not only the objective risk conditions. In this context, questionnaires and collaborative mapping will be employed to explore the perception of safety, not only within the urban parks but also in their immediate surroundings, involving the local community. The aim is to collect qualitative, dynamic, and participatory data directly from the community, which will provide a more comprehensive understanding of local issues, actual needs, and solutions proposed by residents, offering an experiential measure of environmental quality.

This approach will enable the formulation of appropriate, shared strategies through community participation, fostering truly inclusive urban planning that strengthens social cohesion and improves the livability and accessibility of public spaces.

References

Bailey, R.G.: Problems with using overlay mapping and their implications for geographic informations systems. Environ. Manage. **12**(1), 11–17 (1988). https://doi.org/10.1007/BF01867373

Bignani, F.D.: Protezione civile e riduzione del rischio disastri. Maggioli editore, Milano (2010)

Bonnes, M., Uzzell, D., Carrus, G., Kelay, T.: Inhabitants' and experts' assessments of environmental quality for urban sustainability. J. Soc. Issues **63**(1), 59–78 (2007). https://doi.org/10.1111/j.1540-4560.2007.00496.x

Calcaterra, D. (a cura di): La geomorfologia di Napoli. In: Manuali (Scienze e Tecnologie), Università la Sapienza, pp. 14–15 (2023)
Chiesa, C., Palme, M.: Valutare la vulnerabilità urbana ai cambiamenti climatici e alle isole di calore urbano. In: TECHNE, 15 (2020). https://doi.org/10.13128/Techne-22086
Chiesa, G., Simonetti, M., Ballada, G.: Potential of attached sunspaces in winter season comparing different technological choices. In: Central and Southern Europe, Energy and Buildings, vol. 138, pp. 377–395. Elsevier (2017). https://doi.org/10.1016/j.enbuild.2016.12.067
Chiesi, L.: Le inciviltà. Degrado urbano e Insicurezza. Il Mulino, Bologna, pp. 129–140 (2004)
Comune di Napoli. https://www.comune.napoli.it/flex/cm/pages/ServeBLOB.php/L/IT/IDPagina/13115. Accessed 24 Aug 2024
Coppola, E., Musto, F.M., et al: Le aree di rigenerazione urbana nella città metropolitana di Napoli. In: Gis Day 2022, Aracne Editrice, pp. 77–91, Aracneeditrice, Napoli (2022). https://doi.org/10.53136/97912218101035
Coppola, F., Grimaldi, M., Isidoro, F.: Spazi urbani sicuri. fedOAPress, Napoli (2021)
Coppola, F.: Un modello risk-based per la prevenzione ambientale del rischio da criminalità. In: Tesi di dottorato in Urbanistica e sicurezza, Università degli studi di Salerno, Dipartimento di Ingegneria civile (2021)
Coseo P., Larsen L.: How factors of land use /land cover, building configuration, and adjacent heat sources and sinks explain urban heat islands in Chicago. Landsc. Urban Plan. **125**, 117–129 (2014). https://doi.org/10.1016/j.landurbplan.2014.02.019
Cozens, P.: Planning, crime and urban sustainability. In: WIT Transactions on Ecology and the Environment, vol. 102, pp. 187–196, A.G. Kungolos, Seville (2007). https://doi.org/10.2495/SDP070181
Dessi, V., Astolfi, L.: Qualità vs quantità. È possibile quantificare la qualità dello spazio pubblico? In: TECHNE, vol. 19, SITd A, Napoli (2020)
Dewberry, E.: Designing out crime: insights from Ecodesign. SecurityJournal **16**(1), 51–62 (2003)
Du Plessis, C.: The links between crime prevention and sustainable development. In: Lawrence, R. (ed.) Sustaining Human Settlement: a challenge for the new millennium, pp. 239–270. Urban International Press, North Shields (2000)
Hillier, B., Sahbaz, O.: High resolution analysis of crime patterns in urban street networks: an initial statistical sketch from an ongoing study of a London borough. In: van Nes, A. (ed.), Proceedings of the 5th International Space Syntax Symposium, TU Delft, Delft, 13–17th June 2005. Delft, Techne Press. (2005)
il sole 24 ore. https://lab24.ilsole24ore.com/indice-della-criminalita/. Accessed 14 Feb 2025
ISPRA: Pericolosità ambientale (2011)
Jacobs, J.: Vita e morte delle grandi città. Einaudi, Torino (1969)
Jeffery C.R.: Crime Prevention Through Environmental Design. Sage Publications, Beverly Hills (1971)
Leone, U.: Sicurezza ambientale. Guida, Napoli (2006)
Matteoli, L., Pagani, R. (eds.): Cityfutures. Architecture Design Technology for the Future of the Cities, Hoepli, Milano (2010)
Mine Crime. https://www.minecrime.it/. Accessed 28 Aug 2024
Morris, C., Simmonds, I.: Associations between varying magnitudes of the urban heat island and the synoptic climatology. Int. J. Climatology **20** (2000). https://doi.org/10.1002/1097-0088(200012)20:15<1931::AID-JOC578>3.0.CO;2-D
napoli today. https://www.napolitoday.it/cronaca/indice-criminalita-napoli-milano-roma.html. Accessed 14 Feb 2025
Newman, O.: Defensible Space-Crime prevention through urban design. Macmillan Pub, Co, (1972)
Pinna, S.: Rischi ambientali e difesa del territorio. FrancoAngeli, Milano (2002)

Sampson, R.J., Raudenbush, S.W.: Neighborhoods and violent crime: a multilevel study of collective efficacy. Science (1997). https://doi.org/10.1126/science.277.5328.918

Protezione civile. https://www.protezionecivile.gov.it/it/approfondimento/ispra---istituto-superiore-protezione-e-ricerca-ambientale--ex-apat/. Accessed 13 Feb 2015

Progetto CLARITY. https://www.cmcc.it/it/report-napoli

Santamouris, M.: Using cool pavements as a mitigation strategy to fight urban heat island – a review of the actual developments. Renew. Sustain. Energy **26**, 224–240 (2013). https://doi.org/10.1016/j.rser.2013.05.047

Santamouris, M.: On the energy impact of urban heat island and global warming on buildings. Energy Build. **82**, 100–113 (2014). https://doi.org/10.1016/j.enbuild.2014.07.022

Sicurella, S., Bianchini, E: Progettazione dello spazio urbano e comportamenti criminosi. Rivista di criminologia, Vittimologia e Sicurezza **VI** (1), 74–90 (2012)

Skogan, W.: Disorder and decline: the state of research. In: Welsh, B.C., Farrington, D.P. (eds.) The Oxford Handbook of Crime Prevention (1990). Oxford University Press (2012). https://doi.org/10.1177/0022427815577836

Taleb, D., Abu-Hijleh, B.: Urban heat island: potential effect of organic and structured urban configurations on temperature variations. Renew. Energy **50**, 747–762 (2013). https://doi.org/10.1016/j.renene.2012.07.030

Treu, M.C.: Città, Salute, Sicurezza. Maggioli Editore, Milano (2009)

Voogt, J., Oke, T.: Thermal remote sensing of urban climates. Remote Sens. Environ. **86**, 370–384 (2003). https://doi.org/10.1016/j.renene.2012.07.030

Wood, E.: Housing Design: A Social Theory, Citizens' Housing and Planning Council of New York. NCJRS Virtual Library, New York (1961)

Wilson, J., Kelling G.: Broken windows. In: Atlantic, pp. 29–36 (1982)

INU: XXVIII Congresso dell'INU-Città come motore di sviluppo del paese. Planum (2013)

Fasolino, I., Coppola, F., Grimaldi, M.: La sicurezza urbana degli insediamenti. Azioni e tecniche per il piano urbanistico. Franco Angeli (2018)

Sampson, R.J., Stephen, W.R.: Systematic social observation of public spaces: a new look at disorder in urban neighborhoods. Am. J. Sociol. **105**(3), 603–651 (1999). https://doi.org/10.1086/210356

A Model Based on Environmental Quality Indicators to Support the Assessment of the Safety Perception of Urban Parks

Emanuela Coppola(✉), Chiara Mastrorilli, Maria Simioli, and Michelangelo Russo

University of Naples Federico II, Naples, Italy
{emanuela.coppola,chiara.mastrorilli,maria.simioli, michelangelo.russo}@unina.it

Abstract. Expectations, needs, and motivations of individuals serve as the backdrop to the complex interaction between mental frameworks and physical data provided by the environment. The research within the SETUP Project "Security Town through Urban Planning" (SeTUP), funded by the PRIN PNRR2022 call, aims to investigate the environmental quality and how the perceived characteristics of the environment generate relationships with the satisfaction and well-being of users for the purpose of evaluating the safety perception.

The model, applied to a public park in the metropolitan city of Naples, is distinguished by its innovative approach, which integrates quantitative indicators derived from sector-specific technical literature and qualitative data collected through surveys administered to a sample of the population living in and using the park. The data examine the morphological-spatial, and perceptual characteristics of both the park and its surroundings (within a proximity radius of 500 m), and highlight its environmental characteristics, accessibility, livability, and safety features by analyzing spatial, human-social, and functional aspects. The data derived from the distribution of questionnaires are intended to systematize the various indicators based on the evaluations of the environments by their users. The organization into a relational geo-database of synthesis has allowed for the identification of critical issues, also through participatory mapping, and, effectively, structure a model to support policies aimed at enhancing the quality and safety of a park area.

Keywords: Perceived safety · urban parks · environmental quality indicators

1 Introduction

In Europe, in the last twenty years, the green has become an essential element of planning both on a metropolitan and municipal scale. While the London Green Infrastructure Plan (2011) was the first European experience, a greater awareness of climate change had already taken place with the United Nations Conference on the human environment (Stockholm 1972), the first conference in history that has as its object the debate concerning the climate system at a global level. Later, it was the Paris Climate Agreements

E. Borgogno-Mondino and P. Zamperlin (Eds.): ASITA 2024, CCIS 2463, pp. 338–353, 2025.
https://doi.org/10.1007/978-3-031-91141-5_23

(2015) that provided that, by 2020, governments should present their National Climate Action Plans, in which they highlight the actions leading to the reduction of greenhouse gas emissions. In Italy, the Ministry of the Environment and Energy Security (MASE), through decree no. 434 of December 21, 2023, approved the national Plan for adaptation to climate changes. In this document, the so-called "green actions" propose nature-based solutions, "consisting in the sustainable use or management of natural services, including ecosystem services, in order to reduce the impacts of climate change"[1].

With a view to combating climate change and the urban heat island, greening policies will have to be increasingly central, and the security of these areas will be part of that "right to the city" [1], "the conquest of which implies a re-appropriation of the times and spaces of urban living through a new configuration of social, political and economic relations, as well as a drastic change in decision-making processes". The issue of urban security is of great importance in this phase of transition towards the creation of sustainable cities and communities.

In criminal literature, there is a correlation between insecurity and economic growth, the explosion of consumption, and urban expansion, which lead to social disintegration and the alteration of values. These changes are linked to the crisis in Western societies, characterized by family weakening, poverty, social exclusion, and drug addiction, resulting in an increase in crime [2].

In the social sciences there is no single definition of "urban violence" [3] but this seems to have constant elements, namely: " they refer to poorly organized actions; they define, as a frequent object of aggression, physical or symbolic public spaces; the gratuitous nature of the acts, which can take different forms, from vandalism to riots; the fact that they have extensive side effects and, frequently, that they are not directed at anyone concretely" [4].

Security represents a more general guarantee of freedom of use of space "overcoming the inconveniences caused by the growing privatization, segregation and conflict of public space in the contemporary city" [5].

The concept of urban security spans various fields of knowledge, from sociology to criminology, psychology, urban geography, and urban planning, giving rise to numerous theoretical research and operational experiments [6].

The complexity of the issue of space security requires an integrated approach, both in the assessment of security conditions and in the definition of appropriate intervention strategies. The effectiveness of these strategies depends on knowledge of the specific context and on a complete analysis of the risk scenario, which can combine and synthesize all the aspects that contribute to the construction of safety conditions, to define a risk model for green spaces in order to guide urban planning choices.

[1] https://www.mase.gov.it/notizie/clima-approvato-il-piano-nazionale-di-adattamento-ai-cambiamenticlimatici.

As part of the Project of National Interest PRIN 2022 PNRR_SeTUP – "Security Town through Urban Planning", research is being developed that aims to build a model that allows the assessment of the perception of security in urban parks, specifically, and of public equipped green areas, in general.

1.1 The Safe City Starting from Public Space

Cities are the scene of a widespread feeling of fear towards the other, the unknown and the unexpected, which has frequently given rise to a specific request for control policies supported by security rhetoric [7]. Safety measures in urban planning focus on two distinct issues: on the one hand, protection against risks associated with major natural events; on the other hand, the prevention of phenomena of illegality, incivility, violence, and petty crime, which are central to the notion of "urban security" [8].

The perspective of interest that this research aims to target is the connection between the physical configuration of spaces, risk perception, and crime. In particular, this study refers to one of the approaches to international security policies [6] – environmental approach – known as "Crime Prevention Through Environmental Design" (CPTED). This approach focuses on the ability of the urban environment to hinder crime [9], and which represents an urban and architectural design practice that organizes physical space and its uses to prevent criminal acts of a spatial nature.

The first studies that investigated the relationship between social behaviour and the characteristics of the physical and cultural environment emerged in the end of the thirties under the guidance of the sociologist Robert Park and other members of the Chicago School. These studies formalized a systematic approach to the study of urban society, highlighting how deviance phenomena are strongly influenced by the environmental context, according to the model known as "Community Crime Prevention" [10].

The first concrete applications of theories on the relationship between urban design and safety were developed in the 1960s through the work and experiments of two prominent American women: Elizabeth Wood and Jane Jacobs. In 1961, Elizabeth Wood formulated a detailed theory, known as "Social Design Theory", which emphasizes the close connection between urban design and the improvement of the quality of life [11]. At the same time, Jane Jacobs criticized the morphological and formal aspects of the city, focusing on elements such as streets, sidewalks, blocks, density, and architectural variety. Jacobs considered these factors essential for creating safe spaces, with the aim of strengthening and promoting the sense of belonging and care for the territory [12]. Their theories provided a solid cultural foundation for future developments and refinements in the field of urban security. A significant experience in this area was that of CPTED, a multidisciplinary approach devised by criminologist Ray Jeffery in the 1970s. The first architect to concretely translate these theories into urban projects was Oscar Newman, author of the concept of "Defensible Space" in 1972. His approach to crime prevention through urban design was based on principles such as territoriality, natural surveillance, urban image, the "milieu" and the safety of neighbouring areas [13]. In the subsequent years, numerous scholars continued to explore the topic of urban security, conducting empirical research on specific environmental contexts. Among them, the "Broken Windows" theory developed in 1982 by James Q. Wilson and George L. Kelling has gained particular notoriety. This theory argues that the cause of degradation and crime does not lie in social classes, but rather in the neglect and degradation of urban spaces themselves. According to Wilson and Kelling, in order to prevent the environmental deterioration and the onset of criminal behaviour, it is essential to maintain a high level of care and attention to the urban context [14]. The maintenance of open and public spaces, therefore, becomes a central theme in the discussions of urban security, where the presence of well-kept spaces can inspire trust, a sense of belonging and territoriality [15].

The CPTED models, introduced in Europe via the United Kingdom, saw a shift in the approach to security with the founding of the FESU (European Forum for Urban Security) in Barcelona in 1987, emphasising the participation of local communities and interventions in the physical and spatial characteristics of existing public spaces. In Italy, European influences mark the birth of FISU (Italian Forum for Urban Security) in 1996 [16], but, despite this, the Italian urban planning discipline has never explicitly included plans, protocols, or other territorial planning tools oriented towards security that were not interpreted as the implementation of repressive actions. Here urban security policies tend to shape urban spaces that are increasingly exclusive rather than open and inclusive, characterized by physical barriers that quickly transform into conceptual barriers [17]. A security-oriented drift also due in part to the partial failure of welfare policies, which determines new segregative topographies and represents an explicit departure from the principles of sustainable development of a city[2]. Starting from an idea of urban security, no longer understood exclusively as a policy of territorial control and crime repression, but as a "public good - security", for the concrete exercise of everyone's rights to move, access and use basic services, equipment, and public spaces [18], the research focuses on a particular type of public space: urban parks.

The relationship between the presence of urban green spaces and the reduction of crime is still a debated issue, but numerous studies indicate that parks and green areas can significantly contribute to reducing crime, especially violent crime. The redevelopment of marginal or degraded urban spaces, making them more attractive and functional for residents, tends to decrease violence and crime in the surrounding areas, as demonstrated in Chicago [19], New York City [20], Philadelphia, Youngstown, Ohio, and Baltimore. These examples demonstrate how the care and management of urban green spaces can play a crucial role in crime prevention and improving the quality of life in urban communities.

The research focuses on the study of several urban parks in Campania, particularly in the province of Naples, to understand how urban green spaces can improve living conditions and environmental quality in terms of safety, contributing to the definition of "safe urban space" of a city as perceived by citizens, reducing the perception of risk. The research adopts the assumptions developed by the literature of the sector, according to a participatory methodological approach that involves the active engagement of citizens in the co-construction of knowledge about the urban and territorial context. The intangible component, in addition to the physical component of the elements that make up the spatial structure of the park, represents the most significant and innovative aspect of the research, which seeks to focus on this through the identification of safety indicators. In

[2] The SDG 11, "Make cities and human settlements inclusive, safe, resilient and sustainable," among its sub-goals 11.7 aims to "ensure universal access to safe, inclusive, accessible, green, and public spaces".

particular, the paper presents the results of the bottom-up investigation of the first case study examined, the "Parco dei Quartieri Spagnoli" in the Montecalvario district, within the II Municipality of the City of Naples.

2 The Proposed Methodology: Qualitative and Bottom-Up Analysis

The SeTUP research addresses the issue of urban park safety from different points of view. Alongside a top-down analysis of their context, conducted based on quantitative data, that considers environmental risk, related to factors of territorial hazard and vulnerability [21], and criminal risk, directly linked to the anthropogenic component [22], a qualitative investigation is conducted through the study of perceived risk, which is explored in depth particularly in this article.

The proposed study explores the subjective dimension of urban security, which responds to the social perception of it. Unlike the recorded crimes in a given place, which refer to its objective dimension, its intangible aspect, not always tied to material reality, consists of opinions, feelings, perceptions, and attitudes that go beyond the fear of crime. If the latter is understood as a specific form of emotional and physical response caused by exposure to problematic events or a perceived threat [23, 24], the perception of safety refers to a widespread feeling that affects the quality of life and individual and collective well-being [25]. Insecurity limits the use of the environment, affects the cohesion of the inhabitants of a neighbourhood, reduces the sense of community, and increases social disorder [26]. It conditions the use of urban parks, discouraging people from visiting, using, or only recognizing them as places intended for the recreation or leisure of their visitors [27, 28], especially in the presence of conditions perceived as risky, such as overly open spaces, with poor visibility, or isolated areas [29].

If we want to address the issue of the safety of a public space, a fundamental indicator of environmental quality [30–32], it is necessary to adopt multidisciplinary, multi-method, and multi-dimensional approaches in order to overcome the potential divergence between technical and less expert assessments [33]. Therefore, the approach to be used cannot be solely place-based focusing only on the characteristics and potential of the context in which one operates but must also be people-oriented and start from the bottom. The adopted qualitative methodology begins with the identification and selection, based on a review of the relevant literature, of indicators of perceived safety in urban green spaces and their surrounding context. These categories were used to structure the various questions in a questionnaire and to divide the criteria for the perceptual mapping of unsafe areas. The two activities, which were to be presented to the park community under study, form the foundation for conducting an effective perceptual survey of the locations. The tools chosen were applied to the different case studies within the Neapolitan context, with the first being the "Parco dei Quartieri Spagnoli". The analysis of the data obtained from the questionnaires and the organisation of the maps into a relational geo-database allow for the identification of the main issues within the green space and the priority variables that most influence users' perceptions of safety. The aim is to create a more realistic and accurate framework aligned with the experiences of local residents, providing a useful decision-support tool and thus facilitating the definition of policies and interventions that truly address the needs for safety and quality of urban green spaces.

2.1 Perceived Safety Indicators in Urban Parks

Accessibility, Legibility and Orientation. Spatial definition is an important aspect of landscape design that influences preference and perceived security, "thus, indications of the possibility of entering the environment, of acquiring information and of maintaining one's orientation emerge as constantly vital attributes" [34]. The recognition of entry points and escape routes [27, 35], as well as the clarity in identifying pathways and the distinguishability of the functions present, therefore become crucial issues. The feeling of disorientation can lead an individual to fear crime, even in the absence of a potential criminal. Parks equipped with orientation elements, such as clear and sufficient directional signage, will be associated with higher levels of safety [27, 36]. In a legible place, users will find it easy to maintain the ability to orient himself; conversely, a place that is difficult to categorise will arouse a series of negative feelings such as frustration, stress, inadequacy, and rejection [37]. The complexity of form, defined by the lower predictability and the richness of perceptual stimuli of the place, is identified by Jacobs as one of the key characteristics of a highly frequented urban park, a quality that reflects the diverse reasons why people live and use the park. Mystery, another predictor of environmental preference, is clearly distinct from surprise and should never be associated with limited visual access [38]. In fact, the increase in complexity in the spatial configuration, along with an excessive amount of hidden information or mystery, determines a proportional growth in preference and psychophysical activation, up to an optimal level, beyond which there is a progressive decrease in preference indices and an exaltation of the feeling of fear and discomfort [39].

Visibility and Surveillance. A high visual permeability, understood as the degree to which a person can observe the characteristics of an unobstructed environment has a significant effect on perceived safety. The literature, in accordance with the theories of "Eyes on the street" proposed by Jacobs, Newman's "Opportunities for surveillance" and Appleton's "prospect-refuge", emphasises the notions of open vision and visibility: the highest level of fear is often associated with the presence of a low visual openness or perspective, a high level of refuge and a difficult escape [26, 27]; notions related both to the feeling of being seen by others, and to the possibility of seeing around [40, 41]. Natural surveillance can be defined as that generated by individuals who use and frequent urban spaces, as well as that resulting from the morphological dimension of architecture, its orientation, and the openings in the façades of buildings – eyes and ears of the community that allow for both listening and being listened to, seeing and being seen, in a bidirectional relationship that makes the pedestrian an active participant in the events occurring within the spaces of the city [12]. A type of surveillance "permanent in its effects, though discontinuous in its action" [42], whereby the idea of the presence of an observer is as effective as the observer's actual presence [43]. Thus, areas that are overly isolated or hidden within the park are consequently perceived as more dangerous or entirely to be avoided. Below are the subcategories associated with this indicator.

Lighting Level. Night-time environments are generally considered more dangerous than daytime ones due to the difference in lighting intensity, which determines the field of vision [44]. Darkness, and the poor visibility associated with it, can provide opportunities to hide for perpetrators of illicit or criminal acts [25, 27, 41, 45]. Homogeneous and uniform lighting of the park area is a concrete help to make all spaces more monitored [36].

Vegetation. The selection and orderly arrangement of vegetation in a park, as part of a coherent and attractive overall design, influenced users' perception and fear [35]. While the presence of vegetation positively affects the attractiveness and pleasantness of the area [33, 46], the excessive density of it, by reducing visual access and increasing the chances of hiding for potential criminals, tends to increase the fear of crime and the perception of insecurity in the green space [41, 47–49]. It is advisable that plants and shrubs be selected or maintained in a way that does not interrupt the views and allow natural control [35, 36, 45].

Attractiveness of Spaces. Individuals in public spaces also rely on the presence of other people as signals that can increase or decrease the feeling of fear [44, 45]. The presence of others within public parks can encourage safe use [50], making criminal acts more difficult or providing potential rescuers in the event of an assault. When the underutilization of the park is evident, it can indeed become a target for unwanted and illicit people and activities [47]. The provision of different functional areas [51], or the organization of diverse events within a public green area, favours the presence of people of different ages, economic conditions, habits, and modes of transport, thus increasing the attractiveness and liveliness throughout the day and its consequent spontaneous control.

Maintenance and Appearance. Maintenance levels in urban green areas represent an important indicator of perceived safety [13, 35, 49, 52] and is the most significant factor influencing individual daytime perception [44]. The "Broken Windows" theory explores the visible impact that the deterioration and abandonment of a place can have on users' behaviour [14]. Maintenance can configure the perception of the park, making it a place that is not only aesthetically pleasing, but also recognized as a space that receives and deserves attention and protection. Carrying out actions aimed at maintaining or enhancing the value of an environment restores to the community a renewed sense of respect, consideration, and belonging, and the place will, with greater difficulty, be vandalised or perceived as unsafe.

2.2 The Structure of the Questionnaire

To address the perceptual survey of urban parks, it was decided to use the questionnaire tool, which implies a moderate involvement of the participants and allows to systematize the data relating to their evaluations of urban green areas, considering architectural, social, functional, and contextual aspects. The module mostly composed of closed-ended questions, aims to understand how individuals' sense of insecurity in a given public space is associated with the presence or absence of certain physical characteristics, by selecting the safety indicators that can most influence its perception.

The perceiver, the object of perception, and the context are the three groups of factors that influence the impressions and reaction process of users. Individuals face insecurity and fear in different ways depending on their age, gender, lifestyle, social relationships, neighbourhood attachment, socio-economic and cultural background, and previous personal experiences. Therefore, "an environment cannot elicit pleasant or unpleasant stimuli, attract or repel an individual, except in relation to their past experiences and to the present, momentary or permanent goals of the individual himself" [46].

The personal and social variables are investigated in the initial section of the questionnaire, identifying factors associated with personal vulnerability, social support, emotional part, and behavioural control [49, 53]. Numerous studies confirm that the age variable is inversely related to the security perception scale and that the fear of crime tends to increase with advancing age [29, 48, 53]. In addition, fear of crime is more pronounced among women than men, and at night than during the day [24, 27, 45]. The social attributes related to the perception of safety in urban parks are explored in connection to the use of spaces: the frequency of use of them, being alone or in a group, the reasons for visiting, the number of users encountered in the park, familiarity with them, the presence of social incivilities, such as unruly young people, drug addicts, alcoholics, homeless individuals, or beggars [41, 49, 52].

In the second part of the questionnaire and in the final part of it, attention is given to the physical characteristics of the perceived place and its proximity context [41, 53] investigated through the indicators described. Beforehand, the interviewee is asked to define the park with one of the adjectives in the list, based on the "Circumplex Model" of the affective qualities of places [54] and its Italian version [55], which proposes a circular organization of affective states evoked by an environmental experience, to link emotions and environmental preferences.

2.3 Mapping of Unsafe Areas in the Park and Perceptual Data Processing with QGIS Software

The mapping of the places and the relative description of the critical issues encountered by the population allow to carry out a spatial analysis of the perceived safety conditions of the park, of its immediate context, within a radius of 500 m, and of their main physical characteristics, capable of arousing feelings of insecurity and fear [26]. By providing the sample of users with explanations regarding the categories of selected indicators, which have already been explored in the administered questionnaire, they are asked to locate on the map the significant areas of the park, label them according to the indicators, and describe the issues encountered or the suggestions to be made. For this purpose, paper maps were provided, along with an alternative link to the MyMaps tool, a Google application that allows users to easily create personalized maps by adding locations and related descriptions. Based on Google's satellite map, the perimeter of the park and proximity boundary within a five-minute radius were outlined, calculated through the study of isochrones using the open-source QGIS tool. The generation of a shareable link with the sample of users enables each of them to make their own changes and report particular problem areas in terms of urban security. The collected data were exported in.kml format, which can be converted into the shapefile vector format using QGIS for their subsequent processing.

It was decided to conduct the mapping process directly in the field, as responses to a simple site plan could evoke memories or mental images that do not accurately reflect the real feelings of fear in response to the actual site features [25]. Compared to evaluation through photographic images, which are unable to capture the dynamics of a real environment [44], the assessment made by a person actually present in the field allows for the collection of additional information to simple images, including noises and smells [47] which, together with their mutual combinations with sight, represent essential environmental signals capable of triggering a wide range of emotions and different associations [44].

The collection of perceptual data, their georeferencing and systematization through the QGIS software aims to synthesize the key contradictions identified, organizing them into very precise categories, site specific indicators of park insecurity, for which future strategies for the promotion and development of urban security can be implemented. The organization in a synthetic relational geo-database makes it possible to map critical issues and actually structure a model to support policies aimed at increasing the quality and safety of a park area.

3 Case Study and Workshop: The "Parco dei Quartieri Spagnoli"

The first case study addressed within the PRIN SeTUP project is the "Parco dei Quartieri Spagnoli", a green lung in the centre of Naples, a coastal city in southern Italy renowned for its immense historical and cultural wealth. It forms a small part of the larger seventeenth-century complex of the "Santissima Trinità delle Monache", better known for its nineteenth-century destination, as a former Military Hospital, one of the largest abbey complexes in Naples, a monumental site of great historical, architectural, and artistic value. The complex is situated in the Montecalvario district, in the II Municipality of the city of Naples, extending along the slopes of the San Martino hill, just a few steps from the historic city centre, the beating heart of urban life and the main destination of tourist flows. Since the 1990s, the park has been left in complete abandonment, though it represents a significant opportunity for urban regeneration and the reuse of green spaces in a densely populated area lacking in public services [56]. The complex, covering an area of about 25,000 m^2, of which around 16,000 m^2 are occupied by gardens, internal courtyards, and other open spaces, is characterized by a planimetric articulation on several levels with some areas reopened to the public and others still unusable due to ongoing Urbact works.

A series of site visits, workshops, and practical activities have been organised at the park, involving young people, students of the master's degree programme in Architecture 5UE of the University Federico II of Naples, and members of the Community of the "Parco dei Quartieri Spagnoli". In alignment with the Faro Convention, this community is united in the protection, enhancement, and social reuse of the green area, aiming to transform it into an open and collective place, to be cared for, restored, and ultimately returned to the public. The goal was to work on-site and engage both regular visitors and others in the construction of a word cloud, in the compilation of the questionnaire and in the subsequent mapping of the critical places. Following the analysis of the collected data, a visit to the park was proposed through virtual and augmented reality, offering an immersive experience to compare with "real perception" in a research-action approach, thanks to the establishment of a three-dimensional model by researchers from the University of Salerno.

The mapping activity and administration of the questionnaires will be submitted to park users even in phases subsequent to the first, in order to carry out a complete monitoring of the evolution of the spaces and the impact of recreational, social, and cultural events scheduled in the green area, which will certainly clarify the users' experience in the park, included during the evening visiting, currently excluded from the opening hours according to existing regulations (Fig. 1).

Fig. 1. Site visit and perceptual workshops organised at the "Parco dei Quartieri Spagnoli" with students from the Faculty of Architecture at the University Federico II of Naples and the park community. Photographs by the authors.

3.1 Results

The first activity organised at the "Parco dei Quartieri Spagnoli" involves describing the green area using adjectives, from which a real-time word cloud is obtained using the Mentimeter generator (Fig. 2). Analysis of the responses from participants reveals a prevalence of negative issues: the difficulty of access to the site is the most felt concern by the community, together with the lack of maintenance, signage, and its low attendance. In this case, the theme of in/security does not directly emerge, but it can be inferred from the associated variables. Despite its negative aspects, park users appreciate it for its relaxing, quiet, and peaceful character, for its panoramic view and for its impressive endowment of greenery.

The subsequent activity involved the administration of the questionnaire previously described, which received 73 responses, primarily from women (68.5%), with most respondents aged between 18–25 years (79.5%) and 41–60 years (12.3%).

61.5% of the sample perceives the park's context as 'peaceful' due to the absence of vulnerable or criminal individuals, while 70.5% of users associate the perception of insecurity, both inside and outside the park, with its isolation and low levels of foot traffic in these areas. All participants agree that the park is unattractive, primarily due to the absence of adequate facilities (playgrounds, sports areas, drinking fountains) and services (toilets, refreshment areas, socio-cultural activities), so as to affect the low attendance of the areas and the relative absence of natural surveillance.

Fig. 2. Word cloud created from the participants' responses. Processing by the authors using the Mentimeter platform.

The presence of social incivility, as well as illegal or criminal acts, does not represent a real or main park criticality associated with its safety. This confirms the importance of conducting a bottom-up survey to address the possible discrepancy between an exclusively objective assessment of security, investigated on the basis of recorded crimes and criminal risk, and the social perception of it.

The Park is recognized by the entire sample as a place easily accessible on foot, due to its proximity to public transport, or by bicycle, and more difficulty by car, due to the lack of parking in the area. The entire sample recognizes the potential and complete permeability of the complex on three sides, except on the northern area due to the presence of the Montesanto-Morghen funicular, noting the existence of several entrances, though currently closed. The active and accessible entrances to the park are, therefore, currently not easily identifiable and insufficient. A problem identified by 72.6% of respondents is the evident presence of architectural barriers, caused by the malfunctioning of the lifts (escalators and elevators) needed to overcome the level changes to access the park and reach its various terraces. During the site visit, users did not identify any particular complexity in the park's layout that would influence the perception of safety. The sense of disorientation does not only concern the internal surface of the park but is already felt along its access roads due to the lack of any type of indication signalling its presence. Upon entering, even here, there is no appropriate signage that declares the total configuration of the park and its articulation into several levels, which indicates all the functions and activities available within, in addition to the fact that most of the present buildings are inaccessible and in disuse.

A portion of the interviewees believe that there are areas within the park that are too isolated or hidden, which can negatively affect the perception of safety. 82.3% of users detected an insufficient presence of lighting fixtures and a consequent poor visibility in the dark hours. 54.8% of respondents consider the current state of abandonment and degradation of existing green areas, due to the total absence of maintenance, as a negative aspect in terms of perceived safety. In addition to the presence of overgrown vegetation, the poor maintenance and deteriorating condition of the buildings within the complex arouse a feeling of neglect and abandonment in the participants and limit its use. Even street furniture, building walls, and other public surfaces (lamp posts, rubbish bins, etc.) are covered with posters, spray writings, and similar markings, leading 87.5% of respondents to rate the level of urban decorum as medium-low.

The same indicators of perceived safety were adapted and reused to conduct a study of the park's surrounding context. Several locations near the "Parco dei Quartieri Spagnoli" were identified as unsafe: vico Trinità delle Monache, Montesanto steps, via Pasquale Scura, and part of Corso Vittorio Emanuele. The most frequently reported reasons are the presence of steep roads, designed only for vehicles and unsuitable for pedestrians due to the absence of sidewalks, intense and fast traffic, poor maintenance and signage, presence of litter, graffiti, homeless people and uncivilized subjects, poorly lit road sections, and poorly frequented areas at certain times. Unlike the internal areas of the park, considered safe places to stay for 67.5% of the sample, its immediate context was rated negatively by 78.4% of them. These problematic areas, along with those preferred by users, were subsequently marked during the final collaborative mapping exercise, carried out using paper maps of the park and its surrounding context (Fig. 3). In the proximity of the park, no 'heart places' were mapped; however, within the park, all the green areas of the upper garden and the middle level, including the "Bosco dei Tigli" and the multifunctional sports pitch, were repeatedly reported as both a favourite place and a problematic and unsafe space due to its constant need for care and maintenance. The presence of a caretaker and the fence on all sides, which allows children to play freely and away from cars, positively affects the community's perception of safety.

The mapping activity conducted by the younger participants using the MyMaps tool involved categorising the indicators of perceived insecurity into three main categories based on the environmental factors present: lighting, maintenance, and disorientation. The visual representation of these three categories enables the immediate identification of the park's most problematic areas through the georeferencing of the collected data in a summary relational geo-database created using GIS tools.

User suggestions highlight the need to reduce existing architectural barriers, including the refurbishment of mechanical lifts, and to enhance lighting, signage, seating, and maintenance of the green spaces and buildings. According to young people, priority should be given to introducing new functions within the park, which implement the field of use and the duration of attendance: dog areas, spaces for the children's play, study zones, refreshment areas, info-points, as well as frequent social and cultural events, festivals, and local fairs, and the extension of the park's opening hours, especially during the summer.

Fig. 3. Collaborative mapping of unsafe areas and heartlands inside and outside the park. Photographs by the authors.

4 Conclusions

The safety of public spaces, particularly urban green spaces, is a complex issue that requires an integrated methodological approach. This process must include an accurate assessment of the existing safety conditions, combining environmental, social, and urban elements, as well as the definition of targeted intervention strategies. The effectiveness of these strategies depends on a thorough understanding of the specific context and an evaluation of the risk scenario.

The SeTUP research aims to develop a model based on environmental quality indicators, with the goal of supporting the assessment of perceived safety in urban parks and contributing to the formulation of policies to improve their quality and safety. The model, applied to public parks in Naples, stands out for its innovative approach that combines quantitative indicators, derived from technical literature, with qualitative data collected through collaborative mapping and questionnaires administered to the community. The workshops conducted demonstrate that involving the population in a structured analytical process fosters collaboration between researchers and users, aiming to identify safety issues and discuss potential improvements and innovative solutions, in a participatory and "maieutic" process [57]. The data collected allows for the analysis of the morphological, spatial, and perceptual characteristics of the park and its surrounding area, highlighting aspects of accessibility, livability, and safety. The results obtained, particularly for the "Parco dei Quartieri Spagnoli", confirm the reliability of the selected indicators, providing insights into the priority issues related to the theme of perceived safety. The research is ongoing, and the methodology presented can be expanded in future studies, considering additional variables such as residential satisfaction, social cohesion, and urban identity, which are closely linked to the perception of safety [53].

References

1. Lefebvre H.: Le Droit à la ville. Paris, Anthro¬pos, trad. it. 1970, Il diritto alla città. Marsilio, Padova (1968)
2. Coppola E.: Laboratorio Bagnoli. Edicampus Edizioni (2020). ISBN 978-88-7603-145-8. http://www.edicampus-edizioni.it/images/ebook/laboratorio-bagnoli.pdf
3. Lepoutre D.: Cœur Banlieue. Codes, rites et langages. Odile Jacob, Paris (2001)
4. Lourenco, N.: Città, violenza urbana e sentimento di insicurezza. Rivista di Criminologia, Vittimologia e Sicurezza, VI **3**, 149–165 (2012)
5. Acierno, A.: Tra sicurezza virtuale e città reale. TRIA **4**, 243–250 (2009)
6. Cardia C., Bottigelli C.: Progettare la città sicura. Pianificazione, disegno urbano, gestione degli spazi pubblici. Hoepli, Milano (2011)
7. Secchi, B.: La città dei ricchi e la città dei poveri. Carocci editori, Bari-Roma (2013)
8. Selmini, R.: La sicurezza urbana. Il mulino, Bologna (2004)
9. Jeffery, C.R.: Crime Prevention through Environmental Design. Sage Publications, Beverly Hills (1971)
10. Mastronardi V., Ciappi S.: Urbanistica e criminalità (I Parte). Alle origini di un rapporto. Urbe et Ius. Revista de estudio de Criminologia y ciencias penales, 1–17 (2020)
11. Wood, E.: Housing Design: A Social Theory. New York: Citizens' Housing and Planning Counsel, New York (1961)
12. Jacobs J.: Vita e morte delle grandi città americane. Einaudi, Torino (1969); trad. it. di The Death and Life of Great American Cities. Prima edizione 1961, Harmondsworth, Penguin Books, 1977
13. Newman, O.: Defensible Space - Crime Prevention Through Urban Design. Macmillan, New York (1972)
14. Kelling, G.L., Wilson, J.Q.: Broken windows: the policy and neighbourhood safety. Atlantic **249**, 29–39 (1982)
15. Musarra G.: La città "si...cura". Pianificare la sicurezza urbana. Life Saf. Secur. **4**(4), 79–82 (2016)
16. Acierno, A.: Urbanistica securitaria: modelli, limiti e prospettive di ricerca. TRIA **5**, 153–66 (2010)
17. Karrer, F., Santangelo, S.: Pianificazione urbana e sicurezza. Cittalia, Per una città sicura dalle ordinanze agli strumenti di pianificazione e regolamentazione della convivenza cittadina, 71–82 (2012)
18. Bolici R., Gambaro M.: La sicurezza urbana per la qualità dello spazio pubblico. TECHNE **19**, 104–113 (2020)
19. Kuo, M., Sullivan, W.: Environment and crime in the inner city: does vegetation reduce crime? Environ. Behav. **33**, 343–367 (2001). https://doi.org/10.1177/00139160121973025
20. NYRP, New York Restoration Project, Annual-Report (2018)
21. Pinna, S.: Rischi ambientali e difesa del territorio. FrancoAngeli, Milano (2002)
22. Coppola, F.: Un modello risk-based per la prevenzione ambientale del rischio da criminalità. Tesi di dottorato in Urbanistica e sicurezza, Università degli studi di Salerno, Dipartimento di Ingegneria civile (2021)

23. Innes, M.: Signal crimes and signal disorders: notes on deviance as communicative action. Br. J. Sociol. **55**(3), 335–355 (2004). https://doi.org/10.1111/j.1468-4446.2004.00023.x
24. Perez Tejera, F., Anguera, M.T., Guàrdia, J., Dalmau-Bueno, A., Valera, S.: Examining perceived safety and park use in public open spaces: The case of Barcelona. J. Environ. Psychol. **81** (2022). https://doi.org/10.1016/j.jenvp.2022.101823
25. Nasar, J.L., Fisher, B.: 'Hot spots' of fear and crime: a multi-method investigation. J. Environ. Psychol. **13**(3), 187–206 (1993)
26. Nasar, J.L., Fisher, B., Grannis, M.: Proximate physical cues to fear of crime. Landsc. Urban Plann. **26**(1–4), 161–178 (1993). https://doi.org/10.1016/0169-2046(93)90014-5
27. Fisher, B., Nasar, J.: Fear of crime in relation to three exterior site features: prospect, refuge, and escape. Environ. Behav. **24**, 35–65 (1992). https://doi.org/10.1177/0013916592241002
28. Thani, S.K.S.O., Hashim, N.H.M., Ismail, W.H.W.: Surveillance by design: assessment using principles of crime prevention through environmental design (CPTED) in urban parks. Procedia Soc. Behav. Sci. **234**, 506–514 (2016). https://doi.org/10.1016/j.sbspro.2016.10.269
29. Madge, C.: Public parks and the geography of fear. Tijdschr. Econ. Soc. Geogr. **88**(3), 237–250 (1997). https://doi.org/10.1111/j.1467-9663.1997.tb01601.x
30. Carmona, M., de Magalhães, C.: Local Environmental Quality. A New View on Measurement, Department for Communities and Local Government, London (2007)
31. Mehta, V.: Evaluating public space. J. Urban Des. **19**(1) (2014)
32. Clemente, M.: Re-design dello spazio pubblico. Franco Angeli, Milano (2017)
33. Bonnes, M., Uzzell, D., Carrus, G., Kelay, T.: Inhabitants' and experts' assessments of environmental quality for urban sustainability. J. Soc. Issues **63**(1), 59–78 (2007). https://doi.org/10.1111/j.1540-4560.2007.00496.x
34. Kaplan, R.: The analysis of perception via preference: a strategy for studying how the environment is experienced. Landsc. Plann. **12**, 161–176 (1985)
35. Anderson L, Stokes G.: Planting in parking lots to improve perceived attractivness and security. Arboric. Urban For. (AUF) **15**(1), 7–10 (1989). https://doi.org/10.48044/jauf.1989.002
36. Comune di Forlì, Servizio Urbanistica e Edilizia Privata, Unità Strumenti attuativi e urbanizzazioni, Linee guida sulle buone pratiche di sicurezza urbana, approvato con Delibera G.C. n. 92 del 23/04/2013 e s.m.i
37. Kaplan, R., Kaplan, S.: The experience of nature: A psychological perspective. Cambridge University Press, Cambridge, UK (1989)
38. Herzog, T., Bryce, A.: Mystery and preference in within-forest settings. Environ. Behav. **39**, 779–796 (2007). https://doi.org/10.1177/0013916506298796
39. Berlyne, D.E.: Aesthetics and Psychobiology. Appleton-Century-Crofts, New York (1971)
40. Appleton, J.: The Experience of Landscape. Wiley, Londra (1975)
41. Mahrous, A.M., Moustafa, Y.M., Abou El-Ela, M.A.: Physical characteristics and perceived security in urban parks: investigation in the Egyptian context. Ain Shams Eng. J. **9**(4), 3055–3066 (2018). https://doi.org/10.1016/j.asej.2018.07.003
42. Foucault, M.: Sorvegliare e punire: la nascita della prigione. Einaudi, Torino (2005)
43. Bentham, J.: El panóptico. Quadrata, Ciudad Autónoma de Buenos Aires (2016)
44. Zhao, J., Huang, Y.: Physical characteristics of urban green spaces in relation to perceived safety. J. Urban Plann. Dev. **147**(4) (2021). https://doi.org/10.1061/(ASCE)UP.1943-5444.0000742
45. Jorgensen, L., Ellis, G.D., Ruddell, E.: Fear perceptions in public parks interactions of environmental concealment, the presence of people recreating, and gender. Environ. Behav. **45**, 803–820 (2013). https://doi.org/10.1177/0013916512446334
46. Baroni, M.R.: Psicologia ambientale. Il Mulino, Bologna (1998)
47. Schroeder, H., Anderson, L.: Perception of personal safety in urban recreation sites. Leisure Res. **16**, 178–194 (1983). https://doi.org/10.1080/00222216.1984.11969584

48. Jorgensen, A., Hitchmough, J., Dunnett, N.: Woodland as a setting for housing-appreciation and fear and the contribution to residential satisfaction and place identity in Warrington New Town, UK. Landsc. Urban Plann. **79**(3–4), 273–287 (2007). https://doi.org/10.1016/j.landurbplan.2006.02.015
49. Sezavar, N., Pazhouhanfar, M., Van Dongen, R.P., Grahn, P.: The importance of designing the spatial distribution and density of vegetation in urban parks for increased experience of safety. J. Cleaner Prod. **403** (2023). https://doi.org/10.1016/j.jclepro.2023.136768
50. Whyte, W.H.: The Social Life of Small Urban Spaces. The Conservation Foundation, Washington DC (1980)
51. Project for public spaces: Placemaking: What if We Built Our Cities Around Places (2022)
52. Mak, B.K.L., Jim, C.Y.: Examining fear-evoking factors in urban parks in Hong Kong. Landsc. Urban Plan. **171**, 42–56 (2018). https://doi.org/10.1016/j.landurbplan.2017.11.012
53. Carro, D., Valera, S., Vidal, T.: Perceived insecurity in the public space: personal, social and environmental variables. Qual. Quant. **44**(2), 303–314 (2010). https://doi.org/10.1007/s11135-008-9200-0
54. Russell, J.A., Pratt, G.: A description of the affective quality attributed to environments. J. Pers. Soc. Psychol. **38**, 311–322 (1980)
55. Perugini, M., Bonnes, M., Aiello, A., Ercolani, A.P.: Il modello circonflesso delle qualità affettive dei luoghi. Sviluppo di uno strumento valutativo italiano. TPM Testing Psychometrics Methodol. **9**(4), 131–152 (2002)
56. Comune di Napoli, Assessorato al diritto alla città, ai beni comuni e all'urbanistica, Unità di Progetto Interdirezionale "Coordinamento progetti URBACT e Reti per lo Sviluppo di Politiche Urbane Integrate", Strategia di riattivazione del complesso della SS Trinità delle monache; ex ospedale militare, Piano di Azione locale della città di Napoli- 2nd chance, Aprile 2018
57. Dolci D.: L'educazione. Edizioni Comunità, Roma (2020)

Knowledge for Sustainable Planning: UnivAQ's Contribution to the GeoSciencesIR Research Infrastructure

Francesco Zullo, Annamaria Felli(✉), Gianni Di Pietro, Emilio Marziali, Cristina Montaldi, and Chiara Cattani

Department of Civil, Construction-Architectural and Environmental Engineering, University of L'Aquila, L'Aquila, Italy
annamaria.felli@graduate.univaq.it

Abstract. Concepts such as environmental sustainability, sustainability of territorial changes, and achievement of European objectives have been permeating the political agenda at various levels, from the larger level to local planning. As for the latter, many funds disbursed are often linked to achieving objectives that require up-to-date knowledge systems and useful monitoring platforms. Therefore, this requires elaborating comprehensive and exhaustive cognitive frameworks capable of simultaneously analyzing different issues and diagnosing how the identified trends manifest themselves and influence a given territory's social, economic, and environmental development. The GeosciencesIR infrastructure is grafted onto this line of research, which aims to improve geological knowledge of the fragile national territory and to protect and improve soil resources. The proposed work aims to highlight Univaq Operative Unit's contribution to achieving this last important goal. In particular, the article shows how this component of the infrastructure is implemented and what issues are addressed so that administrations, both at the regional and local levels, have a set of data and indicators that allow them to support the process of preparing plans and also any related environmental assessment procedures.

Keywords: Environmental Sustainability · Urban Planning · Monitoring Platform

1 Introduction

Concepts such as environmental sustainability, the sustainability of territorial changes, and the achievement of European objectives have been permeating political agendas at various levels, from the larger scale to local planning, for several years. For the latter, many of the loans disbursed are often linked to the achievement of objectives that require up-to-date knowledge systems and useful monitoring platforms [1, 2]. This requires the creation of a comprehensive and exhaustive cognitive framework capable of analyzing different issues simultaneously and diagnosing how the trends identified affect the social,

E. Borgogno-Mondino and P. Zamperlin (Eds.): ASITA 2024, CCIS 2463, pp. 354–364, 2025.
https://doi.org/10.1007/978-3-031-91141-5_24

economic, and environmental performance of an area [1–6]. The GeoSciencesIR infrastructure builds on this line of research, which aims to improve geological knowledge of the fragile national territory and to protect and enhance soil resources [7]. The GeoSciencesIR project provides valuable support as one of its objectives is to create a new research infrastructure that, in addition to updating geological knowledge on national soils, also aims at sustainable soil management through Work Package (WP) no. 5. The Operative Unit (OU) of the University of L'Aquila is involved in this work package together with ISPRA, the University of Molise and the University of Naples Federico II. The contribution of the Operative Unit (OU) of the University of L'Aquila (Univaq) is crucial to achieve this goal through the updating of geological knowledge and the introduction of tools for sustainable soil management (Fig. 1).

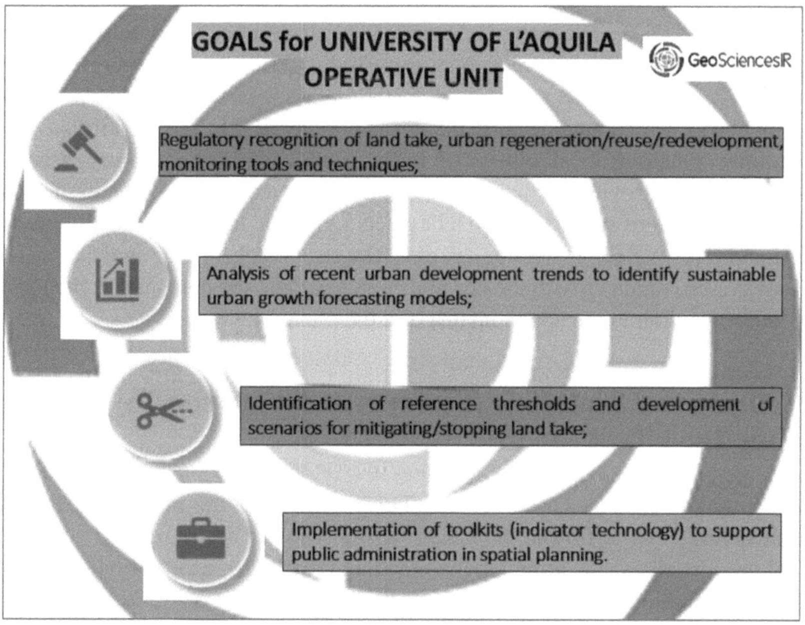

Fig. 1. Goals for the University of L'Aquila Operative Unit (OU).

This work aims to highlight the role of the Univaq OU in creating this component of the infrastructure, detailing the issues addressed to support regional and local administrations. In particular, the data and indicators developed to facilitate the formation of plans and the related environmental assessment procedures will be analyzed. The OU intends to create a decision support system (Dashboard) that allows local administrations (municipal and provincial) to have up-to-date data and information on various issues that influence land use change and especially land urbanization. The dashboard will allow the authorities to know what the trends are (demographic, economic, social, land use, and land take) in progress through the use of graph indicators and appropriate statistical parameters. The indicators will be selected after a careful evaluation process both of the methods of population of the same (temporal continuity) and of their ability to describe the phenomenon analyzed (Key indicators). A fundamental part of this work is dedicated to land take, a crucial issue for territorial planning and environmental sustainability. In addition, the differences between legal and technical definitions of land take are certainly discussed, highlighting how these influence the consistency of regional laws with European objectives [1–6]. The analysis reveals a lack of a uniform definition and regional regulatory variations that undermine the effectiveness of land use containment and reversal policies, highlighting the challenges and opportunities to achieve the ambitious "zero budget" targets set at the national and European levels [8–10]. The variables at play are numerous and it is still difficult to be able to implement territorial evolutionary scenarios with high adherence to the expected configuration. It is also true that a better knowledge of the territory together with the trends of the processes that could certainly play a role in the future structure, represents a fundamental prerogative for the establishment of urban planning tools that are aware and fully responsive to the needs of the communities that inhabit the places [2–6]. The lack of cogency in the planning of a vast area and strategies that are often not linked to the real conditions of the territories have entrusted the plan with objectives that have been disregarded and that have produced negative effects on the national soil, which are still difficult to solve today [2–5]. The toolkit that is being created aims to support local authorities in the knowledge of the territory of action of the plan (regional, provincial, municipal) through the creation of a system of data and information of various origins and on a large enough scale to support the establishment of solid and effective cognitive frameworks. The use of appropriate indicators (for the issues addressed) together with the possibility of graphing the data, makes the tool easy to use and accessible to the actors involved in the planning process.

2 Methods and Materials (Features and Functionality of the Toolkit)

The construction of the GeosciencesIR platform required the integration of data of different nature. The territorial extension of reference is the municipal one, even if the final product allows an administrative reading on a larger scale (province/region), a functional reading of the territory (through the Local Labour Systems), and a reading from an environmental point of view, obtained through the classification of the Italian Eco-Regions.

The first phase of the work concerned the collection of data for the creation of the following databases:

1. Land Take
2. Demography
3. Economy
4. Territorial constraints
5. Real Estate Market
6. Real Estate Assets
7. Road Network
8. Municipal classifications

The final product will contain the union of these databases, to provide a complete overview to the end user of the territory of interest. The analyses were conducted both synchronously and diachronically, finding data from 2001, where available. In this way, the end user will have a complete picture of both the current situation of the territory and its historical trend.

The second phase of the work was to standardize the data with the current configuration of Italian municipalities, which in 23 years has gone from 8101 municipalities in 2001 to 7896 in 2024, following several mergers, incorporations, and demergers. Figure 2 shows that the merger phenomenon has been particularly evident since 2015 following Law no. 56 of 7 April 2014 ("Delrio Law"), which defines new criteria for the union of Italian municipalities.

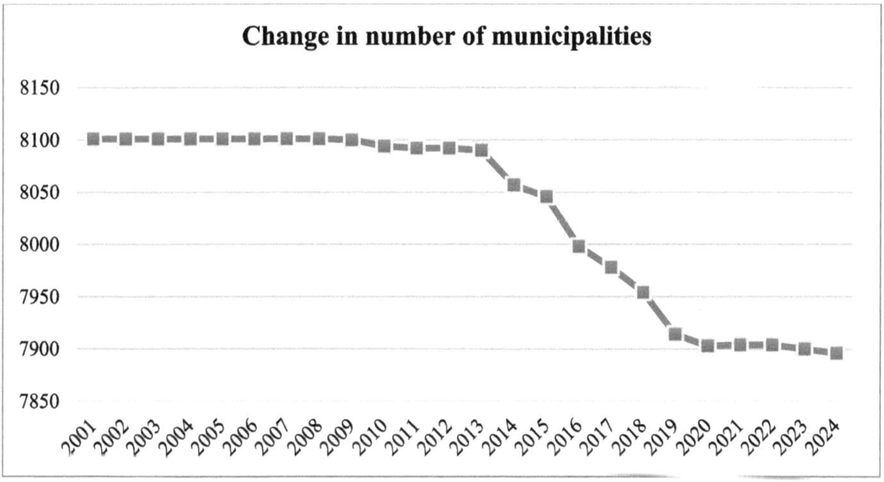

Fig. 2. Change in number of Italian municipalities. (Elaboration of the authors)

The analyzed data concern the following thematic areas: demography, land take, real estate market, real estate assets, the geography of risks (floods and landslides) and values (Protected Areas and Natura 2000 Network), economy, and road network. There are many sources:

1. *National Institute of Statistics* (Istat) [11] for the cartographic base and everything related to demographic aspects (analyzed period 2001 – 2024).
2. *Higher Institute for Environmental Research and Protection* (ISPRA) [12] for data on land take (reference period 2006 - 2022).
3. *Revenue Agency – Real Estate Market Observatory* [13] concerning information on real estate market trends (reference period 2011 – 2023).
4. *Ministry of Economy and Finance* (MEF) [14] for all data relating to the economic variable (reference period 2001, 2011, 2012, 2016 – 2022).
5. *Open Street Map* [15] for the road network (updated July 2024).

6. *Italian National Geoportal* [16] as regards the cartographic bases concerning the geography of areas with different degrees of risk (floods and landslides) and environmental constraints (Official List of Protected Areas and Natura 2000 Network) to assess their coverage on a municipal basis.

The main problem we have encountered concerns the standardization of data after mergers between municipalities. After these mergers, the identification codes of the municipalities (both the Istat numerical code and the cadastral codes of the Revenue Agency) are generated from scratch, which prevents a direct link to the municipalities and therefore to the data before the merger. From an operational point of view, this process leads to a manual merger of 205 municipalities with the sum of all values previously calculated for the existing municipalities before the merger.

The interchange format used is the GeoPackage and all the information/data collected have been standardized according to the INSPIRE Directive (Directive 2007/2/EC of the European Parliament and of the Council of 14 March 2007).

The third phase of the work consisted of developing a set of indicators, both at the level of individual themes and for comparison between different themes. To this end, the techniques of indicator engineering were applied, in which, in addition to the formulation of the individual indicators, the possible relationships are also examined in order to identify a specific set that is effective and efficient for the representation of phenomena and the understanding of the dynamics present.

The different indicators come both from the scientific reading [1–6, 9–16] and from sets created by the different national institutes for monitoring the 2030 Agenda.

Table 1 shows a list of the number of indicators analyzed for each database and the source of the associated data.

Table 1. Overview of Evaluated Indicators by Database and Their Data Sources

Database	Number of indicators computed	Data Source
1 - Land Take	2	ISPRA
2 - Demography	7	ISTAT
3 - Economy	15	MEF
4 - Territorial constraints	8	ISPRA/ISTAT
5 - Real Estate Market	4	Agenzia delle Entrate
6 - Real Estate Assets	1	Agenzia delle Entrate
7 - Road Network	9	Open Street Map
TOTAL	46 indicators	

Table 2 shows, for example, an indicator calculated for each database, through its name, its mathematical formulation, the parameters used in the calculation with the respective units of measurement, and a brief description of its meaning.

Table 2. Example of Indicator Calculation for Each Database

Database	Name	Formulation	Parameters	Indicatos Summary
1 - Land Take	Impermeabilization Density	$Dimp = \frac{Sim}{Su}$	Simp = Impermeabilized Surface [ha] Su = Reference unit surface [ha]	Percentage of total artificial surface, measured in a specific year, compared to the total surface of the territorial area under analysis
2 - Demography	Urbanized Surface Per Capita	$SUpc = \frac{Surb}{Pop\ com}$	Surb = Urbanized Surface [mq] Pop com = Resident Population in the municipality [Nab]	Ratio between urbanized surface and resident population in the municipality
3 - Economy	Taxable Income Per Capite	$Ripc = \frac{R\ imp}{N\ Cont}$	R imp = Taxable Income [€] N cont = Number of Taxpayers [Nab]	Ratio between taxable income and the number of taxpayers for the analyzed municipality
4 - Territorial Constraints	Territorial Constraints Pressure	$Dta = \frac{S\ av}{Su}$	S av = Surface of Restricted Areas [ha] Su = Reference unit surface [ha]	Percentage incidence of restricted areas (Natura 2000 Network, EUAP Sites, PAI Areas, Landslide Areas) compared to the municipal surface
5 - Real Estate Market	Incidence of Residential Transactions	$Itr = \frac{N\ tr}{N\ t\ tot}$	N tr = Number of Residential Sector Transactions N t tot = Total Number of Transactions	Percentage incidence of the number of transactions made in the residential sector on the total municipal transactions

(continued)

Table 2. *(continued)*

Database	Name	Formulation	Parameters	Indicatos Summary
6 - Real Estate Assets	Housing Availability Index	$Vpa = \frac{N\ vani}{Pop\ com}$	N vani = Cadastral Consistency expressed in rooms (Group A - AdE) Pop com = Resident Population in the municipality [Nab]	Ratio between the cadastral consistency expressed in rooms of group A (AdE Classification) and the resident population in the municipality
7 - Road Network	Highway Density	$Daut = \frac{l\ aut}{li}$	l aut = highway lenght [km] li = road network lenght [km]	Percentage ratio between the length of highways present in the municipal territory and the total length of the infrastructures

In the "Municipal Classification" database, no indicators have been calculated, as it only presents information on which the results of the other databases can be read. Among the different classifications proposed, in addition to those previously mentioned in administrative, functional, and environmental readings, we find:

- Altimetric area.
- Degree of urbanization.
- Demographic groups.
- Territorial extension.
- Tourist classification.
- Classification of municipalities according to the National Strategy for Internal Areas (SNAI).

The classifications listed above are proposed by ISTAT, based on data collected during census surveys or coming for example from the Digital Elevation Model – DEM.

3 Results

The first relevant aspect addressed by the Univaq OU concerns the regulatory analysis and critical review of the laws in force in Italy on land take, intending to understand the tools through which it is trying to achieve zero land take, expected by 2030 (National Ecological Transition Plan, in force by March 2022).

The absence of a national control room has created significant discrepancies between regions, both in the definitions of land take and in the methods of containment [17–22]. Regional regulations, which are often ambiguous, introduce exceptions that exclude irreversible transformations from the calculation of land take, creating a substantial ineffectiveness of the rules [2–5, 17–23].

An emblematic case is Veneto, where regional law no. 14 of 2017 establishes a limit on land take until 2050, but with numerous exceptions that include mining and agricultural entrepreneurial activities. Similarly, in Abruzzo and the Metropolitan City of Bologna, regional regulations set a "perimeter of the urbanized territory" that excludes areas that are apparently urbanized, but in reality not taken [3, 5–6, 23–25].

The analysis also finds that setting a containment threshold is not sufficient without considering how new buildings are allocated, a particularly serious problem in Italy, where fragmented urbanization or "sprinkling" [26–30] leads to energy inefficiencies and vulnerability to extreme weather events. Such climatic emergencies, like flood phenomena, are increasingly frequent and aggravate the fragility of the Italian urban structure.

The regulatory complexity and regional discrepancies highlighted in the analysis of land take require effective tools to monitor and manage the territory in a coordinated manner. In this context, the construction of the GeosciencesIR platform, through the integration of diversified databases, offers a complete and multi-scalar view of the territory. However, to facilitate the interpretation and understanding of territorial dynamics, it is essential to identify synthetic indicators that effectively represent the phenomena analyzed.

In this context, seven key indicators will be selected, one for each database (land take, demography, economy, territorial constraints, real estate market, real estate, and road network) that facilitate the interpretation and understanding of territorial dynamics. These indicators will be chosen for three main reasons:

1. Greater representativeness of the phenomenon analyzed.
2. Correlation with the indicators of other databases.
3. Annual data update, to achieve more efficient monitoring over time.

The key indicators are intended to provide an integrated and multi-factorial view of the phenomena analyzed. The choice of a key indicator represents a strategic approach to assess the complexity of territorial phenomena, allowing more detailed and more easily understandable analyses for territorial planning actors (administrators, technicians, citizens).

To correlate data of different natures in a single synthetic measure, a composite indicator will be constructed. Different variables, in fact, such as those analyzed in the GeoSciencesIR platform, to support the territorial planning processes, provide an overall view of the phenomena, but only as a whole are they indicators of the phenomenon under study. To measure these variables, it is desirable to construct a summary indicator, which is not reflected in empirical observation but is the result of logical and/or mathematical operations.

The composite indicator will provide a summary measure of the current state of Italian municipalities. It aims to identify the areas most affected by the correlation of the analyzed phenomena and to facilitate the territorial analysis of these phenomena over time. Additionally, the composite indicator will serve as a useful tool for decision-makers and technical planners.

Figure 3 shows the diagram of the construction of the composite indicator. The indicator will be built through the combination of 7 key indicators, appropriately selected, which describe the main territorial, demographic, economic, and real estate market variables within a municipal entity.

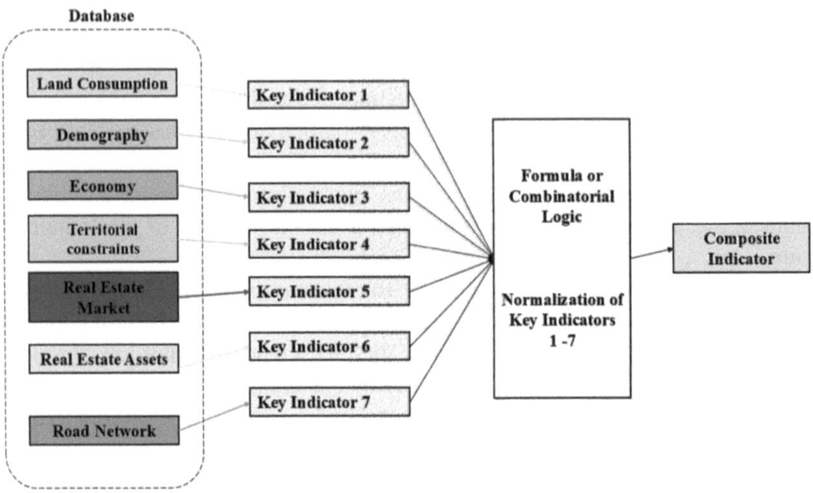

Fig. 3. Diagram of the composite indicator's construction. (Elaboration of the authors)

4 Discussion and Conclusion

The toolkit under development not only provides a clearer and more detailed view of territorial dynamics but also helps identify the responsible parties for each macro-sector and creates a single indicator that synthesizes key factors. One of its innovative features is the ability to interpret the territory both administratively and functionally, using Local Labor Systems (LLS) carried out by ISTAT to offer a broader, more articulated perspective. Additionally, the integration of ISTAT's "Eco Regions" classification enriches the analysis by accounting for environmental characteristics. This multi-level approach, supported by 20 years of historical data at the municipal level, equips planners and decision-makers with tools for more informed and sustainable land management. This platform offers the opportunity to overcome the difficulties related to regulatory fragmentation, helping policymakers and technologists to develop policies and knowledge frameworks that not only consider territorial objectives, but are also in line with ongoing transformations, thus filling gaps in regulatory systems. The use of open data from various sources allows the creation of realistic knowledge frameworks that help prevent uncontrolled urban sprawl and promote diversified economic and social growth strategies. The toolkit offers a platform with certified, aggregated data, enabling clear assessments of territorial challenges and potential, while monitoring trends from the past 20 years. With these features, local administrations can plan more effectively, applying adaptive management techniques to align land use with regulatory limits. The toolkit is not just a decision support system (DSS) but fosters a participatory, bottom-up approach, with data organized in both synchronic and diachronic formats. The goal is to create a comprehensive indicator for territorial planning focused on sustainability and urban regeneration, avoiding uncontrolled expansion.

In the future, the toolkit could incorporate new data, such as Municipal Urban Plans, information on green infrastructure, hydrogeological risk, and climate change impacts. These updates will make the platform an evolving and adaptable system, capable of addressing emerging territorial challenges and supporting long-term sustainability.

Acknowledgments. This contribution is realized within the framework of the PNRR project "Geo-SciencesIR" funded by the European Union Next Generation EU (PNRR "Geo-SciencesIR" – Missione 4, "Istruzione e Ricerca" – Componente 2, "Dalla ricercar all'impresa" – Linea di investimento 3.1, "Fondo per la realizzazione di un sistema integrato di infrastrutture di ricercar e innovazione". Finanziato dall'Unione Europea NextGenerationEU CUP I53C22000800006).

Disclosure of Interests. The authors have no competing interests.

References

1. Munafò, M.: Consumo di Suolo, Dinamiche Territoriali e Servizi Ecosistemici, Report SNPA 37/23, Ispra, Rome, Italy (2023)
2. Felli, A., Zullo, F.: The importance of urban regeneration actions: European and Italian legislative framework analysis. In: 2nd International Conference on Future Challenges in Sustainable Urban Planning & Territorial Management, Universidad Politécnica de Cartagena, Cartagena (2024)
3. Marziali, E., Felli, A., Cattani, C., Zullo, F.: Planning Without Shared Strategies. Impacts and Perspectives Along the Abruzzo Adriatic Coastal Belt. In: Gervasi, O., Murgante, B., Garau, C., Taniar, D., C. Rocha, A.M.A., Faginas Lago, M.N. (eds.) Computational Science and Its Applications – ICCSA 2024 Workshops. ICCSA 2024. LNCS, vol. 14820. Springer, Cham (2024). https://doi-org.univaq.idm.oclc.org/10.1007/978-3-031-65285-1_20
4. Felli, A., Zullo, F.: Legislative foundations: exploring land take laws and urban regeneration policies in Italy and Europe. Land **13**(713), 2024 (2024)
5. Montaldi, C.: Consumo di suolo: Un complesso quadro di politiche, definizioni e soglie. In: Territorio 2023, vol.103, pp. 147–156 (2024)
6. Fiorini, L., Zullo, F., Marucci, A., Di Dato, C., Romano, B.: Planning tool mosaic (PTM): a platform for Italy, a country without a strategic framework. Land **10**(3), 279 (2021)
7. GeoSciences IR Homepage. https://geosciences-ir.it/. Accessed 15 Jun 2024
8. Decoville, A., Schneider, M.: Can the 2050 zero land take objective of the EU be reliably monitored? A comparative study. J. Land Use Sci. **11**(3), 331–349 (2016)
9. Barbier, E.B., Burgess, J.C.: The Sustainable Development Goals and the systems approach to sustainability. Economics **11**(1) (2017)
10. Berisha, E., Cotella, G., Rivolin, J., Solly, A.: Sistemi di governo del territorio e consumo di suolo in Europa. In: TERRITORIO, pp. 123–132 (2023)
11. Istituto Nazionale di Statistica (Istat). https://www.istat.it/. Accessed 25 Mar 2024
12. Istituto Superiore per la Ricerca e la Protezione Ambientale (ISPRA). https://groupware.sinanet.isprambiente.it/. Accessed 15 Mar 2024

13. Agenzia delle entrate. https://www.agenziaentrate.gov.it/portale/web/guest/schede/fabbricatiterreni/omi/banche-dati/stock-catastale. Accessed 28 Mar 2024
14. Ministero dell'Economia e delle Finanze. https://www.mef.gov.it. Accessed 19 Jun 2024
15. Open street map. https://www.openstreetmap.org/. Accessed 21 Jun 2024
16. Geoportale Nazionale Italiano. https://gn.mase.gov.it/portale/home. Accessed 03 Jul 2024
17. Lopatriello, B., Saganeiti, L., Scorza, F., Murgante, B.: Differenze e incongruenze nelle tecniche di monitoraggio del consumo di suolo. In book CONSUMO DI SUOLO, SERVIZI ECOSISTEMICI E GREEN INFRASTRUCTURES: Metodi, ricerche e progetti innovativi per incrementare il Capitale naturale e migliorare la resilienza urbana – CRCS 2022. INU Edizioni srl (2022)
18. Montaldi, C., Di Pietro, G., Romano, B., Zullo, F.: Consumo di suolo: analisi e sperimentazione di soglie funzionali. Atti della XXV Conferenza Nazionale della SIU - Transizioni, giustizia spaziale e progetto di territorio, Planum Publisher e Società Italiana degli Urbanisti, vol. 09, Cagliari, Italy, pp. 137–141 (2024)
19. Montaldi, C., Zullo, F., Munafò, M.: Limit land take. A matter of thresholds? In: International Conference on Innovation in Urban and Regional Planning, pp. 695–705. Springer, Switzerland (2024)
20. Sferlazza, E.: Proposta di un modello vettoriale multitemporale per la rappresentazione e la gestione in ambiente GIS dei PRG comunali. In: Proceedings of the 8th ASITA National Conference, Rome, Italy, pp. 14–17 (2004)
21. Tarsi, E.: I piani regionali in Italia sono pronti ad orientare le sfide della transizione ecologica? Proposta per una metodologia di analisi. In Atti della XXIV Conferenza Nazionale SIU-Società italiana degli Urbanisti-Dare valore ai valori in urbanistica Brescia 23-24 Giugno 2022. Planum Publisher e Società Italiana degli Urbanisti, vol. 3, pp. 48-53 (2023)
22. Zoppi, C.: Valutazione e pianificazione delle trasformazioni territoriali nei processi di governance ed e-governance. Sostenibilità ed e-governance nella pianificazione del territorio. FrancoAngeli. pp. 1–384 (2012)
23. Zullo, F., Montaldi, C., Di Pietro, G., Cattani, C.: Land use changes and ecosystem services: the case study of the Abruzzo region coastal strip. ISPRS Int. J. Geo Inf. **11**(12), 588 (2022)
24. Marucci, A., Fiorini, L., Ulisse, C.: Urban pressure scenario on the protected areas systems. In: International Conference on Innovation in Urban and Regional Planning, University of Cagliari, Cagliari (2019)
25. Città Metropolitana di Bologna. https://www.cittametropolitana.bo.it/pianificazione/osservatorio_metropolitano_consumo_suolo/Consumo_di_suolo_ai_sensi_della_L_R_24_17. Accessed 19 Feb 2023
26. Romano, B., Fiorini, L., Zullo, F., Marucci, A.: Una valutazione delle dinamiche di consumo di suolo in Italia: Gli esiti della ricerca DICEAA. In Caring fo Our Soil: Aver Cura Della Natura dei Territori; WWF Italia Onlus, Rome, Italy, pp. 19–28 (2017)
27. Romano, B., Zullo, F., Fiorini, L., Marucci, A.: Molecular no smart-planning in Italy: 8000 municipalities in action throughout the country. Sustainability **11**(22), 6467 (2019)
28. Manganelli, B., Murgante, B., Saganeiti, L.: The social cost of urban sprinkling. Sustainability **12**(6), 2236 (2020)
29. Romano, B., Zullo, F., Fiorini, L., Ciabò, S., Marucci, A.: Sprinkling: An approach to describe urbanization dynamics in Italy. Sustainability **9**(1), 97 (2017)
30. Romano, B., Zullo, F., Saganeiti, L., Montaldi, C.: Controllo integrato delle dinamiche urbane e demografiche: Un complesso problema di cut-off. Consumo di suolo, servizi ecosistemici e green infrastructures, Rapporto, pp. 63–72 (2022)

Urban Regeneration Using the Sound: The Project Augmented Reality Soundscape (ARS)

Rosa Anna La Rocca[1(✉)], Romano Fistola[1], Ida Zingariello[1], and Filippo Fabbri[2]

[1] DICEA, University of Naples Federico II, Naples, Italy
{larocca,romano.fistola,ida.zingariello}@unina.it
[2] Université Paris-Saclay, Paris, France
filippo.fabbri@universite-paris-saclay.fr

Abstract. The project "Augmented Reality Soundscape" (ARS) deals with the issue of urban regeneration and it represents a first application to test the use of augmented reality applied to the sounds. It is part of a larger research aimed at defining methods to promote Soft Urban Regeneration Actions. Authors intended the term *soft* to underline the possibility to intervene on urban assets using methods and procedures that are based on the involvement of locals act without contrasts. This process develops in three main phases: 1) the sustainability (economic, environmental and social) of the intervention; 2) participatory processes by involvement of locals; 3) evaluation of the effects of the intervention. The use of the soundscape in urban renewal is a still unexplored field of the urban research that can be indagated with the aim of defining shared occasion to transform and use urban public spaces giving them the possibility of acting as a magnet of care and attention for residents and tourists. The paper in the first part introduces to this idea of using also sounds to "augment" the perception of a physical space, in the second part it presents first findings of an application of the ARS in Cachan (France) carried out with the engagement of the students at University Paris-Saclay in Cachan.

Keywords: Soundscape · Urban Regeneration · Augmented Reality

1 Introduction

This study stems from the intention to define a bottom-up urban regeneration process that leverages the latest technological advancements to trigger an attractive reuse of marginal urban spaces. The objective of the research is to point out a procedure that can be applied to different urban contexts across various national settings while respecting their uniqueness.

The proposal of this study, thus, refers to the basic idea that by using advanced technology, particularly augmented reality combined with spatialized sounds, it is possible to envision specific spatial features of the urban context being analyzed. These features will characterize the way in which space is experienced through a dedicated application designed to run on personal mobile phones. Through the creation of a specific soundscape within the urban context of reference, it will be possible to give the space a new connotation without physically intervening on it.

E. Borgogno-Mondino and P. Zamperlin (Eds.): ASITA 2024, CCIS 2463, pp. 365–376, 2025.
https://doi.org/10.1007/978-3-031-91141-5_25

This approach promotes an intervention that is easily implementable and realizable at low costs. The proposed procedure could become a particularly useful practice for administrations seeking to revitalize specific urban areas where the use of dedicated funds is not feasible or where the preservation of environmental specificities prevents spatial modifications. An additional point of interest in this research is the experimentation conducted with students from the University of Paris-Saclay, which served as a particularly valuable test for the calibration and refinement of all phases of the procedure. What stands out as particularly interesting is the new dimension of urban regeneration, traditionally understood as a set of actions aimed at renewing the spatial context, which has often devolved into a generalized urban revamping.

2 Contextualizing ARS Project Objectives: A Literature Review

The concept of urban regeneration is still controverse and still makes the object of the scientific debate.

The initial urban renewal concept -essentially focused on the overall improvement of the physical image of cities- turns, over the years, into a process more attentive also to the social issue connected with the physical decline especially in the peripheric areas of the city. The real turning point occurred from the Nineties onwards, when the focus of regeneration concerns the multidimensional integration of the physical, social, economic, and environmental conditions of the city [1, 2]. The widespread adoption of the sustainability paradigm in its current form dealing with three dimensions (social, environmental and economic) contributed to this radical transition. The Sustainable Development Goals (SDG) of the Agenda 2030 underlined the importance of integration between economic, environmental and social issues (cfr. SDG11 "*sustainable cities and communities*"). Some scholars [3] have investigated the relationship between urban regeneration and SDG highlighting which type of regeneration interventions have the best performance in terms of sustainability. Other research [4–9] has indagated the scientific landscape on urban regeneration and its impacts through the lens of evaluation using bibliometric tools. The concept of urban regeneration encompasses a wide range of interconnected perspectives, such as social, cultural, ethical, legal, technical, and environmental generating also a new research line focused on the "adaptive reuse" [10] most connected with the deindustrialization phenomenon. Among scholars interested in the study of urban regeneration there are also those who underline the lack of research on collaborative decision-making approaches that is gaining attention only in recent few years [11].

Within the scientific debate, a shared point can be individualized in the acknowledgement that the involvement of the social component is central for the success of an urban regeneration process. Dos Santos Figueiredo et al. [12] developed a conceptual model to indicate the interaction between urban regeneration and social innovation articulated in three levels. The first level refers to the factors implied into the regeneration process (economic, environmental, social physical, governmental); the second level indicates the factors relied to the social aspects that promote the urban regeneration (social relations, network, collaboration, sustainability, social cohesion, management, scalability); the third level refers to the external effects of the interaction between social innovation and urban regeneration (human needs, quality of life, empowerment).

Since the 1990s, the relationship between decision-makers and social context has grown increasingly strategic. Following British examples, participative urban regeneration projects have proliferated, inspired by the governance model established in England and spreading across Europe and beyond. Research during this period has shifted to evaluating the effects of engagement and empowerment in decision-making processes, focusing on the efficiency of governance related to regeneration efforts. A significant part of the debate centers on finding a common definition for interventions aimed at reusing existing urban areas. This stems from the recognition that land, energy, and water are finite resources, making it imperative to move away from an "additive approach" to prioritize on revitalizing abandoned or underutilized urban spaces resulting from deindustrialization or misalignment with current city uses. Thus, if these conditions broadly describe the main changes occurred in the last thirty years, present cities are experimenting with methods, procedures, and actions to give "new life" and return to collective use those abandoned urban areas as "common good" [13, 14].

Another aspect that must be considered in this transition from the top-down decision processes to the bottom-up solutions for the general improvement of the urban spaces and their "return to life" for a common use, is the increasing demand for urban quality, despite definition of quality in an urban context is rather subjective and not easily definable. Many studies [15–17] analyzed the concept of quality associated with the urban context stating that to assess the quality of urban spaces it is necessary to consider a holistic approach that expands the sectorial perspective connected to the single terms such as urban environmental quality, livability, quality of life, and sustainability. Very interesting for the aims of our research is the reference to sensory urbanism [18], developed to challenge the ocular-centric focus of much research and practice in urban planning and design. This approach, in fact, allows for the relationship between the urban quality of spaces and the wellbeing of people who live in those spaces.

This is not new, if considering that in 2009 the Commission for Architecture and the Built Environment (CABE) [19] affirmed "Evidence increasingly suggests that the wider environment can reduce stress, encourage exercise and promote good health" (CABE, 2009, p. 4) while the World Health Organization defined health as "a state of complete physical, mental, and social well-being and not merely the absence of disease or infirmity" [20].

The complexity of the relationship between the quality of urban spaces and wellbeing is evident but it is not impossible to find out a procedure for activating urban regeneration processes using intangible tools.

This can be indicated as one of the main objectives of the ARS project. A key objective of the ARS project, in fact, is to recognize that a regenerative urban process should consider also the perceptions of residents, enhancing the transmission of a site's evocative memory that would otherwise be lost. In this regard, the project refers to the use of soundscape as means to improve the perception of natural/artificial elements that concur to the definition of the regenerative project. Yang et al. [21] examined the interrelationships between soundscapes and human connections to place, with a focus on the contrasting perspectives of residents and visitors. They found the pivotal role of soundscapes in shaping human-place relationships, noting that residents and visitors showed a shared inclination towards natural sounds, while a significant divide emerged in the feeling of place attachment: compared to visitors, residents showed a heightened sense of belonging and uniqueness.

For the targets of this research, it is important to differentiate the sentiment of belonging with the feeling evocated by soundscape. Differences between the attachment and the wellbeing of residents have been also investigated in scientific debate demonstrating the importance of soundscape in significantly influencing individuals' perceptions and emotional connections to a specific location [22–25]. In those studies, soundscape has been recognized as "the acoustic environment as perceived or experienced and/or understood by a person or people, in context" [23]. Some scholars [26, 27] also demonstrated the positive impacts of soundscapes on human behavior. For instance, the presence of music in urban open spaces can act to prolong people's stay in a venue, while natural sounds can enhance social interactions within groups in urban parks.

In the wake of this line of research, this study proposes revitalizing urban areas by creating unique augmented soundscapes.

3 Materials and Methods

This research posits that constructing a sound landscape forms the foundation for regenerating and enhancing urban spaces. This process can be achieved through low-impact, bottom-up socio-functional actions, including participatory initiatives involving local urban communities.

The methodology unfolds in several stages, beginning with the theoretical classification of sonic characteristics and physical elements within urban spaces.

The theoretical framework distinguishes between negative sound emissions ("acoustic entropy" or noise) and positive sound emissions ("urban euphony").

Acoustic entropy represents unpleasant sounds pervasive in urban environments, which can adversely affect human health, especially with prolonged exposure [28–30]. Conversely, urban euphony refers to sounds that enhance spatial usability and can include natural elements (e.g., water, wind, trees) or artificial sounds (e.g., music) designed to enrich sensory and physical experiences in urban spaces.

These sounds can transform locations such as historic landmarks and cultural sites into attractions for both residents and tourists, with innovative technologies like augmented and mixed reality further amplifying these effects. The workflow in Fig. 1 can help to better understand the project steps.

During the sound recognition phase, the association between physical and sensory environments is crucial, allowing designers to craft soundscapes informed by the physical elements of a space.

Sound markers that can be identified in an urban space may include:

- Natural Elements, like rivers and trees.
- Artificial Elements, like objects specifically designed to produce sound.
- Digital elements, such as augmented sound, combined via technology.

Euphonic content may consist of:

- Human Voice: Spoken, sung, recited, whispered.
- Nature sounds: Wind, rain, flowing water, etc.

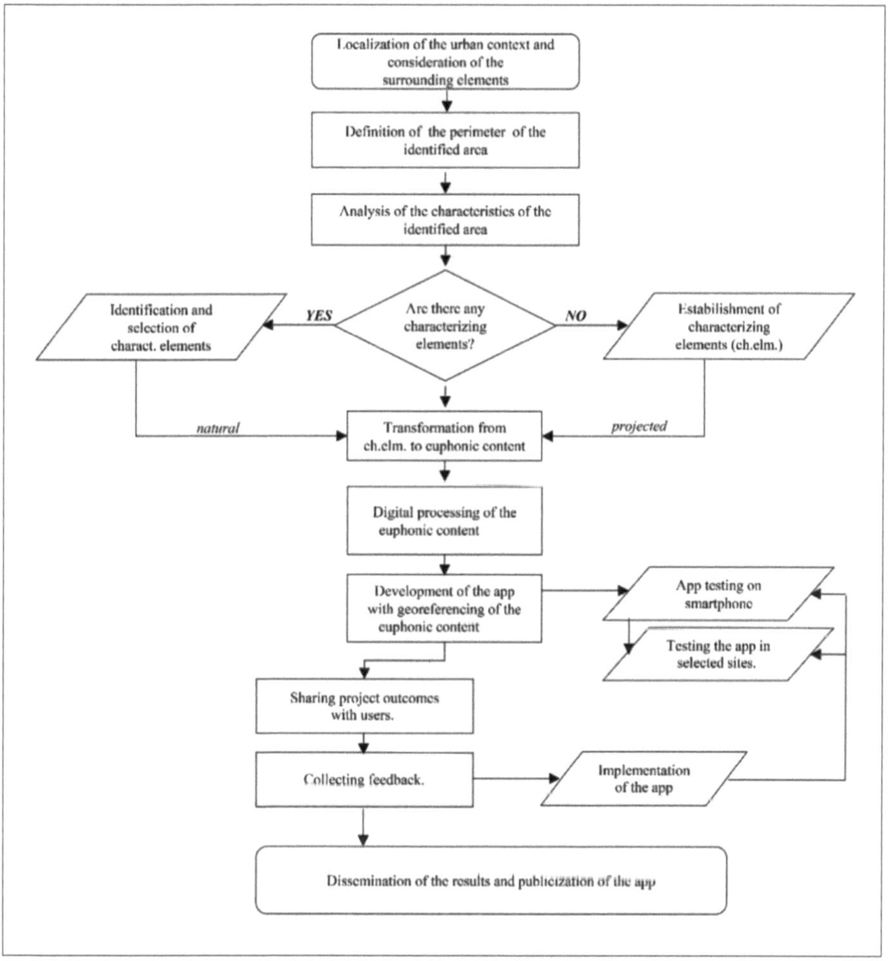

Fig. 1. The methodological structure of the ARS project

– Musical melody: specifically composed.

These elements contribute to designing a conceptual map, highlighting silent, intrinsic sounds, induced sounds, and composed sounds. Silent elements, like arches, require designed soundscapes, while intrinsic and induced sounds may be captured, processed, or enhanced for immersive experiences. Sound installations, digital and physical, such as kinetic sculptures or interactive instruments, further enrich these spaces.

4 Application and Testing: The Case Study of La Biévre in Cachan

4.1 Framing the Urban Environment

Cachan is a small city in the Ile-de-France region belonging to the Paris metropolitan area and to the Métropole du Grand Paris project. It is in the Department Val-de-Marne and has a surface of 2.78 km^2 with a population of about 30.000 inhabitants (2023). It is very close to Paris (2 km distance). In the territorial division of the Métropole du Grand Paris (Greater Paris Metropolis), Cachan is in the current territorial public establishment Grand-Orly Seine Bièvre (GOSB) that is the second largest territory of the Metropolis, after Paris, with 680,000 inhabitants. Its history is very linked to the institution of École Normale Supérieure, located in Cachan after the second world war, that gained to the city the title of university pole in the south of the Paris region. At the beginning of the twenty-first century Cachan is part of a large urban requalification project mainly focused on the realization of green public spaces and public services.

The 2024 Olympic Games marked the beginning of the requalification of the La Bièvre promenade, a long river that runs through Cachan and flows into the Seine in Paris. This area is significant in Cachan's urban history. Historically, artisans like tanners and launderers used the Bièvre river for waste disposal and skin cleaning, leading to severe pollution and the river being treated as an open sewer in the 18th century. Despite its rich historical and natural identity, the river had been underutilized and deemed unhealthy, prompting efforts to revive its ecological and social importance as urban development progressed. At present, in Cachan, the Biévre is partially visible again in pleasant harmony with the surrounding urban context (see Fig. 2).

4.2 The Workshop in the University Institute of Technology in Cachan

A preliminary test of the ARS methodology was conducted during a workshop at the University Institute of Technology (IUT) in Cachan in March 2024. Students from Sound and Image Technologies course were invited to choose an urban site in which they should have applied their own idea of urban regeneration using sounds. The phase of choosing the urban area was conducted under the guide of experts in urban planning (authors) after discussion and debate during the workshop and led to the proposal to apply urban regeneration concepts to the promenade of La Biévre. In a second phase, students were invited to design spatialized soundscapes to evoke the valley's historical activities, such as tanning and laundering, recreating the vibrant auditory scene of the past.

Hence, the selection of the urban area, notable for its unique natural features, stemmed from a perceptual analysis conducted with workshop students. It was deemed ideal for a regeneration project focused on enhancing soundscapes to enrich the location's appeal and attract both residents and visitors. The ARS workshop aimed to create a spatialized soundscape that evokes the historical use of the Biévre river by tanners and launderers prior to its burial. The goal was to revive the vibrant activity of the area through sound, recreating the continuous noise of materials as they were processed, the human voices, the clatter of tools, and the energy generated by human presence and activity. To make this possible it was needed to project a specific application that could associate sounds and ambience together offering users an "augmented dimension" in which sound and history of the place intertwine.

Fig. 2. The area of La Bievre (bounded by a red line) in Cachan in two different years (2000 on the left and 2025 on the right). The watercourse is highlighted with a blue line (source: Google Earth).

4.3 The Augmented Reality Application

The final phase of the ARS workshop (see Fig. 3) involved creating an augmented reality audio application for urban spaces. This application aims to overlay digital audio content onto the real world, enhancing the urban context and enabling a reimagined use of urban spaces.

The AR audio application was developed by the students in Unity, using AR Foundation's tools and Google's ARCore framework for using the application via android smartphones.

The app is designed to be marker based, which means that it exploits AR Foundation's image tracking tools, which allow AR content to be activated after framing an image that works as a marker. Thus, it was important that students in their project not only determine the best position for the marker in the study area but also design a marker graphically appropriate for the correct functioning of the application, because the app recognizes the marker and works in a stable manner (i.e. it does not lose the AR content if user moves away from the marker), if the image of the marker respects some characteristics such as a black and white pattern with geometric references.

Another important step for the development of the app was the choice and design of the sound content that students wanted to associate with the elements they identified as characterizing the urban context of the study area. Students were tasked with creating diverse audio content, including sounds (human, animal, natural, and artificial) and music, that not only described but also explained urban elements, effectively narrating them and providing new insights. Divided into small work teams, the students developed the app using a Unity programming environment. During this phase, students learned to use Unity programming to create a virtual replica of the study area. This replica integrated

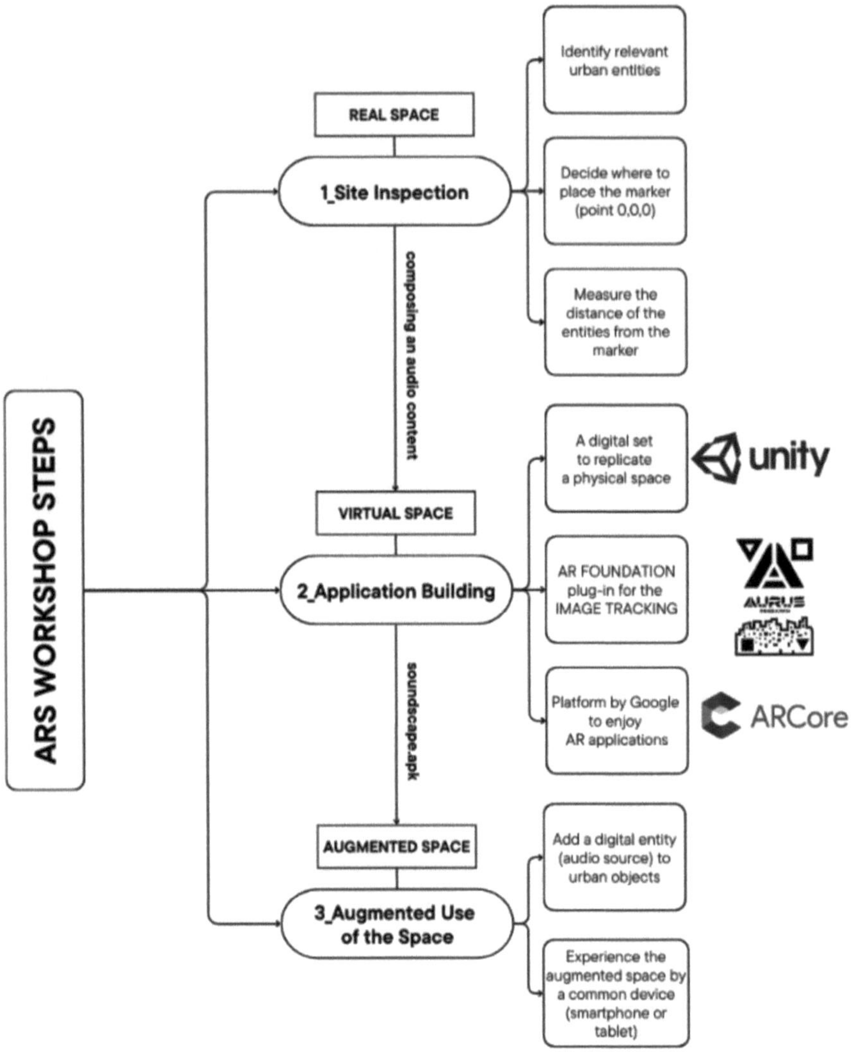

Fig. 3. ARS workshop's workflow. During the workshop three main phases were conducted with the aim of attaining the development of the app for the augmented soundscape of the promenade of Bievre

the identified urban elements with a specifically reconstructed 3D object, which students linked to the designed audio tracks. The audio tracks were set in a loop, with a linear roll of, and the maximum distance beyond which the audio would no longer be audible was defined. Then the image designed as marker was set as AR tracked image and finally the app was exported in.apk format for Android devices supporting ARCore. The final step of the workshop has been the text of the functioning of the projected app in the study area. Students tested their app on-site using their smartphones, moving freely through the urban area while listening to audio tracks they created for each chosen representative element. The application allows users to listen to audio content by approaching the associated urban elements, with spatialized audio that increases in volume as users get closer and decreases as users move away.

The created soundscape merges the elements in augmented reality and euphonic sounds allowing users to enjoy the urban space in a different way in which they have an active role. This result, that certainly needs to be implemented, can be considered as a first step for the active use of both urban spaces and technologies from users. It can also represent a tool to enhance the appeal of urban public spaces which often indicate the overall quality of life in cities.

5 Results and Discussion

The proposition explored in this study was that the use of sounds and augmented reality could help to the diffusion of non-invasive procedure for the requalification of urban spaces making them attractive for residents and tourists. In this sense the ARS project intended to pursue the possibility of Soft Urban Action aimed at transforming urban places without generating conflicts as the involvement of locals in the processes of requalification assumes a central role. The main question of the research has been whether the use of technologies, particularly referring to the use of augmented reality, could be appropriate in proposing a requalification design that could also move using sounds making urban spaces a special site in which the ancient traditions of the city's history could be rediscovered.

Related to these larger objectives, the most significant outcome of the ARS is its easy of realization through an app that can be used on smartphones and for this can have a large diffusion and utilization. The ease of application is linked to a complex structure that requires knowledge of the urban transformation processes. Identifying elements that effectively convey the project's message (characterizing elements) demands a detailed site analysis, for instance including interviews or surveys with locals to grasp the significance of these elements. This stage highlights the necessity of having different expertise for the success of the proposal.

A particular aspect that the ARS project has considered refers to the effort to define educational/training path to transfer the methodology. In this sense, the workshop in Cachan has been an important moment for the project to be tested both as training and as evidence for multidisciplinary and collaborative methods.

The limits of the project mainly stand in being the project itself at a first stage of development as the initial idea developed within a larger project founded by the Italian Ministry of Research of research (INSITE project) focused on the territorial promotion for inner areas - characterized by geo-paleontological sites - also using augmented reality and sounds for their revitalization and basing on interdisciplinary and multidisciplinary approach. Further development of the methodology must be foreseen also considering suggestions and results coming from the first application in Cachan.

6 Conclusions

New technologies have a growing central role in many fields and in everyday life. It is becoming urgent to have knowledge in using their potentialities to improve performance and decisions concerning the urban context.

The conscious adoption of new technologies for activating processes of city regeneration, thus, is a field of great interest for scholars of urban phenomena, experts in innovative technologies, and local administrators. Developing methodologies to quickly define appropriate actions for enhancing urban spaces, which are underused or even considered on the edge of the city, is one of the tasks that should increasingly characterize urban research. Techniques and procedures that can be implemented in projects adding digital sound elements to spatial contexts, uniquely enhancing their use need to be developed.

This study tried to demonstrate that urban regeneration can also be achieved through a limited investments. The ARS project aims at divulgating the potentialities of this concept, offering both a methodology and a technical procedure for urban enhancement using augmented reality with spatialized sound.

The workshop at the University of Paris-Saclay served as an initial opportunity to test this methodology while engaging students in a project focused on urban requalification through augmented soundscapes.

Acknowledgments. This work was developed within the context of the *Progetto di Rilevante Interesse Internazionale* INSITE-INtegrated Shared knowledge: from geo-paleontological herItage to present TErritorial challenges (www.insiteprin2022.org). Although the paper is the result of a joint effort, R.A. La Rocca contributed to the drafting of the paragraph 2; R. Fistola edited the paragraph 3, while I. Zingariello and F. Fabbri drafted the contents of the paragraph 4. The introduction, results and conclusions were written jointly.

References

1. Zheng, H.W., Shen, G.Q., Wang, H.: A review of recent studies on sustainable urban renewal. Habitat Int. **41**, 272–279 (2014)
2. Roberts, P.: The evolution, definition and purpose of urban regeneration. In: Urban Regeneration: A Handbook, vol. 1, pp. 9–36 (2000)
3. Zhao, X., Hu, Y., Xia, N., Li, M., Chen, D., Xu, Y.: Urban regeneration and SDGs assessment based on multi-source data: practical experience from Shenzhen, China. Ecol. Ind. **165**, 112138 (2024)
4. Cerreta, M., La Rocca, L.: Urban regeneration processes and social impact: a literature review to explore the role of evaluation. In: 21st International Conference on Computational Science and Its Applications, ICCSA 2021, Cagliari, Italy, 13–16 September 2021, Proceedings, Part VI 21, pp. 167–182. Springer (2021)
5. Bielinskas, V., Burinskienė, M., Podviezko, A.: Choice of abandoned territories conversion scenario according to MCDA methods. J. Civ. Eng. Manag. **24**(1), 79–92 (2018). https://doi.org/10.3846/jcem.2018.303
6. Calderini, M., Chiodo, V., Michelucci, F.V.: The social impact investment race: toward an interpretative framework. Eur. Bus. Rev. **30**(1), 66–81 (2018). https://doi.org/10.1108/EBR-10-2016-0134

7. Pirlone, F., Spadaro, I., Candia, S.: Metropolitan governance for territorial cohesion. TeMA J. Land Use Mob. Environ. **10**(2), 213–228 (2017). https://doi.org/10.6092/1970-9870/4956
8. Fistola R., La Rocca R.A.: From smart city to artificial intelligence city. Envisaging the future of urban planning. TeMA J. Land Use Mob. Environ. **17**(3), 411–422 (2024). https://doi.org/10.6093/1970-9870/11081
9. Fistola, R., Gaglione, F., Zingariello, I.: The small smart city: renewable energy sources in little town of Italy. TeMA J. Land Use Mob. Environ. **16**(1), 183–199 (2023). https://doi.org/10.6093/1970-9870/9850
10. Vardopoulos, I.: Adaptive reuse for sustainable development and land use: a multivariate linear regression analysis estimating key determinants of public perceptions. Heritage **6**(2), 809–828 (2023)
11. Wang, H., Zhao, Y., Gao, X., Gao, B.: Collaborative decision-making for urban regeneration: a literature review and bibliometric analysis. Land Use Policy **107**, 105479 (2021)
12. dos Santos Figueiredo, Y. D., Prim, M.A., Dandolini, G.A.: Urban regeneration in the light of social innovation: a systematic integrative literature review. Land Use Policy **113**, 105873 (2022)
13. Hussain, W., Kohn, M.: The common good (2018)
14. Jaede, M.: The concept of the common good. PSRP Working Paper, 8 (2017)
15. Adams, M.: Quality of urban spaces and wellbeing. In: Wellbeing: A Complete Reference Guide, pp. 1–21 (2014)
16. Pacione, M.: Urban liveability: a review. Urban Geogr. **11**(1), 1–30 (1990)
17. Porteous, J.D.: Design with people: the quality of the urban environment. Environ. Behav. **3**(2), 155–177 (1971)
18. Globa, A., Wang, R., Beza, B.: Sensory urbanism and placemaking exploring virtual reality and the creation of place. Deakin University. Conference Contribution (2019). https://hdl.handle.net/10536/DRO/DU:30128291
19. CABE (Commission for Architecture and the Built Environment): Future health: Sustainable places for health and well-being. CABE, London (2009)
20. World Health Organization Constitution of the World Health Organization (Forty-fifth edition, supplement, October) (2006). http://www.who.int/governance/eb/who_constitution_en.pdf
21. Yang, L., Liu, J., Albert, C., Guo, X.: Exploring the effects of soundscape perception on place attachment: a comparative study of residents and tourists. Appl. Acoust. **222**, 110048 (2024).https://doi.org/10.1016/j.apacoust.2024.110048
22. Kaltenborn, B.P., Bjerke, T.: Associations between landscape preferences and place attachment: a study in Røros. Southern Norway Landscape Res. **27**(4), 381–396 (2002). https://doi.org/10.1080/01426390220000023943
23. ISO: Acoustics—Soundscape—Part 1: Definition and conceptual framework. International Organization for Standardization, Geneva (2014)
24. Jeon J.Y., Jo H.I.: Effects of audio-visual interactions on soundscape and landscape perception and their influence on satisfaction with the urban environment. Build Environ. **169** (2020). https://doi.org/10.1016/j.buildenv.2019.106544
25. Jo H.I., Jeon J.Y.: Urban soundscape categorization based on individual recognition, perception, and assessment of sound environments. Landsc. Urban Plan. **2021**, 216 (2021). https://doi.org/10.1016/j.landurbplan.2021.104241
26. Aletta, F., Lepore, F., Kostara-Konstantinou, E., Kang, J., Astolfi, A.: An experimental study on the influence of soundscapes on people's behaviour in an open public space. Appl. Sci. **6**(10), 276 (2016). https://www.mdpi.com/2076-3417/6/10/276
27. Chen, X., Kang, J.: Natural sounds can encourage social interactions in urban parks. Landsc. Urban Plan. **239**, 104870 (2023). https://www.sciencedirect.com/science/article/pii/S0169204623001895. https://doi.org/10.1016/j.landurbplan.2023.104870

28. Brown, A.L., Van Kamp, I.: WHO environmental noise guidelines for the European region: a systematic review of transport noise interventions and their impacts on health. Int. J. Environ. Res. Public Health **14**(8), 873 (2017)
29. Clark, C., Paunovic, K.: WHO Environmental Noise Guidelines for the European region: a systematic review on environmental noise and quality of life, wellbeing and mental health. Int. J. Environ. Res. Public Health **15**(11), 2400 (2018)
30. Flanagan, E., Malmqvist, E., Oudin, A., Persson, K.S., Ohlsson, J.A., Mattisson, K.: Health impact assessment of road traffic noise exposure based on different densification scenarios in Malmö, Sweden. Environ. Int. **174**, 107867 (2023)

A Novel Spatial Unit to Improve Representation in Crime Mapping: The Toronto, Canada Example

Yule Lu and Stefania Bertazzon(✉)

University of Calgary, Calgary, AB T2N 1N4, Canada
bertazzs@ucalgary.ca

Abstract. With the development of GIS, and advancement of transparency and open data policy over the years, maps have become an increasingly important tool for communication and distribution of crime related information between police departments and the general public. However, current crime maps exhibit major shortcomings stemming from the methods that yield them. Among them, the use of traditional spatial units, i.e., points and areal spatial units in crime maps has long stood and appears to be an overlooked problem. Conversely, research on novel spatial units has been going on for years, and traditional point-style and areal-style symbolization have been criticized for a long time, e.g., for privacy concerns in point-style maps and calculating crime statistics using population in corresponding visualization in areal spatial units. Nonetheless, crime maps produced by police departments of some major Canadian cities are yet to adopt any novel spatial unit.

This study proposes a novel spatial unit: the street segment, to address some problems of existing crime maps using traditional point and areal spatial units. Our results suggest that using the street segment as spatial unit to present crime statistics mitigates some shortcomings of current crime maps, like overgeneralization and privacy concerns. It provides opportunities like Crime Prevention Through Environmental Design (CPTED) and Route Planning and enhances the practical functionality of crime maps by assisting the general public in daily decision-making.

Keywords: Crime Mapping · Street Segment · Spatial Unit · Toronto

1 Introduction

Improper use of web-maps in disseminating crime information could result in inefficiency, misinterpretation, and potential privacy breaches. This may be exacerbated by the lack of expertise in the GIS field by the general public. Merely visualizing raw data or displaying total crime numbers does not address this issue, as map readers may not be able to relate these numbers to the local context. For example, a higher total crime count in a large community does not necessarily indicate a greater danger than a smaller community with fewer crimes; factors like area size and population are important. Hence, enabling direct comparisons is key to preventing over- or under-estimating the risk of victimization.

E. Borgogno-Mondino and P. Zamperlin (Eds.): ASITA 2024, CCIS 2463, pp. 377–388, 2025.
https://doi.org/10.1007/978-3-031-91141-5_26

Additional concerns in crime mapping, arising from privacy concerns, have been recognized for decades [1] current crime maps do not display location explicitly like the GEODASH crime map [2] by the Vancouver Police Department and TPS Crime map [3] by the Toronto Police Service, however, the privacy issues persist through re-identification risk. Re-identification risk refers to the possibility of individuals or groups being identified from sensitive datasets, even if they were not explicitly identified within them [4]. Even though the TPS Crime Map and GEODASH Crime Map do not explicitly disclose the addresses of incidents, masking data before map release does not eliminate the risk of re-identification[5, 6]. In the context of crime maps, re-identifying victims or vulnerable areas can have serious implications. Criminals can exploit maps prone to re-identification; for example, victims of burglaries may fear being perceived as easy targets, particularly in areas or addresses that have been repeatedly victimized. Consequently, victims may choose not to report crimes to avoid being re-victimized [7].

Some studies suggest re-engineering the original location from masked maps is possible [4, 8]. Therefore, using higher-level aggregation instead of point-style visualization may be beneficial. However, it is difficult to re-engineer a vulnerable victim's location from maps aggregated at the community or neighbourhood level, as seen in Wellbeing Toronto [9] and Calgary's Community Crime Map [10]. Aggregation, as an alternative to the point-style visualization approach, may involve a loss of detailed information that would aid in day-to-day decision-making. This approach also raises concerns such as the Modifiable Areal Unit Problem (MAUP) and ecological fallacy, which can introduce bias due to information loss from aggregation [11]. MAUP occurs when different aggregation methods produce different results, while ecological fallacy assumes that the characteristics of a group apply to every individual.

A standardized representation of crime incidents on the street level could enable more nuanced policy and aid implementation. For example, Crime Prevention Through Environmental Design (CPTED) is a practice that achieves crime prevention by altering the physical environment, especially in urban areas. CPTED focuses on the potential of the physical environment for crime prevention rather than on socioeconomics, which is a more common focus. The first proponent of CPTED, Jeffery [12], argues that the physical environment could provide opportunities for crimes. While Piroozfar et al. [13] reported criticisms to CPTED referring to the high cost of reengineering the physical environment, they also noted the lack of academic research that could back this criticism and compare direct and indirect costs of crime; hence, CPTED could very well be the most cost-effective way to combat crime. Street segment or other micro-unit analysis could facilitate CPTED, by providing analytical results at finer resolution, hence disclosing a closer relationship between crime statistics and the physical environment, especially when street segments are the selected spatial unit. With finer analysis results, the cost of CPTED could potentially be reduced, and resources could be better allocated by prioritizing crime hotspots rather than wasting resources on larger, safer areas. This is an important practical advantage of the analysis and representation of crime at micro-level spatial unit like street segments.

Standardizing crime statistics on the street level also enables crime-aware route planning. Route planning is a well-researched field of study, and many studies have discussed different types of route planning [14, 15]. However, the use of crime statistics for network analysis and route planning is less researched and there are hardly any applications for daily use by the general public. Crime statistics on the street level could be included in the cost travel analysis as a risk factor or in the design of dedicated route planning that analyzes the optimum risk-distance to output the least distance travel while minimizing exposure to crime risk. Much like police portal planning [16], instead of planning toward high-risk areas, it helps the general public to avoid high-risk areas.

With this study, we demonstrate the representation of crime statistics on a novel spatial unit, street segments, compared to more traditional areal units. The study discusses (1) the representation of crime statistics, i.e. raw number of crime and crime rate on street segments, and (2) the implementation of a street segment standardization approach to address the limitations of point-style and aggregated-style visualizations of crime statistics. Toronto downtown is used as an example.

2 Methods

2.1 Overview

The flowchart presented in Fig. 1 summarizes the methodology of the development of crime maps utilizing the novel spatial unit and traditional areal units, as well as the comparison between maps.

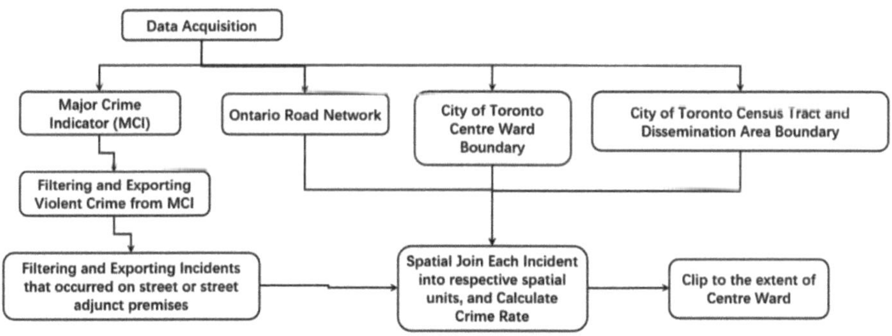

Fig. 1. Methodology Flowchart

2.2 Study Area

The study focuses on the Centre Ward of Toronto, depicted in Fig. 2, chosen for its urbanization level and high crime concentration. As of 2021, the ward covers 5.84 km^2 with a population of 116,930, i.e., the 5th most populated [17] and smallest of all wards, resulting in a population density much higher than the city average. In 2022, the Centre Ward recorded 1621 crimes categorized as Major Crime Indicators (MCI) representing 8.85% of all MCI records, which is the highest among all wards in Toronto. Over 1200 of these crimes were violent, in the Assault and Robbery categories [18].

Fig. 2. Toronto Centre Ward

2.3 Data: Sources and Selection

Datasets utilized in this study were: (1) Major Crime Indicator (MCI), (2) Ontario Road Network, (3) City of Toronto Ward Boundary, (4) Census Tracts (CT) Boundary and population by CT, (5) Dissemination Areas (DA) Boundary and population by DA. The Ward Boundaries dataset, sourced from the City of Toronto [19], comprises vector polygons representing individual wards. The Ontario Road Network dataset, obtained from Statistic Canada [20], encompasses all roads in Ontario organized into segments, represented as line features. The CT and DA boundary, also their corresponding population data came from Statistic Canada [19, 20] as well, which will be later clipped to the extent of the Centre Ward. The Major Crime Indicators (MCI) dataset, provided by the Toronto Police Services [18], comprises crime records that include detailed information of each incident, summarized in Table 1. This information was used to select the study year 2022, the crime location, i.e., crimes that occurred on streets, excluding crimes that happened in houses and apartments for those premises are rather confined and private, and select violent crimes, which are assault and robbery, according to the Toronto Police Service definition [21]. For the resulting record selection, incident coordinates are used to pinpoint the incident for further aggregation.

Table 1. Major Crime Indicator Important Fields

Field Name	Description
OCC_YEAR	Year which incident occurred
PREMISES_TYPE	Premise type of each incident
MCI_CATEGORY	Crime type, example: Assault, Break and Enter
X	Longitude
Y	Latitude

2.4 Spatial Operation and Crime Rates Calculation

The Ontario Road Network and the MCI data, census tracts, dissemination areas and MCI data should be integrated before performing crime rate calculation; however, the MCI data posed some problems, as the coordinates of each record do not correspond to the original occurrence, and multiple records may have the exact same coordinates (typically at intersections). This happens when police departments release crime data publicly and, due to serious privacy concerns, they conceal crime locations to reduce re-identification and re-victimization risks [5, 7]. Therefore, assigning an incident to a particular street segment/DA/CT may be inappropriate, and crime incidents were spatially joined to every street segment/DA/CT within 50/100/150 m.

The typical method of mitigating the effect of population size on the number of crimes is calculating the crime rate, which is the ratio between the number of crimes and the population size, the common equation [22, 23] is as follows:

$$Crime\ Rate\ per\ capita = \frac{RC}{R} * \mathrm{N} \tag{1}$$

RC is a Registered Crime (Or reported crime).

R is the number of residents in the area of interest.

N is the number of residents/population (100, 1,000 or 10,000) for standardization.

The crime rates calculation for census tracts and dissemination areas followed the above equation by rationing between violent crime incidents recorded in MCI and the population of each census tract/dissemination area, then standardized by 100.

However, no population data publicly available corresponds with street segments. Thus, to calculate the crime rate on street segments, there must be a replacement for the population in the equation. The length of each street segment is decided to replace the population in the crime rate equation, alter the equation as follows:

$$\text{Crime Rate per Length} = \frac{RC}{S} * SL \tag{2}$$

RC is a Registered Crime (Or reported crime) on each street segment.

S is the length of each street segment.

SL is the length of street segments (100, 1,000 or 10,000 m) for standardization.

Equation 2 replaces population at both the denominator and standardizer with street segment lengths, and the crime rates will be standardized by 100 m.

The calculation of crime rates will first be performed on the entire City of Toronto, before clipping to the extent of the study area, the Centre Ward. This sequence is to prevent edge effect by first performing spatial operation and crime rates calculation first on a much larger extent than the study area.

3 Results

3.1 Crime Rate Descriptive Statistics: Traditional vs. Proposed Spatial Units

Descriptive statistics of Crime rates in CTs, DAs, and street segments are shown in Table 2, as well as the number of entries of each spatial unit within the Centre Ward. The number of street segments is manyfold higher than the number of CTs and DAs, with 1348 segments, compared to 131 DAs and 26 CTs. No CTs exhibit zero crime rate, while 2 DAs and 508 street segments do.

Table 2. Descriptive Statistic of Crime Rates

	Entries	Min	Median	Mean	Max	Standard Deviation
CTs (per 100 pop)	26	3.6	17.6	22.14	64.69	16.33
DAs (per 100 pop)	131	0	4.08	6.55	135.21	12.71
Street Segments (per 100 m)	1348	0	1.68	6.04	334.4	16.37

3.2 Crime Rate Visualization: Traditional vs. Proposed Spatial Units

Figure 3 shows the crime rates in CTs and DAs, overlayed with crime rates on street segments. The spatial pattern of crime rates in these three different spatial units is similar: high crime rate in the center and the west side of the Centre Ward. DAs, with their finer spatial resolution, can show crime rate variation within CTs, since a single CT normally contains multiple DAs. The variation in crime rates is much higher in DAs than in CTs, as shown in Table 2. The spatial pattern of crime rate on street segments is similar to that shown in Fig. 3: high values concentrated in the ward's center and west side. Importantly, in the crime rate calculation, the standardizer used in CTs and DAs is different from the one used in street segments; thus, the overlay is not meant to compare the value of crime rates across the three units directly, but, rather, to illustrate that crime rate on street segments can vary within DAs, like it varies through DAs within CTs. Hence, street segments can show variations of crime rates even within DA, demonstrating the potential of street segments in presenting crime statistics at even finer spatial resolution than traditional areal spatial units. Figure 4 shows crime rates in the Toronto Centre Ward by street segments with close-ups of the higher crime rate concentration areas. Street segments with high crime rates cluster near the famous Yonge-Dundas Square, also home to a major shopping center. The segments of Yonge Street located within Centre Ward feature mostly restaurants, stores, supermarkets, and fast-food outlets, and no residential areas. Beyond Yonge-Dundas Square, other parts of Yonge Street and Dundas Street feature heavy vehicle and pedestrian traffic. Church Street, also rich in street-side stores and restaurants, hosts nightclubs and bars, resulting in heavy traffic, both day and night.

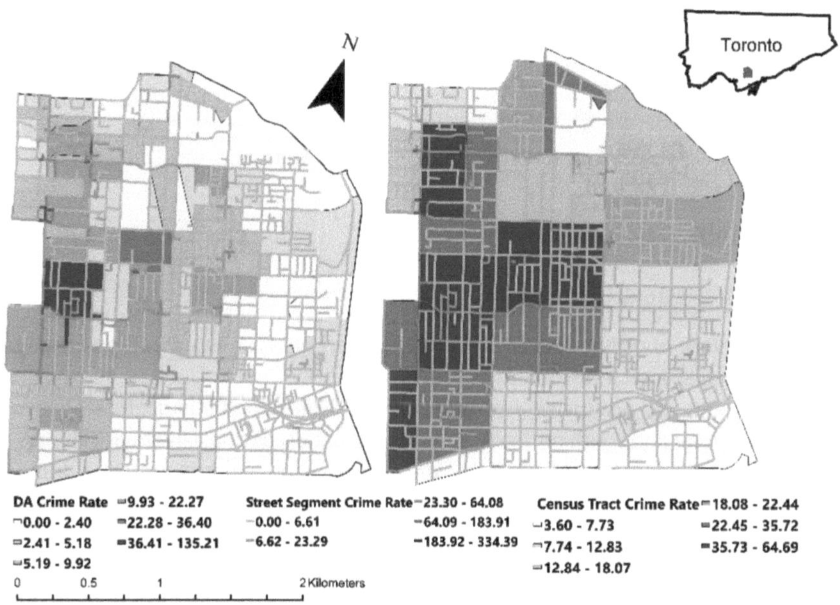

Fig. 3. Crime Rates in CTs and DAs with Street Segments Overlay

Fig. 4. Crime Rates in Street Segments

4 Discussion

4.1 Spatial Pattern of Crime Rates

The spatial pattern of crime rates in street segments (Fig. 4) shows that high crime rates are concentrated around a few major streets (i.e., Yonge, Queen, Dundas, and Wellesley Street) in the west and northwest part of the Centre Ward, gradually decreasing towards the north, northeast and south portions. This spatial pattern is consistent with studies that found associations between higher crime concentration and major roads. High crime rate areas lie within the largest and busiest entertainment and commercial areas of Toronto, like other studies [24, 25] suggesting that commercial and entertainment areas exhibit higher crime risk than other places. The north and northeast areas portions of the Ward, where crime rates are lower, are mostly residential or parks. While residential areas may be less attractive to crimes like assault and robbery, some studies suggest public green spaces and urban parks may also attract crime [26, 27]. These studies suggest that, in the Toronto core, crime concentrations in green spaces and parks pale compared to those in entertainment and commercial districts.

4.2 Assumptions and Limitations

This study calculated crime rates over 2022, overlooking temporal variations in criminal incidents.[28–34] suggest that the yearly scale masks fluctuations at monthly, daily, and hourly scales. For instance, burglary peaks in winter months, while robbery, shoplifting, and drug-related crimes peak in summer months. Disregarding temporal and seasonal variations may weaken the crime rates, especially for cross-comparisons.

An inherent problem that affects the accuracy of crime rates and other crime statistics based on public data is the poor locational accuracy and high location uncertainty of MCI data, stemming from the lack of information on the original crime location. This could alter the perception of safety vs. danger conveyed by crime rates and other crime statistics. Also, poorly located MCI data could potentially aggravate the MAUP. With large spatial areal units, like communities or municipal districts, slight misallocation, e.g., a 50-m shift from mid-segment on the closest intersection in recording an incident, may be a minor problem, potentially further reduced by larger-scale aggregation. Conversely, such differences may have more serious impacts on small spatial units like street segments, like in cases of segments 12 m long and shorter.

This study, like others of its kind, relies solely on reported crime data, therefore missing out on unreported crimes, which are not uncommon. The decision not to report a crime may result from several reasons: Asiama & Zhong [35] suggest that victims may choose not to report crimes to avoid disclosing the circumstances of their occurrence. For example, Masucci and Langton [36] suggest that the hate crimes in United States are unreported in mass, while Semukhina [37] investigates the reasons for not reporting crimes in Volgograd, Russia. Fohring [38] suggests that people in deprivation are less likely to report crime and at higher risk of criminal victimization, and the most at-risk of victimization population may overlap with those who are least willing to report crimes This finding undermines the validity of using police crime record; however, unreported crime is a dilemma that has virtually no solution when dealing with crime data. Thus, even though the problem of unreported crime is nearly impossible to properly address, its impact and limitation on reported crime data cannot be ignored.

4.3 Rationale for Street Segments

In this study, crime rates on street segments show significant variation within other areal units, and most crimes were concentrated on a few segments, and the majority of other segments only have very low or zero crime rates; these findings are consistent with other research [39–41]. While the street segment is a less researched spatial unit, researchers have pointed out the value and benefits of employing such spatial units [42]. On the other hand, academics have criticized the areal spatial unit and the corresponding population as standardizer in crime statistics calculations. Andresen [43, 44] pointed out the different roles of ambient population vs. residential population in different crimes, and the ambient population is the estimation of the population of an area over 24 h. The ambient population model produced a better fit for certain types of crime, and the residential population model was superior for other types of crime. This suggests that the potentially inconsistent results in crime statistics while using population as the standardizer, and compared to constantly changing population, street segments' length is a much less changed feature, which provides temporal stability. Weisburd [40] suggests that only a few streets drive the crime rate in an area. This characteristic is also shown in this study: within an area with a high crime rate, only a few segments have a high crime rate, and others have very low or even zero crime rate, suggesting areal spatial units are often overgeneralizing and street segments as a spatial unit could provide detailed information.

Despite being used rarely [45, 46], street segments as a spatial unit in crime mapping have shown great potential, offering a middle ground between point-style symbolization and areal aggregation, providing a more local focus, more nuanced information, and potentially mitigating ecological fallacy. Also, street segments have coarser spatial resolution than points, naturally embedding additional masking of the original location of incidents, reducing the risk of privacy problems compared to point-style maps.

5 Conclusion

This study explored and discussed the potential of street segments as a spatial unit in crime statistic calculation and representation This goal was achieved by (i) calculating using street segments and their length, and (ii) representing crime rates in street segments and two different areal spatial units, census tracts and dissemination areas, and by comparing the visualization of crime rates in street segments vs. areal spatial units. This study highlighted the benefits of utilizing street segments in crime statistics visualization. These benefits include facilitating further research, policy-making and practical implementation. However, this study also recognizes some disadvantages and limitations of using street segments. In summary, using street segments as spatial units and/or standardizers is a compromise between areal aggregated maps and point style maps in terms of representation and provides different advantages and disadvantages compared to using population as standardizer and areal spatial units in visualization in terms of crime statistics calculations and representation.

Author Contributions. Conceptualization, Y. L.; Formal analysis, Y. L.; Methodology, Y. L.; Supervision, S. B.; Validation, Y. L. and S. B.; Visualization, Y. L.; Writing—original draft, Y. L.; Writing—review and editing, Y. L. and S. B.

References

1. Burrough, P., Craglia, M., Masser, I., Rhind, D.: Decision makers' perspectives on European geographic information policy issues. Trans. GIS **2**, 61–71 (1997). https://doi.org/10.1111/j.1467-9671.1997.tb00005.x
2. GEODASH Crime Map. https://geodash.vpd.ca
3. Toronto Police Service: TPS Crime App (Year-to-Date). https://data.torontopolice.on.ca/pages/maps
4. Curtis, A.J., Mills, J.W., Leitner, M.: Spatial confidentiality and GIS: re-engineering mortality locations from published maps about Hurricane Katrina. Int. J. Health Geogr. **5**, 44 (2006)
5. Cassa, C.A., Wieland, S.C., Mandl, K.D.: Re-identification of home addresses from spatial locations anonymized by Gaussian skew. Int. J. Health Geogr. **7** (2008)
6. Zimmerman, D.L., Pavlik, C.: Quantifying the effects of mask metadata disclosure and multiple releases on the confidentiality of geographically masked health data. Geogr. Anal. **40**, 52–76 (2008)
7. Wartell, J., McEwen, J.T.: Privacy in the Information Age: A Guide for Sharing Crime Maps and Spatial Data. Institute for Law and, Justice, NCJ 188739, Washington DC (2001)
8. Leitner, M., Mills, J.W., Curtis, A.: Can novices to geospatial technology compromise spatial confidentiality? KN J. Cartography Geogr. Inf. **57**, 78–84 (2007)

9. City of Toronto: Wellbeing Toronto. https://www.toronto.ca/city-government/data-research-maps/neighbourhoods-communities/wellbeing-toronto/
10. Calgary Police Service: Community Crime Statistics Map. https://data.calgary.ca/Health-and-Safety/Community-Crime-Statistics-Map/n24v-9r86
11. Openshaw, S.: A million or so correlation coefficients: three experiments on the modifiable areal unit problem (1979)
12. Jeffery, C.R.: Crime prevention through environmental design. Am. Behav. Sci. **14**, 598 (1971)
13. Piroozfar, P., Farr, E.R., Aboagye-Nimo, E., Osei-Berchie, J.: Crime prevention in urban spaces through environmental design: a critical UK perspective. Cities **95**, 102411 (2019)
14. Kunnapapdeelert, S., Johnson, J., Phalitnonkiat, P.: Green last-mile route planning for efficient e-commerce distribution. Eng. Manage. Prod. Serv. **14**, 1–12 (2022)
15. Strasser, B., Wagner, D., Zeitz, T.: Space-efficient, fast and exact routing in time-dependent road networks. Algorithms **14**, 90 (2021)
16. Abhay, D.A., Akash, S., Ashwin, K., Shenoy, A.G., Auradkar, P.K.: Smart policing: using geospatial crime data to plan patrol routes. In: 2023 4th International Conference for Emerging Technology (INCET), pp. 1–7 (2023)
17. City of Toronto: Ward Profile: Toronto Centre. https://www.toronto.ca/wp-content/uploads/2024/01/8c68-CityPlanning-2021-Census-Profile-Ward-13.pdf
18. Toronto Police Services: TPS Crime Statistics - Major Crime Indicators. https://data.torontopolice.on.ca/pages/major-crime-indicators
19. City of Toronto: City Wards. https://open.toronto.ca/dataset/city-wards/
20. Statistic Canada: Census – Road Network File. https://www12.statcan.gc.ca/census-recensement/2021/geo/sip-pis/rnf-frr/index2021-eng.cfm?year=21
21. Toronto Police Service: Glossary of Terms. https://www.tps.ca/data-maps/resources/glossary-terms/#:~:text=Violent%20Crime%3A%20Involve%20the%20use,sexual%20assault%2C%20abduction%20and%20robbery
22. Oliveira, M.: More crime in cities? On the scaling laws of crime and the inadequacy of per capita rankings—a cross-country study. Crime Sci. **10** (2021)
23. Boivin, R.: On the use of crime rates. Can. J. Criminol. Crim. Justice **55**, 263–277 (2013)
24. Townsley, M., Grimshaw, R.: The consequences of queueing: crowding, situational features and aggression in entertainment precincts. Crime Prev. Commun. Safety. **15**, 23–47 (2013)
25. Wheeler, A.P.: Quantifying the local and spatial effects of alcohol outlets on crime. Crime Delinq. **65**, 845–871 (2019)
26. Kimpton, A., Corcoran, J., Wickes, R.: Greenspace and crime: an analysis of greenspace types, neighboring composition, and the temporal dimensions of crime. J. Res. Crime Delinq. **54**, 303–337 (2017)
27. Taylor, R.B., Haberman, C.P., ER, G.: Urban park crime: neighborhood context and park features. J. Crim. Justice **64**, 101622 (2019)
28. Shiode, N., Shiode, S., Nishi, H., Hino, K.: Seasonal characteristics of crime: an empirical investigation of the temporal fluctuation of the different types of crime in London. Comput. Urban Sci. **3** (2023)
29. Linning, S.J., Andresen, M.A., Ghaseminejad, A.H., Brantingham, P.J.: Crime seasonality across multiple jurisdictions in British Columbia, Canada. Can. J. Criminol. Crim. Justice **59**, 251–280 (2017)
30. Cheng, W., et al.: Identifying the spatio-temporal characteristics of crime in Liangshan Prefecture, China. Int. J. Environ. Res. Public Health **19**, 10862 (2022)
31. Nakaya, T., Yano, K.: Visualising crime clusters in a space-time cube: an exploratory data-analysis approach using space-time kernel density estimation and scan statistics. Trans. GIS **14**, 223–239 (2010)

32. Hewitt, A.N., Andresen, M.A., Beauregard, E., Brantingham, P.L.: Dangerous times? A routine activities examination of the temporal patterns of sexual offenses over time. Justice Q. **39**, 113–133 (2020)
33. Brunsdon, C., Corcoran, J.: Unveiling the relationship between land use types and the temporal signals of crime: an empirical decomposition approach. Environ. Plan. B Urban Analytics City Sci. **49**, 847–865 (2021)
34. McLeod, A.I., MacNeill, I.B., Bhattacharyya, J.D.: Seasonal effects in Canadian murders. Canadian J. Stat./La Revue Canadienne de Statistique **13**, 269–275 (1985)
35. Asiama, A.A., Zhong, H.: Victims rational decision: a theoretical and empirical explanation of dark figures in crime statistics. Cogent Soc. Sci. **8** (2022)
36. Lynn, L., Madeline, M., Bureau of Justice Statistics: Hate Crime Victimization, 2004–2015 (2017)
37. Semukhina, O.: Unreported crimes, public dissatisfaction of police, and observed police misconduct in the Volgograd region, Russia: a research note. Int. J. Comp. Appl. Crim. Just. **38**, 305–325 (2014). https://doi.org/10.1080/01924036.2013.872690
38. Fohring, S.: Putting a face on the dark figure: describing victims who don't report crime. Temida. **17**(3–18), 1450–6637 (2014)
39. Sherman, L.W., Gartin, P.R., Buerger, M.: Hot spots of predatory crime: routine activities and the criminology of place. Criminology **27**, 27–56 (1989)
40. Weisburd, D.: The law of crime concentration and the criminology of place. Criminology **53**, 133–157 (2015)
41. Pierce, G., Spaar, S., Briggs, L.: The character of police work: strategic and tactical implications (1988)
42. Rosser, G., Davies, T., Bowers, K.J., Johnson, S.D., Cheng, T.: Predictive crime mapping: arbitrary grids or street networks? J. Quant. Criminol. **33**, 569–594 (2017)
43. Andresen, M.A.: The ambient population and crime analysis. Prof. Geogr. **63**, 193–212 (2011)
44. Andresen, M.A.: Location quotients, ambient populations, and the spatial analysis of crime in Vancouver, Canada. Environ. Plan. **39**, 2423–2444 (2007)
45. Davies, T.P., Bishop, S.R.: Modelling patterns of burglary on street networks. Crime Sci. **2** (2013)
46. Poole, A.T., McCutcheon, J.E., Toohy, K., Burraston, B.: Testing the impact of road network connectivity on criminal lethality. Homicide Stud. **22**, 277–295 (2018)

Satellite Data Analysis and Geographic Information System to Support Urban Planning: State of the Art

Lara D'Ambrosio(✉) and Franco Guzzetti

Department of Architecture, Built Environment and Construction Engineering, Politecnico di Milano, Milan, Italy
{lara.dambrosio,franco.guzzetti}@polimi.it

Abstract. In the modern scenario, urban planning and territorial monitoring have become crucial tasks for regional administrations and local authorities due to rapid city and demographic growth. Combining open data from Earth Observation missions with geospatial data for urban planning, such as geodatabases, orthoimages, and thematic maps, is essential for making well-informed environmental support and natural resource management decisions. This research presents a comprehensive overview of the key topics, approaches, and machine learning applications in urban planning. Reviewing recent literature and EU funding programmes such as Horizon 2020 and the European Space Programme (focusing on the Earth Observation missions Copernicus and IRIDE), we emphasized the significance of integrating and implementing satellite data in the Geographic Information System (GIS) using machine learning for sustainable urban planning and management. Furthermore, the results highlighted the importance of remote sensing, particularly satellite images, in understanding urban forms, territorial planning, and monitoring the evolution of the built environment, nature, and ecosystem.

Keywords: Urban planning · GIS · Earth Observation · remote sensing · satellite data · machine learning · smart city · Copernicus · IRIDE

1 Introduction

The study of urban development focuses on cities' physical and demographic expansion [1]. Uncontrolled population growth impacts the environment through land consumption, soil sealing, deforestation, loss of agricultural resources, ecosystem degradation, pollution, and heat islands [2]. The effects of climate change (e.g., floods, heatwaves) and global events (e.g., the pandemic, energy crisis) require flexible, rapid monitoring. Comprehensive territorial planning is essential to address these challenges.

Local authorities use standard geospatial tools like geodatabases, orthoimages, and thematic maps. Satellite remote sensing can provide additional information on territorial changes, offering more frequent data (every few months) compared to current tools, which take years to update. Monitoring land and ecosystems over time is crucial for sustainable urban development and planning [3].

E. Borgogno-Mondino and P. Zamperlin (Eds.): ASITA 2024, CCIS 2463, pp. 389–404, 2025.
https://doi.org/10.1007/978-3-031-91141-5_27

In this scenario, image processing, whether satellite or aerial, optical or radar, is a central tool in urban planning. Its applications span military, medical, industrial, multimedia, and geospatial fields [4]. Global land management relies on data storage and use, with open data enabling widespread geospatial analysis. High-resolution satellite and aerial imagery, combined with Geographic Information Systems (GIS), form the basis for urban planning, integrating large datasets for study and display [5]. Many local authorities worldwide use GIS to manage land use, infrastructure, and public services effectively [3].

While GIS in planning is well-explored, using optical multispectral and radar satellite images is more recent. Satellite remote sensing improves our understanding of the Earth, monitoring surface, temperature, and atmospheric changes essential for environmental planning and resource management [3].

Advances in remote sensing systems now allow the use of both active (Synthetic Aperture Radar - SAR) and passive (optical, thermal, multispectral, hyperspectral) data [6]. Integrating optical and radar satellite images enables accurate land mapping (LU/LC) using object-based and spectral classification techniques, supporting urban planning, change detection, and hazard monitoring [6].

This paper reviews urban planning using geospatial data integrated with satellite remote sensing and examines the European context of EU funding in the Green Deal. It emphasizes the role of local authorities in sustainable urban planning and ecosystem preservation and the importance of Earth Observation missions like Copernicus and IRIDE for monitoring and future planning.

2 Methods

2.1 Literature Review Process

Central to the methodology used is the collection of the most recent articles that dealt simultaneously with GIS and satellite data for urban planning. The dataset was refined to articles published in the last few years because the field of study is rapidly evolving. Furthermore, artificial intelligence and learning machines have only recently been applied to Earth Observation. To this end, search terms were developed and used to gather data from well-established literature databases: Scopus and Web of Science databases were queried for 2019–2024.

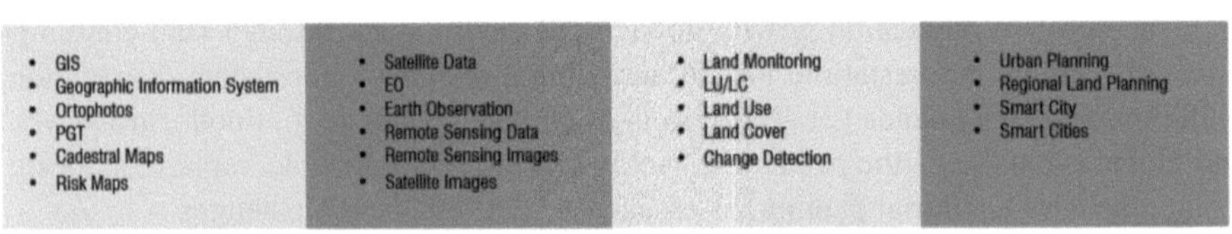

Fig. 1. Keywords definition: synonymous and correlated terms.

The search process used the "TITLE-ABS-KEY" field in Scopus and the "TS" field in Web of Science. Articles were selected using the following query:(GIS)syn AND (satellite data)syn AND (land monitoring)syn AND (urban planning)syn

(GIS)syn AND (satellite data)syn AND (land monitoring)syn AND (urban planning)syn

where "syn" indicates a list of synonymous and correlated terms utilized (Fig. 1). The records were exported to an Excel spreadsheet, duplicates removed, and titles and abstracts reviewed. Articles mentioning satellite data and GIS but not focused on urban planning were excluded. The remaining articles were filtered to include only those using optical data (panchromatic, RGB, multispectral, hyperspectral) and SAR for studying Earth's surface, excluding marine, atmospheric, water resources, and emergency management studies. Ultimately, 43 peer-reviewed articles were retained for the study.

2.1.1 Emerging Trends

An initial bibliographic analysis (Fig. 2) showed the recent rise in satellite data use for urban planning, peaking in 2019 with 24 articles. Given the field's rapid evolution, we focused on articles published between 2019 and 2021. The literature was categorized by country and territory, with India leading (11 articles) and Morocco, Turkey, and China. Only two articles were from the United States (Fig. 3).

By analyzing the 43 research papers selected from Scopus and Web of Science, we deduce that the commonly used datasets in the different research works were Landsat (Landsat-8, Landsat-7, and Landsat-5), Sentinel (Sentinel-2 and Sentinel-1), and IKONOS. Additionally, researchers have employed other datasets such as SRTM (Shuttle Radar Topography Mission), RapidEye, Cartoset, and THEOS (Thailand Earth Observation System) in their investigations. As shown in the figure below (Fig. 4), the dataset used primarily was Landsat-8, used in the research of 27 reviewed articles.

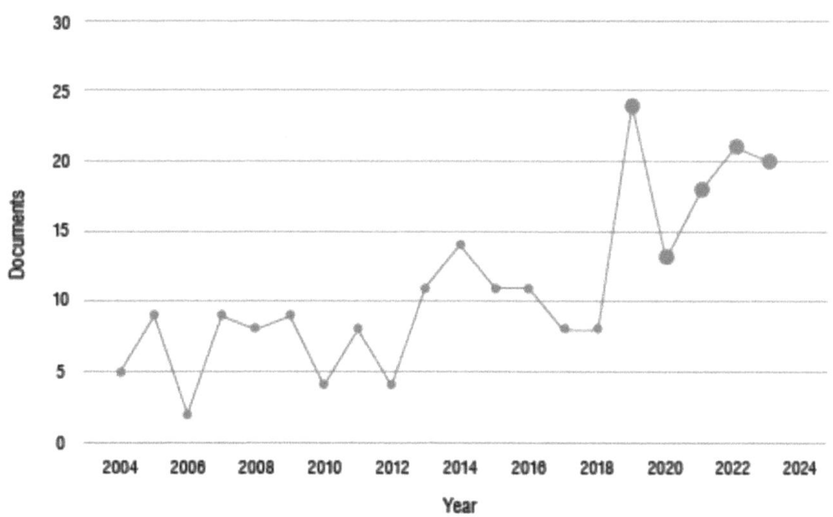

Fig. 2. Documents by year.

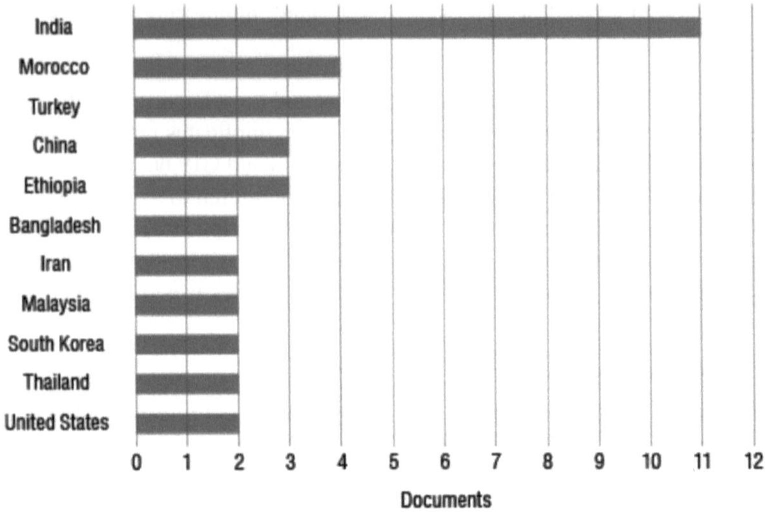

Fig. 3. Documents by country or territory - up to 11 countries or territories.

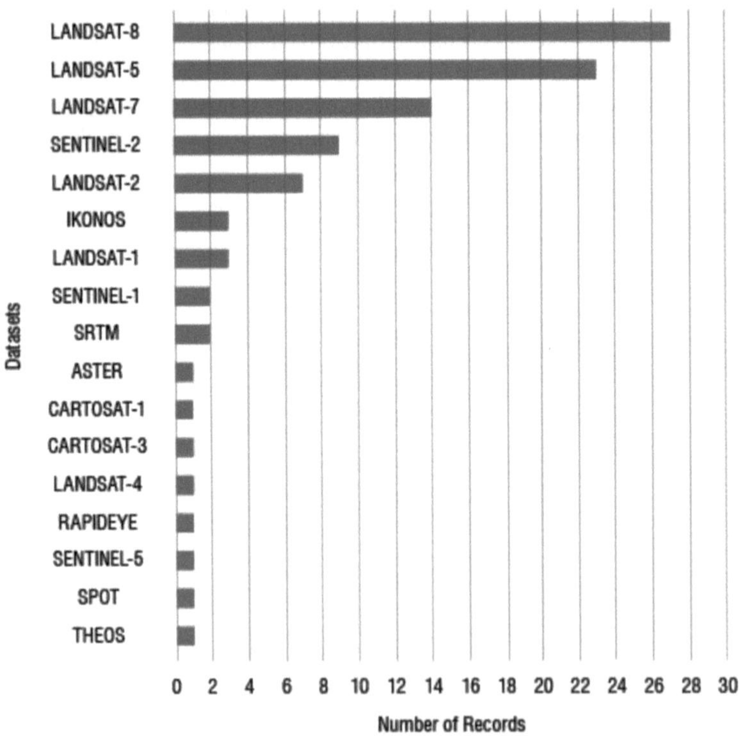

Fig. 4. Analysis based on the datasets employed.

2.2 European Programmes Review Process

As for the literature review process, the same search terms were developed for state-of-the-art research on EU funding programmes for earth observation and urban planning. We identified two programs: Horizon 2020 and the European Space Programme. Within these programmes, after carefully screening the specific topic under analysis and eliminating older programmes (before 2015), we identified three projects within the Horizon 2020 Programme and two missions within the European Space Programme: Copernicus and IRIDE. For the IRIDE program, we analyzed the issue of an Italian geomatics journal, GEOmedia: Nov/Dic 2023 anno XXVII N.6.

3 Findings

The findings from the literature review were categorized and grouped based on two primary recurring themes: land consumption, emphasizing changes in land use and land cover, and heat islands. Meanwhile, European projects and missions were organized according to their respective EU funding programmes: Horizon 2020 and European Space Mission.

3.1 Literature Review Synthesis

3.1.1 Land Consumption

In the panorama of urban growth, land use/land cover (LU/LC) classification is crucial for sustainable urban planning, land use, and resource management [7]. Over 65% of the reviewed articles focused on LU/LC mapping for urban and demographic growth, using satellite datasets like Landsat-8 with Landsat-5 [7–14] and Sentinel-2 [15], sometimes combining both constellations [16–20]. Despite its potential, the synergy between active SAR (e.g., Sentinel-1) and passive remote sensing (e.g., Sentinel-2) remains underexplored [6]. In addition to the previously mentioned satellites, other datasets utilized in the reviewed research addressing land use and land cover changes include Cartosat-3 [21], GaoFen-2 [22], IKONOS [23], and THEOS [24]. The satellite image classification methods literature is divided into pixel-based [25] and object-based classifications [6, 21, 26]; both methods are combined in a few cases [18] (Fig. 5). The first method is based on pixel-by-pixel classification of remote sensing images, using the mixed spectral responses of all pixels in the training set for a given class to decide whether to group different pixels to have similar features [27]. This approach is efficient for low spatial resolution data. However, it could be better for high-resolution satellite data because it cannot distinguish surface features from different objects with the same spectral characteristics [4]. The second image classification method goes through pre-established images of objects after a segmentation process. This process divides the entire image into consistent groups of pixels called segments, to whom is assigned a class according to a set of defined rules [28].

Classification Approches	Attributes				
	Spectral/Color	Form/Shape	Area/Size	Texture	Content
Object-based	✓	✓	✓	✓	✓
Pixel-based	✓	✗	✗	✗	✗

Fig. 5. Attributes used in pixel-based and object-based classification [4].

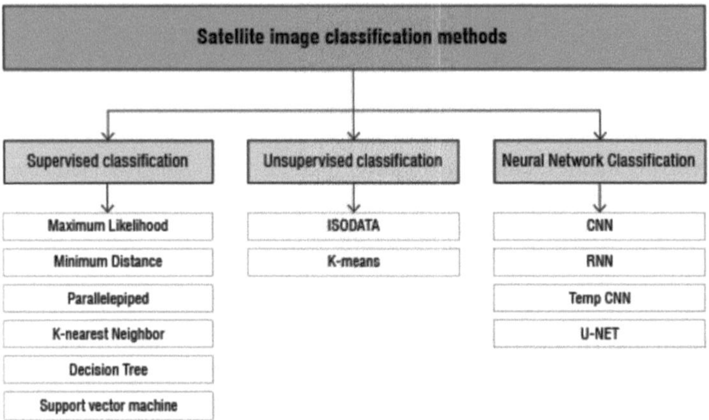

Fig. 6. Satellite image classification methods [4].

The articles reviewed also identify two methods for classifying LU/LC changes: supervised classification [6, 9, 20, 25, 29] and unsupervised classification. Supervised classification uses training samples as a guide during the classification process. The analyst chooses groups of training samples corresponding to the different land use and cover classifications identified. The samples are thus used to train a classifier to categorize the image's pixels into the previously identified classes [19]. Land use land cover (LU/LC) mapping from remote sensing data uses supervised classification algorithms like maximum likelihood [9, 13, 25, 30, 31], minimum distance, support vector machine (SVM) [10, 30], decision tree, and random forest [17]. Unsupervised classification involves grouping pixels in the same image based on spectral characteristics without prior knowledge of the different land use and cover classes.

The analyst chooses the classes he wants to identify before clustering the image pixels, using clustering algorithms such as k-means [26] and ISODATA. Unsupervised classification is less accurate but is more flexible and requires less training data than supervised classification [19].

Recently, a third method for classifying LU/LC changes was developed involving conventional neural networks (CNN) [15], recurrent neural networks (RNN), and generative adversarial networks (GAN). Convolutional neural network-based classification provides new strategies for geospatial data analysis in GIS map updating, such as semantic segmentation, object detection, and image classification.

This deep learning approach accelerates map updates, reduces human labor, and enables more frequent, real-time updates [21] (Fig. 6).

Satellite images from Earth Observation (EO) provide constant information on Earth's subsystems. Surface materials have unique spectral signatures based on their physical properties and interaction with electromagnetic radiation. Specific spectral bands are combined into spectral indices to minimize unwanted effects, offering focused information on materials, processes, or phenomena. Various spectral indices have been proposed for different application domains [32]. The reviewed studies identify several spectral indices in research on land use and land cover. The main ones are Normalized Difference Vegetation Index (NDVI) [3, 16, 17, 31], Normalized Difference Built-up Index (NDBI) [3, 16, 17], Normalized Difference Bareness Index (NDBaI) [16], Built-up Index (BUI) [16], and Built-up Area Extraction Index (BAEI) [3]. Other spectral indices are the Soil Adjusted Vegetation Index (SAVI) [17], Enhanced Built-up and Bareness Index (EBBI) [16], and Urban Quality of Life Index (UQoL) [17] (Table 1).

The articles' most frequently identified land use and land cover (LULC) classes include built-up areas, bare soil/rocks, shrubs/tall herbs, tree/forest cover, grasslands, and cropland [33]. Accuracy evaluation is essential in the classification process, which compares the categorized data with the actual LU/LC classes presented in the primary data. This way, we can precisely evaluate the classification performance, highlighting the variations between the two datasets [19]. The stages of the accuracy evaluation process are different: gathering ground truth data [10, 21, 29], developing a confusion matrix, calculating overall accuracy [13, 17, 26, 34], producer's and user's accuracy [13, 22, 29, 34]. Finally, most studies provide the kappa coefficient [7, 9, 10, 13, 17, 25, 29, 30, 34], which compares the agreement between the observed and reference classification data.

Change detection in LU/LC compares satellite images from different periods and locations, involving preprocessing, registration, change detection method selection, analysis, and accuracy evaluation. Images are preprocessed to improve quality, remove errors, and align with the same geographic system [19]. Algorithms like object-based change detection [21], image differencing, and post-classification comparison enable LULC change detection and measurement.

The most used geographic information and remote sensing software in the studies was Geographic Information System (GIS) [3, 11, 19, 35] by Esri and TerrSet [10, 13, 14, 31] by IDRISI.

Furthermore, some research used cellular automata mathematical models to predict future expansions as a final step in identifying a map of land use and cover changes for sustainable and informed urban planning. CA-Markov [7, 10, 13, 14, 24, 31], Artificial Neural Network (ANN) [29], and the SLEUTH cellular automaton model [20] were the most used models.

Finally, all the research highlighted how the data and results obtained from the classification and mapping of LU/LC changes are indispensable steps for sustainable and conscious urban planning to mitigate the effects of urban expansion and climate change.

Table 1. Table 1.Spectral indices found in the literature review [17].

Name of Index	Author(s)	Formula
The Built-up Area Extraction Index (BAEI)	Ouchra et al. (2022) [3]	$\frac{RED+0.3}{GREEN+SWIR1}$
The Built-up Index (BUI)	Tin et al. (2021) [19]	$\frac{SWIR1-NIR}{SWIR1+NIR} - \frac{NIR-RED}{NIR+RED}$
Enhanced Built-up and Bareness Index (EBBI)	Tin et al. (2021) [19]	$\frac{SWIR-Red}{^{10}\sqrt{(SWIR+TIR)}}$
Normalized Difference Bareness Index (NDBaI)	Tin et al. (2021) [19]	$\frac{D(BAND\ 5)-D(BAND\ 6)}{D(BAND\ 5)+D(BAND\ 6)}$
Normalized Difference Built-Up Index (NDBI)	Ouchra et al. (2022) [3]	$\frac{SWIR-NIR}{SWIR+NIR}$
Normalized Difference Vegetation Index (NDVI)	Alsharif et al. (2022) [34]	$\frac{NIR-RED}{NIR+RED}$
Soil Adjusted Vegetation Index (SAVI)	Yagoub et al. (2022) [20]	$\frac{NIR-RED}{NIR+RED+L}(1+L)$
Urban Quality of Life Index (UQoL)	Yagoub et al. (2022) [20]	$\Sigma^{n}_{1} F_i W_i$

3.1.2 Heat Islands

Urbanization increases impervious surfaces, raising Land Surface Temperature (LST) and creating Urban Heat Islands (UHI), which negatively impact ecosystems, climate, hydrology, biodiversity, and human health [36]. Fifteen reviewed articles focus on how LU/LC classifications influence LST and UHI. Most use multispectral satellite imagery from passive remote sensing, such as Landsat-8 with Landsat-7 [37, 38], and Landsat-8 with Landsat-5 and Landsat-7 [39–41], with some integrating data from both Sentinel and Landsat [36, 42].

In addition to the satellites mentioned, the reviewed studies on heat islands also used datasets like RapidEye [2] and IKONOS [43]. As discussed in Subsect. 3.1.1, analyzing LU/LC changes and their impact on LST involves several phases and methods, starting with classification using pixel-based or object-based approaches [39], which help identify land use and cover variations.

The classification can be supervised [2, 38, 40, 43, 44] or unsupervised, with human operator involvement in the former and automatic algorithms in the latter. The predominant supervised classification algorithms employed in the studies included maximum likelihood [38, 41, 43, 45], support vector machine (SVM) [2], decision tree [36, 40], and random forest [36, 46]. In the analysis process, spectral indices such as the Normalized Difference Vegetation Index (NDVI) [36–44, 46, 47] and the Normalized Difference Water Index (NDWI) [39, 44] were used to identify areas covered by vegetation and water, respectively. These indices provide crucial information about the distribution and health of terrestrial ecosystems.

The data obtained from these analyses were then compared with Land Surface Temperature (LST) [36–47] and Urban Heat Island (UHI) [36, 38–47] measurements to identify correlations between changes in LU/LC and increases in surface temperatures. This approach allows for a better understanding of the impact of environmental transformations on urbanization and the surrounding environment (Fig. 7).

Prediction models like Multiple Linear Regression (MLR) [44] and Autoregressive Integrated Moving Average (ARIMA) [38] were used to estimate future trends in LU/LC changes and thermal parameters. These algorithms leverage historical data to predict future scenarios, helping manage environmental impacts. The articles emphasize how integrating thermal and multispectral satellite data with advanced analysis provides a solid foundation for understanding and addressing environmental changes linked to urbanization and global warming.

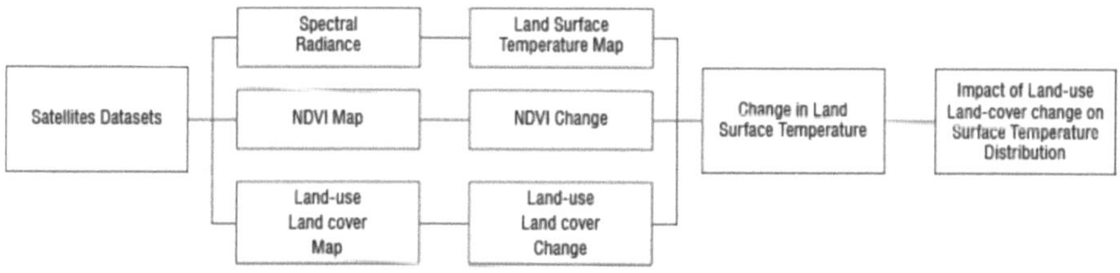

Fig. 7. An example of a methodology flowchart in detective LST changes [40].

3.2 European Programmes Synthesis

3.2.1 Horizon 2020

Remote Monitoring for More Effective Nature-Based Solutions Against Natural Hazards

Sustainable planning must address climate change, uncontrolled population growth, and natural disasters. It is crucial to monitor at-risk areas, prevent construction in such zones, and implement emergency protocols. Constant ground monitoring and remote sensing technologies support informed, sustainable planning.

The Horizon 2020 programme highlighted two significant EU projects: OPERANDUM and RECONECT, published in Earth-Science Reviews. These projects focus on Nature-Based Solutions (NBS) to manage climate challenges such as floods, heatwaves, and landslides. NBS are efficient, sustainable alternatives to traditional structural measures like dams, offering lower costs and greater flexibility in urban settings.

Remote sensing and GIS are pivotal in evaluating NBS interventions using spectral indices like NDWI, NDVI, and LST. These technologies help monitor environmental changes such as flooded areas, agricultural droughts, and urban heat islands, providing insights into the effectiveness of NBS.

OPERANDUM and RECONECT emphasize integrating NBS into urban planning to combat climate change and urban growth. These projects promote green infrastructure, sustainable development, and community engagement, aiming to create resilient, livable cities while preserving natural resources.

Artificial Intelligence: Expanding Scientific Boundaries and Enhancing Innovation

In urban planning, another significant project within the European Horizon 2020 programme is DeepCube. AI is increasingly important in European research, ensuring Europe remains a leader in science and technology. The DeepCube project uses AI and semantic web technologies to analyze Copernicus big data, addressing socio-environmental challenges and terrestrial processes linked to climate change while creating high business value.

DeepCube operates an open, interoperable platform with ICT tools like the Earth System Data Cube (ESDC), Semantic Cube, and Hopsworks for distributed Deep Learning (DL). The platform can be deployed on cloud infrastructures and high-performance computing systems. DeepCube uses these tools to create innovative DL pipelines and develop architectures for non-conventional data such as SAR interferometric and social network data. It combines data-driven deep learning with physical modeling, utilizing explainable AI and causal AI to address complex issues like fire hazard prediction and climate-induced migration.

The project addresses key Earth Observation challenges involving biosphere, atmosphere, and anthroposphere interactions, such as forecasting droughts and heat in Africa, climate-induced migration, Mediterranean fire hazards, volcanic deformation detection, infrastructure monitoring, and sustainable tourism via Copernicus services. Fusing AI with Copernicus open data services is crucial for monitoring urban transformations and climate change impacts and developing adaptation strategies.

3.2.2 European Space Programmes

Copernicus

The EU Space Programme aims to enhance European Earth Observation (EO), Satellite Navigation, Connectivity, Space Research, and Innovation capabilities. It supports the European space industry, promotes innovation, and contributes to the growth of a European 'New Space' ecosystem. A key program component is Copernicus, Europe's Earth Observation system, which provides essential data for environmental management, climate change mitigation, and civil security.

Copernicus, developed by the EU in collaboration with the European Space Agency (ESA), is one of the most ambitious Earth observation programs. It integrates a constellation of Sentinels satellites, ground-based sensors, and data processing infrastructure to provide timely, reliable, and accessible environmental and climate information.

The primary goal of Copernicus is to support decision-making by providing accurate and up-to-date data on environmental parameters such as atmospheric composition, land use, ocean dynamics, biodiversity, and natural disasters. Using advanced remote sensing technologies, Copernicus offers insights into global trends, changes, and emerging risks impacting ecosystems, communities, and economies.

Copernicus's open data policy allows users to freely access satellite imagery and environmental datasets through portals like the Copernicus Open Access Hub.

This unrestricted access fosters scientific research and innovation and supports tackling challenges like climate change adaptation, disaster risk reduction, and natural resource management. Copernicus is divided into six thematic services: Atmosphere Monitoring Service (CAMS), Marine Environment Monitoring Service (CMEMS), Land Monitoring Service (CLMS), Climate Change Service (C3S), Emergency Management Service (EMS), and Security Service (CSS) (Table 2).

Copernicus data is crucial for urban planning, aiding sustainable, resilient city development. Sentinel-2 images, with high spatial resolution and frequent revisit times, are used for land use classification, urban heat island monitoring, and flood risk assessments. Indices like NDVI and BUI derived from Sentinel-2 data help distinguish land cover types [16], while Land Surface Temperature (LST) calculated from thermal bands assesses urban heat islands [36]. Sentinel-1's SAR imagery benefits flood mapping due to its ability to penetrate cloud cover.

Copernicus data supports urban planning by offering vital information for climate adaptation and resilience strategies. It helps prioritize resources, allocate investments, and forecast urban transformations, enhancing cities' resilience and contributing to sustainable development.

IRIDE

The IRIDE programme, funded with 1.1 billion Euros and managed by the European Space Agency (ESA) with support from the Italian Space Agency (ASI), is a major Italian Earth observation initiative. It involves developing 40 satellites by Italian companies like Thales Alenia Space, OHB Italia, Argotec, Sitael, and D-Orbit. These smaller, efficient satellites reflect the New Space Economy's innovations, utilizing modern, cost-effective technologies.

Operating in low Earth orbit (LEO), the satellites will provide extensive Earth coverage with optical, SAR, and multispectral sensors, offering near real-time national monitoring. This data is crucial for civil protection and state institutions, aiding in observing hydrogeological instability, forest fires, and coastal pollution.

IRIDE's challenges include adopting new technologies and adhering to ESA's stringent regulations. Professionals with a comprehensive system vision are essential to overcome these hurdles and ensure timely satellite deployment.

The IRIDE System encompasses processing chains and products across eight Thematic Domains, aiming to supply geospatial products for institutional users. By 2026, 60 Service Value Chains (SVC) and around 300 geospatial products will be operational, following a multi-sensor, multi-mission approach to ensure a user-friendly system.

IRIDE products include: S1 - Coastal Marine Monitoring, S2 - Air Quality, S3 - Ground Movements, S4 - Land Cover, S5 – IdroMeteoClima, S6 - Water Resources Management, S7 – Emergencies, and S8 – Safety (Table 2).

The IRIDE development involves industrial, research, and institutional collaboration to ensure product effectiveness. Over 100 Italian companies contribute, enhancing the national space sector and creating vital geospatial products for public administrations.

IRIDE aims to deepen understanding of urban and environmental dynamics through advanced satellite technologies and data analysis, providing public administrations with essential insights for developing sustainable solutions to urbanization and climate change challenges.

Table 2. Table 2.Comparison of European Space Programmes: Copernicus and IRIDE.

COPERNICUS	IRIDE
esa	esa asi
Born 25 years ago	Born in 2021
First launched in 2014	Yet to be launched (2025)
EU funds	PNRR funds
7 missions known as Sentinels	40 satellites
Open data	For Public Amministration
Services:	Services:
- Atmosphere Monitoring Service (CAMS)	S1 - Coastal Marine Monitoring
- Marine Environment Monitoring Service (CMEMS)	S2 - Air Quality
- Land Monitoring Service (CLMS)	S3 - Ground Movements
- Climate Change Service (C3S)	S4 - Land Cover
- Emergency Management Service (EMS)	S5 - IdroMeteoClima
- Security Service (CSS)	S6 - Water Resources Management
	S7 - Emergencies
	S8 - Safety

4 Discussion

4.1 Critical Evaluation

Strengths

This study confirms the critical role of satellite imagery and GIS data in urban planning, offering insights into ever-changing urban landscapes. The reviewed articles highlight satellite imagery's importance in monitoring land use, heat islands, urban sprawl, deforestation, pollution, and managing natural disasters like floods, landslides, and earthquakes. By applying algorithms, future urban expansion can be forecasted, supporting sustainable urban planning with up-to-date information.

European projects like OPERANDUM and RECONECT promote nature-based solutions (NBS) to mitigate climate impacts, raising awareness among planners and the public about economical, eco-friendly alternatives.

In this complex context, integrating AI with Copernicus' open data services is vital for tracking urban evolution, assessing climate impacts, and developing targeted emergency and adaptation plans. As one of the most comprehensive Earth observation programmes, Copernicus supports resilient and sustainable urban management.

On the other hand, the IRIDE programme stands out for its tailored approach to Italy's public administration, offering innovative solutions for space sector applications in government and land management, emphasizing its strategic significance.

Weaknesses

Urbanization and climate change are among the most pressing challenges for society. While extensively studied, these issues are often addressed in isolation rather than through an integrated approach. A holistic strategy that considers spatial, social, economic, and environmental factors is essential to tackle urban sprawl and climate change. Only by understanding the interconnected dynamics of urban and climate challenges can we devise strategies to mitigate negative impacts and foster sustainable urban development. European research highlights the need for integrated approaches that address the synergies between urbanization, heat islands, deforestation, and natural disasters, ensuring a comprehensive understanding of these complex issues.

4.2 Unexplored Potential

Promoting interdisciplinary research and collaboration among experts is essential for developing integrated decision-making models and tools for future cities. Bridging the gaps between academic disciplines can lead to innovative, sustainable solutions for urban challenges.

Public administrations are key in addressing urbanization and climate change through cooperative, integrated strategies. Understanding urban and environmental dynamics is vital for crafting policies that foster resilient, sustainable cities.

The IRIDE space programme is a pioneer, enhancing the understanding of urban and environmental dynamics and supporting public administration efforts to tackle these challenges. It highlights the need for ongoing research and projects to unlock further potential and refine solutions.

5 Conclusion

In conclusion, this analysis underscores the critical role of satellite imagery and GIS data in modern urban planning. These tools are essential for monitoring urban changes, managing climate impacts, and addressing natural disasters like floods and earthquakes. Satellite imagery offers real-time insights into land use and development trends, aiding in risk mitigation and adaptation strategies. Furthermore, GIS data supports predictive modeling for urban expansion, facilitating sustainable planning.

Promoting interdisciplinary collaboration is vital for developing integrated models to tackle future urban challenges. Leveraging these technologies is key to building safer, more sustainable cities for current and future generations.

References

1. Goodchild, M.F.: Recent advances in geographic information science (2010)
2. El Mjiri, I., Rahimi, A., Bouasria, A.: Remote sensing and GIS at the heart of the smart management of El Jadida City (Morocco) (2021)
3. Ouchra, H., Belangour, A., Erraissi, A.: Satellite data analysis and geographic information system for urban planning: a systematic review. In: 2022 International Conference on Data Analytics for Business and Industry (ICDABI), pp. 558–564. IEEE (2022)

4. Ouchra, H., Belangour, A., Erraissi, A.: A comprehensive study of using remote sensing and geographical information systems for urban planning. Internetw. Indonesia J. **12**, 15–20 (2022)
5. Chang, K.-T.: Geographic information system. In: International Encyclopedia of Geography: People, the Earth, Environment and Technology, pp. 1–10 (2016)
6. Yulianti, E., Na'am, J., et al.: Optical SAR fusion of Sentinel-2 images for mapping high resolution land cover. In: 2018 International Conference on System Science and Engineering (ICSSE), pp. 1–4. IEEE (2018)
7. Kalkhajeh, R.G., Jamali, A.A.: Analysis and predicting the trend of land use/cover changes using neural network and systematic points statistical analysis (SPSA). J. Indian Soc. Remote Sens. **47**(9), 1471–1485 (2019)
8. Haldar, S., et al.: Dynamicity of land use/land cover (LULC): An analysis from peri-urban and rural neighbourhoods of Durgapur Municipal Corporation (DMC) in India. Reg. Sustain. **4**(2), 150–172 (2023)
9. Dhali, Md.K., Chakraborty, M., Sahana, M.: Assessing spatio-temporal growth of urban subcentre using Shannons entropy model and principle component analysis: A case from North 24 Parganas, lower Ganga River Basin, India. Egyptian J. Remote Sens. Space Sci. **22**(1), 25–35 (2019)
10. Atef, I., Ahmed, W., Abdel-Maguid, R.H.: Future land use land cover changes in ElFayoum governorate: a simulation study using satellite data and CA-Markov model. Stochast. Environ. Res. Risk Assess., 1–14 (2023)
11. Khan, B., Rathore, V.S., Krishna, A.P.: Identification of Desakota region and urban growth analysis in Patna City, India using remote sensing data and GIS. J. Indian Soc. Remote Sens. **49**, 935–945 (2021)
12. Hailu, T., Assefa, E., Zeleke, T.: Land use planning implementation and its effect on the ecosystem in Addis Ababa, Ethiopia. Environ. Challenges **13**, 100798 (2023)
13. Aticho, A., et al.: Observed and projected changes in urbanization and nature conservation in a typical fast growing city of Ethiopia, Jimma. Biodivers. Conserv. **32**(12), 4007–4028 (2023)
14. Faichia, C., et al.: Using RS data-based CA–Markov model for dynamic simulation of historical and future LUCC in Vientiane, Laos. Sustainability **12**(20), 8410 (2020)
15. Sawant, S., et al.: Sen-2 LULC: land use land cover dataset for deep learning approaches. Data Brief **51**, 109724 (2023)
16. Tin, S.N., Muttitanon, W.: analysis of Enhanced Built-up and Bare Land Index (EBBI) in the urban area of Yangon, Myanmar. Int. J. Geoinf. **17**(4) (2021)
17. Yagoub, M.M., et al.: Extraction of urban quality of life indicators using remote sensing and machine learning: the case of Al Ain city, United Arab Emirates (UAE). ISPRS Int. J. Geo-Inf. **11**(9), 458 (2022)
18. Szarek-Iwaniuk, P., Dawidowicz, A., Senetra, A.: Methodology for precision land use mapping towards sustainable urbanized land development. Int. J. Environ. Res. Pub. Health **19**(6), 3633 (2022)
19. Patel, A., et al.: Novel approach for the LULC change detection using GIS & Google Earth Engine through spatiotemporal analysis to evaluate the urbanization growth of Ahmedabad city. Results Eng. **21**, 101788 (2024)
20. Mallouk, A., et al.: Using the SLEUTH urban growth model coupled with a GIS to simulate and predict the future urban expansion of Casablanca region, Morocco. Int. Arch. Photogramm. Remote. Sens. Spat. Inf. Sci. **42**, 139–145 (2019)
21. Vasavi, S., et al.: Advancing GIS map maintenance: change detection and update using ResU-Net: a case study on Chandigarh and Hyderabad cities, India. Curr. Sci. (00113891) **126**(3) (2024)

22. Huang, H., Li, Q., Zhang, Y.: Urban residential land suitability analysis combining remote sensing and social sensing data: a case study in Beijing, China. Sustainability **11**(8), 2255 (2019)
23. Henriques, C.D., Correia, E.: Long-term urban land use data in Maputo, Mozambique: A comprehensive dataset covering five decades (1964–2001). Data Brief **50**, 109595 (2023)
24. Chotchaiwong, P., Wijitkosum, S.: Predicting urban expansion and urban land use changes in Nakhon Ratchasima City using a CA-Markov model under two different scenarios. Land **8**(9), 140 (2019)
25. Bhuiyan, M.M.H., et al.: Monitoring dynamic land-use change in rural–urban transition: a case study from Hathazari Upazila, Bangladesh. Geol. Ecol. Landscapes **3**(4), 247–257 (2019)
26. Vu, T.T., et al.: Enhanced urban functional land use map with free and open-source data. Int. J. Digit. Earth **14**(11), 1744–1757 (2021)
27. Uca Avci, Z.D., et al.: A comparison of pixel-based and object-based classification methods, a case study: Istanbul, Turkey. In: Proceedings of the 34th International Symposium on Remote Sensing of Environment, Sydney, Australia (2011)
28. Jawak, S.D., Devliyal, P., Luis, A.J.: A comprehensive review on pixel oriented and object oriented methods for information extraction from remotely sensed satellite images with a special emphasis on cryospheric applications. Adv. Remote Sens. **4**(3), 177–195 (2015)
29. Ganesh, V.N., Sridhar, R.S.: Land-use change detection and assessment for sustainable development of peri-urban areas using remote sensing and GIS: a case study of Coimbatore city, Tamil Nadu, India. J. Environ. Protect. Ecol. **21**(6), 2229–2244 (2020)
30. Baig, M.F., et al.: Comparative analysis of support vector machine and maximum likelihood classifications using satellite images of Selangor, Malaysia. In: 2021 Third International Sustainability and Resilience Conference: Climate Change, pp. 405–409. IEEE (2021)
31. Alsharif, M., et al.: Land use land cover change analysis for urban growth prediction using landsat satellite data and Markov Chain Model for Al Baha region Saudi Arabia. Forests **13**(10), 1530 (2022)
32. Montero, D., et al.: A standardized catalogue of spectral indices to advance the use of remote sensing in Earth system research. Sci. Data **10**(1), 1–20 (2023)
33. Bokhari, S.A., et al.: Assessing land cover transformation for urban environmental sustainability through satellite sensing. Sustainability **14**(2810), 2022 (2022)
34. GebreMedhin, A., et al.: Detection of urban land use land cover dynamics using GIS and remote sensing: a case study of Axum town, Northern Ethiopia. J. Indian Soc. Remote Sens. **47**, 1209–1222 (2019)
35. Yousif, Q.Y., Altaei, M.S.M.: Land use geodatabase of baghdad city creation using geographic information system technology. In: 2023 Al-Sadiq International Conference on Communication and Information Technology (AICCIT), pp. 212–217. IEEE (2023)
36. Furuya, M.T.G., et al.: A machine learning approach for mapping surface urban heat island using environmental and socioeconomic variables: a case study in a medium-sized Brazilian city. Environ. Earth Sci. **82**(13), 325 (2023)
37. imek, Ç.K., Ödül, H.: A method proposal for monitoring the microclimatic change in an urban area. Sustain. Cities Soc. **46**, 101407 (2019)
38. Kesavan, R., et al.: ARIMA modeling for forecasting land surface temperature and determination of urban heat island using remote sensing techniques for Chennai city, India. Arabian J. Geosci. **14**(11), 1016 (2021)
39. Cetin, M.: The effect of urban planning on urban formations determining bioclimatic comfort areas effect using satellitia imagines on air quality: a case study of Bursa city. Air Qual. Atmos. Health **12**(10), 1237–1249 (2019)
40. Gazi, Md.Y., et al.: Spatio-temporal dynamic land cover changes and their impacts on the urban thermal environment in the Chittagong metropolitan area, Bangladesh. GeoJournal **86**, 2119–2134 (2021)

41. Singh, A., Mishra, V.N.: Estimation of changes in land surface temperature using multi-temporal Landsat data of Ghaziabad District, India. Forum geografic **19**(1) (2020)
42. Dhar, R.B., et al.: Impact of land-use/land-cover change on land surface temperature using satellite data: a case study of Rajarhat Block, North 24-Parganas District, West Bengal. J. Indian Soc. Remote Sens. **47**, 331–348 (2019)
43. Karaku, C.B.: The impact of land use/land cover (LULC) changes on land surface temperature in Sivas City Center and its surroundings and assessment of Urban Heat Island. Asia-Pacific J. Atmos. Sci. **55**(4), 669–684 (2019)
44. Ghosh, S., Chatterjee, N.D., Dinda, S.: Relation between urban biophysical composition and dynamics of land surface temperature in the Kolkata metropolitan area: a GIS and statistical based analysis for sustainable planning. Model. Earth Syst. Environ. **5**, 307–329 (2019)
45. McCarty, D., Lee, J., Kim, H.W.: Machine learning simulation of land cover impact on surface urban heat island surrounding park areas. Sustainability **13**(22), 12678 (2021)
46. Khorrami, B., Heidarlou, H.B., Feizizadeh, B.: Evaluation of the environmental impacts of urbanization from the viewpoint of increased skin temperatures: a case study from Istanbul, Turkey. Appl. Geomatics **13**(3), 311–324 (2021)
47. Das, M., Das, A.: Assessing the relationship between local climatic zones (LCZs) and land surface temperature (LST)–A case study of Sriniketan-Santiniketan Planning Area (SSPA), West Bengal, India. Urban Clim. **32**, 100591 (2020)

Assessing the Quality of a Topographic Database Using SLAM Technology: Proposal for an Operational Procedure

Antonio Matellon[1,2], Eleonora Maset[1(✉)], Domenico Visintini[1], and Alberto Beinat[1]

[1] Polytechnic Department of Engineering and Architecture (DPIA), University of Udine, Via delle Scienze 206, Udine, Italy
matellon.antonio@spes.uniud.it, {eleonora.maset,domenico.visintini,alberto.beinat}@uniud.it

[2] Department of Engineering and Architecture (DIA), University of Trieste, Via Alfonso Valerio 6/1, Trieste, Italy

Abstract. This paper investigates the use of point clouds from Simultaneous Localization and Mapping (SLAM) technology as a reference for the quality assessment of a large-scale topographic database. Three distinct approaches are proposed for the comparison between SLAM data and the vector features of the database, evaluating strengths and limitations of each methodology on a study area of the novel topographic database of the Friuli Venezia Giulia region (Italy). The tests carried out show that SLAM-based laser scanners facilitate the acquisition of a reference 3D model at a considerably faster time than the conventional topographic field techniques typically employed in quality control. Furthermore, the results demonstrate that, despite their inferior precision in comparison to traditional surveying, SLAM sensors are still sufficiently accurate to assess the metric quality of databases realized at a scale of 1:1000–1:2000.

Keywords: Topographic Database · Simultaneous Localization and Mapping · Portable Laser Scanner · Point Clouds · Testing

1 Introduction

The availability of complete, consistent, and accurate geospatial data is a fundamental prerequisite for the design, management, and monitoring of the territory. The presence of errors and inaccuracies negatively affect the reliability of spatial analyses based on these data, ultimately influencing the decision-making process in urban and territorial planning. In this respect, official cartography produced by public administrations plays a pivotal role, as it ensures the distribution of high-quality and certified data whose geometric congruence with reality is assessed through appropriate testing procedures [1].

E. Borgogno-Mondino and P. Zamperlin (Eds.): ASITA 2024, CCIS 2463, pp. 405–417, 2025.
https://doi.org/10.1007/978-3-031-91141-5_28

To date, the most common approach to verify the accuracy of map products is based on the use of classical topographic techniques, such as total station and Global Navigation Satellite System (GNSS) surveying, to measure the coordinates of a limited number of highly visible, unambiguously identifiable check points, that are assumed as ground truth. For instance, in photogrammetry the differences between the topographic-measured coordinates and the photogrammetric ones are analyzed to assess the model accuracy [2]. The metric quality of airborne Light Detection and Ranging (LiDAR) surveys, instead, is typically evaluated by comparing the elevation of GNSS-measured check points with the elevation estimated from the LiDAR ground data [3].

In the course of testing a (vector) topographic database, the coordinates of the vertices of the geometric features are compared to those directly measured in the field. This process serves to verify that the discrepancies comply with the requisite tolerances.

The approach based on topographic-measured check points is undoubtedly an accurate and reliable method. Nevertheless, it is also inherently time-consuming in terms of the data acquisition phase and is constrained in its capacity to measure (and thus verify) a large number of points. In this context, novel portable laser scanners based on the Simultaneous Localization and Mapping (SLAM) technology could be a viable alternative for the acquisition of a complete and dense 3D point cloud, which could serve as a reference model in testing operations. Indeed, SLAM-based portable devices guarantee faster data acquisitions in the field, while concurrently preserving a high degree of accuracy. Furthermore, the data obtained are rich in details that would be difficult to capture with a traditional survey (e.g., the height at the foot of the building, the geometry of the eaves line or the sidewalk).

Laser scanning systems based on SLAM technology were introduced to the market a few years ago and rapidly gained popularity, particularly for mapping indoor and underground environments. In fact, the use of SLAM algorithms enables the surveying of the surrounding environment simply by walking trough it, without the need for sensor position data from external sources such as GNSS. Moreover, these devices are well-suited for mapping the outdoor sites in which database testing is often conducted, including urban canyons and historic villages with irregular buildings and narrow streets [4]. In such scenarios, the GNSS signal is frequently unreliable, and the use of alternative static surveying technologies, such as Terrestrial Laser Scanning (TLS), is both time-consuming and susceptible to data gaps and occlusions resulting from complex geometries.

In terms of accuracy, the literature reports a range of results for SLAM systems, with accuracy levels varying from a few centimeters to 10 cm [5,6]. Although these instruments yield point clouds with greater noise than photogrammetry and TLS techniques, several authors concur that a representation scale of 1:100–1:200 can be attained through their use [7–9]. This is compatible with the testing of products such as a topographic database, which is realized at the scale 1:1000–1:2000.

In light of these considerations, in this paper we propose a novel application of portable laser scanners: the use of SLAM-based point clouds as a reference to assess the conformity, completeness and metric quality of a topographic database. Three different approaches, described in Sect. 2, are tested for the comparison between SLAM data and the vector features of the database. The results, reported and discussed in Sects. 3 and 4, show that SLAM technology can be a useful alternative to classical topographic methods also in this context.

2 Materials and Methods

2.1 Proposed Procedure

As previously mentioned, the proposed testing procedure leverages on the strengths of SLAM systems, going beyond conventional point-to-point comparisons between the 3D coordinates obtained from a total station survey and the corresponding vertices of the objects (represented as lines or polygons) belonging to the database. As a matter of fact, the use of a SLAM-based point cloud as ground truth allows great flexibility in the methodology that can be employed for testing a topographic database. In particular, the following solutions are investigated:

1. *Point-to-cloud* comparison: small patches are extracted from the SLAM-based point cloud at the vertices of a certain object and compared with the corresponding vertices of the geometric feature in the database. This implies the calculation of a point-to-patch distance, which is, in essence, a cloud-to-cloud (C2C) distance.
2. *Line-to-cloud* comparison: slices of the point cloud are extracted at the element of interest and compared with the corresponding lines representing the object in the database. To easily compute the distances between the lines and the cropped SLAM data, lines can be converted into sets of points through a high-density sampling process, thus bringing the comparison back to a C2C distance calculation.
3. *Line-to-line* comparison: vector drawings are extracted from the SLAM-based point cloud and subsequently compared with the lines of the database. Also in this case, points can be sampled from the lines, thus enabling C2C distance computation.

Going deeper into the implementation details, in this work the slices of the SLAM point cloud, used in the *line-to-cloud* comparison, were extracted with the tools provided by ReCap Pro software [10], whereas the vectorization process, required in the *line-to-line* approach, was conducted manually in AutoCAD [11]. The selection of the patches for the *point-to-cloud* approach was performed using the open-source software CloudCompare [12]. This software was also employed to sample points along the lines for the second and third methodology, setting a linear density value of 100 points/m, and to calculate the C2C distances. The C2C value is a nearest neighbor distance: for each point of the compared cloud, the nearest point in the reference cloud is searched and their euclidean distance is computed[1]. In the C2C analyses, the objects of the topographic database were assigned the role of *compared*, while the SLAM data was assigned the role of *reference*.

2.2 Study Area

The proposed testing procedure was evaluated on a study area located in the Friuli Venezia Giulia region (Italy). In 2017, the Friuli Venezia Giulia administration launched a substantial mapping programme with the aim of updating the spatial data and cartographic products of the territory [13]. Initially, the entire 7,900 km^2 area of the region was covered with airborne LiDAR, photogrammetric and hyperspectral surveys, which led to the generation of the Digital Terrain Model, the Digital Building Model, and the Digital Surface Model at a resolution of 50 cm/pixel, true-orhophotos with a resolution of 10 cm/pixel and 1 m/pixel hyperspectral rectified images (see [14] for further details).

Moreover, the regional numerical technical map is currently being renewed, converting it into a modern topographic database. To date, the database has been created for the main municipalities and is available at scales of 1:1000, 1:2000 or 1:5000, according to the specific zones. Following the Italian Ministerial Decree 10.11.2011, "Technical rules for the definition of the content specification of the geotopographic databases", which implements an ISO TC211 compliant GeoUML methodology, the topographic database is structured in a hierarchical manner: *classes*, i.e., objects that share common properties, are organized into *themes*, which in turns are grouped into *layers*. All recently developed cartographic products are available for free visualization and download via the geoportal *Eagle.fvg* [15].

In this paper, we chose as case study the Rizzi district in the municipality of Udine, for which the database was created at a scale of 1:2000. The developed testing approaches were applied on eight buildings, distributed homogeneously within the study area, but differing in terms of shape, size and use (Fig. 1). For each building, the vector features belonging to the classes *Building volumetric units* (i.e., the elementary, homogeneous building volume) and *Roofing elements* (i.e., the various roofing parts of a building, including pitches, terraces, domes, etc.) were taken into consideration. As the objects in the *Building volumetric unit* class are not properly 3D features (an object is a horizontal polygon, placed at the same height of the foot of the building), only the planimetric quality assessment was performed for this class. On the contrary, both planimetric and altimetric quality analyses were conducted on the 3D shapes of the *Roofing elements*.

2.3 SLAM Data Acquisition and Validation

The SLAM-based system employed in this work is the Stonex X120^{GO} [16] portable laser scanner (Fig. 2a), which is equipped with a LiDAR rotating head

[1] https://www.cloudcompare.org/doc/wiki/index.php/Distances_Computation.

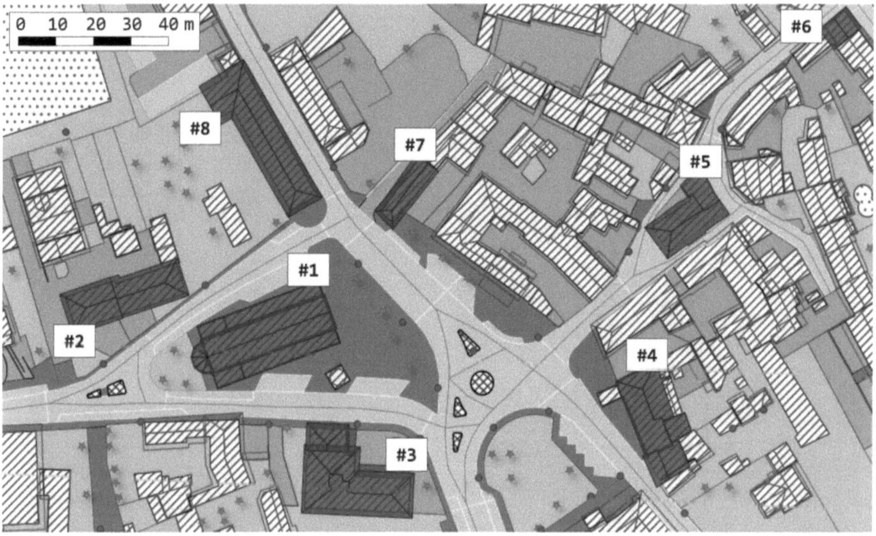

Fig. 1. Topographic database of the study area in the municipality of Udine. The eight buildings selected to evaluate the proposed testing procedures are highlighted in red. (Color figure online)

that acquires 320,000 points/s. The device is capable of measuring distances ranging from 0.5 m to 120 m, with a field of view of 360° horizontally and 270° vertically. The declared relative accuracy is 6 mm. Thanks to three 5-megapixel cameras that allow to capture panoramic images, the point cloud obtained from the instrument can be colored in post-processing. Furthermore, the device can be integrated with the RTK120^{GO} GNSS-module for point cloud georeferencing. The module permits to receive signals from the four GNSS constellations (GPS, GLONASS, Galileo and BDS) and enables real-time connection to the local permanent GNSS network, thus performing Network Real-Time Kinematic (NRTK) positioning. For georeferencing purposes, it is sufficient to receive the NRTK correction for a period of approximately half the duration of the survey. This allows georeferencing to be performed even when part of the data acquisition is conducted indoor or, more generally, in the absence of GNSS signal. To obtain the final point cloud, all data acquired in the field is automatically processed off-line via the SLAM algorithm implemented in the GOPost software [17].

For the survey of the study area, a 20-min data acquisition was conducted along a trajectory of 1.1 km (Fig. 2b). The automatic post-processing phase in the GOPost software took approximately 50 min on a workstation Intel Core i7-9700x CPU @3.00 Ghz, equipped with 64 GB RAM and a Nvidia GeForce RTX 2070 Super GPU. The final point cloud consists of 151M points and was georeferenced in the same coordinate system of the topographic database (EPSG:6708) thanks to the NRTK connection to the regional permanent GNSS network

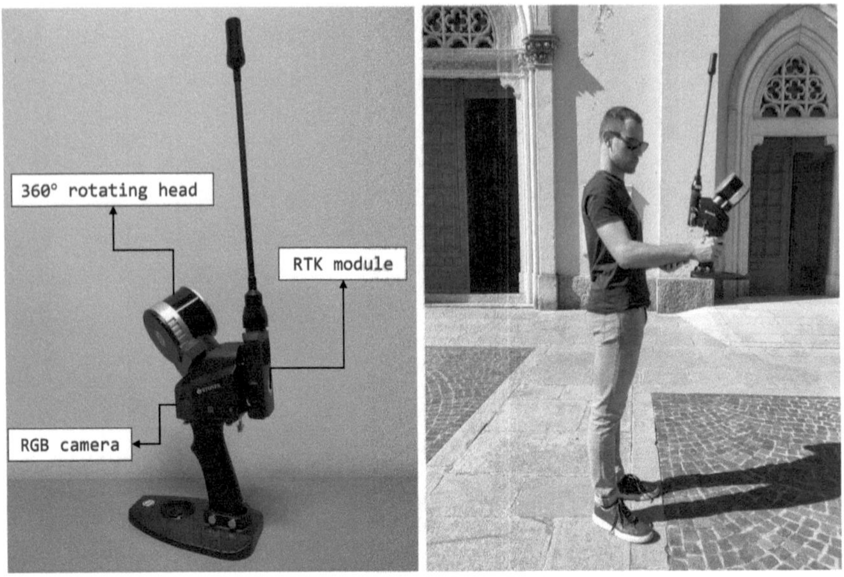

(a) Stonex X120^{GO} (b) Survey with the SLAM sensor

Fig. 2. The Stonex X120^{GO} portable laser scanner used for the reference data acquisition.

"Antonio Marussi". Figure 3 depicts the SLAM point cloud, colored according to the intensity value of the return signal measured by the LiDAR sensor, with the vector data from the topographic database superimposed.

In order to preliminary assess the metric quality of the point cloud obtained from the SLAM device, a comparison was conducted with respect to 75 points measured with a reflectorless total station on the edges of buildings and roofs, regarded as the ground truth. In particular, the validation process followed the *point-to-cloud* approach described in Sect. 2.1, where, in this special case, the points in question are not vertices of the database features, but rather points measured through the topographic survey.

3 Results

As outlined in Sect. 2.1, the three proposed methodologies ultimately entail the calculation of discrepancies in terms of C2C distances. From the C2C values obtained, we computed the Root Mean Square Error (RMSE) as a measure of accuracy, defined as

$$\text{RMSE} = \sqrt{\frac{\sum_{i=1}^{n} d_i^2}{n}}$$

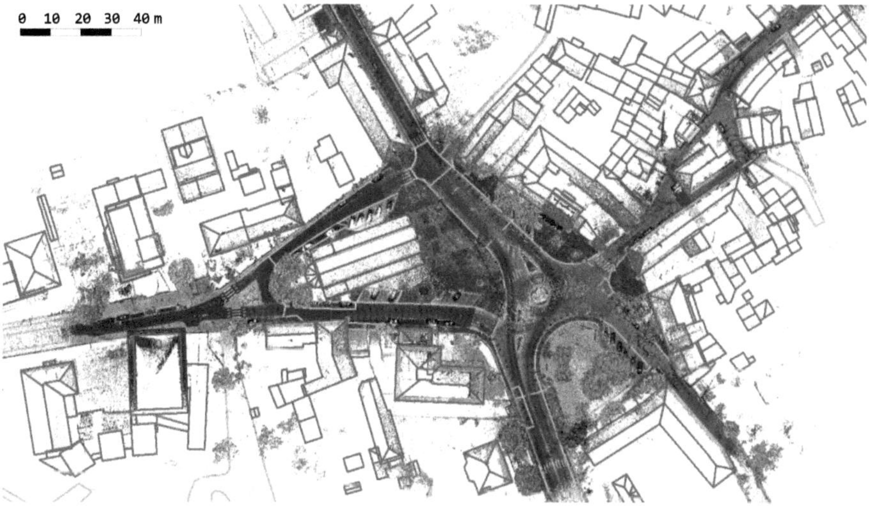

(a) Top view

(b) 3D view

Fig. 3. Point cloud acquired with the SLAM-based portable laser scanner, overlaid with vector data from the topographic database. The line colors encode different classes of objects (*Building volumetric units* (orange), *Roofing elements* (red), *Vehicle and pedestrian areas* (cyan)). Green and pink dots show the points measured with a total station on the eaves lines of the roofs and on the building facades, respectively. (Color figure online)

where d_i is the distance (splitted in planimetric and vertical components) between the ith compared point and the corresponding (i.e., nearest) reference one and n is the total number of evaluated points.

Table 1 shows the results of the SLAM data validation procedure, described in Sect. 2.3. The findings documented in the literature are corroborated in this case study, which demonstrates the accuracy of the SLAM point cloud to be within a few centimeters for both the planimetric and altimetric components. This renders the SLAM data suitable for utilization as a reference point cloud for the purposes of database testing.

Table 1. Results of the validation process conducted on the SLAM data.

Object	$RMSE_{XY}$ [m]	$RMSE_{Z}$ [m]
Building edges	0.044	—
Roof vertices	0.043	0.025

The metric assessment of the database features for each analyzed building, performed according to the three proposed methodologies, led to the values reported in Tables 2, 3, and 4. The aggregated results of the comparison between the topographic database and the SLAM data are presented in Table 5. It is notable that all three approaches produced highly comparable aggregated results. Furthermore, the RMSE values are all below the minimum accuracy threshold required in the technical specifications for the database realization at a scale of 1:2000, namely 0.50 m and 0.40 m for the planimetric and altimetric components, respectively.

Table 2. Results of the *point-to-cloud* testing methodology.

Building n.	*Volumetric units*	*Roofing elements*	
	$RMSE_{XY}$ [m]	$RMSE_{XY}$ [m]	$RMSE_{Z}$ [m]
#1	0.122	0.147	0.094
#2	0.457	0.106	0.134
#3	0.384	0.091	0.112
#4	0.684	0.110	0.067
#5	0.265	0.140	0.115
#6	0.214	0.660	0.268
#7	0.188	0.073	0.064
#8	0.839	0.172	0.153

4 Discussion

The case study demonstrated that the use of SLAM point clouds offers a number of advantages when compared to traditional topographic surveying techniques

Table 3. Results of the *line-to-cloud* testing methodology.

Building n.	*Volumetric units*	*Roofing elements*	
	$RMSE_{XY}$ [m]	$RMSE_{XY}$ [m]	$RMSE_{Z}$ [m]
#1	0.247	0.154	0.130
#2	0.274	0.135	0.132
#3	0.358	0.140	0.126
#4	0.363	0.089	0.085
#5	0.194	0.116	0.115
#6	0.156	0.364	0.254
#7	0.208	0.177	0.104
#8	0.422	0.127	0.120

Table 4. Results of the *line-to-line* testing methodology.

Building n.	*Volumetric units*	*Roofing elements*	
	$RMSE_{XY}$ [m]	$RMSE_{XY}$ [m]	$RMSE_{Z}$ [m]
#1	0.201	0.122	0.242
#2	0.251	0.087	0.172
#3	0.351	0.162	0.173
#4	0.409	0.107	0.103
#5	0.220	0.142	0.146
#6	0.127	0.411	0.320
#7	0.162	0.051	0.096
#8	0.380	0.138	0.172

for the quality assessment of a topographic database. Firstly, the time required for data acquisition is significantly reduced. In this work, the point cloud of an area of approximately 1 ha was obtained in a time period of only 20 min, whereas the topographic survey of the edges of buildings and roofs within the same area required several hours. Moreover, the NRTK module installed on the SLAM device enabled direct georeferencing of the point cloud, thus speeding up the process without requiring additional GNSS measurements, which are instead necessary for georeferencing the survey conducted through the total station. The time needed in the office for data post-processing is comparable for the two surveying techniques.

SLAM technology also proves to offer a significantly more versatile solution for the selection of test areas. Traditional topographical measurements require the control points to be directly visible from the station vertices: this severely limits the choice of control sites, short of onerous traverses. In contrast, SLAM technology allows easy operation even in narrow and winding alleys.

Table 5. Aggregate results of the developed testing methodologies.

	Volumetric units	*Roofing elements*	
	$RMSE_{XY}$ [m]	$RMSE_{XY}$ [m]	$RMSE_{Z}$ [m]
Point-to-cloud	0.412	0.177	0.118
Line-to-cloud	0.315	0.145	0.124
Line-to-line	0.302	0.135	0.187

A further significant strength of the SLAM technology is that it provides a comprehensive and detailed 3D representation of the mapped environment. This permits a preliminary qualitative assessment of the topographic database, not only in terms of its metric characteristics, but also in regard to the completeness of the vectorized objects. As far as the semantic aspects of the database are concerned, their analysis (e.g., verifying that a vector feature is correctly associated with its respective class) is typically performed through field reconnaissance. In contrast, the acquisition of the SLAM data enables this evaluation to be conducted a posteriori in the office.

In regard to the three approaches developed to compare the SLAM point cloud and the features of the database, from this first case study it was observed that, although the outcomes were comparable, the methodologies employed demonstrated distinctive pros and cons. The *point-to-cloud* methodology is analogous to the traditional comparison between a limited number of reference check points and the corresponding database vertices. However, it exploits only small patches extracted from the point cloud, thereby not fully leveraging on the extensive quantity and completeness of the SLAM data. In contrast, the *line-to-cloud* and *line-to-line* approaches examine the vector feature in its entirety, thereby facilitating a more comprehensive assessment of the overall metric quality.

A critical evaluation of the aforementioned two last approaches reveals that the *line-to-line* method, despite needing additional manual effort (and, consequently, a longer processing time), is the most effective method for conducting the comparison between the SLAM data and the vector elements on an equal basis. Indeed, when vectorizing from the SLAM point cloud the lines that serve as reference in the testing process, one can consider that certain minor details are not required to be drawn at the employed scale of representation, in accordance with the technical specifications of the database and, consequently, with the level of detail that characterizes the features being evaluated. Conversely, the *line-to-cloud* approach carries the potential to overestimate database error in cases where complex geometries are present and fully reconstructed in the SLAM point cloud. To illustrate this, consider the example in Fig. 4, which demonstrates how the *line-to-cloud* approach yielded high errors at the church facade (Fig. 4a). However, these errors should not be detected and included in the testing process, as the size of the architectural details is too small to be represented at the scale of 1:2000 of the database. In the *line-to-line* method, instead,

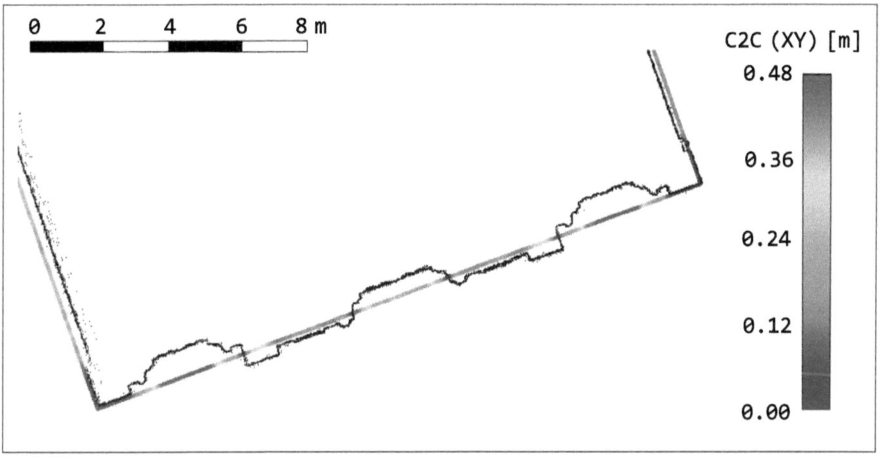

(a) *Line-to-cloud* comparison on building #1

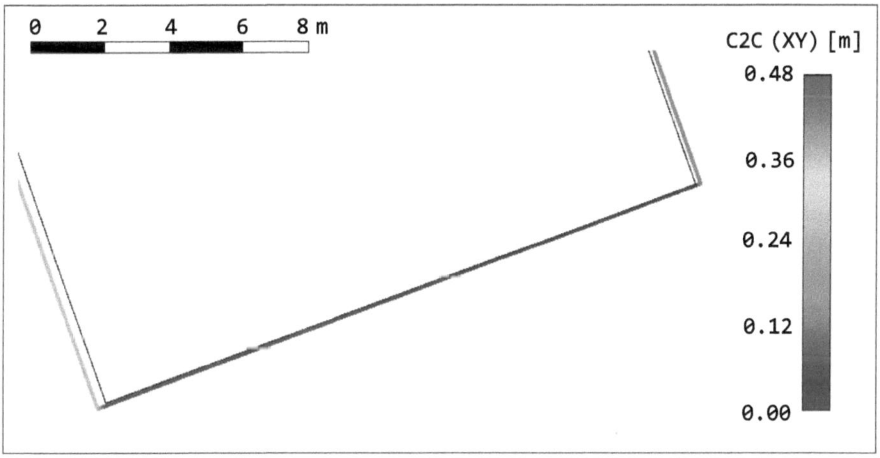

(b) *Line-to-line* comparison on building #1

Fig. 4. An example of the *line-to-cloud* and *line-to-line* approaches. The reference set is shown in black: in (a), it is a slice of the SLAM point cloud; in (b), it is the line obtained from the vectorization step performed on the SLAM data. The vector features of the topographic database, transformed into points, are colored according to the C2C distance (XY component) from the reference.

the reference line corresponding to the church facade is drawn in accordance to the required scale of representation and the discrepancies of the database with respect to the reference are correctly evaluated.

In general, all the three proposed methodologies share a common disadvantage, namely the necessity for manual intervention by the operator. In the future, efforts will be made to automate the process. In this regard, a preliminary semantic segmentation of the SLAM point cloud could prove to be beneficial for subsequent analyses. The utilization of a point cloud that has already been categorized into distinct classes, such as roofing, buildings, roads and other relevant ones, results in substantial simplifications with respect to the management of the entire point cloud. This, in turn, facilitates the analysis of individual buildings. Consequently, the *line-to-cloud* comparison for the *Roofing elements* could be applied directly on the roofing points segmented from the SLAM dataset, without the need to perform all the intermediate, time-consuming manual steps presented above, such as the ad hoc extraction of point cloud slices at the roofing. Furthermore, the implementation of an automatic or semi-automatic vectorization algorithm on the point cloud would serve to further streamline the *line-to-line* comparison.

5 Conclusions

In this study, SLAM technology, which in the existing literature is primarily examined in relation to more accurate surveying techniques, is instead employed as the reference data source for the metric evaluation of a large-scale topographic database. Three distinct methodologies were developed to compare the SLAM point cloud with respect to the vector features of the database. According to the first test carried out on the Friuli Venezia Giulia topographic database, the *line-to-line* method resulted in the most suited approach for this particular application. Although the proposed approach requires further refinements to enhance its efficiency, it is already proving beneficial to complement classical topographic techniques for testing operations, with the potential to supersede them in the near future.

Acknowledgments. The research has been partially funded by the strategic plan of University of Udine within the framework of the project "ESPeRT".

References

1. Franzini, M., Casella, V.M., Monti, B.: The Digital Twin of the metropolitan area of Milan: quality assessment of aerial and terrestrial data. In: Borgogno Mondino, E., Zamperlin, P. (eds.) ASITA 2023. CCIS, vol. 2088, pp. 152–171. Springer, Cham (2024). https://doi.org/10.1007/978-3-031-59925-5_12
2. Casella, V., Franzini, M., Kocaman, S., Gruen, A.: Geometric accuracy assessment of ADS40 imagery under various network configurations. Int. Arch. Photogramm. Remote. Sens. Spat. Inf. Sci. **37**(B1), 627–632 (2008)
3. Liu, X.: Accuracy assessment of LiDAR elevation data using survey marks. Surv. Rev. **43**(319), 80–93 (2011)
4. Di Stefano, F., Chiappini, S., Gorreja, A., Balestra, M., Pierdicca, R.: Mobile 3D scan LiDAR: a literature review. Geomat. Nat. Haz. Risk **12**(1), 2387–2429 (2021)
5. Tucci, G., Visintini, D., Bonora, V., Parisi, E.I.: Examination of indoor mobile mapping systems in a diversified internal/external test field. Appl. Sci. **8**(3), 401 (2018)

6. Maset, E., Cucchiaro, S., Cazorzi, F., Crosilla, F., Fusiello, A., Beinat, A.: Investigating the performance of a handheld mobile mapping system in different outdoor scenarios. Int. Arch. Photogramm. Remote. Sens. Spat. Inf. Sci. **43**(B1–2021), 103–109 (2021)
7. Sammartano, G., Spanò, A.: Point clouds by SLAM-based mobile mapping systems: accuracy and geometric content validation in multisensor survey and stand-alone acquisition. Appl. Geom. **10**(4), 317–339 (2018)
8. Matrone, F., Colucci, E., Ugliotti, F.M., Del Giudice, M.: From an integrated survey with MMS to a Scan-to-BIM process for educational purposes. Int. Arch. Photogramm. Remote. Sens. Spat. Inf. Sci. **48–1**(W1–2023), 279–286 (2023)
9. Matellon, A., Maset, E., Beinat, A., Visintini, D.: Surface reconstruction from SLAM-based point clouds: results from the datasets of the 2023 SIFET benchmark. Remote Sens. **16**, 3439 (2024)
10. Autodesk ReCap Pro. https://www.autodesk.com/it/products/recap/overview?term=1-YEAR&tab=subscription. Accessed 11 Sept 2024
11. Autodesk AutoCAD: https://www.autodesk.com/it/products/autocad/overview?term=1-YEAR&tab=subscription. Accessed 11 Sept 2024
12. CloudCompare. https://www.danielgm.net/cc/. Accessed 11 Sept 2024
13. Crosilla, F., Picech, G., Beinat, A.: Fifty years of the Friuli Venezia Giulia regional technical map: a best practice in the Italian cartographic context. Appl. Geomat. **13**(3), 437–452 (2021)
14. Maset, E., Visintini, D., Beinat, A.: On the role of geomatics and official regional cartography in the Interconnected Nord-Est Innovation Ecosystem. In: Borgogno Mondino, E., Zamperlin, P. (eds.) ASITA 2023. CCIS, vol. 2088, pp. 172–183. Springer, Cham (2024). https://doi.org/10.1007/978-3-031-59925-5_13
15. Eaglefvg Webgis. https://eaglefvg.regione.fvg.it/eagle/main.aspx?configuration=guest. Accessed 11 Sept 2024
16. Stonex X120^{GO} SLAM Laser Scanner. https://www.stonex.it/project/x120go-slam-laser-scanner/. Accessed 11 Sept 2024
17. Stonex GOPost. https://www.stonex.it/it/project/x120go-slam-laser-scanner/#software. Accessed 11 Sept 2024

Correction to: Mapping Burned Areas with Optical and Sentinel-1 Synthetic Aperture Radar Data

Alessandro Gatti, Marco Manzoni, Andrea Monti-Guarnieri, Giovanna Sona, Giovanna Venuti, and Daniela Stroppiana

Correction to:
Chapter 3 in: E. Borgogno-Mondino and P. Zamperlin (Eds.): ***Geomatics for Green and Digital Transition*****, CCIS 2463,**
https://doi.org/10.1007/978-3-031-91141-5_3

In the originally published version of chapter 3, in page 40 there was a formula, which was updated incorrectly. It has been corrected.

The updated version of this chapter can be found at
https://doi.org/10.1007/978-3-031-91141-5_3

E. Borgogno-Mondino and P. Zamperlin (Eds.): ASITA 2024, CCIS 2463, p. C1, 2025.
https://doi.org/10.1007/978-3-031-91141-5_29

Author Index

E. Borgogno-Mondino and P. Zamperlin (Eds.): ASITA 2024, CCIS 2463, pp. 419–421, 2025.
https://doi.org/10.1007/978-3-031-91141-5

MIX
Papier aus verantwortungsvollen Quellen
Paper from responsible sources
FSC® C105338

If you have any concerns about our products,
you can contact us on
ProductSafety@springernature.com

In case Publisher is established outside the EU,
the EU authorized representative is:
Springer Nature Customer Service Center GmbH
Europaplatz 3, 69115 Heidelberg, Germany

Printed by Libri Plureos GmbH
in Hamburg, Germany